Contemporary Social Problems

in North American Society

Shahid Alvi

University of St. Thomas

Walter DeKeseredy

Carleton University

Desmond Ellis

York University

Addison-Wesley

Don Mills, Ontario • Reading, Massachusetts • Harlow, England
Melbourne, Australia • Amsterdam, The Netherlands • Bonn, Germany

Canadian Cataloguing in Publication Data

Alvi, Shahid
  Contemporary social problems in North American society

Includes bibliographical references and index.
ISBN 0-201-61392-1

1. Social problems—Canada. 2. Social problems—United States. 3. Canada—Social
conditions—1991– . 4. United States—Social conditions—1980– . I. DeKeseredy, Walter S.,
1959– . II. Ellis, Desmond. III. Title.

HN103.5.A584 2000   361.1'0971   C99-931618-4

ISBN 0-201-61392-1

Printed and bound in Canada.

1 2 3 4 5   04 03 02 01 00

Vice President, Editorial Director: Laura Pearson
Acquisitions Editor: Nicole Lukach
Developmental Editor: Laura Paterson Forbes
Production Editor: Avivah Wargon
Copy Editor: Muriel Napier
Production Coordinator: Wendy Moran
Permissions/Photo Research: Siobhan Dooley
Art Director: Mary Opper
Cover Design: Anthony Leung
Cover Image: Tony Stone Images
Page Layout: B.J. Weckerle

Photo credits:
Dick Hemingway, pp. 1, 39, 71, 109, 247, 381; David Longstreath/CP, p. 155; © Rob Goldman
1993/Masterfile, p. 195; © Mark Scott 1994/Masterfile, p. 301; © Lester Lefkowitz/Masterfile, p. 347.

Contents

Chapter 2:   Hey Buddy, Can You Spare a Dime?: Poverty in North America 39

Chapter 3:   Get a Job! Unemployment in North America 71

Chapter 4: Is There a Doctor in the House? Health and Health Care in North America 109

Chapter 8:   Drug Abuse in North America 301

Chapter 9: The Information Revolution: Privacy, Pornography, and Alienation 347

Chapter 10: Conclusion 381

PREFACE

Every day, thousands, perhaps millions, of North Americans directly or indirectly experience what sociologists James Coleman and Donald Cressey refer to as a "depressingly long" list of social problems such as poverty, unemployment, violent crime, pollution, and so on. The main objective of this text is to introduce you to the sociological study of these and other contemporary social problems in North America. Following C. Wright Mills, within the context of a pedagogical approach that links personal experience with broader political, economic, social, and cultural forces, our book is specifically designed to help answer important questions such as the following:

➤ To what extent are U.S. or Canadian citizens at risk of suffering from the social problems described in Chapters 2 to 9?

➤ Which groups of North Americans suffer from poverty, unemployment, violent crime, and other social problems?

➤ Which theories best explain the issues described in Chapters 2 to 9?

➤ What are the most effective solutions to the problems covered in this text?

At first glance, our book has much in common with other leading social problems texts. Indeed, most university and college instructors who teach social problems courses adopt books that emphasize developing a **sociological imagination** and cover most of the topics addressed here. As one of our friends who has taught social problems courses in the United States for approximately ten years points out, "It isn't an accident that most social problems books are similar." They cover the issues, theories, and policies addressed by almost every social problems instructor. However, what makes *Contemporary Social Problems in North American Society* clearly distinct from others is our approach.

We provide a comprehensive, comparative, and highly intelligible overview of various social problems. Of course, we could have covered many more social problems, and several other texts do. However, we purposely limited our focus to eight substantive topics—not because we think others are unimportant or of little social consequence. Rather, we decided to replace the standard "cafeteria concept"—covering a little bit of many kinds of social problems—with the concept of *table d'hôte*, presenting a few selected offerings. These are limited in number, so that each topic can be covered in some depth, an approach we believe necessary for acquiring more than a superficial knowledge of it.

We also describe definitions, research, theories, and policies in a way that will make the sociological study of social problems "come alive." For example, each chapter includes the voices of men, women, and children who have experienced one or more of the social problems covered in this text. Further,

➤ Each chapter attempts to engage and involve the reader in a dialog with the authors, with her/himself, with other students, and with the people quoted or referred to in this text. To achieve this goal, discussion questions, problem solving scenarios, and suggestions for workshop or classroom exercises are included at the end of every chapter.

➤ We have included a unique chapter (Chapter 9) on various ways in which North American society has been transformed by the widespread use of computers in everyday life, and more recently, by the Internet.

➤ Each of Chapters 2 to 9 attempts to address the intersection of race/ethnicity, class, and gender. Typically, most introductory sociology and social problems texts offer separate chapters on the experiences of women, the economically disenfranchised, and visible minorities. In sharp contrast to this approach, the concerns and experiences of members of these three social groups are integrated into the entire text.

➤ The extent, nature, and distribution of eight contemporary social problems that exist in both Canada and the United States are described. Although we focus primarily on North American issues, we frequently direct your attention to the social problems experienced by people in other nations, at the same time making clear the linkages between these "foreign" issues and those of the North American context.

➤ The following questions are raised in each chapter: "How do we define the problem?" "What is the extent and distribution of the problem?" "What are the causes?" "What are the solutions?" Again, in-depth rather than superficial coverage of a smaller number of substantive topics is provided.

➤ Each chapter includes up-to-date studies, theories, and policy proposals.

ACKNOWLEDGMENTS

Each of us has always been keenly interested in a wide variety of social problems and we have wanted to write a book such as this for years. However, if it were not for the encouragement and support of Gord Muschette, this project would never have come to fruition. Dave Ward and Brian Henderson provided the support, encouragement, patience, and editorial expertise to help realize the project. We are deeply grateful for their assistance and commitment. We also greatly appreciate the time, effort, and excellent work done by people at Pearson Education Canada, including Nicole Lukach, Laura Paterson Forbes, Avivah Wargon, and freelance editors Muriel Napier and Gillian Scobie.

As always, our families helped us in immeasurable ways. Our intimate partners, parents, and children were always there to cheer us up and to remind us that there is more to life than sociology. The faith, patience, and encouragement of Pamela Corrigan and Megan and Erin Alvi are, as always, deeply appreciated. Special thanks go to Marie Barger, Walter DeKeseredy's mother-in-law, who was always there when Walter and Pat DeKeseredy's work schedules created child-care dilemmas.

If our families and our publishers were central to the completion of this book, the same can be said about our friends and colleagues. The following people took time away from their busy schedules to provide us with comments, criticisms, and other forms of intellectual support: Bruce Arrigo, Gregg Barak, Raquel Kennedy Bergen, Penelope Canan, Meda Chesney-Lind, Wallace Clement, Kim Cook, Daniel Curran, Dawn Currie, Dennis Forcese, Alberto Godenzi, Mark Hamm, Brian MacLean, Linda MacLeod, Dragan Milovanovic, Barbara Perry, Claire Renzetti, Martin Schwartz, Jim Thomas, Andreas Tomaszewski, Kenneth Tunnell, Terry Wotherspoon, and reviewers Robert Adamoski, Kwantlen College; Patricia Atchison, Colorado State University; Brenda Beagan, University of British Columbia; and Rita Duncan, Tulsa Community College. Since many of these scholars disagree with one another, obviously, we are totally responsible for what we took from them. Their input, as well as that of many others we have not named, is greatly appreciated.

Many thanks also go to all the support staff at Carleton University's Department of Sociology and Anthropology. Ann Carroll, Nazira Conroy, Lynn Gunn, Kim Mitchell, and Joel Nordenstrom went out of their way to help us write this book, and we will never forget their assistance and good humor.

ABOUT THE AUTHORS

Shahid Alvi is assistant professor at the University of St. Thomas in St. Paul, Minnesota, where he teaches in the areas of criminology and criminal justice policy. He holds a BA and MA in Sociology from the University of Saskatchewan, and a Ph.D. from Carleton University, Ottawa, Ontario, where he specialized in the political economy of work, occupations, and professions. His current research interests include crime, public housing and social policy, theories of crime, crimes of the powerful, violence in society, and the sociology of work and family issues. He has published scholarly articles and reports in the area of criminology and work-family conflict, and is currently writing a book on youth and the Canadian criminal justice system.

Walter S. DeKeseredy is professor of sociology at Carleton University, Ottawa, Ontario. He has published dozens of journal articles and book chapters on woman abuse and other criminological issues. He is the author of *Woman Abuse in Dating Relationships: The Role of Male Peer Support* and *Women, Crime, and the Canadian Criminal Justice System*; with Ronald Hinch, co-author of *Woman Abuse: Sociological Perspectives*; with Desmond Ellis, co-author of the second edition of *The Wrong Stuff: An Introduction to the Sociological Study of Deviance*; with Linda MacLeod, co-author of *Woman Abuse: A Sociological Story*; and with Martin D. Schwartz, co-author of *Contemporary Criminology, Sexual Assault on the College Campus: The Role of Male Peer Support*, and *Woman Abuse on Campus: Results from the Canadian National Survey*. In 1995 he received the Critical Criminologist of the Year Award from the American Society of Criminology's Division of Critical Criminology. In 1993, he received Carleton University's Research Achievement Award. Currently, he is co-editor of *Critical Criminology: An International Journal* and he serves on the editorial boards of *Violence Against Women: An International and Interdisciplinary Journal* and *Women & Criminal Justice*.

Desmond Ellis is professor of sociology at York University in Toronto, Ontario, and serves on the Executive Committee of the LaMarsh Centre for Research on Violence and Conflict Resolution, which he helped create in 1981. He is a former chair of York University's Department of Sociology. He has written numerous journal articles on woman abuse among separating couples, prison violence, and other forms of interpersonal violence. He is author of *The Wrong Stuff: An Introduction to the Sociological Study of Deviance*; with Walter S. DeKeseredy, co-author of the second edition of *The Wrong Stuff*; and with Noreen Stuckless, co-author of *Mediating and Negotiating Marital Conflicts*. His next research project will be a field experimental study of the effects of power imbalances on the process and outcomes of divorce mediation.

Chapter 1

Social Problems and the Sociological Enterprise

Sociology does not excuse individual failure. It does, however, focus on the larger social forces that shape people's fates. People are indeed responsible for their own lives, but often they do not realize how much the odds are stacked against them or, conversely, the extent to which their social position creates advantages for them and their offspring. The sociological imagination helps one understand the complex interrelationships between individual actions and social forces. (Kornblum, 1997: 31)

OBJECTIVES

In this chapter we focus on the topics
1. What is sociology?
2. What is a social problem?
3. Sociological theories of social problems
4. How do sociologists gather social problems data?

Introduction: The Sociological Enterprise

As quickly as you can, make a list of what you consider to be some social problems confronting North American society today. What does your list contain? Initially, you might have no difficulty stating what these social problems are. Like many North Americans, your "common sense" will probably oblige you to acknowledge that crime, unemployment, and poverty are social problems requiring a serious assessment of their causes, consequences, and potential solutions. But think a little more carefully about your list. What kind of crime are we talking about? Violent crime? Corporate crime? And how much crime is there, really? Why should unemployment be considered a social problem? If people are unemployed, isn't it their fault for not making the right decisions in their lives? And what is poverty? Is it a condition that exists only among certain categories of people, those who are "lazy," "don't want to work," or are "welfare bums"? Doesn't the definition of poverty depend on different perceptions of the "bare minimum" to live on? How much suffering is "enough" to merit calling something a social problem?

As you can see, even defining social problems, never mind doing something about them, can be a complicated task, depending to a great extent on how we have been taught to think about social life. In this text, we introduce you to central sociological perspectives on some important social problems. We draw your attention to the helpfulness of these perspectives in understanding the nature and consequences of, as well as potential solutions to, these problems. In addition, we aim to give you an understanding of the ways in which the practice of sociology—the sociological enterprise—can help us to see the world in ways that differ appreciably from "common sense."

What Is Sociology?

Norbert Elias, author of *What is Sociology?* argued that "sociology...is a relatively autonomous social science" (1978: 45). In other words, **sociology** is an independent discipline and its subject matter—the topics covered in this text—can only be adequately explained by sociology. Other social sciences, however, such as geography, history, political science, and economics have their own specialized subject matter that may be part of sociology, but is not fully sociological.

For example, if society is regarded as a pie, then economists, political scientists, and geographers study slices of it, psychologists and biologists study the individual molecules of which the pie is made, and sociologists study the entire pie—that is, society as a whole. Some common questions sociologists try to answer are

➤ How is social order possible in a society?

➤ How and why do societies change or stay the same?

➤ How and why are societies differentiated by male and female gender roles?

➤ How is society stratified by gender, race/ethnicity, and social class?

Two of the most general and widely used sociological concepts sociologists employ in answering these questions are **culture** and **social structure**.

Culture refers to a shared, symbolic realm. Language such as conversations, jokes, and songs; values such as democracy, material success, and monogamy; and norms (legal and social rules) are all part of culture. What does culture do? It helps us understand each other and our relationship to the social environment. It also makes social interaction possible, and shapes or guides it. Where does culture come from? It is learned during the process of socialization—a process of learning patterns of culture such as norms and values. What happens if an individual is not socialized by his/her parents or others to learn and internalize his/her society's culture? Studies of individuals raised in isolation from others show that they cannot communicate or function effectively as human beings. It is through the process of socialization, then, that we become human, and our culture is so much a part of us that we take it for granted.

Social structure refers to the partly independent and partly interdependent social groupings (e.g., gender, race/ethnic, age, income, educational, religious) and institutions (e.g., legal, economic, familial, governmental, political) that exist in a society. When sociologists talk about the **structural location/position** of individuals, they are referring to membership in social groups and/or participation in institutions, and membership and participation are usually framed in terms of social roles.

With these considerations in mind, sociology may be defined as an independent social science whose subject matter is society, its culture, social groupings, the institutions that form its constituent parts, and its social structure. According to sociologist C. Wright Mills (1959: 11), to possess the **sociological imagination** one must be "fully aware of the idea of social structure," capable of analyzing the many linkages between different structural parts (e.g., membership in a specific race/ethnic group and membership among the unemployed), and adept at tracing linkages between membership in a social grouping and individual suffering (e.g., membership of the female gender group and rape). In other words, exercising the sociological imagination means appreciating that understanding society requires a grasp of the interplay of social structure and individuals, or, as Peter Berger (1963) points out, seeing the general in the particular.

In Mills' idea of the sociological imagination, however, culture is ignored and social structure is emphasized. Thus Mills, and many who followed him, formulated structural explanations of social problems. But other sociologists, such as Kitsuse and Spector (1973), emphasize cultural influences in their **social constructionist theories** of social problems, while some sociologists include both culture and structure in their explanation of social problems (e.g., Dobash and Dobash, 1979). And then there are others, like Giddens (1991) and Messerschmidt (1993), who make room for **human agency** in their theories of society and social problems. For example, they see individuals as agents who actively attempt to resist, evade, avoid, and change cultural and structural forces that they find more constraining than liberating.

As you can see, there are different ways to exercise the sociological imagination, each emphasizing different aspects of the role of culture, individual agency, and social structure in understanding society and its problems.

What Is a Social Problem?

A Common Sense Definition-Image

On the first day of class, when we ask our students to identify some major social problems they usually provide us with a long list of other problems in addition to those mentioned in the introduction to this chapter. These frequently include pollution/global warming, substance abuse, street youth gangs, and AIDS. We then ask students to explain why these are social problems, and to indicate who is responsible for them. The students' usual answer is that the items on their lists should be defined as social problems because of the harm they inflict on large numbers of people, and that responsibility rests with the individuals involved.

Among those they hold responsible for social problems, students typically discriminate between the "bad" (e.g., rapists, polluters, and child abusers) and the "sick" (e.g., drug addicts, alcoholics, and the mentally ill). At the same time, many students attribute some pathology to members of both groups. In other words, they maintain that there is "something wrong" with these individuals. Typical "common sense" responses to our questions, then, yield the following definition-image of a social problem: An event or outcome caused by some pathological individuals who inflict suffering on many people.

Not surprisingly, the notions that pathological individuals are the cause of social problems, and that widespread suffering indicates the presence of a social problem, are central to the definition-image of social problems held by most North Americans. This includes those who are in a position to make and enforce laws (e.g., politicians and police officers), the popular news media, social scientists who attempt to explain human behavior (e.g., psychologists), and those who help individuals who are suffering (e.g., counselors, mental health therapists, and social workers). As you have no doubt guessed already, however, this perspective differs from the approach taken by sociologists.

Social Definitions and Images

Sociologists offer alternative definition-images of social problems. One of the most widely cited appears in C. Wright Mills' (1959) book *The Sociological Imagination*, and includes three noteworthy points. First, Mills distinguished between the suffering of an individual person, which he called a **private trouble**, and the suffering of many individuals, sometimes on a recurring or continuing basis, which he referred to as a **public issue**. For Mills, public issues—not private troubles—are social problems. Thus, while a psychologist would focus on the great stress and personal anxiety experienced by an unemployed person, a sociologist would typically focus on high rates of unemployment, the impact on society of unemployment, and its causes (see Chapter 3). This does not mean that sociologists ignore personal suffering, but rather that they seek to understand the relationship between personal suffering and larger social structures and processes.

This leads us to the second point, that historical, contemporary global, and societal factors are responsible for the presence of public issues (social problems) in societies like ours. Put simply, the causes of social problems are social and not individual.

A third point made by Mills is that power influences the course of history as well as the distribution of income and wealth in society. Specifically, some social groups own or control more resources (such as wealth, political influence, the media, or property) than others, and working together as a "power elite," they help create and maintain unequal social arrangements or conditions that serve their own interests. Hence, social problems are the intended or unintended consequences of these unequal arrangements.

Since 1959, Mills' definition-image of social problems has been accepted and built on by some sociologists, and rejected in favor of an alternative one by others. Let's first of all look at some of the important contributions of those who build on Mills' basic ideas.

Building on Mills: Subjectivity, Inclusiveness, and the Role of the Individual

Sociologists influenced by Mills built on his work by doing three things. They

> included a subjective element in their objective definitions of social problems;

> broadened the idea of power and inequality to include gender and race/ethnicity; and

> avoided the hazard of claiming that social structure determines everything by acknowledging that individuals have the ability to influence events.

Like Mills, the average person and many sociologists associate significant psychological and physical suffering with the existence of a social problem. But as we alluded to earlier in this chapter, this raises the question of exactly how much is significant. In addition, is it possible for most people to agree on the level of harm that should be enough to call something a social problem? Is there such a thing as an objective (meaning neutral or unbiased) definition of social problems?

Certainly sociologists often attempt to make objective measurements of suffering caused by social problems—they count admissions to hospitals, the number of homeless, the number and types of violent crime victims (see Chapter 5), and so on. However, as Eitzen and Bacca Zinn (1997) point out, we must go beyond Mills by acknowledging that even these so-called objective measures contain a subjective element. That is, widespread suffering indicates the presence of a social problem only because it deviates from a social norm or standard that the sociologist embraces and shares with certain others. Widespread suffering indicates a social problem because such suffering violates the moral norm that says there ought to be less suffering in the world. But making a moral decision to call such violations social problems is a subjective process, because it goes on in the minds and hearts of sociologists and those who share their outlook on what society ought to look like. Thus, people from different walks of life, with different values (conceptions of the desirable) and who are guided by different norms (rules or standards) will make different subjective decisions about the amounts and types of suffering they call social problems. We therefore need to keep in mind that the definition of a social problem depends on the moral and social stances of those who do the defining. As such, it is a political undertaking, involving a conscious decision to take a position on what our society ought to look like.

Following Mills, sociologists such as Curran and Renzetti (1996), Eitzen and Bacca Zinn (1997), Wilson (1973), and Ylló (1993) identified power and inequality as societal causes of social problems. However, they have gone beyond Mills' ideas about the nature of power and inequality (discussed below) by asking us to take seriously the role and interplay of factors such as social class, gender, and race/ethnicity in our consideration of social problems. For these scholars, then, power and inequality can take many different, and sometimes complex, forms.

Sociologists such as Eitzen and Bacca Zinn (1997), and Giddens (1985) also argue that human beings are not simply "puppets on a string" manipulated by forces beyond their control. They maintain that we have greater freedom from external (societal) influences on our behavior than Mills thought. That is to say, they allow for human agency in their definition-images of social life generally, and of social problems in particular. Assuming that individuals are agents means assuming that they have plans and motives, that they attribute meanings to actions and events, and that they do not simply experience suffering as a private trouble, but try to do something about it. Doing something about it includes both individual attempts to prevent, alleviate, resist, and avoid suffering, as well as forming or joining social movements which focus on changing the conditions that cause suffering.

Rejecters: Reality Is Socially Constructed

Collectively, rejecters are known as **social constructionists**. In contrast to those who acknowledge that the process of defining and studying social problems involves political decisions, constructionists claim that such decisions should not influence the sociological enterprise. They reject Mills' definition-image of social problems because it places objectively harmful conditions at its core, and ignores the fact that all we know about these conditions is what claims-makers such as the media, government officials, spokespersons for social movements, policy makers, and social scientists tell us about them. In short, they argue that it is more important to study how people "collectively construct" problems and solutions than it is to understand them as objective phenomena. Assuming that knowledge about the social world is socially constructed, then, constructionists

➤ regard objective social conditions as relatively unimportant;

➤ emphasize subjective judgments in the definition of a condition as a social problem;

➤ define social problems as a process of making claims about putative (supposed) social conditions; and

➤ attempt to explain claims and claims-making and not the social conditions referred to by claims-makers.

The above four elements appear in Kitsuse and Spector's (1973) influential social constructionist definition-image of social problems. They focus on the process of defining a condition as a social problem, and are interested neither in whether, nor to what degree, the condition of suffering objectively exists. Thus, Kitsuse and Spector (1973: 409) define social problems as "the activities of groups making assertions of grievances and claims with respect to some putative conditions." The process to which they refer is a subjective one involving the meanings, values, and judgments of those who make claims and those who make conflicting claims. A constructionist theory of social problems, then, attempts to explain the "emergence and maintenance of claims-making and responding activities" (1973: 409). Put differently, constructionist theorists are interested in the process and manner by which people construct images and definitions of social problems.

Official attitudes towards marijuana use during the 1930s provide a good example of the process of defining (or socially constructing) a supposed social condition as a social problem. During the 1930s, a variety of concerns (including organized crime) competed for recognition as social problems, and a number of government agencies (claims-makers) competed for government funds. One of these agencies was the Federal Bureau of Investigation (FBI), which helped make and promote *Reefer Madness*, a film that portrayed the marijuana user as a crazed musician-addict who would kill to satisfy his lust for the "noxious weed" that "destroyed" individuals, families, schools, and communities. Helping to make and promote this film was part of the FBI's strategy to obtain recognition and a larger share of government funding for itself. If suffering was implicated here, it had more to do with the suffering of the FBI (e.g., if its funding was reduced, or its activities taken over by other agencies) than with the suffering of marijuana users and their alleged victims. The FBI "constructed" a social problem for its own benefit, and from the constructionist point of view, what is important is why and how it did so, not whether there was, in fact, a "marijuana problem."

Is it possible to use a definition-image of social problems that integrates the arguments of builders and constructionists? We believe so. However, we think that these two approaches make a greater contribution to understanding different aspects of social problems if they are not integrated. After all, their proponents are interested in different aspects of social problems, and they want to describe, explain, and do something about different kinds of things. For example, those who formulate objective definitions focus on objective conditions of suffering, while those who formulate subjective-process definitions focus on what people (claims-makers) say, how claims emerge, what people (claims-makers) say about social conditions in attempting to transform them into social problems, and what determines the relative success or failure of claims-making activities.

In sum, Mills and those who build on his ideas take the position that a social problem is a condition of widespread suffering whose source can be traced to society's social arrangements. The social constructionists reject Mills' objective definition, and concentrate on the subjective process of defining and creating social problems. We take the view that each definition-image is useful to the degree to which it is appropriate for answering the questions that a researcher asks.

Sociological Theories of Social Problems

Why do the social problems included in this text exist in North America? Your answer to that question will reveal your theoretical perspective on social problems in the United States and Canada. If you say that the problems exist because of inequalities, then your viewpoint is similar to ours. In fact, we take the position that the vast majority of social problems in North America are best understood as stemming from inequality of power. In the following section, we present an overview of the main ideas of this power/inequality perspective. We then provide a summary of some major theoretical approaches in sociology, aspects of which both compete with and enhance the power/inequality position.

We also want to make you aware of an important distinction. Aggregates such as bureaucracies, classes, and gender groups represent a macro-level of reality, while individuals constitute a micro-level of social reality. Thus, power/inequality theories which explain the behavior of individuals in terms of their membership in one or more interdependent aggregates are called macro theories. For example, a macro theory of gender inequality links gender hierarchy in work places (e.g., males earn more and hold higher positions of authority than females) to gender inequality favoring male partners in households, and gender inequality in households to rates of male violence towards their female partners.

Micro power/inequality theories focus on individuals. They attempt to explain how and why individuals take advantage of the opportunities presented by virtue of their membership in one or more interdependent aggregates (e.g., households, workplaces), and resist, evade, avoid, maintain, or try to change their situations if they experience them as harmful or too constraining. Thus, a micro theory of gender inequality links the exercise of greater male power in the home (e.g., control of access to the television set) to the maintenance of gender hierarchy in workplaces and society as a whole. This home-leisure situation is one of many in which males and females interact in ways that help maintain male dominance (Walker, 1996), a problem many sociologists refer to as **patriarchy**, and which is discussed later in this chapter.

A Power/Inequality Perspective

Karl Marx (1818–1883) and Max Weber, (1864–1920) are two of sociology's founding scholars, who influenced the development of several important sociological theories of power and inequality in contemporary societies. It is to Marx's influence that we turn first.

The Influence of Marx

Marx's general sociological theory helps us understand the relation between the economy, class conflict, and a myriad of issues of major interest to sociologists who study social problems.

One important goal of Marx's general sociological theory is to provide a scholarly account of, and to help create, the economic and political conditions necessary for individuals to rediscover and realize their essential selves. This is because he felt, and tried to demonstrate, that **capitalism**, with its major class divisions and antagonistic class relations, inequality, and exploitation of both human labor and nature in the interests of capital accumulation, dehumanizes, alienates, and "denatures" human beings. For Marx, achieving full humanity could only be attained in a socialist society characterized by the absence of private property, the eradication of inequality based on private property, and the replacement of capitalism's highly developed and specialized division of labor with a system in which each individual performs a variety of occupational and other social roles (Marx, 1863). **Socialism** would permit the realization of Marx's image of humanity, whereas capitalism denied this image. Marx's general theory is, among other things, an attempt to replace capitalism with socialism by showing how historical trends and laws make such a transformation inevitable.

Marx's is also a **historical materialist theory**, based on "observations and an accurate description of real conditions" (Bottomore et al., 1983: 206). This approach allows us to grasp the role of historical factors and circumstances that have conditioned social life today.

The starting point of Marx's general social theory is the premise that "man must be in a position to live (obtain food, clothing, shelter) in order to be able to make history" (1939: 7). We must produce to exist, so understanding how we produce, and the relationships we enter into when we produce at any given time in history, are both central to understanding human societies, including the social problems they generate. This premise is the basis of Marx's approach to issues like class formation, class conflict, and social change. Thus, his account is one that explains human nature, the origins and functions of ideas, classes, class conflict, and social problems by pointing to the way an economic system works, and to the consequences for people who live and work within that system.

More specifically, the theory may be stated as follows: scarcity motivates human labor. For much of our early history, human labor did not produce goods and services beyond what people needed to consume. As human skills, knowledge, materials and social organization improved, human labor was able to produce a surplus beyond the needs of immediate consumption. In pre-capitalist or "tributary societies," rulers used force or the threat of force to take the surplus away from those who helped produce it. Gradually, this system gave way to mercantilism, in which rulers were replaced by a new class of people—merchants—who took away such surplus, returned some of it in the form of taxes to the state, and enjoyed the protection of laws guaranteeing the right to private property.

Eventually, mercantilism was replaced by capitalism. Capitalists owned the means of production. These are the types of tools and machines, types of labor (e.g., slaves or wage laborers), and types of institutions (e.g., farms, factories, etc.) found in different economic contexts (Lynch and Groves, 1989). Capitalists appropriated most of the surplus, and used much of it to achieve even greater surpluses in the future by reinvesting it in their enterprises, a process called capital accumulation. The **state** benefited from this by obtaining increased revenues. In return, it coordinated capitalist activities and interests and created and enforced laws supportive of capitalism. What the workers and capitalists thought about their respective situations in life and their relation to each other was determined by where each group stood in relation to the means of production. In addition to the power they gain from their close connections with the state and their control over the means of production, capitalists also rely on their ability to control the means of communication so that they can conceal from the working class (those who do not own the means of production) the real material reasons for their situation in life. Thus, capitalists help to create and propagate **ideological forms of consciousness** (false consciousness) that justify capitalism to capitalists and workers alike.

Ownership and non-ownership of the means of production divides society into two major classes: capitalists and workers. Although Marx did not see any significant role for the middle classes in society, this is understandable since at the time he wrote there was no large middle class. Moreover, he could not have foreseen the growth of a class of people who were neither fully working class, nor fully capitalist. Today, there continues to be debate over whether the middle class is being "pulled" into the working class, is becoming part of the capitalist class, or whether both processes are occurring (Alvi, 1994b). Regardless of the role of the middle classes in capitalist society, for Marx the issue boiled down to the ultimate conflict between the two most important "great hostile camps"—the working class and the capitalist class.

Marx argues, however, that because of contradictions endemic to capitalism, capitalists would become their own grave-diggers.[1] For example, by massing workers in factories, capitalists unwittingly facilitated worker communication and the awareness that they were all in the same situation. With the development of this "class consciousness," conflicts between workers and individual capitalists would be transformed into class conflicts between workers and capitalists generally. Capitalists, Marx predicted, would not voluntarily relinquish control of an economic system that generated massive inequality in wealth and standard of living. They would be willing to use force to prevent social change. For their part, the workers would come to see revolutionary violence as being the only way of creating a radically transformed, more egalitarian, socialist society. The result would be the revolution of the working class, which the workers would eventually win.

Marx's influence is evident in the theories of sociologists who

➤ believe that an understanding of social classes and class interests is central to an understanding of inequality in capitalist societies;

➤ identify ownership/control of economic production as the determinant of social class; and

➤ argue that people are unconsciously influenced and constrained by values and ideas learned in their particular social group and cannot always exercise free will.

Are the two central classes discussed above the only important players in capitalist social systems? According to contemporary sociologists, the answer is no, particularly when we consider the important role played by the state in alleviating (and sometimes creating) social problems. For example, governments, which are one component of the state, create laws, policies, and programs which are usually portrayed as rational responses to social problems. But often, from the point of view of some sociologists, such actions create more problems than they solve. Thus, we need to consider the roles and functions of the state in modern society if we are to have a wider understanding of social problems and what is to be done about them.

Power/Inequality Models of the State

Although he did not offer a systematic study of the state, Marx influenced many contemporary sociologists who do study it. One of his most influential ideas is known as **instrumentalism**, which is rooted in a classic statement made by he and Engels: "The executive of the modern state is but a committee for managing the common affairs of the whole bourgeoisie" (1975: 82). Miliband (1969) is one prominent social theorist who nourished and elaborated upon this assertion. Miliband's starting point is his opposition to the **structural functionalist** model of the state. Structural functionalists think of the state as a neutral referee mediating the competition between a number of interest groups.[2] No single group exerts a predominant influence on the state, because the state itself ensures that power is diffused across various interest groups or power blocs.

In contrast to the structural functionalist perspective, Miliband contends that there is a class grouping in which most power is concentrated, and that the state actively promotes the interests of this group. For Miliband (1969: 54), the state consists of "the government, the administration, the military, the police, the judicial branch, the subcentral government, and parliamentary assemblies. The interrelations among these institutions form "the state system," and the state, or state system, is subordinate to the ruling class. In other words, Miliband views the state as a tool or instrument (hence the term "instrumentalism") used by the ruling class to promote its financial interests and maintain its control over the disenfranchised. The ruling class is "a fact of life in advanced capitalist societies." The "fact" Miliband refers to is this: "The vast majority of men and women are governed, represented, administered, judged and commanded in war by people drawn from other, economically and socially superior and relatively distant classes" (1969: 67). Although few in number, the ruling class owns most of the property, wealth, and income in society. Capitalist societies characterized by a ruling class are also characterized by vast economic, political, and social inequality.

To support their argument that the state works at the command (or behest) of the ruling class, instrumental Marxists such as Miliband (1969) and Quinney (1974) point to the similar social origins of business and state elites.[3] The individuals who run large businesses and state bureaucracies are in many ways the same people. They come from the same privileged backgrounds, intermarry, go to the same schools, share the same ideologies, and have the same financial goals. In short, they belong to the same class—the ruling class. Naturally, according to instrumental Marxists, state elites are going to make sure that the state intervenes in economic affairs in ways that promote the interests of business. This remains so, even when the state passes laws which on the surface may appear to be against business interests, such as workers' compensation laws, or workers' health and safety regulations.

From an instrumental perspective, then, laws, and their origin and functioning, represent ways of protecting and furthering the long-term interests of the ruling class. If the state does not actually act at the behest of the capitalist ruling class, it "does act autonomously on its behalf" (Miliband, 1983: 64).[4]

Some readers, especially if they belong to labor unions or know others who do, are likely to find instrumental Marxist arguments problematic or even extreme. They might be asking themselves why, if the state only serves to protect the interests of the ruling class, so many people have collective bargaining rights, and are allowed to create and join unions. Don't unions and collective bargaining challenge the interests of the ruling class? They certainly do, and thus—contrary to the instrumentalist position—periodically the working class does have considerable influence on the state (Lynch and Groves, 1989).

Another challenge to the instrumentalist position is that, although they are extremely lenient, there are regulatory laws seemingly designed to curb corporate wrongdoing. If the state were truly a handmaiden to the ruling class, such legislation would not exist. Further, in North America, laws exist to safeguard human rights, to set minimum wage standards, to protect the environment, to promote workers' safety, and so on—none of which are in the financial interests of the propertied class (DeKeseredy and Schwartz, 1996). Because of these and other criticisms,[5] instrumental Marxist theories of the state are no longer popular.

In response to the above and other criticisms of instrumental Marxist theories of the state, several theorists developed **structural Marxism**, an alternative Marxist explanation of the state. Structural Marxists, such as Althusser (1971), Poulantzas (1973), Balbus (1977), and Chambliss and Seidman (1982), argue that the state is not simply a tool or instrument of the ruling class. Although they acknowledge some link between the state and the interest of corporate elites, they view the state as relatively independent from individual capitalists. In other words, to protect the long-term interests of capitalism, the state must occasionally act against the short-term interests of particular members of the ruling class (Gold et al., 1975).

We pointed out that some laws work against ruling class interests. For example, health and safety legislation and other laws designed to improve work conditions do, to a certain extent, improve workers' material conditions. However, structural Marxists argue that these laws are primarily strategies used by the capitalist state in its attempt to resolve conflicts between the ruling and working classes, reproduce the existing capitalist system, and maintain social harmony (O'Connor, 1973; Poulantzas, 1973; Smandych, 1985). Moreover, legislation that obstructs the overriding goals of capitalist elites is weak. For example, while there are regulatory laws supposedly designed to curb corporate violence against workers, thousands of people are still either killed or injured in the workplace because corporate executives continue to avoid formal sanctions (Ellis and DeKeseredy, 1996; Frank and Lynch, 1992; Reasons et al., 1981; Reiman, 1998). When business elites are punished, they typically receive fines, which is not an effective means of forcing them to comply with health and safety legislation. Rather, these penalties are viewed as simply the "cost of doing business" (Hinch, 1994).

In sum, structural Marxists contend that to preserve the capitalist political economic order, and also to generate an image of itself as an "honest broker" between the ruling and working classes, the state creates weak laws that give disenfranchised people a sense or impression that their voices are being heard.

However, in reality, such legal reforms offer "no significant impediment to the accumulation of capital and the continuation of the capitalist system" (Hinch, 1992: 279).

Although some variations of the structural Marxist perspective have considerable empirical support,[6] it has several shortcomings. For example, structuralists have not adequately documented the state's short-term neutrality and long-term bias (Sheley, 1985). Further, while structural Marxists use the concept of relative autonomy of the state from the ruling class to explain many things, they have not really explained how it is determined, or what factors create it (Comack and Brickey, 1991).

The Influence of Weber

Weber shared Marx's concern about the negative consequences of capitalism, but felt that there were other factors that should be considered in the analysis of societies and their problems.

The influence of Max Weber is evident in the theories of those who

➤ believe that an understanding of inequality is central to an understanding of capitalist society but who insist that, in addition to social classes, other sources of social inequality such as political, bureaucratic, gender, race/ethnicity, and educational ("credentials") groupings should also be taken into account;

➤ emphasize **verstehen**: an approach to understanding social life which stresses empathy with the individuals being studied. The word itself means "understanding from within," and implies that we can more fully grasp social reality by trying to understand it from the point of view of those who experience it;

➤ see the relative power of social groupings in zero-sum terms; that is, the gains of the more powerful groups are always at the expense of the less powerful groups;

➤ associate the power of a dominant social grouping with its ability to exclude members of subordinate groupings from access to power resources, and the power of a subordinate group with its ability to take or claim such resources; and

➤ emphasize human agency. In other words, they assume individuals have religious and other ideas, as well as values and norms that are independent of their class position, and are human agents who attempt to understand their situation and behave in the light of that understanding.

The theoretical approach used to understand social problems in this text focuses on the nature and consequences of power inequalities in North American society. As Weberians point out, property and credentials are effective weapons in the social struggle to maintain inequality because they are supported by laws and professional rules that governments enforce through policing and licensing. Moreover, while the exercise of power can take many shapes and forms, people are capable of struggling—and often do struggle—either individually or collectively against the forces that constrain and condition their lives.

As Marxists argue, class position, based on the control or ownership of capital that produces goods, services, and jobs is also central to an understanding of inequality in North America. But they also remind us that we must consider the role of the state (which includes, but is not restricted to, government) in reproducing class and other forms of power/inequality by virtue of its commitment to reproducing the social conditions (through law-making or law enforcement for instance) in which inequality may continue.

In concluding this section, we offer the following caution. The power/inequality perspective we have just discussed is obviously not the only theoretical perspective that can be applied to the analysis of social problems. However, our partiality to this perspective stems from the belief that it is sociology's role to reduce, and even eliminate, the harm caused by many social problems, and that a power/inequality framework lends itself well to this task.

In addition, one of the great strengths of sociology is its ability to challenge "common sense" views of social problems by illuminating aspects of society that might otherwise be ignored or undervalued. We contend that a power/inequality perspective supported by quantitative and qualitative evidence can best help us to uncover and understand the too often neglected role of everyday realities, such as gender, race/ethnicity, and social class, in creating and perpetuating social problems.

Nevertheless, other sociologists have applied different perspectives, such as variations of structural functionalism, symbolic interactionism, and feminist theories to the study of social problems, and some of these, particularly feminist theories, have made important contributions to the goal of eliminating the human troubles discussed in this text. In the next few sections we review these three important contemporary sociological perspectives, and in Chapters 2 to 9, we include them where they are noteworthy and relevant. These inclusions broaden your knowledge and provide a sounder basis for critically evaluating theoretical perspectives, both ours and others'.

Structural Functionalism[7]

Emile Durkheim is viewed by many sociologists as the founder of **structural functionalism**. Four ideas are central to Durkheim's sociological perspective. First, human beings are essentially egoistic, that is, their wants always exceed the means available to satisfy them. According to Durkheim (1951: 248), "The more one has, the more one wants, since satisfactions received only stimulate instead of filling needs." Because they are exclusively interested in satisfying their own individual wants and will do anything to satisfy wants that are always increasing, it is not possible to have a stable society composed solely of rampant egoists. They will routinely rob, deceive, and kill each other in order to satisfy escalating psychological and material wants. Imagine what our society would be like if it were composed solely not of patient, trouble-free Maytag salespersons, but only of infants whose every psychological and material want had to be instantly and continuously satisfied without regard for the wants of others.

Second, the basis of social order is shared values and norms. That is to say, egoism is effectively regulated when all of us are assumed to believe that it is wrong to sell crack and to beat, kill, and rob others. These values and norms are learned and preserved through interaction with others who advocate them.

Third, in more or less obvious ways, most, if not all, regularly occurring activities, such as going to church, playing sports, committing crimes, and working, continue to exist in society because they contribute to the stability of society. They are, in other words, functional or good for society as a whole. This is why they continue to exist.

Finally, because Durkheim was a structural functionalist, he viewed society as similar to a biological organism. In a perfectly working body, all of the parts work together to provide health. A great body with a broken-down heart is in big trouble. In the same way, North American society consists of many interdependent parts that give it equilibrium. For example, families, schools, criminal justice systems, churches, and other institutions all help to maintain a balanced system. Changing one or more of these parts will change the others; however, the direction of change is usually towards restoring equilibrium or dealing with the disturbances caused by social change.

Durkheim's functionalism, his consensual assumptions, definitions, theory, and research methods have been subjected to a number of criticisms. For example, some sociologists have attacked Durkheim for viewing people's aspirations as egoistic, contending instead that such behavior is learned. Others find his approach too biological and inherently conservative, and there are those who challenge his emphasis on value consensus (Taylor et al., 1973). For example, research shows many North American citizens are sharply divided on issues such as recreational drug use, restrictive firearms legislation, abortion, capital punishment, and U.S. military involvement in the Persian Gulf (DeKeseredy and Schwartz, 1996). Still, many sociologists have found Durkheim an important resource for developing their own work (e.g., Merton, 1938; Pearce, 1989). Regardless of how sociologists interpret his writings, Durkheim unquestionably influenced some of the contemporary theories reviewed throughout this text.

Structural Functionalist Theory: Some Contemporary Examples[8]

Included among the best known sociological examples of the use of structural functionalist theory to interpret recurring types of social problems are Davis' (1937) work on prostitution, and Polsky's (1969) theory of pornography. The starting point for both is this paradoxical finding: in most societies in which they exist, prostitution and pornography are regarded as stigmatized, illegitimate forms of sexual expression. How can they continue to exist when they are condemned? Because, according to these theorists, they perform an important function for society by permitting the expression of antisocial or illegitimate sex.

Their functional argument proceeds as follows. Men's sexual urges are not inherently social. Rather, they cater to individual satisfaction. Left to themselves, men would flit from one woman to the next, and, with each, they would engage in all manner of sexual acts that would produce pleasure for them, but not necessarily children for society. Children mean responsibilities, and responsibly cared for children ensure the continuance of society. If children are to be properly socialized, something has to be done about regulating man's egotistical sexual inclinations.

Their societal solution is to connect sexual inclinations and social, familial responsibilities by making a broad distinction between legitimate and illegitimate sex. Legitimate sex is confined to a married partner and (within marriage) to sexual activities that are most likely to lead to procreation. But man's quest for new partners and novel sexual experiences remains as strong as ever. These illegitimate forms of sex also need to be expressed. They help "drain off" antisocial urges, and in this way enable men to bear the social burdens imposed on them by confining legitimate sex to the "missionary position" with a married partner. While prostitution provides directly for sex with other women, pornography provides for the vicarious enjoyment of various kinds of forbidden but desired sexual activities. In sum, prostitution and pornography are functional for society because, by permitting the expression of antisocial sex, they act as a safety valve and so help keep families together.

This analysis, offered by two male sociologists, might suggest that prostitution and pornography are not really functional for society as a whole, but only for half of it—the male half. This may be true; however, some feminists have extended the functional analysis of pornography to include women. Consider Gronau (1985), a feminist scholar who asserts that feminists should not support censorship of pornography, even its violent forms. Rather, they should be strongly against it. Why? Because pornography is functional for women. According to Gronau (1985), it serves to remind them of the rampant sexism that victimizes and exploits them. If pornography is censored, the evidence of sexism is hidden. It is more difficult to mobilize women to fight against hidden sexism than it is to fight the obvious and extreme form of sexism manifested in pornography. Pornography, then, is functional for women. Censorship has harmful consequences and is therefore "dysfunctional" for them. It should be noted, however, that this functional conception of pornography as being of benefit to women represents a minority view among feminists who have written on the topic.[9]

Symbolic Interactionism[10]

Some of the theories described in this text (e.g., Becker's labelling theory) are derived from **symbolic interactionist theory**, a major sociological school of thought developed by George Herbert Mead (1934). Whereas Durkheim answered the question "How is society possible?" by identifying the social control of rampant egoism as a necessary condition, Mead and other interactionists' answers emphasize shared meanings. Symbolic interactionists argue that

"Human actions are best understood in terms of the meaning that those actions have for the actors, rather than in terms of pre-existing biological, psychological, or social conditions. These meanings are to some extent created by the individual, but primarily they are derived from intimate personal interactions with people" (Vold and Bernard, 1986: 250).

According to Mead, via the process of socialization, human beings gradually learn the meanings, the descriptions, and evaluations that constitute their symbolic universe. Central to this process is the emergence of the social self or "self-as-object-to-itself." Socialized individuals, those in whom this kind of self has emerged, have acquired the ability to describe and evaluate themselves in the same way that others describe and evaluate them. The source of the social self, then, is the reaction of others—we tend to see ourselves as others see us. Moreover, the way we see ourselves influences the way we behave. Usually, individuals tend to behave in ways that are consistent with their self-images.

We can use the metaphor of multi-player games such as ice hockey, football, or soccer, to better understand symbolic interactionism. Mead's game has one important and distinctive property: in the course of interacting with each other, self-images and the rules of the game may be changed. New self-images and rules may be created, some rules applied, others not. Thus, Mead's game is flexible and has a creative, evolving quality to it. Simply examining the game's rules as they appear in the Rule Book will not tell you very much about how the game is actually played or the course of the game. Games like ice hockey have an emergent quality to them, and the process of emergence must be studied directly. The game's structure, its rules, and its competitive values should be taken into account, but the primary focus of analysis is the process of symbolic interaction. The large, many-player game called society emerges out of, and can be changed by, the symbolic interaction that takes place among individuals in such small scale settings as homes, schools, workplaces, churches, and so on. Indeed, as symbolic interactionists concentrate on such small scale settings, their approach falls into the category of micro sociology.

Most sociologists who adopt a social-psychological, symbolic-interactionist approach to the study of social problems in these settings work with a set of sensitizing concepts bequeathed them by Mead. These include interaction, symbols, meanings, process, emergence, and self-concept. A few have borrowed concepts formulated by other theorists, and some have tried to combine Mead's micro-sociological approach with a macro-societal one.

Symbolic Interactionist Theory: A Contemporary Example

Edwin Lemert's (1951) perspective on primary and secondary deviance is one of the most widely read and cited examples of a symbolic interactionist theory, an approach that emphasizes the consequences of labelling or stigmatization. According to Lemert, primary deviance is "situational" or opportunistic, and everyone, at one time or another, commits primary deviant or criminal acts. Not only does primary deviance occur occasionally, but it is also regarded as excusable by the individual who engages in this behavior either because it is just one of those things that sometimes happens (like getting drunk) or because it's just something that goes with the job or other perfectly acceptable social roles. Consider police officers who occasionally accept free coffee and meals from restaurant owners in their patrol areas. The officers know that accepting free gifts is prohibited by police rules, but they accept them anyway, because "all the guys do it." They also believe that it is little enough to accept, in return for putting their lives on the line to protect the restaurant owner's property (Sherman, 1974). Because these deviations are dealt with as functions of a socially acceptable role, they constitute primary deviance.

Now, suppose a citizen and a regular patron of one of the restaurants serving free meals to police officers reports the matter to the police chief and gets his or her complaint published in the local newspaper. Consequently, three police officers are fired, and two are convicted of accepting free meals as bribes for overlooking the restaurant owner's illegally parked car and his serving beer to minors. Their criminal conviction prevents them from obtaining jobs with other police forces or private security firms. So, they use knowledge gained as police officers to plan and execute their own burglaries and car-theft operation. Following a few arrests and trials but no convictions, they gradually come to see themselves as criminals and construct a number of justifications for their full-time criminal careers. They are now secondary deviants. According to Lemert (1951: 77), their deviation is secondary because they "employ (their) deviant behavior or a role based upon it as a means of defense, attack, or adjustment to the overt and covert problems created by the consequent societal reaction" to their behaviors.

Lemert (1951: 75) contends that sociologists who study deviant behavior should concentrate on secondary deviance and deviants because "deviations are not significant until they are organized subjectively and transformed into active roles and become the criteria for assigning social status." The successful crooked police officers referred to above had a very high status among professional crooks, but very low status among the rest of conformist society.

The differentiation in status referred to here covers both social and moral aspects. In other words, conformist members of society won't socialize with career criminals because they believe it is just wrong for some individuals to make a living using criminal means while most people make a living in an honest way. The social and moral differentiation of secondary (career) deviants from primary or occasional deviants (e.g., most of us) is the outcome of societal reactions to deviance, reactions that result in restricted educational and occupational opportunities and the acquisition of a criminal self-identity.

One of the most outstanding contributions of Lemert's theory and other interactionist perspectives on social problems described in this text is that they invert the "deviance leads to social control relation" (Ellis, 1987). For example, many sociologists contend that imprisonment and other means of punishment are caused by deviance, while interactionists contend that social control is a major cause of deviance. In reversing the traditional view of the deviance-control relation, interactionists opened the way for a sustained examination of a neglected partner in the production of crime and deviance—those who make and enforce the rules.

Still, some sociologists criticize Becker (1973), Lemert (1951), and other interactionists for assuming that societal reactions to deviance, crime, and other social problems occur in vacuums. In other words, they do not explicitly describe the broader structural and cultural forces that influence the criminal justice system's and various other social control agencies' labelling process. Taylor et al. (1973: 168-169), for example, contend that Lemert and other labelling theorists do not "lay bare the structured inequalities in power and interest which underpin processes whereby laws are created and enforced."

Feminist Theory

If you have never taken a sociology course and if this is the first sociology textbook chapter you have ever read, by now you might be saying to yourself, "The sociological study of social problems seems to be dominated by white European or

North American men." This is true. In fact, sociology in general is both **eurocentric** and **androcentric**. The former refers to emphasizing issues that are of primary concern to European and Western societies, while the latter refers to writing and research done from a "male-centered" perspective (Renzetti and Curran, 1998). Nevertheless, since the 1960s, a growing number of sociologists have, and still are, making important feminist contributions to the study of social problems described in this text and other sources. Before we describe some of these contributions, which, by the way, are often grouped by other sociologists under the heading "power/inequality perspectives," it is first necessary to define **feminism**.

What is feminism? Heavily influenced by the media, religious groups, and conservative politicians, many people equate feminism with demonizing or hating men, not shaving one's legs and armpits, going bra-less, being gay or lesbian, and being pro-choice. Of course, some feminists belong to one or more of these groups; but many men and women are feminists. In fact, we, the authors of this text, define ourselves as pro-feminist men. We and other feminists are united by a commitment to put **gender** at the forefront of our analyses of social problems, and by our efforts to eliminate gender inequality. Here, following Schur (1984: 10), gender "refers to the sociocultural and psychological shaping, patterning, and evaluating of female and male behavior." Further, the goal of feminist scholars is "not to push men out so as to pull women in," but rather to "gender" the study of social problems (Renzetti, 1993: 232).

There is no united feminist perspective on social problems and thus it is incorrect to paint all feminists with the same brush. For example, Tong (1989) identifies eight distinct types of feminism, and there are major debates within each brand (Schwartz, 1991). For the purpose of this text, however, we offer Daly and Chesney-Lind's (1988: 502) definition, which refers to feminism as "a set of theories about women's oppression and a set of strategies for change." Feminist perspectives on social problems can be distinguished from nonfeminist or "male-stream" perspectives on the basis of the following shared attributes:[11]

➤ Gender and power are key elements of social problems.

➤ Sex and gender are distinct. Sex is determined by bio-physiology, and the concepts "men" and "women" are used in referring to sex differences. Gender, however, is socially constructed, and the concepts "male" and "female" are used in referring to gender differences.

➤ Gender inequality is viewed as the major cause of the continued oppression and marginalization of women.

➤ Scholarship and research should be used to support women.

➤ Gender and gender relations order social life and social institutions in fundamental ways.

➤ Women should be at the center of the study of social problems, not peripheral, invisible, or appendages to men.

➤ Male social constructions of gender and gender relations, which are unauthentic but useful props for gender inequality, should be replaced with authentic social constructions supporting gender equality.

Again, at least eight variants of feminist theory exist, each of which takes a distinct approach to understanding gender issues, asks different types of questions, and offers different theories of social problems and their control (Beirne and Messerschmidt, 1995). Most textbooks, however, limit their reviews to four widely read and cited perspectives: liberal feminism, Marxist feminism, radical feminism, and socialist feminism. Each of these is briefly described here.

Of all the feminist theories developed so far in North America, liberal feminism is the most widely recognized. **Liberal feminists** assert that women are discriminated against on the basis of their sex, so that they are denied access to the same political financial, career, and personal opportunities as men (Messerschmidt, 1993). Liberal feminists further assert that this problem can be eliminated by removing all obstacles to women's access to education, paid employment, political activity, and other public institutions; having women participate equally with men in the public sphere; and enacting legal change (Daly and Chesney-Lind, 1988: 537).

Marxist feminists contend that class and gender divisions of labor determine male and female positions in any society. But the gender division of labor is viewed as the product of the class division of labor. Since women are seen as being dominated primarily by capital and secondarily by men, the main strategy for change promoted by Marxist feminists is the transformation from a capitalist society to a democratic socialist society (Daly and Chesney-Lind, 1988; Messerschmidt, 1986).

Radical feminists see male power and privilege as the "root cause" of all social relations, inequality, and other social problems. According to radical feminists, "The most important relations in any society are found in patriarchy (institutionalized male dominance which includes masculine control over the labor power and sexuality of women); all other relations (such as class) are secondary and derived from male-female relations" (Beirne and Messerschmidt, 1991: 519). Some strategies for change advanced by radical feminists are overthrowing patriarchal relations; developing biological reproduction technologies that enable women to have sexual autonomy; and creating women-centered social institutions and women-only organizations (Daly and Chesney-Lind, 1988: 538).

Socialist feminism contains some elements of Marxist and radical feminism. For example, class and patriarchy are considered key variables in socialist feminist analyses of social problems. However, neither class nor patriarchy is presumed to be dominant. Rather, class and gender relations are seen as equally important, "inextricably intertwined," and "inseparable," and they interact to determine the social order at any particular time in history (Jaggar, 1983; Messerschmidt, 1986). Socialist feminists argue that "to understand class...we must recognize how it is structured by gender, conversely, to understand gender requires an examination of how it is structured by class" (Beirne and Messerschmidt, 1991: 520). In sum, socialist feminists contend that we are influenced by both class and gender relations, and that strategies for change should simultaneously focus on transforming patriarchal and class relations (Daly and Chesney-Lind, 1988).

Feminist Theory: A Contemporary Example

Russell (1990) is one of many North American feminist scholars who has devoted a substantial amount of time and energy to studying and explaining the abuse of women in intimate, heterosexual relationships. She contends that the primary cause of wife rape in the United States is the unequal division of labor in the patriarchal family. In such a family, the wife is economically dependent on her husband, often even if she has paid employment outside the home. This dependency is exacerbated for women with children and/or for women who lack marketable job skills. If their husbands leave them, they will probably fall into poverty because they are unable to support themselves and their children financially. Consequently, many economically vulnerable women have unwanted sexual relations with their spouses because they fear being abandoned. As Messerschmidt (1986: 142) points out, "A husband may threaten 'his wife' with divorce if she does not 'put out' when he wants her to, and the wife may conclude that unwanted sexual intercourse is not as harmful as the alternative, economic poverty and distress."

Like all the other theoretical perspectives described throughout this text, feminist theories have been criticized on several grounds, and they have been attacked from the left and the right. For example, Gelles (1980), and Gelles and Cornell (1985), refer to radical feminist theories as single-factor explanations that have very little explanatory value in social science.[12] Moreover, Levinson (1989) views theories of patriarchy as political agendas rather than social scientific theories. He also contends that these perspectives are difficult to verify.

Some left-wing scholars have criticized radical feminist theories for assuming a "universal dimension of men's power" (Rice, 1990: 62). For example, some radical feminists see all men as being equally likely to assault female intimates. Although woman abuse certainly occurs in all classes and in all occupations (DeKeseredy and MacLeod, 1997; Schwartz, 1988), most of the empirical literature shows that some groups are more likely than others to produce wife rapists, wife beaters, date rapists, and so on.

Despite the above and other criticisms of feminist theories of social problems, feminist scholars have made many important contributions to the sociological study of social problems, including uncovering and explaining the alarming amount of male-to-female violence and sexual harassment that occurs in North American families, formal institutions, and in public settings. Further, feminists provide a much needed challenge to the ways in which "male stream" sociologists think about their research subjects, as well as the subject of their research (Currie and MacLean, 1994).

How Do Sociologists Gather Social Problems Data?

If you are a sociology major, you will undoubtedly be required to take a methods course. Based on our experience teaching this course, we fully expect you to approach it initially "with the enthusiasm of a recalcitrant patient in a dentist's office. Even if the experience is not going to be painful, it most certainly is not anticipated to be exciting or interesting" (Hagan, 1993: 1). Now, you are probably saying to yourself, "Oh no! What am I in for? Maybe I should change my major." Please don't, because gathering and analyzing social problems data can be fun, exciting, and interesting. In fact, there is nothing that pleases the authors of this text more than "getting our hands dirty" with all kinds of data. Indeed, we always look forward to analyzing the results of our research the same way most people look forward to holidays.

Our goal here is not to make you an expert or an enthusiastic methodologist, but simply to introduce you to the strengths and weaknesses of several sociological research methods. These are: field experimental research; field research; surveys; official or government statistics; historical research; and historical-comparative research. Before we describe and evaluate these methods, however, it is first necessary to describe the criteria sociologists use to assess the soundness of data collection methods.

Reliability and Validity

A reliable method of data collection is one that produces similar results when it is used repeatedly under similar conditions by the same researcher or by different researchers. Consistency is the defining attribute of reliability. Thus, a properly balanced bathroom scale is a reliable measure of the weight of individuals if it yields very similar weight values (pounds/ounces or kilograms/grams) when each person weighs himself or herself on a number of different occasions during the day. Here, replication yields highly consistent results, and, as the scale was properly balanced, the results (weight values) are also highly valid.

A method of data collection which has high validity is one that accurately measures exactly what it is supposed to measure. Thus, an improperly balanced bathroom weigh scale is an invalid method of determining your weight. This remains true even though it may yield very similar weight values when you weigh yourself at different times of the day. In this case, replication yields consistent results, but your true or actual weight is consistently shown to be pounds/kilograms more or less than your actual or true weight.

The reliability and validity of data collection methods in sociological research on social problems can be illustrated by considering the methods used to collect data on childhood aggression. Such validity is determined by consensus. For example, if most researchers who study this topic agree that the method measures both what childhood aggression truly is and its essence, then the method tends to be regarded as having high validity.

What is the core or essence of childhood aggression? What do most people, parents, or researchers point to when they say a child is behaving aggressively? In 1963, two psychologists named Bandura and Walters published the results of a number of experiments on the aggressive behavior of children who were exposed to films with aggressive content. Their hypothesis was that children imitate the aggression they observe. They found that children who observed films with aggressive content were more likely to engage in aggressive behavior than children who did not watch such films. Their measure of the children's aggression was "hitting, punching, or pushing Bobo the Clown."

One major criticism of these experiments was that hitting, punching, or pushing a Bobo the Clown doll was not a valid measure of aggressive behavior. The critics contended that the children who engaged in these activities were not behaving aggressively. Rather, they were only playing. The essence of aggressive behavior is the "intention to hurt or harm," and this, critics stated, could not be inferred from either the children's behavior and demeanor, or the remarks they made while they were "playing with" Bobo the Clown.

Internal and External Validity

The laboratory experimental study of childhood aggression, or any other phenomenon, can be used for the purpose of identifying and differentiating between two important types of validity. These are internal and external validity (Campbell and Stanley, 1963). **Internal validity** refers to research design, methods of data collection, and the measurement and types of data analysis used in a specific study. External validity refers to the generalisability of the findings obtained from a specific study to other individuals, groups, and populations. These two types of validity are related to each other in the following way: methods of study that are high on internal validity tend to be lower on external validity, and methods of study that are high on external validity tend to be lower on internal validity.

Laboratory experimental methods, such as those used by Bandura and Walters (1963), have higher internal validity than non-experimental (e.g., survey) methods because of the high degree of experimenter control over the experimental situation. Thus, they can randomly assign subjects to experimental and treatment groups (thereby eliminating the confounding effects of initial differences between subjects), design and manipulate the treatment variables such as exposure to films with aggressive content, and observe and/or videotape the behavior of the subjects.

On the other hand, the artificiality of the laboratory experimental situation decreases its external validity. Thus, children's aggressive behavior in settings like school playgrounds may be far more strongly associated with what other children do or say to them, or said or did to them earlier in the day, their physical characteristics, whether they have desired money, food, and so on, than on what they saw on television the previous evening.

One way of increasing the validity of the method of collecting data on children's aggression following exposure to films with aggressive and non-aggressive content, would be to show the films at school, just before recess, and then observe and videotape hitting and punching among the children during the recess break. Of course, this would be an unethical thing to do if the researcher believed that exposing children to films with aggressive content would increase the likelihood that they could be injured as a result of being hit or punched.

A survey of a probability (random) sample of school children, using a questionnaire that includes questions on television viewing habits and aggressive behavior would have higher external validity than a laboratory experimental study, because the data collected refer to behavior in natural settings. Moreover, if the sample was randomly selected, the results could be generalized to other groups of children within statistically measurable degrees of error. On the other hand, survey researchers cannot randomly assign subjects to experimental and treatment groups, and they cannot control the exposure of children to films with aggressive content. Hence, they tend to use statistical methods of controlling for factors other than exposure to films with aggressive content, which may account for differences in the frequency and seriousness of children's aggression. Statistical methods of control are not as effective as random assignment in controlling for alternatives to the hypothesized cause of children's aggressive behavior.

Methods of collecting data on violence, poverty, unemployment, health, families, environmental degradation, drug abuse, and technology are described in the chapters that follow, and questions about their reliability and validity may occur to you as you read them. Each study you read should motivate you to ask: "What are the major findings and how were the data collected?"

Field Experimental Research

Psychologists such as Bandura and Walters (1963) and Milgram (1963) conduct laboratory experiments, while sociologists who undertake experimental research tend to carry out **field experimental research**. This type of research is done in natural settings, using an experimental design. Like the laboratory experimenter, the field experimental researcher also uses an experimental design, but usually does not have as much control over the experimental situation. After all, it is easier to control what goes on in a university's psychology department laboratory than in schools, factories, streets, and homes.

During the past 25 years, the results of a number of sociological studies have influenced social policy. Sherman and Berk's (1984) field experiment has had a major influence upon law enforcement policy. This study was specifically designed to test the hypothesis that husbands who had been arrested for committing less serious (misdemeanor) assaults against their wives are less likely to assault them during the six months following their arrest than violent husbands who were not arrested by the police. Instead of arresting them, the police asked one of them, usually the husband, to leave the residence for eight hours or so, or the police gave both the husband and the wife advice (counseling) at the scene of the assault.

Field experimental research like Sherman and Berk's requires that the researcher

➤ undertake research in natural (field) settings;

➤ deliberately and thoughtfully introduce an intervention or change; and

➤ randomly assign interventions to research subjects, or research subjects to interventions.

Sometimes important and interesting results are reported by researchers who do field research and who, for theoretical and/or practical reasons intervene in the lives of their research subjects or participants, but do not randomly assign subjects to interventions. Such researchers are doing quasi (almost) field experimental research. One widely cited study conducted in this manner is Sherif's (1966) work in inter-group conflict, that is, conflict between youth gangs and other social groupings. "The Robbers' Cave" was designed to test "The Hypothesis of Superordinate Goals,"—goals "that are compelling for the groups involved, but cannot be achieved by a single group through its own efforts" (1966: 88).

Note that Sherman and Berk used random assignment in order to eliminate possible biases resulting from administering specific interventions to specific types of wife assaulters. Sherif, however, used "matching" in an attempt to make members of the two subject groups very similar to each other, so that initial differences in the composition of these groups did not play a part in accounting for the findings. In evaluating field experimental studies, you should always try to find out how subjects were assigned to interventions, or interventions to subjects, because the answer has direct implications for both their internal and external validity.

Ethical questions should also be prominent in your evaluation of any research project involving human beings, animals, or the environment, but they are especially salient in field experimental research where the researcher actively intervenes in the lives of human beings.

Advantages and Disadvantages of Field Experimental Research
Advantages include

- ➤ producing findings with relatively high internal and external validity;
- ➤ contributing to the cumulative development of knowledge by providing researchers with studies whose external validity would be well worth checking out because their internal validity has already been established; and
- ➤ producing findings that are more likely to be accepted by policy makers because of the aura of "the scientific method" that surrounds them.

Disadvantages include

- ➤ practical difficulties associated with actually carrying out field experimental research as designed (e.g., Sherman and Berk reported difficulties getting police officers to administer the interventions on a strictly random basis); and
- ➤ ethical considerations which require field experimental researchers to avoid interventions that harm, or may harm, participants in the short or longer run (thus, cocaine cannot be administered to some subjects and marijuana to others to study their relative addictive power, or whether use of the latter leads to use of the former).

Field Research
Field research refers to research conducted in natural settings such as hospitals, schools, families, pool halls, dance clubs, streets, business corporations, courts, army units, and public washrooms. When is it appropriate to use field research? Like any other method, it depends on the types of questions you want answered.

Lofland and Stark (1965), for example, used it in a study of religious conversion. They believed that an adequate test of a theory attempting to explain "what really happens" during the process of religious conversion requires field research on members and prospective members of religious groups in the natural settings (communities, neighborhoods) in which they live, work, socialize, attend meetings, worship, and go to school.

Field research includes two major methods of research—**case studies** and **observation**. Case studies are detailed studies of specific outcomes, events, or processes that occur over varying periods of time. Usually a single case is studied. A variety of data collection methods may be used in conducting case studies and field research generally. These include listening to and engaging in casual conversations, conducting more focused in-depth interviews, reviewing statistics, making tape recordings, taking photographs, making maps, and reading local newspapers, community notices, and records.

Field researchers also observe people, events, and processes. In fact, observation is a data collection method that is used by most, if not all, of them. All field researchers however, do not use the same method of observation. Specifically, some adopt the role of **non-participant observer**—and remain detached from the people, events, and processes they observe. They also value scientific objectivity and believe that remaining detached, that is, adopting the role of a neutral, emotionally uninvolved, outsider, helps them achieve this goal.

Participant observers are researchers who actually participate, albeit to varying degrees, in the lives of the small community or group they are studying. They value the collection of valid data that reveals meanings, feelings, conduct, and codes that constitute the lived experience of the persons they are studying. According to anthropologists Spradley and McCurdy (1975: 59), involvement in the lives of the people being studied helps the field researcher "look at life through their eyes," and to "detach oneself from one's own perspective but not from that of persons whose culture you are studying." Detachment, then, is involved in both non-participant and participant observation, but in a fundamentally different way. In the latter, detachment from one's own perspective and biases facilitates the collection of authentic or valid data. In the former, detachment from the lives of the persons being studied facilitates the collection of more reliable data. Non-participant and participant observation can be, and often are, used sequentially.

According to Spradley and McCurdy (1975), **ethnography** is a third part in the sequence of field research methods that field researchers should, but do not always, use. Instead, they do observation and call it ethnography. Davidson and Layder (1994: 164) define ethnography as being "concerned with the 'discovery' and description of the culture and structure of particular social groups." Ethnographers do at least four things that observers are unlikely to do:

➤ They define as their goal the discovery of the values, norms, and meanings that members of a small community, village, or social group use to organize their relationships with other human beings and the environment. They also use this information to describe how different kinds of relationships (economic, political, familial, religious, legal) are interrelated to form a whole.

➤ Ethnographers rarely, if ever, impose their own meanings, perceptions, values, and norms on members of the communities and groups they are studying.

➤ They are far more likely than observers to be **social cryptographers**, who seek to discover the codes people use in organizing and explaining their behavior.

➤ Ethnographers routinely use observation, especially participant observation, as a research tool to produce ethnographic research reports, but the opposite cannot be true because observation always precedes ethnography.

Field researchers tend to select **non-probability** or **judgmental samples**. This involves gathering, for theoretical or other reasons, in-depth data from members of a specific kind of social group or small community. We cannot statistically measure the degree of error involved in generalizing the findings from non-probability or judgmental samples. Findings based on the use of non-probability samples have lower external validity than those based on the use of representative samples. On the other hand, the intensive analysis of in-depth data on behavior and subjective states (e.g., emotions, meanings, attributions) confers higher internal validity on findings from field research studies using non-probability samples, than on findings from surveys using representative national, regional, or city-wide samples. In evaluating different samples, it is important to approach them with the concept of appropriateness to the problem being studied, instead of the concept of a "winner" in a Best Method context.

Advantages and Disadvantages of Field Research

Advantages include

- offering an understanding of a small social group or community from the per-spective of its members;
- providing in-depth data on complex subjective states and patterns of social in-teraction that cannot be obtained through surveys;
- using it, not only to test theory, but also to develop theories grounded in find-ings with high internal validity; and
- yielding findings whose vividness and graphic detail provide a significant amount of support for useful interventions.

Disadvantages include the facts that it is difficult for the researcher

- to generalize from sample findings to the populations from which the samples were selected;
- to use a larger number of groups or communities to test theory grounded in field research done on one similar group or community; and
- to conduct multivariate statistical analyses requiring a large sample size.

Surveys

What is a **survey**? We define it as a systematic method of collecting data from a relatively large number of individuals. Surveys are widely used, and you have probably participated in at least one at some time. In fact, the survey is the most widely used method in social science (Stark, 1985). The United Nations, national governments, political parties, radio and television stations, trade unions, community groups, business corporations, and university researchers all fund or conduct surveys. The survey is the method most frequently used to collect data on the social problems that we focus on in this text.

Sociological survey researchers start, or should start, with a clearly formulated research problem, one that can be empirical and/or theoretical. Empirical problems are those that can be solved by collecting descriptive survey data, while theoretical problems can be solved by collecting explanatory survey data. Descriptive data are provided by answers to such questions as "who, what, when, where, how often," and "with whom." Explanatory data are provided by answers to "why" and/or "how" questions.

In Chapters 2 to 9, descriptive answers are presented statistically as averages (means, medians), rates (prevalence and incidence), percentage differences, and frequency distributions (see Box 1.1 for how they are calculated). For example, in Chapter 7, Table 7.4 (p. 286), shows that Mexico's annual population growth rate is twice that of the United States; China's population is over four times greater than that of the United States and 10 times greater than that of Mexico; and that the percentage of the population in poverty in the United States is 11 percent, while in Mexico it is 33 percent.

Table 7.4 also gives the findings of a descriptive survey on the use of contraceptives (prevalence rate) in various nations. Here we discover that the Nigerian rate is more than 13 times lower than the Chinese rate, 12 times lower than the rate in the United States, and over 8 times lower than the rate of Mexico.

Advantages and Disadvantages of Surveys
Advantages include

> providing quantitative (numerical) descriptions of society, or segments of it, that help governments make policy decisions, businesses market their products, activist organizations design their reform strategies, and academics interested in undertaking descriptive and explanatory research;

> being more likely to be funded because they yield "hard" (numerical) data favored by funding agencies;

> providing quantitative data revealing broad, society-wide patterns that cannot be discovered by observational studies using qualitative methods; and

> promoting the cumulative development of knowledge when they are used to test theories suggested by qualitative (observational) research, and/or confirm the findings of such research.

Disadvantages include

> the difficulty of establishing causal relations in research into the causes of social problems;

> their relatively high cost;

> their susceptibility to different kinds of error at the design, instrument construction, sampling, data collection, coding, data entry, and data analysis stages;

> the high level of organizational skill needed to carry them out effectively;

> their inappropriateness when the researcher is interested in asking questions that respondents are likely to answer dishonestly because of their feelings of guilt, shame, or anxiety; and

> the relatively superficial data on verbal and non-verbal forms of communication, intentions, motives, contexts, and plans that they produce in comparison with observing, listening and asking questions of participants in natural settings.

BOX 1-1

Rates: Function, Calculation, Definition, Measurement

Function

Rates are often used by social scientists because they help them compare societies or other social groupings that vary in the size of their populations. Specifically, rates take these differences into account.

Calculation

Divide the act, event, or outcome by the population and multiply by a constant. Thus, the formula for calculating a country's crude death rate—a significant source of suffering—is

Death rate = Number of Deaths in 1998 / Population X 1,000

Types of Rates

The *incidence* rate indicates how many new acts, events, or outcomes occurred during a given time period, such as 6 or 12 months.

Example: A survey question measuring the incidence of "date rape."

Question: Did you experience one or more of the following sexual experiences [list of 10] during the past 12 months?"

The *prevalence* rate indicates the total number of persons who reported experiencing specified acts, events, or outcomes during a particular time period.

Example: A survey question measuring the prevalence of "date rape."

Question: Have you experienced one or more of the following [list of 10] sexual experiences since the age of 14?"

Source: Koss (1989: 151–154). From *Violence in Dating Relationships: Emerging Social Issues*, edited by Pirog-Good and J.E. Stets. Copyright © 1989 by Praeger. Reproduced with permission of Greenwood Publishing Group, Inc., Westport, CT.

Official (Government) Statistics

Official statistics are statistics collected, coded, tabulated, and disseminated by agencies of national (federal) and local (state, provincial) governments. Statistics published by the governments of Canada, Mexico, and the United States are the major sources of data on social problems in North America. In fact, these governments publish statistics on all of the social problems covered in this text.

In analyzing and evaluating findings and conclusions based on government statistics, it is important to remember that such data, like other statistics, are socially produced. That is to say, government statisticians talk to each other and to agencies that provide them with the raw data about what a particular issue (e.g., health) is, what should be counted, and how it should be classified or categorized. Any given statistic, then, is the result of interaction between representatives of agencies engaged in its production.

The interaction that produces government statistics is strongly influenced by the organizational and other objectives of the agencies that provide the information, and the policy objectives of the government. For example, hundreds of local police forces provide crime data to the federal governments of Canada, Mexico, and the United States. The statistics collected by police forces are related to the organizational objective of allocating police resources efficiently. These statistics can also be used by governments to show that their crime control policies are working (political objective) and/or to divert resources from fighting one type of crime to fighting another (e.g., from youth crime to cigarette smuggling).

The statistics produced by governments can be classified as primary or secondary data, depending on whose interests they serve and whose conceptions and theoretical assumptions influenced their collection. For governments and government agencies, government statistics are primary data. They were produced and paid for by them, for their own purposes. For non-governmental users, including most social scientists, they are secondary data. That is to say, they did not pay for them directly (only indirectly via taxes), and their intellectual and other interests played a minimal or secondary role in deciding what data to collect, how to collect and classify it, or why it should be collected.

Using secondary data limits our ability to answer certain questions. For example, what are the consequences of social class position for aging parents whose children are members of different social class groupings? We cannot answer this question because the Canadian, Mexican, and American governments do not publish statistics on the social class positions of their citizens. Consider another example. What physical attributes (e.g., sex, race/ethnicity, age, obesity) or social factors (e.g., social support—or lack of it—by family members, employment status), in addition to the severity of their physical or mental condition, influence the decision to admit an individual to hospital? As MacFarlane points out, the only relevant statistics hospitals publish are on diagnoses (1990: 56).

The secondary nature of government statistics is one major disadvantage for the sociologists who use them. Their exclusion from the social production of government statistics prevents or decreases their opportunity to challenge, at an early stage of the data collection process, the decisions of more powerful individuals within the government who "set the agenda and decide which social phenomenon will and will not be monitored and measured numerically" (Davidson and Layder, 1994: 62). This is not a trivial concern, because the policy and planning decisions of governments, based on the statistics they collect, directly influence the daily lives of all Canadians, Mexicans, and Americans.

On the other hand, members and representatives of these governments would say that they were democratically elected and that they have a country to govern. Governing means making administrative, policy, and planning decisions. They collect data that helps them make these decisions. Thus, when they became aware of the aging population (e.g., a larger proportion of older folk), they redirected more resources towards assisting the elderly.

The reality is this: only governments have the resources (money, people, authority) to collect the kinds and quantity of statistics they gather on a regular basis and, not infrequently, for specific purposes. If the government did not collect statistics, we would have to deal with the problem of no data or very little data, rather than secondary data on the social problems we deal with in this text. On balance, the trade-off is worth it, at least until such time as academics are permitted to be full partners in the production of the statistics by government agencies.

Advantages and Disadvantages of Official Statistics

Advantages include the facts that

➤ government statistics are quantitative.

➤ they are systematically collected.

➤ the data are collected on a recurring basis every few months, year, or set number of years.

➤ they are readily available.

➤ they are either available free or at relatively low cost.

➤ the statistics constitute an empirical basis for the government's administrative, policy, and planning decisions.

➤ they cover society as a whole.

➤ they affect the daily lives of all individuals living in the society.

Disadvantages include the fact that

➤ they are collected primarily to serve the interests of governments and government agencies, and only secondarily the interests of scholars and other non-governmental users.

Historical and Historical-Comparative Research

According to Giddens (1996: 3), thinking sociologically means taking "the broader view." This means that sociologists must show how existing social problems have been influenced, not only by contemporary societal/global (structural and cultural) factors, but also by historical forces. They must collect data on more than a single case and present descriptions and explanations based on a comparison of them. Historical research that takes the broader view of the social problem being studied partially meets these requirements, but historical research that ignores the problem's structural and cultural context, does not. Historical-comparative research that shows how taking the broader view into account increases our understanding of social problems fully meets these requirements.

Historical Research

Historical research is aimed at describing and explaining changes in society, its institutions (e.g., law), and social groupings (e.g., social classes, achievements, or problems) over time. E. P. Thompson's (1977) study is an outstanding example of historical research. He studied a major eighteenth century social problem—the significant escalation in the use of the death penalty by England's property-owning political leaders (Hanoverian Whigs), who were core members of a subculture of corruption. Thompson used state papers published by the Public Records Office; private papers (Collections) of the landed gentry and business magnates; court (Quarter Sessional) records; and pamphlets, and newspapers, publications describing the thoughts and activities of forest farmers, priests, parishioners, and schoolmasters in parishes adjacent to the Windsor and Hampshire forests where poaching and other activities prohibited by the government's new draconian law, *The Black Act*, occurred.

Historical-Comparative Research

Historical-comparative research is research aimed at developing and/or testing theories using historical data on two or more societies, institutions, movements, or social groupings within the same society. The historical-comparative research on capitalism conducted by Max Weber provides a good example of this kind of research.

Weber described capitalism as "the most fateful force in modern life," and he defined it as involving the quest for "forever renewed profit, by means of continuous, rational, capitalistic enterprise" (1956: 17). He looked at Calvinism, an ascetic religion based on the teachings of John Calvin (1509-1564). Capitalism's spirit (a set of religious ideas and values of great motivational significance) was not to be equated with the unbridled, irrational greed for money. If this link between a religious ethic and capitalism makes sense to you, Weber would say that his explanation was logically adequate.

Weber's next step was to find out if his explanation was also causally adequate. To this end, he conducted historical-comparative research using historical data and economic systems in a variety of countries. The results of his research on Western Europe indicated that modern capitalism was more highly developed in countries where Calvinism was established (e.g., England, France, the Netherlands) than in those where religions such as Methodism, Catholicism, or Lutheranism were established (e.g., Spain, Poland, Germany). Second, his review of the proceedings of congresses, the Catholic media, and occupational statistics, revealed that business leaders were "overwhelmingly Protestant" (1956: 35).

Third, his detailed historical studies of the religions of Western Europe, Israel, China, and India, indicated that modern capitalism did not develop where religions other than Calvinism were established (e.g., Judaism, Hinduism, Buddhism). On the basis of these historical-comparative findings, Weber concluded that his explanation was also causally adequate.

Advantages and Disadvantages of Historical and Historical-Comparative Research

Advantages include the following:

➤ It provides answers to interesting questions about origins that cannot be adequately answered by other research methods.

➤ By making comparisons across time (earlier with later years) and across space (different societies and social groups within the same society), it is well-suited to test causal theories of social problems and other social phenomena.

➤ The lessons we learn from history may help us to avoid repeating past mistakes.

Disadvantages include the following:

➤ Most, if not all, researchers doing historical research identify missing data as a problem.

➤ Many historical researchers also identify biased data as a problem.

➤ The possibility of confusing an account of the origins of a social problem with an explanation of it is a potential drawback.

Summary

In this chapter, we provided you with widely read and cited answers to several important questions, such as "what is sociology?" and "what is a social problem?". We also described several major theoretical perspectives on social problems, but emphasized our preference for the power/inequality model in covering the social problems in Chapters 2 to 9.

Many sociologists who study various social problems do much more than simply define and explain them. They also gather and analyze data derived from a wide range of sources, such as surveys, field research, and so on. It is important to keep in mind that all the research methods described here have strengths and limitations, and that you should choose one (or more) that best helps you to answer your research questions. As many methods instructors correctly point out to their students, the type of research problem you choose to study should always determine the method or methods you select.

An Important Note

Before we begin the sociological enterprise of analyzing some contemporary social problems we must address an important issue here. Throughout this text we examine social problems in North America, which we have chosen to define mainly as Canada and the United States. Why did we focus on these countries?

First, Canada and the United States share more than the longest unguarded border in the world. Both countries also share an enormous amount of trade and commerce. In fact, the volume of goods, services, and investment income flowing between Canada and the United States constitutes the largest two-way exchange in the world. In 1997, for example, transactions between the United States and Canada reached $387 billion, while Canada's purchases of U.S. merchandise amounted to about $5,263 per person in the same year (Embassy of Canada, 1997).

One could argue, as many have, that economic interdependency also means shared social experiences. Thus, the nature and causes of many social problems in both countries are generally the same, although in some cases they take a different form or magnitude. As well, Canada and the United States have much in common culturally. Although many Canadians and Americans will argue enthusiastically that their cultures are independent, there are important aspects of culture expressed in books, television and radio, and public opinion which are shared by both nations. This is especially true given that globalization—the increased economic, cultural, and political interdependence of nations and the rise of the global "world community"—is now a fact of life in our world. Canada and the United States are, in effect, inextricably connected.

As well, one of the strengths of comparative approaches to social issues is that it allows us to put our own nations in perspective, and to learn from the experiences of others. Again, the fact that Canada and the United States are more alike than not, makes us feel comfortable with our choice of these two countries as the basis of comparison.

KEY TERMS

Androcentric
Capitalism
Case studies
Cultural capital
Culture
Eurocentric
External validity
Feminism
Field experimental research
Field research
Gender
Historical research
Historical-comparative research
Historical materialist theory
Ideological forms of consciousness
Human agency
Internal validity
Liberal feminism
Marxist feminism
Non-participant observer
Observation

Official statistics
Participant observer
Patriarchy
Private trouble
Public issue
Radical feminism
Social closure
Social constructionist theories
Social cryptographers
Social structure
Socialism
Socialist feminism
Sociological imagination
Sociology
State
Structural functionalism
Structural location/position
Survey
Symbolic interactionist theory
Verstehen

DISCUSSION QUESTIONS

1. What is the sociological imagination?
2. What are the strengths and limitations of objective definitions of social problems?
3. What is the difference between structure and culture?
4. Describe how our power/inequality model is influenced by the work of Max Weber.
5. What is the difference between radical feminism and Marxist feminism?
6. What are the limitations of structural functionalism?
7. What is Mead's answer to the question "How is society possible?"?
8. Why would you use a survey?
9. What are the strengths and limitations of surveys?
10. In designing a research project, is it more important to focus on internal validity than on external validity? Why or why not?
11. When and why would you use ethnographic research techniques?
12. What are the strengths and limitations of historical methods?

PROBLEM SOLVING SCENARIOS

1. Sexual assault is a problem on your campus and you have been asked to design a research project that will yield findings relevant to its prevention or reduction. Describe the research method(s) you will use, and the rationale for its (their) use.
2. You are Max Weber and you are involved in a debate with Karl Marx on the relevance and importance of culture for an understanding of the social problem of poverty. Describe and defend your reply to Marx, who insists that you only need to study the economy and jobs.
3. Child abuse is a problem in the United States and Canada. You have been asked to design a study that will yield findings relevant to its prevention or reduction. Describe the research methods you will use, and the rationale for their use.
4. In a group, identify some major problems with the ways in which newspapers and television news shows report survey data. How would you minimize or overcome these problems?
5. Select one or two sociological studies that interest you and, based on what you have read in this chapter, identify the strengths and limitations of the methods used in these studies.
6. Try to explain homicide by using our power/inequality model.
7. Attempt to explain wife abuse using a variant of feminist theory.
8. In a group, debate the structural functionalist theory of pornography and prostitution.

WEB EXERCISES

1. Visit the following Web site. Examine the chart carefully, then write a three-page mini-essay on the ways in which this data might be interpreted by at least two different theorists.

   http://www.trinity.edu/~mkearl/fam$coll.jpg

2. To learn more about chance, probability, and sociological methods, visit the following Web site and try some of the exercises.

   http://www.dartmouth.edu/~chance/chance_news/current_news/current.html

SUGGESTED READINGS

Babbie, E. *The Practice of Social Research*. Belmont, CA: Wadsworth, 1983.
One of the most widely used methods texts in sociology, this book describes experimental, survey, field research, and historical-comparative research methods in detail. It also covers sampling and methods of data analysis in a relatively straightforward manner.

Coser, L. *Masters of Sociological Thought* (2nd edition). New York: Harcourt Brace Jovanovich, 1977.
This book provides an excellent overview of the main ideas of Weber, Marx, and other sociological theorists discussed throughout our text.

Gray, G., and N. Guppy. *Successful Surveys*. Toronto: Harcourt Brace, 1994.
This is one of the most easily understood and comprehensive books on the design, data collection, data analysis, and publication phases of survey research.

Messerschmidt, J. *Masculinities and Crime: Critique and Reconceptualization of Theory*. Landham, MD: Roman and Littlefield, 1993.
This widely read and cited criminology text provides an excellent overview and critique of the feminist theories described in this chapter and elsewhere.

Mills, C.W. *The Sociological Imagination*. New York: Oxford University Press, 1959.
Defined by most sociologists as a classic, this book is a "must read" for anyone seeking to develop a rich understanding of what it means to possess the sociological imagination described in this chapter and elsewhere.

Sampson, R. "The Promises and Pitfalls of Macro-Level Research," *The Criminologist*, 14: 6-11, 1989.
This is a relatively short, first-rate discussion of the strengths and weaknesses of macro- and micro-level sociological theorizing.

Webb, E., D. Campbell, R. Schwartz, and L. Sachrest. *Unobstrusive Measures: Non-Reactive Research in the Social Sciences*. Chicago: Rand McNally, 1966. This is a well-written, easily-understood, first-class book on how to do field research in a way that increases the internal validity of the findings.

ENDNOTES

1   On page 53 of The Communist Manifesto (1872), Marx states "But not only has the bourgeoisie forged the weapons that bring death to itself; it has also called into existence the men who are to wield those weapons, the working class."

2   Some of the widely cited theorists who popularized this perspective are Emile Durkheim, Roscoe Pound, Talcott Parsons, and Jerome Hall.

3   Other lines of evidence are that the members of the ruling class have participated directly in the state system. For example, they have helped regulate, govern, administer, and so on. In addition, there are strong personal and friendly relations or ties between members of the ruling class and those who run state bureaucracies (Miliband, 1969).

4   This represents a reformulation of Miliband's (1969) earlier "crude view of the state as a mere 'instrument' of the ruling class obediently acting at its dictation" (Miliband, 1983: 64).

5   For more in-depth criticisms of instrumental Marxism, see Comack and Brickey (1991), DeKeseredy and Schwartz (1996), Gold et al. (1975), Greenberg (1981), Lynch and Groves (1989), and Shoham and Hoffman (1991).

6   See, for example, Smandych's (1985) analysis of the early Canadian anti-combines legislation.

7   This section includes modified sections of material published previously by Ellis (1987).

8   This section includes modified sections of material published previously by Ellis (1987).

9   For a non-functional, anti-censorship, feminist approach to pornography see Vance (1984).

10   This section includes modified sections of material published previously by Ellis (1987).

11   See Bograd (1988), DeKeseredy and MacLeod (1997), DeKeseredy and Schwartz (1996), Ellis and DeKeseredy (1996), Maguire (1987), Saunders (1988), and Yllö (1993) for more detailed descriptions of the principles included in this list.

12   They were referring more specifically to the work of radical feminists Dobash and Dobash (1979).

Chapter 2

Hey Buddy, Can You Spare a Dime? Poverty in North America

There is an ugly smell rising from the basement of the stately American mansion. (Myrdall, 1987: 156)

OBJECTIVES

In this chapter we focus on the topics

1. What is poverty?
2. What is the extent and distribution of poverty in North America?
3. What causes poverty: some theoretical perspectives
4. What is to be done about poverty in North America: progressive ways of overcoming or minimizing the problem

Introduction

On August 25, 1997, Walter DeKeseredy stopped for a coffee and a doughnut at a new Starbucks coffee shop in his neighborhood. Since this popular café was "bursting at the seams" with customers, he had to sit down with a group of five male teenagers. No one said a word to him for about ten minutes and DeKeseredy assumed that they did not want him "hanging out" with them. Suddenly, one young man turned to DeKeseredy and said, "Hey mister, have you seen today's newspaper? Turn to page B5. It really stinks!" Since he hadn't time to read the Ottawa Citizen that morning and didn't have one with him, DeKeseredy asked the teenager to show him the page. He handed it to him and said, "Read it and tell me if you don't think the first letter to the editor doesn't stink! This letter is featured in Box 2.1. What does it smell like to you? Do you detect a distinct odor in the air, one that smells like poverty, misery, hopelessness, and the struggle to survive?

BOX 2-1

Squeegee Kids Deserve More Respect

In regards to the July 30 letter, "Let's rid streets of squeegee kids on welfare," I feel obliged to set the story straight on the true reason why people on welfare need to earn the extra money by means of this service. [T]he writer of the letter seems to believe that $520 a month is enough to survive in today's economy. To be honest, it is not nearly enough to live on even on an extremely tight budget, and I would be interested in watching the writer try to survive on this income. The fact is that there are not enough jobs out there to support everyone... I handed out nearly 30 resumes to many different food and clothing departments and every one of them stated that they were not hiring. Naturally, Lanthier most likely has a decent paying occupation and does not have to worry about finances nearly as much as a person on welfare.

After I have paid for all of my monthly expenses, I find myself to be approximately $163 in debt. I need the money that I earn through my work as a squeegee kid in order to make up for that $163 that I do not have. This does not include the money that I need to spend on clothing, household cleansers, entertainment, school supplies, and cat food.

Lanthier stated that squeegee kids make up to $100 per day washing vehicle windows on downtown street corners. I am not sure how the woman he described could claim to earn $100 a day as a squeegee kid, but I surely do not, and nor do any of the other window washers that I asked. The average daily income of local squeegee kids is $40. Perhaps two years ago one person could have made up to $100 a day washing vehicle windows, but there are simply too many people providing this service now for everyone to earn so much.

Lanthier declared that every squeegee kid spends their earnings on drugs and alcohol, but I know that this is not true. I do not drink alcohol or do drugs. I am not in the position to speak for the rest of the squeegee kids downtown on this matter, but I trust that at least 50 percent of them can honestly claim the same thing.

One comment that really fired the bullet in Lanthier's shots against squeegee kids was that we "do not practice birth control." This comment was highly degrading to myself and other squeegee kids... I do practice safe sex, as a matter of fact, and I strongly believe that this comment was highly out of place.

There are many benefits to being a squeegee kid other than earning money to support ourselves. For one, we learn excellent people skills, common sense, open-mindedness, money management, and life skills much better than we do in school because we are learning through experience. Washing vehicle windows is also much safer and less degrading than prostitution, and we are creating employment for ourselves where the government can not. Being a squeegee kid is not an easy occupation either because we have to put up with the people's ignorance, as well as the aching muscles that we all go home with at the end of each day. To get straight to the point, being a squeegee kid is not all that it is cracked up to be. It is just as strenuous as other normal occupations.

Finally, most of the squeegee kids are homeless, and they need income to support themselves.

I would like to make it clear to the public that our service of washing vehicle windows is a free service and if people wish to make donations then they are welcomed to and are also greatly appreciated.

Squeegee kids deserve more respect from society, and the majority of us are putting the money to good use.

Source: S. LeBlanc, *The Ottawa Citizen*, August 25, 1997, B5.

BOX 2-1

The author of this letter is just one of many North American "disposable children" who are struggling to find solutions to the "seemingly insoluble" challenges of poverty and hunger (Chase-Lansdale and Brooks-Gunn, 1995; Golden, 1997; Kolzon, 1997). By the way, the letter writer receives a monthly welfare check in the amount of US$390, and her expenses, including necessities such as rent, electricity, phone, food, laundry, and so on, add up to a total of US$512.26.

Many North American university students also struggle to "make ends meet." However, their financial problems pale in comparison to the letter writer's, and most university graduates eventually secure and maintain a middle-class occupation (Forcese, 1997). Chances are that people like you will never live in what Wilson (1996: 19) refers to as "new poverty neighborhoods," communities characterized by high levels of joblessness, homelessness, hunger, predatory street crime, hard drug use (e.g., smoking crack-cocaine) and drug dealing, family disruption, and a host of other major social problems that plague "the truly disadvantaged" (Wilson, 1987). Alarming levels of hopelessness and despair are also endemic to these neighborhoods, and as pointed out in Box 2.2, these problems can kill you.

BOX 2-2

Hopelessness Can Kill You, Medical Study Suggests

Despair does as much damage to the heart as smoking 20 cigarettes a day, a new study has found.

After a four-year study of almost 1,000 middle-aged men, scientists from the Public Health Institute in Berkeley, California, have discovered that hopelessness accelerates hardening of the arteries, a major cause of heart disease and strokes.

"It really surprised us that men who had some hardening of the arteries at the start of the study and admitted to hopelessness showed 20 percent faster progression than men who did not," said Dr. Susan Everson, who led the study.

"That's the same ratio as a pack-a-day smoker. Clearly, in this study, hopelessness had as strong an effect as smoking does."

The study was welcomed enthusiastically by Dr. George Fedor, a specialist at the Ottawa Heart Institute, as "another positive piece of the jigsaw" in predicting cardiovascular risk factors.

"Psycho-social factors are very, very important predictors and more and more data indicates this," he said.

"These papers clearly point to the fact that it (despair or hopelessness) probably would have to impact the equation just like smoking or hypertension. In future we will also need to assess the psychological make-up of people to help us assess cardiovascular risk.

In turn, that means your cardiovascular risk profile would also include relaxation techniques and proper stress-reducing techniques."

In the Berkeley study, two questions were asked to gauge hopeless feelings. The men were asked if they felt it was impossible to reach goals they had set for themselves and if the future was so hopeless that nothing would change for the better.

In addition, ultrasound scans were taken of the blood vessels of each man at the beginning and end of the study to indicate changes.

Progression in arteriosclerosis, or hardening of the arteries, was 20 percent greater in those who had reported a high level of despair.

BOX 2-2

"The message from this is that people must recognize how important their psychological state is in relation to their physical health," says Dr. Everson.

"People should understand that if they've lost hope, there are things they can do to reorganize their lives to become more optimistic.

"They can seek psychological or psychiatric treatment to help them deal with their feelings of hopelessness because certainly this is not a personality trait. It's clearly a response to the environment they live in, or the stressors they experience."

_____

Source: R. Starnes, "Hopelessness Can Kill You, Medical Study Suggests," *The Ottawa Citizen*, August 27, 1997, A1. Reprinted with permission of *The Ottawa Citizen*.

As you can read in Box 2.2, Dr. Everson contends that people should seek psychological treatment to help them deal with feelings of hopelessness, and that this psychological problem is in fact a response to environmental factors. Counseling alone, however, does nothing to alleviate joblessness and other problems that plague impoverished people (Currie, 1985, 1993). Only policies aimed at eliminating poverty can enhance the "severely distressed's" physical and psychological well-being (Kasarda, 1992).

Similarly, psychological treatment will not lower the staggering rate of lung problems found in inner-city ghetto neighborhoods. For example, autopsy data analyzed in the early 1990s show that 80 percent of low-income Los Angeles residents who died as a result of violence or accidents had lung tissue abnormalities; more than one quarter of them had "severe lesions" in their lungs (Mann, 1990: 257). These lung abnormalities are the result of living in the most polluted ghetto neighborhoods, communities where people's general health is already damaged by the effects of gross economic inequality (Michalowski, 1991).

What Is Poverty?

In early September, 1997, Walter DeKeseredy decided to stop in at Carleton University's graduate student pub for a beer after his Wednesday afternoon lecture. The atmosphere was pleasant and the pub was filled with students drinking beer, renewing old acquaintances, discussing intellectual issues, and generally having a good time. Two graduate students in the sociology department saw DeKeseredy and asked him to join them at their table. One said, "Walter, you are always busy. You must be writing something now. What are you up to?" DeKeseredy said that he was trying to complete this chapter on poverty. The other student said, "How depressing! I know what it's like. Sometimes I can't even afford to go out to the pub with my friends." Apparently, for this student, a key indicator of what he defined as "poverty" was not having enough money to buy beer. Does this fit with your own definition of poverty?

As Devine and Wright (1993: 2) point out, "At first blush, defining poverty would seem to be a straightforward, even simple, task." In fact, defining poverty is the subject of much debate and controversy. Even some of the most prestigious and highly regarded statistical agencies in the world[1] admit that they cannot "draw the poverty line" (Beauchense, 1997). Within the sociological literature, however, definitions of poverty typically fall under two broad categories: (1) absolute and (2) relative.

Absolute Poverty

What is **absolute poverty**? Is there a basic, or absolute, standard of poverty in the United States and Canada? Some people view poverty in absolute terms as a family's inability to buy "basic necessities" (e.g., food, shelter, and clothing). The U.S. federal government does not have an explicit definition of poverty, but takes an absolute approach—one that emphasizes the ability to buy the food required for a minimum adequate diet (Ross and Shillington, 1989). This "dividing line" between the "poor" and "non-poor" was developed in 1964, and at that time, the federal government estimated that, in order to purchase other essentials, a family needs an income three times higher than the amount required to buy food. Thus, in 1964, a U.S. family of four with an income of less than $3,000 was officially designated as "poor." Today, the U.S. **poverty line** for an individual is probably about $8,000, and close to $16,000 for a family of four (Lauer, 1998). In sum, according to proponents of absolute definitions, poor Americans are those who cannot meet the above "nutritional milestone" (Devine and Wright, 1993).

What's wrong with this picture? Obviously, an individual's or a family's physical and psychological well-being depends on much more than food. For example, they need clean drinking water, a roof over their heads, and so on (Devine and Wright, 1993). Thus, the U.S. government's official absolute definition excludes many people who cannot afford these basic needs, most of whom we would define as poor (Lauer, 1998). Consider April, a forty-year-old woman interviewed by Harman (1989: 88). Often homeless, April was forced to ride a subway all night to survive. In our opinion, April is poor. What do you think? The following is a brief account of her "underground" experiences.

"...I've done that several times. At least, until the guards tell me to get off, and then I've stayed out for twenty-four hours wandering the streets. I've met some very weird people on the streets at night, some weird men, I've had some terrible experiences. And that night the cops stopped me twice. But when I was on the subway they asked me where I was from and I said I had a terrible room and couldn't sleep and just rode around to have a safe place to sit and they said I would have to get off. They wanted to know what was wrong, why I sat there just staring into space, and I said that I'd had nervous breakdown and that I spent some time in the [psychiatric hospital]...But they still told me I had to get off, that the subway is not to be used for that kind of thing, that you have to have a purpose for riding it."

Let's assume for a minute that people like April eventually become "homeful" (i.e., manage to rent a room, apartment, or house) and can purchase a basket of food. Are they now above the poverty line? Perhaps they are; however, some foods and residences are better than others. What if many people can achieve the "nutritional milestone" described previously and have a roof over the heads, but cannot afford electricity and fresh fruit? Are they poor? Aren't electricity and a healthy dose of vitamin C necessities in contemporary North America? What about other things? According to Devine and Wright (1993: 3), "One might even argue that in North America today television sets and automobiles are necessities of life, even though the vast bulk of the world's population continues to exist with neither." Indeed, it would be easy to construct a very long list of needs.

The most important point to consider here is that it is extremely difficult, if not impossible, to **quantify**, or count, poverty accurately and to determine an absolute minimum level, because definitions of "necessity" or "basic needs" vary across time, place, and social groups (Schiller, 1989; Hurst, 1995). For example, approximately 65 years ago, millions of rural U.S. citizens lacked electricity but were not defined as poor. Most of the world's population still lacks electricity, but most Americans now regard this key source of energy as a necessity (Devine and Wright, 1993). For this and other reasons, some social scientists prefer to use relative definitions of poverty.

Relative Poverty

Relative poverty is defined in relation to a society's mean or median income. So, if your income is at the bottom end of the income distribution, you are poor regardless of your absolute income (Devine and Wright, 1993). What if you are a millionaire? If everyone else in your society makes much more money than you do, then, according to the relative approach, you are poor. Moreover, as the average income of the population changes, so does the poverty line. Poverty and inequality are not considered to be mutually exclusive, and poverty can only be eliminated by eliminating income inequality (Hurst, 1995).

What does the relative approach tell us about North American society? Since we live on a capitalist continent, one that is structured specifically to foster social, economic, and political inequality, the relative approach, by definition, strongly suggests that poverty can never be eliminated—because at least 20 percent of the population will fall in the lowest income category, regardless of their wages. Do you believe that one-fifth of all North Americans are poor? Devine and Wright (1993), two of North America's leading experts on poverty, don't think so, and contend that some relative definitions of poverty are not useful.

Consider relative definitions that emphasize **subjective deprivation** relative to some reference group. Let's return briefly to the graduate student who lamented about not being able to go to the pub with his friends. His reference group was some of his graduate student peers, and his perceptions of them played a key role in his defining himself as "poor." Would he still consider himself poor if his reference group consisted of homeless people? While relative subjective deprivation definitions call attention to the psychological dimensions of poverty and help us understand how people come to view themselves and others as poor, they suffer from major pitfalls, described here by Devine and Wright (1993: 4).

"The problem with the relative deprivation approach is that everyone is deprived relative to someone else, excepting only the single richest person in the world. The Kennedys are deprived compared to the Rockefellers. And likewise, everyone is also comparatively advantaged relative to someone else, excepting only the single poorest person in the world. A homeless man sleeping in the gutter with a dollar in his pocket is, after all, better off than another homeless man, sleeping in the same gutter, but with no money in his pockets at all."

Summary

Absolute definitions focus on a minimum level of income, while relative conceptions define poverty in relation either to society's distribution of income or people's reference groups. What is the best approach? This is a difficult question to answer, especially since both categories have major shortcomings. Devine and Wright (1993) argue that one should not be chosen over the other. Rather, what we need is a definition that is both sensitive to a society's level of economic development and demarcates a truly disadvantaged group of people according to some objective, albeit socially-defined, standard.

The most important point to consider here is that sociologists, policy makers, the general public, and so on will never reach a consensus. This is because defining poverty is a political act that depends largely on people's values and beliefs (Hurst, 1995). As Haveman (1987: 56) correctly points out, "The concept of poverty, like those of unemployment, disability, and well-being is elastic, multidimensional, nonobjective, and culturally determined." Definitions of poverty also influence the ways in which we measure the extent of this problem, an issue addressed in the next section of this chapter.

What Is the Extent and Distribution of Poverty in North America?

There are serious problems with the poverty data generated by North American government agencies such as the U.S. Bureau of the Census. For example, according to the U.S. federal government, the poverty line is defined as three times the cost of a basic nutritional diet and, each year, the poverty level is adjusted to changes in the Consumer Price Index.[2] This official measure has been sharply attacked on several grounds, including the following:

➤ It is based on pre-tax income rather than post-tax income. Thus, estimates of available financial resources are inflated (O'Hare, 1985; Curran and Renzetti, 1996).

➤ It determines a family's economic status by using its income at only one point in time. This "one-year, snap-shot" approach does not allow us to distinguish between those who are poor for only a short period of time, and those who are "persistently poor" (Hurst, 1995: 351).

➤ Using diet as a means of determining poverty levels does not address the nutritional requirements of the poor over time (Curran and Renzetti, 1996).

Despite these and other limitations,[3] the U.S. official statistics presented here reveal that many people are poor, and if the issue of relative deprivation was taken into account, those statistics would likely be higher. When you read official statistics on the extent and distribution of poverty, keep in mind that the only thing we can derive from them is that they are simply counts of those who are officially designated as poor. It is impossible to make conclusions about the respondents' attitudes, beliefs, values, and so on. This is why some researchers such as Curran and Renzetti (1996: 103) assert that "It is time we move beyond simple statistical classifications."

The Extent and Distribution of Poverty in the United States

The data presented here were compiled from data collected in the March, 1996 Current Population Survey (CPS) conducted by the U.S. Bureau of the Census. This is a national representative sample survey of approximately 50,000 households. The following data are for the 1995 calendar year, and are limited to income received before income tax payments and deductions for social security, Medicare, union dues, etc. (U.S. Bureau of the Census, 1996a).

According to the CPS, in 1995 (U.S. Bureau of the Census, 1996b, 1996c)

➤ 13.8 percent of the United States population were poor;

➤ 20.8 percent of children under 18 years of age were poor; the highest rate for any age group. Box 2.3 provides an alarming overview of the many problems poor children face in the United States;

➤ 10.8 percent of U.S. families were poor, as were 5.6 percent of married couples, 14 percent of male householder families, and 32.4 percent of families with a female householder. 20.6 percent of the poor female householders were white, 45.1 percent were African-American, and 49.4 percent were of Hispanic origin;

➤ 8.5 percent of white, 6.4 percent of non-Hispanic white, 26.4 percent of African-American, 12.4 percent of Asian and Pacific Islander, and 27 percent of Hispanic families were poor;

➤ 29.3 percent of African-Americans, 11.2 percent of whites, 8.5 percent of non-Hispanic whites, 14.6 percent of Asian and Pacific Islanders, and 30.3 percent of Hispanics were poor;

➤ of the married couples in the CPS sample, Hispanic couples had the highest rate of poverty (18.9 percent), followed by African-American (8.5 percent), and white couples (5.1 percent);

➤ 13.4 percent of those living in metropolitan areas, and 15.6 percent of the people who lived outside these areas were poor; and

➤ the Southern region had the highest poverty rate (15.7 percent), followed by the West (14.9 percent), the Northeast (12.5 percent), and the Midwest (11 percent).

BOX 2-3

Child Poverty in the United States: Some Basic Facts

One out of every five children in the United States is poor, and one in eight is hungry. In fact, there are approximately 12 million hungry children in the United States (Bread, 1992: 3).

Since 1969, the child poverty rate has increased by 50 percent despite a 50 percent increase in the country's gross national product (Edelman, 1994).

An African-American baby born in the shadow of the White House is now more likely to die in his or her first year of life than a child born in Jamaica or Trinidad (Houston et al., 1994).

According to a United Nations Children's Fund report, the United States has the highest child poverty rate of any rich nation in the world (Bennett, 1993).

One in seven poor children had no health insurance in 1993 (Pence and Ropers, 1995).

Poor children are five times more likely to die from disease and illness, three times more likely to die during childhood, three times more likely to be hospitalized, and two times more likely to have physical or mental disabilities (Garabino and Kostelny, 1994).

Poor children have a four to twenty times greater chance of being born mentally retarded (Edelman, 1995).

Slightly over 50 percent of all U.S. children were fully immunized against preventable childhood diseases in 1992 (McLoyd et al., 1994).

Many more U.S. children live below the poverty line than in the United Kingdom, France, Sweden, and Canada. These countries spend two to three times what the United States does on children and families (Sklar, 1990).

51.4 percent of those who receive food stamps are children, and children receiving food stamps increased by an unprecedented 51 percent between 1989 and 1993.

Over 50 percent of poor children's families have incomes up to $5,700 below the official poverty line.

One out of four reported homeless persons is a child.

Of children in single-parent households (87 percent of which are female-led), 73 percent experience poverty at some time during their lives.

Approximately 40 percent of African-American teenagers are poor, 30 percent of Hispanic teens are poor, and 50 percent of pregnant teens do not receive prenatal health care.

Poor youth between the ages of 16 and 24 are two times more likely to drop out of high school, and half as likely to finish college or university.

75 percent of African-American students and 46 percent of Hispanic students attend schools ranked at the bottom of the socioeconomic ladder.

A 1993 United Nations Children's Fund report, which measured each nation according to the social health and welfare performance it should have achieved based on its wealth, found that "Vietnam had a plus rating of 116 while the United States had a minus rating of 3."

Source: This is a modified version of a box constructed by Golden (1997: 55–56). Reprinted with permission of Wadsworth Publishing, a division of Thomson Learning. Fax 800-730-2215.

BOX 2-3

The Extent and Distribution of Poverty in Canada

There is no "official" measure of poverty in Canada. Nevertheless, Statistics Canada's **Low Income Cut-Offs (LICOs)** is the best known, and has generated much controversy and debate.[4] Statistics Canada does not, and never did, claim to measure poverty. Rather, this federal government agency defines Low Income Cut-Offs as a measure of what it views as "financial difficulty" or "straitened circumstances." As Ross et al. (1997: 1) point out, "The difference between straitened circumstances and poverty is moot, however, and most social policy analysts, politicians and editorial writers treat the cut-offs as poverty lines." Following these people and researchers affiliated with the Canadian Council on Social Development (CCSD),[5] the LICOs presented in this section are treated here as poverty lines because Canadian researchers, not for lack of trying, have not been able to find an acceptable alternative (Beauchesne, 1997).

Recall our previous discussion of absolute and relative definitions of poverty. Since Statistics Canada often updates its poverty lines based on changes in the proportion of average income required to buy basic needs, this agency has standardized a relative conception of poverty (Forcese, 1997), and according to Ross et al. (1996), Statistics Canada appears to view poverty as relative rather than absolute (see Table 2.1).[6]

The bulk of the Canadian data reported here was prepared by the Canadian Council on Social Development's Centre for International Statistics (CCSD, 1997), using Statistics Canada's 1992 LICOs base. Before we review these and other relevant data, it is first necessary to give a brief description of the limitations of the LICOs. Perhaps the most outstanding pitfall, similar to the U.S. Bureau of the Census data described previously, is that Statistics Canada does not report low-income data based on after-tax incomes (Ross and Shillington, 1989). This is not to say that Statistics Canada did not gather such statistics. For example, in 1990, it started to publish low-income measures based on median post-tax incomes. For reasons unknown to us, however, in its most recent annual report on 1992 gross income data, Statistics Canada focuses only on the LICOs, an approach that still

Table 2.1
Canadian Low-Income Cut-Offs (LICOs), 1996

Family Size	500,000+	Population of Community of Residence 100,000– 499,999	30,000– 99,999	Less than 30,000	Rural
1	$17,132	$14,694	$14,591	$13,577	$11,839
2	$21,414	$18,367	$18,239	$16,971	$14,799
3	$26, 633	$22,844	$22,684	$21,107	$18,406
4	$32,238	$27,651	$27,459	$25,551	$22,279
5	$36,036	$30,910	$30,695	$28,562	$24,905
6	$39,835	$34,168	$33,930	$31,571	$27,530
7 +	$43,634	$37,427	$37,166	$34,581	$30,156

Source: Canadian Council on Social Development (1997).

seems to be this government agency's preferred mode of determining Canada's official poverty line (Ross et al., 1996).

Another problem with the LICOs is that Statistics Canada's definition of the basic necessities of food, housing, and clothes is based on all spending in these categories, including buying items like expensive designer clothes and steak. Despite these and other problems with the LICOs, many progressives, including those affiliated with the Canadian Council on Social Development, argue that Statistics Canada's measure "is a reasonable basis for the analysis of poverty in Canada" (Ross and Shillington, 1989: 20). What do you think?

LICOs data show that in 1995, 17.8 percent of all Canadians and 15.6 percent of all Canadian families were poor. However, some people are worse off than others. For example, the rate of poverty among non-elderly,[7] two-parent families (9.7 percent) is markedly lower than that among non-elderly, single-mother families (57.3 percent) and non-elderly, single-father families (25.4 percent). Obviously, single-mother families are "overwhelmingly" struggling with income levels below the poverty line.

Life does not necessarily become better as poor women get older. Unfortunately, female poverty extends into old age because women live longer than men do, and they are less likely to have an old age income. For example, 57 percent of Canadian workers who could not save money for their retirement (because there was little, if anything, to be saved) were women (Forcese, 1997; Maser, 1995).

In 1995, the Canadian elderly poverty rate was 18.7 percent (CCSD, 1997). So much for the "golden years." In fact, this statistic and other poverty data strongly suggest that we should fear, rather than look forward to, retirement. Regardless of whether they have pensions, Canadian seniors often have incomes that barely allow them to purchase the basic essentials, and excluding Native peoples (e.g., Cree, Mohawk, etc.), elderly women are the most impoverished. There are, of course, some "exceptions to the rule," such as well-educated, middle-class women who acquired full-time, "decent paying" jobs which enabled them to save for their retirement and receive pension benefits (Forcese, 1997). As pointed out in Chapter 3, however, part-time, "pink ghetto" work (e.g., cashier, waitress, secretary) is the only kind of work available to most women, especially those with families and/or who lack a university/college education. Thus, they are destined to live in poverty.

Living alone also puts the elderly at greater risk of being poor (Curran and Renzetti, 1996). In 1995, 6.9 percent of the Canadian elderly in families were poor, compared to 45.1 percent of the unattached elderly. Most of the latter group include women who obviously suffer from more than the loss of a husband or cohabiting partner. Elderly women's poverty is often the result of being economically dependent on their husbands. Since many husbands die before their wives, divorce/separate, or abandon their wives, many women are "one man away from poverty" (Orloff, 1993: 319).

Canadian seniors have a high rate of poverty, and the same can be said about children. In 1995, 21 percent of Canadians under the age of 18 were poor (CCSD, 1997). Many of these young people end up becoming "disposable children" (Golden, 1997), youths who experience major threats to their physical and psychological well-being. This can include physical and sexual abuse; homelessness; neglect; hunger; disease; and a host of other tragedies (see Box 2.3).[8]

Which ethnic or cultural group has the highest poverty rate? As a whole, Native or First Nations peoples are Canada's version of those whom Wilson (1987) refers to as "truly disadvantaged." In fact, Native peoples are less likely to have any income, and to have lower-than-average income levels, than Canadians as a whole. Further, in terms of average incomes, all types of Native peoples rank near the bottom compared to the incomes of other ethnic/racial groups (Gerber, 1990; Wotherspoon and Satzewich, 1993). Thus, as pointed out in Box 2.4, it is not surprising that many Canadian Native persons suffer from major health problems.

Poverty also varies in different regions of Canada. For example, of all 10 Canadian provinces, Newfoundland had the highest family poverty rate in 1995 (19 percent), while Prince Edward Island had the lowest rate (9.3 percent). Poverty rates in urban Quebec are high compared to other Canadian cities (CCSD, 1997). The problem of urban poverty is addressed throughout this text because it is strongly associated with a host of other North American social problems, such as violent crime (see Chapter 5) and hard drug use (see Chapter 8).

Summary

What can we conclude from the poverty data presented in this chapter? Some readers might argue that the 1995 Canadian poverty rate (17.8 percent of the total population) is higher than that of the United States (13 percent). Is this really the case? Unless both countries use the same measure, it is extremely difficult, if not impossible, to determine whether the rate of poverty is higher in Canada than in the United States. Perhaps we will see a comparative study in the near future, one that uses one method of determining poverty rates in both countries. In the meantime, however, we can conclude that an alarming number of North American people are poor. We can also conclude that, in both Canada and the United States, the elderly, children, visible minorities, women, and female-headed families are "disproportionately represented among the poor" (Curran and Renzetti, 1996).

BOX 2-4

Native Peoples, Poverty, and Health

It is readily apparent that the health of Native peoples in Saskatchewan, and all across Canada, is closely tied to poverty and living conditions. Abject poverty contributes to dismal living conditions, which make for extraordinarily poor health and high mortality. Therefore, a policy on Native health care is impossible without a policy on alleviating poverty and improving living conditions. A political economy approach to understanding Native health care is absolutely essential.

As the Canadian Institute of Child Health has pointed out, the health problems of Canada's Native children bear a striking similarity to those found in third world countries: "The state of poverty in which they live makes them particularly vulnerable to health hazards. Their powerlessness and social isolation possibly contribute to higher than average suicide rates." Further, "this country cannot ignore the deplorable conditions of Native people.... When you look at the overcrowding, the poor housing conditions, the lack of running water in so many Indian communities, there's no reason [this] should exist in Canada (Struthers, January 27, 1990).

It is quite clear, according to the First Nations Health Commission, why this is a third world health problem right within our society—60 percent of Native households still lack running water or sewage, and over 30 percent of Native children still live in overcrowded homes (Canadian Press, October 11, 1991).

Of course, one possible explanation could be inadequate Native use of available health facilities. But far more attention continues to be directed at the inadequacy of facilities, not to mention poor quality of service. It has recently been pointed out, for example: "that the lack of accessible medical services is particularly hard on elderly Native people, especially in northern Saskatchewan - unable to speak English, and frightened by being removed to a strange and lonely southern hospital environment, they are reluctant in the extreme to move for better health care - they'd rather stay up north...and die" (Mandryk, 1990).

Source: Anderson (1994: 318–319).

The data presented here also tell us that something is seriously wrong with North American society. For example, how can poverty exist in two of the richest nations in the world, and why do the general public, politicians, academics, and so on tolerate it? It seems that two separate "nations" have emerged in both Canada and the United States. One is a nation of wealth and affluence, where people eat good food, live in luxurious houses, and reap many other benefits of material success; the other is one of poverty, characterized by hunger, homelessness, despair, desperation, violence, and drugs. So much for the notion of "one nation under God" (Devine and Wright, 1993).

What Causes Poverty: Some Theoretical Perspectives

Like many other issues addressed throughout this text, the question of what causes poverty generates heated debates, and there are several conflicting answers. The main purpose of this section is to describe and evaluate several social scientific theories of poverty. We begin by reviewing the personal inferiority perspective, a so-called theory that has a long history in North America and is warmly embraced by conservative academics, politicians, and the general public. In fact, this conservative perspective has dominated public discussions on poverty for the last decade.

Personal Inferiority Theory

Occasionally referred to as a genetic or biological argument, the **personal inferiority** thesis is rooted in the writings of nineteenth-century social theorist Herbert Spencer (1820-1903), one of the "masters of sociological thought" (Coser, 1977). Like naturalist Charles Darwin (1968),[9] Spencer was heavily influenced by the doctrine of "survival of the fittest," and argued that only those with superior intelligence could succeed in the struggle to survive. For Spencer, the poor were poor because they were "unfit" and lacked the intelligence necessary to succeed. Spencer also sharply attacked government social welfare programs for the poor because they would distort what he viewed as the "beneficial processes of natural selection" (Coser, 1977: 101). For example, according to Spencer (1851: 151):

"That rigorous necessity which, when allowed to operate, becomes so sharp a spur to the lazy and so strong a bridle to the random, these paupers' friends would repeal....Blind to the fact that under the natural order of things society is constantly excreting its unhealthy, imbecile, slow, vacillating, faithless members, these unthinking though well-meaning, men advocate an interference which not only stops the purifying process, but even increases the vitiation - absolutely encourages the multiplication of the reckless and incompetent by offering them an unfailing provision, and discourages the multiplication of the competent and provident by heightening the difficulty of maintaining a family."

Does this argument sound familiar? Readers who watch the Rush Limbaugh television talk show have probably heard arguments similar to Spencer's. However, these and other contemporary personal inferiority perspectives on poverty are not restricted to television and radio talk shows. They are endemic to our society and appear in scholarly publications, such as the widely read and cited, albeit highly controversial, 1994 book *The Bell Curve: Intelligence and Class Structure in American Life*. The authors, the late Richard Herrnstein and Charles Murray, contend that broader social forces, such as class, gender, and ethnic inequality, do not cause poverty. Rather, based on their analysis of "scientific" data generated by the Armed Forces Qualifications Test (AFQT), Herrnstein and Murray contend that low intelligence or "cognitive ability" is the main cause of social problems such as crime, poverty, etc. They also oppose early intervention programs (e.g., Head Start) for economically disenfranchised children because, in their opinion, they do not deal with the problem of low intelligence.

It is true that the test scores of children who participated in Head Start programs are not much different from the scores of those who did not attend. Referred to as "fade-out," this problem does not surprise William Julius Wilson, one of the world's leading sociological experts on the plight of inner-city ghetto residents. However, his interpretation of the convergence of the above test scores is fundamentally distinct from Herrnstein and Murray's. For example, according to Wilson (1996: xv–xvi):

"Anyone familiar with the harsh environment of the inner-city ghetto should not be surprised by the research findings on the Head Start fade-out. It would be extraordinary if the gains from Head Start programs were sustained in some of these environments. The children of the inner-city ghetto have to contend with public schools plagued by unimaginative curricula, overcrowded classrooms, inadequate plant and facilities, and only a small proportion of teachers who have confidence in their students and expect them to learn. Inner-city ghetto children also grow up in neighborhoods with devastating rates of joblessness, which trigger a whole series of other problems that are not conducive to healthy child development or intellectual growth. Included among these are broken families, antisocial behavior, social networks that do not extend beyond the formal confines of the ghetto environment, and a lack of informal social control over the behavior and activities of children and adults in the neighborhood."

How can we expect poor children to do well in school if they have to deal with the above problems? Moreover, most geneticists do not draw a line separating biological influences from environmental influences. Thus, it is "intellectually irresponsible" to blame poor children's scholastic abilities on low intelligence (Wilson, 1996). Such an approach is tantamount to **victim blaming**, a discourse that claims that those who have been harmed by crime, poverty, and many other social problems have contributed to their own downfall (Karmen, 1996).

The policy implications of the personal inferiority perspective are, to say the least, simple: do nothing. After all, if you believe that poor people are intellectually deficient and therefore unable ever to succeed, then there is no point providing them with any type of social assistance. In fact, Charles Murray (1984) once argued that social programs only make matters worse. He states that increasing rates of poverty and high rates of joblessness, crime, and a host of other social problems that currently plague the poor are the function of the "misguided" liberal welfare programs implemented in the 1960s. Nothing could be further from the truth. In fact, Murray's argument is little more than conservative ideology "dressed up in social scientific regalia" (Devine and Wright, 1993: 125).

What Murray and those who share his views on poverty fail to recognize is that increased spending on social programs did not lead to more poverty and a subculture of dependency and welfare. Rather, poverty rates stayed high between 1968 and today because unemployment rates are at least twice as high now than they were in 1968 and real wages have fallen (Greenstein, 1985). Unfortunately, when unemployment rates (see Chapter 3) increase, so do poverty rates (Wilson, 1987, 1986). Moreover, we are currently witnessing the **contraction of the welfare**

state (Devine and Wright, 1993). In other words, in Canada and the United States, federal, state, provincial, and local governments are cutting or reducing social programs, political actions that only exacerbate the problems identified here and in other chapters (Alvi and DeKeseredy, 1997; Wilson, 1996). What would poverty rates be if there were no social assistance programs like those attacked by Murray and other conservatives? They would probably be much higher (Wilson, 1987).

Unfortunately, things are not likely to improve in the near future because: (1) work is rapidly disappearing in many inner-city communities (Wilson, 1996) and (2), as stated previously, the personal inferiority perspective described here is embraced by many politicians, journalists, and the general public. For example, in 1996, U.S. President Bill Clinton signed a regressive welfare reform bill into law, one that "drove the nation's welfare policy off the edge of a cliff" (Wilentz, 1996: 7). This bill severely restricts poor people's welfare benefits to a life-time maximum of five years and, according to Wilson, "The worst thing we could do is impose time limits and then expect people to sink and swim once they move off welfare" (cited in Wilentz, 1996: 7).

The Culture of Poverty Theory

The **culture of poverty** theory, developed by Oscar Lewis in 1966, is a variation of the personal inferiority thesis and is also widely accepted and promoted by conservatives. Proponents of this theory contend that middle-class and lower-class values are distinct. For example, according to Banfield (1974: 61), "The lower-class individual lives from moment to moment....Impulse governs his behavior, either because he cannot discipline himself to sacrifice a present for future satisfaction or because he has no sense of the future." Lewis, Banfield, and other culture of poverty theorists argue that the poor are poor because, unlike middle-class people, they lack the moral fiber and discipline to get an education, to get jobs, defer gratification, and so on. This theory is flawed for several reasons, but despite its major shortcomings, it is broadcast locally and nationally by leading radio and television personalities.

For example, on September 19, 1997, Walter DeKeseredy decided to listen to Lowell Green's radio talk show on 580 CFRA, an Ottawa radio station. Mr. Green was sharply critical of liberal welfare policies, and argued that the main reason people are poor is because they sit at home all day long watching television, drinking beer, and smoking cigarettes. He said, "There are plenty of jobs out there if you want one. Just get off your butts and go look for them." If only it was that easy! Chapter 3 shows that getting a job is much harder than you might think, especially if you lack an educational background that prepares you for the changing nature of work (e.g., rapid technological change).

The truth is that the poor and affluent have the same goals and values (Cook and Curtin, 1987; Goodwin, 1969; Wilson, 1996). Both groups want to be happy, have jobs, decent standards of living, a warm and loving family, a safe neighborhood, and so on. However, only the affluent have the legitimate means of achieving the "American Dream" and its related status (Merton, 1938; Messner and Rosenfeld, 1997). What happens to many people who live in an inner-city ghetto characterized by joblessness and the myriad of social problems strongly associated with unemployment? Perhaps the best answer to this question is provided by Wilson (1996: 52):

"[W]here jobs are scarce, where people rarely, if ever, have the opportunity to help their friends and neighbors find jobs, and where there is a disruptive or degraded school life purporting to prepare youngsters for eventual participation in the workforce, many people eventually lose their feeling of connectedness to work in the formal economy; they no longer expect work to be a regular, and regulating force in their lives. In the case of young people, they may grow up in an environment that lacks the idea of work as a central experience of adult life—they have little or no labor-force attachment. These circumstances also increase the likelihood that the residents will rely on illegitimate sources of income, thereby further weakening their attachment to the legitimate labor market."

Is "proper socialization" (i.e., teaching lower-class and under-class people to strive for the American Dream and to defer immediate gratification), a solution proposed by Banfield (1974), going to solve these problems? Many progressive sociologists doubt it. Only the policy proposals briefly outlined in a subsequent section of this chapter and in other sources (Devine and Wright, 1993; Golden, 1997; Wilson, 1996) can make a difference. For example, economic success and/or escaping poverty is not purely a function of an individual's "desire," "merit," or "hard work." Throughout North America, poverty is similar to a bathtub that continually overflows. Asking the victims to mop harder will slightly reduce the amount of water on the floor, but it does not close the faucet (Currie, 1985). What needs to be shut off here are the broader social, political, and economic forces that perpetuate the alarming levels of poverty described previously.

Here's another challenge to the "proper socialization" thesis. You can provide poor people with all the counseling, "rehabilitation," and job training in the world, but if they have to return to jobless communities, what difference will this type of socialization make? Remember, most poor people share the same values as the middle and upper class, and there is no hard evidence showing that most jobless people don't want to work and ultimately improve their quality of life. How can you achieve economic success if there are no legitimate opportunities to do so?

It should also be noted that some culture of poverty theorists like Banfield argue that poor people are more prone to engage in deviant behaviors, such as violence and drug dealing, because they cannot control their basic drives. Contrary to popular belief, most poor people are not criminals (Lea and Young, 1984); however, data presented in Chapters 5 and 8 and elsewhere show that poor people report higher rates of predatory street crime, drug use, drug dealing, and criminal victimization. This is not to say that these and other criminal behaviors are "ghetto-specific" (Wilson, 1996). In other words, they are not found only in poor communities. For example, for two years, William Chambliss (1973) observed two groups of high school students. One he called the Saints, and the other he called the Roughnecks. The Saints came from middle-class homes, while the Roughnecks were the children of lower-class parents. Despite this social class difference, over the two-year period, Chambliss found that the rate of delinquency in both groups was roughly equal. Nevertheless, whereas not one Saint was arrested for criminal activities, the Roughnecks were constantly in trouble with the police and community.

Although violent crime and involvement in the drug world are widespread in North American society, these and other types of illegitimate behaviors are more frequent in inner-city ghettos, such as those found in Chicago, East St. Louis, and New York. Nevertheless, "deviant values" do not explain this problem. Rather, the social constraints on the choices economically impoverished people can make, and their limited, or non-existent, job opportunities shape and provide the context for "ghetto-related" behaviors, such as crime (Tomaszewski, 1997; Wilson, 1996). Being jobless increases the likelihood that poor people will turn to illegitimate means of income (e.g., stealing, drug dealing), thereby further weakening their attachment to the conventional social order and the legitimate labor market (Wilson, 1996).

In sum, crimes committed by the truly disadvantaged are "common behavioral responses to curiously grotesque conditions" (Devine and Wright, 1993: 128). If you want to change these behaviors, then you must change the conditions that foster them. Harsh punishment, inadequate job training, and other attempts to "repair deficient or deviant values" haven't worked (Currie, 1985, 1993; Devine and Wright, 1993). Isn't it about time we developed more effective solutions— progressive initiatives that address the broader social forces which create poverty, unemployment, and the ghetto-related behaviors discussed here? Some sociologists have developed what Wilson (1996) refers to as a "broader vision," and one salient example of a theory that recognizes the ways in which structured social inequality contributes to poverty is described next.

Structural Theory

What or who is deficient? According to Wilson (1996), the answer to this question is: definitely not individuals. Rather, he and other progressive sociologists (Piven and Cloward, 1979; Golden, 1997) contend there are serious problems with the way North American society is structured, and they offer a variation of the power/inequality perspective discussed in Chapter 1. Indeed, this chapter and Chapter 3 show that North American society is characterized by gross economic inequality, and economic inequality and poverty go hand in hand. Even the U.S. general population's "brazen conviction of equal opportunity has wilted" (Forcese, 1997: 209). For example, 64 percent of Illinois residents polled by the Chicago *Tribune* in 1996 didn't believe that a good education and hard work guarantees a good life.[10] They are right! For example, we are experiencing a new conservative political economy, one that has resulted in "deficit mania" (McQuaig, 1987), and corporate and government downsizing. Deficit mania and downsizing mean lost jobs, and since 1980, more than eight million industrial jobs have been lost in a land that newspaper and magazine columnist Allan Fotheringham refers to as the "Excited States" (Forcese, 1997).

Like many victims of downsizing, William Julius Wilson (1996) is deeply concerned about jobs, and joblessness is a central component of his theory of urban poverty. Urban poverty, for him, is an alarming consequence of what happens "when work disappears." As he correctly points out, "For the first time in the twentieth century most adults in many inner-city neighborhoods are not working in a typical week" (1996: xiii). Inner cities have always had high rates of poverty; however, the current North American rate of joblessness is shocking (see Chapter 3). To understand inner-city poverty, according to Wilson, we have to understand the conditions that generated recent escalating rates of joblessness and social disorganization problems in urban ghetto neighborhoods.

Wilson argues that many inner-city people are poor because economic globalization, the "suburbanization" of employment, rapid technological change, and the recent shift from a manufacturing to a service-based economy led to a sharp decline in the number of low-skilled jobs (mainly in the industrial sector) available in U.S. inner cities. Cities were once "centers of goods processing." (Kasarda, 1992). Now, they are centers of "information processing" and those lacking computer and other "high tech" skills are left out of the picture. Obviously, many different people suffer from the effects of these economic transitions, but low-skilled, inner-city African-Americans suffer the most. For example, between 1973 and 1987, the number of African-American males aged 20 to 29 employed by manufacturing industries fell from three out of every eight to one in five (Wilson, 1996).

You don't have to have a Ph.D. or be a world-renowned sociologist like Wilson to recognize the ways in which these factors have contributed to joblessness. For example, consider the following statements made by some of the African-American, inner-city Chicago residents interviewed by Wilson and his colleagues (1996: 36–37):

"Chicago is really full of peoples. Everybody can't get a good job. They don't have enough good jobs to provide for everybody. I don't think they have enough jobs period...And all the factories and the places, they closed up and moved out of the city and stuff like that, you know. I guess it's one of the reasons they haven't got too many jobs now, 'cause a lot of the jobs now, factories and business, they're done moved out. So that way it's less jobs for peoples." (41-year-old African-American woman who is a nurse's aide.)

"The machines are putting a lot of people out of jobs. I worked for Time magazine for seven years on a videograph printer and they came along with the Abedic printer, it cost them half a million dollars: they did what we did [in] half the time, eliminated two shifts." (33-year-old janitor from the South Side of Chicago.)

"You could walk out of the house and get a job. Maybe not what you want but you could get a job. Now, you can't find anything. A lot of people in this neighborhood, they want to work but they can't get work. A few, but a very few, they just don't want to work. The majority of them want to work but they can't find work." (29-year-old African-American male who is unemployed and lives in one of the South Side of Chicago's poorest neighborhoods.)

"Well, most of the jobs have moved out of Chicago. Factory jobs have moved out. There are no jobs here. Not like it was 20, 30 years ago. And people aren't skilled enough for the jobs that are here. You don't have enough skilled and educated people to fill them." (41-year-old hospital worker from a poor section of Chicago's South Side.)

In addition to breeding poverty in inner cities, Wilson contends that concentrated joblessness in ghetto communities destroys community-based networks of informal social control, disrupts families, contributes to high levels of crime, precludes adequate access to prenatal and child care, and destroys neighborhood businesses. In sum, the "real problem" for Wilson is not that poor inner-city people don't want to work. It's that there is no work to be found (Wilentz, 1996).

Wilson's widely-read and cited theory is an important sociological contribution to theoretical work on urban poverty. However, his work has been criticized on several grounds. For example, Tomaszewski (1997) argues that although Wilson correctly emphasizes the negative impact of global restructuring on low-skilled workers, he does not take into account the complex relationship between the government and free market forces. For example, Wilson does not adequately answer an important question: "What complex role does the U.S. federal government play in perpetuating and legitimizing the broader social forces that generate joblessness, poverty, and the other social problems that plague the truly disadvantaged?" Some Marxist political economists (Miliband, 1969; Panitch, 1977) would argue that the state or government can, and often does, help corporations achieve goals—such as lowering minimum wage levels—that are detrimental to economically disenfranchised groups.

Tomaszewski (1997) further argues that Wilson's theory would benefit from a more in-depth analysis of the U.S. political economy. For example, heavily informed by Marxist theory, Tomaszewski contends that capitalism generates structured social inequality and poverty, an issue conspicuously absent from Wilson's perspective. According to Tomaszewski (1997: 4):

"It is in the interest of those who benefit most from this very economic system to ensure that these inequalities remain by guaranteeing the persistence of a 'reserve army of labor' which helps to ensure that wage levels are minimized. Given that Wilson's solutions are located in the welfare state, we should keep the argument in mind that welfare is not intended to alleviate the effects of inequality, but merely to pacify the truly disadvantaged and prevent civil disorder."

Despite these limitations, Wilson's work sensitizes us to the fact that structural forces contribute much more to poverty than do individual or cultural deficiencies. Although many liberal and radical sociologists, community activists, and other progressives are seriously thinking about and debating Wilson's work, his theory and progressive policy proposals have "cut little ice" in the place that counts the most—the White House (Wilentz, 1996: 7).

What Is to Be Done About Poverty in North America: Progressive Ways of Overcoming or Minimizing the Problem

Most of the topics included in social problems texts elicit highly politicized conceptions and definitions. This is certainly true of the topic covered in this chapter, poverty. If, as Sartre (1969: 29) suggests, "all writing is political," then conceptions and definitions of poverty are political in a more primal sense, that is they precede research and theory and so focus attention on certain aspects of the social world while diverting attention from others (Ellis, 1987). Thus, a sociologist who conceives of poverty as a function of cultural inferiority will call for coercing the "damnable lassitude" out of the poor and divert attention from the broader social forces that foster economic inequality. In sum, the sociological study of social problems and the advancement of political views and policy proposals go together.

"Whose side are we on?" (Becker, 1967). By now, you probably have the answer to this question. Throughout this chapter, we have strongly emphasized the ways in which broader social forces in general, and economic inequality in particular, contribute to poverty. We have strongly suggested that conservative theories (e.g., structural functionalism) and policies are inadequate. Thus, not surprisingly, we will propose several progressive policies here and in other chapters that call for overcoming or minimizing the staggering levels of social, economic, and political inequality endemic to North America. Before we describe what we consider to be effective means of curbing poverty, it is first necessary to evaluate one highly controversial conservative strategy, because it is currently dominating public discourse on poverty.

A Conservative "Solution"?

Today, in both Canada and the United States, the affluent enjoy their social, political, and economic advantages, while the poor suffer the "structural violence" inherent in North America's system of institutionalized inequalities. Unfortunately, there is little chance that we will see drastic attempts to eliminate the North American class structure, and needless to say, the ruling class is not likely to contribute to the development and implementation of strategies aimed at eroding its advantages (Forcese, 1997; Messerschmidt, 1986).[11] This does not mean that conservative defenders of the capitalist status quo completely ignore the poor. In fact, the truly disadvantaged are seen by many ruling and economic elites as a passive threat to the dominant social order. Referred to as "social junk" because they are not formally attached to the capitalist economy, the poor are seen by the ruling class as requiring discipline. Thus, the "invisible hand" of the capitalist market is replaced by the "visible fist" of the government. For example, the government intervenes to ensure that the process of capital accumulation is not hindered by these potential troublemakers (Spitzer, 1975). Workfare is one of the resources the government uses to deal with the poor surplus population, and it to this strategy that we now turn.

Workfare

Again, many North Americans, including some academics and politicians, regard the poor as being "lazy and shiftless," and they strongly advocate **workfare** as a means of coping with the "unpleasantry of disadvantage" (Forcese, 1997).[12] In the United States, workfare was introduced in the 1980s, but was only recently introduced in parts of Canada, such as Ontario. Put simply, workfare requires poor people to work for their welfare checks.

Those who support workfare contend that it has the following benefits and they use the jargon described in Box 2.5 to justify it:

➤ People willing to work clearly have need, so workfare weeds out those who try to exploit or "rip off" the welfare system, such as those some people claim are sitting at home all day watching television, drinking beer, and smoking cigarettes.

➤ Making welfare recipients work lowers the costs of welfare.

➤ Workfare helps people acquire or enhance skills that can lead to full-time employment.

➤ Workfare makes the welfare system more equitable. For example, able-bodied people should not be treated the same as those who are unable to work (Lauer, 1998: 241).

Those opposed to workfare argue that (Lauer, 1998: 241):

➤ Income support programs should not be abandoned because they are more effective in the long run in reducing poverty.

➤ People on workfare learn little, if anything, that will make them more marketable.

➤ Many people are poor for only short periods of time and thus need support during that time rather than a job that delays their search for new and unsubsidized work.

➤ The economic costs of running workfare programs are higher than the alternatives because the administrative expenses outweigh whatever is saved having people do menial, and often degrading, types of work.

➤ Workfare jobs do not provide an income that enables people to escape from poverty, and they do not lead to jobs that will help them achieve this goal.

Regardless of whether you personally agree or disagree with workfare, you, like many others, probably want to know whether it works. Consistent with many other flawed "band-aid" or "quick formula" money-saving strategies, it doesn't (Curran and Renzetti, 1996). Keep in mind too, that simply having a job does not necessarily help people escape poverty, and contrary to popular belief and to what some conservative politicians, academics, and journalists say, many poor people are working. For example, in 1990, approximately 60 percent of the U.S. poverty households had at least one resident who held a job for at least part of the year. Furthermore, about 18 percent of all poor households had more than one worker (Devine and Wright, 1993). So much for the "shiftless, lazy bum" theory of poverty.

BOX 2-5

Workfare Jargon

The following jargon is used by workfare supporters to help convince people that workfare actually benefits those who receive welfare and unemployment insurance.

Active, Not Passive, Social Programs

People who use this phrase claim that existing welfare programs make people lazy. This phrase implies that training and prodding people to get off welfare will create jobs for them.

Breaking the Cycle of Poverty

"Lurking behind" this phrase is the theory that children are socialized to be poor by poor parents. They then pass this preference for poverty on to their children. However, no one is exhorted to "break the cycle of wealth" where rich people pass their wealth on to children who pass it on to their children, perpetuating inequality of income distribution. This shows the double standard of media and social policy makers.

Bring Social Programs into the Twenty-First Century

This generally means "cut and slash" social programs so that people will have to work at low-wage jobs in order to compete with Mexican workers who make $5.00 a day.

Discouraging Dependence

This term implies that welfare and unemployment insurance create "dependent" people. According to this theory the programs have to be changed so that people don't use them. The reality, again, is that people will automatically take jobs when they provide decent wages.

Disincentive to Work

The direct opposite of "incentive to work." Used in sentences such as "Welfare is a disincentive to work," this phrase implies that people would rather collect welfare than work at paid jobs. In the vast majority of cases, this is untrue. Increasing the minimum wage to $10.00 or $11.00 an hour would eliminate virtually any "disincentive" to work and it wouldn't cost the taxpayers a cent.

Ejection Seat

This phrase refers to the policies of Alberta and Michigan, where people are simply ejected off welfare into destitution and homelessness.

Hand-Up, Not Hand-Out

This term originated in the United States and is currently coming into use by Canadian social policy makers. It implies that social programs as they exist always keep people from getting work. If programs are changed to provide counseling, money-management skills, and training for low-wage jobs, the theory goes, then people will get off welfare. The reality is that people on welfare and/or who receive unemployment insurance will take available jobs when wages are high enough to sustain them. No prodding is necessary.

Incentive to Work

This phrase is often used in sentences such as: "Cutting unemployment insurance or welfare to provide an incentive to work." The incentive is desperation. If people can't rely on unemployment insurance or welfare, they will be so desperate that they will have to take any job, no matter how ill-suited it is to their skills or how low the pay.

Poverty Culture

Another phrase which implies that poor people like to be poor and that they need counseling from middle-class professionals to help them choose another "culture," presumably one that provides more money.

Reform

This term used to mean "to make things better." Now, when applied to social programs, such as the unemployment insurance system, it almost always means "to make things worse for low income people."

Self-Esteem

Bandied about in sentences such as, "People need work to build their self-esteem," this implies that a single parent must build self-esteem at a low wage, exploitative paid job, rather than by staying at home to raise children who will be good citizens.

Training for the Jobs of the Future

This phrase is used to imply that if only we got ourselves trained as computer programmers or air traffic controllers, we could get off welfare. In fact, we don't need millions of North American people in "high tech" jobs, and training does not create jobs.

Most of the available jobs provide low wages and tens of thousands of people are trained and then can't find work. They are pushed out into the labor force to compete with those who do have jobs and pull wages down because they are trained for exploitation.

BOX 2-5

BOX 2-5

Trampoline Effect

This phrase recognizes that North America is going to lose many jobs. Social programs, it implies, should be designed to bounce people back into jobs, which still don't exist.

Truly Needy

This phrase is used to justify cutting universal social programs, or programs to the "merely" needy. It implies, for example, that people on unemployment insurance, who may get more money than people on welfare, should have to give up their unemployment insurance so that the government can cut the deficit and maintain payments to the "truly needy." Lost in the dialogue is the status of the truly greedy, who continue to use their tax breaks and incentives to accumulate wealth.

Source: Swanson (1997: 152–155). "Resisting Workfare," pp. 149–170 in *Workfare: Ideology For New Underclass*, edited by E. Shragge. Toronto: Garamond Press. Reprinted by permission of Garamond Press.

Another point to consider is that having a job does not mean that you will have a decent income, clean place to live, warm clothes, proper medical care, or healthy food. Consider homeless people. Many of them wash dishes and sweep floors in exchange for a warm meal and/or a place to sleep. They may not be officially employed but they are working (Barak, 1991; Devine and Wright, 1993). Furthermore, as stated previously, many poor people lack the necessary educational background to get jobs that enable them to acquire the above basic necessities. Why, then, according to Devine and Wright (1993: 60), "do we even expect people to work when the earnings from many jobs will not suffice to keep a family out of poverty?" Clearly much more than work is needed to help people escape poverty.

Progressive Alternative Solutions

Obviously, poverty and joblessness are directly related. Poverty is also a powerful determinant of many social problems discussed throughout this text, such as violent crime (see Chapter 5) and drug abuse (see Chapter 8). If we can eliminate or minimize poverty, we will ultimately overcome or minimize many other problems that plague our society. How can we achieve this goal?

The following are some examples of **progressive policy proposals** that are addressed in much greater detail in subsequent chapters of this text. We invite you to read these chapters and to think seriously about how and why poverty is strongly associated with health problems, violence, drug dealing, and so on. After you read the relevant chapters, we invite you to discuss and debate the effectiveness of the following strategies, advanced by many progressive sociologists, policy analysts, community activists, and so on:

➤ job creation and training programs, including publicly supported community-oriented job creation;

> higher minimum wage level;

> day care;

> housing assistance;

> introducing entrepreneurial skills into the high school curriculum; and

> creating linkages between schools, private business, and government agencies.

Those people caught up in "deficit mania" (McQuaig, 1987) would probably ask "What would all this cost?" (Devine and Wright, 1993). This is a logical and fair question. These and other strategies advanced in this text would probably cost billions of dollars. However, the cost of poverty and related social problems is much higher (Currie, 1985, 1993). For example, Devine and Wright estimate that the direct and indirect cost of poverty in the United States is half a trillion dollars a year. Can we afford this? We don't think so, and, like other sociologists, we contend that spending billions of dollars to solve poverty and the other social problems discussed in this text is a solid investment. As pointed out in Chapter 8, "the urban underclass is a time bomb ticking. It would be prudent...to defuse the bomb while there is still something to save" (Devine and Wright, 1993: 217).

Summary

In this chapter, you have read about poverty, a major symptom of social, economic, and political inequality. The data presented here show that both Canada and the United States have high levels of poverty; however, these statistics constitute just the tip of the iceberg, because many poor people (e.g., the homeless) are excluded from data sets generated by government agencies. In fact, the ways in which Statistics Canada and the U.S. Bureau of the Census measure poverty have several major pitfalls.

Why are people poor? Many people answer this question by offering personal inferiority or culture of poverty theories. Many sociologists contend that these perspectives are flawed, and that they are little more than ideological statements dressed up as social science. If only a handful of North Americans were poor, it would be easy to accept inferiority theories. Unfortunately, poverty is deeply entrenched in our society; we are currently experiencing unprecedented levels of poverty and joblessness in many parts of North America (Forcese, 1997; Wilson, 1996). Therefore, sociologists like ourselves ask how, given the endemic nature of poverty and its related problems (e.g., predatory street violence), we can maintain that they are caused by genetic or psychological factors. Even if this were the case, one would have to spend a great deal of time looking at the social structure of a continent that produces a substantial number of inferior people (DeKeseredy and Schwartz, 1996). Because North America has astoundingly high rates of poverty, individualistic perspectives have little to offer.

We need to develop what C. Wright Mills (1959) calls the sociological imagination. As described in Chapter 1, this perspective, like Wilson's (1996) structural theory, calls for an understanding of the ways in which private troubles are related to public issues. Private troubles are just what you might think. If you are poor, you have a problem and you have to deal with it. You may need unemployment insurance, welfare, government housing, or any of a number of other forms of aid discussed throughout this text. However, the data presented here show that many people are suffering from the exact same personal problem at the same time. Why? Mills would argue that there is something about the broader social, political, and economic forces that allows so many North Americans to be poor. To be able to look beyond the private troubles of one or two poor people and see the broader problem of poverty in North America is to possess the sociological imagination.

What is to be done about poverty? The answer is definitely not workfare and government cutbacks. We need more progressive strategies, such as creating jobs that provide a decent wage. Can we develop and implement the policies briefly advanced in this chapter and discussed in greater detail in later chapters? The good news is that we can if we want or have to. In fact, "Employers can, if obliged, produce jobs as well as products. Educational institutions, if obliged, can generate mobility. Political parties, if obliged, can legislate benefits" (Forcese, 1997: 215). What do you think about this, and what role do you see yourself playing in the struggle to eliminate or overcome poverty?

KEY TERMS

Absolute poverty
Contraction of the welfare state
Culture of poverty
Low Income Cut-Offs (LICOs)
Personal inferiority
Poverty line
Progressive policy proposals
Quantify
Relative poverty
Sociological imagination
Subjective deprivation
Victim blaming
Workfare

DISCUSSION QUESTIONS

1. What are the strengths and limitations of absolute and relative definitions of poverty?
2. What are the limitations of official measures of poverty, such as those used by the U.S. Bureau of the Census?
3. What are the limitations of the personal inferiority theory?
4. Why are so many elderly people and children poor?
5. Why do many progressive sociologists oppose workfare?

PROBLEM SOLVING SCENARIOS

1. When you watch television and/or read the newspaper over the next week, note the ways in which the news, movies, etc. depict poor people. Do the media present a picture of poor people similar to the sociological one provided in this chapter?
2. As a class, divide up into groups of six people and debate the value of workfare.
3. In a group, discuss ways in which you could develop measures of poverty that are superior to those used by Canadian and United States government agencies.
4. Generate a group discussion on how university and college students can help overcome or minimize poverty in North America.
5. Create your own theory of poverty, one that takes into account the data presented in this chapter.

WEB EXERCISES

1. Create a model illustrating the ways we can connect structural analyses of poverty interpretations that favor the actions and attitudes of individuals. Start your research at

   http://cpmcnet.columbia.edu/dept/nccp/

2. Compare and contrast the two approaches to solving poverty in North America that are given at the following websites. You will have to do some browsing within each website to gather the information you need.

   http://www.fraserinstitute.ca/ and http://www.foodfirst.org/

SUGGESTED READINGS

Devine, Joel A. and James D. Wright. *The Greatest of Evils: Urban Poverty and the American Underclass.* New York: Aldine de Gruyter, 1993.
Like *When Work Disappears*, this book provides a comprehensive sociological overview of U.S. urban poverty and its related problems, and also provides some progressive answers to the question "What is to be done about poverty?".

Forcese, Dennis. *The Canadian Class Structure* (4th edition). Toronto: McGraw-Hill Ryerson, 1997.
This book provides students and researchers with a comprehensive critical overview of class-based inequalities in Canada, including poverty. It will be of special interest to people concerned about gender, age, and racial/ethnic variations in the Canadian class structure.

Golden, Renny. *Disposable Children: America's Child Welfare System.* Belmont, CA: Wadsworth, 1997.
What role does the child welfare system play in perpetuating and maintaining child poverty? In this book, Golden provides compelling answers to this question and suggests several alternative methods of helping disenfranchised children.

Shragge, Eric (ed.) *Workfare: Ideology for a New Underclass.* Toronto: Garamond, 1997.
This book provides a collection of readings on the major limitations of workfare, and compares Canadian workfare programs with similar ones found in the United States.

Wilson, William Julius. *When Work Disappears: The World of the New Urban Poor.* New York: Knopf, 1996.
In this book, Wilson presents a powerful challenge to conservative perspectives on poverty, such as personal and cultural inferiority theories. Moreover, he makes explicit the devastating consequences of joblessness in United States inner-city communities.

ENDNOTES

1   One example of such an agency is Statistics Canada (Beauchense, 1997).
2   The Consumer Price Index measures the costs of products, services, and other items (e.g., fuel, electricity, etc.) that are essential to everyday life. In other words, it measures the cost of living (Curran and Renzetti, 1996).
3   See Beeghley (1984), Curran and Renzetti (1996), Duncan, (1984), Hurst (1995), and Plotnick and Skidmore (1975) for more detailed information on problems with the U.S. federal government's official measure of poverty.

4   To calculate LICOs, Statistics Canada estimates the percentage of gross (before tax) income that the average Canadian family spends on basic needs, such as food, clothing, and shelter. Then, it arbitrarily marks the percentage up by 20 percentage points, and the final percentage corresponds on average to a given household income level which becomes the LICO for that year (Ross et al., 1997). In sum, the LICOs reviewed in this chapter represent incomes below which families "spend a significantly higher proportion of their incomes on necessities than Canadian families as a whole" (Evans and Chawla, 1990: 33; Spector, 1994: 269-271).

5   See, for example, Ross et al. (1996).

6   This table was constructed by the Canadian Council on Social Development (1997).

7   The "elderly" are referred to here as people 65 years of age and older (CCSD, 1997).

8   See Golden (1997) for more detailed information on these and other dangers that poor youth and children face in contemporary North American society.

9   Charles Darwin's *The Origin of Species* was first published by John Murray in 1859.

10   See Forcese (1997) for more information on this study.

11   The ruling class is defined here as consisting of the dominant few elites who successfully govern, represent, administer, judge, and command the subordinate many. Among the elites that collectively make up the ruling or dominant class, economic elites appear to constitute a dominant faction (Ellis, 1987; Miliband, 1969).

12   See Shragge (1997) for a more in-depth critique of workfare.

Chapter (3)

Get a Job!
Unemployment in
North America

The signs are, to put it bluntly, that there are not going to be enough conventional jobs to go around—not full-time, lifetime jobs with an employer who pays you a pension for the ten years or so of your retirement. That is going to be true no matter which Government is in power over the next twenty years.
(Handy, 1984: 1)

OBJECTIVES

In this chapter we focus on the topics

1. The meaning of work
2. Defining unemployment and understanding why it is a problem
3. Making sense of unemployment and work issues as social problems
4. What is to be done about unemployment?

Introduction

A multinational Canadian bank recently produced a television commercial which, to the tune of folk singer Bob Dylan's "The Times they are a Changin'," depicts "ordinary people" rejoicing in the fact that they can now pay bills over the Internet. The bank could not have chosen a more ironic theme. In the 1960s, when Dylan wrote this song, jobs were relatively plentiful, the North American economy was booming, and unemployment was low. Thirty years later some momentous and painful changes have indeed occurred. The banking industry provides an excellent example of these changes—it is part of a sector, services, that now dominates modern capitalism. It has implemented new technologies such as Internet banking and automated teller machines (ATMs) to reduce costs and improve service and, in the process, eliminated 37 percent of its workforce between 1983 and 1993. Dylan's song urges us to "start swimmin' or....sink like a stone." For many North Americans, fundamental shifts in the nature of the economy have meant that when it comes to employment, more are sinking and fewer are swimming. Indeed, for them, these basic economic changes have meant that unemployment has become a personal and social problem of often catastrophic proportions.

The Meaning of Work

Few of us would disagree with the notion that work is central to our lives. Most of us need "work to live" although probably far fewer would say that they "live to work." In general, the meaning of work is different for different people. For many, work is sometimes unhealthy, dangerous, boring, repetitive, or otherwise unfulfilling. It is, as economist John Kenneth Galbraith points out, "a stint to be performed." He goes on to say that for a minority of people, "work, as it continues to be called, is an entirely different matter. It is taken for granted that it will be enjoyable" (quoted in Ehrenreich, 1989: 261).

The notion that work is experienced differently is not particularly insightful. For the most part, however, our understanding of the opposite of being employed—unemployment—is not so commonplace. In this chapter, we argue that unemployment is both a private trouble and a public issue, which is generally misunderstood. More specifically, we illustrate that unemployment in modern North American society is increasingly problematic for the following reasons:

➤ Many experts agree that there are no longer any guarantees that we will actually have well-paying, fulfilling jobs (Aronowitz & DiFazio, 1994; Rifkin, 1996).

➤ Researchers have documented many adverse psychological effects of unemployment. These include financial anxiety, loss of variety (in terms of things to do), loss of structure in life, reduced scope for decisions (because of fewer options), less skill development, social rejection, reduced interpersonal contact, substance abuse, marital discord and abuse, depression, and loss of status (Warr, 1983; Grant and Barling, 1994).

➤ Unemployment is a social and personal problem in itself, but is also strongly related to other social ills, such as crime, imprisonment, and mental or physical illness (Lynch and Groves, 1989). Moreover, unacceptable rates of unemployment do not permit us to achieve a just society.

➤ Despite massive changes in the nature of work and increasing knowledge of problems associated with unemployment, many North Americans continue to believe that "work is always there for those who want it badly enough." However, uncritical acceptance of this belief is based on an unrealistic picture of the nature of the economy, and is grounded in assumptions that were probably more appropriate shortly after World War II.

To understand why this social problem persists, we need to answer some basic questions about work and employment. In the next section, we look more closely at the questions: "What is work?," What is unemployment?," and "In what ways does unemployment constitute a social problem?"

Defining Unemployment and Understanding Why It Is a Problem

A useful way of understanding unemployment as a social problem is to think about what it means to be employed. To some readers, it may seem frivolous to think about defining **employment**, particularly since many of us tend to think about employment in very superficial terms—one either has a job or hasn't. Yet when we think critically about work some interesting insights and important sociological questions arise. For instance, from a sociological perspective, we need to consider whether we are referring to paid or unpaid domestic labor.[1] Another important question arises when we think about those instances where people are "working" (and so are officially employed) in low-paid, dead-end, part-time jobs. If people are working in jobs which keep them below the poverty line, or hold no promise for personal or career development, in what sense can they really be said to be "employed"? Definitions of employment and unemployment are not simple issues, and for this reason questions about what it means to work and to be unemployed are important ones for sociologists.

Most of us would probably be comfortable with a **relational definition of work**; that is, describing it in terms of the relationship between an employer and employee. The former provides the latter with work for wages or salary in exchange for the employee's capacity to produce goods. At the most basic level, then, to be employed is to provide work or services in exchange for a wage or salary. The law has institutionalized this definition. In legal terms, work in industrial societies is usually defined as a "master-servant" (or "owner-worker") relationship, which gives us some sense of the unequal relationship between workers and employers.

Although straightforward, such definitions tell us little of what it means to work or, conversely, to be out of work. Nor do they provide any information on the meaning and impact of work or non-work in our lives.

When we ask North Americans whether they work to live, or live to work, we find that their answers are related to the nature of the work they do as well as its occupational status. The bulk of people who work in higher status, reasonably well-paying and interesting jobs are more concerned with the capacity of work to enrich their lives than its ability to line their pockets. Conversely, the lower the job in the occupational hierarchy, the more likely the worker is to view the work as "just a job" providing a paycheck and little else (Fox, 1980). Indeed, according to many analysts, most workers want jobs that are interesting and meaningful—although the desire for high income runs a close second in the hierarchy of meaningful job characteristics (Weaver and Matthews, 1996).

Most North Americans want interesting jobs, adequate autonomy to get their work done, and a chance to develop their personal capacities (Lowe and Krahn, 1984; Feldman, 1996). Although most would like to work in interesting, motivating jobs, the majority are not lucky enough to do so. This is illustrated by a 1990 opinion poll that found that only 10 percent of Americans are satisfied with their jobs (Simon, 1996: 6). Clearly, for most of us, work is much more than something we do to put food on the table. It is a fundamental part of our existence because it is instrumental to our personal makeup. This is illustrated when we examine North Americans' concerns about the possibility of being unemployed. In Canada, the percentage of people who thought that "unemployment is the most important problem facing the country today" jumped from 12 percent in 1981 to 50 percent in 1985, despite the fact that the official unemployment rate rose only two percentage points (from 8 to 10 percent) in that same time frame.

Some commentators maintain that work is central to our existence, and that "we are shaped, molded, regulated, even assimilated by our work. Work is our behavioral product, but so, too, are we and our lives in many ways the products of our work" (Bryant, 1972: 32). Others, such as Jeremy Rifkin (1996) argue that work is in effect "anthropologically necessary," that it is a central fact of what makes us human. We can also see the centrality of work in our lives in the time we spend working. Despite the arguments of researchers some years ago that we would have more leisure time because of the liberating effects of technology in work, today North Americans are working harder than ever before. Indeed, Americans now work about 140 hours more per year than they did a decade ago, and Canadians rank third in the world (behind the Japanese and Americans) in terms of highest number of hours worked per year.

Why do we work so hard? Quite simply, families are finding that they have to work harder than they have in the past to make ends meet. Two-thirds of Canadian families now depend on two incomes to maintain standards of living they held in 1980. In the United States in 1979, the average weekly wage for blue collar workers was $387. Ten years later it had dropped to $335. In the 20 years between 1973 and 1993, American blue collar workers lost 15 percent of their purchasing power. At the beginning of the 1980s, most U. S. families conformed to the "traditional" nuclear family model, with the husband going to work and the wife staying at home. By the end of the decade, nearly half (46 percent) of all married couples were working to support their families, and only a third (34 percent) were still one-earner married couples (Rifkin, 1995: 172). In addition to the increased participation of women in the workforce for personal and career reasons, these families are dual-earners because they need two incomes to survive. There can be little disagreement that work is important to us because we need to work to live.

Obviously, work as it has evolved in our societies is something we need to do for both personal and financial reasons. Being employed is much more than a necessary condition of existence in terms of earning money to buy life's needs; it is central to our definition of ourselves as human. It follows that being unemployed is not only difficult in terms of people's diminished abilities to purchase life's necessities, it is also dehumanizing. Accordingly, we would agree with Schwarzer et al., (1994: 76), who argue that employment is "the basis for earning one's living and for being respected in a Western society characterized by high material and economic values. Thus the impact of unemployment goes beyond direct economic costs."

Counting the Unemployed: How Many and Who?

Both the Canadian and U. S. governments conduct periodic surveys of the general population to determine the number of people who are officially out of work. **Unemployment** is officially defined as the number of individuals who are out of work and actively looking for a job during a period of time before the survey of employment is conducted (two weeks in Canada, four in the United States). According to the Population Division of the U.S. Bureau of the Census (Rawlings and Saluter, Household and Family Characteristics: March 1994), unemployed persons are those who

"...during the survey week, had no employment but were available for work and (1) had engaged in any specific job-seeking activity within the past 4 weeks, such as registering at a public or private employment office, meeting with prospective employers, checking with friends or relatives, placing or answering advertisements, writing letters of application, or being on a union or professional register; (2) were waiting to be called back to a job from which they had been laid off; or (3) were waiting to report to a new wage or salary job within 30 days.

Furthermore,

All those who are not classified as employed or unemployed are defined as "not in the labor force." This group who are neither employed nor seeking work includes persons engaged only in own home housework, attending school, or unable to work because of long-term physical or mental illness; persons who are retired or too old to work, seasonal workers for whom the survey week fell in an off season, and the voluntary idle. Persons doing only unpaid family work (less than 15 hours) are also classified as not in the labor force."

The **unemployment rate** therefore, is the number of people capable of, and willing to work, but unable to find employment, divided by the total number of persons available for employment at any time (Gilpin, 1977: 230). As we will see, for a number of reasons, these official definitions do not permit us to understand the full extent and nature of unemployment.

The International Labor Organization recently estimated that, worldwide, there are one billion people, amounting to about one-third of the employable workforce, who are unemployed today. While this is a striking number, one of the most important sociological issues associated with unemployment is that we have only a rough sense of exactly how many unemployed people there are in North America. We do know, however, that official statistics on the unemployment rate in both Canada and the United States grossly underestimate the real proportion of people who are unemployed. There are several important reasons for this:

1. Many individuals who become unemployed simply do not register with official state agencies as being unemployed, and are therefore "invisible" to the system.

2. Some people do not officially look for work until they feel that the labor market has improved.

3. It is difficult to count those who are unemployed over longer periods of time, since temporary employment schemes often give the illusion that such workers are employed when in fact they are seasonally or temporarily employed.

4. Official statistics do not take into account the number of young people who are in school but would rather be working, or the number of women who would be working if they could afford adequate child care.

5. Official statistics do not provide us with a sense of the number of people who have dropped out of the labor force and have stopped looking for work; often referred to as "discouraged workers."

6. Underemployment—the phenomenon in which people's skills, training, experience, and education (their **cultural capital**) are not made use of in the jobs they are in—is an increasingly common feature of modern working life.

While people employed in such **"McJobs"** as described in point 6 are technically "employed," for most, such short-term, low wage jobs are probably not meeting their personal or financial needs. One good indicator of this is the increasing proportion of people working in "non-standard" jobs such as part-time, short-term, and voluntary work. According to a recent study of the Canadian workplace, nearly one-third of all jobs fit into one of these non-standard categories. The same study reports that involuntary part-time employment (those individuals who are working in part-time jobs but would rather be working full-time) accounted for 36 percent of all part-time employment in 1993 (Betcherman et al., 1994: 76–77).

Another important aspect of counting unemployment is the assumption made by governments and the public that as long as the official unemployment rate falls within an "acceptable" range, there is nothing wrong with the employment situation. The difficulty with this view is that it does not account for the realities described above, namely, that many of those who are employed are likely to be underemployed. Furthermore, the notion as to what is an "acceptable" unemployment

BOX 3-1

"Discouraged Workers" To Be Counted in Jobless Surveys

Carol Howes, Southam Newspapers

CALGARY—Anger boils to the surface whenever Margaret reads Canada's monthly unemployment statistics. Her 48-year-old husband was laid off from his job as a mechanical engineer in the oil patch two years ago and has had to return to school.

All efforts to find another job failed, so he opted to move into a different field in a last-ditch effort to create a new life for himself. Money is tight, friends have stopped calling and relatives in Central Canada are puzzled.

"Our family sees the low unemployment numbers here and they say, 'Calgary is so hot, why can't your husband get a job?'"

Margaret (who asked that her last name not be used to avoid embarrassment for her husband) says she would love to tell a few statisticians what to do with their numbers. Her husband doesn't count in their books because he's back at school. But in her books, he's as unemployed as it gets.

There's a lot of people like him out there—people who just don't take a paycheck home," says Margaret. "They just don't show up in those statistics."

She's right. And the statisticians know it too. Margaret's husband is a member of that growing segment of Canada's population referred to as "discouraged workers" who are not measured in the country's official unemployment rate.

In order to be counted, they have to be out of work, but looking for work or available for work. Simply giving up doesn't fit into the description.

The reason is that Canada's unemployment rate is based on a definition that has been used for years—long before workers became "discouraged"—and for international comparisons by the International Labour Organization.

But Statistics Canada says the agency now wants more Canadians on the periphery of the labor force, like Margaret's husband, to stand up and be counted.

So it's making changes. The official unemployment rate will be measured the same as always, but the agency will produce alternative figures that paint a different—but some would argue more accurate—picture.

Over the next six months, Statistics Canada will phase in a redesigned questionnaire to the 52,000 households it surveys each month in order to collect its labor force data.

The last set of revisions was in 1976 and "since then an enormous amount of the labor force has changed" says Deborah Sunter who is heading the changes.

The new questionnaire will not only get a better measurement on the number of Canadians who are not part of the labor force because they can't find work, but those also doing contract work, seasonal, and involuntary part-time jobs.

BOX 3-1

"You're going to have a fuller picture of quality of employment," says Sunter.

Historically, Statistics Canada has done this kind of research on an ad hoc basis. But, with the speed at which the Canadian labor market is changing, the public could do with more timely and consistent data, she says.

A new addition to the survey will be questions about wages. With that kind of information, the federal agency will be able to follow compensation trends, measure who is getting paid for overtime, or how wages compare regionally or by industry.

Likewise, with more people telecommuting, for the first time Statistics Canada will measure each month where Canadians actually conduct their work.

The changes are sure to be welcomed by Statistics Canada critics who have argued that by overlooking a huge group of people who have given up looking for work as well as those who have been forced into part-time work, Canada's labor market is even more dismal than it appears.

One critic, the Bank of Nova Scotia, has put Canada's jobless rate, which has been officially running between 9 and 10 percent, at closer to 13 percent by counting in all those who have opted out of the labor force since 1990.

Sunter argues the new data will likely only push the "unofficial" unemployment rate up by one percentage point. After all, not everyone who has left the workforce in the past six years have done so against [his/her] will, she points out.

Regardless of the outcome of the new survey, it's all academic for people like Margaret. She will still have trouble trying to explain to relatives back home why her husband can't find a job in a city that boasts an official 6.9 percent unemployment rate.

Source: *The Ottawa Citizen*, Saturday, November 2, 1996, reprinted from *The Calgary Herald*. Reprinted with the permission of *The Calgary Herald*.

rate has changed many times over the last 60 years. In Canada for example, at one point an unemployment rate of 5 percent was considered to be scandalous; now, the official rate of approximately 10 percent is considered to be "normal."

According to the U.S. Department of Commerce (1994), for individuals to be counted as unemployed, they must meet the Labor Department's specific requirements regarding employability. The danger of relying on data generated within the parameters of this definition is that a good proportion of people who do not fit these requirements will not be counted among the unemployed, even though they may, in fact, be unemployed.

The difficulties associated with accurately calculating unemployment should make us skeptical about official pronouncements regarding unemployment. As we write this text, unemployment rates in the United States have officially decreased in the last year. However, if we were to include those individuals who have given up looking for work, are invisible to the official counting system, or who are under-employed, we would see that the real rates of unemployment and under-employment are actually quite high. Put differently, although unemployment in the United States is currently fairly low (about 5 percent) such statistics may be misleading because we are not sure to what extent such jobs are well-paid, secure, and full-time. Nor do they tell us the extent to which workers are holding more than one job, or how much overtime work they do. Because they take such factors into account, many social scientists argue that actual unemployment rates are probably higher than those commonly declared by official state agencies.

Unemployment, Race, Class, Gender, and Age

One of the more persistent myths associated with the unemployed is that they are lazy or unwilling to work. The flip side of this coin is the assumption that those who are motivated and intelligent enough will get well-paying "good" jobs on their own merit. This perspective, also known as the **human capital approach**, assumes that people rationally invest in themselves—their education, skills, work experience, and so on—to increase their chances of getting good jobs. When these skills and experience are no longer appropriate to the changing work context, unemployment occurs. A core assumption of the human capital approach is that our society is a **meritocracy**—a society in which everyone has an equal opportunity to get ahead (or get a job) because institutional arrangements such as the educational system (which is crucial to getting a job) or the labor market constitute a "level playing field." This assumption is problematic because when we examine data on the kinds of people who are unemployed, it is clear that not everyone has equal access to the training, education, and resources necessary to become gainfully employed. In North America, this is especially clear when we look at the experiences of visible minorities, African-Americans, Hispanics, Native (Aboriginal) peoples, and women.[2] In other words, when we look at how jobs are organized and distributed according to characteristics such as race, class, and gender, it is very clear that unemployment in North American society is unequally experienced and unevenly structured.

The fact that class, race, and gender are important factors in structuring the labor market is illustrated by data on who does what kind of work in North America. In the United States, women are more likely to occupy the lowest-paying jobs in society, hold only 15 percent of management positions, one percent of senior management positions, and are outnumbered by men 600 to 1 in the top jobs within Fortune 500 companies (Caston, 1998). Similarly, Table 3.1 shows that in Canada, 60 percent of all women working in 1996 were concentrated in two occupational groups—the business, finance, and administrative sector where they tend to perform mostly secretarial or clerical jobs, and the retail sales and service sector. Moreover, 50 percent of women in North America work in only 20 occupations (Richmond-Abbott, 1992). This high concentration of women in a few low-paying and career-limited occupations has the important effect of driving down their wages because the labor supply is so high. In addition, consider the following statistics from the Canadian Labour Congress (1997) and Statistics Canada (1995):

➤ Only 20 percent of women have full-time, full-year jobs, which pay more than $30,000 per year, compared to 40 percent of men.

➤ Canada has the second highest incidence of low-paid employment for women, (34.3 percent) among all industrialized (OECD) countries. Only Japan (37.2 percent) was worse.

➤ While women account for less than 20 percent of those in the top ten paying job categories, they represent more than 70 percent in the lowest-paying jobs.

➤ The unemployment rate for young women (under 24)—15.6 percent; for "visible minority" women—13.4 percent; for Aboriginal women—17.7 percent; and for women with disabilities—16.6 percent. Research produced by the Disabled Women's Network of Canada shows that 65 percent of women with disabilities who were unemployed wanted to work.

➤ In less than 20 years, the number of female part-time workers has increased by 200 percent. Throughout that period, women made up 70 percent of the part-time workforce. Over a third of part-time workers wanted to work full-time, but could only find part-time employment.

➤ One in ten jobs is now temporary. Over a period of 15 years, the number of women working more than one job increased by 372 percent.

Clerical and service occupations are among the lowest-paid jobs available; they are also the most vulnerable in that it is in these sectors that employers tend to substitute new technologies for human labor (for example, word processing has replaced the traditional "secretarial pool"). In addition, because they continue to have greater domestic and family responsibilities than men, women are more likely to seek employment that affords them the time to manage conflicting work and family obligations (Clement and Myles, 1994; Alvi, 1994). This largely means that part-time work is the only kind of employment realistically available to many women with families. However, most part-time jobs are in what is often called the "pink ghetto,"—jobs such as secretaries, cashiers, and waitresses, concentrated in the service and white collar areas and typified by low wages, poor working conditions, minimal benefits, and reduced or non-existent career options. In addition, for reasons discussed further below, many of these jobs will probably vanish in the coming decades.

This is not to suggest that the labor market for women has not improved since World War II, only that in terms of accessing the most financially rewarding jobs, most women still find that the "deck is stacked" against them. As one Canadian report notes,

"Although the employment rate of women increases dramatically with educational attainment, women with post-secondary training are still somewhat less likely than their male counterparts to be employed. In 1994, 77 percent of female university graduates, versus 82 percent of male graduates, were employed. Similarly, among those with other types of post-secondary qualifications, 65 percent of women, compared with 76 percent of men, worked for pay or profit" (Statistics Canada, 1995).

Gender differences are also evident within the workplace. Sexual stereotypes, although under challenge, are still major obstacles for many women. But perhaps

Table 3.1
Percentage of Labor Force Participants, by Major Occupational Group and Sex, Canada, 1996

	Males	Females
Management occupations	11	6
Business, finance, and administrative occupations	10	29
Natural and applied sciences and related occupations	7	2
Health occupations	2	8
Occupations in social science, education, government service, and religion	5	9
Occupations in art, culture, recreation, and sport	2	3
Sales and service occupations	20	31
Trades, transport and equipment operators, and related occupations	24	2
Occupations unique to primary industry	7	2
Occupations unique to processing, manufacturing and utilities	10	5

Source: Statistics Canada, 1996 Census, Catalogue No. 93F0027XDB96007

the most telling difference between the employment experiences of men and women is in income. In spite of the fact that women have almost achieved equality in educational achievement, women in the United States earn substantially less than their male counterparts regardless of educational credentials (see Table 3.2). Similarly, a recent Canadian report on the status of women states that "At all levels of educational attainment, women's earnings are lower than those of men. Even female university graduates employed full-time, full-year, only earned 75 percent as much as their male colleagues in 1993, while the figure was 74 percent for women with a non-university post secondary certificate, and 72 percent for high school graduates" (Statistics Canada, 1995).

These differences in income provide some evidence for the substitution of cheaper female labor for male labor as a fundamental strategy for reproducing the capitalist economy in North America.[3] To some extent, it also partially explains the dramatic increases in female labor force participation in both Canada and the United States over the past few decades. It is clear that the use of female labor has been advantageous for capitalists in North America because it is cheaper and, since women continue to be the "last hired and first fired," more able to meet the needs of an economic system that demands a flexible, and expendable, workforce. Essentially, these data demonstrate that job security is enjoyed only by a minority of North Americans, and that job security depends greatly on gender.

When we look at racial differences with respect to employment and unemployment, the conclusions we must draw are also striking. According to Hacker (cited in Walker et al., 1996: 65), "a greater proportion of Black Americans lack regular employment [today] than at any time since the 1930s Depression."

Table 3.2

Average Incomes of Persons 18 Years Old and Older by Education and Sex, United States, 1996

Educational Level	Women	Men	Percent Difference
Less than 9th grade	$10,414	$16,540	37
Without High School Diploma	$10,423	$18,453	44
With High School Diploma	$16,161	$27,642	42
With Bachelor's Degree or higher	$32,715	$56,277	42

Source: U.S. Department of Commerce, Economics and Statistics Administration, Bureau of the Census, September, 1997

Looking at data on employment rates as a proportion of the total African-American and white employed labor forces, we can also see that African-Americans are far more likely to be employed in different ways than their white counterparts (see Table 3.3). One of the most disheartening aspects of this differential employment is the fact that highly educated African-American men are only slightly more likely to be employed than if they had only a high school degree. Well-educated African-American women fare slightly better, since those with college degrees make up 14 percent of the entire African-American female labor force, compared to only 9 percent of African-American women who had less than a high school education. Compare this with the experiences of white males and females. In 1994, white males with a college degree were nearly three times as likely to be employed as their counterparts with less than a high school degree, and white females with college degrees were more than three times as likely to be employed as their peers who had less than a high school education.

What do these figures tell us about the work and education experiences of African-Americans compared to whites? It appears that getting more education does not guarantee a job as much if you are African-American compared with if you are white. As William Julius Wilson (1987) remarks, "gaining an education does not account for the effects of discrimination that might occur when people of color apply for jobs."

Wilson also reminds us that much of the unemployment experienced by African-Americans in the United States can be attributed to the fact that many such individuals are schooled and socialized to accept low-skill, low-wage positions within the economy. This socialization effect can also be generalized to the experiences of visible minorities, Native peoples, and women. As these jobs disappear, either because they have become obsolete, or because such industries have moved to new parts of the country or abroad, it becomes very difficult to find gainful employment in one's own community. In addition, "the growth of a non-working class of prime-age males along with a larger number of those who are often unemployed, who work part-time, or who work in temporary jobs is concentrated among the poorly educated, the school dropouts, and minorities" (Wilson, 1996: 26). As modern day capitalism in North America has shifted from

Table 3.3
Occupations of the Employed, by Selected Characteristics, U.S.A: 1994 (thousands)

Sex, Race and Educational Attainment	Total Employed	Total Civilian Racial Labor Force	Employed as Percent of Total Racial Labor Force	Percent in Category					
				Management/ Professional	Technical/ Admin.	Service	Precision Production	Operators/ Fabricators	Forestry, Farming, and Fishing
White Males < High School	5 242 000	60 700 000	9	0.4	0.6	0.9	2.5	3.2	0.9
White Males College	14 227 000	60 700 000	23	15.6	5.2	0.7	1.0	0.6	0.3
African-American Males < High School	787 000	7 100 000	11	0.4	0.7	2.1	2.0	5.0	0.9
African-American Males College	950 000	7 100 000	13	7.5	3.0	1.0	0.8	0.9	0.0
White Females < High School	2 969 000	50 300 000	6	0.3	1.3	2.2	0.3	1.6	0.2
White Females College	10 619 000	50 300 000	21	14.9	5.0	0.8	0.1	0.2	0.1
African-American Females < High School	641 000	7 400 000	9	0.3	1.0	4.8	0.3	2.1	0.1
African-American Females College	1 047 000	7 400 000	14	9.7	3.4	0.7	0.1	0.2	–

Source: Calculated from The National Data Book, Statistical Abstract of the United States 1995, 15th edition, Maryland, Bernan Press, 1995, pp. 399 & 416 (U.S. Bureau of the Census).

a goods producing to a service based economy, there has been a simultaneous shift in the kinds of skills required to get and keep a job, and many such skills are not accessible, particularly if they involve access to, and knowledge of, new technologies such as computers (Wilson, 1987: 39). One extraordinary illustration of this can be found in Table 3.4. Here, we can see that white youth are approximately three times as likely as African-Americans and Hispanics to have access to a computer, and are more likely to use computers in school and in the home. If one of the new "tools of the trade" in today's economy is the computer, it is clear that many African-Americans and Hispanics are at some disadvantage when it comes to the prospect of acquiring and utilizing the skills that will help them find and keep jobs.

Table 3.4
Access to, and use of, Computers in the United States by Age and Race, 1993

	3-17 years	Over 18
White		
Access to a computer	35.8	26.9
Use home computer	75.3	66.7
Use computer at school	62.7	53.1
Use computer any place	61.4	37.5
Use computer at work	–	47.1
African-American		
Access to a computer	13	13.8
Use home computer	67.3	56.8
Use computer at school	50.9	54.8
Use computer any place	45.6	25
Use computer at work	–	36.1
Hispanic Origin		
Access to a computer	12.1	12.9
Use home computer	68.4	61.3
Use computer at school	45.5	22
Use computer any place	–	29.3
Use computer at work		

Source: Education and Social Stratification Branch, Population Division, U.S. Bureau of the Census, 1993

In Table 3.5 we see that both male and female African-Americans and Hispanics are twice as likely to be unemployed as whites. Table 3.6 shows that African-Americans tend to remain unemployed for longer periods of time, particularly in the categories of moderate length of time unemployed (11-20 weeks), and in the high length of time unemployed (52–99 weeks) categories.

Table 3.7 illustrates the bleak reality of unemployment for young people, particularly if we control for race. When we examine employment statistics for different age groups between 1955 and 1984, it is easy to agree with Wilson's

Table 3.5
Percent of Civilian Labor Force Unemployed, by Sex and Race, United States, April, 1998

	Male	Female
White	2.9	3.4
African-American	7.4	8.2
Hispanic (males and females)	6.5	–

Source: Bureau of Labor Statistics at http://stats.bls.gov/news.release/empsit.t02.htm

Table 3.6
Ratio of Duration of Unemployment for African-Americans and Whites, United States, 1996

Duration of Unemployment	Number of Whites	Percent Whites	Number of African-Americans	Percent African-Americans	Ratio of African-American-to White Unemployment Duration
Low 0–5 weeks	214 862 122	98.480	32 686 478	95.008	1:1
6–10 weeks	936 212	0.429	307 857	0.895	2:1
11–20 weeks	1 105 039	0.506	1 105 039	3.212	6:1
21–30 weeks	660 822	0.303	111 177	0.323	1:1
31–52 weeks	475 352	0.218	99 945	0.291	1:1
High 52–99 weeks	139 956	0.064	93 257	0.271	4:1
Totals	218 179 503	100	34 403 753	100	

Source: Bureau of Labor Statistics, Ferret tables

assessment that unemployment for African-American youth has, "reached catastrophic proportions" (Wilson, 1987: 43).

The general patterns identified with regards to race are similar in Canada. That is, certain of Canada's visible minorities experience differential access to the labor market, and tend to fall into certain job categories.

Table 3.8 shows that with the exception of Japanese, Chinese, and South East Asians, unemployment rates for visible minorities can be up to twice as high as those for other adults. At the same time, and similar to the situation in the United States, possession of a college or university education does not guarantee a high-paying job. According to 1991 Census data, slightly more than 50 percent of visible minorities between the ages of 25 and 44 with university degrees worked in professional or managerial jobs, compared with 70 percent of other adults (Kelly, 1991). In addition,

Table 3.7
Employment-Population Ratio for Civilian Males Aged 16 to 34, by Race and Age, 1955, 1984, and 1998, United States.

Race and Age	1955	1984	1998
African-American & Other Races			
16–17	41.1	16.2	
18–19	66.0	34.0	29.0 (both sexes, 16 to 19)
20–24	78.6	58.3	
25–34	87.6	76.3	67.4 (African-American males over 20 only)
White			
16–17	42.2	37.8	
18–19	64.2	60.1	45.7 (both sexes, 16 to 19)
20–24	80.4	78.0	
25–34	95.2	89.5	74.7 (males only 20 and over)

Source: U.S. Department of Labor, Employment and Training Report of the President (Washington, D.C.: Government Printing Office, 1982) and Employment and Earnings, 32 (January, 1985), cited in Wilson, 1987: 43; and The Employment Situation, Bureau of Labor Statistics at http://www.bls.census.gov/cps/pub/empsit_0498.htm, April, 1998

Table 3.8
Age-Standardized Unemployment Rates of Visible Minority Groups, Canada, 1991

Group	Percent
Latin Americans	19
South East Asians	17
South Asians	16
West Asians and Arabs	16
African-Americans	15
Chinese	10
Filipinos	8
Koreans	8
Pacific Islanders (1)	7
Japanese	6
Visible minorities	13
Other adults	10

Sources: Kelly, 1991, Statistics Canada at: http://www.statcan.ca/Documents/English/SocTrends/vismin.html

"...manual labor jobs were relatively common among highly-educated South East Asians and Latin Americans who worked in the 18 months before the 1991 Census. Among those aged 25 to 44, about 25 percent of South East Asians and Latin Americans with some postsecondary education were in manual labor jobs, as were 11 percent of Latin Americans

with a university degree. Overall, 12 percent of visible minorities aged 25 to 44 with a postsecondary education, and 4 percent of those with a university degree had such jobs. Among other adults that age, 8 percent of those with some postsecondary education and 2 percent of university graduates were manual laborers."

Of all the minority groups in Canada, the Aboriginal population experiences the highest unemployment rates. According to the 1991 Aboriginal Peoples Survey, the unemployment rate for Aboriginal people is nearly 25 percent (Statistics Canada, 1991). Moreover, most of those reporting difficulties finding work stated that the main reason for lack of employment was that there were few or no jobs in the areas where they lived, and one in ten felt that the major obstacle to their employment was the fact they were Aboriginal (See Table 3.9).

Table 3.9
Barriers to Employment, Adult Aboriginals, Canada, 1991

	Number	Percent
No jobs in area where they live	83 685	39
Education and work does not match job	52 410	24
Child care problems	10 760	5
Not enough information about available jobs	33 440	16
They were Aboriginal	20 770	10
Other reasons	12 975	6
Total	214 040	100

Source: Statistics Canada, 1991 Aboriginal Peoples Survey, Schooling, Work and Related Activities, Income, Expenses and Mobility

When we look at the reasons the unemployed give for how they lost their jobs in 1994, we see that, in general, the majority became unemployed due to factories or plants closing. African-American men and women as well as Hispanic women are more likely to be the victims of closed factories than whites of both genders (See Table 3.10). On the other hand, white men and women report higher incidences of insufficient work or an abolished shift or position than African-Americans and Hispanic women.

Finally, the experience of unemployment will often mean making a transition from full-time work, to no work, to part-time work, and this is especially true the longer a person remains unemployed between jobs. A recent study conducted by the U.S. Bureau of Labor Statistics found that "the characteristics distinguishing contingent workers from other workers were that they were disproportionately young and attending school full-time, female, and black" (U.S. Bureau of Labor Statistics, 1996).

The differential experiences of the unemployed described here beg the important questions of not only why there is unemployment, but why unemployment looks the way it does. It is to these questions that we turn next.

Table 3.10
Reason for Work Displacement, by Race and Gender, United States, 1994 (in Percent)

Race and Gender	Plant moved or closed down	Insufficient work	Position or shift abolished
White Men	40	33	27
White Women	43	26	31
African-American Men	52	23	25
African-American Women	52	25	23
Hispanic Men	45	42	13
Hispanic Women	58	22	20

Source: Office of Employment and Unemployment Statistics, Bureau of Labor Statistics at
http://stats.bls.gov/blshome.html

Making Sense of Unemployment and Work Issues as Social Problems

Unemployment presents a number of serious difficulties to both the researcher (because it is difficult to make an accurate count of the unemployed), and the "researched" (since it is also a difficult experience with which to live). So how can we understand unemployment in sociological terms? We can only do this if we have a clear sense of the strengths and limitations of the dominant explanations for unemployment discussed in this chapter. But even before we can address these issues, we need to understand the social and economic context in which unemployment has taken place since the beginning of industrial capitalism and, particularly, in the past few decades. In other words, we need to understand the forces and trends that have shaped a society in which unemployment seems to be taken for granted.

To begin to do this we must understand that North America, as well as the rest of the industrialized world, is undergoing a fundamental change in the way work of all types is organized, due mainly to basic shifts in the structure of advanced capitalism as well as demographic trends. One of the most important trends affecting work and unemployment has to do with the changing nature of industry. The term that is usually used to characterize this transformation—**post-industrialism**—describes a drift in modern capitalist society away from jobs requiring manual skills, such as those in traditional manufacturing plants, towards work emphasizing knowledge and services (See Table 3.11). When we look at the United States for instance, projections regarding the 10 fastest growing occupations all fall within the category of service and knowledge-based work (see Table 3.12).

In Canada, between 1979 and 1989, service industry employment grew by 29 percent while employment growth in goods producing industries was a mere

Table 3.11
Changes in Distribution of Major Occupational Groups, Canada, 1911–1991

Occupational Group	1911	1931	1951	1971	1986	1991
Services	9	10	11	12	14	35
Commercial/finance	6	7	8	11	10	6
Manufacturing/mechanical	16	13	18	20	16	17
Professional	4	7	8	14	16	18**
Clerical	4	8	12	18	19	
Agriculture	38	32	17	7	4	4
Other*	23	24	28	19	21	20

* includes managerial, transportation, construction, forestry, fishing and mining occupations
** grouped professional and clerical occupations

Source: Statistics Canada, Census of Canada and Catalogue 93-151; Canada Year Book, 1994: 208

Table 3.12
Projections of 10 Fastest-Growing Occupations 1994–2005, United States

Occupation	Projected Percent Change	Rank
Homemaker-home health aides	107	1
Computer scientists and systems analysts	91	2
Physical therapy assistants and aides	83	3
Occupational therapy assistants and aides	82	4
Physical therapists	80	5
Human services workers	75	6
Services sales representatives	72	7
Occupational therapists	72	8
Medical assistants	59	9
Paralegals	58	10

Source:Bureau of Labor Statistics Occupational Outlook 1994–1995 edition, Bureau of Labor Statistics, Washington, D.C.

four percent. Services now employ more than two-thirds of all workers in Canada and the United States (Statistics Canada, 1994: 258; Curran and Renzetti, 1996).

This transformation has had major implications for North Americans. Traditional mass manufacturing has become less reliant on manual skills and more dependent on technological innovations such as computerization. This results in the displacement of workers by technology, which in turn creates a "reserve" population of workers who no longer possess the right "tools" for new jobs. At the same time, good service and knowledge jobs increasingly rely on our capacity to access and utilize particular kinds of knowledge and skills. For example, it could be argued convincingly that the trend towards using computers in work means that the collective knowledge of many workers increasingly resides on hard drives all over the world. The implications of this are profound, for it is not difficult to imagine a day soon when fewer workers are needed because the knowledge required to produce a product or deliver a service is already available to workers who have access to such information on corporate computer networks. One frequently mentioned solution to this phenomenon is the "retraining" thesis, which states that if people are displaced by technology or new forms of work requiring new skills, the logical solution is to retrain them for such work. Today, many people are told that they can no longer expect to have jobs or careers for life, and that they should expect to experience periods of employment interspersed with periods of unemployment during which they can learn new skills for new jobs. However, increasingly there are fewer such jobs and there is evidence to suggest that "retraining does not significantly affect the re-employment rate for the unemployed and constitutes a significant expense" (Dickinson, 1995: 315).

Another phenomenon that affects the experience of employment and unemployment is that of the **runaway plant**. This term refers to the tendency for employers to move their operations to other areas inside and outside the continent. The key reasons for this are discussed in more detail below, but in general, the main explanation is that this has become one of the most effective ways of maintaining or growing a business. Yet while such motives may prove beneficial for the company and, to some extent, for the newly employed workers in areas where the firm has moved, the implications for those workers left behind can be devastating.[4] Aside from the often sudden plunge into unemployment of those workers employed by the migrating company, frequently the "trickle down" effects— the impact on related industries, businesses, and communities—can create enormous personal, social, and economic upheaval. Indeed, whole towns and cities are often devastated as a result of corporate exodus. As one author (Grayson, 1983: 286) points out,

"The consequence of shutdowns, unemployment, can have devastating effects on employees and their families. Apart from the economic consequences, loss of self-respect, insomnia, strained family relations, domestic violence, depression, alcohol abuse, and even suicide are well-documented reactions to job loss. Although some would like to believe that 'economic adversity brings us together,' in general, this is not the case."

In addition, the organizational structure of work is changing from hierarchical bureaucracies to networks, partnerships, and "flattened" organizations, all of which are supposed to enhance the business's efficiency in producing goods and services. As organizations "de-layer," "re-engineer," or "downsize" their employees, the unemployment rate goes up. The difficulty with this "corporate anorexia" is that no one is quite sure as to whether such re-configurations of organizational structure are in fact doing what they are supposed to do. Management experts have long argued that the workplace should be "re-invented" to provide workers with greater autonomy to do their jobs and a larger stake in the process and results of working life. Yet, despite a great deal of fanfare and emphasis on worker "empowerment" the basic relationships between employer and employee have remained the same for decades.

Another trend that warrants scrutiny is job security. Increasingly, workers in both Canada and the United States are finding that there are very few "jobs for life." Rather, average workers will soon find themselves changing jobs, and even careers, quite often. According to the U.S. Bureau of the Census, one-third of those who left a job between 1990 and 1992 were unemployed the following month. Perhaps more striking, "just under 1 in every 4 people had stable incomes....this means that the large majority (about three-fourths) are subject to some kind of economic fluctuation from one year to the next *regardless of the state of the economy*" (U.S. Bureau of the Census, 1995a: 2, our emphasis). On average, these individuals were unemployed for 2.4 months, an increase from 1.8 months in 1987-89 (U.S. Bureau of the Census, 1995a), and as Wilson (1996: 25) points out, "In 1987–89, a low-skilled male worker was jobless eight and a half weeks longer than he would have been in 1967-69. Moreover, the proportion of men who 'permanently' dropped out of the labor force was more than twice as high in the late 1980s than it had been in the late 1960s."

Explaining Unemployment: Sociological Perspectives

One of the most curious aspects of unemployment is the way in which North Americans try to make sense of this phenomenon. Many Canadians and Americans subscribe to an ideology (a particular way of thinking about and acting on things) of work and employment that has prevailed for some time. In essence, this ideology is that the individual is to blame for his/her unemployment. The enduring strength of this belief is illustrated by Aronowitz and DiFazio (1994) who point out that even though a third of the U.S. labor force was out of work during the Great Depression, they still blamed themselves for their situation. The modern day equivalent of this ideology is that unemployment is a necessary evil. The argument here is that without a group of unemployed people, capitalists would not be able to be effective and therefore the economy (and thus the nation) would slide into economic obscurity. In other words, unemployment is viewed here as functional for society. However, Charles Handy (1984: 179) maintains that we have become very successful at conditioning ourselves to believe that people who don't work simply don't want to work (those whom we sometimes refer to as "scroungers"), do not need to work (married women and older men), or do not deserve to work (the unskilled and untrained).

The realities of unemployment are, of course, quite different from these perceptions. Indeed, it can be argued convincingly that the dominant ideology associated with the causes of unemployment is more along the lines of myth than reasonable explanation.

Nearly 20 years ago, economist Cy Gonick (1978) undertook to dispel several of these myths about unemployment that bear repeating in the 1990s:

➤ One popular myth is that anyone could get a job if they really tried. While there are certainly people who are neither capable nor willing to find work in North America, the reality is that the number of full-time job vacancies simply does not match the number of people "officially" looking for work.

➤ Another myth is that unemployment is so high because of unemployment insurance. Here, the implication is that people on unemployment insurance are pampered, lazy, or otherwise enjoying the fruits of a generous something-for-nothing policy. Again, the facts do not support these assertions. Most North Americans want to work and, for them, unemployment insurance (or welfare) is an ongoing humiliation. Moreover, unemployment insurance benefits are hardly generous. In the United States, only about one-third of all poor people receive cash welfare or unemployment benefits (Renzetti and Curran,1996: 102). Moreover, the level of welfare or unemployment insurance compensation for most individuals is far below the poverty line.

➤ Another common explanation for unemployment is that high wages are pricing Canadian and United States goods and services out of the market. This argument is often advanced in opposition to unions, who, through collective bargaining, have historically managed to sustain reasonable wages and job security for workers. Today, unions are generally in decline and so cannot really be held responsible at the same time as employers and governments are launching strategies of wage and benefits cuts and rollbacks. Moreover, as Fry (1984) reminds us, we must ask why it is always wages and benefits that are deemed to be overpriced, and not refrigerators, stoves, and television sets.

➤ Another myth is that high minimum wages contribute to unemployment. Yet employers have consistently focused on maintaining low labor costs by encouraging part-time work. Although it is true that increases in the minimum wage can cause some enterprises difficulties, according to Gonick, the real increase in unemployment due to increased minimum wage is negligible.

➤ In the 1970s, many people argued that there simply weren't enough educated and skilled people to fill available jobs. But recent trends in downsizing across the continent have shown that there are many highly educated and skilled individuals who are currently unemployed. For instance, two and a half million American workers fell victim to corporate restructuring between 1991 and 1995, even though this period of time was largely thought to be an economic recovery. As we have already shown, for many such workers the chances of taking a new job at similar or higher rates of pay are diminishing.

➤ Given the transformation of families from single earner to dual earner couples across the continent, it is often argued that the higher family income means unemployment isn't so tough. However, as we pointed out earlier in this chapter, it is clear from the evidence that most families need two incomes to survive, mostly because real wages have not increased since the mid 1980s.

➤ Finally, there is the contention that unemployment figures are not valid measures of hardship because they take into account so many "secondary" wage earners such as women and young people without family responsibilities. While it is clearly no longer the case that women can be regarded as "secondary" wage earners, it is still sometimes argued that women should busy themselves in "traditional" family relationships (one earner and one stay-at-home homemaker) so that they do not "take away jobs from men," and that their "unnatural" participation in the labor force is at the root of inflated unemployment figures. This contention is, quite simply, ludicrous. The entrance of women into the paid labor force has been a historical necessity. Women's paid and unpaid (domestic) labor has been essential to economic growth in both Canada and the United States. Furthermore, the purported relationship between unemployment and women's labor force participation rates is not supported by the experience of other countries, where women's participation is higher than in both Canada and the United States—yet unemployment rates are lower.

Why is it so important to examine these myths? When members of societies such as ours are inclined to view the world based on incorrect assumptions, it is not surprising that our social and economic policies tend to be ineffective at worst, and inconsequential at best. As the following section illustrates, the dominant explanation for unemployment fails to provide appropriate and effective solutions precisely because many of its assumptions are false or outdated.

Explanations for Unemployment

It is always difficult to reduce complex social phenomena to one or two simple theories, but in general, it can be argued that there are two dominant explanations for unemployment: neo-conservative and neo-Marxist. We have chosen to discuss explanations of unemployment in this way because, in our view, the bulk of current public, economic, and political debates on the unemployment issue (and other issues) generally fall into some variant of these two camps.

Neo-Conservative Explanations

Neo-conservative explanations generally fall into the structural functionalist camp of sociological theories discussed in Chapter 1. Neo-conservatives argue that unemployment is a function of cyclical fluctuations in the economy. Two types of unemployment are often highlighted. **Cyclical unemployment** refers to unemployment experienced by individuals according to the cycles of the economy. According to this view, in a recession or economic downturn, the unemployment rate would naturally tend to increase as the market readjusts. Once the downturn in the cycle is over for a sufficiently long period, any unemployment that remains is referred to as **structural unemployment**. Moreover, it is assumed that such unemployment is not temporary (i.e., it will go away or be reduced after the cycle is over) but that it is endemic (part of the very structure) to the system. Thus, the solution to unemployment in this framework lies in waiting for the down cycle to be over, or engaging in measures (such as limited government intervention) to reduce the time between down cycles and normal periods in which full, or near full, employment levels prevail. The essential assumptions of this perspective are based on the classical economic theories of Adam Smith which assert that competition in the market regulates profits. In other words, if profits are too high, other capitalists will compete to drive profits down. If profits are too low, capitalists will reinvest in other, more profitable areas of the economy. Similarly, competition will keep wages fair since workers will move into better paying jobs if wages are too low (Hale, 1995: 215).

To summarize, then, neo-conservative perspectives contend that free market economies are cyclical in nature, and that troughs and peaks in the supply and demand of goods and services are natural phenomena. The logic of the system is such that any shortcomings in supply or demand will eventually play themselves out and the system will correct itself. Consequently, neo-conservative thought is largely against state interference in the market since government policies are liable to upset the delicate natural balance of supply and demand. In this scenario, commodities that do not sell (because of poor quality, high prices, inefficiency within companies, or other reasons) result in job losses.

Neo-conservatives typically argue that the current unemployment situation is a temporary, although decade-long, effect of fundamental shifts in the nature of capitalism. They find evidence for this contention in history, pointing out that the first industrial revolution displayed very similar symptoms which were due to basic structural changes in the way things were produced. For instance, they point to the rapid decline since the beginning of the 1900s of the number of farmers in North America. Most importantly, they argue that such structural changes, while devastating to the millions of people they displace, will right themselves once the structural changes are complete—just as displaced agricultural workers eventually found employment in factories.

In addition, many utilizing this explanation argue that the demographic structure of North America is such that fewer young people are entering the workforce, which means that there will eventually be a shortage of skilled labor. To some extent this is true, but it still poses the problem of how people, particularly those in disadvantaged social groups, are to gain the advanced skills that will be required in the new economy once things turn around.

Another explanation advanced by the neo-conservative camp has to do with the impact and cost of social programs designed to alleviate the negative consequences of capitalism. Here, the argument is based on the perception that a large and growing number of North Americans do not want to work because they can easily collect unemployment benefits. The solution, then, is to cut social programs and force people to work at menial jobs in order to reinstate equilibrium between supply and demand.[5]

In such accounts of the way societies work, phenomena such as work and unemployment would be explained by thinking about the ways in which work and non-work contribute to reproducing our social system. For example, a neo-conservative explanation would assume that certain jobs (let's say managerial, professional jobs) need to be eliminated in today's workplace because they no longer fulfill their purpose (their function) in those workplaces—they have become obsolete. The flip side of this argument would be that some jobs (for instance research and development jobs in bio-technology, or computer programming) are more important than ever before because they are meeting the functional needs of today's market system. The point here is that if people cannot make the right decisions as to what occupations or fields to train for, or if they are unwilling or unable to upgrade their skills and qualifications to meet rapidly changing standards, they will experience unemployment.

It is not hard to see that this perspective tends to blame individuals or institutions such as schools or families that are responsible for training and socializing people for their unemployed status. The unemployed are considered to be, in some way, unwilling or unable to adapt to the changing nature of market economies. This argument makes sense within the structural functional sociological framework when we consider that these theories assume that societies are already fairly well integrated and that, in terms of social structure (the ways in which societies are put together and the relationships between the elements that make up society), there really are not that many problems. Put differently, for structural functionalists, social problems like unemployment should be blamed on individuals and, if there is any attention paid to the nature of social structure, it is only in the sense that elements of the structure are perhaps "dysfunctional" and in need of repair. Consequently, since very little attention is directed to the underlying logic of the social system itself, solutions to social problems tend to be piecemeal and short-term. Because they only examine the surface appearance of unemployment, the neo-conservative explanation ignores an analysis of the nature of the social system itself (the relationship between the elements) to understand social problems like unemployment.

Another consequence of conceptualizing unemployment in this way is that it tends to ignore the role of market systems in general, and employers in particular in creating unemployment. From a structural functionalist point of view, if unemployment is defined in structural terms, then you can look for structural causes among the elements of society that might appear to cause it. Some of these structural explanations were discussed when we looked at Gonick's myths. The most important aspect of the structural functionalist analysis is that, while it may seem very compelling and believable to politicians and the public, it is not a very satisfactory explanation of unemployment. Accordingly, because it fails as an explanation for North American society's increasing failure to provide employment for all, it cannot provide us with workable solutions to the problem. Indeed, by emphasizing the increasing role of structural forces as opposed to cyclical factors in explaining unemployment, governments are able to argue that there is really nothing they can do to change the direction of the job market and provide more employment opportunities for the populace.

Instead, governments and employers suggest that current trends in employment are related to the globalization of the economy, a phenomenon in which the global market is opened so that capital, labor, and information are exceptionally mobile and thus able to travel wherever labor costs are lowest and profits highest. In the true spirit of Adam Smith, defenders of globalization argue that opening up markets will impose a "healthy discipline" upon national economies. In essence, the assumptions are that the advanced industrialized nations must be competitive, that they have so far lacked the vigor and will to meet the competitive challenge, and that the solution is to drastically cut the cost of labor and social/economic programs—i. e., the welfare state, (Laxer, 1993). As we might expect, those making this argument state that the pain and suffering that many people will experience in the process of restructuring the economy for the global stage is merely short-term, that it is for our own good, and that eventually, the invisible hand will triumph. In many ways the ideology of globalization plays a central role in the current trend towards large-scale elimination of jobs in the private and public sectors.

One indicator of this phenomenon is the runaway plant, in which companies and sometimes whole industries leave locations for areas with potentially higher profit margins because these locations offer cheaper labor, lower taxes, better regulatory policies, or cheaper raw materials. Importantly, governments in North America have embraced rather than criticized globalization, thereby making them accomplices in the job loss scenario. One important illustration of this is the relatively recent North American Free Trade Agreement (NAFTA) which allows for the free movement of goods, capital, and services, but which, in Canada at least, has probably resulted in more jobs lost than created (Storey, 1991).

In addition, corporations have fostered a work climate in which those with jobs are told that they are fortunate to have jobs, and that the price of admission to the ranks of the employed is to work harder and smarter with less. This strategy not only allows neo-conservatives to blame the unemployed for their plight, but also provides employers with a tool for the ongoing discipline of the employed to increase productivity or reduce expectations. While such a strategy may increase profits in the short term, the long-term effects are sobering, because overwork and stress are increasingly becoming major problems in North American work cultures. Indeed, Statistics Canada estimates that stress related disorders due to overwork cost Canadian businesses $12 billion per year (Statistics Canada, 1992). In the United States, the figure is around $200 billion (International Labor Organization, 1993).

A major failing of the neo-conservative explanation is its inability to account for the serious differences in unemployment experienced by minorities and women. If the market has a natural logic that will eventually solve problems like unemployment, why has it not done so? Why do African-American males continue to experience differential employment relative to white males? Why do many people of color continue to earn less than whites despite their increasing educational attainments? And why, despite increasing educational parity between men and women, do women continue to earn less than men? None of these questions can be adequately answered by the neo-conservative approach precisely because its assumptions do not really permit an adequate understanding of the real relationships between employers, the employable, and the economic structure in which they are embedded. Thus, it can provide us with very little in the way of workable long-term policy solutions to unemployment. Despite these failures, this perspective continues to be the dominant approach to solving unemployment issues in North America. This is in part because it has so far worked for a relatively small but powerful segment of the population (the capitalist and affluent middle classes), but is also because the major changes that would be required to change the way we understand and deal with employment issues represent a major threat to a world view that has become ingrained. To paraphrase C. Wright Mills (1959), many North Americans seem to be fairly comfortable in placing the blame for unemployment on individuals rather than looking beyond the "personal milieux" towards structural change.

The Dual Labor Market or Labor Segmentation Thesis

Another perspective which falls under the category of structural functionalist theory is known as the dual labor market or **labor market segmentation thesis**. It is commonly presented as an explanation for the difficulties faced by certain types, or segments, of workers. Essentially, those utilizing this perspective argue that a two-tiered labor market has emerged, consisting of primary and secondary sectors. Primary markets consist of jobs falling into the professional and managerial class of occupations within large competitive firms. Workers in this sector tend to receive high wages, usually possess high skills, are unionized, and enjoy promotions and prominent status. Work in the secondary market is marked by non-unionization, low rates of pay, lower skill requirements, and high labor turnover, and tends to occur in smaller firms (Das Gupta, 1996: 6). For the most part, women and people of color are more likely to be found in secondary labor markets, whereas workers in the primary market tend to be white males. For many individuals, movement between the markets is hampered by social, economic, or geographic factors, as well as the interests of unions or professional associations which often seek to maintain occupational barriers (Curtis and Tepperman, 1988).

Dual labor market theorists tend to assume many of the same things as neo-conservatives, in that while they can describe the differential placement of individuals into primary and secondary labor markets, they have difficulty explaining how these workers come to be in these markets in the first place. In effect, they tend to ignore the social structural processes by which groups such as minorities or women end up in low-paying, dead-end jobs (Gordon, Edwards, and Reich, 1982).

A different type of segmented labor market theory is offered by economist and demographer David Foot (1996: 57–79). He argues that employment opportunities are changing because of economic and demographic changes. More specifically, he believes that the future of work will increasingly be composed of the following four career streams:

1. the linear path, or the traditional career path of upward mobility towards the top;
2. the spiral path, in which an employee spirals up the corporate structure by mixing lateral moves (involving a change of occupation) with promotions;
3. the steady-state path, where a person has one career for a lifetime (such as a lawyer or doctor); and
4. the transitory path, which is taken by workers who will essentially "adopt whatever occupation is necessary to get a job."

Foot argues that the fastest growing jobs in the future will be the spiral and transitory types, primarily because organizations are flattening their structures. Therefore "spiralists" will be making many lateral moves within organizations or industries. In addition, organizations are downsizing. Although this means reducing the labor force, employers still need to get work done and this work will be performed mostly by transitory workers. The implications of his analysis are that people preparing to enter the job market will be more successful if they have a range of skills which can be transferred from job to job, and if they are flexible enough to adapt to rapidly changing job circumstances.

A Neo-Marxist Explanation

Neo-Marxist explanations for unemployment begin with the assumption that work in capitalist society is essentially exploitative. Because this relationship implies inequality, neo-Marxist theories are a variant of the power/inequality perspective. Neo-Marxists maintain that work is exploitative in the sense that workers come to the plant or company gates with nothing to sell but their labor power or capacity to work. The capitalist buys this labor power and pays for it in the form of wages or salary in what appears to be a fair exchange of labor power for money. However, if the exchange were simply an equal one, the capitalist would never make any profit. Profit has to come from somewhere, and it is in the concept of capacity to work that we find it. Put simply, when the capitalist purchases labor power, he/she is buying the workers' ability to produce more than they are worth, in terms of wages or salary. In other words, it is only the workers who have the capacity to produce value greater than what they are paid in return for producing that value who are useful to a capitalist. This surplus value, or profit, is really the value created by unpaid work, and it is in this sense that work in capitalist societies is exploitative.

Capitalists are faced with a difficult problem. They must maximize profit, and indeed make increasing levels of profit if the company is to grow, and they must do this in the face of increasing pressure from competitors who may have a better, cheaper, or more attractive product. There are many ways they can do this. For instance, they can expand their sphere of sales to other markets in different regions and countries. As the company's sales grow the firm expands to meet the increased demand for products. More labor may be hired to meet increased production requirements, or to manage the increasingly complex division of labor within the firm. Hence, at the beginning of a firm's expansion phase, or when new industries emerge, workers are in demand.

This traditional approach to explaining unemployment is based on something called Say's Law, which basically states that supply creates its own demand (See Figure 3.1). The main idea here is that when capitalists produce goods or services, they generate demand for those products. In turn, this produces income, a part of which is reinvested in the company, which leads to more production and therefore more jobs. The main problem with this formula is that it assumes that people will always consume what is available in the marketplace (the demand side of the equation). In fact, as many economists are now pointing out, consumers often feel they should hold back in purchasing goods or services, especially when economic times are tough.

In general, the history of North American capitalism has followed the path described here. New industries were created at the beginning of industrial capitalism in the United States, as they were in Canada, although with a different focus and trajectory. In the United States, continuous and rapid economic growth coupled with the opportunities afforded by World War II have created the largest and most powerful economy in the world. Canadian development was slightly different, relying mostly on the extraction and processing of raw materials for foreign markets. But in addition, a high proportion of Canadian industries has always been foreign-owned. Prior to 1900, Canada was the eighth largest manufacturing country in

FIGURE 3.1
Say's Law

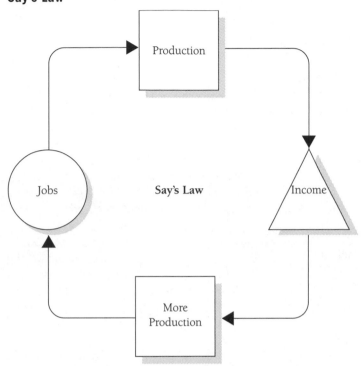

Source: Adapted from Handy, 1984: 4

the world, with a well-educated labor force and high standard of living. This environment attracted foreign (mostly U.S.) investors, so that by 1983 the value of foreign investment in Canada was the highest in the world (Laxer, 1989). According to Brym (1996: 220) there were three main consequences of this phenomenon, all of which have contributed to Canada's long-term rise in unemployment:

1. Much of the capital that could be reinvested in Canada to create jobs goes to U.S. based multinational industries in the form of profits, management fees, royalties etc.

2. Much of the assembly that has occurred in Canadian branch plants is from parts made elsewhere.

3. The mandate of Canadian branch plants involved in manufacturing has usually been just to service the Canadian market, not to expand internationally.

As capitalism developed in North America, unemployment fluctuated wildly, according to the conditions of the economy. In the United States for instance, during the twentieth century, the annual average unemployment rate reported by the Bureau of Labor Statistics varied between 1.2 and 24.9 percent (Vedder and Gallaway, 1994). But, despite these variations in unemployment, there has always been faith that things would get better. In response to public outcry about the unemployment situation in Canada and the United States, governments, economists, and captains of industry could reply confidently that new industries would develop, new markets would be found, and people could be retrained for new jobs. "Not to worry," they said, "the market will take care of things in the end."

The problem with this argument is not that it was never true, but that it was true for a period of time in the development of capitalism and is probably no longer valid today. What has happened recently to make the situation so different?

Those critical of the neo-conservative model would agree that the three decades following World War II were the most prosperous for North Americans, primarily because markets were expanding and foreign competition was minimal. Accordingly, jobs were relatively plentiful. By the 1970s, increased competition from Europe and Japan fostered the decline of industrialism in the United States. The Midwest started to degenerate into what is sometimes referred to as a rust belt. Several financial crises also occurred, including the bailing out of Savings and Loans companies, culminating in significant downsizing efforts by major corporations.

In addition, according to the neo-Marxist critique, capitalists became too efficient. Remember that one of the purposes of the capitalist economic system is to accumulate capital. Given this fundamental aspect of the system, it's not surprising that capitalists have invented numerous ways to reduce their costs while maximizing the productivity of their workers. One way to do this is for the company to "run away" as explained earlier in this chapter. But there are other ways. For example, given that profit derives from workers producing more than they are worth (in terms of wages or salary) in a given time period (the workday), profit could be increased by lengthening the working day or making employees do more in a shorter period of time. Another way would be to replace human workers with technologies such as automatic assembly machines or, more recently, computers. All of these methods have been used by capitalists in North America with, on the whole, and from the perspective of capitalists, good results. However, the substantial gains in productivity made by U.S. and Canadian corporations in the last 40 years or so have accrued mainly to upper managers and executives, not workers. As Bartlett and Steele point out (1992: 19-20),

➤ In 1953, executive compensation was the equivalent of 22 percent of corporate profits. By 1987 it was 61 percent.

➤ In 1988, the average CEO was making 93 times the earnings of the average factory worker, up from 29 times in 1979.

➤ Between 1977 and the beginning of the 1990s, the salaries of top U.S. executives rose by 220 percent.

➤ At the time John F. Kennedy came into office, the typical CEO of a Fortune 500 company was earning $190,000 a year. By 1992, the average annual compensation topped $1.2 million.

With the advent of production methods such as the assembly line (pioneered by Henry Ford), the utilization of more efficient management techniques, and the replacement of human beings with technology, it became possible to produce more products in a shorter time period for less. But the downside has been what is referred to as recurrent crises of overproduction in which there are too few dollars chasing too many goods. In such a situation, the production process has become so efficient that it is possible to produce more goods and services than people can consume, hence the notion of overproduction.[6]

The implications of this situation for employment are profound. Think of it this way. If employers are able to produce goods and services more efficiently than ever before, and if the main ways they accomplish this are to use technology to replace human beings, or to employ cheaper workers in cheaper locales, then logic tells us they will be reluctant to hire more employees in local communities. As well, as new industries emerge in the service sector, they are likely to utilize the most sophisticated technologies available to reduce costs from the very beginning of the enterprise, and will therefore be unlikely to hire employees in the same quantity as industries 30 years ago that were engaged primarily in manufacturing. This has in fact been the case in most industrialized countries, where there has been a gradual fall in the numbers of workers employed in manufacturing-based industries and a corresponding massive growth in output in these same sectors (Jones,1982: 62). The essence of the neo-Marxist explanation, then, is the notion that it is the nature of capitalism, its structural logic, that entails job loss.

This perspective also lends itself more readily than neo-conservatism to explaining the differential employment rates and experiences of women, African-Americans, Hispanics and visible minorities. We have seen that despite a narrowing of the historical gap between such individuals and whites in terms of educational attainment, occupational position and earnings, unemployment for many of these groups is persistently higher than white unemployment. According to some (Wilson, Tienda and Wu, 1995) the explanation for this can only be found in the concepts of differential access to employment opportunities by region, occupational placement, labor market segmentation by race, and labor market discrimination. While the gender gap can be explained in terms of the cheap labor and flexibility argument developed earlier in this chapter, the racial gap in unemployment can be explained by referring to data showing that many African-Americans still encounter overt and institutionalized racism when confronted with the problem of finding work (Badgett, 1994). Essentially, many people of color in North America suffer discrimination in the labor market due to the "stigma" of color, and because they have historically existed in inferior class or economic positions (Franklin, 1991).

Moreover, neo-Marxists have provided considerable insight into the relationship between the structure and logic of capitalism and women's experiences in the labor force. As mentioned earlier in this chapter, they argue that because women are often placed in low-paying, dead-end jobs, they constitute a pool of cheap and dispensable labor—precisely what is needed for late capitalist societies to remain competitive. They also contend that women are at a distinct disadvantage in the labor market because they are educated from an early age to see themselves in more "caring," "nurturing," or otherwise supportive jobs.[7] Such institutionalized streaming has made it very difficult for women to enter traditionally male dominated fields. As well, "women seldom have the full information or mobility needed to choose jobs" (Richmond-Abbott, in Kourany et al., 1992: 139). In some ways, employment opportunities are getting better for women; they are entering traditionally male fields, are achieving educational parity, and are being promoted slowly. Nevertheless, the nature of capitalism and the "old boys network" that sustains it will continue to pose a major challenge for women entering the labor force.

In summary, those employing a neo-Marxist explanation of unemployment argue that capitalism has a destructive and contradictory side where labor is always forced into an unequal relationship with capital. Moreover, the logic of this economic system forces employers to make decisions about production which will, in most cases, force many people out of work and, just as important, will preclude the re-entry of displaced workers into the workplace because they have become permanently redundant.

One of the most important outcomes of this situation is that workers who are displaced and who are looking for work will increasingly find it as part-time workers, in labor- (and to a lesser extent technology-) intensive jobs. Much of this reality is masked, however, by governments who are somewhat reluctant to admit publicly that part-time labor is the reality faced by many workers in North America. For example, the federal government announced that 1,230,000 jobs had been created in the United States in the first half of 1993. But they did not mention that 60 percent of them were part-time, and that most were in the low-wage service sectors (Rifkin, 1995:167). In Canada, the percentage of part-time workers increased from 12.5 percent in 1973 to 18.6 percent in 1993. Of these workers, however, the proportion who preferred full-time work increased from 10.6 percent to 31.9 percent in the same time frame (Ottawa Citizen, July 20, 1996: B5).

What Is To Be Done About Unemployment?

Solutions to the problem of unemployment and underemployment depend on our perspective on their causes. We have seen that there are two general perspectives in this regard, and that while they share some assumptions, they are essentially quite different. This means that the policies that might emerge will also be very different. Keeping in mind again that it is always dangerous to oversimplify, there seem to be two possible outcomes of current trends in unemployment in North America.

Assuming that the neo-conservative structural/cyclical approach is valid, we could argue that unemployment will correct itself because the logic of the market economy will eventually triumph. Thus, policies directed at changing the situation, such as government make-work programs or incentives to employers to provide jobs, will necessarily be short-lived solutions, since they do nothing to change the powerful invisible hand that supposedly rules market economies. The solution here, then, is to do as little as possible in the way of government policy.

Alternatively, but still within the assumptions of neo-conservative thought, it could be argued that some people will be out of work, that this condition is permanent, and that there is nothing we can do about it. In effect, the polarization of the labor market would be seen as natural. The implications of this are rather grim, for if governments wish to ensure that the top 20 percent of the population keeps its wealth, they will have to create increasingly oppressive social control practices to guard against an increasingly dissatisfied and politically dangerous mass of people who cannot find meaningful and remunerative work. To some extent this may be happening now as many communities of "haves" are springing up in the United States and Canada, designed specifically to bar the disenfranchised. In effect, if neo-conservative thinking on economic policy continues to prevail, we may see an economic crisis of unprecedented proportions, resulting in the creation of more prisons to house the disenfranchised, massive waste of human potential, and a continued degeneration of the social fabric.

The neo-Marxist alternatives also suggest two separate paths. One is very similar to the neo-conservative view in that it entails the natural working out of the logic of the economic system. Here, since capitalism is assumed to have a contradictory logic, it is accepted that that system has sown the seeds of its own destruction. The only thing to do is to wait for the economy to destroy itself, then rebuild it on different assumptions. Of course, the danger of this approach is that it seems blind to the fact that capitalism has historically been remarkably resilient. Moreover, there is likely to be continued and even enhanced suffering if the system is left to its own devices. Thus, the "wait for the end strategy" is problematic since it is difficult to imagine when the end will come and what will happen in the meantime.

Another, more realistic, set of options is presented by those critical of capitalist logic but aware of the importance of political and economic resistance to the system by subordinate groups (such as the unemployed). Such realist neo-Marxists might suggest that alternatives to the current suffering of the unemployed are possible, but depend greatly on political will. It is possible that governments and industry could engage in new social and economic policies that essentially involve rethinking the nature and purpose of work. Several of the following possibilities could occur in this scenario:

> Government, industry workers and their representatives could cooperate to shorten the workweek, thereby increasing employment opportunities for those currently experiencing unemployment or underemployment.

> Jobs could be rationed.

> Earlier retirement could be made a condition of employment.

> A value added tax could be created, thus increasing the tax revenue base to create or sustain social programs that act as a buffer to those who fall through the employment cracks.

> Since technology is replacing jobs, there may be some positive social outcomes available in taxing industries employing such labor saving technologies again to increase the tax base.

> North America and other industrialized nations may have reached a stage in their development where it is imperative to rethink what it means to work. In other words, it may no longer be possible to think of work only as something that we do to put food on the table, but to think of it as something we do to contribute to the communities in which we live. In this regard, some have suggested that we need to create a social economy consisting of volunteer, community service, for which governments pay a "shadow" wage.

To be sure, if the neo-Marxists are correct in their assessment of the causes of unemployment and underemployment, North Americans' expectations of the meaning and purpose of work must change. Put simply, in the future, work is just not going to be the way it has been in the past, and there are no new industries on the horizon with the potential of picking up the slack in job creation.

Summary

This chapter has documented the importance and centrality of work to our financial, physical, and mental well-being. It has also shown that the right to work is something that is not enjoyed by everyone. Two competing theories of unemployment were highlighted. Neo-conservative theories tend to be dominant today and are based on the natural justice of the free market system as expressed in Adam Smith's notion of the invisible hand. However this approach fails to explain persistent phenomena, particularly the differential employment of women, minority groups, and people of color. Moreover, its assumptions tend to lead to uncritical acceptance of current and projected levels and types of unemployment and underemployment, which, in turn, have major implications for North American society.

Neo-Marxist theories maintain that unemployment is part of the structural logic of capitalism and that solutions to this social problem must therefore be grounded in fundamental structural and ideological change. They maintain that we can either wait for the system to fall apart and rebuild society from the shambles, or that we can, through political and economic pressure, change the way that we think about, manage, and distribute work in contemporary society. The challenge for those utilizing this perspective is in determining effective strategies for political and economic resistance to the imperatives of late capitalism.

KEY TERMS

Cultural capital
Cyclical unemployment
Employment
Human capital approach
Labor market segmentation thesis
McJobs
Meritocracy
Post-industrialism
Relational definition of work
Runaway plant
Say's Law
Structural unemployment
Unemployment
Unemployment rate

DISCUSSION QUESTIONS

1. How does the human capital approach regarding employment fit with the two major theories of unemployment discussed in this chapter?
2. In what ways are neo-conservative and neo-Marxist theories of unemployment different and similar?
3. What factors do you think would account for women's differential treatment in the labor market? What kinds of similarities with that of African-Americans or visible minorities do you see in women's experiences?
4. What kinds of strategies can you think of for distributing work more evenly? What would be the social, political, and economic implications of your strategies?
5. In what ways do the historical development of the Canadian and U. S. economies contribute to employment patterns in these countries?

PROBLEM SOLVING SCENARIOS

1. How would you go about researching the experiences of the unemployed in your community? What questions would you ask, and to what issues would you have to be sensitive?
2. If you were in charge of government procedures regarding the collection of data on unemployment what changes would you make to current policies and procedures on gathering such information?
3. Working in groups of four, determine the gap between average unemployment insurance payments per month and what it costs to feed, house, and clothe a family of four in your state or province.
4. Examine at least three different media accounts of the lives of the unemployed, as well as economic issues related to unemployment. What similarities, differences, and issues are raised by these portrayals of the lives of the unemployed?
5. With your classmates, debate whether North Americans are working to live or living to work.

WEB EXERCISES

1. One of the most important demographic trends discussed in this book is the aging of the North American population. Write a paper on the linkages between aging and unemployment. Begin your research by pointing your browser at

   http://www.trinity.edu/~mkearl/ger-econ.html

2. Based on data from the General Social Survey (GSS), write a brief, persuasive argument regarding some aspect of the issue of employment and unemployment. For instance, you could focus on the effects of unemployment, people's attitudes towards being unemployed, or what people want in a job. You can access the GSS data tables at

http://www.icpsr.umich.edu/gss/module/work.htm

SUGGESTED READINGS

Aronowitz, S., and W. DiFazio. *The Jobless Future: Sci-Tech and the Dogma of Work.* Minneapolis: University of Minnesota Press, 1994.
This book provides an analysis of the interplay of contemporary class structure in the United States, gender, race/ethnicity, technology, science, and the alienation and exploitation of modern workers. It also discusses the political and philosophical consequences and potential solutions to the dilemmas posed by a jobless future.

Handy, C. *The Future of Work.* Worcester: Basil Blackwell, 1984.
Written 15 years ago, this is still a classic statement on the nature and future of work.

Laxer, J. *False God: How the Globalization Myth Has Impoverished Canada.* Toronto: Lester, 1993.
Laxer offers a penetrating analysis and critique of globalization and its impact on the Canadian economy.

Rifkin, J. *The End of Work: The Decline of the Global Labor Force and the Dawn of the Post-Market Era.* New York: Tarcher/Putnam, 1996.
Rifkin's book provides an excellent analysis of work in historical context, speculates about the future of work given current trends, and offers alternative ways of thinking about work.

Wilson, W. J. *The Truly Disadvantaged: The Inner City, the Underclass and Public Policy.* Chicago: University of Chicago Press, 1987.
Wilson examines the causes and potential cures for inner-city poverty with particular reference to the plight of African-Americans.

ENDNOTES

1   There are many women who would argue (and they would be right) that the work they do at home is unpaid labor but ought to be remunerated because the care and raising of a family and the maintenance of a household is absolutely central to maintaining people who do work for pay. At the same time, women's participation in the labor force has increased dramatically in North America yet, in the United States in the last two decades, working women have nearly doubled their hours at work while the number of hours they devote to household labor has decreased by only 14 percent. At the same time, the total hours put in by men at work and at home fell by 8 percent (Mason, 1988: 38). Canadian data show clear similarities. Statistics Canada estimated in 1993 that, despite men's increasing sense of responsibility for household tasks, Canadian women (whether they have children or not) spend approximately twice as much time doing unpaid household chores compared to men (Statistics Canada, 1993). Clearly, the notion of work means different things to different people.

2   Here, the term "visible minority" refers to "a group of people who are singled out for unequal treatment on the basis of their physical and cultural characteristics and who regard themselves as objects of collective discrimination" (Henslin and Nelson, 1997: 196-7).

3   However, the "cheap labor" argument presents something of a paradox for neo-Marxist analyses of women's underemployment and unemployment: if women's labor is cheaper for capital, then why are they not hired in all kinds of sectors? That is, why do they continue to be segregated in the low-wage industries? The answer is related to the fact that women constitute a very flexible, or elastic, labor force which, in addition to experiencing a historical devaluation of their work, is vulnerable to forces which might compel its members to return to the home to perform domestic labor when job markets contract. Importantly, much of this phenomenon is seen as being the "natural" state of things (Marchak, in Maroney and Luxton, 1987).

4   We should note that when companies move to other locations, they often do so to employ and exploit a labor force that is politically and economically weak.

5   In Ontario, the conservative provincial government has done just this by implementing a system of workfare which demands that welfare recipients work at menial, low-paying jobs at the same time as they collect benefits.

6   Importantly, many of those who are able to consume are doing so by incurring high debts (in the form of credit cards for instance). In a credit-oriented society such as ours, losing a job can lead to devastation.

7   For example, Graham Lowe (1987) has shown how the work of male clerks became increasingly mechanized and then was "redefined" as women's work in the early 1900s.

Chapter (4)

Is There a Doctor in the House? Health and Health Care in North America

We now better understand the relationship among economic growth, prosperity, and health and well-being, and the need for a long-term integrated perspective on the determinants of health and economic growth. Can we, as societies, make intelligent and wise use of this understanding? (Frank and Mustard, 1995)

OBJECTIVES

In this chapter we focus on the topics
  1. What is health and what is illness?
  2. Sociological theories of health
  3. How many North Americans are not in "good health?"
  4. Who has major health problems and who does not?
  5. How is health care structured and delivered in North America?
  6. The social determinants of ill health
  7. Get well soon! What is to be done about the sick?

Introduction

Achieving and maintaining good health is probably one of the most important issues in North Americans' lives. A majority of both Canadians and Americans indicate that they are willing to pay higher taxes to preserve universal health insurance (in Canada), or to obtain universal and permanent health coverage (in the United States) (Wilson, 1996: 205). Most of us have been sick at some point in our lives, and we all know how good it feels to become well again. We are so focused on our health that we spend billions of dollars every year on exercise equipment, health club memberships, diets, proper foods and, not least of all, on health care providers such as physicians and nurses.

But it is not just the personal experience of health that is desirable—there are social costs to ill health as well. In fact, the cost of poor health to North American society as a whole is quite extraordinary. For example, data on the costs of "unintentional injuries" alone, cited by the National Safety Council (1994) for the United States (all figures in U.S. dollars) show that

- The total financial loss in terms of wage and productivity losses was $227 billion.
- The costs of medical expenses amounted to $77.8 billion.
- The administrative expense was $70.1 billion.
- The costs to employers totaled $18.7 billion.
- The costs due to motor vehicle damage were $18.7 billion.

As we will see further in this chapter, and as noted in Box 4.1, many illnesses, diseases, and life-threatening or debilitating conditions are in fact the unhappy outcomes of social, economic, and political structures that make it very difficult for individuals to live healthy lifestyles (Bolaria and Dickinson, 1994). Yet despite the fact that health seems to be both a social and individual responsibility, to a large extent our sense of health reflects our individual behavior because we tend to believe that achieving or sustaining good health is one's personal responsibility. As C.W. Mills might have argued, we generally act as if health and illness are purely "personal issues," unrelated to the nature and structure of the society in which we live.

It is certainly true that we can improve our psychological and physical well-being by taking personal precautions and by living well. But how often do we really think about the "social" causes of disease? Why do we hold individuals responsible for their well-being? And who benefits from the individualistic focus on health? These and related questions are the subject matter of the sociologies of medicine, and health and illness. Each of these related fields examines the structure of medical care (sociology of medicine), and the social causes and consequences of illness (sociology of health and illness). This chapter draws on insights from both fields to provide readers with a sense of the major debates and problems characterizing the field of health and health care.

BOX 4-1

Poverty, Homelessness, and Health

Valarie Tarasuk works at the Ontario Workers' Compensation Institute in Toronto. She conducted a study of critical health issues facing adult homeless people who attended a drop-in center in downtown Toronto, and some of her results are described here.

Members' income and housing situations were key determinants of the nature of their daily lives. Many wandered daily between soup kitchens, social service agencies, temporary employment agencies, and hostels or other forms of shelter. Their impoverished circumstances invariably necessitated a dependence on charitable food assistance programs for the bulk of their food. This pattern of food acquisition may have compromised the nutritional quality of individuals' intakes, placing them at increased risk of ill health. Poverty also meant additional health risks for members with drug and alcohol addictions as they sought out less and less expensive intoxicants. The consumption of potentially lethal substances such as non-beverage sources of alcohol was common among some members. Others were known to inhale gasoline or glue—substances which can cause serious neurological damage.

Source: Tarazuk (1994: 60).

What Is Health and What Is Illness?

When most of us think about our health, we typically define it in negative terms— that is in terms of the absence of disease. We hold images of illness as chronic, debilitating conditions such as cancer or heart disease. We also tend to view the solution to health problems as residing in "cures" for disease. Those who study health, however, often have different perceptions of what constitutes health and illness. Medical professionals, for instance, tend to view health in terms of the absence of physical or psychological abnormalities. Others, such as some sociologists, have a much broader view of health and illness. They contend that health is a "total state of well-being" involving one's physical, psychological, and even spiritual health (Navarro, 1976). In taking this approach, sociologists are trying to highlight a key health issue—that being ill is not just a consequence of "catching a disease" or engaging in "dangerous lifestyles," but is also fundamentally related to the social and physical environment around us. In other words, they maintain that health is "socially determined."

Sociologists are not alone in this broader approach. In fact, as early as 1958, the World Health Organization (WHO, 1958: 459) pointed out that negative definitions focusing only on the absence of physical and mental ill health do not allow us to account for the social aspects of health. Following WHO, this chapter employs a definition of health that includes physical, psychological, and socio-economic components. Thus, the following **holistic definition of health**, while broad, takes account of the linkages between factors such as a satisfactory lifestyle, a safe environment, particular biological risk factors, and health. Health, then, is a state of complete physical, mental and social well-being, and not merely the absence of disease or infirmity.

This approach also allows us to de-emphasize the individualistic nature of how we go about accounting for our health. As we pointed out in Chapter 1, C.W. Mills argued that one of the great challenges facing contemporary societies is our ability and willingness to link private troubles with public issues. Put in the context of our interests in this chapter, Mills' comments remind us that we should resist the tendency to blame ourselves, or more usually, our unhealthy lifestyles for our health problems. To be sure, eating a high fat, low fiber diet, washing down our food with copious quantities of alcohol, and smoking a few packs of cigarettes a day are all individual behaviors that can (and probably will) affect our health. However, we also have to be aware of the relationship between factors such as stress at work, domestic violence, unemployment, poverty, addiction, and mental or physical illness. For example, approximately 46 million Americans smoke cigarettes, a habit that is well-known for its devastating health consequences. It is also well-known that quitting is very difficult because nicotine is as addictive as cocaine or heroin (Lyman and Potter, 1996: 40). Thus, quitting is not simply a matter of making a personal decision and commitment to stop. Moreover, thinking about the health consequences of smoking only at the level of individual behavior tends to ignore the fact that tobacco companies vigorously engage in advertising and sponsorship campaigns to maintain their market, all in the name of profit (see Box 4.2). As such, this is a structural issue requiring some appreciation of the social, economic, and cultural problems that surround smoking (Lyman and Potter, 1996: 39-42). To use only a negative and narrow definition, then, means that we do not account for the myriad individuals who are experiencing poor health but are still functioning in everyday society, and for those people who cannot find a "cure" for their ailments, because the causes lie in broader social factors over which individuals or medical professionals have no control.

If the narrow-negative model of health is inadequate, why do most of us (including medical professionals) continue to think about it in these terms? To answer this question, we must first examine some sociological theories of health, after which we will turn to the history of medicine.

Sociological Theories of Health

How do people come to be healthy? Why are some people healthier than others? To answer these questions, we review three basic sociological approaches to understanding health: conflict theory, feminist theory, and structural functionalist theory.

BOX 4-2

Excerpts from the "Marlboro Man" Lawsuit

On August 30, 1996, the widow of the "Marlboro Man" filed suit against the tobacco industry, alleging that its fraud and deceit contributed to David McLean's death from lung cancer. McLean was featured in a long-running campaign for Philip Morris' most popular brand of cigarettes. McLean's widow alleges that he routinely smoked as many as five packs of cigarettes a day in the course of shooting print and television commercials.

Nature of the Case

In the early 1960s, Philip Morris, Inc., came up with perhaps the most famous advertising image ever created—the Marlboro Man. The portrait of a rugged, adventurous cowboy smoking a cigarette while sitting astride his horse, against a scenic mountainous backdrop is used effectively to this day, making Marlboro the best-selling cigarette in the world. But while the prominent image of the Marlboro Man lives on, David McLean, the actor who originally portrayed the Marlboro Man, has died of lung cancer. Cigarettes killed the Marlboro Man.

By this action, Plaintiffs LILO MCLEAN, the wife of David McLean, and MARK HUTH, AKA MARK MCLEAN, the son of David McLean, seek damages for wrongful death and personal injuries to David McLean based on common law theories of fraud and deceit, negligent misrepresentation, misrepresentation to consumers, breach of express warranty, and breach of implied warranty.

FACTUAL ALLEGATIONS

A. David McLean's Use of Cigarettes.

David McLean began smoking cigarettes at the age of 12 and was almost immediately addicted to the nicotine in tobacco. Because of his addiction to nicotine, Mr. McLean continued smoking cigarettes until he died at age 73.

Due to his addiction to nicotine, David McLean smoked cigarettes every day. Although he tried to quit smoking numerous times, his addiction to nicotine prevented him from doing so.

During the time he became addicted to the nicotine in cigarettes, David McLean did not know the adverse health consequences of smoking. Until 1964, cigarette packages and advertisements contained no warning of the adverse health effects of tobacco. David McLean was led to believe that smoking cigarettes was not harmful to his health or addictive.

During his long history of smoking, David McLean primarily smoked Marlboro and Chesterfield brand cigarettes.

In the early 1960s, already a smoker for over twenty years, David McLean was hired to portray the Marlboro Man in television and print advertising. During the taping of the commercials, David McLean was obligated to smoke Marlboro cigarettes. The commercials were very carefully orchestrated, and David McLean was required to smoke up to five packs per take, in order to get the ashes to fall a certain way, the smoke to rise a certain way, and the hand to hold the cigarette in a certain way.

Even after his portrayal of the Marlboro Man, David McLean continued to smoke Marlboro cigarettes, and he continued to receive boxes of Marlboro cigarettes as gifts.

In approximately 1985, David McLean began to suffer from emphysema due to smoking.

In approximately 1993, during a pre-operative check-up for back surgery, David McLean's doctors found a tumor in his right lung. After further review, David McLean was diagnosed with lung cancer. Later that year, he underwent surgery to remove the tumor and part of the lung.

Initially, doctors believed that the tumor had been fully removed. But in 1995, doctors discovered that cancer was still present in his right lung. Later that year, doctors discovered that the cancer had spread to his brain and his spine. Chemotherapy and other treatments administered to David McLean were unsuccessful.

In October of 1995, due to cancer caused by long years of smoking cigarettes, David McLean died, leaving a widow and fatherless son.

B. The Industry Conspiracy On Smoking and Health: Deceiving the Public About Disease and Death.

Through a fraudulent course of conduct that has spanned decades, Defendants have manufactured, promoted, distributed, or sold tobacco products to millions of consumers, including David McLean, knowing, but denying and concealing, that their tobacco products contain a highly addictive drug, known as nicotine, and have, unbeknownst to the public, controlled and manipulated the amount and big-availability of nicotine in their tobacco products for the purpose and with the intent of creating and sustaining addiction.

The Tobacco Companies reap enormous profits from their manufacture and sale of cigarettes to consumers throughout the United States, including the State of Texas. The Tobacco Companies' earnings for the last year alone exceeded six billion dollars (U.S.). The Tobacco Companies, make, advertise and sell cigarettes despite their knowledge of the following facts: More than 10 million Americans have died as a result of smoking cigarettes; almost one death in every five is due to a smoking-related illness; the leading cause of preventable death in the United States today is smoking cigarettes; smoking causes cardiovascular disease and is responsible for approximately one third of all heart disease deaths; smoking causes almost all lung

BOX 4-2

and throat cancer deaths; smoking causes various pulmonary diseases, including emphysema; smoking causes stillbirths and neonatal deaths among the babies of mothers who smoke; and cigarettes may contain any number of approximately 700 additives, including a number of toxic and dangerous chemicals. Despite the overwhelming weight of scientific evidence that smoking cigarettes and using smokeless tobacco pose serious health risks, and despite the gruesome statistical legacy left by the tobacco industry, approximately 50 million Americans continue to smoke cigarettes, including 3,000 new teenage smokers daily, and millions more continue to use smokeless tobacco because they are addicted to these products. More specifically, they are addicted to nicotine, the drug in tobacco that causes an addiction similar to that suffered by users of heroin and cocaine.

BOX 4-2

Source: http://www.courttv.com/library/business/tobacco/marlboroman.html. Reprinted by permission of the Courtroom Television Network.

Structural Functionalist Theories: Health and Illness as the "Capacity to Perform"

The dominant perspective in the sociology of health has historically been structural functionalism. As you will recall from previous chapters, functionalists maintain that society and its systems are the most important objects of inquiry for social scientists. More specifically, they argue that social systems are composed of inter-related parts (such as health care institutions, governments, and medical schools) that operate together to make society function properly.

You can probably see that this perspective lends itself quite well to certain models of health and disease. In fact, most perspectives on health in North America today are based on a functionalist model. Like the functional model of society, the body is seen as a system with inter-dependent parts, which tend naturally to exist in balance, or equilibrium, with one another. When one part (such as the lungs or the brain) is not working properly, it is said to be dysfunctional, requiring some form of medical intervention. Perhaps the most influential of functionalist theorists, Talcott Parsons (1972: 117), argued that health is equivalent to "the state of optimum capacity of an individual for the effective performance of the roles and tasks for which he [sic] has been socialized." Notice that in Parsons' definition, what is important is the "performance of roles and tasks" and not the experience of ill health itself (Dickinson and Bolaria, 1994). Moreover, for Parsons, illness is not the responsibility of the individual who is sick, but of a medical system that is presumed to be neutral and unbiased. In effect, the approach taken by such functional models relies on a very mechanical conception of health and illness—the individual is seen as the proverbial cog in a wheel, in that the experience of illness is reduced to a problem of, and for, social systems.

Generally, this approach is the essence of what is called the **allopathic model** of medicine. Allopathic medicine treats illness by attempting to create a state of well-being in the body that is opposite to the state of illness (Clarke, 1990). It is based on post hoc intervention, or, put another way, attempts to intervene in the dysfunctional body system, after the system is sick or infected.

It is very important here to state that despite its post hoc nature, allopathic medicine is often very effective in successfully treating many medical conditions. It is surely true, for instance, that many couples who suffered from infertility only 20 years ago would today have an excellent chance of conceiving children through the technology of in-vitro fertilization (the "test-tube" baby). It is also true that modern medicine can indeed often appear to have worked "miracles." The problem is not that medicine is ineffective all the time, but that functionalist approaches often do not place health and illness in broader social contexts. Instead, they focus on individuals (in terms of their role in the system) and medical institutions (the system itself). In Parsons' approach for example, illness is viewed as a type of "deviant" behavior, in need of the social control that comes from modern scientific medicine (Carpenter, 1980). One very good example of this "control the individual but ignore the context" strategy comes from a study conducted in 1977, which showed that an astonishing 42 percent of elderly women (between 65 and 74 years old) received mood-modifying drugs in the province of Saskatchewan. In addition to experiencing health problems, many of these women also suffered from profound poverty. Yet instead of dealing with the linkages between ill health, class, and poverty directly, the strategy seems to have been to provide a medical "solution." In effect, their health problems were dealt with medically rather than socially (Harding, 1986) (See Box 4.3 for another example).

In general, then, from a functionalist perspective, modern technological advancements in medicine have been central to creating healthier individuals. Thus, they would emphasize discoveries like those of Louis Pasteur who determined that micro-organisms cause disease, or Roentgen who discovered X-rays, and Lister's recognition of the importance of antiseptics (Weiss and Lonnquist, 1997). However, these are relatively new developments. In fact, the medicine practised by early physicians was often no more effective than that of competitors such as homeopaths or chiropractors (Shortt, 1983). How, then, did we come to rely on the scientific functionalist model of health? The answer lies in the history of the medical profession itself, which, as we shall see, was extremely successful in dominating, and later excluding, alternative models of health and health care delivery.

Conflict Theories: "Health Care and Capitalism Are Dangerous to Your Health"

Conflict, or critical, approaches emphasize relationships of power among various groups in society. They question who has power over whom, and how it is maintained and lost. Within the sociological study of health and illness, this perspective has only recently started to have a major impact on the ways in which we think about and deal with illness. Probably the earliest critical approach to illness and health, however, comes from the work of Frederick Engels, who in his *The Condition of the Working Class in England* (1845) portrayed the horrible consequences of early capitalist production on the health of factory workers in England. Not only did he show that work could be hazardous to one's health, he also demonstrated that the larger social consequences of capitalism (such as

BOX 4-3

The Rush to Ritalin

By Sharon Kirkey: Southam Newspapers

OTTAWA — A trip to the principal's office used to mean big trouble. These days, more kids are showing up in the school office just to get their midday dose of Ritalin.

Ritalin, the drug used to treat hyperactivity in children, is being seized on by a generation worried about controlling inappropriate behavior. But some doctors think Ritalin is being prescribed to children who are simply having trouble in school. The numbers suggest they have good reason to worry. The number of prescriptions for Ritalin increased four-fold from 1990 to 1995, making the stimulant one of the most prescribed drugs in the country. Ontario and British Columbia lead the country in Ritalin sales. Even the federal government is alarmed.

Earlier this month, Health Canada's Health Protection Branch convened some two dozen child psychiatrists, psychologists, teachers and parents to look at the growing use of Ritalin in Canada. "They wanted to know whether they should be concerned about this. I think they should be," said Dr. Normand Carrey, a child psychiatrist at the Royal Ottawa Hospital, who participated in the meeting.

The group recommended the government look at how Ritalin is being prescribed, and by whom. And they want to make doctors better aware of standards and guidelines for diagnosing attention deficit-hyperactivity disorder (ADHD).

No one knows exactly what's behind the surge in Ritalin use, but experts speculate it's due to everything from increased awareness of attention disorders in schools to teachers and parents becoming less tolerant of unruly behavior. There's also concern that some doctors aren't doing a thorough enough assessment before prescribing Ritalin.

"ADHD has become too much of an easy diagnosis," Carrey said. Some local school offices have become virtual noon-time pharmacies. At one Ottawa-area board of education, the number of medications dispensed to students by office administrators has increased 20 percent over the past 18 months. A good chunk of those pills is Ritalin.

"We always worry that we're a half-step away from giving someone the wrong dosage," says John Beatty, the board's superintendent of school operations. At some schools, children as young as seven are asked to take their Ritalin themselves. The little blue pills have become so common in schoolyards that some kids are reportedly selling their spare Ritalin to friends, who take it in the hope of getting a buzz.

"Every parent wants their child to be at the top of the class," says Dr. André Coté, clinical director of the Children's Mental Health Treatment Centre at the Royal

BOX 4-3

Ottawa Hospital. "What we might be seeing is that people are trying to improve their kids' performance by giving them medication."

Others worry that Ritalin has become an easy answer for busy families trying to cope with a hyperactive or aggressive child on their own. Even proponents of Ritalin fear that normal, rambunctious children may be being labelled with a disease for which there is still no clear test.

"I do believe that we have less tolerance of deviant behavior," says Carrey. "Johnny might have been disruptive a couple generations ago, but maybe the extended family was around to support parents more. Now parents are left to cope with the behavior themselves and they might grab on to (a diagnosis of ADHD) and say, 'This explains it.'"

Source: Kirkey, Sharon. "The Rush to Ritalin," excerpted from *The Ottawa Citizen*, June 1, 1996. Southam Newspapers. Reprinted by permission of *The Ottawa Citizen*.

widespread migration, low pay, and inadequate shelter) could result in epidemics such as tuberculosis and typhoid (Navarro, 1986). One of the central themes of Engels' work was that capitalism fosters social and economic conditions that create dangerous conditions for working people. Importantly, this theme has continued to dominate research and discussion on health within the conflict framework.

One of the most vocal advocates of the idea that people are often "sick of work" in more ways than one is Vincente Navarro. He argues that even though living and working conditions have improved since the era in which Engels wrote, capitalism has created new health problems for modern populations. He points to the fact that the foremost goal of capitalists is, of course, to make as much profit as possible, and that this imperative drives capitalists to ignore the health consequences of the profit motive, either deliberately or unintentionally. Consider the link between job stress and poor health for example. Numerous studies have shown that there is a strong positive association among stresses such as the inability to do one's job properly, low autonomy, and time pressures, and outcomes such as high blood pressure, headaches, and depression (Gutierres, Saenz and Green, 1994; Beehr and Bhagat, 1985). The most important aspect of this relationship for conflict theorists is the fact that job stress is directly related to the need for capitalists and managers to increase the speed and efficiency of work in order to improve productivity and thereby maximize profits.

Another good example of the link between profit motive and poor health is evident in the problem of workplace safety. Consider the following figures:

➤ It has been estimated that since 1976 more than a million Canadian workers have been injured in work-related accidents (Labor Canada, 1991).

➤ Between 1979 and 1989, there were nearly 12,000 work-related accidents resulting in death (Statistics Canada, 1992).

➤ Similarly, in the United States, it has been estimated that between 50,000 and 70,000 workers die from occupational disease every year (Corporate Crime Reporter, 1988).

➤ Each year in the United States, occupational diseases cause 350,000 new illnesses (Corporate Crime Reporter, 1988).

It is also important to note that statistics on occupational disease and injuries are probably underestimates, since both employers and employees have a vested interest in not reporting their incidence. This is because many employees will suffer financially if forced to take workers' compensation payments that are below their normal salaries and wages. In addition, because employers must pay workers' compensation insurance and health insurance premiums, they are often reluctant to report incidents for fear that their premiums will increase. From their point of view, this would eat into profits, and in fact, it already does. For example, in the United States between 1991 and 1994, private employers' health insurance costs per employee-hour worked increased by 24 percent to US$1.14 an hour (National Center for Health Statistics, 1994).

While some workplace incidents are truly accidental, it is clear that many companies and organizations are more interested in extracting high levels of performance from employees than they are in investing in safety equipment, proper safety protocols, or non-toxic working environments (Frank and Lynch, 1992).

Another key set of arguments made by conflict theorists is directed at the nature, structure, and delivery of health care itself. In particular, theorists such as Illich (1976) argue that one of the major obstacles to achieving good health for all is health care providers themselves. Illich contends that contemporary medical practice is iatrogenic: a term he uses to denote medically induced disease or ill health. He outlines three kinds of **iatrogenesis**:

1. Clinical iatrogenesis occurs when patients die as a result of medical care. The focus is on medical practice by health care workers, practitioners, or the institutions (such as hospitals) in which they work

2. Social iatrogenesis happens when health policies reproduce or buttress organizations which generate ill health. The central issue here is medical or health policy and its role in medicalizing so many aspects of our lives.

3. Structural iatrogenesis takes place when "medically sponsored behavior and delusions restrict the vital autonomy of people by undermining their competency in growing up, caring for each other and aging" (Illich, 1976: 165). The key factor here is the role of medical ideology in reproducing our dependence on medical institutions while at the same time diminishing our sense of personal and social responsibility for good health.

There are many examples of the negative influence of medical practice, policies, and ideology over health. Most of us have heard the old (but not very funny) joke about the operation being a success, but the patient dying. In some ways, this quip captures the essence of clinical iatrogenesis very well, because it illustrates that while the objective of medical care is to "do no harm" (as the Hippocratic oath states), there are often many negative, unintended consequences of medical practice. For example, prescription drugs are widely used in medical practice today, and in fact, North American physicians are among the highest prescribers in the world (Alvi, 1994). Although it may well be true that certain drugs have benefits for certain patients, it is also true that the tendency towards "prescription based" medicine has created negative consequences such as drug dependency, suffering from side effects, long-term health complications arising from inadequate knowledge of the drug's impact, dangerous drug interactions, and even suicide and death. The striking symbiotic relationship between pharmaceutical companies and physicians can be seen in the following facts:

➤ In 1992, Canadians used over CAN$7 billion worth of prescription and non-prescription drugs (Fulton, 1993).

➤ There are currently 16,000 pharmaceutical products on the market, and approximately 500 new drugs are approved each year.

➤ According to a poll conducted in 1991 by the Medical Post, physicians receive information on prescription drugs directly from the pharmaceutical industry through advertising and direct sales visits 66 percent of the time.

➤ A study conducted by the Annals of Internal Medicine (June, 1992) found that, despite the fact that 92 percent of the ads potentially violated at least one Food and Drug Administration regulation, 59 percent of advertisements would not lead to proper prescribing, while another 50 percent were judged to have little or no educational value.

➤ Americans spend an estimated 50 million days in hospital every year as a result of adverse drug reactions (York, 1987).

➤ In Canada, the combined expenditures of the pharmaceutical industry on attempts to influence physicians' prescribing patterns range from CAN$6,000 to CAN$10,000 per year, per physician. (Drug Programs Reform Secretariat, 1992).

➤ Canadian physicians have the highest prescription rate in the world, but also spend the least time interviewing patients. On average, they write 4,000 to 5,000 prescriptions per year, with the highest average among family physicians (most often the first point of contact in the medical system) who write 6,000 to 8,000 prescriptions per year—or 25 to 30 prescriptions each working day (Drug Programs Reform Secretariat, 1992).

Some additional examples from the work of York (1987) point to the iatrogenic potential of doctors' work and the hospitals in which they work:

➤ In the United States, about a quarter of a million patients die during surgery or shortly after surgery every year.

➤ When the doctors of Los Angeles County went on strike in 1976 there was a 50 percent decline in the number of operations—and an 18 percent drop in the county's death rate.

➤ A study conducted in a teaching hospital in Boston found that 36 percent of the hospital's patients had illnesses caused by the medical system, and 9 percent had an iatrogenic disease that prolonged their disability or threatened their lives.

For Illich, social iatrogenesis represents the negative impact on our physical and psychological well-being of the presence of medicine in nearly every aspect of our daily lives. For example, throughout the course of our lives, we are exposed to medical technology, medical ideas about what is "normal" and "abnormal," and medical solutions to everyday problems. Think of your own life. The chances are very good that you were born in a hospital, under the care of doctors and nurses, that later you received pediatric care, that you currently go to the doctor for various ailments, or to make sure you are still healthy, and that when you are older, you will receive geriatric care. For Illich, this is proof positive that North Americans are addicted to the medical model of health, despite the fact that many researchers have shown that a good portion of physician-patient interactions are unnecessary (Anderson, 1981). It is also true that many medical technologies have not proven to be entirely successful (See Box 4.4).

For example, Deber and Thompson (1992) note that many hospitals have invested heavily in lithotriptor machines (used to shatter gallstones) despite the fact that there is insufficient data on their performance and effectiveness as compared to traditional treatment of this ailment. It is also significant that, as with pharmaceuticals, the main source of information used in making decisions regarding the acquisition of new technologies is the manufacturer.

In Illich's view, structural iatrogenesis involves the removal of responsibility for health from the individual. For him, this is a negative outcome, since he feels that it is important for human beings to experience disease, pain, and suffering because these factors are so central to the development of one's full humanity. To illustrate, think about the increasing tendency to utilize drugs during the birthing process. It has been said that giving birth is probably the most incredibly painful, but rewarding, experience a woman can have. For Illich, those women who are choosing to give birth with the "benefit" of pain-killing drugs will miss out on a very important aspect of human existence.

To summarize, then, Illich's arguments (particularly in his aptly titled book *Medical Nemesis*) are critical of modern medicine's historical ability to become the "only way" of dealing with illness and disease, its pretense in holding all the answers, and its capacity actually to cause as many health problems as it solves.

While Illich's arguments have been major influences on critical approaches to health and illness, his work has been open to some criticism. One of the most important of these stems from the work of Vincente Navarro (1986) and others (Waitzkin, 1983; Doyal, 1995) who argue that though Illich has provided an important critique of the nature of medicine in industrialized societies, he does not provide an adequate analysis of the context in which modern medicine operates. In other words, the argument that physicians and the medical system can themselves be dangerous to your health is one thing, but we must also ask how it is that this came to be so. For those who pursue such questions, the answers lie in the linkages between modern day medical practice and the socio-economic context.

BOX 4-4

Body Works

By Wallace Immen: Medical Reporter

If only fixing a defective gene were as simple as changing a spark plug, we could use our growing knowledge about inherited genetic risks to head off disease.

It may eventually come to that, but don't hold your breath. Despite enthusiastic predictions, gene therapy today is at about the level of a medieval barrage: Everything is thrown at the target, in this case bits of genetic material at a cell, in the hope that something will hit the spot. Meanwhile, a healthy lifestyle is still the best defence.

That said, the spinoffs from research on how things go wrong with genes are providing insights into the many ways the body has to keep things going right. So even if you've been dealt a bad hand in gene rummy, there may be ways to head off your risk of developing a particular disease.

There are a few well-publicized hereditary genes that by themselves make a small part of the population vulnerable to breast cancer or Huntington's disease. But in many cases, it is not the aberrant gene but the disorder it allows to happen in the body that brings on the disease.

While genes are often called the body's blueprints, they're hardly static line drawings. They're more like contractors who organize the body's building and repair or managers who oversee production and maintenance within cells.

The spiral arrangement of genes at the centre of each cell makes sure the specific genes that define what a cell does are switched on while the rest are switched off. This makes the cell act in very specific ways. But if the switches aren't working or are improperly turned on, the result is a cell out of control.

There are many places where things can go wrong. So far, about 42,000 genes have been identified in the human code and researchers have estimated that there could be between 60,000 and 150,000. Fortunately, we're learning that a single bad gene may only marginally increase the risk of conditions such as high blood pressure, asthma or cancer.

However, the combined effect of a number of very small genetic abnormalities can lead to a serious susceptibility to a disease, according to Dr. Robert Hegele, an endocrine researcher at St. Michael's Hospital in Toronto.

For instance, when studying high cholesterol levels among Alberta's Hutterites, he found eight inherited genes that increase cholesterol levels in members of the religious sect. Almost everyone in the close-knit community inherits one of the genes, which on its own raises cholesterol production a mere 3 or 4 percent above average. But some people inherit several, and the cumulative effect is a cholesterol level as much as 25 percent above normal. This poses a definite risk of heart disease.

Fortunately, genes appear to work in the other direction as well. Even if several genes are operating abnormally, others that can perform similar functions will keep things running.

A gene known as APOE-2 reduces cholesterol even as other factors raise it. Dr. Hegele suggests this may explain why a few lucky people can avoid heart disease even though they are overweight, smoke, and never exercise.

One day, doctors may be able to administer such a cholesterol-lowering gene to someone developing heart disease, or switch on an anti-cancer gene to counteract one that's promoting a tumor. But don't count on it soon. The task of screening and repairing is huge. Dr. Hegele believes genetic screening tests for predisposition to heart disease may have to look at 40 or 50 genes to get the total picture.

The good news is there's no need to wait for such technology. For instance, Dr. Hegele estimates that genes contribute no more than 40 percent of our cholesterol production. So even if you have this genetic predisposition, you can still greatly reduce your risk of heart disease by altering your lifestyle—stopping smoking and lowering fat in the diet.

Lifestyle factors can also increase a predisposition towards cancer. A recently announced long-term study by the U.S. National Cancer Institute found that people with the highest genetic risk—those with an extensive family history of colon cancer—could dramatically reduce their likelihood of developing tumors by lowering their intake of beef and alcohol while keeping their weight under control and not smoking. Genetically prone people who ate a lot of meat were as much as five times more likely to develop cancer as those who ate little meat. Meanwhile, the people who ate the highest amount of fruit had fewer tumors than people who ate very little meat but also little fruit.

So we don't have to be victims of our genes. If you can see a collision coming, it makes sense to try to avoid it.

BOX 4-4

Source: Wallace Immen, "How and Why Things Happen," *The Globe and Mail*, "The Middle Kingdom: Body Works," May 28, 1997. Reprinted with permission of *The Globe and Mail*.

We have already seen in some of the examples given here that there are clearly some people who benefit from the medical model of illness (pharmaceutical companies, and physicians themselves for example). For those who wish to advance Illich's arguments, it is important therefore to understand that "difficulties in health and medical care emerged from social contradictions and rarely can be separated from those contradictions" (Waitzkin, 1983: 5). If we take this position seriously, then it is obvious that we need to link concepts such as race, gender, and class inequality in broader society with problems of health. Those studying one of the most important of these concepts, gender, have made important contributions to our understanding of health and illness.

Feminist Perspectives: "The Medicalization of Women's Lives"

Feminist sociology highlights the importance of seeing the world from the point of view of women. In feminist research on health and health care, the dominant theme has been the **"medicalization"** of women's lives (Pescosolido and Kronenfeld, 1995). Medicalization can be defined as a process in which a condition or situation comes to be defined as an illness. The main argument here is that a good portion of women's lives has been defined as "medical issues." Here, the social control aspects of medicine are emphasized by showing how women's "place in the home" is reproduced by constructing women mainly in terms of their reproductive roles (Walters, 1994; 1991). If we think about pregnancy again, this point becomes clearer when we understand that the medical profession essentially defines pregnancy as a "condition" in which the fetus/child is a "parasite" feeding off the mother's body. Other examples include the ways in which women's reproductive life (menstruation, menopause, pregnancy and childbirth, and in/fertility) are dealt with by organized medicine. But reproductive issues are obviously not the only ones concerning women. Indeed, there is some evidence that stress, concerns about body image, and problems like migraines, arthritis, and chronic headaches are more problematic for many women (Walters, 1994).

A second issue concerning feminists interested in health issues is the problem of inequalities in health between women and men. Some data on these inequities are presented later in this chapter, and elsewhere in this text. What concerns us here are the ways in which feminist theorists explain these inequalities. The main explanation boils down to the fact that for feminists, gender inequalities in health are reflections of broader inequalities between women and men. Basic socio-economic differences, however, also combine with the fact that women's health is affected by their unequal access to quality health care. There are several reasons for this. First, although women are major health care users as well as providers, they are under-represented in health care decision making. Second, although women and men have different health needs, the medical establishment tends to ignore these differences; in other words, the gendered nature of health is not taken into account (Vanwijk, Vanvliet and Kolk, 1996). As Findlay and Millar (1994: 277-278) point out, the reasons underpinning these realities are rooted in history:

"As medicine began to emerge as a profession in its own right, the lives of ordinary women were of little concern to doctors and other powerful groups, a situation which reflected women's inferior status. Instead, their health needs and other major social events in their life (notably pregnancy and childbirth) were left to other women in the community....But instead of working to improve the skills and training of traditional female healers and midwives, the young, overwhelmingly male medical profession moved to usurp their role in the management of women's health. After a long struggle—and despite the fact that midwives regularly achieved lower maternal mortality rates than physicians—doctors succeeded in discrediting women's traditional expertise (as 'ignorance,' 'superstition,' and 'incompetence') and by the early twentieth century, in driving them from the field."

Of further concern to feminist researchers are the negative health experiences of women as workers, both inside and outside the medical arena. For instance DeKeseredy and Hinch (1994), point out that employers often perpetrate violence against women, expose them to health risks that specifically concern women, and often "look the other way" when women are subjected to harassment. In addition, many research studies point to the inequitable nature of the medical profession itself, in which women have traditionally worked in medical specialties such as nursing and midwifery—defined as "subordinate" to those (such as physicians) that have historically been occupied primarily by men (Findlay and Millar, 1994; Coburn, 1993).

For feminist researchers, then, the patriarchal structure of society, in combination with the social and cultural context in which women work, live, and play, are key factors in the perception and determination of women's health. At the same time, despite the fact that women make up the majority of health care providers, they have historically been excluded from decision making within health care research and practice. Accordingly, most feminist perspectives on health call for a gendered approach to understanding and acting upon health issues.

How Did Physicians Become So Powerful?

Physicians directly or indirectly control the bulk of health care resources (York, 1987). As feminist and conflict theorists point out, one of the most important ways of understanding why health care is the way it is in North America is to ask how physicians became so powerful. To answer this question, we must go back two centuries.

In both Canada and the United States, in the mid-eighteenth century, an elite group of physicians began lobbying governments to create laws barring those who did not fit into the allopathic model of health. There were, in fact, many such individuals. For instance, allopathic physicians faced tremendous competition from health practitioners (called "irregulars") such as Aboriginal healers, homeopaths, chiropractors, Thomsonians, herbalists, and midwives who provided medical relief to the bulk of the population, particularly to the poorer classes. As far as allopathic physicians were concerned, if their brand of medicine was to survive and prosper then the irregular practitioners must be destroyed or controlled. Moreover, the difficulties involved in excluding other practitioners (and thereby controlling the market for services) were compounded by the fact that there was little unity among allopaths themselves. There could be no way of demonstrating the superiority of regular medicine until there was a relatively homogeneous group of regular practitioners united against what they considered to be "quackery."

Initially, allopaths attempted to influence politicians to create laws that would sanction those unwilling to join their own group of medical "experts." These doctors relied heavily on their connections with the ruling classes of the day, as well as on the fact that they tended to be part of the ruling classes themselves. And, while it was not easy to persuade politicians about the effectiveness of allopathic medicine, eventually they succeeded in eliminating most of the competition from those practising alternative approaches to the traditional medicine they thought so effective. They accomplished this by embarking on a strategy involving the identification, persecution, and prosecution of those practitioners who did not comply with rules set out by elite medical societies. Some of this legislation was quite punitive, at times setting ridiculously high fines as a deterrent to "illegal" practice. In other cases physicians championed legislation which resorted to the legal (and often lucrative) payment of informers whose function was to expose anyone who was not properly licensed.

These political efforts were combined with a public campaign to discredit alternative approaches to healing. In Canada for example, as early as the 1700s, an elite group of physicians, mostly ships' doctors, argued that they should be given professional status so that the public would be protected from the uncontrolled acts of "unscrupulous charlatans."[1] The most important characteristics of these early bids was the attempt to exclude other forms of health practices from the market for health care and the simultaneous attempt to advance a model of allopathic medicine as "science."

The wish to exclude such undesirables was founded on the belief that untrained and unqualified men and women were giving what was considered to be scientific medicine a bad name, and that such people were causing more harm than good in the community. While this may have been true of a number of practitioners, it is also clear that many allopaths were by no means innocent of quackery themselves. They were more concerned with persuading the government as well as the public that their knowledge was unique and special, and as such, warranted special political and economic treatment. And, as Shortt (1983: 60) argues, "....what is of paramount importance...is the manner in which physicians used, not the content, but the rhetoric of science."

The strategy of tarnishing the reputation of alternative health practitioners, while legally barring them from competition worked very well indeed for allopathic practitioners. Control over entrance to the profession by upper-class, male-dominated physicians became entrenched as medical schools in American and Canadian universities adopted restrictive and discriminatory entrance policies (de la Cour and Sheinin, 1990). By the 1920s, a hospital-based, allopathic, and technology-oriented system of health care, with doctors in control, had become firmly established.

The history of North American medicine and health is therefore not so much about the triumph of science as it is the growth and dominance of a profession. As well, it is clear that the allopathic perspective on health is by no means the only viewpoint, and that even within it, it is unclear what "normal" health status actually is. For instance, the medical profession by no means agrees universally on what "normal" blood pressure is, or on the kinds of personality characteristics that should merit a diagnosis of "personality disorder" (Fulton, 1993).

In summary, physicians in North America were able to advance their model of health to the exclusion of others by deliberately excluding other, non-allopathic practitioners. At the same time, public belief in the effectiveness of science underpinned the rise to prominence of the functionalist, allopathic health model at the expense of other approaches. What is important here is the fact that this did not emerge because it is the only or most effective approach to dealing with health and illness. Rather, it is the way we "think about" health because most of us, including the medical profession, tend to believe in its effectiveness uncritically. Moreover, it is important to realize that this perspective emphasizes after the fact, individual responsibility for health rather than societal-based, preventive approaches.

Summary

We have seen that conflict and feminist theories about health challenge those posed by functionalists in several ways. Functionalists argue that the body is a system of interdependent parts. This model has evolved into an approach that emphasizes a narrow focus on the patient's organs, body parts, or illness, as opposed to the "whole person." Furthermore, functionalists maintain that the proper issues for social scientists to study are the impact of the social system (including, of course the health care system, the medical profession, hospitals and the like) on people's attitudes, behaviors, or feelings. In doing so, they tend to uncritically accept the relations of power that exist in any given social system.

In contrast, conflict and feminist theories do emphasize power relations. For conflict theorists, understanding the impact of the profit seeking, bureaucratic, and efficiency driven world we live in is crucial for understanding the structure and impact of the North American health care system. As such, they seek to place health and the health care system in context, and to provide linkages between social, economic and political factors, and health issues. For feminists, the central concern is to examine the history, nature, and structure of male power, and the impact of such power on women's health and their role as health providers.

Having looked at theoretical issues that tend to dominate the field of health, what, then, can we say about North American's health status? How healthy are we? What are the issues associated with measuring health? It is to these questions that we now turn.

How Many North Americans Are Not in "Good Health"?

Our theoretical perspective on health very much conditions the kinds of questions we ask about health. For instance, our understanding of how many North Americans are in good or bad health is greatly influenced by different ideas about what a good measurement of health actually is.

Measures of Health

Usually, we measure health and illness by relying on several types of official data collected by governments and other agencies responsible for health. There are many such measures, but the following five are commonly used.

1. **Infant mortality rates**, which are defined as the number of children under the age of one year who die per 1,000 live births.

2. **Mortality rates**, broken down by cause of death, to give the number of deaths from various causes in proportion to a given population.

3. **Life expectancy**, which is defined as the average number of years of life remaining to an individual at any given age.

4. **Morbidity**, or "sickness," tells us the number of people who are sick and from what they're suffering.

5. Figures that tell us how much we spend on health care as a nation, or how many health care workers per population there are in a country.

Like all measures, each of those listed has limitations as to what it can tell us about the health status of populations. Infant mortality rates are a good indicator of health because they focus on children who are very sensitive to bad health practices and various types of disease. Mortality rates are useful because they tell us how people die, their age, race, gender, and a host of other important variables. Life expectancy is calculated from mortality rates and is a good indicator because most of us believe that longevity is a sign of good health (Marmot, 1994). And morbidity rates provide us with important information regarding the prevalence of certain forms of illness.

On the other hand, numbers focusing on health care are not good indicators of health. It is important to understand this distinction because very often North Americans are told that the nation is spending billions of dollars on health care, and that they should therefore not panic when cutbacks, hospital closures, or other changes to the health care delivery system occur or are proposed. Particularly today, it is not unusual to hear that the health care system is a financial liability, that "health care costs are spiraling out of control," and that this requires serious cutbacks in health care resources.

Whether there is a financial crisis in health care funding in North America is actually a matter of debate, depending on how much we are willing to spend in return for healthy societies. But for our purposes, the most important issue is that information on the amounts of money and labor power that exist within a health care system is not a good indicator of health because it does not focus on the outcomes of health practices of health care institutions such as hospitals. In addition, the number of people in a health care plan, or the amount of money spent on prescription drugs may be interesting if we want to know how financial resources are distributed, but they tell us nothing about the impact of using such drugs on people's health. A good example of the difference between health care spending and actual health can be seen when we realize that the United States spends more per person on medical care than any industrialized nation in the world, yet ranks lower than those nations in measures like infant mortality and longevity (Chappell, 1995).

Finally, like the definitions of health discussed here, these measures are essentially negative approaches to determining the health of the nation. On one hand, they are negative in the sense that they deal with rates of death (never a pleasant topic) or how long we can expect to live. But in another way, while each of these measures does tell us something about the health of a nation, they are not very good measures if we take a holistic approach to health and illness. For instance, none of these measures tells us much about the relationship between unemployment and cardiovascular disease, or the level of health as measured by suicide or homicide rates. And none of them tells us anything about the extent to which illness or deaths are caused by factors such as iatrogenesis, or unhealthy working and living environments. Accordingly, such commonly used measures possess significant limitations. Keeping these issues in mind, what can we say about the number of North Americans who are in good or bad health?

The Health of Nations

We examine data on the indicators discussed above in two ways. We compare Canada and the United States to other industrialized nations, and we look at changes in the indicators over time. By taking this approach, we not only get a sense of how we compare to other societies, but can also assess the extent to which we have improved or deteriorated over time. Table 4.1 provides a comparison of infant mortality rates in Canada, the United States, and three other industrialized nations. Compared to these industrialized countries, Canada and the United States rank about the same as other industrial nations, with the exception of Japan.[2] However, according to data from the U. S. Bureau of the Census (1994), if we compare Canada and the United States with countries whose population is more than 5 million, Canada ranks tenth in infant mortality rates, while the United States ranks eighteenth (Weiss and Lonnquist, 1997: 45).

There can be no question that the health of North Americans has improved over time. In Table 4.2 we see that between 1921 and 1990 the infant mortality rate for both the United States and Canada fell dramatically, with the most significant drops occurring between 1931 and 1951. Moreover, we can also see from these data that the rate of improvement in infant mortality in both Canada and the United States has slowed and has been quite stable in the past few decades. This raises the question: "What factors contributed to the massive decreases in infant mortality rates during the 1920 to 1950 period, and why have there been so few significant improvements since?"

Table 4.1
Infant Mortality Rates Among Selected Nations per 1000 live births, 1980–1996 (projected to year 2000)

Country	1980–82	1983–85	1986–87	1993	1996	2000
Canada	10	8	8	7	6	6
United States	12	11	10	9	7	6
Japan	7	6	5	4	4	4
Germany	10	9	8	–	6	5.7
United Kingdom	12	10	9	10	6	6

Source: World Health Organization, Geneva, 1991 (cited in Fulton, 1993: 221); Population Reference Bureau, 1993 World Population Data Sheet (Washington, DC: Population Reference Bureau Inc. 1993); U.S. Bureau of Census; National Center for Health Statistics, 1996.

Table 4.2
Infant Mortality Rate per 1,000 Live Births: Canada and United States, 1921–1990

	Canada			United States	
Year	Rate	Change	Year	Rate	Change
1921	102.1	–	1900	100	
1931	86	16.1		No data	
1941	61.1	24.9		No data	
1951	38.5	22.6	1950	29.2	70.8*
1961	27.2	11.3	1960	23	6.2
1971	17.5	9.7	1970	20	3
1981	9.6	7.9	1975	16.1	3.9
1986	7.9	1.7	1986	10.4	5.7
1987	7.3	0.6	1987	10.1	0.3
1988	7.2	0.1	1988	10.0	0.1
1989	7.1	0.1	1989	9.8	0.2
1990	6.8	0.3	1900	9.2	.06

* from 1900 to 1951

Sources: Canada Year Book, 148; Health Aspects of Pregnancy and Childbirth: United States, 1982-88, National Center for Health Statistics.

If we take a "technological functionalist" approach, we might simply answer that the major improvements were due to the positive effects of new medical technologies inserted into the process of having children. For instance, physicians and the health care system in general have started to pay more attention to pre-natal care, pregnancy, and childbirth than ever before. The argument might continue that better diagnostic techniques, more successful surgical procedures, and overall increased "scrutiny" by the medical profession has resulted in lower infant mortality rates. However, if we take a more critical perspective, the answer to the question would also rest with factors such as better nutrition, education, and awareness for couples having children since the 1920s. Indeed, according to the National Center for Health Statistics (1995), the dramatic decline in infant mortality rates is due primarily to the decreased impact of diseases such as pneumonia, influenza, respiratory distress syndrome, prematurity, low birthweight, congenital problems, and accidents.[3] More broadly, a study conducted by the U.S. General Accounting Office (1991) found that the majority of premature deaths can be attributed to unhealthy lifestyles, environmental factors, and biological factors.

What diseases do we die from in North America? Table 4.3 shows death rates by causes of death in North America and selected countries. From this data we can see that the three leading causes of death in these countries are heart disease, cerebro-vascular disease and cancer. Moreover, we can see that Japan has a very low incidence of heart disease compared to other industrialized nations, particularly the United Kingdom, which has a rate of death from heart conditions more than 13 times that of Japan. Canada and the United States are not much better, with four

Table 4.3
Death Rates by Cause and Country: Age Standardized Death Rate per 100,000 Population

Country	Ischemic Heart Disease	Cerebro-vascular Disease	Cancer: Lung Trachea, Bronchus	Cancer: Stomach	Cancer: Female Breast	Bronchitis, Emphysema, Asthma	Chronic Liver Disease and Cirrhosis	Motor Vehicle	Suicide and Self-inflicted Injury
Canada (1992)	147	47	53	7	32	7	8	11	13
United States (1991)	170	48	58	5	32	9	11	16	12
Japan (1993)	34	78	28	32	9	10	12	10	15
Germany (1993)	158	85	36	15	32	19	22	11	14
United Kingdom (1992)	446	190	120	24	77	19	14	16	18

Source: World Health Organization, Geneva, Switzerland, World Health Statistics Annual, 1993.

and five times Japan's death rate from heart disease. On the other hand, North Americans are less likely to die from stomach cancer, bronchitis, emphysema, asthma, liver disease, and self-inflicted injuries than Japanese. Overall, North Americans tend to die of the same causes as people in other industrialized nations, and tend to rank near the middle (that is, not the worst, but not the best either) in terms of death rates from these causes.

North Americans' ranking in terms of life expectancy compares favorably with other countries (Table 4.4), although several European countries not shown in the table, such as Sweden, Italy, and Holland, have higher life expectancies. Once again, Japan has the highest life expectancy.

All of these figures seem to show that North Americans have a decent standard of health compared to other nations, and that we are gradually improving. We are living longer, our children are healthier, and, though we die of some horrible diseases, at least we know that the "enemies" (such as cancer and heart disease) are consistent killers, and that we can greatly improve our chances of not contracting these diseases by modifying our lifestyles. On the face of it, then, we might conclude that North America is a healthy continent, and its health care systems are working.

Table 4.4
Life Expectancy at Birth (Years), 1993, 1996, and projected to year 2000

Country	1993	1996	2000
Canada	77	79	80
United States	75	76	76.3
Japan	79	79.6	80
Germany	*	76	76.7
United Kingdom	76	76.4	77.1

* figures not available

Source: Population Reference Bureau, 1993 World Population Data Sheet (Washington, DC: Population Reference Bureau Inc. 1993).

Table 4.5
Health Expenditures by Country: 1985 and 1995

Country	As Percent of Total Gross Domestic Product		Percent of GDP spent on public health	
	1985	1995	1985	1995
Canada	8.4	9.6	6.4	6.9
United States	10.7	14.2	4.3	6.6
Japan	6.7	7.2	4.7	5.7
Germany	8.5	10.4	6.6	8.2
United Kingdom	5.9	6.9	5.0	5.9

Source: Organization for Economic Cooperation and Development (OECD) Health Data 97, Paris, 1997 available at: http://www.oecd.org/publications/observer/figures/heal_a.pdf. Reprinted with permission.

However, our optimism would be shaken when we take into account that Canada and the United States spend more money on health care than most of our comparison nations (Table 4.5). This fact tells us two things. First, it is likely that our approach to spending on health care is inefficient in the sense that we are not getting enough "bang" from our health care dollars. Second, the reason for this is probably rooted in the types of things that we buy when we spend on health care.

For example, Figure 4.1 shows that in 1993, Americans spent most of their health care dollars on hospitals, physicians' services, and drugs, while the lowest two categories of spending were on home health care (an alternative to institutionalized medicine) and public health (which focuses on prevention). The situation is the same in Canada, where less than one percent of the health care dollar goes towards the prevention of ill health.

As you will recall, the functionalist model of health might explain these numbers in terms of the important positive functions played by hospitals and doctors in creating and maintaining health. On the other hand, conflict theorists would interpret the figures differently, arguing that the large sums of money Canadians and Americans spend on health system intervention would probably be better spent on preventive measures. They might point to evidence suggesting that nearly 80 percent of ill health is related to the lifestyle choices of individuals, and that effective strategies for dealing with ill health should therefore be focused on prevention and education. Finally, given their suspicion of the "free market," they

FIGURE 4.1
Spending on Health Services and Supplies Per Capita by Type of Expenditure, United States, 1993

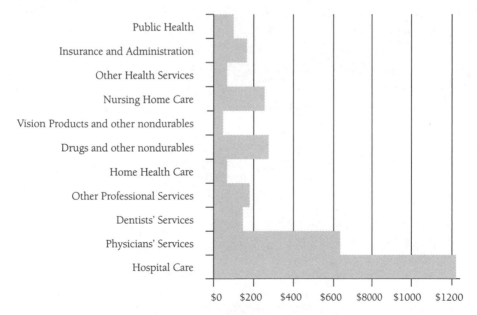

Source: U.S. Health Care Financing Administration, *Health Care Financing Review*, Fall, 1994

would point out that those who stand to make the most financial gains from the way the present system allocates dollars are physicians, and pharmaceutical and medical technology companies. In the words of one doctor interviewed for a study conducted by one of the authors of this book "quite simply, there is no money in preventive medicine."

Who Has Major Health Problems and Who Does Not?

Being "healthy" in North America depends on one's personal characteristics and economic circumstances. Numerous studies have shown that there is a strong link between poverty and ill health, for example (Manga, 1981; Hill, 1978; Wilkins and Adams, 1981). Other studies, such as *The Black Report* conducted in 1982 in the United Kingdom, have shown that social class differences in levels of health have persisted for more than 40 years. In fact, the most consistent findings in analyses of health data show that level of income as well as education, gender, race, and age can all predict the level of health or the kinds of health problems we might experience (See Box 4.5).

One of the most striking factors predicting health is race. In Canada, detailed data on the health status of various racial and ethnic groups is not available. However, we do know something about the health status of Aboriginal peoples. Unhappily, it is difficult to disagree with Fulton's assertion that "the health status of our native population is a disgrace to the nation" (1993: 221). She goes on to point to the following startling statistics:

➤ Suicide levels for Aboriginal people between 15 and 24 are six times the national average.

➤ Violence is the cause of 35 percent of all deaths.

➤ Inuit women have lung cancer rates 15 to 30 times higher than that of other Canadians.

➤ In 1985, the infant mortality rate for Native peoples was 50 to 60 percent above the national rate.

If we look at the information presented for the United States in Table 4.6, we can see further evidence that causes of death vary according to racial background. For most racial groups in the table, the top causes of death are related to diseases which are related to genetic, behavioral, or environmental factors. What is extraordinary, however, is the fact that homicide and deaths due to "legal intervention" rank as the third most common killer of African-American males in the United States. In fact, homicides rank among the top ten killers of all non-white males and females covered in the table.

Can we reduce these different experiences of health to factors such as biology and personal behavior? Certainly, for some differences, biology and socialization patterns are important explanatory factors. For instance, when we compare the experiences of women and men, we see that there are important gender differences

BOX 4-5

Family Environment Affects Health of Family Members

January 1, 1997

A new report from the National Center for Health Statistics, Centers for Disease Control and Prevention examines the relationship between health status and family characteristics and finds that such family traits as education, income, marital status, and family size have an important impact on the health of family members.

In general, the report found that people living with a spouse, children in two-parent households, and those in families with higher education and income were the healthiest. "Health and Selected Socioeconomic Characteristics of the Family: United States, 1988-90" is a comprehensive analysis of 11 separate health variables, from the extent of disability to the incidence of acute conditions. While other NCHS reports—some using later data—have examined one or more family traits by selected health outcomes, this is the first report to cover many health traits and an array of health status indicators.

Highlights of the report show that:

Married men and women in all age groups are less likely to be limited in activity due to illness than single, separated, divorced, or widowed individuals.

Middle-aged adults who live alone have higher rates of doctor visits, acute conditions, and short- and long-term disability.

Children living with a single parent or adult report a higher prevalence of activity limitation and higher rates of disability. They are also more likely to be in fair or poor health and more likely to have been hospitalized.

Never-married persons under 25 years of age living with both parents had lower than average levels of activity limitation, fair or poor health, and hospitalization in direct contrast to never-married persons living with their mother.

Children living in the poorest families report a higher level of activity limitation, poor or fair health, and hospitalization than those in families with higher incomes.

Adults show a similar impact of income with those in the poorest families more likely to have activity limitations, poor or fair health status, bed disability, acute conditions, and hospitalization.

Children under 18 years of age report higher rates of hospitalization where the responsible family member had less than 12 years of education than in families where the responsible adult was better educated. Marital status, income, and education may affect health characteristics in several ways. Higher income and education may provide family members with more knowledge of good health habits and better access to health and preventive services. Persons living with a spouse are likely to have better health profiles because of lifestyle differences (such as better eating habits, someone to share a problem with) and higher incomes.

The report includes these health indexes: percent limited in activity; percent with fair or poor respondent-assessed health status; restricted activity days; bed disability days; work-loss days and school-loss days; percent with a physician contact in the past year; number of annual physician contacts per person; percent with a hospital episode in the past year; days per short-term hospital stay; and incidence of acute conditions.

Data in the report "Health and Selected Socioeconomic Characteristics of the Family: United States, 1988-90," by John Gary Collins and Felicia B. LeClere, are based on household interviews with a sample of the nation's civilian, non-institutionalized population.

For more information or for a copy of this report, contact the NCHS Public Affairs Office (301) 436-7551 or by e-mail at: paoquery@nch10a.em.cdc.gov. A copy of the full report can be viewed or downloaded from the NCHS home page at http://www.cdc.gov/nchswww/nchshome.htm

Source: For Immediate Release (301) 436-7551, National Center for Health Statistics at: http://www.cdc.gov/nchswww/releases/97facts/97sheets/famhealt.htm

Table 4.6
Leading Causes of Death, According to Sex and Race: United States 1991

White Male
1. Diseases of heart
2. Malignant neoplasms
3. Unintentional injuries
4. Cerebro-vascular diseases
5. Chronic obstructive pulmonary diseases
6. Pneumonia and influenza
7. Suicide
8. Human immunodeficiency virus infection
9. Diabetes mellitus
10. Chronic liver disease and cirrhosis

White Female
1. Diseases of heart
2. Malignant neoplasms
3. Cerebro-vascular diseases
4. Pneumonia and influenza
5. Chronic obstructive pulmonary diseases
6. Unintentional injuries
7. Diabetes mellitus
8. Atherosclerosis
9. Septicemia
10. Nephritis, nephrotic syndrome, and nephrosis

Table 4.6 *continued*

African-American Male
1. Diseases of heart
2. Malignant neoplasms
3. Homicide and legal intervention
4. Unintentional injuries
5. Cerebro-vascular diseases
6. Human immunodeficiency virus infection
7. Pneumonia and influenza
8. Certain conditions originating in the perinatal period
9. Chronic obstructive pulmonary diseases
10. Diabetes mellitus

African-American Female
1. Diseases of heart
2. Malignant neoplasms
3. Cerebro-vascular diseases
4. Diabetes mellitus
5. Unintentional injuries
6. Pneumonia and influenza
7. Certain conditions originating in the perinatal period
8. Homicide and legal intervention
9. Chronic obstructive pulmonary diseases
10. Nephritis, nephrotic syndrome, and nephrosis

American Indian or Alaskan Native Male
1. Diseases of heart
2. Unintentional injuries
3. Malignant neoplasms
4. Suicide
5. Homicide and legal intervention
6. Chronic liver disease and cirrhosis
7. Pneumonia and influenza
8. Cerebro-vascular diseases
9. Diabetes mellitus
10. Chronic obstructive pulmonary diseases

American Indian or Alaskan Native Female
1. Diseases of heart
2. Malignant neoplasms
3. Unintentional injuries
4. Diabetes mellitus
5. Cerebro-vascular diseases
6. Chronic liver disease and cirrhosis
7. Pneumonia and influenza
8. Chronic obstructive pulmonary diseases
9. Homicide and legal intervention
10. Certain conditions originating in the perinatal period

Asian or Pacific Islander Male
1. Diseases of heart
2. Malignant neoplasms
3. Cerebro-vascular diseases
4. Unintentional injuries
5. Pneumonia and influenza
6. Chronic obstructive pulmonary diseases
7. Homicide and legal intervention
8. Suicide
9. Diabetes mellitus
10. Human immunodeficiency virus infection

Asian or Pacific Islander Female
1. Malignant neoplasms
2. Diseases of heart
3. Cerebro-vascular diseases
4. Unintentional injuries
5. Pneumonia and influenza
6. Diabetes mellitus
7. Chronic obstructive pulmonary diseases
8. Homicide and legal intervention
9. Congenital anomalies
10. Suicide

Source: Centers for Disease Control and Prevention, National Center for Health Statistics: Vital Statistics of the United States, Vol. II, Mortality

in the understanding and experience of ill health. Scholars like Verbrugge (1985) have pointed out that

⮞ women seem to suffer more mild illnesses than men (although men are more likely to contract fatal or serious conditions);

⮞ women are more likely to see themselves as sick than men;

⮞ women tend to take better care of themselves when they are sick; and

⮞ as a whole, women's greater willingness to take preventive and healing actions mean that their health problems tend not to become as severe as men of the same age.

As for the explanations of these differences, Verbrugge (1985) contends that they can be ranked as follows:

1. Differences in lifestyle
2. Psychosocial differences in acknowledgment of the signs and symptoms and associated behaviors
3. Prior medical care
4. Biological differences
5. Willingness to talk about illness
6. Differing responses of doctors to males and females.

As for the explanation of the different health experiences between other kinds of groups organized along racial or class differences, it is difficult to believe that there is something inherently different about these groups that predisposes them to the kinds of health problems described here. In this text, we favor structural explanations that focus on the social relationships and conditions experienced by various social groups in North America. In effect, it is not race, but racism, that matters so much in determining health. It is a fact that many Canadian Native peoples or African-Americans have different life chances. It is related to these groups' different access to adequate nutrition, education, and employment opportunities, which in turn creates less healthy circumstances in which to live (Whiteis, 1997). Consider the plight of Canadian Native children described in Box 4.6.

The data presented in this and the preceding section also provide strong evidence for the argument that good health is dependent on much more than a well-financed and technologically sophisticated health care delivery system. One of the key things the data tell us is that while the health of North Americans has improved as a whole, there are still major differences between various groups in our society. Thus, while there is little doubt that absolute poverty is deleterious to health, it is also likely that relative deprivation (the perception that others are better off than oneself or one's social reference group) is a major correlate of ill health (Marmot, 1994; Wilkinson, 1986). More specifically, when social groups, which can be defined in terms of racial, class, or gender differences, possess "less" than the group above it (think of the example of working-class versus

BOX 4-6

Health Problems Among Canadian First Nations Peoples

[H]ealth problems among First Nations peoples are...a consequence of poverty and socioeconomic conditions. Leading causes of death among Indian infants include respiratory ailments, infectious and parasitic diseases, and accidents, all of which are indicators of inadequate housing, sanitary conditions, and access to medical facilities (Department of Indian Affairs and Northern Development, 1980: 16, Muir, 1991: 16). Poverty contributes to infant mortality and other health problems among mothers and young children. Wilkins, Sherman and Best (1991: 28) conclude from their analysis of health conditions for children in urban Canada that, "infants from poorer neighbourhoods were 30-50 percent more likely to be born too small, too soon, or with growth retardation, they were two-thirds more likely to die before their first birthday, and more than twice as likely to die in the post-neonatal period (28-364 days)." Similarly, Muir (1991, 14) observes that probability of infant mortality and other health risks is associated with poverty through the interaction of poor nutrition, high stress, obstetric complications, smoking, alcohol and drug use by the mother during pregnancy, and other problems in the mother's health status.

_____

Source: Wotherspoon (1994: 250). Reprinted with permission of Fernwood Publishing Co., Ltd.

middle-class people), their levels of health will vary according to the magnitude of the differences (Marmot, Davey-Smith, Stansfeld et al., 1991; Wilkinson, 1986).

Much of the variation in the experience of health in the United States results from another structural issue: lack of access to health insurance. As Table 4.7 shows, since 1987, fewer people have had access to health care insurance in the United States. In addition, access to health insurance depends on race, age, and gender; there are more men than women covered by health insurance, more whites than African-Americans and Hispanics, and more older people than the very young (18 and under to 34 years old).[4]

Summary

We can conclude, then, that not only is there a gap in the health status of various categories of people in North America, but that, at least in the United States, the gap is widening. Another important issue that emerges from the data is that the most disadvantaged groups in society tend to be those who have the least access to medical care. For example, those with lower education are less likely to have coverage, as are African-Americans and Hispanics. As we have seen in other chapters, it is important to understand that the roots of inequality in access to health stem from social factors such as racism, unequal access to higher education, gender bias, and unemployment. Moreover, disadvantaged groups are far more likely to experience high rates of interpersonal violence, poor eating habits, and dangerous environmental conditions, all of which contribute to higher rates of morbidity and mortality.

Table 4.7
Health Insurance Coverage Status by Selected Characteristics, United States, 1987 to 1994, in percent

Characteristics	Private	Medicaid	Not covered by Health Insurance
Year			
1987	75.5	8.4	12.9
1988	74.7	8.5	13.4
1989	74.6	8.6	13.6
1990	73.2	9.7	13.9
1991	72.1	10.7	14.1
1992	70.7	11.5	15.0
1993	70.2	12.2	15.3
1994	70.3	12.1	15.2
Gender			
Male	70.6	10.3	16.6
Female	70	13.7	13.7
Race			
White	74	9.4	14.0
African-American	51.1	26.9	19.7
Hispanic	42.7	22.6	33.7
Age			
Under 18	65.6	22.9	14.2
18 to 24	61.7	12.6	26.7
25 to 34	68.6	9.1	22.0
35 to 44	76.2	6.9	16.0
45 to 54	81	4.9	12.8
55 to 64	75.8	6.2	13.9
65 and older	68	9.2	0.9
Education			
High School			9.0
High School, No College			5.6
College (one or more years)			2.8

Source: U.S. Bureau of the Census, March Supplement to the Current Population Survey, Unpublished data

But to understand the problems of unequal access and treatment with respect to health and health care, we must examine the structure of health care systems in North America. This is the focus of the next section.

How Is Health Care Structured and Delivered in North America?

Particularly in the last few decades, public discussions of the state of health care in North America have been associated with perceptions that both Canada and the United States are facing a "health care crisis." The nature of the crisis varies. It is often argued that there are not enough health care resources to go around, and that people should be more responsible for their own well-being; that too many individuals are in poor health; that the structure of the health care system is increasingly determined by corporate interests, or that demographic changes mean a greater proportion of elderly people in the future, which in turn, means increased costs.

More commonly, especially in the 1990s, government officials in both Canada and the United States maintain that health care costs are "spiraling out of control," and that fiscal restraint is necessary. It is true that health care costs have increased dramatically in both countries. In 1961, the United States spent US$121 billion on health care, but by the year 2000 it is projected to spend $1.3 trillion (Congressional Budget Office, 1995). Canada has not fared much better, seeing an increase in spending from CAN$12.3 billion in 1975 to nearly $67 billion in 1991 (Health Information Division, 1993).[5]

An additional concern revolves around the effectiveness of current health care models, and, related to the cost cutting issue, the drive to make the system more efficient. Finally, particularly in the United States, there has been major concern over improving access to health care, especially in light of the data presented earlier in this chapter. To provide you with a better understanding of these issues, in this section we concentrate on the structure of health insurance in Canada and the United States.

Health Insurance in Canada and the United States
The Canadian Model
There are very important differences between Canada and the United States in the ways in which health care is structured and delivered. The main one is that Canada possesses a "single payer" national health care scheme (often called Medicare) paid for mainly through taxes, while the United States does not. Like many other commentators on Canadian health care, Naylor (1986) argues that the Canadian health care system is one in which a system of "private practice and public payment" prevails. Put differently, Canadians pay for the bulk of health care costs through taxes, but most of the actual care is delivered by physicians who are mostly in private practice. In effect, Canadian doctors are "quasi-employees" of the state. This arrangement, which has been in full effect since the early 1970s,

has unquestionably contributed positively to Canadians' health, because such a system provides greater access for more people. However, Medicare is under increasing pressure from the Canadian federal and provincial governments as well as employers.

To understand why, we must realize that the development of national health insurance in Canada was the result of a long drawn-out process in which the federal and provincial governments often fought bitterly among themselves and with the medical profession over issues such as the costs of delivering such a service, autonomy (physicians did not want to be treated as "government employees"), and administrative responsibilities. By the time it was fully implemented across the country, it was clear that it had been introduced only with the understanding that physicians could keep their fee-for-service payment system as long as care was delivered to all Canadians under the principle of non-profit insurance (Crichton, 1976). The system that resulted is composed of five parts:

1. Public Administration. The public insurance plan must be operated on a non-profit basis, and accountable to the province.
2. Universality. All eligible residents of a province must be entitled to coverage by public health insurance.
3. Accessibility. Insured health services must be reasonably accessible, i.e., have no financial or other impediments.
4. Portability. The public insurance plan must cover eligible residents while they are temporarily absent from the province.
5. Comprehensiveness. Medically necessary health services must be covered by public health insurance.

For nearly three decades, these basic principles of delivering health care to Canadians have worked reasonably well. However, the shifting social and economic context within which health policy is made is placing increased pressure on the system. One of the most important of these pressures comes from the need for employers to remain competitive. While approximately 72 percent of Canada's health care system is publicly funded, the remaining 28 percent of costs are paid privately, either by the individual concerned or by an employer as part of employee benefit plans. Employers contribute significantly to the cost of Canada's health system through payroll and income taxes, and by providing their employees with health benefit plans.

The trouble is that Canadian governments have been concerned with reducing the large debts they have accumulated since World War II. In the context of this fiscal crisis, many employers anticipate that their costs will increase given that the portion which used to be funded by government, may, in the future, increasingly be re-directed to the private sector. If they are forced to cover what provincial plans drop, the costs of benefit plans—a significant competitive edge in seeking skilled labor—would increase. Since employers now have a very large role in paying for health, it is not surprising that they argue that the health care sector—hospitals, physicians' practices, and other health care institutions—should become more efficient and cost effective. Some of the most important ways in which governments have responded to this have been to

> intensify pressure on physicians to become more cost effective and more efficient. This is being attempted through the use of work protocols, monitoring systems, and increased physician accountability;

> close hospitals and other health care institutions;

> limit the number and types of services to which Canadians can have access without paying the health care provider directly. For example, certain services (such as plastic surgery) and some drugs are being "delisted" in Canada;

> centralize the administration of health; and

> educate the public that while the system appears to be "free," in fact it is not, with funding coming from tax dollars that are increasingly scarce. The idea here is to encourage the public to be more responsible in using medical services, particularly since many physicians maintain that about half the cases they see are trivial (Alvi, 1994).

In sum, Canadian governments are attempting to establish the conditions whereby "value for money" will become the overriding principle of a publicly financed system within which most physicians will continue to practice privately. And, as Medicare comes under increasing financial pressure, many are calling for the introduction of private care. Although the privatization of the health care system in Canada appears attractive to some politicians, physicians, and investors, many experts maintain that such a strategy could very well lead to the demise of the five principles of the system and a move to a more "Americanized" approach to health care (Gordon and Berger, 1996). What, then, does the American model look like?

The American Model

As noted above, the United States has a different system of health insurance from Canada. Americans experimented with the idea of national health insurance during the 1930s and 1940s (Starr, 1982). As the economy expanded after World War II, a shortage of skilled labor and the need to attract and retain good employees prompted employers to offer health insurance as part of their benefits packages. At the same time, calls for a system more along the lines of the Canadian approach were lobbied against by groups such as physicians who opposed government control of their work, and insurance companies who felt there was more money to be made via a private system. By 1954, the employer based approach had become entrenched, with nearly two-thirds of Americans having some type of hospital insurance, half having surgical insurance, and a quarter possessing medical insurance (Anderson and Feldman, 1956).

Thus, the most significant aspect of the U.S. model is that health insurance is tied to employment (Jecker, 1994). Most Americans have access to private health insurance paid for by employers as a part of benefits packages. Predictably, U.S. employers are experiencing the same kinds of pressures to sustain profit levels as their Canadian counterparts. Thus, many employers in the United States are shifting increasing health benefit costs to employees by requiring them to pay a greater proportion of their insurance premiums, by making them pay higher deductibles and copayments, and by reducing the pool of money available for wages to pay for health care costs (Cantor, Barrand, Dsonia, Cohen and Merrill, 1991; Uchitelle, 1991) There is, however, another problem with this approach: it does not include many individuals who are unemployed, poor, or old.

To deal with these problems, in 1965, President Johnson passed the Medicare and Medicaid bills providing insurance to those who were unable to access private employer based health insurance. Medicare is primarily designed to address the needs of people over the age of 65. It is divided into two parts, one providing insurance for hospital services, and the other providing coverage for other medical services such as physician services or lab tests.

Medicaid is a public assistance program designed to assist those individuals who do not meet the criteria for Medicare, are poor, are unable to find employment, or for whom Medicare is insufficient to meet their needs.

The main problems associated with these programs are that

➤ many businesses simply cannot afford to provide health insurance for their employees. In addition, those who are self employed may find it difficult to afford insurance;

➤ the very stringent eligibility requirements for Medicare and Medicaid mean that many individuals do not qualify for these programs. Since such individuals are unlikely to be able to afford private insurance, they end up uninsured. Currently, about one in six Americans has no insurance whatsoever;

➤ some physicians refuse to treat Medicaid patients because of the paperwork involved and frequent delays in payment (Terry, 1991); and

➤ for many people, Medicare is not free. Many who use it (those above a certain income level) must pay a deductible before they can utilize medical services, and payment for a portion of the services delivered is required (the principle of coinsurance).

One important conclusion we can draw from these points is that access to adequate health care is both a political and economic issue in the United States. As already mentioned, health insurance is tied to employment. Thus, many of the unemployed and those whose employers do not provide health insurance as a benefit are forced to pay from their own pockets or hope that they do not become ill. Even those who qualify may find that assistance in the form of Medicaid or Medicare is often inadequate for their needs, and that physicians, hospitals, and other providers are reluctant to accept public assistance patients because doing so is not profitable (Freund and McGuire, 1995; Albrecht, 1992). In addition, programs such as Medicaid are very expensive, and access to health care via such programs varies by state definitions of poverty or need (Weiss and Lonnquist, 1997).

At the same time, political controversy over whether these groups should get more adequate health insurance is based primarily on the interests of some physicians, insurance companies, and various others who believe that like any other business, health should be distributed according to market forces.

Ironically, in some ways, the U. S. and Canadian health care insurance systems seem to be converging. Canadians are debating the merits of moving to a privatized system driven by better efficiency, while Americans continue to struggle with the problem of partial coverage and glaring inequality. Many observers contend that U.S. policy makers are seriously considering adopting aspects of the Canadian system to increase accessibility and possibly reduce costs (Thorpe, 1994). On the other hand, as Canadian employers are being asked to pay for a larger portion of the health care bill, pressure is mounting to curb what is perceived to be "excessive" spending and to increase efficiency. Many assume that the private sector has the most experience in cutting costs and improving efficiency. Given this, and in light of increasing commitments to the ideology of the free market, it is possible that Canada may increasingly adopt an approach resembling aspects of the U.S. model. In both countries, the impact of these changes on the population's health remains to be seen.

The Social Determinants of Ill Health

We have already seen in this chapter that using a broad definition of health (such as the one advocated by the World Health Organization) means that we have to take into account the impact of social factors in creating health and ill health. Many of these factors have already been discussed. However, in this section we want to emphasize the fact that improving the health of North Americans depends greatly on our willingness and ability to deal appropriately with the social determinants of health.

By now you will have realized that there are important links between established indicators of health such as morbidity, mortality, and life expectancy, and factors such as race, class, gender, poverty, and unemployment. In the remainder of this section, we want to emphasize the importance of two other social determinants: changes in the experience and nature of work, and the relationship between health, changing demographics, and the family.

Work

There is powerful evidence that the social, cultural, and economic environments in which people live are powerful determinants of their health, yet neither Canadian nor American health care systems have attempted to deal meaningfully with these larger social issues. For instance, recent literature in both the human resources and health promotion fields has noted the growing awareness among organizations that social, economic, and work environments are the prime determinants of health (see Chapter 3).

Most of the interest in work as a social determinant is reinforced by findings from studies in Sweden and elsewhere, showing that people who work in demanding jobs and who have little control over their work are more prone to coronary heart disease than people in demanding jobs with high levels of control (Karasek and Theorell, 1990; Marmot and Theorell, 1988). Yet few employers have examined the impact of their work policies on health, or re-evaluated the goals of their corporate health programs (Marshall, Brandenburg, and Lippmann,

1994). In one conference attended by one of the authors of this text, a well-known expert in the field stated that "the link between social support and health is stronger than evidence for linkages between smoking and lung cancer." Social support refers to relationships with others that make up the "many different resources that aid persons in times of crisis and help them cope with life (Freund and McGuire, 1995: 114). Despite evidence that social support buffers work-related stress (Hibbard and Pope, 1993), few employers have taken a proactive, preventative stance to workplace stress and fewer still have recognized the important stress-preventing role of social support in the workplace.

While many health care providers have become convinced of the important linkages between health and the environment, and despite the overwhelming evidence that comprehensive and proactive approaches to workplace health are effective, corporations themselves have, by and large, not been so easy to convince. Very few businesses in Canada or the United States have taken proactive steps to develop workplace policies that address employee health because they are not aware of the short- and long-term benefits of such an approach, and because they fear that proactive strategies entail high costs which will eat into profit margins. Moreover, developing proactive workplace health programs integrated with corporate strategy may well entail changing management style, the organization of work, and corporate culture. In light of the major organizational and management challenges associated with these factors, corporations have been slow or unwilling to change. Thus, while prevention-oriented workplace health programs hold much promise in curbing stress and enhancing health, the harmonization of these policies with corporate strategy—i.e., the attempt to create a "wellness culture" within the organization—is a relatively new phenomenon.

Indeed, it would seem that many employers would rather pay lip service to the notion that "healthy employees mean healthy companies." Recently, one of the authors of this book met with a colleague who had given a talk to corporate executives about the negative consequences of stress in the workplace. The talk had emphasized that there are optimal levels of stress, during which workers are performing at their peak levels (just think of exam time!). However, she also pointed out that after a certain point, stress becomes counterproductive, and has a strong negative impact on the health of the worker. What is striking about this example was the response given by the executives—they wanted to know how much stress they could get away with imposing on their employees before those individuals would collapse or degenerate into an unproductive state. Apparently, for these executives, the bottom line is more important than the health of their workers.

More broadly, a long period of "downsizing" and "corporate re-engineering" in North America has created not only unemployment, but also a worker population who, because they did not lose their jobs, are often referred to as "survivors." Many of these workers face difficulties dealing with the increased volume of work for which they are now responsible, and operate with the uneasy feeling that perhaps "they will be next" to lose their jobs. Moreover, such workers are also much more reluctant to report difficulties with their mental and physical health given a prevailing culture that says, "you must suffer in silence" for fear of repercussions.

Fiscal and revenue crises have also underpinned shifts in corporate direction and values which, in many public and private sector organizations, means taking a closer look at the prerequisites and conditions necessary for competitiveness. Usually, a heightened focus on competitiveness means heightened expectations of employees. For the most part, employees are willing to respond to such expectations. But their capacity to respond will be conditioned by their level of mental and physical well-being. Thus, if the employer can provide employees with a work environment that promotes and fosters health then employees are more likely to be able to meet the employment challenges necessary in the new context. Since there has been a shift in the employment contract from the notion of a "fair day's pay for a fair day's work" to the concept of "mutually beneficial partnerships," part of the employer's responsibility will be to provide the healthiest environment possible.

In summary, workplaces that do not provide employees with a range of possibilities for managing and controlling the pace and nature of work and little social support tend to have employees with reduced well-being and increased health risk (Gaillard and Wientjes, 1994). At the very least, the physical and mental stresses emerging from lack of control and diminished social support translate into higher health benefits costs for employers.

The experience of work in industrialized societies has always been conditioned by the nature of the economic environment in which work takes place. Computers, faxes, and other communication technologies have dramatically altered the ways in which people work by isolating them from fellow workers and by increasing the pace of work. Today's fast-paced global economy has also fostered a dramatic increase in the pace of work, in part because of the need to produce goods and services "just in time" with fewer human resources. Indeed, it is becoming commonplace to hear that employees are being asked to "do more with less." The nature of work has also changed from the production of goods and raw materials to a concentration on services and, in particular, to a focus on harnessing research and development to the needs of industry. In this new context, meeting the objectives of wealth generation and excellence requires a committed, energized, and productive workforce. However, at the precise moment that such employees are required, the pressures and stresses on employees have never been higher. As employees of the "new age" organization struggle to stay healthy, they are looking for a commitment on the part of their employers to create healthy working environments. The question is, will they get one?

Demography, Health, and Families

Changing demographics is also an important social determinant of health. One of the most important of these changes to occur in the last 50 years in North America has been the influx of women into the workforce. One of the key sources of stress for many working women comes from their participation in the "double day." Despite the fact that men are taking more time to spend on family and non-work obligations such as housework, in most cases the bulk of such caregiving and domestic labor duties still falls to women (de Koninck, 1984) Accordingly, these women rank among the most stressed of all workers. Based on data from a host of studies, they will also tend to exhibit greater chances of becoming ill.

Another important set of mental and physical stressors is related to the demography of aging. In Canada, the proportion of the population over the age of 65 will have increased from just 6 percent in 1931 to 19 percent by 2021. Currently, about 40 percent of Canadians over the age of 65 have a permanent disability, and, in 1989, about 41 percent of women over the age of 65 lived in poverty (deWolff, 1994). According to Riley (1994), the trends in the United States are similar. If these trends continue, many of these individuals will require significant levels of economic support as well as help with day-to-day activities (Kornblum and Julian, 1995).

Improvements in public health and medical technology have also contributed to North America's aging patterns by decreasing mortality rates. For instance, in Canada, since 1970, fertility rates have dropped to below the replacement level (the level required to maintain the current size of the population without immigration), and this trend is likely to continue (Canadian Social Trends, 1994).

Taken together, these tendencies mean that although we are living longer, there are increasingly fewer of us to provide support and care for the elderly. By extension, these facts strongly suggest that the families (most often the working daughters) of these individuals will face significant financial and logistical problems if they do not already do so.

The shape of families has also changed dramatically in the past 50 years. Dual income families are now the norm in Canada and the United States In earlier family structures, care for dependent individuals was performed almost exclusively by women who provided such care in conjunction with other household labor as part of the function of maintaining families, and family responsibilities were carried out primarily by women separated from the workplace both in time and in place.

For workers with family obligations, these changes mean that work tasks and family-related activities are no longer sequential but have become increasingly interwoven—a phenomenon that can lead to lowered mental and physical health, higher employer health costs, and greater long- and short-term disability claims for employers (Alvi, 1994).

Put simply, today's work and non-work obligations place high levels of stress on workers, their families, and their employers. Indeed, there is plenty of recent research pointing to strong clear relationships between family stress and ill health (Duxbury, Higgins and Lee, 1992; Paris, 1989). Not surprisingly, these studies have also pointed out that flexibility in work arrangements, supportive supervisors, and responsive family leave policies would dramatically reduce stress and improve health for the bulk of employees.

As you will see in Chapter 6, the overall social, emotional, and psychological health of the family has profound effects on individual well-being. According to McDaniel, (1997), the ways in which families and health are linked can be described as follows:

➤ Families have various health-related functions, including the provision of health, health promotion, and health education. When they cannot success-fully carry out these functions, families can obstruct good health.

➤ Family health is affected by the interaction of health policies, social policies, and economic policies.

➤ Family status and family relations are perhaps the key determinants of the health and well-being of families.

Furthermore, the distribution of resources such as access to adequate jobs, child care, and even time can have a crucial impact on individual health. For example, think of the health problems associated with poor quality child care. What kinds of health problems do you think a child might develop as a result of inadequate attention or supervision? How about insufficient nutritious food? And what happens when families cannot get access to adequate advice and treatment before, during, and after pregnancy? How do we go about dealing with sexual and other forms of abuse within families? What will we do when our aging parents (who are living longer than ever before) require care that we cannot afford?

These are some of the many questions that need to be answered if we are to provide a more healthful society for families. But before we can do so, we need to recognize and take seriously the fact that the family dynamics are a major determinant of health. At the very least, such questions should remind us to address the complex and controversial issues that link ill health as a private experience with its "public" qualities.

In summary, employers, policy makers, and researchers need to recognize not only that people, over the course of their lives, will face new challenges to sustaining or improving their physical and mental well-being, but also that the demographic factors that seem to be driving increased stress and associated health problems are largely irreversible.

Get Well Soon! What Is to Be Done About the Sick?

In our classrooms, students often tell us that sociology seems to be very good at exposing truths, criticizing what exists, or at least providing another way of looking at social reality. But they also point out that sociology seldom offers good solutions to the problems it uncovers. In part, they are right. It is difficult to provide solutions when the sociological analysis and evidence seem to indicate that the problem in question requires changes rooted in the very foundations of society. For instance, in this chapter, we have shown that sociological evidence on what determines health points to the role of medicine itself in creating health or illness. But it has also shown that health is dependent on factors like quality and nature of employment, demography, the politics of health insurance, social support, education, and the environment (Pappas, Queen, Hadden and Fisher, 1993). It follows, then, that answers to the question "What is to be done about the sick?" generally fall into two categories:

1. Short-term solutions that tend to be dependent on the politics that prevail in society at any given time.

2. Long-term solutions that focus on fundamentally altering the structure of society.

Both approaches can improve our health, but it is important to recognize that short- and long-term strategies ought to be linked to one another. It is possible, for instance, to attempt to change population health through incremental, or gradual, approaches. Such a strategy requires making connections between a long-term strategy (let's say providing safe meaningful employment for all) and short-term tactics (such as providing support to reduce the stresses of unemployment).

We discuss many of these long-term goals (such as increasing employment, eliminating poverty, or improving race relations) in other chapters. Here, we will concentrate on a few incremental policies that emerge from recognizing that health is socially, not individually determined (Evans, Barer and Marmor, 1994).

First, there is very little public awareness of the link between health and the social context despite the overwhelming evidence that such relationships exist. Thus, one important and very low-cost strategy is to increase public awareness through public relations campaigns, neighborhood information sessions or classroom education. The goal here is to help people redefine health to include socio-economic factors. In Canada at least, the federal government has begun to embrace a broader vision of illness causation and treatment and is starting to recognize the importance of health education and promotion, and community development (Clarke, 1990).

A second policy implication is related to the recognition that particular segments of the population are more unhealthy than others. This implies a strategy of income redistribution so that these individuals and families can have adequate financial resources to meet their daily needs. Perhaps this can be accomplished through more equitable taxation policies in both Canada and the United States. In the United States, unequal access to health care would also suggest implementing a national health program that would provide care for the nearly 35 million Americans who are uninsured (U.S. Bureau of the Census, 1990). As William Glaser (1994) points out, America created a successful social security system by learning from other countries, and health insurance, financed by payroll taxes and supplemented by government subsidies, should be added now. Americans are seriously looking at other nations' experiences in this regard, but within Canada, the policy issues seem to be revolving around privatization of the system. Thus, Canadians will need to focus on ensuring that the basic principles of their health care system (regarded by many as one of the best in the world) remain intact.

A third tactic that would have many positive implications for North Americans' health would rest on reallocating resources away from the medical profession, towards making changes in the physical and social environment.(Corin, 1994). More generally, this would include more research on the limitations of the medical model of illness and health, and identification of the barriers to health policy change.

Finally, North Americans must resolve whether they can afford to allow health care to be dominated by corporate interests. In 1993, the Clinton administration attempted to implement reforms to the health care system through a proposal called "managed competition." This scheme was notable for its attempt to provide universal health care to all Americans, while addressing the concerns of other powerful stakeholders in the health arena. However, because taxes would have to increase to finance the program, small businesses, as well as liquor, beer, and cigarette manufacturers opposed managed care. As well, middle class voters were concerned about the possibility of increased taxes. In addition, the American Medical Association, the American Hospital Association, and various pharmaceutical companies opposed limits being placed on their fees and prices. Not surprisingly, the bill was defeated in 1994 (Weiss and Lonnquist, 1997).

As we have seen in this chapter, corporations can either directly or indirectly create healthy or unhealthy populations. As Whiteis (1997) reminds us, corporate control of the economy has been a major factor in maintaining the inequitable distribution of health resources, in contributing to declining public health conditions, and in creating poor, disenfranchised communities. While we are certainly not going to get rid of corporations, there is much potential in encouraging employers to become more involved in improving the health of their workers (by improving working conditions for instance) and the communities in which they live (for example, by creating secure jobs or contributing financially to community development). And employers should be made aware that such programs could, after all, contribute to their own financial health.

Ultimately, given the relationship between economic growth, prosperity, health, and well-being, perhaps North America should focus its political and economic resources on the health of its people, and not just the bottom line.

Summary

A central objective of this chapter is to illustrate the difficulties associated with defining health in terms of the traditional medical model. Though this model should not be rejected, we point out that it has limitations, and that a more holistic or broader approach to defining health is needed if we are to truly improve the health of North Americans.

The chapter also provides an overview of levels of health, and a snapshot of who is healthy and who is not. The two key issues emerging from this discussion are the poor health performance of North America relative to other countries which spend less on health care, and the continued differences in levels of health or access to health care experienced by certain segments of the North American population.

We also review theories of health, pointing to the differences between technological-functionalist approaches and more critical theories. The central idea here is that while modern medical technology has made important contributions to health, it is by no means the only, nor even the most important, determinant of health. In addition, women's health concerns are shown to be dominated by a mostly male-oriented medical profession which has "medicalized" women's health. The chapter also provides some discussion of how physicians became the dominant players in the health care arena.

Finally, we review some policy directions based on the view that it is really important to "shake the foundation" of underlying belief systems about health, and question (and hopefully change) the interests of corporations and institutionalized medicine.

KEY TERMS

Allopathic model
Holistic definition of health
Iatrogenesis
Infant mortality rates
Life expectancy
Medicalization
Morbidity
Mortality rates
Social support

DISCUSSION QUESTIONS

1. What kinds of problems do you see arising from using definitions of health based on the medical model? What are the strengths and limitations of employing a broader definition?
2. What are the major differences between conflict and functionalist theories of health and illness?
3. What are some examples of the "medicalization" of women's lives?
4. What are some of the most important reasons for differences in the health levels of African-Americans and whites?
5. What are some of the most important social determinants of health, and how do they make an impact on health?

PROBLEM SOLVING SCENARIOS

1. Set up a debate among your classmates on the question: "Should the United States move to create a health care system based on the Canadian model?"
2. How would you go about determining the health of students at your school? What methods would you use? What kinds of questions would you ask?
3. Assume you and your classmates are in control of some of the nation's wealthiest corporations. What kinds of policies would you implement to create better health in the workplace and in the community? What challenges would you face in doing so?
4. Design a public education campaign to promote the idea that health is more than a personal responsibility.
5. Looking at your own family and friends, identify several everyday actions or beliefs that might contribute either to good or to poor health.

WEB EXERCISES

1. Start by pointing your browser at the following website, and compare different articles on one particular health problem (such as breast cancer) that are good examples of the medical model of health and disease and the social determinants of health model.

    http://www.medscape.com/

2. There is some controversy over the view that AIDS, Ebola, and other diseases were actually created by humans. Look at this website and provide an assessment of this viewpoint.

    ftp://ftp.tetrahedron.org/pub

SUGGESTED READINGS

Bolaria, B. S. & Dickinson (eds.), *Health, Illness and Health Care in Canada*, (2nd edition), Toronto: Harcourt Brace, 1994.
This is a good collection of readings on the major theoretical approaches in medical sociology, Canadian health care, various substantive issues in the field of medical sociology, and the politics and economics of health care in Canada.

Freund, Peter E.S. and McGuire, M.B., *Health, Illness, and the Social Body; A Critical Sociology*. 2nd ed. Englewood Cliffs, N.J.: Prentice Hall, 1995.
A very good review of the critical approach to health and illness.

Morone, J. A. and Belkin, G. S. (eds.), *The Politics of Health Care Reform: Lessons from the Past, Prospects for the Future*, Duke University Press, 1994.
This book helps to place current debates about health care in the United States in context while shedding light on possible scenarios for the future. It also provides comparisons with other nations' experiences.

Naylor, C. D., *Private Practice, Public Payment*, Kingston: McGill-Queens University Press, 1986.
A book similar to Starr's, but for those interested in how Canadian doctors rose to power and how the Canadian health insurance scheme (Medicare) developed.

Starr, Paul, *The Social Transformation of American Medicine*, New York: Basic Books, 1982.
Although this is an older book, there is still no better analysis of the development and rise to power of the medical profession in the United States. It won the 1984 Pulitzer prize for general non-fiction.

ENDNOTES

1   For a superb analysis of similar historical developments in the United States, see Paul Starr, *The Social Transformation of American Medicine*, 1982.

2   We have chosen to focus on countries in the Organization for Economic Cooperation and Development (OECD). The countries we have highlighted are widely agreed to be North America's main economic competitors, and therefore serve as a useful gauge for comparative purposes.

3   The most critical determinant of infant death is low birthweight (NCHS, 1995).

4   In Canada, where health insurance is universal, the problem of access does not present itself as starkly as it does in the United States.

5   However, the rate of increase in Canada has been much slower than in the United States (Evans, Barer and Hertzman, 1991).

Chapter (5)

It's a Jungle Out There: Violent Crime

No one living in a major American city needs convincing that despite more than a decade of ever-"tougher" policies against crime, the United States remains wracked by violence and fear. Criminal violence is woven deeply into our social fabric—a brutal and appalling affront to any reasonable conception of civilized life. (Currie, 1985: 4)

OBJECTIVES

In this chapter we focus on the topics

1. What is violent crime?
2. The extent and patterns of violent crime in North America
3. Why are people violent?
4. What is to be done about violent crime in North America?

Introduction

North Americans who watch television, read newspapers, or watch Hollywood movies are bombarded with numerous fictional and nonfictional images and stories of violent street crimes such as muggings, bank robberies, homicides, etc. (Marsh, 1991; Surette, 1998). What the media show or report, however, typically does not reflect the reality of violent crime. For example, the media devote a substantial amount of attention to murders involving adolescents and young adults; however, less than one-fourth of an American citizen's lifetime homicide risk is experienced before the age of 25 (Reiss and Roth, 1993: 62). Moreover, the media "exaggerates the most terrifying crimes and misleads people into thinking of the predatory stranger as the typical criminal" (Scheingold, 1984: 55). In sum, for these and other reasons too numerous to describe here, the mass media clearly paint a distorted picture of violent crime in both Canada and the United States.[1]

This is not to say that violent crime is not a major problem for many people, especially those who are socially, politically, and economically disenfranchised—the unemployed, for example. For them, and others at the bottom of North America's socioeconomic ladder, violent crime is not primarily a product of moral panics or societal reaction. Rather, they view homicide, armed robbery, mugging, domestic violence, and so on as some of society's "greatest of evils" (Devine and Wright, 1993). In fact, many disenfranchised North Americans are currently experiencing what Currie (1993) refers to as "the American Nightmare." In his path-breaking analysis of inner-city drug use and violent crime, Currie correctly points out that

"Americans living in the worst-hit neighborhoods still face the reality of drug dealers on their doorsteps and shots in the night; many fear for their lives, or their children's lives, and sense that their communities had slid downward into a permanent state of terror and disintegration. Even those fortunate to live in better neighborhoods cannot pick up a newspaper or watch the news without confronting story after story about the toll of drugs and drug-related violence on communities and families" (1993: 9).

Canadians who read the above observation are probably saying to themselves, "I can't relate to Currie's statement. I live in Canada and we are much safer here." This point is well-taken and has empirical support. Even so, like their disenfranchised U.S. counterparts, many poor, female, and Aboriginal Canadians (e.g., Cree, Huron, Mohawk) do not regard their country as a "haven in a heartless world" (Lasch, 1977). For example, an alarming number of Canadian women are physically and sexually assaulted by their intimate male partners. In fact, some Canadian surveys (Brinkerhoff and Lupri, 1988) suggest that Canadian women are at greater risk of experiencing spousal violence than those in U.S. marital/cohabiting relationships. Thus, it is not surprising that a large number of Canadian women have a "well-founded fear" of crime, and are deeply concerned about their personal safety (Hanmer and Saunders, 1984; Kelly and DeKeseredy, 1994).

The shocking number of injurious male-to-female violent acts described in this chapter fosters an atmosphere of fear and insecurity, and serves as a powerful means of social control (DeKeseredy and Schwartz, 1998a; Hornosty, 1996). Thus, for many people, such as the women who participated in two large-scale, representative sample surveys (DeKeseredy and Kelly, 1993a; Statistics Canada, 1993a), Canada is hardly a "peaceable kingdom."

What Is Violent Crime?

Defining violent crime is the subject of much debate and discussion. In fact, a review of the existing social scientific literature on violence reveals a myriad of definitions. For the purpose of this chapter, however, following Reiss and Roth (1993: 35), we limit our focus to acts of **interpersonal violence**. This is referred to here as "behavior by persons against other persons, that intentionally threatens, attempts, or actually inflicts physical harm." More specifically, the behaviors discussed here are: homicide, assault, sexual assault, and robbery. This is not to say that we do not view other highly injurious behaviors or incidents as violent.

Consider acts of **corporate violence**. Although these major threats to our well-being are not dealt with by criminal law, and are for the most part trivialized by the media, policy makers, and many members of the general population, they are significantly more economically, socially, physically, and environmentally harmful than street crimes (Reiman, 1998). What is corporate violence? According to DeKeseredy and Hinch, this variant of "suite crime" is

"... any behavior undertaken in the name of the corporation by decision makers, or other persons in authority within the corporation, that endangers the health and safety of employees or other persons who are affected by that behavior. Even acts of omission, in which decision makers, etc., refuse to take action to reduce or eliminate known health and safety risks, must be considered corporate violence. It is the impact the action has on the victim, not the intent of the act, which determines whether or not it is violence" (1991: 100).

The following are examples of corporate violence:

> In 1985, Stefan Golab died after exposure to a cyanide solution used in the Illinois Film Recovery Systems factory. He and his co-workers were not given the proper equipment to protect themselves, and were required to work in plant air that was filled with a "yellowish haze" of cyanide fumes (Frank and Lynch, 1992).

> In early 1989, Denis died of lung cancer (mesothelioma) at the age of 55. For many years, working as a plumber, he had had repeated exposure to asbestos.

> Anne was only 27 when she died in mid-1990. While employed as a store clerk, she had opened a mislabeled carton of hazardous material and accidentally inhaled the fumes. She died one month later.

> Mike was cleaning a fiberglass tank with acetone when a fire broke out. He died as a result of severe burns to 68 percent of his body (Canadian Labour Congress, 1993a: 6).

These "atrocity tales" are not rare (Goffman, 1961). For example, according to the American Federation of Labor and Congress of Industrial Organizations (AFL-CIO), in the United States, close to 10,000 people die in the workplace each year because of traumatic injuries, and about 100,000 workers die each year from the long-term effects of occupational diseases (1993: 1). Further, approximately 16,000 workplace injuries occur each day in the United States, and around 60,000 workers are permanently disabled each year.[2]

In Canada, according to the Canadian Labour Congress: (1) annual deaths from workplace injuries average approximately 1,000; (2) there are close to 1,000,000 Canadian workplace injuries every year; and (3) one Canadian worker is killed every two hours of each working day (1993b: 2). These data constitute only the tip of the corporate violence iceberg because it is very difficult to generate accurate incidence and prevalence data. For example, acts of corporate violence are rarely committed in public. In fact, they tend to be intricate, complex, and highly sophisticated law violations (Clinard and Yeager, 1980). Further, only after a great deal of accumulated damage is done do people realize that they were victimized by their employers, who purposely created dangerous working conditions to lower production costs and increase profits (DeKeseredy and Goff, 1992; Katz, 1978). It should also be noted that some workers do not report occupational injuries because their employers bribe them to "keep quiet" (Galloway, 1996).

Despite the methodological problems associated with counting corporate violence, if you compare the data given here and other corporate violence statistics[3] with the interpersonal violence data presented later in this chapter, you will discover that: (1) the corporate death rate is more than six times greater than the street death rate (Ellis and DeKeseredy, 1996; Frank and Lynch, 1992), and (2) the rate of nonfatal assault in the workplace is more than 30 times the street assault rate.

Unfortunately, corporate violence and other types of corporate crime are dealt with by civil or administrative law, with penalties such as fines but not prison. Interestingly, persons who accidentally kill while committing a street crime are typically found guilty of murder. A quick check of your local prison will reveal a number of people incarcerated for long terms for exactly this crime. Yet, death in the workplace caused by criminal negligence has not strained the prison budget of any North American jurisdiction (DeKeseredy and Schwartz, 1996).

Consider a statement made by *Rolling Stone* journalist William Greider at the time of the 1996 World Series: "For street criminals, three strikes and they're out. For corporations, it's a whole different ballgame" (1994: 36). If corporate executives who make decisions that threaten workers' physical safety are exempt from the purview of the law, the same can be said about another group of violent people—hockey players who fight on the ice.

Think about the following examples of professional hockey violence. Should those who engaged in these acts be labeled violent criminals? Or, are their highly injurious and potentially lethal behaviors "just part of the game"? Are you one of the many North Americans who "like to see fighting at a hockey game" and who do not believe that such behavior is either criminal or deviant? (Grescoe, 1972; Hallowell and Meshbesher, 1977; Smith, 1983).

➤ In 1969, Boston Bruins' "Terrible" Ted Green and Wayne Maki of St. Louis engage in a stick duel during an exhibition game in Ottawa. Green is struck on the head by a full-swinging blow. His skull fractured, he almost dies.

➤ Boston's Dave Forbes and Minnesota North Stars' Henry Boucha engage in a minor altercation for which both are penalized. Forbes threatens Boucha from the penalty box; then, leaving the box at the expiration of the penalties, he lunges at Boucha from behind, striking him near the right eye with the butt end of his stick. Boucha falls to his knees, hands over face; Forbes jumps on his back, punching until pulled off by another player. Boucha is taken to hospital, where he receives 25 stitches and the first of several eye operations (Smith, 1983: 15–16).

Only a small number of cases such as these have resulted in litigation. Thus, it is fair to conclude that despite the life-threatening nature of some "punch-ups," many North Americans see nothing wrong with "hockey fisticuffs" (Smith, 1983). Similarly, many people, including some who belong to the "power elite" (Mills, 1956), see nothing wrong with slapping or spanking a child (Straus, 1991). In fact, a substantial number of North Americans regard these behaviors "as necessary, normal, and good" (Straus et al., 1981) even though many physicians, community-based activists, front-line workers, academics, etc. define these behaviors as abusive or violent. See Box 5.1 for differing views on spanking children.

We could provide a much longer list of injurious behaviors that many people do not regard as violent. However, the most important point to consider here is that, like other social problems examined in this text, violence is often "not a quality of the act the person commits, but rather a consequence of the application by others of rules and sanctions to an offender" (Becker, 1973: 9). Nevertheless, there is considerable agreement among North Americans about the seriousness of the violent behaviors discussed in this chapter.[4] In other words, the violent activities examined here are "consensus crimes." This means that members of all or most North American social groups share norms and values that legally prohibit these forms of conduct, and impose the most severe penalties on those who violate laws relating to them (Ellis and DeKeseredy, 1996; Hagan, 1994).

BOX 5-1

Don't Spank Your Children, Pediatric Society Tells Parents

Adults Should Use Other Forms of Discipline, Doctor Tells Parents

Skip the rod and spare the child, the Canadian Pediatric Society says.

Spanking should be used only in rare cases where a child has placed himself or herself in danger, the society suggests in a position paper released Monday.

Most spanking is abuse even is there is no injury, spokesman Emmett Francoeur said at a news conference.

"Spanking doesn't work," said Francoeur, a pediatrician and director of the society's psychosocial pediatrics committee.

He said there are much better means of discipline, such as placing a child alone for a few minutes.

Francoeur said many adults suffer low self-esteem because they were spanked as children, and he does not believe a child should even be tapped with an open hand.

But the association does not call outright for a ban on spanking.

Nor does it advocate repealing a section of the Criminal Code that says parents and guardians of children may use reasonable force in performing their duties.

If that section were repealed, parents who spanked their children could be open to criminal charges.

Francoeur said the society will approach the Justice Department to discuss rewriting the controversial section.

Leon Benoit, a spokesman for the Reform Party, does not think governments should try to stop spanking.

"It's up to parents to decide how they're going to raise their kids," Benoit said outside the Commons.

"I certainly spanked my children on rare occasion(s)."

Jim Sclater of Vancouver-based Focus on the Family said spanking is the most effective means to deal with a defiant child.

"We recommend it. If parents don't realize that a defiant child will soon be running the household and soon become a problem to teachers and even police and others, then we're missing something important here." Several studies have found that adults who were subjected to corporal punishment as children are more likely to engage in violence and abuse.

But most of the anti-spanking literature does not distinguish between spanking and abusive acts like kicking, punching and hitting, says Den Trumbull of the American Academy of Pediatrics.

Writing in the U.S. academy's journal, Trumbull says so-called disciplinary spanking, which does not cause physical injury, can be an effective disciplinary method.

"Studies have found disciplinary spanking to be a component of parenting styles with excellent outcomes."

BOX 5-1

Source: Reprinted in *The Ottawa Citizen*, October 8, 1996. Reprinted with permission of The Canadian Press.

The Extent and Patterns of Violent Crime in North America

Contrary to popular belief, violent crime is not an insurmountable problem. In fact, at the time of writing this chapter, in both Canada and the United States, the probability of becoming a victim of violent crime is declining (Canadian Centre for Justice Statistics, 1996; Curran and Renzetti, 1996; Silverman and Kennedy, 1993). Consider homicide. The data presented next show that the rate of this type of victimization has dropped over the last few years. Homicide is defined here as lethal interpersonal violent acts by persons with no legal mandate to use violence, and these behaviors are legally designated as criminal homicides (Gartner, 1995). It is to "deadly deeds" committed in the United States that we now turn.

Homicide in the United States

Obviously, victimization surveys tell us nothing about the extent, distribution, and sources of homicide. Therefore, in this section, we must rely on official statistics generated by the Federal Bureau of Investigation (FBI) Uniform Crime Reports (UCR). Over 16,000 law enforcement agencies participate in this program, and they voluntarily supply their crime statistics to FBI officials who compile and publish the UCR. At the time of writing this chapter, the FBI released their 1994 homicide data and these statistics are described next (FBI, 1995, 1996: 4):

➤ In 1994, 23,305 people were murdered. The rate was 9 per 100,000 U.S. citizens; this is the lowest count since 1989.

➤ Supplemental data received by the FBI showed that 79 percent of the victims were male; 88 percent were 18 years of age or older; 51 percent were African-American; and 47 percent were white.

➤ Data based on a total of 25,052 offenders show that 91 percent were males; 84 percent were 18 years of age or older; 56 percent were African-American; and 42 percent were white.

➤ 47 percent of the murder victims were related to (12 percent) or acquainted with (35 percent) their assailants, and among all female homicide victims in 1994, 28 percent were killed by their husbands or boyfriends.

➤ Only 3 percent of all male victims were killed by female intimates.

➤ 28 percent of the murders resulted from arguments and 18 percent from felonious activities such as robbery, arson, etc.

➤ 7 out of every 10 murders reported in 1994 were committed with firearms.

What can we conclude from these statistics? Perhaps Gartner (1995: 199-200) provides us with the best answer to this question:

"[T]he highest rates of victimization and offending occur among persons who are disadvantaged in status, power, and economic resources... Often these disadvantages are associated with ascribed characteristics, such as age, race/ethnicity, and gender."

Where do most of the homicides occur? FBI (1995) data show that some places are more or less "safer" than others. As you might guess, large metropolitan areas are more dangerous than small cities and rural areas. For example, in 1994, there were 11 homicide victims per 100,000 in some of the largest U.S. cities, while in small cities and rural counties, there were only five victims per 100,000, and less than two per 100,000 in the most rural states (Barkan, 1997; FBI, 1995).

There are also key variations in homicide rates within cities. Urban areas characterized by high levels of poverty and racial inequality report higher levels of homicide than do more affluent communities (Crutchfield, 1989). In fact, African-American homicide rates are consistently higher in urban areas marked by strong racial segregation (Peterson and Krivo, 1993). Why are those whom William Julius Wilson (1987) refers to as the "truly disadvantaged" at greater risk of killing or being killed? Research shows that they more likely to be involved in murder because they experience some or all of a wide variety of problems strongly associated with all kinds of predatory street crime. These are: high rates of family disruption; inadequate access to prenatal counseling and child care; low infant birth weight; breakdown of community-based networks of informal social control; unemployment and underemployment; lack of employment prospects; extreme poverty; and other major devastating economic changes.[5]

The deep south of the United States has higher levels of inequality (Blau and Blau, 1982; Loftin and Hill, 1974; Parker, 1989) and thus it is not surprising that this region has the highest rate of homicide. For example, research consistently shows that the southern United States has about 40 percent of the nation's murders (Holmes and Holmes, 1994).

If homicide is patterned geographically within the United States, the same can be said across nations. In fact, in the last two decades, U.S. homicide rates have remained considerably higher than those of any other industrialized nation. For example, several studies show that during this time period, the U.S. homicide rate has averaged between eight and 10 per 100,000, while the average rate for other industrial nations has been between one and three per 100,000 (Archer and Gartner, 1984; Barkan, 1997; Bennett and Lynch, 1990; Kalish, 1988).

Why is the United States the homicide center of the world? Are Americans genetically predisposed to killing people? Well, so far no one has been able to find a specific gene responsible for conformity or criminal conduct. In fact, that is not how genes work (Currie, 1985). Rather, the United States is more violent than other nations because it is a country characterized by very high levels of poverty, unemployment, and racial and gender inequality. Also, compared to other industrialized nations such as Canada, the United States provides its citizens with extremely inadequate health care, income support, and social services (Currie, 1993).

There is no reason to believe that things are going to get better in the immediate future. Approximately 10 years ago, Elliott Currie made a powerful statement about violence in U.S. inner-cities and, unfortunately, nothing has changed. According to Currie,

"To live in the urban United States in the 1980s is to feel that the elementary bonds of society are badly frayed. The sense of social disintegration is so pervasive that it is easy

to forget that things are not the same elsewhere. Violence on the American level comes to seem like a fact of life, an inevitable feature of modern society. It is not. Most of us are aware that we are worse off, in this respect, than other advanced industrial countries. How much worse, however, is truly startling" (1985: 5).

Despite the fact that Canada is a patriarchal capitalist country characterized by high levels of economic, gender, and racial/ethnic inequality, Canadians are at much lower risk of being involved in homicide. For example, the murder rate is three to four times lower than that of the United States (Johnson, 1996a).

Homicide in Canada

The homicide data summarized in this section are derived from the Canadian federal government's Homicide Survey. The Survey has gathered rich information from the police on all homicides across Canada since 1961. In 1991, the Survey was modified to add some new data elements and to improve some existing ones. One homicide is counted for every victim, and the data in this chapter are current as of June, 1996 (Johnson, 1996a: 22).

The Canadian homicide rate has declined over the past two decades, and in 1994, it reached its lowest level in 25 years. There were 596 Canadian homicide victims in 1994, 34 less than in 1993. It should also be noted that in 1994, the homicide rate was 2.04 per 100,000, and that this rate is 6 percent lower than the 1993 rate (2.18), and 51 percent lower than the 1975 rate (3.02); only the United States, Northern Ireland, and Italy reported higher homicide rates than Canada; and 33 percent of all the homicides that occurred in 1994 in Canada were committed with firearms (Johnson, 1996a). These statistics do not answer some key questions about the patterns of homicide in 1994. Thus, we must turn your attention to other Homicide Survey data analyzed by Wilson and Daly (1994) and Silverman and Kennedy (1993), four of the world's leading experts on spousal homicide. They analyzed Statistics Canada's Homicide Survey data and found that the following information held true between 1974 and 1992 (1994: 1-12):

> The 1,435 women killed by their husbands constituted 38 percent of the total number of adult female homicide victims over 15 years of age.
> The 451 men killed by their wives constituted just 6 percent of all adult male homicide victims.
> A registered-married Canadian woman is nine times more likely to be killed by her spouse than by a stranger.
> 23 percent of the women killed by their registered-married husbands were separated at the time of the event, and three percent were divorced.
> Compared to co-residing couples, separation entails a six-fold increase in risk to wives.
> 32 percent of murdered wives were killed by common-law husbands.
> Rates of spousal homicide have remained constant over this 19-year period, with an average of 13 wives and 4 husbands per million couples in the

Canadian population killed each year. Also, 3.2 women have been killed by their husbands for each husband killed by his wife.

➤ 87 percent of spousal homicides occurred in a private residence. In 1991, 97 percent of the spousal homicides that occurred in these settings took place in the home of the wife and/or husband.

➤ The highest rates of spousal homicides were in the western provinces (e.g., Alberta) and territories, while the lowest were in Newfoundland and Prince Edward Island.

➤ In 1991-1992, 37 percent of slain wives and 82 percent of slain husbands were noted by the police to have consumed alcohol, within the 174 cases (80 percent) for which data on alcohol consumption was recorded.

➤ Firearms constituted the most frequent means of spousal homicide. However, this accounted for less than one-half of all cases. Also, men were more likely than women to beat or strangle their partners to death, and a higher percentage of women stabbed their husbands.

➤ Young wives are at the greatest risk of being murdered by their partners. The risk to both men and women decreases with age.

Silverman and Kennedy (1993) analyzed 12,828 victim-incidents that occurred between 1961 and 1990. They found the following:

➤ Murders are committed mainly by young, single, male Caucasians.

➤ Friend/acquaintance murder represents only 24 percent of all murders.

➤ Native people kill other family members more often than do non-Native people (24 percent compared to 16 percent of all murders).

➤ Stranger murders account for only 7 percent of all murders, and are typically a male domain.

➤ 794 murders involved offenders under the age of 18. Eighteen percent of these "deadly deeds" involved children under 15 years of age, and close to 30 percent of the perpetrators under 15 and between 15-17 were First Nations youth.

➤ Only 2.5 percent of all the murders that occurred between 1961 and 1990 involved offenders aged 65 and over, and most of the victims were spouses or lovers (56 percent). Eleven percent involved other family members and the remaining 27 percent were perpetrated against their friends and acquaintances. As expected, most elderly murders (96 percent) are committed by males, and only 5 percent of elderly murders are committed by First Nations people.

➤ Canadian Native peoples are involved in murderous events in proportions that are five times their proportion in the whole population. Further, the rate of Native murder has been as high as ten times that of the rest of the Canadian population.

Canadian small towns and large cities have the highest homicide rates. Moreover, the region with the highest homicide rates is the prairies (Ellis and DeKeseredy, 1996). This region encompasses Alberta, Saskatchewan, and Manitoba.

In sum, Canadians are much less likely to be killed than U.S. citizens; however, "this protection is not equally distributed among Canadians" (Gartner, 1995: 213). For example, as in the United States, those who are socially and economically disadvantaged (e.g., African-Americans) experience the highest rates of lethal victimization. Similarly, those who are disenfranchised in both Canada and the United States are at great risk of experiencing non-lethal physical assaults.

Assault

Here, we present data on the extent and distribution of non-lethal and non-sexual physical assaults. Examples of these behaviors are beatings, punches, kicks, etc. However, some of these actions involve weapons, and some can cause death. Many take place "behind closed doors" (Straus et al., 1981) in family/household settings, and a substantial number occur in public "hot spots" of predatory street crime such as bars, taverns, etc. (Sherman et al., 1989). In order to get accurate data on these social problems, sociologists and/or criminologists typically use **victimization surveys**. There are many different such surveys, conducted in many different ways, but all of them ask people to provide information on crimes that have been committed against them. While the interviewers have their "feet in the door," they may also ask about fear of crime, the effects of victimization (such as injury), reasons that the crime wasn't reported, and so on (DeKeseredy and Schwartz, 1996).

There are two broad types of victimization surveys. Generally, government-sponsored surveys seek data on the extent, nature, and consequences of assault and other types of property and predatory street crime. These include the U.S. National Crime Victimization Survey (NCVS) and Statistics Canada's General Social Survey (GSS). Put simply, these surveys ask a large number of people, scientifically chosen from across the country and representing most types of citizens, questions about the same events covered in official police statistics such as the American Uniform Crime Reports and the Canadian Uniform Crime Reporting Survey, to see if additional information can be obtained. As stated previously in this chapter, of course, murder is not part of victimization surveys.

A growing number of other surveys focus on more specific violent behaviors, such as wife-beating, date rape, anti-gay violence, child abuse, etc. Different methodological procedures are used in these studies; however, the one thing all victimization surveys have in common is that they ask people to describe their own experiences (DeKeseredy and Schwartz, 1996).

Many victimization surveys are accused of underreporting even fairly major assaults, as people in general tend to hold back information when the assailants were friends or family members (Hagan, 1993). For example, over the past two decades, one criticism of government-sponsored victimization surveys has been that respondents were told that the survey was a measure of crime. If they do not understand that violence or rape by a husband is a crime, and if the questions are not designed to point this out to them, they may not disclose these events (Straus, 1989).[6] This is why we have divided our description of assault data into two sections. The first includes data generated by government crime surveys, while the other includes spousal violence data generated by surveys specifically designed to measure this problem.

The Extent and Patterns of Assault in North America: Results from Large-Scale Crime Surveys

The U.S. data presented below are derived from the U.S. Department of Justice's National Crime Victimization Survey (NCVS), a telephone survey administered twice a year to a nationally representative sample of roughly 49,000 households comprising approximately 100,000 persons. NCVS data for 1995 show that 38.9 percent of the respondents stated that they were assaulted, 9.3 percent of the respondents reported being victims of aggravated assault,[7] and 29.6 percent stated that they were victims of simple assault.[8]

Who is most likely to be victimized by these crimes? Generally, African-Americans are more likely than whites, and Hispanics more likely than non-Hispanics to be victims. However, these general racial/ethnic differences do not apply to simple assault (Barkan, 1997). In fact, the risk of simple assault is about the same for these ethnic groups (Reiss and Roth, 1993). Furthermore,

> ▶ The risk of being assaulted is greater for young people, especially those who are 16 to 19 years of age.

> ▶ Except for partner assaults, the risk of women being assaulted is much lower than for men.

> ▶ The risk of being assaulted by a friend, acquaintance, or intimate partner is higher than the probability of being attacked by a stranger.

> ▶ Low family income is a key predictor of being assaulted (Reiss and Roth, 1993).

> ▶ The Southern U.S. states account for the most aggravated assaults.

> ▶ Rates of aggravated assault are highest in metropolitan areas and lowest in rural areas.

In Canada, according to data generated by the 1993 GSS,

> ▶ There were 6,700 assaults per 100,000 Canadians at least 15 years of age (1 for every 15 individuals) (Gartner and Doob, 1994).

> ▶ Slight majorities of those who were assaulted one or more times were women, single, had a personal income of less than $15,000 per year, and were working at a job.

> ▶ Seven out of 10 victims were younger than 30 and a slight majority of them were under the age of 20 when they were assaulted.

> ▶ Eighty percent lived in urban areas, 74 percent were childless, and 60 percent lived in households consisting of three or fewer members.

> ▶ About half of the victims reported being assaulted in 30 or more evening activities outside the home per month, and another 3 out of 10 engaged in between 15 and 29 such activities.

> ▶ More than 4 out of 5 assault victims reported that they were assaulted by a lone offender, while most of the other victims stated that they were attacked by two offenders. However, 10 percent stated that there were three or more offenders.

➤ Thirty-eight percent of assault victims reported that the offenders were strangers, while roughly as many victims stated that their assailants were acquaintances.

➤ Nineteen percent of the assailants were defined as relatives, and 5 percent were unknown.

➤ According to respondents, most of the assaults occurred in public settings. For example, 10 percent occurred in bars or restaurants, 24 percent in other types of commercial locations, and 27 percent in other public places, such as parks, parking garages, and on streets.

➤ Of those who were assaulted in residences, half lived with perpetrators, and approximately two-thirds of the assailants were let into the residence by someone (Gartner and Doob, 1994; Koenig, 1996: 398-401).

These North American victimization survey data show that Canadians are much less likely to be assaulted than U.S. citizens. It is true that in public places, Americans engage much more often in sub-lethal forms of violence than their Canadian counterparts (Silverman, 1992; however, this is not the case in intimate contexts, such as marriage and cohabiting relationships. In fact, survey data presented in the next section show that more Canadian women "suffer in silence" (Pizzey, 1974) or "behind closed doors" (Straus et al., 1981).

Assaults Against Female Marital/Cohabiting Partners[9]

The best way to determine the extent, distribution, and sources of assaults on female marital/cohabiting partners is to conduct representative sample self-report and/or victimization surveys specifically designed to collect data on male-to-female violence. Again, most government victimization surveys do not include well-crafted measures of "intimate intrusions" (Stanko, 1985), and thus their estimates of wife-beating and other types of domestic violence greatly underestimate the number of women who are victimized by their male partners.

North American researchers use different ways of collecting data on non-sexual violence among intimates, but the most common measure is the Conflict Tactics Scale (CTS). Developed by University of New Hampshire sociologist Murray Straus (1979), this quantitative procedure has appeared in hundreds of scientific journals and at least ten books (Straus, 1990). The CTS generally consists of 18 items that measure three different ways of handling interpersonal conflict in intimate relationships: reasoning, verbal aggression,[10] and physical violence. The items are ranked on a continuum from least to most severe, with the first ten describing nonviolent tactics, and the last eight describing violent strategies. The last five items, from "kicked," "bit," or "hit with a fist" to "used a knife or a gun," make up what Straus et al. (1981) refer to as the "severe violence index." Only the physical violence incidence and prevalence data generated by the CTS is presented here. Incidence refers here to the percentage of women who were victimized in the past 12 months. Prevalence is the percentage of male-to-female assaults that occurred over a longer time period (e.g., "ever").

In the United States, Straus and Gelles' (1986) National Family Violence Resurvey generated an 11.3 percent annual incidence rate. This figure is slightly

Table 5.1
North American Wife Abuse Surveys

	Description of Surveys					Abuse Rates			
Survey	Survey Location & Date	Sample Description	Interview Mode	Measure Abuse	Abuse Past year (%)	Severe Abuse Past Year (%)	Abuse Ever (%)	Severe Abuse Ever (%)
Straus et al. (1981)	U.S. National 1975	2,143 married or cohabiting men and women	Face-to-face	CTS (aggregate)[1]	12.1	3.8	–	–
Schulman (1979)	Kentucky 1979	1,793 presently or formerly married and cohabiting men and women	Phone	CTS[2]	10.0	4.1	21.0	8.7
Strauss & Gelles (1986)	U.S. National 1985	3,520 presently or formerly married or cohabiting men and women	Phone	CTS (aggregate)	11.3	3.0	–	–
Brinkerhoff & Lupri (1988)	Calgary 1981	526 men and women	Face-to-face and self-administered questionnaire	CTS (men only)[3]	24.5	10.8	–	–

Study	Location/Year	Sample	Method	Instrument				
Kennedy & Dutton (1989)	Alberta 1987	1,045 men and women	Face-to-face and phone	CTS (aggregate)	11.2	2.3	—	—
Lupri (1990)	Canada National 1986	1,530 married or cohabiting men and women	Face-to-face and mail questionnaire	CTS (men only)	17.8	10	—	—
Smith (1986)	Toronto 1985	315 women aaged 18–55	Phone	CTS/open questions and 1 supplementary question	10.8	—	18.1	7.3
Smith (1987)	Toronto 1987	604 presently or formerly married or cohabiting women	Phone	CTS & 3 supplementary questions	14.4[4]	5.1	36.4[5]	11.3
Statistics Canada (1993)	Canada National 1993	12,300 women 18 years of age and older	Phone	CTS[6]	3.0	—	29.0	—

[1] Men-as-aggressors and women-as-victims from different couples.
[2] Women-as-victims.
[3] Men-as-aggressors.
[4] Past year rates based on CTS alone.
[5] Abuse ever rates based on CTS (25.0, 7.8) plus supplementary questions.
[6] Includes a sexual assault item.

Source: DeKeseredy and MacLeod (1997). Reprinted by permission of Harcourt Canada, Ltd.

lower than the 1975 rate (12.1 percent) reported by Straus et al. (1981) who conducted a similar national representative sample survey. In sharp contrast to these figures, Table 5.1[11] shows that one national study, one city-wide survey, and one provincial inquiry report higher Canadian CTS-based rates. For example, Lupri (1990) obtained an 18 percent annual incidence rate of husband-to-wife violence. Even more significant is Brinkerhoff and Lupri's (1988) Calgary estimate (24.5 percent). Thus, when it comes to interacting with female marital/cohabiting partners, Canadian men are more likely than American males to assault them.

National Canadian surveys conducted by Lupri (1990) and Statistics Canada (Rodgers, 1994) produced data on geographic variations. Lupri found that the western and Atlantic provinces had the highest rates of physical violence against female spouses. A western province, British Columbia, had the highest overall rate (24 percent); in second place was the Atlantic region (24 percent). Quebec had the lowest provincial rate (13 percent). Ontario, one of the most heavily populated provinces, recorded a figure (17 percent) very close to the national average (18 percent).

Using similar measures,[12] Statistics Canada's Violence Against Women Survey (VAWS) asked women who have ever been married or involved in common-law relationships to report how many times they had been assaulted in their lifetime. Approximately 29 percent of all the respondents 18 years of age and older stated that they had been victimized, and those who lived in British Columbia (36 percent) and Alberta (34 percent) reported the highest lifetime rates. Participants from Newfoundland (17 percent), Prince Edward Island (25 percent), and Quebec (25 percent) reported the lowest rates. Furthermore, in contrast to Lupri's (1990) findings, the VAWS found that the risk of assault increases as one moves from east to west (Rodgers, 1994).

DeKeseredy and Schwartz (1997) contend that Western Canadian rates are higher than those of Eastern and Central Canada because Western Canadians are, in some ways, more conservative and patriarchal (Forcese, 1997). These researchers further argue that Western men are more likely to be influenced by sexist male peer groups. For example, several neo-Nazi white supremacist groups (e.g., Heritage Front, Aryan Nations, etc.) are based in the West (Kinsella, 1994). The right-wing federal Reform Party is also firmly grounded there and has received considerable support from Western voters, especially from farmers (Harrison and Krahn, 1995). The Reform Party attracts many racists (Kinsella, 1994) and is strongly opposed to day care and other state-sponsored services that could help economically disadvantaged mothers obtain full- or part-time jobs. In fact, Reformers want mothers to stay at home and look after their children. The Reform Party is now so strong that it has become Canada's Official Opposition Party, despite the fact that it did not manage to elect a single federal Member of Parliament east of Manitoba during the 1997 federal election.

Statistics Canada also found no difference in wife abuse rates between women living in large urban centers[13] and those in the rest of Canada. Lupri (1990), on the other hand, found that violence against female marital/cohabiting partners seems to be more common in urban areas. For example, towns with less than 5,000 people had the lowest rates (12 percent). Medium-sized towns and metropolitan areas accounted for a significantly greater share of violence (20 percent and 23 percent respectively).

While homicide rates vary greatly across different American regions, the incidence of male-to-female violence in marital/cohabiting relationships evidently does not. In fact, based on their analysis of the First National Family Violence Survey, Straus et al. state that "although we anticipated that there would be family violence in each region of America, we did not expect to find so little variation between regions" (1981: 127). Similarly, the rate of violence in large American cities is the same as the rural rate—both are 5 percent. Small cities and suburban areas recorded only slightly lower rates (4 percent and 3 percent respectively). Unfortunately, more up-to-date U.S. geographic data were not reported by researchers involved with the National Family Violence Resurvey of 1985 (e.g., Straus and Gelles, 1996).

What are the key **risk markers** or attributes associated with an increased probability of male assaults on female marital/cohabiting partners? Research shows that alcohol consumption,[14] unemployment, low family income, and low occupational status,[15] age,[16] and ethnicity[17] are strong correlates. So are men's adherence to the **ideology of familial patriarchy** and **male peer support** (DeKeseredy and Kelly, 1993b; DeKeseredy and Schwartz, 1998a; Smith, 1990a). Relevant themes of familial patriarchal ideology are an insistence on women's obedience, respect, loyalty, dependency, sexual access, and sexual fidelity (Barrett and MacIntosh, 1982; Dobash and Dobash, 1979; Pateman, 1988). Male peer refers to "the attachments to male peers and the resources that these men provide that encourage and legitimate woman abuse" (DeKeseredy, 1990: 130).[18]

Many North American women are also at great risk of being physically assaulted by their dating and estranged marital partners (DeKeseredy and Schwartz, 1998a; Ellis and DeKeseredy, 1997; Ellis and Stuckless, 1996; Pirog-Good and Stets, 1991). Space limitations preclude a review of the research on this topic here; however, the extant literature on these variations of woman abuse and male violence against marital/cohabiting partners clearly shows that

"[f]or women, the home, not the street, poses the greatest threat and, as all the evidence suggests, domestic threat and crime is least likely to be reported to official agencies whose data is used to calculate risk of falling victim to crime" (Stanko, 1995: 161).

In addition to experiencing high rates of non-sexual assault in intimate relationships, many women are at great risk of being sexually assaulted by their male partners. Next, we examine the extent and patterns of this major North American social problem.

Male-to-Female Sexual Assaults

As is the case with many types of crimes, methodological and conceptual differences preclude reliable comparisons of most Canadian and U.S. survey data on male-to-female sexual assaults, such as rape, attempted rape, and other types of illegal unwanted sexual contact (DeKeseredy et al., 1993; Ellis and DeKeseredy, 1996). Perhaps, then, the best comparisons can be made by examining the results of the International Crime Survey (ICS) (van Dijk and Mayhew, 1992). However, data generated from other surveys are also presented in this section.

In 1989 and 1992, women from several countries were asked the following question:[19]

"Firstly, a rather personal question. People sometimes grab, touch or assault[20] others for sexual reasons in a really offensive way. This can happen either inside one's house or elsewhere, for instance in a pub, the street, at school, on public transport, in cinemas, on the beach, or at one's work place. Over the past five years has anyone done this to you? Please take your time to think about this" (van Dijk and Mayhew, 1992: 28).

For all sexual incidents taken together, Canada had a higher one-year victimization rate (4.1 percent) than the United States (3.7 percent). In fact, of all the countries included in the sample, Canada had the second-highest rates (Australia ranked first, at 5.6 percent). Data on "more serious" forms of sexual assault, such as rape, attempted rape, and indecent assault, show that the Canadian rate (1.8 percent) is slightly higher than the American one (1.5 percent). Van Dijk and Mayhew state that these figures should be read cautiously because the responses may have been influenced by interviewers' communications skills or gender and/or variations across groups and countries, in the definitions of unwanted sexual incidents and in the willingness to disclose these incidents to an interviewer. Despite these cautionary notes, it seems that Canadian women are more likely than their American counterparts to experience sexual assault.

Where are women most likely to be sexually assaulted? In the United States, as you might expect, cities are much more risky than smaller areas. For example, NCVS data show that central city women are twice as likely to experience rape as their suburban or rural counterparts. NCVS data also show that most of the non-stranger rapes take place at or near the victim's home, and at or near a friend's home. On the other hand, most of the stranger rapes occur in open or public areas, and at or near a friend's home. Further, most rapes recorded in the southern states, and most of the stranger and non-stranger rapes occur at night (Bachman, 1994). Similarly, in Canada most sexual assaults occur at night or in the early morning hours (Ellis and DeKeseredy, 1996).

As in the United States, sexual assault is patterned geographically in Canada. For example, 1994 UCR data show that Atlantic provinces report rates of sexual assault above the national average; Western provinces report relatively high rates of sexual assault, however, the Yukon and Northwest Territories report sexual assault rates much higher than the national average; and Quebec scores lowest on sexual assault (Johnson, 1996a).

Statistics Canada's VAWS also provides some data on the location of sexual assault. Of the adult lifetime sexual assaults committed by men other than marital partners: 50 percent occurred in the home of the victim, offender, or another person;

one in six sexual attacks[21] took place "on the street," and one in five occurred in a car; and unwanted sexual touching[22] equally occurred on the street, in the victim's workplace, in a public building, or at a bar or dance (Roberts, 1994: 4–5).

A rapidly growing body of empirical research shows that North American university and college students—especially those in dating relationships—are at great risk of being sexually assaulted, and survey data generated by several sources show that most of these incidents occur off- rather than on-campus (see Bohmer and Parrot, 1993; Elliot et al., 1992; Finkelman, 1992; Koss, 1989; Warshaw, 1988).[23]

What are the social patterns of sexual assault in North America? Below is a list of some answers to this question generated by large-scale victimization surveys:

➤ Most victims know their offenders. For example, a recent NVCS found that 82 percent of the women who reported they were sexually assaulted stated that they knew their assailants, and only 18 percent reported that they were attacked by strangers (Bachman and Saltzman, 1995).

➤ A large number of sexual assault victims were attacked by a boyfriend, date, or marital partner. For example, the National Women's Study (NWS), a longitudinal telephone survey conducted in the United States, found that of the 714 women who stated that they were raped some time in their lifetime: 9 percent were attacked by their husband or ex-husband, and 10 percent were raped by a boyfriend or ex-boyfriend (National Victim Center, 1992).

➤ In Canada, Randall and Haskell's (1995) Toronto survey found that 30 percent of all sexual assaults that took place after a woman turned 16 years of age were committed by husbands, partners, and boyfriends.

➤ Only a few U.S. studies have examined racial/ethnic variations in sexual assault, and most of them found no statistically significant variations across different groups (Ageton, 1983; Bachman and Saltzman, 1995; Hall and Flannery, 1984; Koss, 1989; Rouse, 1988).

➤ To the best of our knowledge, only one Canadian study has examined ethnic variations. In Winnipeg, Brickman and Briere (1984) found that the majority of victims and offenders were white.

➤ Sexual assault cuts across all socio-economic categories; however, young women who live in lower-class communities are at greater risk of being victimized (Beirne and Messerschmidt, 1995).

The preceding discussion identified some key correlates of sexual assault (e.g., marital status, economic inequality etc.). The following are other key risk factors identified by sexual assault researchers such as DeKeseredy and Hinch (1991), Messerschmidt (1986, 1993), Schwendinger and Schwendinger (1983), Schwartz and DeKeseredy (1997), and Schwartz and Pitts (1995): male peer support; age (e.g., young women are at greater risk than older women); alcohol consumption; and men's adherence to the ideology of familial and/or social patriarchy.

The Personal Aspects of Physical and Sexual Violence Against Women Statistics

Many feminist scholars correctly point out that one of the most important limitations of statistics presented in the two previous sections of this chapter (as well as in other sections) is that they frequently appear to ignore real women who experience real pain. In other words, statistics on male-to-female victimization and other types of interpersonal violence have the power to reduce living human beings to abstract clusters of symbols (DeKeseredy and MacLeod, 1997). Thus, like other feminist sociologists who study woman abuse, we would like you to try to view the violence against women statistics presented here through the eyes of those who are abused. The key point to consider is that each data set discussed in this chapter is intensely personal, and is a document of people's pain.

Consider the pain and suffering described below by one female victim of dating violence:

"I went to the drive-through window at the bank to cash a check and he followed me in his car. He got out and started telling me what a cunt I was and how nobody would ever love me. I was really embarrassed. Everyone was watching me through the bank window. When they sent my money out, he took it and my driver's license. We argued and he called me names. I grabbed my driver's license and he started to crack it, and I turned to run. He grabbed me by the hair and slammed my head into the top of the car. A bunch of my hair ripped out. I fell back against the car. Everything was blurry. He shook me saying, 'Why do you make me hurt you?'" (Stone, 1991: 30).

Robbery

Following the Federal Bureau of Investigation (1995), robbery is defined here as "the taking or attempting to take anything of value from the care, custody, or control of a person or persons by force or threat of force or violence and/or by putting the victim in fear." Although robbery is considered a violent crime, it is a much rarer crime than assault (Koenig, 1996).

In the United States, recent NCVS and UCR data show the following facts:[24]

➤ There were 1.3 million robberies in 1992.

➤ Persons under the age of 25 account for almost two-thirds of all arrests.

➤ Robbery is more common in large urban areas.

➤ Robbery rates are highest in the Northeast. The West is a "close second," followed by the South and Midwest. Thus, the geographic patterning of robbery differs from that of other violent crimes (Barkan, 1997).

➤ Compared to other violent crimes, such as assault and homicide, robbery is mainly an interracial crime.

➤ Men and African-Americans are much more likely to be robbery victims than whites and women. However, NCVS data show a race-gender interaction for African-American women. For example, they are robbed less often than African-American males, but more often than white men. Also, Hispanics are robbed more often than non-Hispanics.

➤ NCVS data show that most people (80 percent) are robbed by strangers. However, approximately 35 percent of female robbery victims know their assailants, while only 10 percent of male victims know who "ripped them off." In sum, "female robbery victims are...three times as likely as male victims to be robbed by someone they know" (Barkan, 1997: 274).

➤ Weapons were involved in 52 percent of all robberies. 50 percent of those who used weapons used handguns and one fourth used knives.

In Canada, the 1993 GSS found that[25] there were 900 attempted or completed robberies per 100,000 Canadians 15 years of age and older; males were twice as likely as women to be victimized by robbery or attempted robbery, and single men reported a rate of victimization more than three times higher than the norm; most robberies or attempted robberies were committed by strangers (67 percent); and the majority (57 percent) occurred outside a residence.

The 1993 GSS also found the following facts:[26]

➤ Single offenders accounted for 54 percent of robberies (including attempted robberies), and 44 percent were committed by multiple offenders.

➤ Approximately two of three victims stated that a weapon was used.

➤ Young people, especially those 15-24 years of age (23 per 1,000), were the main victims.

➤ Most robberies (including attempted robberies) occurred in urban areas.

➤ Almost 90 percent of the victims were childless, and 60 percent lived in residences consisting of no more than three people.

➤ Half of the victims had an annual personal income of less than $10,000.

➤ Two out of three victims thought that their robbery was either drug- or alcohol-related.

➤ The vast majority of robberies occurred between 6 p.m. and 6 a.m.

Other Canadian studies found that Quebec accounts for about 60 percent of all armed robberies in Canada. Thus, it appears that French-Canadians are more likely to commit this crime than members of other racial/ethnic groups. Further, most robbers are socially and economically disenfranchised (Desroches, 1995; Gabor et al., 1987).

Summary

What can we conclude from the four types of violence data presented in this chapter? Perhaps the two most obvious conclusions are: (1) except for male violence against female marital/cohabiting partners and sexual assault, U.S. rates of interpersonal violence are higher than those of Canada, and (2) disenfranchised people (e.g., African-Americans, women, lower-class people, etc.) are at the greatest risk of experiencing violent crimes. Another important conclusion worth noting here is that violence rates in Canada and the United States vary with places, time, substances, and relationships, and age.

By now, many readers are probably asking themselves, "Why is the United States by and large more violent than Canada?" After all, most Canadians and

Americans live in close proximity to each other, listen to the same music, etc. This question was addressed in the section on homicide; even so, in Box 5.2, Barkan (1997: 262-263) provides some other compelling answers to this question.

Some of the points raised in Box 5.2 are subject to much debate. For example, while Canadians do not have a "Wild West tradition of settling differences," some scholars contend that they have a long history of violent labour disputes, such as the 1919 Winnipeg General Strike (Tunnell, 1995), and there were frontier rebellions such as the ones led by the Métis in 1869-70 and 1885 (Gurr, 1995). These are hardly examples of "accepting authority and expecting the government to look out for the greater good." It should also be noted in passing that although some Canadian rates of violence (e.g., homicide) are markedly lower than in the United States, Canada is one of the most violent countries in the world. For example, international crime survey data reviewed by Johnson (1996a) show that Canada ranks fourth in homicide rates, and among the highest in non-lethal violence compared to other Western countries (e.g., Norway, Sweden, and Scotland). In sum, Canada does have a serious violent crime problem, and it is by no means a "peaceable kingdom." Nevertheless, it is considerably safer in many respects than the United States.

Why Are People Violent?

Although there are many theories of violence, we will only discuss the most widely read and cited contemporary perspectives, especially those relevant to the data presented in previous sections of this chapter. We begin our review by describing Blau and Blau's (1982) inequality and violence thesis.

Inequality and Violence

As William Julius Wilson (1991: 1) correctly pointed out in his 1990 Presidential address to the American Sociological Association:

"Poverty in the United States has become more urban, more concentrated, and more firmly implanted in large metropolises, particularly in the older industrial cities with immense and highly segregated black and Hispanic residents. For example, in Chicago, the poverty rates in the inner-city neighborhoods increased by an average of 12 percentage points from 1970 to 1980. In eight of the ten neighborhoods that represent the historic core of Chicago's "Black Belt," more than four families in ten were living in poverty by 1980."

If poverty is a major characteristic of many U.S. inner-cities (see Chapter 2), the same can be said about violent crime. In fact, poverty and economic inequality are two major predictors of violence. This is not to say that "sheer poverty" or the absence of "glittering prizes" (e.g., car, house, color television, etc.) alone motivate disenfranchised people to beat or kill people (Young, 1992). In fact, most socioeconomically disadvantaged inner-city residents are law-abiding people (Lea and Young, 1984). What, then, is the connection between being "truly disadvantaged" (Wilson, 1987) and committing violent crimes?

BOX 5-2

Why Is Canada Less Violent Than the United States?

Because Canada is just to the north of the United States, its much lower violent crime rate is particularly illuminating. In many ways the two countries are very similar. They share roughly the same tastes in cars, music, and fast food, and they both have a long history of immigration and ethnic conflict. Despite its similarities to the United States, however, Canada remains, as one observer put it, "a remarkably peaceable kingdom planted [next] to one of the most murderous nations on earth" (Nickerson, 1994: 24)...[T]he U.S. homicide rate is about 4.5 times higher Canada's, its aggravated assault rate 44 times higher, and its robbery rate about 2.5 times higher. The homicide difference between the two nations is even more striking when we compare four large cities, two from each country, ranging in size from 2.8 million (Chicago) to 4.1 million (Toronto)...[T]he 1993 homicide rate per 100,000 in the two U.S. cities was some 10 to 15 times higher than that in their Canadian counterparts.

Several reasons account for these differences. Canada has much less inequality than the United States, and a handgun ownership rate that is only one-seventh that of the United States. An historical reason is Canada's lack of the frontier tradition of lawlessness and vigilante justice, which highlights U.S. history. The settlement of the West in Canada was instead led by the Canadian Northwest Mounted Police, who made sure it proceeded in an orderly and lawful fashion. As one observer summarizes this historical difference between the two nations, "Our [the United States'] heroes...were grimy, hard-driving, dusty gunmen; theirs were groomed, shaven, disciplined troops with shiny brass buttons. We had people before there was law, while they had law before there were people" (in McCaghy and Capron, 1994: 141). As one Canadian criminologist argues, "The United States is a society of confrontation, a country born of violent rebellion against authority...with a Wild West tradition of settling differences with guns. Canadians have never seen themselves as a nation of Davy Crocketts. Canada is a country of compromise that evolved peacefully. We have no tradition of revolution or civil war. We do have a tradition of accepting authority and expecting government to look out for the greater good" (Nickerson, 1994: 24).

Source: Barkan (1997: 262–263).

According to Blau and Blau (1982), robbery and other types of predatory street violence are products of **relative deprivation**. In other words, "under-class" and other disadvantaged people kill and rob because they harbor the following deep feelings generated by the inequalities they regard as unjust: despair, frustration, hopelessness, resentment, and alienation. For example, in advanced capitalist societies such as the

United States, impoverished African-Americans are told that "all men are created equal"; however, they can clearly see the economic inequalities associated with their racial status, along with the financial prosperity of others. This glaring contradiction generates deep hostility and weakens bonds to conventional social norms that restrain this attitude, which ultimately can lead to violence.

In sum, economic inequality is a major determinant of violence. Nevertheless, when you factor in racial inequalities, a new dynamic is created, one that is much stronger than the effect of economic inequality alone. Thus, according to Blau and Blau, "High rates of criminal violence are apparently the price of racial and economic inequalities" (1982: 126). Moreover, these and other forms of structured social inequality are found in metropolitan communities described above by Wilson (1991) and therefore it is no surprise that these communities report high rates of lethal and non-lethal violence.

The Neighborhood Family Structure Model

Similar to Blau and Blau's perspective, Sampson's (1986) neighborhood family structure model places a strong emphasis on the ways in which inner-city community structural characteristics contribute to violent crime. According to this model (see Figure 5.1), economically disadvantaged African-American and Hispanic people tend to live in ghetto poverty areas, an argument strongly supported by a growing body of research (e.g., Wacquant and Wilson, 1989; Wilson, 1987, 1996). Unfortunately, these people's economic marginality is strengthened by various conditions in the neighborhoods in which they live (Wilson, 1991, 1996), such as overcrowded housing, family disruption, and residential mobility (e.g., families moving from one residence to another). These three conditions disrupt the community, which in turn decreases the effectiveness of both formal social control (e.g., policing) and informal social control (by neighbors and friends). Also, family disruption decreases the effectiveness of informal (parental) social control. Thus, ineffective formal and informal social control increases the risk of violent victimization.

Heavily informed by Marxist perspectives on the alarming conditions of the "ghetto poor" (Wilson, 1991), Michalowski (1985) makes a similar argument in his attempt to explain why economically marginalized violent offenders attack members of their own socioeconomic group rather than more affluent people who play a key role in perpetuating and legitimating the conditions that oppress them. According to Michalowski:

"Humans do not generally attack or steal the property of those with whom they feel a sense of moral community. Moral community refers to the body of people toward whom we feel a sense of obligation and human concern. Inequality tends to narrow people's moral community by creating material and social barriers between different segments of society and by placing individuals in competitive rather than cooperative relations as a result of the struggle to improve personal position in a world of inequalities. As individuals, particularly the least well off, come to feel that the deprivations and disappointments in their lives are proof that people in general care little about what happens to them,

FIGURE 5.1
Sampson's Family Disruption Model

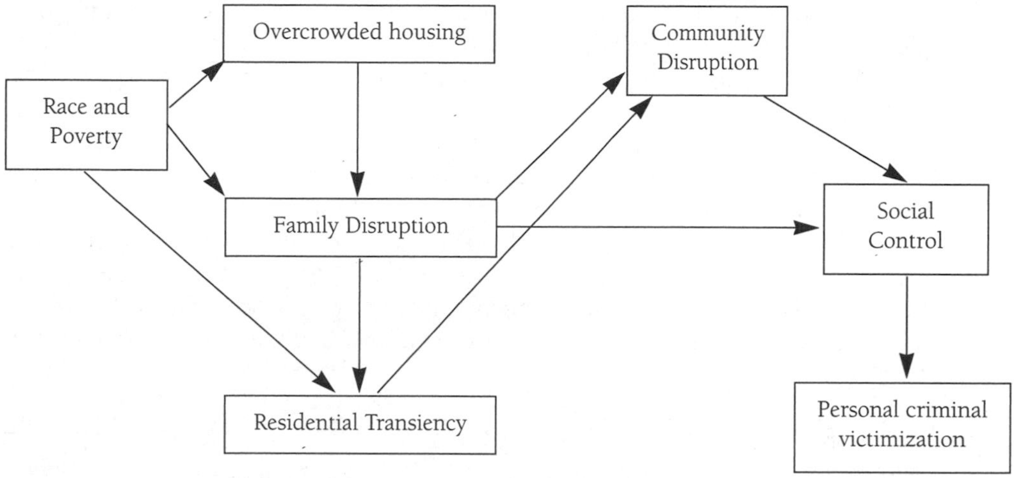

Source: Sampson (1986). Reprinted with permission of Springer-Verlag New York, Inc.

their sense of shared obligation with those others tends to weaken. This weakening of a felt sense of moral obligation towards others makes committing crimes against them much easier" (1985: 408-409).

The Subculture of Violence

You are now aware that some cities, regions, provinces, states, and other geographic areas have higher rates of violence than others. Consider homicide rates in the United States. Most of the murders and manslaughters occur in many large cities, with New York, Dallas, Washington, DC, Philadelphia, New Orleans, and San Antonio "leading the pack" (DeKeseredy and Schwartz, 1996). Why are these and other cities so violent? According to Wolfgang and Ferracuti (1967), they have high rates of violence because a **subculture of violence** exists in these metropolitan areas.

In such a subculture, violence is learned behavior. Also, members of this subculture share some of the values and norms of the mainstream culture; express violence in many, but not all, social situations; expect violence to occur under some circumstances and are willing to take part in it; receive strong positive support for committing violent acts and strong disapproval for not doing so; adhere to pro-violence norms that are in conflict with the anti-violence norms of mainstream society; learn pro-violence norms and values through the process of differential learning, association, or identification; and, of course, view violence as legitimate (Wolfgang and Ferracuti, 1967: 158-160).

Although the subculture of violence theory "seems clear and quickly catches attention," it is at best a "plausible" thesis (Smith, 1983: 40). Simply put, "No one has yet been able to find the subculture of violence—and not for the lack of trying" (Currie, 1985: 164). However, the lack of empirical support doesn't bother Wolfgang and Ferracuti, who argue that "basic evidence of a subculture of violence is still missing or tautological" (1967: 312). Still, some have found support for the "generic" form of the violent subculture hypothesis. For example, Smith's (1979) study of hockey players provides evidence of a violent occupational subculture, composed primarily of older male youths in highly competitive leagues, where professional standards of behavior are in force.

Despite the above pitfalls, this theory was instrumental in generating a national debate in the United States on the causes of violent crime in inner-cities. Furthermore, despite the lack of empirical support, to this day, the subculture of violence theory is widely and uncritically accepted by many academics, government officials, and members of the general population (Smith, 1983).

This is not to say that we should totally reject the concept of violent subculture because it has the potential to help explain why some men abuse their marital/cohabiting partners and dating partners. In fact, Lee Bowker (1983) provides some evidence of a patriarchal subculture of violence and it is to his perspective that we now turn.

The "Standards of Gratification" Thesis[27]

So far, we have reviewed theories that focus primarily on predatory street violence. However, data presented in a previous section of this chapter show that most adult female victims of violence are victimized by their male partners. Why do men beat their wives/cohabiting partners? Well, Bowker (1983) is a feminist sociologist who found that a line from a popular Beatles' song describes the ways in which men are motivated to assault their female partners: "with a little help from my friends."

For example, based on data gathered from the reports of a sample of battered women, Bowker found that the more contact there was between wife batterers and their male friends, the more frequent and severe the beatings of their wives would be. He explains this association by describing a social psychological process in which male batterers develop "standards of gratification" which dictate that they should dominate their spouses and children. When male domination is threatened, or is perceived to be challenged, psychological stress is experienced. Consequently, men react with a contrived rage to re-establish domination patterns that meet their standards of gratification. These standards are developed through childhood exposure to their mothers being dominated by their fathers, and by the men themselves being dominated in their family of orientation.

Standards that lead men to wife-beating are fully developed in men who are heavily integrated in male peer groups that continually reinforce standards of gratification through male dominance. For Bowker, these all-male networks constitute a patriarchal subculture of violence. He also states that the more fully men are integrated into this subculture, the greater the probability that they will beat their wives. The subculture is not restricted to a single class, religion, occupational category, or ethnic group, and it socializes married members to believe in the subordination of women and the use of violence to maintain their control.

Bowker's perspective has influenced the theoretical and empirical work of several male peer support theorists, such as DeKeseredy and Schwartz (1993). Unfortunately, like Wolfgang and Ferracuti's (1967) contribution, thus far it remains without strong empirical support and, therefore, speculative. Bowker admits that his study did not focus directly on a male subculture of violence. In his own words, "one can only guess at its broad outlines" (1983: 136). His study shows only that the frequency and severity of wife-beating is positively associated with wives' reports of husbands' contacts with their male friends. Since no males were included in the sample, there are no measures of husbands' friends' adherence to patriarchal attitudes and beliefs, or the degree to which abuse-facilitating values and norms are actually shared by these men. In fairness to Bowker, he is sensitive to these weaknesses, and contends that interviews with wife beaters are needed to adequately discern whether there is a relationship between wife-beating and a male patriarchal subculture of violence.

Another problem with Bowker's perspective is that it views pro-abuse male peer support as a constant rather than a variable (Schwartz and DeKeseredy, 1997). In other words, he regards it as a "universal risk factor" in that all men receive this support regardless of their place on the economic, political, or social ladder of society. Of course he is correct in arguing that this male patriarchal subculture is not restricted to one specific time, place, or sociodemographic group. But, however seductive it is to see all women as a class, and all men as equally affected by the effects of patriarchal capitalism, there is neither theoretical nor empirical evidence to support this formulation (Schwartz, 1988). Both the amount and types of violence may vary by class in most societies, including our own (Messerschmidt, 1993).

Summary

The main objective of this section was to review several widely used and cited sociological perspectives on violence. Whether we like it or not, theory is "a fundamental part of our everyday lives" (Curran and Renzetti, 1994: 2). Some people, however, contend that sociological theories such as those reviewed here, and university/college courses that survey various perspectives on violence are not practical, or are of little value. For these and many other people, such as conservative criminologist James Q. Wilson (1985), the question of what is to be done about violence is more important than why or how people engage in this brutal behavior.

Contrary to popular belief, as Curran and Renzetti point out:

"Without the generalizable knowledge provided by theories, we would have to solve the same problems over and over again, largely through trial and error. Theory, therefore, rather than being the ethereal mass that many of us conceive it to be, may be quite practical. It is useable knowledge" (1994: 2).

For example, before we can develop effective policies to curb violence, we must first determine what causes or motivates people to beat, kill, sexually assault, and rob. Unfortunately, despite decades of qualitative and quantitative research on the sources of violent crime, we don't have one definitive or "pat explanation." We still only have bad, good, and better theories of violence. As you progress through your post-secondary school education, you will find out that every perspective on every social problem, such as violence, is wanting on some grounds (Curran and Renzetti, 1994: 4–5). So are the progressive policy proposals described in the next section.

What Is to Be Done About Violent Crime in North America?

Space limitations preclude a detailed discussion of the ways in which the types of violence examined here can be prevented or controlled. In fact, one could write, and several people have written or edited, entire books on control and prevention issues surrounding violence (e.g., Hampton et al., 1996; Howell et al., 1995). Before we suggest a few of what we and other progressive scholars believe to be effective means of curbing violence in North America, it is first necessary to critique prisons, an approach called for by a substantial number of North Americans.

"Get Tough on Violent Crime": The Failure of Prisons to Curb Violence

Like it or not, prisons don't work. They only deter those currently locked up in jails and prisons from hurting members of the general population (Currie, 1985). Regardless of what conservative talk show host Rush Limbaugh says, prisons aren't **general deterrents**. Those who contend that they are, predict that if the general population hears about your sentence for beating up an elderly man in a bar, particularly if combined with fictional and non-fictional media stories about the "pains of imprisonment" such as prison rape, bad food, and lack of freedom, (Johnson and Toch, 1982), most people are not likely to commit violent crimes for fear of going to prison. Well, for several reasons presented here, it doesn't work that way.

Consider the United States. While data presented in this chapter show that it is an extremely violent country, it is also the most punitive country in the industrialized world (Selke, 1993). Furthermore, the United States is currently experiencing an "imprisonment binge." For example, Irwin and Austin (1994: 1, 4-5) found the following facts:

➤ The number of incarcerated people on any given day per 100,000 population increased between 1980 and 1992 from 138 to 329, as compared to only 26 in 1850.

➤ About one out of every four (23 percent) African-American men aged 20-29 is either in prison or jail, or on probation or parole on any given day.

➤ Approximately one out of every 10 Hispanic men (10.4 percent) aged 20-29 is either in prison or jail, or on probation or parole on any given day.

➤ Approximately one out of every 16 white men aged 20–29 (6.2 percent) is either in prison or jail, or on probation or parole on any given day.

➤ The number of young African-American men under the control of the criminal justice system (609,690) is greater than the total number of African-American men of all ages enrolled in college as of 1986 (436,000).

➤ Approximately 60 years ago, less than one-fourth of prison admissions were non-white. Today, nearly half are non-white.

Obviously, the United States is tough on crime. Why, then, aren't prisons working? Simply put, these penal institutions do not address the broader social, economic, and political forces—such as racial, class, and gender inequality—that motivate people to commit violent crimes. For example, most predatory street offenders are unemployed, underemployed, or members of the under-class (Reiman, 1998). Since a substantial amount of their violent conduct is caused by conditions such as unemployment, a lack of adequate housing, and an absence of future prospects, prisons do nothing to alleviate these problems. Furthermore, when people are released from prison, most of them typically return to the same economically deprived inner-city neighborhoods where they committed these crimes in the first place. Indeed, "it doesn't take long for them to pick up where they left off" (DeKeseredy and Schwartz, 1996: 454).

What's also important to note here is that for many under-class people who face great difficulties surviving on a day-to-day basis, prison may represent a higher standard of living. Although they have to endure many and often terrifying hardships in prison, these people also have a roof over their heads, three meals a day, membership in a peer group, and better medical attention (DeKeseredy and Schwartz, 1996). Compare this young African-American inmate's attitude (as told to Claude Brown) to the plight of the newly released inmate with no resources:

"Now if I get busted and end up in the joint pullin' a dime and a nickel, like I am, then I don't have to worry about no bucks, no clothes, I get free rent and three squares a day. So, you see, Mr. Brown, I really can't lose" (cited in Irwin and Austin, 1994: 164).

We could provide you with many other reasons that prisons don't work. However, the most important point to consider here is that if you want to lower the rates of violence described in this chapter, you must target the key sources of violence, a point completely ignored by "law and order" advocates. As Irwin and Austin point out:

"Reducing crime means addressing those factors that are more directly related to crime. This means reducing teenage pregnancies, high school dropout rates, unemployment, drug abuse, and lack of meaningful job opportunities. Although many will differ on how best to address these factors, the first step is to acknowledge that these forces have more to do with reducing crime than escalating the use of imprisonment" (1994: 167).

Unfortunately, more for political and ideological reasons than because people and politicians think it will work, the typical response to the failure of imprisonment described here is to call for more of what has already been done—build more prisons and lock more people up. For example, in their critique of prisons, DeKeseredy and Schwartz (1996: 450) contend that

"It is rather extraordinary that in the country that already hands down the harshest prison sentences in the world, many people have come to believe that we are 'too soft' on crime and that we must 'up the ante' or increase the costs of breaking the law. When we discover that people commit crimes without paying the slightest attention to the potential penalty, we increase the penalty. Then we find that people are still not paying attention

to the possible penalty, so we increase it again. When do we come to the conclusion that people are committing crime without paying attention to the possible penalty?"

In sum, for those who regard prison and other draconian measures (e.g., the death penalty) as the only solutions to violent crime, any talk about alternative strategies is viewed as outrageous. Well, an outrageous social problem such as violent crime requires outrageous proposals (Gibbons, 1995), some of which are briefly suggested in the next few sections of this chapter. Heavily informed by criminologists such as Messerschmidt (1986), Currie (1985, 1993), and DeKeseredy and Schwartz (1996) who call for strategies that "chip away" at the broader social, political, and economic determinants of violence, we contend that the following initiatives are necessary to curb the alarming rates of violence described in this chapter: (1) job creation and training programs, and (2) adequate social services.

Job Creation and Training Programs

If the mass media were your only source of information on violent crime, chances are that you would probably regard violent offenders as inherently evil, or as antisocial beings who totally reject the norms and values of conventional society. In reality, most predatory street offenders, such as gang members, do not have a "wicked" human nature, nor have they rejected conventional values. In fact, they would accept decent jobs if they were available (Hagedorn, 1994). Unfortunately, the unemployment rate in both Canada and the United States (see Chapter 3) is high, and many inner-city people are permanently unemployed because of changes in the economy since 1970, including the shift from goods-producing to service-producing industries; innovations in technology; relocation of manufacturing industries out of the central city; and periodic recessions (Wilson, 1991: 7). For these and other reasons, there are no jobs today, and there will be no jobs tomorrow for most inner-city youth, especially those who are African-American, Native, and Hispanic. Thus, we should be surprised that the violent crime rates in North American inner-cities are not even higher!

How do we deal we deal with the above problems that breed violent crime? Below are some recommendations proposed by Michalowski (1983: 14-18) and Currie (1985, 1989, 1993):

➤ Government laws requiring retraining and job placement for all workers displaced by new technology.

➤ A minimum wage level that is approximately 50 percent higher than the poverty level.

➤ Publicly supported community-oriented job creation.

➤ Upgrades in the quality of work available to disenfranchised people.

➤ Intensive job training and supported work designed to help prepare the young and disabled for stable careers.

➤ Job creation in local communities.

➤ A "solidaristic" wage policy that narrows the inequalities in wages within and between occupations.

➤ Disincentives for companies to replace higher paying jobs in the United States and Canada with lower-paying ones in other countries such as Mexico.

If other capitalist nations such as Germany, Japan, and Switzerland can use these strategies, so can the United States and Canada. But, economic and political elites strongly oppose these and other progressive economic policies because they don't want to give up the financial gains they have made under the current system (Barak, 1986). Corporations and governments have the money to improve the social and economic environment of inner-cities, they just don't want to spend it. In other words, "it isn't so much economic obstacles as ideological obstacles that account for our failure to mount a massive campaign to expand and upgrade the labor force" (DeKeseredy and Schwartz,1996: 467).

Adequate Social Services

State-sponsored social services did little to curb violent crime rates in the 1960s, a point successfully exploited by conservative politicians and academics such as former U.S. Senator Bob Dole and James Q. Wilson (1985). Why didn't strategies like early childhood education, remedial education, and welfare work? The answer is that they were not sensitive to the powerful influences of the economy and labor market (Currie, 1985). In other words, why bother increasing people's "human capital" by training them for jobs that don't exist? For example, Walter DeKeseredy has a friend who worked as a secretary and lost her job due to financial cutbacks. She knew how to type, but she didn't know how to use up-to-date word-processing software. So, in her struggle to get a new job, she took a computer course and successfully completed it. However, there was no secretarial job to be found in her community. Now, she is in New Zealand and still can't get a job. What does this tell you about the contribution of remedial education?

According to Currie (1992), in order to avoid the mistakes of the sixties, progressive social services must be integrated into a plan to eliminate unemployment and subemployment. With this cautionary note in mind, we suggest the following two strategies to help lower the rates of predatory street crime and family violence: day care and housing assistance.

Day Care

Many parents who go to school or hold full- or part-time jobs find it extremely difficult to balance these responsibilities with child care obligations. Indeed, dozens of articles, scholarly studies, and monographs show that work-family conflict is a serious issue for many parents.[28] Two concepts used to understand the conflicting relationship between work and non-work obligations are overload and **role interference**. Overload refers to a situation in which the daily workload is too much for an individual to handle, resulting in tiredness and burnout. Role interference is a concept denoting the phenomenon in which the social roles played by individuals (such as worker and mother) overlap and conflict (Duxbury et al., 1992; Greenhaus and Beutell, 1985; Jones and Butler, 1980; Kopelman et al., 1983).

These and other problems are more acute for low-income families who cannot afford babysitters or other types of child care. For example, disenfranchised parents who are forced both to work long hours and to raise children are at great risk of either taking drugs or abusing their children because of extreme stress (Currie, 1993). Others adapt to the situation by leaving their children unsupervised, which can lead to participation in street crimes (DeKeseredy and Schwartz, 1996).

Other disenfranchised parents simply stay at home in order to avoid the problems associated with inadequate child care. They are forced out of the labor force because child care costs greatly exceed their weekly or monthly income. Single parents are especially prone to this problem, and thus, many reluctantly rely on meager welfare support. For example, in Canada, 56 percent of single-mother families are poor compared to only about 12 percent of two-parent families (Statistics Canada, 1996). Although some of their problems can often be avoided through affordable day care programs, the United States has fewer such state-supported programs than virtually any other advanced industrial nation, and many Canadian day care programs are closing down or are at great risk of closing due to government cutbacks.

Unfortunately, many conservative people believe that day care is a waste of the taxpayers' money, a view recently expressed in Canada by the ultraconservative Reform Party. Based on their review of unpublished data gathered by an equally conservative research agency, the National Foundation for Family Research and Education, several Reform Party members argued that day care causes crime. They also claimed that day care increases the likelihood of clinical depression and increases personal stress. Moreover, they maintained that day care leads to an increased demand for social services and law enforcement.

Nothing is further from the truth! Like eating Quaker Oats, day care is "the right thing to do" because low-income and unemployed parents can either work or look for jobs without experiencing the high levels of physical and psychological stress associated with worrying about their children's well-being; day care greatly reduces the risk of drug use, child abuse, child neglect, and gang participation; and it enables people to obtain jobs and feel as if they are part of the North American mainstream (Currie, 1993).

In sum, providing disadvantaged people with day care creates a situation in which "the most alienated groups develop the same kind of "investment" in leading legitimate lives that has led middle-class drug-users to moderate their use and keep the social problems they generate to a tolerable level" (Alder, 1994: 263). Of course, not any type of day care will do. Simply having someone watch or be near a child does not guarantee that he or she will not grow up to be violent. Rather, it is the quality of day care children receive that determines whether or not they will end up being violent, do poorly in school, or experience health problems. A quality day care center, for example, is one that is clean, has a sufficient number of workers, and employs skilled and well-trained people who are deeply concerned about children's emotional and physical development.

If governments and corporations should sponsor quality day care, the same can be said about other means of supporting low-income and under-class families, such those provided by the Center for Family Life in Brooklyn, New York. According to Currie (1993: 315–16), this agency offers the following services that prevent child abuse and delinquency, and buffers parents from the life-events stress associated with the trials and tribulations of raising their children:

> A play group for children 6 months to 3 years and a simultaneous support group for parents.

> A weekly group to help mothers of children age 3 to 4 improve their parenting skills.

> Extensive help for parents in dealing with schools and other community agencies to ensure that they get the educational, financial, housing, child care, vocational, and homemaking help they need.

> Comprehensive after-school, five-day-a-week child care.

> A two-night-a-week program of recreation, dramatic arts, and tutoring for children.

> Community-wide forums and workshops on various parenting issues and concerns.

In this age of neo-conservatism, chances are that politicians and many members of the general public will strongly oppose the strategies proposed here. These proponents of "rugged individualism" are also opposed to housing assistance, despite the fact that it can make a positive difference.

Housing Assistance

United States housing policy has promoted homelessness. Therefore, it is not surprising that many violent street criminals and battered women are homeless (Barak, 1991; Harman, 1989). Moreover, the highest rates of illegal drug abuse are found among the homeless (Currie, 1993). It should also be noted that many battered women stay with their abusive partners because they know they cannot afford another place to live. If they leave, their only choice is to live on the streets with their children. Of course, this is no choice at all, because few homeless shelters will take in children (Liebow, 1995), and social service agencies commonly place in foster care children found living with their mothers on the street (Pitts, 1996).

The lack of affordable housing has been closely associated with increased crime problems for many years. Reformers believed that if only slums could be bulldozed under, better housing would magically arise, and the poor would have nice places to live. But, life doesn't work that way. Unfortunately, there is also a relationship between homelessness and violent victimization. Those living on the streets also have a much higher rate of victimization than the general population. In fact, "street peoples'" rate of victimization is three times higher even than for those living in extreme poverty but with homes (Fitzpatrick et al., 1993).

What, then, is to be done? In response to this question, some readers may be saying to themselves, "Let's provide more government-sponsored housing." This point is well taken; however, simply doing this is not enough. For example, it hardly benefits society to create "vast new fortresslike housing projects that jam the disorganized poor together in impoverished isolation" (Currie, 1993: 319). Both the public and private sectors should donate money to refurbish old and deteriorating buildings, houses, and apartments so that they can be occupied by the homeless and other disenfranchised people.

In 1995, the Smithsonian magazine highlighted an excellent model for achieving this goal. In an impoverished section of the South Bronx, "one of America's absolutely worst neighborhoods" (DeKeseredy and Schwartz, 1996), a progressive coalition of people reclaimed apartment unit by apartment unit. Amazingly, new single-family housing for working-class and under-class minority families is currently being built where fields of rubble were all that could be seen a few years ago (Breslin, 1995). This initiative also helps create new construction jobs, which is an example of what Schwendinger and Schwendinger refer to as "the multiplier effects of crime prevention" (1993: 439). This employment policy helps people to engage in various activities that support prosocial behavior and good child-rearing practices, as well as training them for highly skilled employment.

Summary

In this section, we have described several progressive and highly effective ways of reducing violent crime. We emphasized these approaches because a safer tomorrow for all—perpetrators and victims alike—begins with policies that reduce the absolute and relative levels of deprivation experienced by families and others at the bottom of the economic and status hierarchies. These and other progressive formal and informal policies too numerous to mention here should be national in scope and implemented right away. As Currie correctly points out:

"A chance this good may not come again. We must not let it pass by...We have, after all, been trying the alternatives for forty years. We have tried moral exhortation. We have tried neglect. We have tried punishment. We have even, more grudgingly tried treatment. We have tried everything but improving lives" (1993: 332).

Summary

In this chapter, you have read about violent crime, one of North America's major social problems. Unfortunately, sociological research shows that the violent crimes discussed here constitute just the tip of the iceberg. Many other types of violence are endemic to North America, such as corporate violence, sports violence, and child abuse. If we are to "build a society that is less dangerous, less fearful, and less torn by violence" (Currie, 1985), then these and other types of "everyday violence" (Stanko, 1990) must also be taken more seriously by researchers, policy makers, the mass media, and members of the general public.

Data reviewed throughout this chapter show that the United States is, for the most part, more violent than Canada. However, Canadians have nothing to brag about. For example, compared to other Western countries, Canada's homicide rate is relatively high, and Canada ranks among the highest in non-lethal violence. Moreover, it seems that Canadian rates of sexual assault and male-to-female violence in marital/cohabiting relationships are higher than U.S. rates. These and other findings seriously challenge the notion of Canada as a "peaceable kingdom."

If violent crime is endemic to North America, so are three key correlates of this problem—class, racial/ethnic, and gender inequality. The theories reviewed here emphasize the influence of one or more of these variables. These perspectives, and the data that inform them, sensitize us to the fact that we must develop a complex analysis of violence that takes into account structured social inequality in the richest continent on Earth, in an atmosphere that denies equal opportunity and blames those who are shut out for their failures (DeKeseredy and Schwartz, 1996).

What is to be done about violent crime? There is "no magic bullet" (Brandt, 1985); however, research shows that much of what we are doing today, such as locking up people and throwing away the key, doesn't work. This is not to say that we are opposed to using the criminal justice system. However, it is only one part of society and we cannot expect it to effectively "clean up the mess" created by other institutions and social forces (Currie, 1985). Indeed, what is needed is a "multi-agency response" (Jones et al., 1986), one that targets the leading causes of violent crime such as poverty, unemployment, homelessness, and inadequate child care. Thus, to reduce violent crime, we need to promote the initiatives proposed in this chapter.

Eliminating these problems will not be easy and there will be much resistance. Nevertheless:

"... if we continue to tolerate the conditions that have made us the most violent of industrial societies, it is not because the problem is overwhelmingly mysterious or because we don't know what to do, but because we have decided that the benefits of changing those conditions aren't worth the costs" (Currie, 1985: 19).

KEY TERMS

Assault
Conflict Tactics Scale (CTS)
Corporate violence
Familial patriarchy
General deterrence
Homicide
Interpersonal violence
Interracial crime
Male peer support
Overload
Relative deprivation
Robbery
Role interference
Sexual assault
Specific deterrence
Victimization surveys

DISCUSSION QUESTIONS

1. Why are many highly injurious and lethal violent acts, such as sports violence, trivialized or ignored by the mass media, policy makers, and many members of the general population?
2. Why is the U.S. homicide rate higher than Canada's?
3. Why are women at greater risk of being victimized at home than on the street and in other public contexts?
4. What are the major limitations of the subculture of violence theory?
5. Why are inner-city, disenfranchised people more likely to commit violent crimes than their more affluent counterparts?
6. Why is imprisonment an ineffective way of curbing violent crime?

PROBLEM SOLVING SCENARIOS

1. Suppose your university/college, a government agency, a community group, or your employer gave you money to conduct a study on violent street crime. In a group, develop a research strategy.
2. When you watch television over the next week, keep a pen and paper handy and note the ways in which the news, movies, etc. depict violent offenders. Do these shows present a realistic picture of violent crime and the key determinants of this problem?
3. Generate a group discussion on the practical value of theorizing violent crime.
4. Suppose you were given money to test Blau and Blau's (1982) theory. How would you do it? What research methods would you use and where would you test their perspective?
5. Create your theory of violent street crime, one that takes into account the data presented in this chapter.
6. Imagine that you work for the government. You have been asked to design a series of meetings and consultations across your state, province, city, town, or territory to get some fresh ideas about how to prevent violent crime. Develop a plan of action, identifying who you would include in these consultations; the kinds of meetings or consultations you would hold (e.g., size of meeting, in what kind of places it would be held, and the people you would invite to each meeting); and the issues you would want to discuss.

WEB EXERCISES

1. Download the complete report on the victims of serious violent crime that you will find at the following address. Then provide a critical sociological analysis of the findings.

   http://www.acsp.uic.edu/oicj/pubs/cjfarrago/agepatterns.cfm

2. Beginning at the website below, read the argument presented on rape, violent crime and firearms. Using your favourite search engine to look for different perspectives on these problems, assess whether possessing a firearm would reduce rates of rape and other violent crimes.

    http://www.nfa.ca/reports/women.html

SUGGESTED READINGS

Currie, Elliott. *Confronting Crime: Why There Is So Much Crime in America and What We Can Do About It.* New York: Pantheon, 1985.
In this widely read and cited book, Currie attempts to explain why violent crime rates in the United States are much higher than in any other industrialized nation. He also shows the major limitations of harsh "law and order" policies, and offers several short-term prevention and control strategies that are highly sensitive to the ways in which family structure, the labor market, and community dynamics influence rates of violent crime.

DeKeseredy, Walter and Linda MacLeod. *Woman Abuse: A Sociological Story.* Toronto: Harcourt Brace, 1997.
This book offers an in-depth analysis of the extent, distribution, and sources of male-to-female violence in intimate relationships. The strengths and weaknesses of various policies designed to prevent and control this problem are also addressed.

Mann, Coramae R. *Unequal Justice: A Question of Color.* Bloomington: Indiana University Press, 1993.
Mann provides a comprehensive, critical overview of the empirical, theoretical, and policy issues surrounding African-Americans involved in homicide and other violent crimes.

Reiss, Albert J. and Jeffrey A. Roth. *Understanding and Preventing Violence.* Washington, DC: National Academy Press, 1993.
This book is an excellent resource for those seeking an interdisciplinary approach to understanding various types of violent crime in the United States

Ross, Jeffrey I. (ed.) *Violence in Canada: Sociopolitical Perspectives.* Toronto: Oxford University Press, 1995.
This book provides a good collection of articles on various types of violence in Canada, such as homicide, non-lethal violence against women in intimate relationships, etc.

ENDNOTES

1   See Barak (1995), and Surette (1992) for a review of studies that support this argument.

2   See DeKeseredy and Schwartz (1996), the National Safety Council (1992), and the U.S. Department of Labor (1992) for more information on these and other American corporate violence statistics.

3   See Ellis and DeKeseredy (1996) for a comprehensive review of the literature on the incidence and prevalence of corporate violence.

4   See Hagan (1985) for a review of these studies.

5   For more empirical and theoretical information on the contribution of these factors to homicide and other violent street crimes, see Blau and Blau (1982), Currie (1985); DeKeseredy and Schwartz (1996), Messner and Tardiff (1986); Reiss and Roth (1993); Sampson (1985, 1987), Sampson and Groves (1987); and Smith and Jarjoura (1988).

6   It should be noted, however, that in response to this criticism, the National Crime Victimization Survey now asks more direct questions about sexual assault and family violence (Bachman and Taylor, 1994).

7   In the United States, the Uniform Crime Reporting Program defines aggravated assault as "the unlawful attack by one person upon another for the purpose of inflicting severe or aggravated bodily injury."

8   For the purpose of this chapter, we use the NCVS definition of simple assault. It is referred to here as an "attack without a weapon resulting either in minor injury or in undetermined injury requiring less than two days of hospitalization."

9   This section includes modified sections of work published previously by Ellis and DeKeseredy (1996).

10   Several researchers (e.g., DeKeseredy and Kelly, 1993a; Honung et al., 1981) refer to the verbal aggression items as psychological abuse measures.

11   This is a modified version of tables constructed by Ellis and DeKeseredy (1996) and Smith (1989). Except for Brinkerhoff and Lupri's (1988) study, all of the Canadian surveys described in this table include separated and divorced respondents.

12   Statistics Canada included an item on sexual assault. See Rodgers (1994) and Johnson (1996b) for a detailed discussion on the ways in which Statistics Canada measured violence against women.

13   Statistics Canada defined large urban centers as "census metropolitan areas which have core populations of 100,000 or over" (Rodgers, 1994:4).

14   For comprehensive reviews of the research on the association between drinking and violence against women, see DeKeseredy and Schwartz (1993), Hotaling and Sugarman (1986), Kaufman Kantor and Straus (1990), and Schwartz and DeKeseredy (1997).

15   See Johnson (1996), Kennedy and Dutton (1989), Lupri (1990), Schwartz (1988), Smith (1990b), and Straus et al. (1981) for more detailed information on the contribution of these risk markers.

16   For example, young men are more likely to assault their female partners than are older men (Johnson, 1996).

17   For example, Aboriginal men and African-American men seem to be more abusive than white men.

18 ˙ See Schwartz and DeKeseredy (1997) for a comprehensive review of the theoretical and empirical literature on the ways in which male peers perpetuate and legitimate woman abuse.

19   Data collected from 20 countries are presented in van Dijk and Mayhew's (1992) report. Surveys were conducted in 1989 and 1992; however, only eight nations participated in both sweeps of the study. For these countries, an average of the 1988 and 1991 rates is presented.

20   The word "assault" was excluded from the 1989 questionnaire.

21   Estimates of sexual attacks were obtained by asking, "Has a stranger, date or boyfriend, spouse or other man ever forced you or attempted to force you into any sexual activity by threatening you, holding you down or hurting you in some way?"

22 The extent of unwanted sexual touching was measured by asking, "Has a stranger or man other than a spouse or boyfriend ever touched you against your will in any sexual way, such as unwanted touching, grabbing, kissing, or fondling?"

23 See Schwartz and DeKeseredy (1997) for a comprehensive review of the North American survey data on the incidence and prevalence of sexual assault on North American post-secondary school campuses.

24 For more information on these U.S. findings, see Barkan, (1997), Bastian and DeBerry (1994), Federal Bureau of Investigation (1995), and Maguire and Pastore (1995). It should be noted that this list is informed by data generated by these researchers.

25 This section includes findings reported by Gartner and Doob (1994), Koenig (1996), and Wright (1995).

26 These data are described in greater detail by Gartner and Doob (1995), Koenig (1996), and Wright (1995).

27 This section is a modified version of work published previously by DeKeseredy (1996), DeKeseredy and MacLeod (1997), and Schwartz and DeKeseredy (1997).

28 See ALVI Social Research (1996) for a review of this literature.

Chapter 6

There's No Place Like Home?
Families in Modern North American Society

The romantic belief in the golden past is not unlike the common view, especially among white-, middle-class North Americans, that life in earlier generations was similar to what was represented on popular television shows such as Ozzie and Harriet *or* Leave it to Beaver. *Of course, we know that relatively few families (even middle class) were like the Nelsons or Cleavers. (Schwartz and DeKeseredy, 1997:9)*

OBJECTIVES

In this chapter we focus on the topics
1. What is a family?
2. Changing demographic and social trends and their relationship to North American family life
3. Family problems
4. Sociological theories of the family
5. What is to be done about enhancing the quality of family life in North America?

Introduction

In the fall of 1989, four months after his wedding, Walter DeKeseredy went to his hometown of Oakville, Ontario to visit his two best friends. They were engaged to be married and were deeply concerned about their future. One friend asked DeKeseredy, "What's marriage like? Do you argue more than you used to? Do you have less time to spend with your friends? What are you going to do when you have children?" These are common and legitimate questions, and they reflect the fact that DeKeseredy's friends were sensitive to what Fox (1995) refers to as the "dilemmas of contemporary family life." Other people, however, have an idealized image of the family, similar to what is depicted in the television shows mentioned in the above quotation. In these "sitcoms," the parents rarely argued, the children received full-time mothering, the fathers were the main "breadwinners," and the families lived in middle-class suburbs.

This chapter shows that, unfortunately, very few North American families are conflict- or hassle-free, and some are much worse off than others, especially those who reside in inner-city ghettos (Wilson, 1996). For example, some of the data reviewed in Chapter 5 show that a substantial number of marriages and cohabiting relationships are "hot spots" of brutal forms of male-to-female violence. Many families also experience great difficulties coping with conflict between work and family obligations, divorce/separation, and a host of other stressful life events. Indeed, much of the sociological work reviewed here challenges Lasch's (1977) notion of the family as a "haven in a heartless world." In fact, as described in Box 6.1, many people find some elements of family life, such as child care, so stressful that they seek refuge in their workplace.

BOX 6-1

There's No Place Like Work

Parents Flee to Office to Escape Children's Cries for Time and Attention

It's an early June morning at the Spotted Deer day care and the reluctant charges begin filing in. One little girl arrives with her thumb stuck in her mouth, a five-year-old is carried in by his mother. Four-year-old Cassie arrives hoisting a Fudgsicle in triumph, a sweet score on her mother's guilt for the 10 hours she's about to spend parked in a day care.

The parents hurry their children to the Cheerios-and-milk table, do their obligatory wave at the "waving window" that overlooks the sidewalk to the parking lot and, as soon as they're out of sight, break into a mad dash for their cars.

They arrive at work to drink fresh coffee, swap gossip with their co-workers, like neighbors over a front-yard hedge, check the day's schedule, then hunker down to a job that, for the most part, leaves them satisfied and rewarded.

Social historian Christopher Lasch once described home as a "haven in a heartless world," our nightly refuge from the soulless, crushing world of work.

But as Arlie Russell Hochschild suggests in these opening scenes of her controversial new book *The Time Bind*, the worlds of home and work are becoming reversed.

A professor of sociology at the University of California, Berkeley, Hochschild spent three years shadowing employees in the chrome-and-glass headquarters of a company she calls "Amerco," a Fortune 500 international firm based in "Spotted Deer" somewhere in rural U.S.A.

She interviewed top salaried managers and factory laborers, traveled from executive suites and emerald golf courses to trailer homes where children darted in and out of ripped front screen doors. Mornings and evenings, weekends and holidays, she camped out on the lawn by the company parking lot to watch when people came to work, and when they went home.

What she discovered was a curious paradox: while employees, white collar and blue, male and female, declared they were strained to the max juggling work and home, only three percent took advantage of programs offering part-time or reduced hours to give them more of the time they claimed they wanted at home.

In fact, during the three years of Hochschild's research, American parents began putting in longer hours at work, and fewer hours at home. Not because they needed the money. Not because of Dickensian bosses. Not for fear of being passed over for promotion, laid off, labeled "uncommitted" or put on the mommy track to unfulfilling work if they asked for reduced hours. Many did it because they wanted to.

According to Hochschild, the concept of more time for family life "seems to have died, gone to heaven and become an angel of an idea."

What she discovered was that, like generations of men before them, women were handing in their pink slips at home for the "reliable orderliness, harmony and managed cheer of work."

As one overloaded Amerco worker told Hochschild: "I get home and the minute I turn the key, my daughter is right there. Granted, she needs somebody to talk to about her day...The baby is still up. He should have been in bed two hours ago, and that upsets me. The dishes are piled in the sink. My daughter comes right up to the door and complains about anything her stepfather said or did, and she wants to talk about her job. My husband is in the other room hollering to my daughter, 'Tracy, I don't ever get any time to talk to your mother, because you're always monopolizing her time before I even get a chance!' They all come at me at once."

At work, "we sit, we talk, we joke. I let them know what's going on, who has to be where, what changes I've made for the shift that day. We sit and chitchat for five or 10 minutes. There's laughing, joking fun."

BOX 6-1

Men have been fleeing home for the "sweet joy of work" for decades, Hochschild writes. What's new here, she reports, is that women are as likely as men to leave behind a sink piled with dirty dishes and family conflicts to get to work early and call out "Hi fellas, I'm here!"

What has sparked this cultural reversal of home and work?

Hochschild says work is becoming increasingly feminized thanks to deliberate and calculated attempts by companies to create a homey atmosphere, all carefully designed to make employees feel like a member of the corporate family at a time when divorce and mobility are undermining our own sense of community and family.

Meanwhile, the real home front has become masculinized, a place where parents watch the clock and, consciously or not, use time-management tricks from the office to maximize profits and ensure efficient use of time.

We squeeze two tasks into one (carting the cell phone into the bathroom for bath time), carve out rigid blocks for homework time and dinner time, and "outsource" parental duties—flash-frozen dinners, homeworker helpers, after-school programs.

We ease our guilt by sanctimoniously protecting quality time, that notion that we can somehow make up for the 10 hours we're away from our kids with one (usually less) quality hour.

"Quality time," Hochschild writes, "holds out the hope that scheduling intense periods of togetherness can compensate for an overall loss of time in such a way that a relationship will suffer no loss of quality. But this is just another way of transferring the cult of efficiency from the office to home."

Worse, we rush through the things that help give our children some semblance of security and balance and normalcy—family routines and dinner hours and chores— just so that we can give them more "quality time."

How are children reacting to this frenetic, efficient, assembly-line family life? "Children dawdle. They sulk. They ask for gifts. They tell their parents by action or word, 'I don't like this.'"

Many working mothers I approached with Hochschild's seemingly alarmist thesis freely admitted that there are mornings when the office beckons, where they can collapse into a chair at their desk and read the paper for five minutes over a cup of coffee that hasn't already been nuked four or five times, where there are adults and established order and the chance to be focused on one task instead of having demands coming from all sides.

Really, should it come as any surprise that, with working mothers still shouldering most of the housework (1.7 hours a day more than their male partners, a disparity Hochschild explored in her earlier book *The Second Shift*), some moms actually look forward to the chance to "relax" at the office?

Source: Kirkey (1997: 11). This is a slightly modified excerpt of Kirkey's review of Hochschild's (1997) *The Time Bind: When Work Becomes Home and Home Becomes Work*. New York: Metropolitan Books. Reprinted with permission of Henry Holt and Company, LLC.

What is to be done about the situation described in Box 6.1? When we asked some "unattached" graduate students this question, they said in jest, "Don't get married and don't have children." If only life was that simple! Other people are deeply disturbed by the problems raised in Box 6.1 and contend that we can solve them by returning to "good old fashioned family values." These conservatives want to bring back the "glory days," when people lived like the Cleavers and Nelsons. They also want to eliminate day care centers and force women to give up their jobs and stay at home with their children (Fox, 1995). The advocates of "traditional family values" want to go back to a place in time that never really existed. For example, many of the family problems described in this chapter are not new (e.g., violence). This is not to say, however, that we should not consider new and more progressive ways of dealing with them. For reasons outlined later on in this chapter, going back will do little, if anything, to improve the quality of North American family life.

What Is a Family?

Many people would have no hesitation in providing you with a "common sense" definition of the family similar to the quotation starting this chapter. They are likely to say that the family consists of a legally married man and woman, perhaps with some children, where the woman's primary responsibility is to take care of the children while the male's is to be the "breadwinner." Others may say that such a definition of the family is outmoded. They would point to the fact that about half of all families in North America are actually "dual income" couples, and that many are choosing to have fewer or no children. Indeed, because the family is something so basic to society, most people have an opinion (and usually a strong one) on what a family is. However, there are many different types of families. According to the Vanier Institute of the Family (1994), some of these family types include the following:

➤ **nuclear families** composed of two parents and their one or more biological or adopted children, living together—when the nuclear family was led by a male wage-earner, it was the conventional family of the 1950s, although now it is only one of many types of family;

➤ **extended families** composed of parents, children, aunts, uncles, grandparents, and other blood relations living together, or not;

➤ **blended** or **recombined** or **reconstituted families** composed of parents who have divorced their first spouses, remarried someone else and formed a new family that includes children from one or both first marriages, and/or from re-marriages;

➤ **"childless" families** consisting of a couple;

➤ **lone-parent families** composed of a parent, most often a mother, with a child or children;

➤ **cohabiting couples** and **common law marriages**—family arrangements that resemble other forms, but without legalized marriage; and

➤ **traditional families**—a confusing term that reflects the changing nature of North American families in that people tend to use it to refer to their own families, or to the family type that they have encountered most often.

The great variety of family forms makes sense given that North American society has changed dramatically over the last 100 years. For instance, most of us would agree that as our society has changed, families have become more complex to adapt to such changes. But while the shape of the family may have changed, can we also say that that the essence of what families do has changed at all? Does the fact that there are so many different family forms mean that certain forms are "abnormal?" Does the great diversity in family forms mean that we are in danger of losing "traditional family values"? If so, what are the "traditional family values" being referred to here? Can we solve these puzzles by simply offering one sociological definition of the family and sticking to it?

If you have been reading other chapters in this book, you might be expecting us to now offer a widely accepted sociological definition of the family, since this is what we have tried to do with other concepts throughout the text. In fact, we do offer such a definition at the end of this section. But we want to point out that the family is yet another one of those areas in sociology that seems to generate constant debate regarding appropriate definitions. And this is by no means a sociological or academic debate, because some type of definition of the family is necessary if we are to create the social and legal policies that will directly affect the millions of individuals making up families in North America (Richardson, 1996). For example, assume for a moment that the only kind of "real" family is a mother and father who are legally married with their own (natural) children. Assume also that only these types of families are eligible for income and child support, health care, and other rights. By making these assumptions you would in fact be closely approximating the actual circumstances of many families today, since in many states and provinces, only these types of families are eligible for such support. Now think about the implications of this situation for same sex (homosexual) couples. What about couples that adopt children? How about people who live together, but are not legally married? Should we treat such groupings differently just because they do not fit "traditional" notions of the family? Should North American society restrict the benefits we offer to so-called "traditional" families while ignoring other family forms? On what basis can we justify defining the family only in traditional terms?

To answer these questions we need to think about how "common sense" definitions of the family are constructed and by whom. For some people, the family should be defined in terms of a **Judeo-Christian** perspective, one that upholds the idea of the family as "divinely sanctioned" and patriarchal (as described above). While there are certainly examples of such families in North America today, it is important to point out that just because something is prevalent in society does not mean it should become the "yardstick" by which all other things should be judged. "Common sense," after all, also tells us that there are many adults and children who share other kinds of relationships, and for whom these arrangements are "familial" (see Table 6.1).

Table 6.1
Images of the Family

Traditional Judeo-Christian Image	Other Possibilities
Married heterosexual couples	Remarriage, divorce, same sex couples
Love	Tension, abusive partners
Permanence	Short-lived
Children	Childlessness
Sexual exclusivity	Multiple sexual partners
Homemakers	Dual Income Couples, dual careers
Legal unions	Common-law, or cohabitation
Intergenerational continuity	Intergenerational disruption

Source: Adapted from Eshleman, 1997: 4

The point is that any attempt to reach a conclusive definition of the family will meet with resistance from numerous people who claim that their own definition is better than any other. More important, it is difficult to produce one definition of the family since family forms keep changing. In effect, there are many definitions, each reflecting the wide variety of moralities, beliefs about lifestyle, and norms that characterize North American life. Moreover, since society is always changing, it makes sense that the nature of the family is as well. Consider, as described in Box 6.2, how the disappearance of work has affected many African-American and other families that live in U.S. inner-city ghettos.

If the form of the family has never really been stable, is it possible to arrive at "the" definition of the family? The answer to this is quite simply that we cannot

BOX 6-2

Joblessness and Inner-city Ghetto Families

As the disappearance of work has become a characteristic feature of the inner-city ghetto, so too has the disappearance of the traditional married-couple family. Only one-quarter of the black families whose children live with them in inner-city neighborhoods in Chicago are husband-wife families today, compared with three-quarters of the inner-city Mexican families, more than one-half of the white families, and nearly one-half of the Puerto Rican families.... And in census tracts with poverty rates of at least 40 percent, only 16.5 percent of the black families with co-resident children are husband-wife families.

Source: W.J. Wilson, *When Work Disappears* (1996: 87-88). Reprinted with permission of Alfred A. Knopf, Inc., a Division of Random House, Inc.

claim that there is one essential definition that can stand the test of time if we only base our definition on what we imagine that they "should" look like. As Eichler (1997: 164) argues: "Old family structures have fractured, and no amount of nostalgic wishing is going to change this fact." Given this, a more fruitful approach to defining the family should be based on what families actually do (Gubrium and Holstein, 1990). Put differently, if we want a useful definition of the family, we need to look carefully at the functions families perform. Eichler (1988) proposes that among the most important of these functions would be emotional involvement, procreation, socialization, economic support, and sharing of resources and residence. Another definition, offered by the Vanier Institute of the Family (1994: 10), is

any combination of two or more people who are bound together over time by ties of mutual consent, birth and/or adoption/placement and who, together, assume responsibility for variant combinations of some of the following:

➤ *physical maintenance and care of group members;*

➤ *addition of new members through procreation or adoption;*

➤ *socialization of children;*

➤ *social control of members;*

➤ *production, consumption, and distribution of goods and services; and*

➤ *affective nurturance—love.*

Since this functional approach seems an adequate reflection of the many roles families carry out and avoids the dilemmas associated with providing a single definition, we will use this framework for understanding the family throughout this chapter. The next section considers the following two questions:

➤ What kinds of changes have occurred in families?

➤ What sociological factors have conditioned these changes?

Changing Demographic and Social Trends and their Relationship to North American Family Life

Social scientists interested in the family have demonstrated that the traditional nuclear family is no longer the norm, and that North American society is characterized by a diversity of family forms. But they are divided on what this increasing variety means. Some argue that the abundance of new family forms indicate that the family is adapting to change (Skolnick, 1991; Hayford and Crysdale, 1991). Others, such as Popenoe (1994), view recent changes in the family negatively, in that "the demise" of the traditional family creates a serious threat to the well-being of children. In this section we want to provide you with a sense of the key changes in the family that have occurred in the twentieth century.

On examination, one of the most important of these changes turns out to be not much of a change at all. It is the idea that families have mutated from the "extended" (where two or three generations live in the same household) to "nuclear" form, and is one of the most common myths about change in the family. Hareven (1982), for instance, has shown that the United States has never witnessed significant numbers of extended families, while Nett (1981), and Katz (1975) have pointed out that such large family forms would have been difficult to sustain in Canada because in the early part of this century people simply did not live long enough to create families in which two or three generations would be alive at the same time, under the same roof. Moreover, most people could simply not afford to live in large families. All of this means that the nuclear family has in fact been the dominant form for approximately 100 years. But it also points to the importance of factors such as social class in the formation of families. We discuss more about the influence of such factors later in this chapter, as we want to concentrate here on the influence of population demographics.

A colleague of ours is fond of saying that when it comes to the family, "demography is destiny." Demography, the study of human populations, can tell us much about the problems currently affecting North American families, and in many ways can help us to predict the kinds of social problems they might experience. In addition, since some commentators argue that demographic shifts are responsible for an "erosion of family values" (Richardson, 1992), we need to be aware of what these trends are and how they may affect families. What, then, are the most important of these demographic and social trends? Most sociologists would agree that the following should be included on any such list:

➤ the declining fertility rate and changes in the size of the family;

➤ shifting norms regarding the role of marriage and children;

➤ the increase in divorce rates;

➤ population aging; and

➤ women's entry into the paid workforce.

Declining Fertility Rates and Family Size

One of the most important demographic shifts to occur in North America has been the steady decline of fertility rates. Fertility rates as they are used in this chapter, measure the total number of children born per thousand women of a given group of women (called a cohort) at the end of their childbearing years (around age 44).[1] At the moment, the fertility rate in North America is less than 2.0 (Eshleman, 1997). Some of the most important reasons for the decline in fertility in North America (and indeed around the world) are that

➤ the incidence of sterility in couples has increased. No one is really sure why this is happening, but some scientists have speculated that the phenomenon is related to environmental issues;

➤ many people are choosing not to have children; and

➤ contraceptive usage has increased.

Though we have some sense of why couples are having fewer children, what is equally important are the social implications of this trend. Consider the following example. Obviously, people are born, grow old, and die. For a nation to replace its population, it would have to have a replacement fertility rate (the level of fertility needed so that a child is born to replace each person in his or her parents' generation) of 2.1 or more, meaning that the average family in these nations is not only reproducing itself (the mother and father), but also adding to the population. So far so good. But our ability to replace ourselves is not the only issue here. There are other important implications of declining fertility for family life. These include the following:

> Increasingly, many couples must struggle to have children, or are unable to have children. This means that many families must deal with the heartache of being unable to conceive, which in turn can add stress and conflict to family relationships.

> The use of new reproductive technologies is becoming increasingly common in North American life, adding to the financial burden of many families, while raising ethical issues surrounding the medicalization of pregnancy and childbirth (see Chapter 4).

What implications does this trend have for family size? Obviously, families are getting smaller. But we know that smaller families have important effects. For instance, a smaller family means fewer interactions between members (and thus fewer opportunities to disagree), and therefore has implications for how well people get along in families (Eshleman, 1997). In addition, as Gee (1992) has pointed out, one's experiences as an only child are significantly different from those of individuals with many siblings. Similarly, Downey (1995) notes that the larger the family, the less likely a child will be to graduate from high school and the lower their educational performance, primarily because large families have fewer resources (e.g., money, time, opportunities for interaction etc.) than do smaller ones.

Shifting Norms Regarding Marriage and Children

While the majority of births in North America still occur within married couples, this appears to be changing rather quickly. The number of children born to couples out of marriage has increased dramatically. In Canada for example, the percentage of children born out-of-wedlock increased from just four percent between 1931 and 1960, to 27 percent in 1991 (McKie and Thompson, 1990: 128).[2] Similarly, in the United States, 26 percent of births are out-of-wedlock (Bureau of Census, 1995). In addition:

> Many people are delaying marriage till later in life. In the United States, for instance, women today are marrying around the age of 25 and men at age 27. But in 1970 women were marrying at age 21 and men at age 23 (Bureau of Census, 1995).

> Since many of these couples may in fact no longer live together, one very important implication is that some families only exist as such in terms of the children's perspectives, while for the parents there may be no such sense of "family unit." As Eichler (1997: 31-32) puts it, we are increasingly seeing a discrepancy between "marital and parental roles....two parents [may still be] parents to the children, but are definitely no longer a couple, nor do they belong to the same family. The children form a family both with their mother and

with their father, and thus have a double family membership, but the ex-spouse are no longer members of each other's families."

Divorce Rates

The rate of divorce commonly indicates what social scientists call "family stability"—the probability of marriage lasting till one of the partners dies, and that children will grow to adulthood with both parents present (Bystydzienski, 1993). This is not to say, of course, that divorced parents are any less likely to provide a loving, nurturing environment in which children can grow up. Nor does a measure of divorce suggest that fewer or more marriages are unhappy unions. This is because statistics on divorce rates can only tell us what has happened as a consequence of divorce laws, not what has happened "inside" the marriage. Keeping this in mind, one's chances of remaining married in North America has decreased over the years. In comparison with Canada, the United States has always had a higher divorce rate (See Figure 6.1), although it appears these rates are converging.

The main reason for lower divorce rates in Canada is not that Canadians are in any sense "more committed" to their spouses. Rather, divorce in Canada has historically been harder to obtain. In fact, until the late 1960s, Canadians could only

FIGURE 6.1

Divorce Rates for the United States and Canada: Number of Divorces per 1000 population, 1880–1988

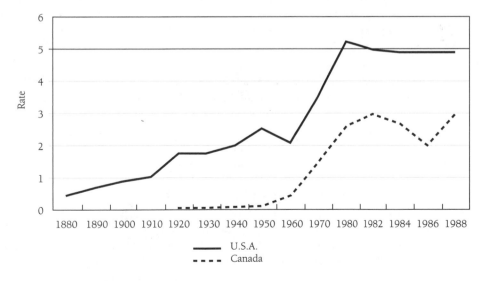

Source: Adapted from Bystydzienski, 1993

get a divorce if they could prove that there had been mental cruelty, adultery, or desertion in the marriage (more than likely, this explains the sudden jump in divorces for Canada you see in Figure 6.1).

Regardless of the differences between the two countries, the main reasons for increasing divorce rates are related to the changes in the nature of the economy, as well as cultural and legal norms (Crysdale, 1991). In the case of the economy, social scientists such as Scanzoni (1982) point out that family income is the strongest predictor of marital success. Given that it has become increasingly difficult for people to maintain decent incomes in the "new economy" (see Chapter 3), it makes sense that some couples find it difficult to maintain a marriage on "love alone."[3] Conversely, marriage rates tend to increase when the economy is stable or booming, reflecting the increased confidence with which young people feel able to start adult life (Glick and Norton, 1977).

There are also implications of divorce for family life after a marriage has ended. For instance, research in both Canada and the United States has consistently shown that women fare far worse economically than men after divorce, and that in fact, the economic status of males after divorce actually improves (Finnie, 1993; Smock, 1993, 1994). Thus, the experience of divorce is economically gendered. Another consequence of the unequal experience of divorce is that many single parent female-headed families experience high rates of poverty (Casper, McLanahan and Garfinkel, 1994). This means that both the children and female parents in such families are extremely disadvantaged compared to most dual income or two parent families. Indeed, according to Eshleman (1997: 241):

"Single parent families are characterized by a high rate of poverty, a high percentage of minority representation, more dependents, relatively low education, and a high rate of mobility...psychologically, single parents are more depressed, are more anxious, have poorer self images, and are less satisfied with their lives. In short, single parents have little equity or stature in U.S. society."

It might seem obvious that children are adversely affected by divorce. However, there is some controversy over this view. It is true that divorce has negative economic and social consequences for children. For instance, as Eshleman (1997) points out, adolescents from divorced homes are less likely to graduate from high school, have a lower probability of ever marrying, and greater chances of getting divorced themselves. In addition, there is some evidence to suggest that children from such homes are more likely to commit crime, and experience problems in relating to peers (Wells and Rankin, 1991). What is uncertain is the extent to which such problems actually come from the relationships between family members during the marriage. It may be, then, that parental conflict, abuse, or persistent economic stress may actually be the factors that influence children in negative ways, and not the actual strain of divorce and separation itself.

Population Aging

As we saw in Chapter 4, one of the most widely used measures of the health of a nation is life expectancy, which measures the average age at which we die. In this regard, both Canada and the United States fare reasonably well. In short, our populations are living to a ripe old age (See Figure 6.2).

But while it is certainly good news that we are living to an older age, there are important implications of this trend for families. One effect that has intrigued many researchers is the impact of declining fertility in combination with the increasing average age of the population. In both Canada and the United States, people are living longer due to better medical treatments to preserve longevity, the elimination of many childhood infectious diseases, and healthier lifestyles (McKie, 1990: 4).

One problem, however, is that older people tend to need more care than other age groups (Alvi, 1995; U.S. Bureau of the Census, 1995). Although not all require expensive medical treatments or hospitalization, many elderly people need daily assistance with everyday tasks (See Figure 6.3). This raises an important set of questions. Who will care for these elderly individuals, given that there will be fewer young people around in the next century? To take the point further, if there are fewer taxpayers (either because there are fewer people of working age and/or because there are fewer jobs), who will pay for the care of the elderly? As we will

FIGURE 6.2
Percentage of the Population Aged 65 and Over, by State, 1993

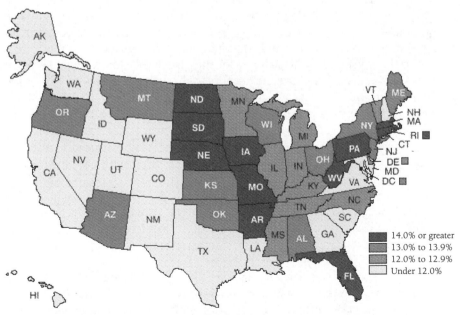

Source: U.S. Bureau of the Census, Statistical Brief 95-8, 1995

FIGURE 6.3

Percentage of Persons Needing Personal Assistance with Everyday Activities by Age, 1990–91, USA

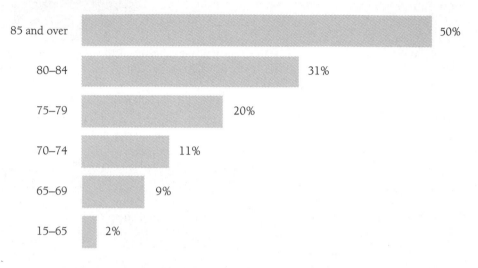

85 and over	50%
80–84	31%
75–79	20%
70–74	11%
65–69	9%
15–65	2%

Source: U.S. Bureau of the Census, Statistical Brief 95-8, 1995

see later in this chapter, the likely answer to the first question is women, but many of these women who are involved in careers and having young children later in life (part of the declining fertility phenomenon), will experience tremendous stress deriving from the dual pressures of caring for elderly relatives as well as their own (often young) children. These people have been given a name—"the sandwich generation"—because they are "sandwiched" between the demands of caring for elderly and young dependents and will often hold full-time jobs as well.

As to the question of who will pay for the care of the elderly, it is likely that cutbacks in health care, and the privatization of health care in general (discussed in Chapter 4), will change the face of the health care delivery system in North America. Some key questions that need to be addressed in relation to this transformation are: Will certain income groups (particularly the elderly) be less able to afford health care? Will they be able to purchase health insurance, and will they face less problems of accessibility to good quality health care institutions (such as nursing homes)? We do not really know the answers to these questions, but in light of trends occurring in the larger social context, we can say that at the moment, North Americans seem completely unprepared for the impact of the explosion in the elderly population that will occur in a few decades.

Women's Entry into the Paid Workforce

At least since the 1930s, single women have always participated in paid labor in both Canada and the United States. However, since World War II, married women have entered the paid workforce at a record rate. In Canada, a mere 5 percent of women participated in the paid workforce in 1941. By 1991, 61 percent of married women were engaging in paid work. According to the U.S. Bureau of Labor Statistics, nearly half, or 48 percent, of all workers, come from dual-earner couples. Only 9.4 percent of workers come from so-called "traditional families," with a male breadwinner and female homemaker. By the year 2000, it is estimated that two-earner couples will rise to the majority, 51 percent of all families, up from 41 percent in 1980.

There are several reasons for this trend. First, as social norms surrounding women's roles have changed, particularly in conjunction with the rise of the feminist movement, women have entered the workforce to realize goals and aspirations which differ from those that have traditionally been prescribed for them, such as "wife" and "mother." Second, today's families require two incomes to survive. As Figure 6.4 shows, family incomes in both Canada and the United States (controlling for inflation) have actually remained stagnant since about 1980. In short, many families are "running on a treadmill" to keep up with their expenses. Third, today's husbands have significantly more positive attitudes towards their spouses' employment (Glass, 1988; Scott, Alwin and Braun, 1996).

FIGURE 6.4
Average Incomes of Families in Canada, 1951–1995 (in 1995 dollars) and in the United States, 1967–1993 (in 1993 dollars)

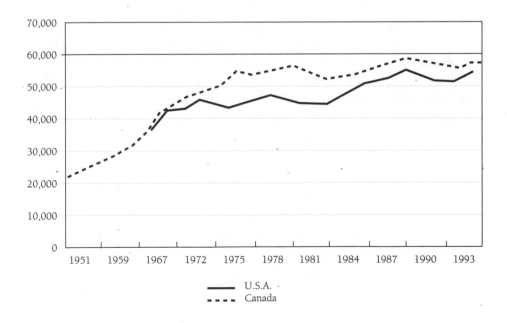

Source: Statistics Canada, *Income Distributions by Size in Canada*, 1995, catalogue no. 13-207-XPB; U.S. Bureau of the Census CD-ROM, *Income and Poverty: 1993*.

BOX 6-3

Clintons To Tackle Child Care Issues

By Mimi Hall

WASHINGTON—As if on cue to illustrate the problem Hillary Rodham Clinton was describing, secretary and single mom Paula Broglio stood up and presented herself to the first lady as a living example of a working woman who can't make it on her own.

On a $25,000 salary and with no child support from her ex-husband, Broglio lives with her 4-year-old son in the guest bedroom of her parents' house so she can afford $200-a-month subsidized child care at a Catholic school while she's at work.

"If I did not have that, and I didn't have my parents, I would probably have to quit my job and go on welfare, because who would watch my child during the day and how could I afford to live in an apartment?" Broglio asked earlier this month at the University of Maryland, where the first lady was speaking about her latest effort to influence public policy.

"That is the problem," Clinton answered. "I could not more vividly describe it."

But Clinton couldn't say how the White House Conference on Child Care, which she and President Clinton will host Thursday, might help the 38-year-old Adelphi, Md., secretary and her little boy, Vincent.

"Your child will be in school before we probably get much of the changes that I would like to see happen," she said.

White House aides are being deliberately vague about what the Clintons have in mind to address the problems of affordability, availability and safety in the nation's child-care industry.

During the 1993-94 health-care debates, they learned that large-scale proposals can bring protest from those who see big government taking over a responsibility that should be left to families and private businesses.

"If you're having a White House conference, I suspect you think there's a government solution," says Gary Bauer of the conservative Family Research Council.

In an interview with USA TODAY on Tuesday, Hillary Clinton wouldn't say what the administration will propose.

"What I'm interested in is putting the spotlight on this issue and using the White House to ... ignite a national conversation," she said.

The goal, she said, is to "call national attention to an issue that political leaders and policymakers should focus on but which has often been ignored."

She wouldn't talk specifics, and her aides said she is not necessarily backing ideas she has mentioned recently: creating a national registry of child-care workers who have been convicted of crimes, for example, or offering protection for caretakers who fear being sued over minor accidents.

In her book *It Takes a Village*, Clinton said child care "is an issue that brings out all of our conflicted feelings about what parenthood should be and about who should care for children when parents are working or otherwise unable to."

Children's issues have been a passion for Clinton since the early 1970s, when she worked as a lawyer at the Children's Defense Fund, a liberal advocacy group. Now she is wading back in to help tackle what the president calls "the next great frontier" in his effort to help working families.

In a recent speech at a Newark church, he ticked off a list of large and small initiatives he already has promoted: a new TV rating system to alert parents about violent or sexual content, a tobacco settlement that aims to stop smoking among children, a $500-per-child tax credit for working families and a balanced federal budget that increases funding for health care for low-income children.

"But we still have to make sure that our parents have access to quality, affordable child care," he said. "That's the great, big hurdle left."

Richard Stolley, president of the Child Care Action Campaign, hopes Thursday's conference can help convince businesses that helping employees find child care helps productivity. "Business needs to be convinced there is a bottom-line benefit," he says.

But the nation's child-care system is in such bad shape, he says, that "we're deluding ourselves if we think this is going to make an enormous difference."

BOX 6-3

The impact of this trend on families has been profound. As we will see later in this chapter, in addition to the treadmill effect, such families must cope with less time to spend with their children and on leisure activities, as well as problems associated with finding, keeping, and being able to afford quality child care arrangements while both parents are at work (See Box 6.3). In addition, as we have pointed out elsewhere in this text, although the participation rates of men and women in the paid work force are becoming equal, women in North America still only earn approximately 70 percent of what men do. This disparity in income worsens the financial situation faced by many families in relation to all kinds of expenses, including child care. In 1991 in the United States for example, about 19 million employed women had children under the age of 15 living with them. These women paid approximately seven percent of their monthly family incomes towards the cost of child care. Poor women, however, paid twenty-seven percent of their incomes towards child care (U.S. Bureau of the Census, 1995).

Another important effect of women's labor force participation is that the North American economic system is highly dependent on women's labor. Again, however, we must be conscious of the fact that while employers rely on women to do paid work, families rely on women (for the most part) to perform unpaid domestic labor. The consequences of this are discussed further later in this chapter.

Summary

The trends described in this section should be kept in mind as you read the rest of this chapter, because they will provide you with a sense of the social and demographic backdrop in which family problems occur. Many of the trends interact in complex ways to create difficulties for families. Once again, this illustrates the ways in which social structural conditions interact with personal lives. Above all, you should understand the importance of social class, economy, inequality, and poverty in shaping family structure, family relationships, and the relative power and situation of family members (Richardson, 1996). Moreover, the preceding sections should sensitize you to the fact that rather than talking about the "demise of the family," it is more useful to think about how families are successfully or unsuccessfully adapting to change. In what follows, we provide an overview of some of the more significant problems families are coping with today.

Family Problems

Work-Family Balance

In Chapter 4, we briefly discussed an emerging field in sociology that links health, family obligations, and the realities of today's workplace. In this section, we provide you with a discussion of an issue that is of increasing importance to North Americans—work-family balance. Also known as "work-life" balance, "work-leisure" balance, or some variant of work and non-work relations, for at least 20 years employers and employees have been examining this issue with varying degrees of interest. One of the most useful and perhaps most important contribution to the field comes from the work of sociologist Rosabeth Moss-Kanter, who first discussed the issue in her path-breaking book *Men and Women of the Corporation*. In her 1989 book, *When Giants Learn to Dance*, she argued that we could no longer afford to think of work and family as unlinked "separate spheres." Moss-Kanter was attempting to alert readers to the fact that while we have traditionally seen the family as something Dad comes home to at the end of a hard day's work, this is merely an image of reality. In fact, it is virtually impossible to separate our work from our non-work activities, primarily because work is so central to our everyday lives (See Chapter 3), that it virtually defines our personalities. In what follows, we want to show why the relationship between work and family has become of so much concern to many people, and what we can do about it.

We have seen that both families and workplaces have transformed dramatically in the past 100 years. Along with shifts in fertility rates, changes in the age composition of the population, and other demographic trends, we have seen that women have entered the paid workforce in large numbers since World War II. This has created a situation in which the majority of families in North America are dual-earner couples. In addition, as Chapter 3 illustrated, there have been profound changes in the structure and nature of work, particularly in the last 20 years.

As we already pointed out, many dual-income couples must work in these arrangements because they require two incomes to survive. However, what is less well known, is that the intersection between work and family responsibilities has created immense pressures and stresses for a great many families (Duxbury et al., 1991; Bolger, DeLongis, Kessler and Wethington, 1989; Frone, Russell and Cooper, 1991; Kanter, 1977; Kirchmeyer, 1992; Staines, 1980; Jackson, Zedeck and Summers, 1985).

Let's illustrate this by way of an example. Think about the "average" day of the typical middle class family of 20 years ago, especially as it might be portrayed in an older television sitcom. The morning would probably consist of mother and father rising and getting ready for the day's work and family responsibilities. The father would gather his work materials, get dressed and showered, and perhaps help mother with readying the children for school. Mother might prepare for her day, which might consist of grocery shopping, cooking, cleaning, mending, driving children to activities or a myriad of other tasks, which make up domestic labor. When father came home around five o'clock, he would, in this idealized world, enjoy a home-cooked meal, engage in conversation with his children and spouse, perhaps help the children with homework, watch a little television, and retire to bed after the news.

Although this is a fictional example, it is nevertheless important because it illustrates that most families, and certainly most organizations, have traditionally structured "the day" between the hours of 9 a.m. and 5 p.m. In addition, notice that the example focuses on the life of a typical middle-class family, an approach we have chosen deliberately because there is so little known about the work-family experiences of working-class and single-parent families. Equally as important are the things that are implied in this scenario. For instance, we might assume that in such a situation, the (usually male) breadwinner would be free to travel on an unlimited basis, relocate at will, or, more typically, work extended hours. The homemaker, on the other hand, would very much be structured by her husband's day. In addition, both parents, but more typically the mother, would be "bounded" by the 9-to-5 day with respect to the services offered by banks, grocery stores, and the like. In other words, if you could not do your shopping or banking between the hours of nine a.m. and five p.m. on a weekday, or on a weekend, you would not get it done at all.

Consider for a moment today's situation for a similar, but dual-income middle-class family. Now, instead of the parents engaging in different activities, both work in the paid labor force. The children may have to get ready for school themselves. A debate starts over who will cook dinner tonight. If any banking or grocery shopping must be done today, someone will have to make time during the lunch hour. Worse, if a child falls ill one parent must stay at home, which means that someone will miss work. If a parent must work overtime, special arrangements must be made by the entire family to deal with that individual's absence. To accommodate the demands of the new workplace, one or both spouses may have to bring work home, which means taking time from family activities such as homework and leisure. At work, both spouses may encounter resentment from co-workers if they "sneak out early" or arrive at work late to deal with family responsibilities. Bosses may tell either partner that "family problems should be left at home where they belong" so as not to interfere with work. Either or both spouses may turn down promotions, or extra responsibilities because they know they cannot afford the time. After a trying day dealing with multiple demands, both parents arrive home tired. They throw something together for dinner. They try valiantly to give their children and each other the time and patience required to sustain good relationships by focusing on "quality time" (See Box 6.1). At the end of the evening, they fall into bed exhausted, hoping the next day will be easier.

The impact of the realities discussed in this chapter does not only apply to the experiences of families. Work itself may, and frequently does, suffer (Glass and Estes, 1997). For example, employees may not be as productive as they could be since they are concerned about the children, or are "stressed out" from the difficulty of balancing work and family obligations. Some workers may not feel that it is important to remain behind at work to finish tasks on various projects. They may also be unwilling to take promotions that would require them to travel, work longer hours, or attend meetings that would interfere with their family life. Finally, as Chapter 4 showed, they may also suffer serious health consequences.

As you can see, the new "facts of working life" faced by many working couples have implications for both employers and employees. More broadly, as Lewis and Lewis (1997) argue, we can no longer take any roles, family or work-related, for granted. For Lewis and Lewis (1997: xiv) the implications are clear:

"The workplace is not isolated from society. People do not leave their problems at home when they cross the threshold at work. If employees are to perform to their maximum potential for the benefit of their employers, then they have to be seen as rounded personalities, not as one dimensional entries on a balance sheet."

As noted earlier in this section, there is a great deal of sociological evidence for the problematic outcomes of work-family conflict. Consider the following data:

➤ In a 1991 survey of 6,000 employees in the Canadian public sector, 32 percent of dual-income mothers reported high work-family conflict (Duxbury, Higgins and Lee, 1991).

➤ According to Lero and Brockman (1993), 27 percent of employed single mothers with children under age 13 experience "severe" work-family tension on a day-to-day basis, compared to 18 percent of employed married mothers.

➤ In a U.S. survey conducted by Rodgers and Associates (1995) for the Dupont company, two-thirds of employees reported difficulty in "getting everything done" for work and family.

> The same survey found that women with a working spouse continued to bear a disproportionate burden for child care and household tasks, spending 103 hours per week (out of a total of 168 hours in a week) on a combination of work, commuting, child care, household, and personal chores.

Duxbury (1992) and her colleagues have shown that work and family conflict is a bi-directional phenomenon. In other words, work can interfere with family life and vice versa. There are two central concepts that allow us to understand the relationship between work and family conflict. The first, **overload**, refers to the problem of having too much to do in a given time. Thus, a person experiencing overload would have difficulty completing the many tasks that might have to be accomplished in a relatively short period of time, which frequently results in tiredness and burnout. The second concept is **role interference**, which refers to a situation in which the social roles played by individuals (such as worker and mother) overlap and conflict (Greenhaus and Beutell, 1985; Kopelman et al. 1983; Jones and Butler, 1980; Duxbury, Higgins, and Lee, 1992). Table 6.2 illustrates the extent to which different types of workers experience overload and interference in their everyday work.

Table 6.2
Percentage of Employees Experiencing Overload and Interference Due to Work-Family Conflict by Type of Worker and Sex, Canada, 1992 (n = 27,000)

	Overload	Work Interferes with Family	Family Interferes with Work
Managers and Professionals			
Males	46	30	22
Females	60	34	15
Non-Management Workers			
Males	33	32	22
Females	51	76	12

Source: Duxbury, Higgins and Lee (1992). Reprinted with permission.

We can see that many individuals experience work-family stress. In addition to the high levels of stress, lowered job commitment, increased absenteeism, and lowered job and life satisfaction experienced by those who have strong work-family conflict, one thing appears very clear—the majority of those experiencing the most negative consequences are women. There are good reasons for the lop-sided effects of work-family conflict on women. The most obvious, of course, is that women are the primary caregivers in our society and, despite some indications that things are changing, still perform most of the domestic labor. Another issue however, stems from the type of work women tend to do. Most women work in service-type jobs that tend to be "routinized," low-paying, "de-skilled," and part-time with little chance of advancement. In effect, they already experience high stress and burnout associated with the demoralizing nature of their work, and are paid less than men and a few other women to endure it. It is not surprising, then, that many experience more difficulty dealing with the stresses of everyday employment and family obligations.

Having considered the more serious implications of work-family conflict, particularly for employers, it may seem strange that more corporations and organizations have not tried to keep pace with today's realities. Indeed, recent studies have shown that with the exception of a few "superstar" companies, the vast majority of corporations seem to be ignoring the issue (Haas and Hwang, 1995; Brannen et al., 1994; Galinsky, Hughes and David, 1990). While some superstar companies are attempting to become more "family friendly," a recent article in *Fortune Magazine* (1997: 73) points out that programs such as flexible work scheduling, job sharing, personal leaves, and even personal valet services

"....relieve some symptoms of the work and family dilemma, (but do not) alleviate the structural problems: the hierarchical and often unforgiving way in which work is organized; the pace of the managerial career path, which requires the highest investment of time just when child rearing is most intense; the emphasis on face time as a measure of dedication and commitment."

In effect, while it may seem "politically correct" to openly discuss the work-family issue in the work environment, the majority of companies seem to view the worker's family as a liability, and remain uncommitted (or pay lip service) to resolving the problems their employees are experiencing. One reason for this is that currently there is a surplus of skilled workers, as Chapter 3 pointed out. Put simply, if employers are not interested in hiring more workers, they will certainly not direct attention to the stresses and difficulties faced by their employees, particularly if they feel that doing so will cost them money. As well, many corporate managers assume that employees experiencing difficulties with the dual demands of career and family are simply incapable of "managing their time properly," thus placing the blame on the individual and not the structure in which work relations occur. Indeed, if an employee cannot properly juggle competing demands, there are bound to be people on the unemployment line who can.

As Gonyea and Googins (1997) point out, particularly in the United States, employers understand that much of what they do for employees is part of a "corporate welfare system" that tends to focus on the well-being of the individual rather than the structure of organizations. Accordingly, they are much more inclined to offer programs and company benefits aimed at improving an individual employee's life (such as flexible work arrangements) rather than changing the very nature of the workplace itself.

Finally, work-family balance has always been seen as a "woman's issue." While it is true that work-family conflict disproportionately affects women, the fact that family care is still viewed as a "woman's role" often prevents the issue of work and family conflict from being viewed as an issue for working parents of both genders. Moreover, if work-family conflict continues to be seen as a "women's issue" there is a danger that because women use family friendly policies (such as special leave or flexible work arrangements) they will be viewed as "on the mommy track," or not as committed as colleagues who do not use such benefits.

Ultimately, these assumptions illustrate the need for employers to maximize profits at all costs, and the view that employees are not people with lives but merely "factors of production." But it is also an illustration of the extent to which traditional assumptions about the separation of work and personal life remain deeply embedded in the minds of employers and even employees (Lewis, 1997). Moreover, it is difficult enough to change an individual, let alone the entire organizational culture we have come to take for granted in North America.

Another important reason that employers seem to be ignoring the new realities stems from a trend discussed extensively in Chapter 3, namely, technological development and the globalization of work and markets. As technology has eliminated the need for many jobs (mostly of a routine nature), it has also blurred the boundaries between work and non-work time. Increasingly, employees are able to choose where and when they may work, although the extent to which alternative work arrangements such as "telework" (or working from afar using computers, e-mail, and fax technology) actually benefit the employee and his or her family, is a matter of debate (Alvi and DeKeseredy, 1996).

Finally, we must consider the fact that many employees fear losing their jobs and are therefore reluctant to complain about working conditions and demands. The prospect of unemployment means that many are often reluctant to take advantage of benefit programs offering more flexibility in work arrangements for fear of appearing uncommitted or "ungrateful" to the organization.

Clearly, employers and, to some extent, employees must face the new facts about work and family conflict. In the concluding section of this chapter, we offer some suggestions as to what can be done about this issue.

Family Violence[4]

A substantial number of North Americans watch popular television shows such as *NYPD Blue, New York Undercover, Cops,* and *America's Most Wanted.* As Taylor (1983: 92) correctly points out:

"Day in and day out, these programs portray an image of urban life in North America as a dangerous human jungle, where the prospect of criminal assault and homicide is almost random and immediate. Human life is seen to be threatened, in particular, by the presence (especially "on the street" but also in everyday business and personal relationships) of psychopathic individuals intent on murder and general mayhem."

If the North American media are instrumental in shaping people's fear of "stranger danger" on our streets (Sacco and Kennedy, 1994), the same can be said about some crime prevention literature, such as the Solicitor General of Canada's crime prevention booklet *Woman Alone* (1990). The authors of this booklet suggest that women take several self-help precautionary measures. Some examples of these actions follow:

➤ Never remain alone in an apartment laundry room, mailroom, or parking garage.

➤ Do not put your first name on your mailbox or in the telephone book.

➤ Try to avoid isolated bus stops.

➤ Do not overburden yourself with packages and a bulky purse.

Such advice influences many people, especially women, to alter their daily lifestyles and routines by staying indoors, changing their style of dress, or revising their route to and from work (DeKeseredy et al., 1992). These strategies, unfortunately, only increase rather than reduce fear of crime (Walklate, 1989). Furthermore, these measures do little, if anything, to deter those who are most likely to physically harm us—family members (Stanko, 1995).

While public places are typically portrayed by the media, criminal justice officials, and some government agencies as "hot spots" of violent behavior, the family is, on the other hand, characterized as a peaceful, loving group of people. In other words, family members are characterized as altruistic, caring individuals who provide us with various types of social support (e.g., affection, shelter, education), and who protect us from physical, psychological, and economic threats posed by the street, workplace, school, etc. This notion is supported by conservative criminologists such as Felson, who argues that "time spent in the family and household settings is less risky than time spent away from those settings" (1994: 39).

This section on the "dark side" of family life challenges arguments such as Felson's. For many North Americans, especially women and children, the family is not the "most nurturing" and loving of all social groups (Miller, 1990; Sacco and Kennedy, 1994). As Gelles and Straus point out in their commentary on fear of violent street crime, "You are more likely to be physically assaulted, beaten, and killed in your own home at the hands of a loved one than anyplace else, or by anyone else in society" (1988: 18).

In the discussion that follows, we describe the sociological patterns of several salient examples of "not the way to love" (Fitzpatrick and Halliday, 1992), such as child abuse, sibling violence, and elder abuse. Since violence against female marital/cohabiting partners was addressed in Chapter 5, sociological research on this social problem is not reproduced here. Nevertheless, we will briefly discuss female-to-male violence in marital/cohabiting relationships, because it is currently the subject of much debate among researchers, women's groups, journalists, policy makers, and the general public. Before we do, however, it is first necessary to define family violence.

What Is Family Violence?

For some people, the answer to this question is simple: an intentional physical act such as a punch, kick, or bite that causes physical pain and suffering, or even death, committed by a family member. For example, the popular magazine *Sports Illustrated*, in the midst of a media frenzy over controversial U.S. Olympic figure skater Tonya Harding, stated that although she had divorced her husband and obtained restraining orders against him, there was little "hard evidence" that she was abused because she did not have "broken bones or black eyes" (Swift, 1994: 90). Many people still share this definition of violence because they believe that if a person does not require stitches, that individual is not hurt.[5]

Many researchers, clinicians, and shelter workers reject the above and similar narrow definitions because they exclude a wide range of behaviors that many family members regard as equally, if not more, injurious. Based on their readings of feminist qualitative studies (e.g., Kelly, 1988; Stanko, 1990), and conversations with victims/survivors, offenders, and a host of others, a growing number of social scientists now recognize that family violence is "multidimensional in nature" (DeKeseredy and Hinch, 1991). In other words, the lives of many North American children, adult women, and elderly persons exist upon what Stanko (1990) refers to as a "continuum of unsafety" that includes a broad range of emotionally and physically threatening behaviors.

The "continuum" ranges from non-physical acts such as insults, to acts such as beatings and rapes.[6] Although the idea of a continuum is often used to portray moving from the least serious to the most serious, family violence researchers who employ this concept regard all of these behaviors as serious. None is automatically considered more injurious than another, and they recommend that researchers, criminal justice officials, social workers, and others not create a hierarchy of abuse or violence.

There are valid reasons for using broad definitions. For example, Kirkwood (1993), found that some of her female respondents who experienced abuse in their marital relationships were drawn into a web of long-term terror through a barrage of psychologically injurious events that many North Americans are likely to term minor, and in some cases of severe psychological abuse, survivors were never physically harmed. Kirkwood also found that emotional abuse generates fear, destroys women's self-esteem, creates intense isolation, and in extreme cases, immobilizes women and makes them unable to function. Additional support for broadening the definition of violence is provided by Walker (1979), who found that most of her female respondents described incidents of psychological humiliation and verbal harassment as their worst abusive experiences, regardless of whether they were physically attacked. So did one of Kirkwood's (1993: 44) respondents:

"I used to say I found verbal abuse much worse than the physical abuse. Even though the physical abuse was terrible. Because I suppose it was only—only!? God—once, twice a year. It was the constant verbal barracking that used to get me down more than anything. Cause that's how you lose your self-esteem. But the violence is awful, the violence is terrible. I think you've got to take that, though, as part of it. If you're constantly being told you are a useless jerk, to be thumped out just...compounds it."

In sum, restricting definitions of violence to physical assaults does not reflect the brutal reality of many North American family members' lives, and it sets up a hierarchy which insists that physical harm is worse than psychological harm (Breines and Gordon, 1993; DeKeseredy and MacLean, 1990; DeKeseredy and MacLeod, 1997). While it is important to recognize the multifaceted nature of family violence in North America, due in part to space limitations and in part to the shortage of sociological empirical and theoretical work on other acts that can be considered violent or abusive, we focus here on non-lethal physical assaults (i.e., behaviors that do not result in death).

This is not to say that homicide in family settings is a trivial issue. However, since this topic was addressed in Chapter 5, it is not discussed at length here. It should be noted in passing, however, that many wives and cohabiting partners who were killed by their spouses also endured extreme forms of non-lethal physical, sexual, and psychological abuse. Again, as pointed out in Box 6.4,[7] North American family violence is multidimensional in nature.

BOX 6-4

Ann's Story

What I am about to tell you is the truth as I know it. Some things are my observations, but most was written down by Ann the week preceding her death. To protect my grandchildren and family, I am using the name "Ann" in place of my daughter's real name and I ask that my name not be made public.

On March 15, 1988, Ann was murdered by her husband during an arranged meeting while she was residing in a shelter for women. She was shot twice in the head.

In her early twenties, Ann met the man she was to marry. He was very attentive, bringing her gifts constantly, giving her cars and jewelry, and showering her with attention. She fell in love. In the summer of 1983 they decided to live together and moved out west. As soon as they crossed the Ontario border, the beatings began. In the months that followed, he totally isolated her from me. Ann was pregnant at the time.

In her writings, Ann tells of being beaten about the head, with chunks of flesh being torn from her chin. She tells of screaming for help and no one coming to her aid. She also tells of the deep embarrassment she suffered when forced to go out after such a beating. Ann tells of being beaten to unconsciousness, of being boxed about the ears until one went deaf, of being pummeled on her pregnant abdomen. She wrote of long rides in the country where he would leave her stranded on some country road for hours and she dared not move. She tells of a booby-trapped house where she couldn't use the phone or open the doors when he was away, of not even being allowed to go to the bathroom by herself, and of the degradation she felt at such times.

She writes of the pain of being forced to disown her mother, and his telling her that if she tried to leave he would have her family killed; and she believed this. She had good reason to believe him. She told of one incident when he took her into the basement and sat her on a stool. He then placed a loaded gun in her mouth. He fixed up a string with one end tied to her toe, and tied her up in such a way that if she moved, she would blow her head off. This tortuous incident lasted for two days, during which he sat on the basement stairs, taunted her, insulted and humiliated her, and laughed at her. She tells of having severe rope burns after this.

In the spring of 1984, they married and she became pregnant again. She told me he repeatedly raped her until she became pregnant. These were particularly brutal rapes. In the spring of 1985, they moved back to his hometown in Ontario. The beatings had stopped and now the mental abuse came in full force. Ann tells of her feelings like this: "The physical abuse was over and the scars had healed some, but the mental abuse will be with me forever." She tells of how he made her feel like dirt and those feelings were still with her when she died.

She was told repeatedly how dumb, stupid, brainless she was and she began to believe it. Ann contemplated suicide on many occasions, but the thought of what would happen to her children always stopped her. Inside, she was a mess.

In the summer of 1986, he allowed her to contact me again, and so I went to see her. When I saw her I cried; she looked awful—thin, pale, with large circles under her eyes and tremors. She explained these symptoms away as P.M.S. I knew differently, but was also a hostage of fear—fear of what he might do to her next, fear that any form of confrontation would surely mean she would be isolated from us again.

The mental abuse continued to her and the children. He forced them to watch horror movies and told them as they watched "This is what I am going to do to you if you don't behave." She writes of his constant criticisms of other people, his hatred of women, the deep depressions, never knowing what she'd have to listen to over and over again, the fear in her children's eyes from living in a no-win situation.

We began to have weekly contact by phone. Her main concerns were for her children, who were constantly sick and would fall asleep for a few minutes only to wake screaming from nightmares. One child had ground his teeth down to nubs. She never spoke of her husband or very little. Then one night she phoned and asked to come home.

I could not believe my eyes when she walked in my door. She looked terrible and so very old and beaten. She was shaking like a leaf and I feared she would collapse. I held her as if she was my baby again. I had seen her fear before, in my work at the hospital, from women who had been abused—one whose husband had sodomized her with a knife, and one who was beaten so badly that only the palms of her hands were not bruised. But the fear I saw in my daughter's eyes far outweighed either of these. She was terrified. She feared for her safety and ours, once he learned she had left. We decided she should go to a shelter for abused women.

When we arrived at the shelter, there was no room and Ann's fear and trembling were intense. The staff working there seeing this quickly made room for her and the children. I do not know what he did to her in their bed or bedroom, but for the short month she had left to live, Ann slept on the living room floor of the shelter because she could not go near a bed—the fear and horror were too great.

During the month she was at the shelter, Ann made great strides; her pride of appearance came back and she looked and acted like she could look the world in

BOX 6-4

the face again. The fears and self-doubt were still there, but she could think and act coherently and for this I thank the staff at the shelter.

During that month at the shelter, she disclosed many of the details of her life with this man. The violence and degradation she experienced were as bad as any prisoner-of-war accounts ever heard. She began to talk of the life she had lived, and also of the life she had planned for herself and her sons—a good life, a healthy life, a life free of abuse.

She made many decisions during that month. She also experienced something she hadn't had in many years: a place where she could talk openly, where she shared friendships and a bond with other women, where she even laughed, and where she was able to make plans for her future.

Ann had clearly decided to leave her husband. Her mind was made up and she had taken steps to secure housing and was putting furniture together, making plans for her sons' schooling, and taking legal action to finalize the separation. While determined about there being no possibility of reconciliation, Ann wanted to meet with her husband to finalize details of the separation. She wanted to help him understand why she was leaving him and what those years of abuse had done to her. She felt it was important that he understand these issues; and she had written him a lengthy letter outlining all of these things to him. She also did not want to refuse his requests to visit their sons, as long as the visits were supervised and controlled.

At his fourth and last visit to Ann, he was finally convinced that she was leaving him and that he no longer had power or control over her. She was determined, brave, courageous, and clear-headed when she faced him that day. He shot her twice, at very close range. She died shortly after being shot, despite extensive medical attempts to save her life.

He was charged with first-degree murder, but it was plea bargained down to second-degree and he received a life sentence, with 14 years before full parole. Fourteen years for one life and the tearing apart of many others. My grandchildren will never know the loving person who was their mother or her love.

This man owned his own business and never drank or used drugs, as far as I know.

Source: Crawford and Gartner (1992: 131–135). Reprinted with permission of the Ontario Women's Directorate.

Obviously, not all abused women end up like Ann. Some carefully plan their escape and eventually lead "normal lives" (Ellis and DeKeseredy, 1997). Others, after their first abusive experience or after many beatings, rapes, and the like, erupt in anger at what has been done to them. For example, one woman told Walter DeKeseredy and Martin Schwartz (1996: 326) the following:

"After 15 years of physical and mental abuse, I turned into 'Lorena Bobbitt.' I had cajoled and done everything I could over the years to help my husband's weak self-esteem and finally one night I snapped. I grabbed my 6-foot, 200-pound husband, flung him on the floor (all 5 foot, 95 pounds of me). He was so shocked, he laid there and took it. It was a great triumph for my self-esteem and the realization that my husband was the one with the problem, not me. Empowered, I divorced him quickly before I changed my mind, and left Youngstown to be with my family where I could get support."

Are women like the one interviewed by DeKeseredy and Schwartz just as violent as men? Does her behavior constitute "husband abuse" or "mutual combat?" In our current political atmosphere Susan Faludi (1991) terms the "backlash," there is an enormous audience for people who contend the violence in marital or common-law relationships is sexually symmetrical. It is to this issue that we now turn.

"But Women Do It Too": Female-to-Male Violence in Intimate Relationships

The following comes from John Fekete (1994: 88), one of several conservative scholars who has no background or expertise in the area of family violence, has never conducted a woman abuse survey, and prior to the publication of his book *Moral Panic: Biopolitics Rising*, had never revealed any sophisticated knowledge of intimate violence:[8]

"[W]omen in relationships with men commit comparatively as many or more acts of physical violence as men do, at every level of severity. It is not a case of friendly slap against vicious beating. It is slap for slap, beating for beating, knifing and shooting for knifing and shooting, on the evidence of women's own self-reports."

There has never been any question that women strike men, sometimes with the intent to injure. That there are battered husbands should not be a subject for disagreement (DeKeseredy and MacLean, 1997; Pagelow, 1985; Schwartz, 1988). The main points of contention are whether women primarily use violence as a means of self-defense, and whether the presence of male victims mitigates or changes the meaning of the fact that women are overwhelmingly the predominant victims of marital violence (Schwartz and DeKeseredy, 1993).

Several studies show that female violence in adult, heterosexual relationships, even with the intent to injure, is used in self-defense (DeKeseredy et al., 1997; Saunders, 1986, 1988). On the other hand, some scholars have attempted to challenge the validity of this research by providing data which they claim demonstrate that marital violence is a "two-way street," and that many men experience "husband abuse" (e.g., McNeely and Robinson-Simpson, 1987; Sommer, 1997; Steinmetz, 1977-78; Stets and Straus, 1990). In 1989, Murray Straus tried to resolve this debate by presenting findings from a 1985 National Family Violence Resurvey conducted in the United States. Based on his analysis of Conflict Tactics Scale (CTS) self-report data obtained from husbands and wives (see Chapter 5 for a description of the CTS), Straus (1989: 9) contends that

"Regardless of whether the analysis is based on all assaults or is focused on dangerous assaults, about as many women as men, according to their own report, attack a spouse who does not hit back. This casts doubt on the "self-defense" explanation of the high rate of assault by women."

Do Straus' data negate the self-defense argument? For many scholars, including the authors of this text, the answer is no, because Straus' data were gleaned only from the CTS. The CTS alone cannot accurately determine gender variations in intimate violence because

➤ males are more likely to underreport their violence (Browning and Dutton, 1996; Edleson and Brygger, 1996; Ellis, 1995; Jouriles and O'Leary, 1985);

➤ it only measures **conflict-instigated** violence and thus ignores male assaults that "come out of the blue" and the fact that men are far more likely than women to use **control-instigated** violence (Browne, 1987; DeKeseredy et al., 1997; Ellis, 1995);

➤ it excludes acts of sexual violence and other highly injurious assaults on women, such as scratches, burning, suffocation, etc. (Smith, 1986); and

➤ it ignores the contexts, meanings, and motives of violence (e.g., the CTS does not measure self-defense) (Breines and Gordon, 1983; DeKeseredy et al., 1997; Dobash et al., 1992).

It should be noted in passing that there is now a new rendition of the CTS—the CTS2. Developed by Straus et al. (1995), the CTS2 addresses some of these and other criticisms of the CTS. For example, it includes more physical and psychological abuse items (e.g., "I called my partner fat or ugly"), and it measures seven types of sexual assault. Also included in the CTS2 are several injury or outcome measures, such as "I needed to see a doctor because of a fight with my partner." These are positive revisions; even so, like the CTS, the CTS2 only situates abuse in the context of settling disputes or conflicts (see the CTS and CTS2 preamble) and thus excludes many types of control-instigated abuse and physical and psychological assaults used in self-defense (DeKeseredy and Schwartz, 1998b).

In fairness to Straus (1989), after presenting what we regard as a flawed interpretation of his CTS data, he admits that his female respondents may have acted in self-defense (1989: 9). Following this statement, he presents data elicited from what he views as a "more direct" measure of self-defense in marital relationships. Participants were asked, "Let's talk about the last time you and your partner got into a physical fight...In that particular instance, who started the physical conflict, you or your partner?" (1989: 9). Of the 428 women who answered this question, 52.7 percent said they hit first. Straus concludes that "These assaults do not support the hypothesis that assaults by women on their partners primarily are acts of self-defense or retaliation" (1989: 11).

Some researchers, including Walter DeKeseredy (DeKeseredy, 1992), contend that these data do not cast doubt on the self-defense explanation, for the following reasons. First, consistent with the CTS, Straus' initiation measure does not measure the contexts, meanings, and motives of wife-to-husband violence. Schwartz and

DeKeseredy (1993), argue that if Straus had asked women about their reasons for initiating attacks, he probably would have found that many women hit first because of a "well-founded fear" of being beaten or raped by their husbands (Hanmer and Saunders, 1984; Saunders, 1989). Male physical and sexual assaults are often preceded by name-calling and other types of psychological abuse (Browne, 1987). Hence, these early warning signs may have prompted many women to hit first in order to deter their partners from hitting them (Saunders, 1989). Thus, most assaults initiated by women may actually be acts of self-defense (DeKeseredy et al., 1987; Walker, 1984).

Second, some respondents may have thought that the initiation measure asked who started the argument rather than who hit first (Saunders, 1989; Stets and Straus, 1990). Third, Straus' measure characterizes marital violence as mutual combat (e.g., "Let's talk about the last time you and your partner got into a physical fight...") (Saunders, 1989). Hence, it may obscure the fact that most violence in spousal relationships involves men beating or raping their partners (Okun, 1986; Dobash et al., 1992).

In sum, both of Straus' arguments are considered by several critics to be incorrect because they are based on data elicited from problematic measures. As pointed out in Box 6.5, however, the problems with Straus' research can be avoided by including two identical sets of questions about motives, meanings, and contexts in different sections of the CTS and CTS2.

Summary

Certainly, some women "do it too," and female-to-male violence must be dealt with before North America can be considered violence-free. Nevertheless, the above critique of Straus' (1989) research and the data summarized in Box 6.4 challenge the common and erroneous assertion made by Fekete (1994) and other "people without data" that violence in intimate, heterosexual relationships is sexually symmetrical—that women and men are equally violent. Intimate homicide data, some of which were presented in Chapter 5, also challenge the sexual symmetry perspective. For example, research reviewed by Dobash et al. (1992: 81) shows that:

"Men often kill wives after lengthy periods of prolonged physical violence accompanied by other forms of abuse and coercion; the roles in such cases are seldom if ever reversed. Men perpetrate familicidal massacres, killing spouse and children together; women do not. Men commonly hunt down and kill wives who have left them; women hardly ever behave similarly. Men kill wives as part of planned murder suicides; analogous acts by women are almost unheard of. Men kill in response to revelations of wife infidelity; women almost never respond similarly, though their mates are often more adulterous."

Unfortunately, as we rapidly approach the end of this century with a wealth of data that clearly demonstrate women to be the primary victims or survivors of violence in dating and marital/cohabiting relationships, many people are still involved in a battle over the nature of women's behavior and its role in woman abuse (DeKeseredy and MacLean, 1998; Schwartz and DeKeseredy, 1993). The

BOX 6-5

Women's Use of Violence in Canadian University/College Dating Relationships: the Results of a National Representative Sample Survey

Why do women use violence in post-secondary school courtship? To answer this important question, Walter DeKeseredy, Daniel Saunders, Martin Schwartz, and Shahid Alvi analyzed the responses to the following three questions developed by Saunders (1986) that followed the first three and the last six violence items in the Conflict Tactics Scale used by DeKeseredy and Kelly (1993a) to measure the prevalence of violence in Canadian university/college dating.

On items...what percentage of these times overall do you estimate that in doing these actions you were primarily motivated by acting in self-defense, that is protecting yourself from immediate physical harm?

On items...what percentage of these times overall do you estimate that in doing these actions you were trying to fight back in a situation where you were not the first to use these or similar tactics?

On items...what percentage of these times overall do you estimate that you used these actions on your dating partners before they actually attacked you or threatened to attack you?

DeKeseredy and colleagues (1997) did not find support for the sexual symmetry thesis. Rather, their data show the following.

Only a small number of women initiated a physical assault since leaving high school. For example, 37 percent of the women who used "minor" forms of violence initiated an attack at some time, and 43 percent initiated "severe" violent acts at least once. Even so, only 7 percent of the women who used "minor" violence 100 percent of the time attacked first, while only 10 percent of those who used "severe" violence were always the ones who initiated an attack.

A large amount of the total violence reported by women was in self-defense; however a majority of women did not report using "minor" (61 percent) or "severe" acts (56.5 percent) of violence in self-defense. Although not the case for most acts, many women's violent acts are either self-defensive or "fighting back." Furthermore, within each level of violence severity, self-defense and "fighting back" were positively and significantly correlated with each other.

Among those women who used violence at all, the ones who report higher levels of self-defensive violence also report higher levels of violence committed against them. For example, about 50 percent of the women who were physically assaulted by their male dating partners since leaving high school reported that their own violence was in self-defense. But, when those women who claimed that 100 percent of their violence was in self-defense were questioned further, higher rates of victimization emerged. About 75 percent had been threatened, and over 85 percent had been pushed, grabbed, or shoved. Also, over 50 percent of the women who used "severe" violence to defend themselves had been choked and kicked, or hit with a fist. About one quarter of these women had been threatened with a weapon.

Women using self-defense violence experienced much higher rates of sexual abuse than other women in the survey. Also, the women who report that their violence was always in self-defense were about twice as likely to be upset because their partners tried to get them to engage in behavior they had seen in pornographic media.

Women who experienced psychological abuse, threats, and physical abuse in combination since leaving high school were much more likely to respond with self-defensive violence (about 80 percent, compared with 36-42 percent of all other victimized women).

These and other findings uncovered by DeKeseredy et al. (1997) are consistent with data from Saunders' (1986) sample of battered women, and it is hoped that they will help resolve the controversy surrounding the issue of whether dating violence is "mutual combat."

How often have you heard of women doing what Ann's husband did to her (see Box 6.4) and what Sylvie Boucher's estranged husband did to her (see Box 6.6[9])? Other data worth noting are the following.[10]

90–95 percent of the requests for police assistance in domestic violence are from or on behalf of women.

Women are much more likely to be injured than are men in disputes or conflicts involving violence.

Even when both men and women are injured, women's injuries are about three times as severe as men's.

Hospital data show women to be overwhelmingly the injured parties in domestic assaults.

Source: Includes modified sections from DeKeseredy and Schwartz (1998a) and DeKeseredy et al. (1997).

BOX 6-5

BOX 6-6

Sylvie Boucher's Violent Death

Former Gatineau, Quebec resident Sylvie Boucher felt that she and her husband Ron Fleury were growing apart. So, on Saturday, November 2, 1996, she moved in with her parents and left her 12-year-old son Francis with Ron. Ron was, to say the least, deeply distressed by the separation. He kept phoning Sylvie and threatened to quit his job and lock himself in the house for the rest of his life if she didn't come back.

On Friday, November 8, Sylvie took time off work so that she could spend the day with Francis, whom she had not seen for an entire week. She arrived at her former house at 8:30 a.m. Shortly after she arrived, Ron's neighbors said that they heard a heated argument and gunshots. That fatal morning, Ron did much more than argue and try to get Sylvie to move back in with him. He killed her and Francis. After doing so, he called the police and said, "I have shot my son and my wife and I'm going to kill myself." By the time the police arrived, he was dead (Campbell and Mercer, 1996).

After reading about this terrifying incident in the *Ottawa Citizen*, all I could say was, "Not again!"

Source: DeKeseredy (1997a: 563). Copyright © 1997 by Sage Publications, Inc. Reprinted by permission of Sage Publications.

anti-feminist crusade briefly addressed in this chapter and elsewhere (Renzetti, 1994; Sanday, 1996; Stanko, 1995), is not likely to stop soon. Nevertheless, as Stanko (1995: 167) correctly points out, "The retort—some men experience violence at the hands of their partners—is not sufficient to diminish the lessons learned about women's experiences of domestic violence."

Spare the Rod and Spoil the Child: Child Abuse

"Sometimes, if they're bad, I slap and spank my children. Am I abusive?" We think so; however, as pointed out in the previous chapter (see Box 5.2), many North Americans strongly disagree with us. In fact, there is little consensus on the meaning of physical child abuse. For example, some people contend that any form of physical punishment is abuse, while others assert that physical punishment should be regarded as abuse only if it harms or threatens a child's physical or mental health.[11] What do you think? How would you define each of the three situations described in Box 6.7?

Based on our own personal and research experiences, as well as a careful reading of the extant sociological literature on child abuse, we suspect that most readers probably view the first two vignettes described by Barnett et al. (1997) as abusive, while the latter is probably considered to be "appropriate" or "normal"

BOX 6-7

Child Abuse or Normal Discipline?

Three-year-old Jimmy was playing with his puppy near a pond in his backyard. He tried to make his puppy drink from the pond by roughly holding his face to the water. Jimmy's father saw him forcing the puppy to drink and yelled at him to stop. After Jimmy did not respond, his father pulled Jimmy away from the dog and began holding his head under water to "teach him a lesson" about the appropriate way to treat his dog.

Angela's baby, Maria, had colic from the day she was born. This meant that from 4:00 in the afternoon until 8:00 p.m., everyday, Maria would cry inconsolably. No matter what Angela did, nothing would help Maria to stop crying. One evening, after Maria had been crying for three straight hours, Angela began shaking Maria out of frustration. The shaking caused Maria to cry more loudly, which, in turn, caused Angela to shake the 5-month-old more vigorously. Angela shook Maria until she lost consciousness.

Ryan and his brother Matthew were playing with their Power Rangers when they got into a disagreement. Both boys began hitting each other and calling one another names. Alice, the mother of the boys, came running into the room and pulled the boys apart. She then took each boy, pulled down his trousers, put him over her knee, and spanked him several times.

Source: Barnett et al. (1997: 42-43). Reprinted by permission of Sage Publications, Inc.

discipline. For example, Murray Straus (1991), one of the world's leading experts on child abuse, found that a very large number of Americans see nothing wrong with what the mother of Ryan and Matthew (see Box 6.7) did to them. But doesn't spanking cause pain, and aren't people who spank children condoning the use of violence to resolve conflicts or to "get one's way" (Barnett et al., 1997)? Isn't spanking strongly associated with other forms of family violence, such as wife abuse and sibling violence? Although several studies show that the answer to these questions is "yes" (Straus, 1991, 1994; Straus et al., 1981), many people refuse to view spanking as deviant behavior. Why should they? After all, many American states exclude corporal punishment from child abuse laws (Barnett et al., 1997).

It is beyond the scope of this text to resolve debates surrounding spanking and other violent means of disciplining children. Perhaps they will never be resolved. For the purpose of this chapter, however, we define physical child abuse as any type of intentional parent-to-child violence—because almost all violent behaviors result in some degree of pain and suffering (DeKeseredy, 1996a). We leave it up to you to discuss and debate this definition in class, with your friends and co-workers, and with your relatives.

What is the extent of physical child abuse in North America? In the United States, the most accurate answers to this question are provided by two national family violence surveys that used renditions of the CTS to measure parent-to-child violence. Conducted in 1975 by Straus et al. (1981), the first survey produced the following data elicited from a random sample of parents:[12]

➤ Three percent of the parents interviewed stated that they kicked, bit, or punched their referent child in 1975, and approximately eight percent of the respondents reported having committed these acts at least once while their child was growing up.

➤ Slightly more than 10 parents in 1,000 reported having beaten their child at least once a year, and slightly more than 40 in 1,000 said they had ever beaten their child.

➤ Approximately 30 children in 1,000 were threatened with a weapon while growing up, while roughly 1 in 1,000 had a parent who shot or stabbed, or tried to shoot or stab, the child.

➤ Responses to the "child abuse index" (e.g., violent acts that could result in an injury) show that 3.6 percent of the parents surveyed reported an abusive act of violence (Gelles and Straus, 1988; Straus et al., 1981).

Administered in 1985, Straus and Gelles' (1986) National Family Violence Resurvey generated the following self-report data:

➤ Approximately 75 percent of the parents in their sample reported at least one violent act.

➤ About two percent of parents engaged in one act of abusive violence (e.g., a high probability of injuring a child).

➤ Nearly 1.5 million children are seriously injured each year.[13]

➤ Each year, 6.9 million children are "abused" (includes being hit with an object).

Are Canadian parents "kinder and gentler?" Not according to data generated by MacMillan et al.'s (1997) representative sample survey of 9,953 Ontario residents aged 15 years and older. These researchers found that 31.2 percent of the males, and 21.1 percent of the females in their sample reported physical abuse while growing up. They also found that 10.7 percent of the males, and 9.2 percent of the females reported having been severely physically abused while growing up.[14] Chances are these rates would be much higher if MacMillan et al. had asked questions about spanking and slapping. Nevertheless, these findings are similar to prevalence rates reported in many other countries using similar definitions of child abuse (Cole, 1997). Still, it is difficult to clearly determine whether Canadian parents are more or less violent than their U.S. counterparts because different measures, samples, and time periods were used in the above North American surveys.

According to Straus et al. (1981), physical punishment and growing up in a household where parents physically assault each other trains people to abuse their children. However, people also learn to hit, beat, etc. their children from external influential sources, such as the media, peer groups, and jobs involving violence (e.g., the military) (DeKeseredy, 1996a; Thorne-Finch, 1992). Siblings may also teach people to be violent. As stated on the cover of the May/June, 1994 issue of the *Utne Reader*, "Don't blame your parents! Your brothers and sisters made you who you are." It is to the problem of sibling violence that we turn next.

"A Normal Part Of Growing Up": Sibling Violence[15]

The rapidly growing amount of media, public, and professional attention given to both wife and child abuse has led many North Americans to believe that violence against wives and children is the most common form of family violence (Barnett et al., 1997; DeKeseredy, 1996a). However, U.S. national survey data show that sibling violence occurs much more frequently than husband-to-wife assaults and parent-to-child violence. In fact, sibling violence is the most common and most overlooked form of family violence in the United States (Gelles and Straus, 1988), and according to Straus and Gelles (1996), children are the most violent members of all American families. Does the following incident sound familiar to you?

"I can't remember a time when my brother didn't taunt me, usually trying to get me to respond so he would be justified in hitting me. Usually he would be saying I was a crybaby or a sissy or stupid or ugly and that no one would like me, want to be around me, or whatever. Sometimes he would accuse me of doing something, and if I denied it, he would call me a liar. I usually felt overwhelmingly helpless because nothing I said or did would stop him. If no one else was around, he would start beating on me, after which he would stop and go away" (cited in Barnett et al., 1997: 50).

If sibling violence is so common, why has it received widespread "selective inattention" (Dexter, 1958)? Before we answer this important question, it is first necessary to define sibling violence.

Sibling violence, like the other types of family violence, is multidimensional in nature. In other words, it includes a wide range of highly injurious physical, sexual, and psychological behaviors (Wallace, 1996). While it is important to recognize that many siblings experience many different types of abusive behaviors, only non-lethal physical assaults are discussed here, since most of the research has focused on these behaviors.[16] Thus, for the purpose of this chapter, sibling violence is defined as any form of intentional physical violence inflicted by one child in a family unit on another.[17] It should be noted in passing that children do not have to be related by birth in order for their physically injurious acts to be considered violent. There are many cases where children from different marriages or cohabiting relationships end up in the same household and physically hurt each other (Wallace, 1996). Sibling violence is overlooked in North America for the following reasons outlined by Gelles and Cornell (195: 85):

- Siblings hitting one another is so common that few people regard these behaviors as violent or deviant.

- Most parents consider conflict among siblings an inevitable part of growing up and rarely discourage their children from engaging in violent behavior with siblings. In fact, most parents typically try to ignore violent interactions and only intervene when "minor" situations are perceived as escalating into major conflicts.

➤ Sibling rivalry is defined as a "normal" part of sibling relations, and many parents believe that such rivalry provides a good training ground for the successful management of aggressive behavior in the real world.

➤ Social norms encourage expressions of aggressive behavior among siblings and thus hinder the recognition of sibling violence as deviant and worthy of serious concern.

Some U.S. researchers have also contributed to the belief that sibling violence is acceptable behavior. Consider Bank and Kahn (1982), who contend that there are five "positive" aspects of sibling aggression:

1. Aggression can be reassuring when parents are emotionally or physically unavailable.

2. It forces children into a social "laboratory" where they can learn how to manage and resolve disputes, and aggression fosters the development of competence, morality, courage, and creativity.

3. Sibling aggression teaches children skills that can be used in other relationships, such as the ability to deflect aggression and to defeat another without humiliation.

4. Sibling aggression promotes feelings of loyalty.

5. Sibling aggression enables children to "displace" their aggression to a more appropriate target.

To the best of our knowledge, no one has been able to provide empirical support for Bank and Kahn's (1982) arguments. While they and many other people regard sibling violence as inevitable and acceptable, it is not a trivial issue, especially when you consider that the U.S. News and World Report (1979) found that 138,000 American children aged 3 to 17 used a weapon on a sibling over a one-year period.

Several other U.S. studies show that sibling violence is a major social problem. For example, data derived from Straus et al.'s (1981) national representative sample of parents who had two or more children at home between the ages of 3 and 17 show that 83 percent of their survey participants stated that at least one incident of sibling violence occurred during the year before the study. In addition, consider the following facts:

➤ Seventy-two percent of Steinmetz's (1977) undergraduate student respondents reported experiencing sibling violence.

➤ Between 63 and 68 percent of the adolescent siblings in Steinmetz's (1982) sample of families used physical violence to resolve conflicts with their brothers or sisters.

➤ 88 percent of the males and 94 percent of the females in Roscoe et al.'s (1987) sample of 244 junior high school students stated that they were victims of sibling violence in the year before the study. Similarly, 85 percent of the males and 96 percent of the females stated that they were the perpetrators of sibling violence during the same time period.

There is very little Canadian sociological research on sibling violence. This is not surprising given that the general public, academics, and a host of others have devoted little, if any, attention to the physical pain siblings inflict on each other. To the best of our knowledge, only two Canadian sociological studies have been done. The first, conducted by two co-authors of this text, Desmond Ellis and Walter DeKeseredy (1994), was exploratory and focused primarily on the prevalence of sibling violence in a non-probability sample of southern Ontario respondents. The second, conducted by Bly (1994), examined the risk markers associated with sibling violence; however, due to space limitations, only Ellis and DeKeseredy's work is briefly reviewed here.

Ellis and DeKeseredy administered self-report questionnaires to a non-probability sample of 215 undergraduate students, and conducted face-to-face interviews with 34 learning-disabled children aged between 6 and 11.[18] Rather than define sibling violence for both sets of respondents, Ellis and DeKeseredy simply asked them to describe what happened when they "got into fights," "had problems getting along with their brothers and sisters," "did or had done to them things they did not like," and "hurt their feelings or hurt their bodies (e.g., bruises, bumps, and cuts)." These methods generated the following data. Of the university students, 47.8 percent reported that they had been physically victimized by their sibling; 100 percent of the learning-disabled children stated that they were physically victimized.

Based on a comparison of the above findings with those produced by U.S. researchers, it is extremely difficult, if not impossible, to determine whether U.S. siblings are more violent than their Canadian counterparts for the following reasons outlined by DeKeseredy (1996a), and Ellis and DeKeseredy (1994):

➤ Different measures were used. For example, Straus et al. (1981) employed the Conflict Tactics Scale.

➤ Different siblings were the focus of the measures used. For example, Straus et al. (1981) collected data on offenders, while Ellis and DeKeseredy gathered data on victims' experiences.

➤ Different types of behaviors were measured. For example, Straus et al. (1981) counted an act as violent no matter whether it actually hurt another sibling, while Ellis and DeKeseredy measured only conduct which actually hurt another sibling.

➤ Some U.S. researchers (Straus et al., 1981) limited their definition to violence associated with sibling conflicts, while Ellis and DeKeseredy used a broader definition: hurtful conduct that was not limited to conflicts between siblings.

➤ Different time periods were used (e.g., "during the past 12 months" and "ever").

➤ Different sampling procedures were used.

Regardless of these differences, Ellis and DeKeseredy's exploratory study suggests that sibling violence is a major Canadian social problem which warrants much more attention. The above statistics are alarming, and even higher rates could be obtained by using a superior research design proposed elsewhere by DeKeseredy and Ellis (1998). Moreover, Ellis and DeKeseredy's prevalence rates are significantly higher than the estimates of male-to-female violence in adult, heterosexual relationships generated by Canadian national representative sample surveys conducted by DeKeseredy and Kelly (1993a), and Statistics Canada. Therefore, it is logical to assume that, as in the U.S., sibling violence is probably the most common form of family violence in the Canadian context.

"Granny-Bashing": Elder Abuse

Like the other variants of family violence addressed in this chapter, the physical abuse of elderly family members is not a new social problem. In fact, it is a "perpetual feature" of North American social history (Stearns, 1986). Nevertheless, prior to the 1980s, elder abuse received little sociological attention in both Canada and the United States (Barnett et al., 1997; DeKeseredy, 1996a). Today, the physical abuse of the elderly is defined by many family researchers, medical professionals, social workers, and so on, as a major type of family violence, and the recent interest in this problem is the product of at least four factors:

1. There is a rapidly growing number of North Americans over 70 years of age (Barnett et al., 1997), and this demographic change has increased awareness about their problems (Gelles and Cornell, 1985; Trevethan, 1992).
2. Since people are living much longer than their ancestors, more middle-aged children than ever before are required to look after their elderly parents (Brillon, 1987; Gelles and Cornell, 1985).
3. A higher proportion of the elderly than members of other age groups vote in elections (Gelles and Straus, 1988).
4. There is growing professional interest in the criminal victimization of the elderly (Barnett et al., 1997; Leroux and Petrunik, 1989).

How many elderly North Americans are physically abused by their children and other family members? It is extremely difficult, if not impossible, to determine the exact extent of this problem for two key reasons. First, unlike younger family members, elderly victims/survivors of intimate violence rarely leave the house (Barnett et al., 1997), and they are typically disconnected from social networks such as workplaces, schools, and recreational centers (DeKeseredy, 1996a). Thus, the elderly are often referred to as "hidden victims" of family violence. For example, if a battered child attends her mathematics class with bruises and cuts, her parents' violent conduct is likely to be detected by her teacher. On the other hand, a battered elderly person is probably confined to his or her house without anyone but the abuser observing (Gelles and Straus, 1988).

The precise measurement of elder abuse is also hindered by the victims' reluctance to report violent events (Barnett et al., 1997). According to Gelles and Straus (1988: 62-63), the elderly's unwillingness to disclose abusive incidents is a function of one or more of the following factors.

➤ The most common victims are those who are frail and who suffer from physical and psychological disorders. Hence, they may be unable to report their experiences or even leave home.

➤ Victims who do not have physical and psychological problems may fear being blamed for their victimization or fear retaliation from their abuser.

➤ Victims may accept or tolerate physical assaults as preferable to perceived dangers or life-events stress associated with alternative living arrangements (e.g., nursing home).

Despite these problems, several North American researchers have tried to generate reliable data on the extent of elder abuse. For example, in the United States, Pillemer and Finkelhor (1988) surveyed 2,000 elderly Boston-area respondents aged 65 and older who lived alone. Sixty-three (3.2 percent) of those who completed Pillemer and Finkelhor's modified rendition of the CTS stated that they were physically or verbally abused, and 2 percent stated that they were physically abused since turning 65.

U.S. national representative sample survey data produced by the National Crime Victimization Survey (NCVS) show that, compared to other age groups (26.7/1,000), elders are at much lower risk of being physically assaulted (2.3/1,000). However, for some time periods (e.g., 1987 to 1990), when they were assaulted, elders (13 percent) were markedly more likely to be attacked by family members than people younger than 65 (9 percent) (Bachman, 1993).

The most widely read and cited Canadian survey of elder abuse was done by Podnieks (1990). She used telephone survey technology to gather data from 2,008 elderly people living in private dwellings. Her data elicited from a modified version of the CTS show that approximately 5 per 1,000 of her respondents, or about 0.5 percent of the sample, reported having been harmed by physical abuse. If you compare Podnieks' data with Pillemer and Finkelhor's findings, at first glance, it seems that Canadian elders are less likely to be abused by family members than are their U.S. counterparts. However, this may be an erroneous conclusion because of methodological differences. More research and similar methods, then, is needed to make accurate comparisons.

Summary

The family violence research reviewed here, although hardly exhaustive, shows that families are not as safe as many people believe. In North America, as elsewhere, family violence is increasingly demanding the attention of social scientists, the media, medical personnel, criminal justice officials, policy makers, and the general public. For example, academic and government researchers are currently developing a substantial body of knowledge on the extent, causes, distribution, and consequences of the violent behaviors addressed in this chapter. They have also attempted to demystify some injurious popular myths about these four social problems (DeKeseredy, 1993). Still, much more work has to be done to minimize or overcome the "intimate intrusions" described here (Stanko, 1985). Moreover, there are many more issues related to family violence that require greater attention, such as those described by Barnett et al. (1997: 294) in Box 6.8. Unfortunately,

BOX 6-8

Family Violence: Old Questions—New Frontiers

Legal Frontiers

1. **Children who kill.** A child kills an abusive parent after years of abuse and is tried for murder. What should be society's response?

2. **Elder care responsibility.** Who is responsible for ensuring the well-being of parents, especially abusive parents?

3. **Battered women's rights.** Can battered women, as a class, be denied health care or insurance? Can battered women be fired because of their abuse?

4. **Child molesters' continued incarceration.** Is it legal for a panel of experts or a jury to determine that a molester is too dangerous to be released to society after he or she has served a prison term for conviction?

Ethical Dilemmas: Conflicts Related to Parent-Parent or Parent-Child Rights

1. **Parental kidnapping.** One parent kidnaps a child from the other. A child is taken without prior knowledge or consent of the custodial parent.

2. **Adoptive versus biological parents' rights.** A biological parent tries to reclaim a child after abandonment and subsequent adoption of the child (Alexander, 1996).

3. **Conception rights.** A woman conceives under unusual circumstances, such as by using sperm from a sperm bank. A surrogate parent gives birth to a nonbiological child.

4. **A child's rights to adoption after abandonment by a biological parent.** A biological parent prevents a child he or she has previously abandoned or been unable to care for from being adopted or from having an adoptive family.

Lesser-Known Frontiers

1. **Sibling abuse.** Brothers and sisters abuse each other. Very little is known about sibling abuse. Should society overlook sibling abuse as normative?

2. **Adolescent physical and sexual abuse offenders.** An adolescent in the family physically abuses or sexually molests a younger relative.

3. **Child-to-parent abuse.** An adolescent physically abuses a parent.

_____

Source: Barnett et al. (1997: 294). Reprinted by permission of Sage Publications, Inc.

family violence is a "never ending and constantly evolving issue" (Ledwitz-Rigby, 1993: 93).

Sociological Theories of the Family

How do social scientists explain the family problems discussed above? As has been our practice in other chapters, we will answer this question by reviewing several major approaches to studying the family—feminist theories, which are a variant of the power-inequality perspective, interactionist theories, and functionalist theories.

Structural Functionalist Theories

We begin with a review of structural functional theories of the family because, like many other issues in sociology, this theoretical perspective has dominated the field for so long. As you have probably gathered by now, the basic argument of structural functionalism is that various structures in society (like the family, the police, or government) exist because they serve an important function. In fact, if they did not play an important role in society, they would not exist at all. In thinking about the family, one of the most important functionalists of all, Talcott Parsons, and his colleague Robert Bales (1955), argued that there are basically two kinds of functions performed by the family. First, the family is responsible for the **primary socialization** of children, that is, the training, care, and other tasks designed to help children take their proper adult roles. Second, when people do become adults, the family helps to stabilize the roles into which they grow, such as "mother," "father," or "breadwinner."

So much for what families are supposed to do. But Parsons goes further by stating that families (like societies) are composed of interdependent parts which interact to produce particular patterns across and within different cultures. These result in particular "shapes" of the family, and in specific functions performed by the family. Let's illustrate this by way of example. In some cultures, having a number of wives is not only permissible but encouraged. In such societies, having many wives would obviously result in a family structure very different from the North American nuclear family, but for such a society, this would be quite normal.

Functionalists maintain that functions can be of two basic kinds, **manifest** or **latent**. Manifest functions are outcomes that are intended—such as socialization, shelter, or reproduction. Latent functions are unintended consequences (and for this reason are often not recognized), and could include socializing children to become abusive, or to reproduce gender roles in society. Thus, the main concern in structural functional perspectives is the relationship between the structure of the family (its shape) and its function (what it does as a consequence of its shape).

One of the main difficulties of this approach to studying the family (and it is a difficulty with structural functionalism in general) is that the theory tends to assume that certain structures, such as particular family forms, only exist because they have important functions. However, as Merton (1957) pointed out, this implies that a particular family form, such as the nuclear family can only play their functional roles in one way.[19] Think of it this way. A structural functionalist approach to the role of families in socializing children would imply that, although this is an important function, there is only one way to socialize children. Does this make sense to you? Is it not the case that families can socialize children in different ways?

Another common criticism of functionalist theory is that it is circular in its reasoning. You can understand this better if you think of the following dilemma— do families look the way they do because they play an important function, or could it be that the function determines the shape of the family?

Finally, because this theoretical orientation tends to "romanticize" the traditional nuclear family, critical social scientists have criticized functionalist theories for their **monolithic bias**—the assumption that the dominant family form has always been a husband and wife living in a monogamous relationship with their biological children (Eichler, 1988). As we have seen, this is obviously no longer the case. Basically, then, this theoretical approach can provide us with tools to understand what families do by emphasizing structure, function, stability, and consensus. However, because it cannot account for changes in the nature of the family it is inherently conservative. Furthermore, the implications of a conservative perspective on the family and other institutions is that such a perspective will often stereotype people into specific roles which may no longer be valid. For example, if the functionalist approach maintains that the primary role of women in the family is to reproduce the family, then obviously this completely misrepresents the reality of many women's family lives today.

The Contribution of Symbolic Interactionists

Symbolic interactionist (or interactionist) theories of the family focus on the ways in which family members interact with one another, inside the family unit itself. Like structural functionalism, the interactionist perspective is one of the most widely used conceptual frameworks for analyzing families. Essentially, interactionist theories are "micro" because they focus on small groups of people and the ways in which they interact with one another. Thus, the usefulness of this perspective comes from its ability to tell us about family dynamics.

One of the most important proponents of this perspective was George Herbert Mead, who argued that human behavior is a response to stimuli. The stimulus is recognized, interpreted by the individual, and influenced by their social attitudes and values. In addition, the behavior is influenced by the anticipated reactions of other people in the environment. Interactionists maintain that the **symbolic language system** is the most important aspect of human behavior. In fact, they feel that language is what distinguishes us from lower animals, and that we can only become human through interaction with others using some kind of symbolic language system. Now of course this does not mean that only those who can speak are in any sense truly human. Notice that they stress language is a system of symbols which do not necessarily have to be speech. In other words, symbolic interactionists recognize that we can communicate with one another via body language, signs, and various other **social acts**. It is through such communication that people come to develop a sense of self, and, because communication is a process that involves two or more individuals, one's sense of self will reflect the attitudes of others. According to Mead, it is through our relationship with "significant others" (such as parents or peers) that children develop a sense of self worth. As children grow, they learn to take on the roles of people outside their immediate family environment, such as "police officer," "teacher," or "figure skater." Mead calls this set of roles the "particular other." In the final stage of development, the child begins to take on the role of the "generalized other," in which the roles and norms of society and culture become part of the individual's personality.

As you can see from this brief description, symbolic interactionists are very interested in the ways in which people learn, by taking the viewpoints of other people, how to take on "social roles." It is not surprising, then, that other concepts related to "roles" are central to symbolic interactionist investigations of the family. For example, interactionists might use the concept of "role expectations," to determine how marriages fall apart by looking at the extent to which husbands and wives have the same or different expectations about marriage. Similarly, as we saw in the section on work and family conflict, symbolic interactionist theory is useful in understanding how "role strain" (the level of discomfort associated with conflicting roles) affects dual-income families (Menaghan, 1991).

For these reasons, this theoretical perspective has been very useful in giving us insight into the "inner workings" of families. However, if this is symbolic interactionism's biggest advantage, it is also its most important weakness. Put simply, precisely because symbolic interactionism focuses on the micro level of the family, it almost always tends to ignore the social-structural factors that occur "in the background." For example, interactionist theories do not concern themselves with factors in the wider society (such as racial discrimination or poverty) that act in very important ways to condition modern family life. Thus, although symbolic interactionism can tell us much about how working mothers respond to work-family conflict, it can tell us very little about the influence of factors such as the changing nature of work, the trend towards longer working hours, or the lack of government policy on work-family balance.

The Power-Inequality Approach: A Focus on Feminist Theories

Contrary to many people's assumptions, there are many types of feminist theory. For example, liberal feminists argue that inequality between men and women can be resolved by creating a society that eliminates particular barriers for women. Such barriers might include entrance requirements to professional schools (e.g., law and medicine), or access to higher management positions in the workplace. Socialist feminists argue that simply creating a "level playing field for women" will not eliminate the structural barriers to women's equality. They contend that the fundamental structural issues that need to be dealt with are patriarchy and the class structure. Radical feminist perspectives emphasize that gender roles are critical to understanding women's subjugation in society. They therefore focus on the role of patriarchy, and the roles that historically have been artificially constructed for women by men. In particular, radical feminist perspectives have been important in highlighting the incidence, prevalence, and devastating consequences of violence and abuse within families. In this section, we emphasize the common ground shared by these three variations of feminist theory, which in themselves constitute a type of power-inequality theory, and discuss the contribution of feminist thought to the study of family life.

What all these feminist perspectives have in common is a concern with women's place in society in comparison to men, and the recognition that contemporary society is dominated by male ideas and social structures. Put differently, all feminist perspectives ask one fundamental question—what about women's experiences? According to Linda Thompson (1992), in answering this very broad question, feminist perspectives tend to split between those that focus on sociological research on women, and those concerned with research for women. Social scientists working in the former tradition take the view that it is important to systematically **document and correct** for sexism, whereas those in the latter maintain that it is important to make a conscious effort to **emancipate** women.

The contribution of feminist perspectives on the sociology of the family has thus been substantial in two ways. First, it has highlighted women's experiences of and in the family. By this we mean that historically, women's experiences within the family have been largely trivialized or ignored. For example, the insight that women in families are not only consumers of goods and services but also producers, has only surfaced relatively recently. Second, feminist research has pointed out the importance of **women's perspectives** on the family and other social institutions, such as work, education, and the justice system. As we have shown earlier in this chapter, one of the most important outcomes of this focus has been more intensive scrutiny of family violence issues, as well as a re-examination of how resources are allocated, and power relations within families (Fox, 1997).

What Is to Be Done About Enhancing the Quality of Family Life in North America?

Throughout this chapter, we have emphasized only a few of the many social problems that affect families. Obviously, we have left out a great deal in the hope that presenting a lot about a little is more useful than glossing over the range of issues faced by families in North America. In part, however, many such issues are covered in other chapters, such as the ones on poverty and work. Nevertheless, we feel a bit uncomfortable talking about "what is to be done" only in relation to the issues covered in this chapter. To a large extent, many of the social policy issues discussed in other chapters would have an important effect on families. Creating better job opportunities, for instance, would certainly benefit the many poor families who struggle to maintain a living every day. Similarly, providing family members with better access to higher education would go a long way towards alleviating many of the social problems associated with inadequate literacy and numerical skills. In effect, enhancing the quality of life of families in North America really depends on taking a wide view of social policy issues as opposed to narrow, "program" oriented approaches. For while such programs may provide relief for some families, they reproduce the tendency to ignore the influence of the wider social context.

Keeping these comments in mind, in this section we provide you with a sense of the kinds of specific "micro" policies that may enhance the well-being of families as well as the larger "social" issues that need to be addressed.

Because violence is a multidimensional problem, North American policy makers and other stakeholders must realize that there are no simple solutions to this issue (DeKeseredy and Schwartz, 1998a). Recognizing the complex nature of family violence, and based on the arguments of DeKeseredy and Schwartz (1996), we offer the following policy suggestions:

> ➤ We know that growing up in a violent family atmosphere is a strong predictor of becoming violent later on. Therefore, we need to focus on creating policies that will enable family members to deal with family conflict in a non-violent manner.

> ➤ We need to create better access to the institutional "shields" that are available for women and children who are battered.

> ➤ We need to develop and implement community education on the issue of family violence, focusing on facts, myths, and linkages to other social problems.

> ➤ We have to encourage men and women to speak and act out against family violence, and to confront those engaging in such acts.

Another important strategy is to conduct more research. Although we are beginning to get more good information on the incidence and prevalence of family violence, we have much to learn when it comes to examining and doing something about the causes of this behavior. As we pointed out, for instance, we know that sibling violence is a common occurrence, but we have paid "selective inattention" to this issue, in part because we have tended to define it as "normal" behavior. Similarly, we need to look more closely at the correlates of elder abuse.

Research should not only focus on the causes or correlates of family violence, but also on the effectiveness of policies already in place. In taking this approach, we can learn much about "what works and what does not," and redirect resources accordingly.

In Box 6.8, we highlighted some of the most important questions requiring debate in relation to family violence. These questions have policy implications. For example, in some Canadian provinces, governments are closing shelters for battered women in order to save money. Yet, in a society in which it is so clear that battered women require some form of post-abusive care, how can such a strategy be justified? More fundamentally, should we not be constructing social policies that address both the outcomes and the causes or risk factors associated with family violence?

A similar concern with research motivates our policy concerns with respect to work and family conflict. We have only begun to understand how dual-earner households cope with the demands of two careers, how workplaces can operate taking into account the new social reality of North American families, and how communities can provide the infrastructure needed to support both the families and workplaces. Obviously, then, one of the first things we need to do is to gain a more complete understanding of how dual-career families in all social classes cope with work and family conflict. But this is not all. We cannot confine our investigations to the lives of dual-income earners. We need to know more about the experiences of single mothers and fathers, poor families, the "sandwich generation," and other groups traditionally excluded from mainstream research, despite the fact that such groups are the most vulnerable in society.

We also need to determine what employers of all kinds can do to help employees deal with the tremendous stresses being experienced by many families. Currently, we know that large organizations have made some inroads in this area, but smaller ones, which typically do not have the resources or the inclination to become "family friendly" remain unresponsive.

As far as communities are concerned, stress for many families could probably be alleviated if services such as banks and grocery stores would make their hours more flexible. Obviously, nationally funded child care programs would make a big difference, not only for working families, but for those whose work opportunities are limited or non-existent because of child care requirements. Indeed, the United States has a long way to go to match the state support for child care enjoyed by other industrialized nations (Currie, 1993). In Canada, federal government promises to create a nationally funded day care program have never been realized.[20]

As Thomas and Ganster (1995) point out, family supportive workplaces can be divided into two categories—those with family supportive policies, and those with supportive supervisors or managers. This distinction helps to remind us that it is not just the structure of the workplace that must change, but also the attitudes of managers. As you can imagine, even if a workplace publicly states its intention to be family friendly, if management does not "buy in" to this policy, change is unlikely. According to the U.S. Conference Board (1993), "supportive supervisors" typically

➤ have a wide knowledge of work-family policies, within their organizations and in general;

➤ apply policies without favoritism;

➤ show flexibility when work-family problems arise; and

➤ believe in the legitimacy of work-family policies as part of the workplace.

One goal, then, should be to educate managers and supervisors as to the realities being experienced by today's working families, and to provide them with appropriate tools to become more effective in managing these realities.

In addition, we can learn much from the experiences and policy strategies of other countries, most notably Sweden. Particularly in terms of the experiences of women, there are important similarities between the United States, Canada, and Sweden (Lundgren-Gaveras, 1996). In Sweden, there has traditionally been strong government support for a "social safety net" that supports working parents with family obligations, including generous leave policies and state-supported child care programs.

Finally, although it is important to provide some programs within organizations that help employees address non-work obligations (anything is better than nothing), such programmatic approaches are not enough. If families are to truly benefit from more caring employers, there will have to be large-scale organizational change. For instance, the culture of the workplace has to become more responsive and accepting of family members' needs. In addition, the very structure of work (e.g., the pace, hours, and expectations) needs to become more accommodating to families.

Although much of what we say in this text is critical of the ways in which employers treat employees, the work-family issue is one in which it is possible to argue that both employers and employees will benefit if a more "family friendly" approach to conducting business is taken. To a large extent, this explains the strategy of many experts of writing about work-family issues as a "strategic tool for enhancing competitiveness."

Summary

In this chapter we have provided you with a sense of how central the family unit is to the study of society and social problems. In addition, we have pointed out that families are diverse, complex, and much like a "rubber band" in that they are constantly "stretching" to meet the demands of a rapidly changing society. In addition, the chapter has provided you with information on the main types of changes that have occurred in North America, and their real and potential impact on family life.

In the context of these complex and rapid changes, there continues to be debate as to what exactly a family is "supposed" to look like. This chapter has shown that taking this approach to defining "the" family is probably not as useful as examining the family from the point of view of the positive things families do, and the barriers that exist to doing them well.

We have tried to show that, contrary to popular and neo-conservative images, the family is often not a "safe place" where we might take refuge from the problems of everyday life. In fact, as our discussion of family violence has shown, the family is probably the most violent place in our society.

Our focus on the relationship between work and family life debunks the myth that these are "separate spheres." Rather, people's experiences of work and family life are very much intertwined, a fact that still seems to escape many individuals, but particularly employers. The negative consequences of overload and interference need to be addressed not only to benefit families, but their employers as well.

We also provided you with a discussion of some important theoretical frameworks for understanding family life. Though each of these approaches offers insight into family problems, it seems clear that research in the future will draw upon the insights synthesized from multiple perspectives.

Finally, we have discussed some policy solutions to the problems presented here. However, the complexity of family life and the fact that families exist in a social, political, and economic context, mean that effective solutions will require a multidimensional and holistic strategy.

KEY TERMS

Blended families
Continuum of unsafety
Extended family
Fertility rate
Functional definition of the family
Manifest and latent functions
Nuclear family
Overload
Role interference
Sandwich generation
Sexual symmetry perspective

DISCUSSION QUESTIONS

1. In what ways will macro-structural (societal) changes occurring now affect families in the future?
2. Given the wide range of family forms, what kinds of functions do you think are essential for modern families?
3. Discuss the following statement: "The phenomenon of women in the workforce is here to stay."
4. What are the strengths and limitations of the definition of family violence used in this chapter?
5. Discuss the following statement: "As women rise in the ranks of management, there will be more corporate action on the work-family concerns faced by their employees."

PROBLEM SOLVING SCENARIOS

1. In groups, discuss strategies that students can engage in to prevent family violence.
2. Many researchers argue that corporal punishment of children for disciplinary purposes does not work. Debate alternative strategies for disciplining children.
3. Approach a business in your community and ask them if you can interview six (or more) employees on what it is like to balance work and family life. What differences do you see between men and women?
4. Make a list of things which would have no or minimal cost, that companies could do to help employees to cope with work-family conflict.
5. Debate the ways in which one's theoretical perspective on the family determines the kinds of policies we might make on the family.

WEB EXERCISES

1. Provide a critical evaluation of the arguments on the effects of divorce on children made at

   http://www.theatlantic.com/atlantic/election/connection/family/danquayl.htm.

2. Beginning at the website below, gather as much information as you can to support or disprove the notion that "work-family conflict disproportionately affects women."

   http://ucaswww.mcm.uc.edu/sociology/kunzctr/

SUGGESTED READINGS

Barnett, Ola W., Cindy L. Miller-Perrin, and Robin D. Perrin. *Family Violence Across the Lifespan: An Introduction.* Thousand Oaks, CA: Sage, 1997.
   Written by two psychologists and a sociologist, this book provides students and researchers with a comprehensive overview of the most important conceptual, empirical, theoretical, and political issues surrounding various types of family violence, including those covered in this chapter.

Eichler, Margrit. *Family Shifts: Families, Policies and Gender Equality.* Toronto: Oxford University Press, 1997.
   This book takes a historical look at the evolution of the family and family policies over this century. It focuses on the impact of various trends, past and present, on the shape and nature of families, and discusses the relationship between policy and various models of the family.

Lewis, Suzan, Jeremy Lewis, (eds.)*The Work-Family Challenge: Rethinking Employment.* London: Sage, 1996.
   This edited collection of readings provides an excellent overview of the main issues affecting working families today. It takes a comparative international perspective and discusses the context of work-family issues, policies, practices, and the problem of cultural change within organizations.

ENDNOTES

1   There are other ways of measuring fertility than the one used here which is Total Fertility Rate (TFR). In general, there are two kinds of measures of fertility: Period measures examine birth rates for a cross section of the population at a given point in time. Cohort measures try to examine the same but for a group of women sharing a characteristic, such as year of birth. Within these two categories, demographers often talk about different types of fertility measures such as General Fertility Rate, Age Specific Fertility Rates, Net Fertility Rates and Gross Reproduction Rates. Students interested in the differences should consult any standard demographics text.

2   There are also some interesting regional variations in Canada. In Quebec for instance, 46 percent of all children are born out of the traditional marriage bond.

3   There are, of course, other predictors of divorce success, including teenage marriage, brief acquaintance, and dissimilar background (Boyd, Goyder, Jones, McRoberts, Pineo and Porter, 1985).

4   This section includes modified sections of an article published previously by DeKeseredy (1996a).

5   This definition is cynically called the "stitch rule" by many women who work in battered women's shelters (DeKeseredy and Schwartz, 1996).

6   For example, Russell (1975: 82-83) describes a case in which a man spent an entire day insulting his girlfriend. Following this, he beat and sodomized her.

7   This case is a slightly modified version of a intimate "femicide" victim's story described by her mother to Crawford and Gartner (1992: 131-135).

8   See DeKeseredy (1996b), and DeKeseredy and MacLeod (1997) for in-depth responses to Fekete's sexual symmetry thesis.

9   This is a slightly modified section of DeKeseredy's (1997a) Guest Editor's Introduction to a special issue of the journal *Violence Against Women*. This issue focused primarily on the extent, distribution, and sources of post-separation woman abuse.

10 See DeKeseredy and MacLeod (1997), Kurz (1993), and Stanko (1995) for more information on these data.

11 See Barnett et al. (1997), Gelles and Cornell (1985), Utech and Garrett (1992), and Wallace (1996) for reviews of some of the key debates surrounding definitions of child abuse.

12 It should be noted that Straus et al. (1981) state that it would have been too time-consuming to ask the respondents to report the use of violence on each of their children. Instead, these researchers "randomly selected one referent child in each family to be the focal point of discussion." Thus, the data reported here are accounts of violence committed by one parent against one child.

13 These data do not include assaults with objects such as a stick or a belt.

14 MacMillan et al. also gathered data on child sexual abuse.

15 This section includes modified sections of work published previously by DeKeseredy (1996a), DeKeseredy and Ellis (1998), and Ellis and DeKeseredy (1994).

16 See Barnett et al. (1997), Wiehe (1990), and Worling (1995) for reviews of research done on sexual and emotional abuse between siblings.

17 This is a slightly modified version of Wallace's (1996) definition of sibling abuse.

18 Ellis and DeKeseredy were fully aware of the fact that data provided by learning-disabled children do not provide a valid basis for generalizing to all children. However, these children were not sampled for this reason. Rather, they were selected because Ellis and DeKeseredy wanted to obtain data on the patterning of hurtful sibling interactions among children. Therefore, they had to select a group in which such interactions occurred relatively infrequently. A teacher who specialized in teaching learning-disabled children suggested that they would likely meet Ellis and DeKeseredy's criterion. She was right, and the literature supports her (e.g., Olweus, 1980).

19 Merton called this the "fallacy of functional indispensability."

20 Since 1987, Canada has provided tax deductions to parents with children in daycare.

Chapter (7)

Population and Environment

Had we been so careful all along, we might not be so worried today about groundwater pollution. The vast majority of us have safe drinking water, but our supplies are not so well distributed that we can afford to add hazardous waste to them, already burdened with highway de-icing salts, farm sprays and fertilizers, and seepage from gasoline and septic tanks. (Boraiko, 1985: 334)

OBJECTIVES

In this chapter we focus on the topics
1. A theory of population and the environment
2. Research on environmental degradation
3. Population, environment, and the human condition
4. What is to be done about population and the environment?

Introduction

Why are people who poison or otherwise damage the environment unwilling to practise self-regulation even though their actions harm themselves and others? Our search for an answer to this question suggested the presence of a motivational structure that is common to all of the recurring, environmentally damaging activities described in this chapter, such as polluting, emitting noxious gases, and creating more people than available resources can sustain. Thus, the presence of a common motivational structure is the first theme of this chapter.

Serious damage to the environment has been going on for a very long time. How long? Some readers, such as those who have read the Bible would probably say since the water problem that Noah anticipated and responded to by building an ark. If you are a student of Medieval (fourteenth century) European history, you might also cite "rains [in 1315] so incessant...they were compared to the Biblical flood, crops failed all over Europe, and famine, the dark horseman of the Apocalypse, became familiar to all" (Tuchman, 1978: 24). Then there are other readers who are likely to point out that the Little Ice Age started during the early years of the fourteenth century, and it caused seriously damaging climatic changes. For example, the Baltic Sea froze on a number of occasions between 1303 and 1307, major blizzards and storms frequently occurred, and there was a significant decrease in the temperature which resulted in a shortening of the growing season (Tuchman, 1978).

If we focus on Europe and forget the Biblical flood and the meteor strike that allegedly wiped out the dinosaurs millions of years earlier, we may conclude that environmentally damaging events have occurred during the past 700 years. For most of this period (660 years), unfortunately, environmental damage was not defined as a social problem. In fact, it was not until the publication of Rachel Carson's book, *Silent Spring* (1962) that the first steps towards defining environmental harm as a social problem were taken (Hardert et al., 1984).

Carson's attempt was relatively successful because it focused, not on natural causes such as the advancing polar and alpine glaciers that caused the Little Ice Age, but on human activity and technology as causes. For example, she described the damage being done to the environment by pesticides. She further argued that if human activity was the problem, then human activity could also help solve it. This possibility, one that does not apply to natural causes, made the public, politicians, and scientists more receptive to her definition of **environmental degradation**, caused by human activity, as a social problem.

A second factor increasing the receptivity of Carson's message was the seriousness of the problem. For example, the Industrial Revolution had started over two hundred years before *Silent Spring* was published, and the cumulative effects of chemical and other pollutants associated with industrial and agricultural production were much more evident during the 1950s then they were in earlier periods. During the 1990s, environmental problems have become serious enough to jeopardize the quality of life of North Americans, and perhaps threaten the very survival of human beings everywhere (Beck, 1992; Postel, 1992).

Thus, the second theme of this chapter is this: human activity is a significant cause of both environmental degradation and the definition of environmental degradation caused by human activity as a social problem. Without the latter (definitional) activity, environmental degradation can exist being defined as a social problem.

Greenpeace, an activist environmental social movement, has played a significant part in helping define species survival and environmental degradation as social problems. One of their more recent media contributions (constructions) is presented in Box 7.1. The newspaper article serves to highlight considerations that should be kept in mind as you read this chapter. First, a multi-causal theory, one that integrates the human and natural causes identified by different scholars (e.g., greenhouse gases, regular cyclical climate changes, El Niño), is more likely to be valid that a mono-causal or single factor theory.

BOX 7-1

A Crack at the Bottom of the World

by Roger Atwood, Reuters, Cormorant Island, Antarctica

The warming of Antarctica, once a vague prediction by researchers, is now a reality. Receding glaciers, milder winters and dramatic changes in wildlife populations are all sure signs.

...There may still be debate about why the Antarctic climate is changing: Is it because of man's greenhouse gases, a natural cyclical up-swing or some combination? But there is no doubt it is changing. The mean temperature on the Antarctic Peninsula has risen by about one degree since 1950.

Worldwide, 1995 was the warmest year on record. Last year was slightly cooler but still well above the average since 1961, indicating that global warming is happening, reports the British Meteorological Society.

About 140 countries have ratified the 1992 Climate Change Convention committing them to stabilizing emissions of gases believed to cause global warming, a phenomenon linked to changes in weather patterns, rising sea levels and disruption in weather patterns.

In Antarctica, climate change is being felt in unexpected ways. Winter pack ice, which in extremely cold winters can cover the ocean almost halfway across the Drake Passage (between Antarctica and South America), is covering less and less area.

In the 1950s, about four out of five winters saw extensive seasonal pack ice, according to various studies using NASA satellite data. Now the rate is one or two out of every five years and that change is having a crucial effect on the way wildlife reproduces, scientists say. Among seals, for example, Weddell and Crabeater seals, which depend upon pack ice, are declining; species such as the fur seal, which avoid pack ice, are increasing. Almost exterminated by hunters in the 1800s, fur seals have multiplied in the South Georgia Islands to levels exceeding those seen before they were hunted, British studies show.

The continent's few hardy plant species simply shut down in warm air. "Corn and soy beans love it but if you increase the air temperature to 12C or 15C, these plants die," says Xiong Fusheng, a botanist at the U.S. National Science Foundation's Palmer Station.

A vast glacier covering Anvers Island, where the station is located, has receded over the past 20 years, leaving in its wake new islands gradually being colonized by seabirds and seals.

Glacial movements take years to reveal patterns and scientists do not fully understand the effects of naturally occurring cyclical changes on climate and sea ice. Wildlife populations will also take years of study before conclusions are possible.

Researchers are also careful not to shoehorn all changes into the context of global warming. However, studies by David Karl of the University of Hawaii and others suggest links between the extent of Antarctic sea ice and El Niño, the warm ocean current that pounds the coasts of Ecuador and Peru with rain every six or seven years.

Source: R. Atwood, Reuters, Cormorant Island, Antarctica. Copyright Reuters Limited, 1999.

Second, the outcome (environmental degradation) that the theories attempt to explain is complex because the environment is made up of complex land, water, and atmospheric systems that are part of a larger, highly complex system characterized by the presence of feedback loops and threshold effects.[1] The complexity increases when technology and sociological variables such as culture, social structure, and economies are added to the explanatory model.

Third, parts of a system, or any system, are by definition, interdependent. This means that intended changes in one part (e.g., atmospheric changes) often lead to unintended changes in another (e.g., rising sea levels, warmer land masses). Sociologist Robert Merton drew attention to the social and sociological significance of the unintended consequences of intended human actions, calling them "unwitting regularities" (1957: 60). This chapter bears testimony to the wisdom of his observation.

A Theory of Population and the Environment

Commons Theory

Once upon a time in England, the patchwork of tree- and shrub-lined hedgerows that enclose agricultural and grazing land did not exist. During Medieval times, for example, and as recently as the 1840s, there were no hedgerows. Grazing pastureland was unfenced and open to all persons with herds of cattle. These common grazing pastures or **commons**, were, in earlier times, that portion of the lord's estate that had not been cultivated. His tenants as well as other common people were free to graze their herds of cattle on the commons.

Until the mid-eighteenth century, the rural population remained relatively low and stable, and there were fewer cattle than the commons could support. Each individual herd owner could increase the size of his herd and thereby increase the quantity of milk the cows produced, with no cost to the rest of the common people using the pasture. During the 1750s, however, the rural population and the number of tenants on the lord's estates increased, bringing about a marked increased in the number of cattle.

Soon, there were too many grazing cattle for the pasture to sustain and replenish itself. Each individual herd owner could increase the size of his herd by adding another cow, but only by burdening all others with the cost of his animal's feeding on, and trampling, the grass. Thus, the profit from an additional cow went to the individual herd owner, but the cost had to be shared by all herd owners using the pasture. Unfortunately, as each herd owner pursued his individual interest by adding to the size of his herd, the common pasture was eventually destroyed and all herd owners were ruined.

The tragedy of the commons, then, describes a situation in which there is a conflict between individual and collective, or social, good. More specifically, given a fixed resource (grazing pasture), individuals who are exclusively motivated to achieve their objectives by using as much of it as they can, and who are not aware of, or don't care enough about, the consequences unless they immediately and visibly harm them, soon use up and/or destroy the resource. This leads to the ruin and suffering of all of them and the community in which the resource is located.

The conflict between individual and societal interest is fundamental to sociology. It has engaged the attention of philosophers such as Thomas Hobbes (1665), and major sociologists such as Durkheim (1893), Adam Smith (1776), Herbert Spencer (1906), Talcott Parsons (1937), and Dennis Wrong (1994). According to Schelling, (1893: 110), the tragedy of the commons "describes a motivational structure that is pervasive [in society]." Further, this motivational structure pervades any situation in which a country, collectivity (e.g., business corporation), or an individual prospers or in many cases merely survives, by passing on to others (community, national, and global public), the short-run economic costs of producing goods and services that damage the environment.

A significant proportion of a finite Planet Earth's land, water, and air resources form contemporary global and national commons. That is to say, within countries, individuals and collectivities (e.g., governments and business corporations) have free access to land, water, and air resources that are owned by everyone in general, and no one in particular. More specifically, these resources are "owned" by national publics if they fall within a country's air, land, and sea space, and by global publics if they fall outside any country's air, land, and sea space. Thus, an individual automobile manufacturer may increase its return on investment and keep shareholders happy by producing over 3,000 pounds of waste for every 100 pounds of product (the front and rear seats) it produces. However, if all manufacturers of cars and other products produced the same ratio of usable to waste product, and a competitive edge could be achieved by increasing the waste to usable product ratio, eventually waste will, if unchecked, destroy the resources on which living systems depend (Hawken, 1994). As manufacturers themselves also depend on these systems, their unrestrained, wasteful practices will eventually not only harm national and global publics by degrading the environment, but they will also harm themselves as individuals and as manufacturers of goods and services. In a capitalist society bankruptcy is, after all, a form of capital punishment.

Power and inequality are also implicated in commons theory. In the commons tragedy described by Hardin (1968), the estate-owning nobility responded to the destruction of the commons by privatizing and enclosing them. In short, they practised social closure. Commoners no longer enjoyed free access to portions of estates formerly designated as (unfenced) commons. The law of the land (e.g., the coercive power of the state) stood behind them, even if **social custom** did not. Social custom was on the side of the many who were powerless (tenants and villagers); the law was on the side of the powerful few (the lords), and the few won. In the process, the many suffered, the few prospered, and the commons were saved.

Within the United States and Canada, power and inequality, as well as purely economic considerations, are reflected in the non-random pattern of toxic and other waste dumps (Walsh et al., 1993). Unlike the Medieval commoners, we now appear to have a situation in which a few, relatively powerful manufacturers prosper, many communities suffer, neither the law nor custom protects the many who are relatively powerless, and the environment is degraded. Environmental protection collectivities, such as community organizations and **social movements**, may therefore be viewed as attempts by relatively powerless publics to achieve their objectives by attempting to balance power imbalances through the use of social constructions, politics, organization, knowledge, media, and the law as resources.

Contemporary national and global commons continue to be used in ways that degrade the environment, partly because of a motivational structure today's degraders share with destroyers of the Medieval commons, and partly because in developed countries that contribute disproportionately to their degradation (e.g., the United States and Canada), the state depends upon them for the revenue it needs for defence, social programs, and other necessary expenditures (Parkin, 1979). In addition, major industrial degraders and their hosts (the states and provinces who court them in order to improve their economies and provide jobs) in these countries, control political and economic resources which could be used to exclude (social closure) governments that attempt to effectively regulate them (e.g., via taxation on waste) from forming the next government. Finally, the state itself associates international political "clout," or power, with economic strength, and economic strength with unfettered capitalist enterprise (Joffe, 1997).

An integrated commons/power and inequality theoretical perspective is, in our view, an appropriate theoretical perspective to apply to the sources of environmental degradation described in this chapter. However, as sociologists, we believe it is necessary and appropriate for us to emphasize the cultural and structural sources of both the motivational structure central to commons theory and power/inequality. Eitzen and Bacca Zinn (1997: 97–104) do a good job of describing these sources of environmental problems in the United States, and we build upon their work by making the linkages described above.

Environmental Degradation: Cultural and Structural Sources

Ideologies are part of culture. More specifically, they refer to a set of ideas or conceptions that are used to legitimize or attack existing social arrangements and activities. Eitzen and Bacca Zinn identify a dominant ideology that legitimizes extremely wasteful and environmentally damaging activities. Specifically, individuals and collectives in the United States who degrade global, national, and community commons share a dominant ideology that includes the following specific elements:

> As the environment belongs to no one in particular, all people have a right to exploit it in ways that benefit them.

> Nature represents a challenge to be overcome, and technology can conquer nature as well as solve any problem associated with attempts to master and exploit the environment.

> Success means acquiring earlier in life, more and better quality material things than others acquire.

> Success and failure are based on individual talent and effort, and the material rewards for personal achievement should go to individuals who merit them rather than to someone else or some larger group.

> In a competitive capitalist society, where success and failure are based on individual talent and effort, material success favors an individual (self) orientation rather than a collective (community, societal, or global) orientation.

Structural sources of environmental degradation include the following:

> a capitalist economic system, primarily driven by shareholders' expectations of an increasing return on their investment, and only secondarily by consideration of the consequences of this orientation for the environment.

> a political system in which lobbyists for industries that degrade the environment influence governments to make political decisions that favor them. An example is President Clinton's (October, 1997) decision to delay until the year 2012 cutting back greenhouse gas emissions to 1990 levels, even though the United States signed a climate change treaty at the 1992 Earth Summit in Brazil, agreeing to achieve 1990 levels by the year 2000.

➤ the concentration of over 75 percent of the population in a relatively few large metropolitan areas located on or adjacent to lakes, rivers, and seas. This concentrates and intensifies the degradation of the surrounding land and water into which pollutants and toxic waste are dumped.

➤ a stratification system in which the economically and politically powerful collectives, such as the automobile and fossil fuel producing industries, degrade the environment; relatively affluent members of the middle-class form, join, and lead environmental social movements; and the poor—those who own neither property nor credentials—pay a disproportionately large amount of their meagre incomes in the form of higher prices for environmentally friendly products and higher taxes designated for cleaning up the environment (Turner, 1997: 414).

Prior to the advent of capitalism, social custom (e.g., cultural norms and traditional practices) was on the side of the relatively powerless commons. For example, custom required the land-owning nobility to provide free access to their commons. Overuse of the land by commoners, to the point where grass would no longer grow, was due mainly to a self-interested focus, a short-run orientation, and ignorance of the harmful longer-run consequences of overgrazing. In contemporary capitalist societies such as the United States and Canada, cultural and structural factors permit, and may even invite, degradation of global, national, and community commons by those who own or control productive property, even though the long-run consequences of polluting, emitting noxious gases, carelessly dumping hazardous waste, and so on are well-known.

At this point you may ask, "But didn't the rich and powerful landed nobility act to protect the environment when they enclosed (fenced) the land, thereby preventing overgrazing by commoner's cattle?" They did, but it was their own land they were protecting. Can you imagine poor commoners persuading parliament to pass a law permitting them to enclose and use land that the land-owning aristocracy had customarily used for fox hunting? When their own land is involved, then, members of economically and politically powerful groups take swift and effective action to prevent or stop its degradation. At the same time, when they degrade land, water, and air to which everyone has free access, they persuade governments not to pass and/or enforce laws regulating their activities. This is as true today as it was in seventeenth century England.

Our commons/power and inequality perspective described here is applicable, as we indicated earlier, to the varied sources of environmental degradation described in this text. In addition, a number of more specific theories are applied to other sources of degradation they were designed to explain. For example: Beck's (1992) **risk society theory** is applied to environmental discrimination in the United States; Malthus' (1798, 1830) **principle of population** is applied to overpopulation; Homer-Dixon's (1991) **scarcity thesis** links overpopulation, food, land, water scarcity, and violent conflict; and Davis' (1945) **demographic transition thesis** is applied to decreasing the growth of populations.

Research on Environmental Degradation

The Significant Six

A review of the relevant literature reveals the existence of the following six significant interrelated environmental problems.

1. Global warming
2. Ozone layer depletion
3. Acid rain
4. Deforestation
5. Overuse/poisoning of the land
6. Overuse/poisoning of water resources

The causes, mechanisms, effects, and consequences of these major environmental problems are presented in Table 7.1. The public's fear and anxiety about these environmental problems is generated and maintained in part by popular media stories with headlines such as the following:

➤ "St Lawrence Belugas Doomed"
➤ "We're Killing the Planet Even Faster Than Feared: UN"
➤ "Fear Spawns Actions on Greenhouse Effect"
➤ "Earth Under Dire Stress"
➤ "The Sea: Tears for Neptune"
➤ "Threats to Species Growing"
➤ "The Air: Hot Times All Around"
➤ "Environment Linked with Strife on Globe"
➤ Ozone Hole Alters Antarctica"

A 1996 Gallup survey of selected countries indicates that a majority of the individuals in most countries believe their health has been adversely affected by environmental problems. Moreover, although the size of the increase varies across countries, the percentage of individuals who felt this way increased in all of them. Thus, between 1992 and 1996, the percentage increase for Chile was 28 (56 percent to 84 percent), Germany 3 (69 percent to 71 percent), United States 2 (67 percent to 69 percent), United Kingdom 7 (53 percent to 60 percent), Canada 7 (52 percent to 59 percent), Switzerland 31 (28 percent to 59 percent), Japan 19 (32 percent to 51 percent) and the Netherlands 5 (35 percent to 40 percent).

These sources of information (Table 7.1, media headlines, and Gallup surveys) are interesting and relevant, but they suffer from two defects. First, they do not adequately convey the complex interrelationships among the causes, effects, and consequences of any single environmental problem, never mind the complex interactions among the causes, effects, and consequences of all six. Second, they divert attention from the fact that individuals are not only harmed by environmental problems caused by the activities of other individuals, but they actively resist their

Table 7.1
Six Major Environmental Problems—Causes, Mechanisms, Effects, and Consequences

Problems	Cause(s)	Mechanism	Effects	Consequences
Global warming	Emission of greenhouse gases* by: • automobiles • burning forests • cattle farting • coal burning homes/industrial plants • burned/cleared soil	Trap sunlight and warm the earth.	• melting of polar ice • rise in sea levels • changes in climate patterns	• poverty • hunger/famine • extinction of species • disease/epidemics
Ozone depletion	Emissions of ozone depleting chemicals: • refrigerators (CFC's) • aerosol sprays • foaming agents in plastics	Increase in harmful ultraviolet-B radiation	• crop damage • loss of habitat • warming of the earth's surface	• starvation • skin cancer, cataracts, immune system damage • extinction of species • hunger, especially for people who eat mainly fish
Acid rain	Emissions by: • automobile exhausts • industrial smoke stacks • burning of coal and shrubs	Harmful levels of sulphur and nitrous oxide deposited on earth's surface	• loss of habitat • disrupted ecosystems, especially mountain areas • air pollution	• extinction of species • adverse health effects

Problems	Cause(s)	Mechanism	Effects	Consequences
Deforestation	Burning/clearing forests	Greenhouse gases (e.g. CO_2) Soil exposed to wind, rain	Global warming Soil erosion and exhaustion	• poverty • hunger • extinction of species • violent inter-group conflicts
Degradation of arable land	Urban development Chemical pollution Desertification	Reduction in amount of arable land Poisoning of soil Overuse of arable land Salinization Soil compacting	Security of land available for growing food Migration of "environmental refugees"	• violent inter-group conflicts • hunger/famine • poverty
Overuse/poisoning of water resources	Agriculture Industry	Pollution Irrigation Dams Diversion Increasing use of water	Scarcity of water Loss of aquatic habitat	• hunger/famine • poverty • extinction of species • violent inter-group conflicts

*Carbon dioxide, nitrous oxide, methane, ozone

prospective or continued victimization by organizing and forming social movements. The three case studies described in the next section remedy both defects.

Case Studies

Southern Florida

The problem of "sustaining mountain peoples and their environments" is not a major one in southern Florida. The biggest "mountain" in this region is Miami's garbage dump. Smaller "hills" are formed by garbage dumps lining the back roads. Between 1960 and 1992, Florida's annual population growth rate was the same as the rate for Sub-Saharan Africa, 2.8 percent, and higher than that of Bangladesh, 2.5 percent. The major cause of Florida's high rate of population growth and the absolute size of its large population (13 million), is immigration. Associated with relatively rapid increases in the population of Florida generally, and southern Florida in particular, is a rapid expansion in agriculture, industry, and development. The increased demand for water has been met by diverting freshwater flows from their natural courses through wetlands, marshes, and forests, to unnatural courses that satisfy the needs of people, industry, and the agri-business. As a result, **ecosystems** in the Everglades, as well as other wetlands and marshes have been disrupted or destroyed.

According to Erhlich and Erhlich (1991: 130), "only 10 percent of bird populations remain in these areas." Now, Great White Herons that once survived by catching and eating fish have become "bird bums," whose survival rests on the fish they are offered by residents and tourists. Further, fauna, flora, deer, cougars, and some nesting birds are either extinct, or on their way towards becoming extinct. Loss of habitat, in short, has resulted in a marked reduction of biodiversity in southern Florida.

In addition to the increased consumption of freshwater resources, loss of habitat has been caused by suburban development encroaching on the Everglades. Human activity is also responsible for the heavy pollution of Lake Okeechobee. The worst, however, may be yet to come. Of all the states in the United States, Florida is most vulnerable to the increases in sea level induced by global warming. By the year 2050, human activity in Florida, North America, and other parts of the world may cause the sea level to rise by as much as two or three feet. If this does happen, and other things remain constant, much of Florida will be flooded, because it is flat and its land surface is very close to sea level. Further, more frequent and severe hurricanes will cause massive flooding reaching all the way to Orlando and other areas located relatively far away from the sea shore. Water supplies would be contaminated by salt because Florida's porous limestone shelf would allow salt water to reach aquifers both near to and far from the sea levels. Salinization of aquifers can occur when fresh water flows on the surface of the land are diverted. For all the reasons described here, but especially because of the predicted disastrous effects of the combination of extreme climatic changes and rising sea levels, Erhlich and Erhlich (1991: 131) conclude that "Florida, even more than California, is on the 'edge of history'."

Grassy Narrows

Grassy Narrows is a First Nations (Ojibwa) reserve in northern Ontario, located above the 50th parallel, north of Lake Superior. The town of Dryden is situated approximately 80 miles south-east of Grassy Narrows. The English-Wabigoon river runs upstream through Dryden, downstream to Grassy Narrows. A pulp and paper mill, owned by Reed Paper Limited, is located in Dryden. Dryden Chemicals Limited (a subsidiary of Reed Paper Limited), based in Dryden, uses mercury in its chloralkali plant, which produces products such as chlorine and caustic soda for the pulp and paper mill. In the process of production, significant amounts of methyl mercury were "lost" in the plant's wastewater that was discharged into the English-Wabigoon river. Specifically, between 1962 and 1970, 20,000 pounds of mercury were dumped into the river as effluent.

Consequently, the river, all three hundred miles of it, was poisoned. So were the fish and all other living things whose habitat was the river. Although the Ontario government was aware of the possible/probable health risks associated with exposure to methyl mercury some years earlier, it was not until 1970 that it finally decided to order Dryden Chemicals Limited to stop dumping mercury into the English-Wabigoon river. By this time however, damage to the environment was complete and irreversible.

You probably know that methyl mercury is a deadly poison. In Minamata, a fishing village in Kyushu, Japan, over a hundred villagers died and several hundreds suffered serious brain damage as a result of eating poisoned fish and shellfish. The source of the poison was the Chisso Chemical Company's giant petrochemical plant. Over the years, it had discharged great quantities of mercury-laced effluent into the bay (Ellis and DeKeseredy, 1996).

The acute effects of methyl mercury poisoning (**Minamata disease**) among the residents of Grassy Narrows are indicated by reports of numbness in feet and hands, painful joints, improperly working eye reflexes, high blood mercury levels, impaired hearing, tremor, feelings of listlessness, and loss of energy. Based on the results of a health survey he conducted, a Japanese specialist in the study of methyl mercury poisoning concluded that "methyl mercury poisoning must be suspected whenever there is a high incidence of visual fields and sensory disturbance, especially when the same symptoms are prevalent in families" (cited in Shkllnyk, 1985: 195). To this we would add, especially when these symptoms and blood levels of mercury are highest among those who eat the most fish—tourist fishing guides and their families.

The chronic effects of methyl mercury poisoning were long-lasting consequences that helped destroy the community itself. Shkllnyk (1985), describes the poisoning of the atmosphere and of the English-Wabigoon river system as "the last nail in the coffin" of the Grassy Narrows reserve community. Indicators of a community in crisis include an 80 percent high school drop out rate; marked increases in the number of children placed in foster homes and/or adopted; for persons aged 15 to 44, a violent death rate five times greater than the rate for Canada as a whole; a suicide rate six times greater than the average for Canada as a whole; massive unemployment; extreme widespread poverty and a rampant sense of powerlessness; hopelessness, alienation, loss of personal and communal identity and sense of solidarity (Shkllnyk, 1985: 234-235).

The poisoning of the environment is not the only cause of the harmful effects described here. The history of the Grassy Narrows band is replete with examples of harms inflicted upon them by colonialism and modernization. In a statement presented to Justice Patrick Hartt, Chair of the Royal Commission on the Northern Environment, Chief Fobister identified a few of these as follows:

▶ the intentional undermining of our religion and our way of life from the Treaty to the present day by the Roman Catholic church, the Royal Canadian Mounted Police, and the Government;

▶ the loss of income from diminished muskrat trapping due to hydro flooding;

▶ the Jones Road breaking the isolation factor which helped in the preservation of a way of life;

▶ the progressive addiction due to alcohol made readily available by tourists, outfitters, and taxi-drivers;

▶ the interdependency and introduction of a foreign value system;

▶ the loss of commercial fishing due to mercury;

▶ the loss of employment and income when Barney Lamm's Ball Lake Lodge closed due to mercury;

▶ the easy availability of welfare [which] discouraged men from working; and

▶ the Chief and Council's incapability to amend the mercury situation and to provide alternative employment (cited in Shkllnyk, 1985: 224).

To this list, Anastasia Shkllnyk adds relocation. For example, a few years prior to 1962, the Canadian federal government relocated the band in its present (Grassy Narrows) location in order to facilitate the delivery of services to it at minimal cost, and relocation undermined communal solidarity and a sense of personal identity. The Grassy Narrows band had already suffered a number of grievous blows when, in a weakened state, it was afflicted with methyl mercury poisoning. The cumulative result was "the total physical, mental, [social] and spiritual breakdown" of members of this reserve community.

Carver Terrace: Resistance to Environmental Injustice

During the 1980s, Carver Terrace, a housing development within Carver City, Texas, was one of the most contaminated places in the United States. In 1984, the U.S. federal government identified it as a Superfund site. A Superfund site is one that is marked for an accelerated or emergency clean-up program.

Contamination of the land on which Carver Terrace stands began in 1910 and ended in 1961. During this 50-year period, two wood-treating companies produced such highly toxic chemicals as creosote and arsenic, and disposed of them into the soil. Local government officials interested in providing jobs and collecting taxes issued permits for the two companies to operate on the site. In 1967, they issued a zoning permit for a developer to build houses on the site. Houses and streets were built close to the contaminated soil, and most of Carver

Terrace's homeowners were middle-class African-Americans who were unable to purchase homes in white neighborhoods because of racial discrimination.

Residents of Carver Terrace were not aware of the extreme toxicity of the soil adjacent to the land on which their houses were built, but they gradually acquired this information. Sometime prior to 1979, the United States Congress asked 50 of the largest companies producing and disposing of toxic chemicals to report sites that contained hazardous waste. Koppers, one of the companies operating on the Carver City sites, identified it as a hazardous site. The Texas Department of Water Resources recommended that Carver Terrace be declared a Superfund site, and in 1984 the EPA did so. In 1987, residents who had experienced health problems for some time sued Koppers. They were unsuccessful, but some of them reached an out-of-court settlement with the company. Then, in 1988, the Environmental Protection Agency (EPA) recommended that the site be cleaned up using a technique known as soil washing/filtering. Relocating the residents was also considered. However, the EPA felt that the level of toxicity was not high enough to justify recommending this more expensive, but safer, alternative.

Local environmental and health groups, the developer of the residential community, and the EPA offered different interpretations of: the malodorous air; formerly healthy individuals becoming sick and/or dying; and stunted and otherwise deformed animals and plants. Not knowing what to make of different estimates of the health risks associated with the contamination, the Carver City residents decided to take matters into their own hands. In 1988, they formed the Carver Terrace Community Action Group (CTCAG) and a coalition with a local environmental group called Friends United for a Safe Environment (FUSE). Between 1988 and 1992, "a successful repertoire of direct action strategies supported by an environmental [justice] frame [a social construction]" resulted in the federal government buying out and relocating the residents, even in the face of opposition by its own Environmental Protection Agency (Capek, 1993: 14).

The social struggle between the EPA and CTCAG took the form of claims and counter-claims-making. Capek (1993) attributes the success of CTCAG to the fact that it derived its claims (rights to information, compensation, hearings at which their testimony would be taken seriously) from a specific interpretation of the situation which she calls the environmental justice frame. In addition to its claims-making contribution, this social construction also attributed blame to CTCAG's opponents.

At the same time of its formation, 1988, CTCAG members were unaware of the environmental justice frame, or its relevance as a weapon in their social struggle. Through their association with FUSE, a Texarkana city environmental group with connections to other local and national environmental social movement organizations (e.g., Greenpeace) and persons (e.g., Lois Gibbs of Love Canal, Buffalo, N.Y.), they learned about it at conferences and meetings, they embraced it, and were guided by it. The adoption of the environmental justice frame, together with a "racism frame" (Carver Terrace residents were mainly African-Americans who were aware of the fact that residents in a mainly white community were relocated with far less fuss when their housing tract was contaminated), helped politicize the struggle and garner national support for their plight. The federal government's decision to relocate them was a decision influenced more by political considerations than the testimony of Koppers', the EPA's or the local city council's experts—persons with relevant technical credentials.

Here it is relevant to note that "social closure" was practised by CTCAG's opponents. For example, information about sources and levels of contamination and their impact on the health of Carver Terrace residents was not communicated to them. Since they could not afford to hire their own experts, they had to rely on danger estimates provided by their opponent's experts. Moreover, information provided by independent experts (e.g., Reports) was withheld from them. During the early stages of the struggle, that is before CTCAG successfully claimed its right to information, knowledge was a power resource possessed mainly by their opponents. Their successful claim helped equalize the distribution of this resource.

Direct action strategies were also part of the social struggle. CTCAG members, as well as members of local, state, and national groups marched, demonstrated, held press conferences, and participated in other activities that engaged the attention of the media and disseminated information about their plight and the justice of their case.

In addition to the successful construction of the conflict as one between environmental-racial justice/injustice, and participation in political (direct action) activities, the outcome of social struggle between CTCAG and the EPA was also influenced by decisions make by the EPA itself. Declaring Carver Terrace a Superfund site (e.g., including it in a list of the country's 50 most hazardous sites requiring emergency action) and then deciding to deal with the problem by merely washing the soil, created an obvious contradiction that its opponents exploited. The EPA, in short, contributed to its own defeat.

Human Development Index

The case studies presented here describe environmental degradation in two rich, developed countries. The degree of inequality between the United States, Canada, and poorer countries is revealed by the United Nations' (1995) **Human Development Index**. Together with other information, a detailed examination of the factors included in the Index suggests that a relatively small number of high human development countries, the world's "top-dog" countries, make a disproportionately large contribution to the environmental degradation of the world (global commons), their own countries, and other less well developed countries.

One of the case studies described here suggests that the same thing happens within countries. For example, a relatively few powerful social units (e.g., businesses) contribute disproportionately to the degradation of the country's environment (national commons), as well as the environment of communities and neighborhoods (local commons). Power and inequality, as well as a primarily self-interested, short-run oriented motivational structure are, in our view, clearly implicated in the destruction of global, national, and local commons. The statistical data presented can be appropriately interpreted using the specific "commons," and the more general "power/inequality" theoretical perspectives described earlier.

Global Environmental Degradation

Erhlich and Erhlich (1991: 123) use the following formula to assess the impact of human activity on the environment: I = PAT or, Impact = Population, multiplied by Affluence, multiplied by Technology. Energy, its mobilization and use, is an important indicator of affluence. Mobilizations of energy include damming and diverting water systems, and deforestation. Energy use produces such material things as highways, telephones, computers, homes, airports, plastics, air conditioners, and automobiles. Environmental destruction and degradation occur when mobilization effects are multiplied by use effects.

For example, a forest is razed in order to strip-mine for coal, a significant source of carbon dioxide. Coal-using power plants are inefficient energy users (the technology factor) that contribute to global warming by emitting high volumes of carbon dioxide into the atmosphere. The larger the number of people dependent on the products of coal-using power plants, the greater the harmful impact on the environment (the population factor).

Affluent (developed) countries with large, high-consumption populations are the major source of emissions (carbon dioxide, nitrogen oxide, methane) that cause global warming and acid rain. The United Nations Human Development Report (1995) reveals that, even among "high development countries," the United States (ranked number two), makes a disproportionately large contribution to polluting the environment. Thus, of the 36 high human development countries for which data are available, the United States accounts for approximately 45 percent of carbon dioxide emissions (mobile sources, energy transformation, and industrial uses) and sulfur and nitrogen emissions. With a rate of 8.95 it ranks second, after Luxembourg (11.41), in greenhouse gas emissions per capita. Although Luxembourg's rate is higher, its contribution to environmental pollution is infinitesimal compared with the United States because Luxembourg has a population of 0.4 million, while the U.S. population stands at 275 million (estimates for the year 2000). The U.S. rate of 8.95 is one and a half times greater than the rate (5.90) for the 23 high human development countries for which information was provided (1995: Table 36).

Data on environmental pollution for poorer, "low/lowest human development" countries was not included in the UN 1996 Report. Presumably, it was not available. For this reason, comparisons between high and low human development countries cannot be made. However, some idea of the magnitude of the difference is suggested by comparisons between the highest and lowest ranked (HDI index) countries for which data are available.

Table 7.2 shows that Canada's greenhouse gas emissions per capita were almost twice as high as Poland's, and Canadian hazardous waste production was 95 times higher than Poland's. Comparable figures for the United States and Poland are over twice as high and 281 times higher, respectively. North America's greenhouse gas emissions per capita were over twice as high as the European Union's, and North America's hazardous waste production was slightly more than that of the European Union even though it has 54 million fewer people.

Table 7.2
Greenhouse Gas Emissions and Hazardous Waste Production in Selected Countries

Country	HDI Rank	Population (millions 1992)	Greenhouse Gas Emissions per capita 1990	Hazardous Waste Production in metric tons 1990
Canada	1	31	7.10	6 080
United States	2	275	8.95	18 000
Poland	51	39	3.56	64
European Union	–	370	4.3	21 520
North America	–	306	8.8	24 080

Source: United Nations (1995), Human Development Report, Table 36.

So far, we have presented evidence indicating that highly developed countries such as the United States and Canada are significant sources of global environmental degradation. As pointed out in the next section, these countries also degrade their own environments, with members of some social groups being exposed to greater risks of harm than others.

Environmental Discrimination

In 1992, Ulrich Beck, a German sociologist, published his political ecological theory of the risk society that focused on the harmful global-environmental impact of modernization. Industrial production is the engine that drives modernization, and hazardous wastes and chemical pollutants are by-products of industrial production. Industrial plants are part of a system that includes technology, science, the law, and business corporations: technology creates the risks; scientific experts underestimate or do not recognize the threat they pose to the environment; environmental protection laws are either absent or created long after major damage is done, or are so fall of loopholes as to be virtually useless; and business corporations profit from the production of materials that degrade and destroy the environment. Beck's theory identifies modernization as the general cause of environmental destruction/degradation, but his focus on global consequences tends to divert attention from the problem of environmental discrimination within societies.

Central to Beck's risk society thesis is the hypothesis that the industrialization of the world threatens the world itself, all its trees, plants, non-human and human animals. "All life on Earth," he says, "faces the threat of self-destruction" (1992: 21).

The harmful consequences of global warming and ozone layer depletion caused by unintended self-destructive human activity are symmetrically distributed. That is to say, all people in all of the countries of the world are exposed to the same risk of being harmed. Within any given industrialized or industrializing society, however, the destruction of health and other risks associated with modernization may be asymmetrically distributed. For example, members of some social class and race/ethnic groups may be exposed to far greater risks of being harmed by the location of toxic waste dumps and industrial plants producing hazardous waste products. Therefore, we can supplement Beck's global risk society theory by an examination of "environmental discrimination" within highly industrialized societies such as the United States.

A review of the history of environmental discrimination in the United States reveals a number of brutal apogees or "high points." One of them is vividly described by Gallagher (1994) in her book *American Ground Zero*. She shows and tells about the poisoning of the environment, and the killing and maiming of human beings and wildlife associated with the above-ground testing of nuclear weapons. As she explains, nuclear clouds covered most of the United States east of the Nevada test site. Overrepresented among those who were killed by cancers of one kind or another, or who became seriously ill and remained so for the rest of their lives, were people described by a high ranking military officer as members of "a low use segment of the population" (1994: 11). These included members of lower-class groupings and American Indians. The bombs were exploded closest to their habitats. They were treated as experimental subjects by senior military personnel and scientific experts who suspected, but did not reveal to them, the likely consequences of exposure to high doses of radiation. Here, the most serious health and quality of life costs were inflicted on the poor and members of a specific visible, indigenous, minority group, while the benefits were experienced by a much larger group, members of "the Free World."

Other significant cases of environmental discrimination against members of lower social class and visible minorities who are poor and politically powerless, is provided by a review of the siting of hazardous waste products dumps. To a disproportionate degree, these are located closest to the homes and workplaces of "low use segments of the population" (Commission for Racial Justice, 1987).

"You show us a community whose population is 75 percent or more black and/or poor, where the land is cheap, where the rate of unemployment is high, and the ability to move to another community where jobs are available is low, and where the residents are relatively powerless politically, and we will show you a community in which hazardous waste management dumps and processing plants are either presently located, or are most likely to be located in the future" (Alario, 1995: 12).

In return for the employment income they obtain from working in toxic waste management related jobs and the local taxes they pay, poor communities frequently accept siting offers. It's a choice between desperately needed jobs/taxes and environmental/personal health. Often, however, offers that the community can accept or reject are not made. Instead, the siting of commercial hazardous waste management facilities is simply imposed on poor communities on the basis of the scientific and economic assessments. Taken together, siting decisions are an outcome of control of property and cultural capital, class and race/ethnic discrimination, and purely economic considerations.

The weight given to each of these factors varies across different communities. Sumter County (Alabama), Scotlandville (Louisiana), and Kettleman (California), are all examples of "poor and high proportion of black or Hispanic residents/large toxic waste management facility, communities." Above all others, Morrisonville (Louisiana), a riverside community of approximately 300 mainly African-American residents, stands out as a "sacrificed community, within a larger sacrifice zone" called Cancer Alley, U.S.A. (Bowermaster, 1993). See Box 7.2 for more information on this problem.

Economic considerations are primarily responsible for the siting of thousands of U.S. and Canadian corporate business outlets which environmentalists accuse of degrading global and national commons. Some of the environmentalists contend that a significant amount of the environmental pollution/degradation caused by human activities in richer and poorer countries has its source in the demands of consumers in those nations for hamburgers.

The Hamburger Connection

As you know, hamburgers are made of beef, which is produced by cattle. What you may not know are the following cattle facts:

> There are 1.28 billion cattle living on the earth.

> Their combined weight is greater than the total weight of the earth's human population of approximately 6 billion people.

> They graze on almost one-quarter of the earth's land surface.

> They eat enough grain to feed hundreds of millions of people, consuming over 70 percent of all the grain produced in North America (Rifkin, 1994).

Along with Jeremy Rifkin's (1994) "cattle culture" facts, we present the following "hamburger culture" facts. In North America, the hamburger really has lots of "economic sizzle." A report by Environment Canada, the federal ministry, reveals that 1,600 Canadian outlets selling hamburgers accounted for about $2 million in sales annually. Almost all adults (close to 95 percent) have eaten a hamburger at least once (Environment Canada, 1996).

BOX 7-2

A Town Called Morrisonville

Only 40 years ago Louisiana was a simple, beautiful place, a "sportsman's paradise," boasting clean air and water. The landscape was flat, subtropical, marked by huge sugarcane plantations. The people along the river lived off fish plucked from its waters, game trapped in the bayous, and vast gardens.

In the 1930s Louisiana first offered tax exemptions to entice petrochemical companies and oil refineries to locate along the Mississippi River. They came, lured by the state's vast natural resources of oil, gas, brine, and surface water. By the 1970s the stretch between Baton Rouge and New Orleans was home to more than 100 chemical makers and refineries and became known as the Chemical Corridor. Today it is better known as Cancer Alley, with the highest concentration of manufacturers, users, and disposers of toxic chemicals in the United States. Included among them is Dow Chemical. Its plaquemine plant, situated adjacent to Morrisonville with its 98 homes occupied by 87 families, opened in 1958 and is flourishing. It employs 2,100 people and annually produces 16 billion pounds of chemicals. It reportedly generates 10 percent of Dow's worldwide sales of almost $19 billion. Each year it also generates more than 3.3 million pounds of toxins —from acetaldehyde to xylene— that have gone directly into the local air, water, and ground.

As a result the air is a toxic gumbo of manmade chemicals that mix and react in ways scientists concede they don't fully understand. (Federal researchers have studied extensively very few of the 60,000 chemicals in commerce.) Millions of pounds of toxic chemicals go directly into the Mississippi each year. Millions of pounds of toxic debris have been buried, dumped in landfills, stored in surface pounds, or injected through underground metal pipes deep into the earth.

People suffer too. The Green Index, published last year by the Institute for Southern Studies, ranks Louisiana 49th among all states in environmental health. Toxic fumes from waste sites cause nausea, headaches, and vomiting in workers and residents. Parishes along the river rank among the highest in the nation in deaths caused by cancer of the lung, stomach, gallbladder, intestine, liver, pancreas, bladder, thyroid, esophagus, and skin. One environmental-health specialist defined living here as "a massive environmental human experiment." Others call the region "a Bhopal waiting to happen."

But another, more singular kind of death haunts those living close to the plants. In the past five years a number of communities along the river have been swept aside by industry, literally wiped off the map: Reveilletown was bought out by Georgia Gulf, Good Hope uprooted by a refinery in St. Charles Parish, Sunrise squeezed out by the Placid oil company. Dow bought Morrisonville in 1989 and relocated its residents.

BOX 7-2

What makes Morrisonville's buy out and razing special is its preemptiveness. The community's 300 residents had made no formal complaint about health problems, nor had an accident at the plant killed or hurt any of them. Dow bought the community before any of that could happen.

Environmental specialist Foutenot suggests the company's motives were dollars and cents. "The onus should be on the company [Dow] to clean up its act, not just move the people out of the way." "It was cheaper than pollution control equipment" said an employee of the Department of Environmental Quality. Jack Martin, a Morrisonville resident and deacon at Naharene Baptist church states that "Dow didn't exactly ask for our input. They just came and told us what they were going to do. I guess Dow is the plantation now."

Source: Bowermaster, (1993).

Hamburgers, millions of them, are sold by national and multinational corporations. Prominent among them is McDonald's. In a house publication entitled *Welcome to McDonald's* (1995: 11), the reader is informed that "A new McDonald's restaurant opened somewhere in the world every 17 hours." In 1995, there were "more than 18,000 restaurants in 89 countries" and by the following year, they expect to be operating "20,000 restaurants in over 100 countries," over 11,000 in the United States, and more than 1,600 in Canada (See Box 7.3). During the first six months of 1996, McDonald's reported a total revenue of US$5,091.1 million, and total assets of US$16,021.4 million (McDonald's Corporation Mid-Year Report, 1996). Based on figures presented in *Welcome to McDonald's*, we estimate that by the year 2000, McDonald's will serve over 6 billion hamburgers around the world. If they were equally distributed, everyone in the world could eat at least one hamburger during the year.

About four years ago, McDonald's, a Goliath among fast food producers and servers all over the world, became involved in a social struggle with David in the form of two unemployed Britons, a male and female whose combined income during the first six months of 1996 we estimate (based on unemployment income) at less than $30,000. David Morris and Helen Steel were environmental activists who published and distributed a leaflet accusing McDonald's of

➤ increasing the scarcity of water (through excess water use for cattle and other livestock);

BOX 7-3

Canadian McFacts

Close to two million Canadians visit McDonald's every day.

There are more than 900 McDonald's in Canada including traditional restaurants and non-traditional restaurants such as WalMart McDonald's, McDonald's Express and oil alliances.

McDonald's and its Franchisees employ more than 70,000 Canadians, making it the fifth largest employer in Canada and the largest employer of Canadian youth.

As of year end 1995, McDonald's Canada had grown to a $1.7 billion business with average restaurants sales of $2,054,000 per year.

In 1995, McDonald's Canada purchased over:

> 50 million pounds of beef
>
> 100 million pounds of fries
>
> 3.8 million dozen eggs
>
> 32 million dozen buns
>
> 23 million pounds of chicken
>
> 3.2 million pounds of fish
>
> 9 million pounds of lettuce

Source: *Welcome to McDonald's*, McDonald's, Toronto.

➤ polluting water supplies (through organic waste—cow dung—and the use of chemical fertilizers to produce feed for livestock);

➤ desertification (each hamburger patty costs approximately 35 pounds of eroded topsoil);

➤ fossil fuel depletion (it takes about a gallon of gas to produce a pound of grain-fed beef in the United States, and the average American family requires more than 260 gallons of fuel and releases 2.5 tons of carbon dioxide into the atmosphere);

➤ global warming (cattle and beef production is a significant factor in the emission of three of the four global warming gases);

➤ chemical damage to the environment (through manufacture and disposal of paper and plastic);

➤ causing health/nutrition problems (serving foods associated with cancer, heart disease, and obesity); and

➤ exploiting children (through advertising showing that Ronald loves McDonald's and McDonald's food, offering toys, linking birthdays with McDonald's food).

McDonald's responded to these accusations by suing Steel and Morris for libel, for defaming Ronald's favorite restaurant. During the course of the trial, a number of experts joined the side of David against Goliath. One of the experts who testified for Steel and Morris was Professor Hecht, who has been studying the social and biotic consequences of land use in Amazonia for over 20 years. She has published six books on this tropical region, is a professor at the University of California, Los Angeles, and is the Associate Director for Research of the Center for Latin American Studies. She has also specialized in the study of the relationship between cattle ranching/raising and the Amazonian environment, especially its tropical forest.

Hecht's research indicates that cattle ranching is a major cause of deforestation. The average deforestation (1,000 hectares per year, 1980-1989) for all developing countries is 868. The comparable figure for Brazil is 3,650 (United Nations, 1995: Table 17). The links between the demand for beef and deforestation are described in these terms: cattle ranching requires large areas of pasture.

For example, forests are cleared in order to meet the increased demand for grazing land. As ranching is not sustainable (e.g., after a few years the quantity and quality of grass will decrease), additional forest must be cleared for pasture. Engaged in by many ranchers, this process of encroachment leads to the deforestation of vast areas of tropical Amazonian forest and results in "tribal cleansing." In other words, the forest habitats of a number of indigenous tribes were destroyed and they were forced to move elsewhere, as the number of cattle increased, from 200,000 to 1.5 million during the 1960s, 1970s, and 1980s in just two *municipios*. This, in turn, resulted in a marked increase in methane gas (cattle flatulence) emissions. The combination of a finite supply of the most economically desirable land, raising cattle, and a high short-term rate of profit, led to the widespread land conflicts in which "more than 3,000 persons died during the past five years" (Hecht, 1996: 3).

The harmful environmental and social consequences of the linkages described by Hecht (1996) include global warming (deforestation and methane emissions), soil erosion, the destruction of indigenous peoples, and inter-group violence. All of these consequences are associated with the demand for hamburgers. In so far as this demand originates in North America, it is, according to Jean Carriere, another defence witness, a case of "economic imperialism."

These accusations led the Canadian government to undertake a comprehensive study on the *Life Cycle of the Hamburger* (1996). One of their major findings was that hamburgers sold in Canadian fast food outlets, including McDonald's, did not come from beef "produced on land once covered by tropical rain forest." Instead, they came from cattle raised on land that was "only suitable for grazing."

McDonald's was also accused of escalating the demand for a product—meat—that requires "between 10 and 20 times more fossil-level energy per edible tonne than grain production." This charge, the study found, has merit.

On its Web site, McDonald's has published its own statement of "Our Commitment to the Environment," which deals with issues such as waste reduction (www.mcdonalds.com/community/environ/info/commit/index.html).

In June, 1997, the judge in the case ruled that some of the accusations made by Davis and Steel were defamatory, but others were not because they were based on fact. Included among the latter are

> the exploitation of children;

> the cruel treatment of some animals;

> the autocractic and unfair nature of McDonald's management; and

> the fact that a consistent diet of McDonald's food increased the risk of heart disease.

Does this verdict mean the social struggle was clearly won by McDonald's? Yes, because this company was awarded partial damages. But collecting the monetary awards from two unemployed persons is bad publicity and therefore bad business. And how much money can the company collect from them anyway? At the time of writing, Morris and Steel are appealing the verdict. Moreover, in so far as the two activists used the media to socially construct McDonald's decision to sue them as an attempt by a large multinational corporation to wield its growing power to prevent criticism against it, McDonald's clearly lost the struggle. Indeed Klein (1997) reports that far more copies of the original Morris/Steel leaflet were distributed after the verdict than were distributed before or during the long trial. Finally, whereas previous conferences called by Steel and Morris were poorly attended by the world's media, their post-verdict conference was well attended by journalists. David, it seems, lost, but he also won more than Goliath did. Note too, political activities (direct action) were more effective than legal intervention or the testimony of experts in bringing about a Pyrrhic victory for McDonald's.

In our evaluation of the charges and rebuttals, we took into account the self-interested and social-responsibility motives of the Canadian government for whom year-round employment and economic activity are predominant objectives, and McDonald's, for whom a high return on investment is the bottom line. We also took into account the sensation seeking, publicity generating activities and pronouncements of environmental activists and vegetarians, and the published research of scholars. Unlike the judge, we concluded that the findings and conclusions of academic researchers are more supportive of many of the charges of activists/vegetarians than are the evidence and arguments presented by governments and McDonald's. Having read the information presented by both sides, you can reach your own conclusions.[2]

One conclusion that you have already reached is that one of McDonald's main products, hamburgers, are eaten mainly by people. Some **neo-Malthusian** population researchers say that if the human population continues to grow at the present rate, there will not be enough hamburgers, grain, or other staple foods to feed them all (Brown, 1995; Erhlich and Erhlich, 1991). Others believe that long before this extreme point is reached, acute inter-group violent conflicts will kill thousands, leaving the winners with adequate food resources and the losers without them. Still others, the optimists, contend that the threat of severe food shortages will instigate creative problem solving that will markedly increase the supply of food, bringing food resources into balance with the demand for them (Simon, 1981; 1995).

Population, Environment, and the Human Condition

With the death rate held constant, the size of the human population can ultimately be traced to human agency, that is, to couples making decisions about whether they should have children and, if they decide to do so, how many, over what period of time. The motivational structure central to commons theory is implicated in their decisions. Specifically, beyond an optimal level, decisions to have children, which benefit individual couples, impose a burden on the resources available to support those who make such decisions, the children they produce as a result of them, as well as others who produce no children (Erhlich and Erhlich, 1992; Schelling, 1978). Here, millions of intended individual (couple) decisions have the unintended consequence of producing a harmful collective outcome: a global commons whose food and water resources cannot adequately sustain the number of people who need and want them.

The relationship between **population size**, food, water resources, and human welfare has been a significant concern of scholars and activists for a long time. Of all the theories that have been published, few have generated as much acrimonious debate as that published by Thomas Malthus in 1798. He was a moralist/social scientist, and formulated a relatively simple yet powerful theory. Since this theory has often been misinterpreted by critics and supporters alike, we present it in his own words:

"Population increases in geometric ratio...Subsistence increases only in an arithmetical ratio. A slight acquaintance with numbers will show the immensity of the first power in comparison of the second.

By that law of our nature which makes food necessary to the life of man, the effects of these two unequal powers must be kept equal.

This implies a strong and constantly operating check on population from the difficulty of subsistence. This difficulty must fall somewhere; and must necessarily be severely felt by a large portion of mankind...

This natural inequality of the two powers of population, and of production in the earth, and that great law of our nature which must constantly keep their effects equal, form the great difficulty that to me appears insurmountable in the way to the perfectibility of society" (Malthus, 1798: 13-16).

Malthus' theory or **principle of population** can be illustrated as follows. Let's suppose that each person needs a bushel of corn in order to survive, and that the number of bushels produced by the available land increases arithmetically. Thus, in a given period of time, this piece of land produces 1 + 2 + 3 + 4 + 5 = 15 bushels of corn. Now, let's suppose that the population dependent on the land for food increases geometrically over the same period of time, that is, 1 + 2 + 4 + 8 + 16 = 31 persons. If it were divided equally, then each person would have half a bushel of corn. If the bushels of corn and people series continued through three more iterations (e.g., 6 + 7 + 8 = 22 bushels and 32 + 64 + 128 = 224 persons), each person would now have 0.2 bushels of corn if the corn was divided equally. At this point, or some time before it was reached, hunger, disease, famine, infanticide, force, and fraud would reduce the number of persons, bringing it into balance with available food resources. These consequences "prematurely shorten the duration of life" and are referred to by Malthus as **positive checks**.

Population growth and available food resources can also be balanced by the operation of preventive checks that include such "vices" as homosexuality, adultery, birth control, abortion, and the virtue of producing fewer children by delaying the age at which people get married. Malthus was against the "vices" and for "prudential restraint" on age at marriage.

The two kinds of checks were associated in the following way—if preventive checks were not adequate to bring population size and food resources into balance, then positive checks would come into play. Famine and war were the ultimate positive checks. Figure 7.1 describes the interrelationship among the variables in Malthus' theory.

FIGURE 7.1
Malthus' "Principle of Population" Theory

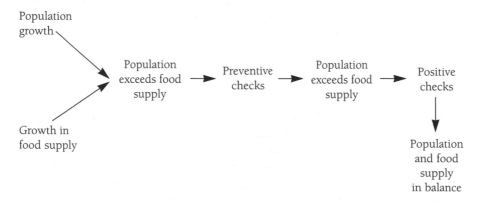

Malthus' theory, as well as predictions derived from it, have been subjected to a number of criticisms. First, Malthus believed that people would foresee the consequences of a negative imbalance between population size and resources (numbers exceed resources needed) and would engage in activities bringing population and resources into balance (e.g., delaying marriages, having fewer children, and remaining celibate until marriage). This has not happened everywhere (Keyfitz and Kindahl-Kiessling, 1994: 23). Even where birth control devices are freely available, the motivational structure described earlier appears to be uninfluenced by it.

Second, at that time he would have been unaware of the impact of artificial methods of birth control (contraception, abortion) on population growth rates, and the impact of the "green revolution" on increasing the supply of food resources.

Third, although the "fertility decisions" (number and spacing of children) were central to his theory, he did not actually study the way in which individuals actually make such decisions. Had he done so, says one of his earliest critics, he would have discovered that people have some knowledge about how much it costs to bear and rear children (their "price"), and what they obtain in exchange in the present and the future. Moreover, they do what they can to lower the price and increase the present and future benefits of having children (Rothschild, 1995: 354).

Thus, while there may be laws governing changes in large numbers of births, deaths, and marriages, this does not mean that the "natural law of populations" forces individuals to behave in ways that conform with Malthus' version of it. Individuals are active agents with free wills, and they make individual/household fertility decisions based on their "intelligence and self-interest" (Ensor, 1818: 207). Unfortunately, intelligence used in the service of short-run self-interest jeopardizes the health of the global commons.

Fourth, Malthus ignored the influences of social, political, and economic institutions, factors of great significance to sociologists. An institution, such as law or the family, is a complex, interrelated set of roles and norms (rules) with which members of these institutions are expected to conform because society as a whole has legitimized them. Thus, George Ensor, an early critic of Malthus, searched, but could not find, "any nation which possessing confirmed liberty and equal laws has become miserable merely by the excess of its people (1818: 308). Here, egalitarian political and legal institutions improve the otherwise harmful impact of overpopulation. In sum, the possible effects of over-population can be evaded, avoided, or muted by the presence of institutions that ensure or help promote three outcomes: (1) equality of opportunity generally and the empowerment of women in particular; (2) equality of condition (distribute resources required for a decent living more equally); and (3) values and life-styles that are inconsistent with "an ethic...of wasteful consumption" (Rothschild, 1995: 358).

Fifth, it is difficult to find compelling evidence supporting predictions derived from Malthus' theory. Thus, the Sahel tragedy is often cited as providing support for his excessively rapid growth/population collapse prediction, but more detailed analyses indicate that this did not happen. For example, Northern Sahel's population was growing, and periodic droughts did lead to a population collapse. But population growth was kept in check mainly by high mortality unrelated to droughts, and longer birth intervals due to breastfeeding (Pederson, 1995: 126).

Contemporary scholars who have been influenced by Malthus are aware of many of the shortcomings noted here. In particular, they have improved on Malthus' theory focusing on "the principle of population" by incorporating population, technology, resources, and consumption into theirs. Specifically, they have replaced a theory driven by the principle of population, by a multi-factor, ecological model. Thus, they may be referred to as "ecological Malthusians."

Ecological Malthusians include those who accept the validity of the following hypothesis:

"the absorptive capacity of the [environment] is already damaged and would be damaged further, in a possibly catastrophic way if world population continued to increase beyond the lifetime of our children, and, if the damage imposed on the [environment] per capita by the population of poor countries were to increase to the level now imposed per capita by the population of rich countries" (cited in Rothschild, 1995: 353).

The contemporary ecological Malthusians whose contributions we review next focus on the links between population growth, food production, and the quality/duration of human life.

Population Growth

By the year 2000, the world's population is estimated to reach 6.12 billion. At 1992 rates of population growth, the world's population is estimated to double in 38 years, i.e., by 2030. Developing countries (n = 123) however, are estimated to double their populations in 32 years, least developed countries in 27 years. Sub-Saharan Africa includes a number of the poorest developed countries—the least among least developed—and its population is estimated to double in only 23 years (UN 1995, Table 16).

Acutely aware of the link between rapid population growth and the scarcity of food resources, delegates to the International Conference on Population and Development (Cairo, 1994), decided to devise a plan that, if successful, would stabilize the world's population at approximately eight billion by the year 2050. The figure of eight (possibly nine) billion people represents a threshold which, if crossed, would, predicts Brown (1995), "exceed the (food) carrying capacity of the land in many countries, leading to environmental degradation, economic decline, social disintegration."

Food Production

As early as 1971, population biologists Erhlich and Erhlich concluded that the world's population of 4.6 billion was more than three times the number that the world can support on a sustainable basis. In a presentation to the American Association for the Advancement of Science (Baltimore, 1996), ecologist William Rees predicted that by the year 2040, two Planet Earths would be required to maintain all 174 countries in the UN report (1995), at current, highly unequal, standards of living. If we wanted developing countries to have the same standard of living as high human development/highly industrialized western societies, then he says we would need five Planet Earths, because "consumption [and] waste output by the present population exceeds the long-term carrying capacity of the planet we now live on" (Baltimore, 1996: 7).

Food and water scarcity is the ultimate determinant of the number of people for whom the earth can provide sustainable food resources. Brown identifies three of Earth's natural limits that are decreasing the global production of food. The first is "the sustainable yield of oceanic [and freshwater] fisheries." Based on his review of the evidence, Brown concluded that a combination of pollution, overfishing, and the introduction of alien fish species has resulted in a stable decline in the supply of seafood per person (1995: 5). The Chesapeake Bay Oyster Catch decline shown in Figure 7.2 is illustrative of the process of slowing fish food production all over the world.

FIGURE 7.2
Chesapeake Bay Oyster Catch, 1880-1993

Thousand tons

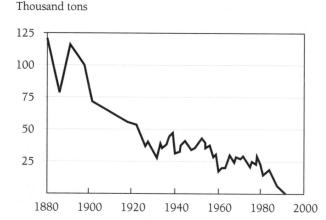

Sources: Maryland Department of Natural Resources, Va., Marine Resource Commission

The amount of available fresh water is the second of the earth's natural limits. The hydrological cycle supplies us with fresh water from rivers and underground aquifers. In various parts of the world, population growth and its concentration in cities has led to a decrease in the supply of water available for agriculture and, therefore, for the production of food. Table 7.3 describes the depletion of groundwater resources in various regions of the world.

Table 7.3
Groundwater Depletion in Major Regions of the World, Circa 1990

Region/Aquifer	Estimates of Depletion
High Plains Aquifer System, United States	Net depletion to date of this aquifer that underlines nearly 20 per cent of all U.S. irrigated land totals some 325 billion cubic meters, roughly 15 times the average annual flow of the Colorado River. More than two-thirds of this occurred in the Texas High Plains, where irrigated area dropped by 26 per cent between 1979 and 1989. Current depletion is estimated at 12 billion cubic meters a year.
California, United States	Groundwater overdraft averages 1.6 billion cubic meters per year, amounting to 15 per cent of the state's annual net groundwater use. Two thirds of the depletion occurs in the Central Valley, the country's vegetable basket.
Southwestern United States	Water tables have dropped more than 120 meters east of Phoenix, Arizona. Projections for Albuquerque, New Mexico, show that if groundwater withdrawals continue at current levels, water tables will drop an additional 20 meters by 2020.
Mexico City and Valley of Mexico	Pumping exceeds natural recharge by 50-80 per cent, which had led to falling water tables, aquifer compaction, land subsidence, and damage to surface structures.
Arabian Peninsula	Groundwater use is nearly three times greater than recharge. Saudi Arabia depends on nonrenewable groundwater for roughly 75 per cent of its water, which includes irrigation of 2-4 million tons of wheat per year. At the depletion rates projected for the nineties, exploitable groundwater reserves would be exhausted within about 50 years.
African Sahara	Vast nonrecharging aquifers underlie North Africa. Current depletion is estimated at 10 billion cubic meters a year.
India	Water tables are falling throughout much of Punjab and Haryana states, India's breadbasket. In Gujarat, groundwater levels declined in 90 per cent of observation wells monitored during the eighties. Large drops have also occurred in Tamil Nadu.

Table 7.3 *(continued)*

Region/Aquifer	Estimates of Depletion
North China	The water table beneath portions of Beijing has dropped 37 meters over the last four decades. North China now has eight regions of overdraft, covering 1.5 million hectares, much of it productive irrigated farmland.
Southeast Asia	Significant overdraft has occurred in and around Bangkok, Manila, and Jakarta. Over-pumping has caused land to subside beneath Bangkok at a rate of 5–10 centimeters a year for the past two decades.

Source: Global Water Policy Project and Worldwatch Institute, Washington, D.C. Reprinted with the permission of the Worldwatch Institute. For more information, visit their Web site at www.worldwatch.org.

The earth's third natural limit and "an even broader threat to world food expansion" to meet the needs of a growing population, is diminishing returns to fertilizer use. It seems that existing varieties of such staples as wheat, rice, and corn have reached the point where the application of even more nutrients does not increase their yield. For example, during the period 1950–1990, fertilizer was used as a substitute for land, and its application doubled the production of food. Since 1990, however, fertilizer has no longer been used as a substitute for land (see Figure 7.3). According to Brown, the trends depicted in this figure "capture the human dilemma" we face at the end of the twentieth century. Think about this—if food output cannot be increased by the use of fertilizers, and the amount of grainland per person is decreasing, how are we going to produce enough food to feed a rapidly growing population?

A rapidly growing population is implicated in this problem because fertilizer invention and use is, in part, a scientific response to the need for increased food production. If food production falls to the point where the demand for food exceeds its sustainable supply, then, says Brown, instability and violent conflicts are probable consequences.

Quality and Duration of Life

For a considerable proportion of Sierra Leone's population, life is nasty, brutish, and short. Of the 174 countries ranked by the United Nations according to their level of human development, Sierra Leone ranks 173 (Chad, also in Africa, is 174). Death comes early in Sierra Leone. For example, life expectancy at birth is 39 years, lowest of all 174 countries. On a variety of other quality of life indicators—daily calorie supply per person, crude death rate, access to safe water, access to public health services—Sierra Leone ranks among the five lowest ranked countries (UN, 1995).

Kaplan (1994: 4) implicates "overpopulation" in Sierra Leone's "coming anarchy." For example, the absolute size of Sierra Leone's population is not large, at 5.1 million, but it exceeds the ability of the land to provide enough food to feed everyone adequately on a sustainable basis. The country's land area is 27,925

FIGURE 7.3
World Fertilizer Use and Grainland Area Per Person

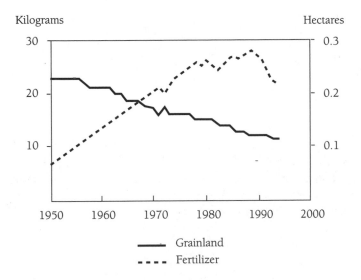

Source: Brown, (1995: 7). Reprinted with the permission of the Worldwatch Institute. For more information, visit their Web site at www.worldwatch.org.

square miles (73,326 square kilometres), but only 7.5 percent of this (2095 square miles/5500 square kilometres) is arable land. This means that approximately one million people must be supported by 380 square miles, or 1,000 square kilometres, of arable land.

In 1961, when Sierra Leone became independent, 61 percent of the country was covered in rain forest. By 1994, the demand for hardwoods for export, firewood for home use, and land to grow food, reduced this figure to six percent. Deforestation was followed by soil erosion that in turn decreased the productivity of the soil, and also permitted flooding. Flooded areas attracted mosquitoes that spread diseases such as malaria. Kaplan notes that "almost everyone...has it" (1994: 48). Scarcity of land and food in Sierra Leone and neighboring Liberia exacerbated violent inter-group conflicts that led to the creation of environmental/war refugees from Liberia to Sierra Leone and vice versa.

The process that resulted in such a poor quality of life for the people of Sierra Leone is described in Figure 7.4.

Based on his study of a number of West African countries (e.g., Benin, Togo, Niger, Ivory Coast, Guinea, Ghana, Nigeria, Sierra Leone), Kaplan reached the following conclusion: "It is Thomas Malthus, the philosopher of demographic doomsday, who is now the prophet of West Africa's future...and West Africa's future eventually, will also be that of the rest of the world" (1994: 48).

FIGURE 7.4
Population, Environment, and Conflict in Sierra Leone

Thomas Homer-Dixon, professor and Coordinator of the University of Toronto's Peace and Conflict Studies Program, formulated a theory linking population size/growth, environmental changes, and acute conflicts that improves on Kaplan's account in two important ways. First, he emphasizes "threshold effects" of environmental changes (1991: 80). For example, when large numbers of people collectively engage in activities that change the environment for the worse, these changes do not occur gradually and cumulatively over a long period of time. Instead, the environment (or parts of it) changes abruptly, leading to unpredictable **threshold crossings** that have significant, harmful, global consequences.

Second, population (size/growth/density) is one important cause of environmental scarcities that lead to acute conflicts, but it is not the only major cause. In this connection, consider the "soccer war" between El Salvador and Honduras in 1969.

William Durham (1979), identifies population growth/density and "land stress" as two ecological factors contributing to the soccer war. Homer-Dixon describes El Salvador as, "the most densely populated country in the Western Hemisphere (190 people per square kilometre)...[with]...a population growth rate of 3.5 percent per year (representing a doubling time of 20 years) (1991: 80).

In addition to these two ecological factors, land scarcity was also caused by a political/economic factor: largely, wealthy landowners in El Salvador used the absence of legal protection and their competitive advantage to squeeze small farmers off their land. This resulted in an increasingly large proportion of the land being owned by a relatively small number of large landowners, leaving many El Salvadorans landless. Land scarcity in El Salvador, then, was associated with both population density and political/economic factors that influenced the acquisition and distribution of land. The scarcity of land created refugees who migrated from El Salvador to Honduras. Viewed as unwanted competitors for resources that were already scarce in their own country, relations between Hondurans and the migrants from El Salvador were far from pleasant. A large number of supporters from both groups were present at the soccer match between Honduras and El Salvador. The co-presence of large numbers of supporters from these two countries at the soccer match merely precipitated hostilities that had been simmering for some time.

The "soccer war" incident is important for two reasons. First, it reveals that both population density and land distribution policies/practices can be significant causes of environmental scarcities that lead to acute inter-group conflicts. Second, it

FIGURE 7.5
Environmental Change and Acute Conflict

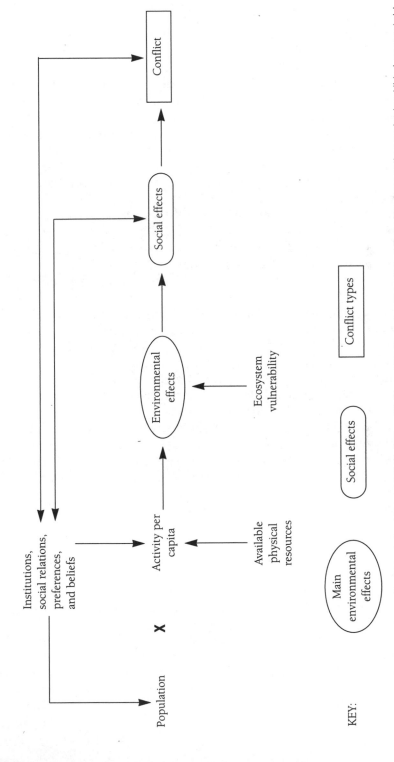

KEY:

Main environmental effects

Social effects

Conflict types

Source: Homer-Dixon (1991: 86). © 1991 by the President and Fellows of Harvard College and the Massachusetts Institute of Technology. Some portions previously published; some material reprinted by permission of the Canadian Institute for International Affairs, 5 Devonshire Place, Toronto, Ontario.

shows how migration mediates the impact of population density and land distribution policies/practices on conflict.

Lessons suggested by Durham's analysis of the soccer war are evident in Homer-Dixon's explanation of how environmental changes lead to acute conflict. Figure 7.5 describes interrelations among ecological, economic, and social variables in the "how theory" applied to developing countries.

This theory says that the size and **composition of a country's population** is influenced by a variety of cultural/structural factors. These factors, as well as the physical resources available, influence the level and kind of human activity per person. The size of the population and the amount/kind of activity per person causes environmental changes. Certain kinds of changes are harmful in and of themselves, and also add to their "natural" harm by causing inter-group conflict. These include greenhouse warming, ozone depletion, acid rain, deforestation, degradation of agricultural land and overuse, and pollution.

The harmful environmental changes described here cause social changes that are themselves causes of conflict. Identifiers of four major social effects are: decrease in agricultural production (food scarcity); economic decline (unemployment, income scarcity); displacement of population (environmental refugees); and disruption of stable, legitimate, authoritative institutions and social relations (families, governments, churches, schools). These social effects cause scarcity conflicts (e.g., probable "water war" between Turkey and Syria over Turkey's plan to dam and divert water from the Euphrates), group identity conflicts (the Bodo/government of India conflict in Assam), and inequality (relative deprivation) conflicts. It should be noted that inequality conflicts can occur in any country in which people believe that their actual level of economic achievement has, because of the country's rapid economic decline, suddenly fallen to a level they believe to be lower than it ought to be.

Like Malthus, the ecological Malthusians include decreases in the annual rate of population growth and population shrinkage in their policy suggestions. Critics of their population reduction policies point out that the ecological Malthusians tend to ignore the contribution made by: (1) economic institutions such as the market, and (2) natural processes such as the demographic transition, towards bringing population and resources into balance.

The Market

Julian Simon (1981, 1996), is prominent among **Cornucopian** (optimist) theorists.[3] Cornucopians are convinced that human ingenuity has contributed towards the progressive improvement in the quality of life in the past and will continue to do so in the future alongside continued growth in the size of the world's population. This counter-intuitive conclusion is derived from the following theory.

"More people and increased income cause problems in the short run—shortages and pollution. Short-run scarcity raises prices and pollution causes outcries. Those problems present opportunity and prompt the search for solutions. In a free society solutions are eventually found. In the long run the new developments leave us better off than if the problems had not arisen" (Simon, 1996: 358).

The solutions that are found are bought and sold, and return on the investment of time, effort, ideas, and the demand for them determines their market price. A "political-social-economic system that provides freedom from government coercion is a crucial element" in bringing population and resources into balance via the mechanism of the free market. Products and practices that contribute to a safer, self-sustainable environment will be produced if there is a profit (sufficiently high return on investment) to be made from their production that is greater than producing environmentally harmful products (Simon, 1996: 359).

During the past 25 years, the market has operated to increase the production of environmentally friendly "green stuff" (e.g., catalytic converters, air conditioners that do not use freon gas, recycled paper). On the other hand, market mechanisms clearly operated to maintain, if not increase, the production of environmentally harmful gases and other toxic substances during this period. Data from three separate sources—Worldwatch Institute, World Resources, and the United Nations—all indicate that environmental degradation and pollution increased between 1970-1995.

This finding does not necessarily disconfirm the "market-as-solution" thesis, because its advocates may say that environmental degradation and pollution have not yet reached the point where it is profitable for investors to invest in, and producers to produce, environmentally friendly products because most consumers demand them and are willing/able to pay for them. Once we have crossed the threshold beyond which consumers and producers, especially in affluent societies, clearly perceive the strong link between their activities and their health, standard of living, and quality of life, then the market will make a much more significant contribution towards improving the quality of the environment.

One problem with this line of argument is that serious, perhaps irreversible, damage may be done to the environment before market mechanisms begin working effectively. Moreover, some of the more significant, environmentally friendly changes that occurred during the period 1970–1995 were initiated by governments rather than markets (e.g., U.S. federal legislation prohibiting the use of freon gas in refrigeration units, laws prohibiting the use of leaded petrol).

The "capitalist-market-as-solution" thesis has also been criticized by scholars who draw attention to the limitations and harmful unintended consequences of relying on "the market" to produce a healthier, self-sustaining environment. According to Soros (1997), the capitalist market is driven by self-interest rather than the common interest. Left to itself, self-interest becomes rampant, and rampant self-interest eventually leads to "intolerable inequities and instability." Without effective government regulation, highly competitive markets will markedly increase and solidify the gap between richer and poorer groups within societies, and between the world's richer and poorer societies. Soros predicts that markets driven by "excessive individualism" will eventually undermine "the values and institutions of a free society" (1997: 48). In a similar vein, political scientist David Marquand offers this warning: "Sooner or later...we shall...have to choose between the free market and the free society" (cited in Gwyn, 1997: 10).

To some degree, criticisms of the market as solution are undermined by a free market that is becoming a potent force for preventing further damage to the environment. The insurance market is the one we have in mind. Weather-related disasters associated with global warming could, in the words of the President of the Reinsurance Association of America, "bankrupt the [insurance] industry" (Flavin, 1996: 34). Industries and other policy-holders that contribute to global warming, face the prospect of paying extremely high premiums for insurance, or reducing, if not eliminating, practices that damage the biosphere. The insurance market then, can make a significant contribution towards reducing the risks of climate change (Flavin, 1996: 34).

The Demographic Transition

Population and resources can be brought into balance by decreasing the size of the former and/or increasing the latter. Demographic transition theory links material prosperity (e.g., increased quantity and quality of resources) with population balance. A balanced population is one in which birth and death rates are approximately equal, and migration (in or out) is not a significant factor. In emphasizing the contribution made by material prosperity towards bringing populations into a positive imbalance with their resource base (e.g., more resources are available than are needed to satisfy basic biological and social wants), demographic transition theory identifies a mechanism, a "positive check," that Malthus did not take into account.

The demographic transition that operated as an effective positive check in Europe and other highly industrialized societies, including the United States, occurred in three stages.

In this model, material prosperity, the positive check that Malthus did not take into account, led to the two positive checks he explicitly acknowledged and favored. These were celibacy and delaying the age of marriage. As the relative size of the middle-classes increased, the number of persons adopting these positive checks also increased. Birth control (artificial contraception) was a positive check that Malthus opposed. Hence, he did not identify it as a positive check. Note that it follows and does not precede material prosperity. In this connection, Hardert et al. note that "Family size began to shrink in Europe and in the United States long before birth control pills or family planning campaigns existed" (1984: 341).

Those who support the demographic transition solution to the contemporary population-exceeds-resources-available problem afflicting many developing countries believe that history will repeat itself. Specifically, they believe that the history of industrialized societies will be repeated by developing societies. Industrialization depends on the production of an agricultural surplus that releases agricultural workers for work in cities and towns (Hardert et al., 1984: 342). The most industrialized societies, those with the highest levels of affluence, produce enough food for their populations with ten percent or less of their labor force in agriculture. The United States, for example, has five percent (or less) of its labor force in agriculture. The remaining eight most populated developing countries, however, have significantly higher proportions of their labor force in agriculture (See Table

Table 7.4
Top Ten Most Populous Countries by Selected Demographic Transition Relevant Factors

HDI Rank[1]	Country	POPULATION Size (millions) in 2000	1992 base: doubling time in years	Contraceptive prevalence rate, any method 1986–1993 (per 100 couples)	People in poverty[2] %	% Labour force in agriculture 1990–1992	Population in cities of 750 000+ as a % of the urban population
111	China	1284.6	62	83	n/a	73	38
134	India	1022.0	36	43	43	62	36
2	U.S.A.	275.1	91	74	11	3	76
141	Nigeria	128.8	23	6	n/a[3]	48	27
104	Indonesia	212.7	45	50	18	56	38
128	Pakistan	161.8	24	12	25	47	49
63	Brazil	174.8	40	66	52	25	42
146	Bangladesh	134.4	32	40	53	59	52
53	Mexico	102.4	34	53	33	23	41
120	Vietnam	82.6	31	53	n/a	n/a	33

[1] Human Development Index, *Human Development Report*, United Nations, 1995.

[2] The income or expenditure level below which a minimum, nutritionally adequate, diet plus essential non-food requirements are not affordable. *Human Development Report*, 1995: 223.

[3] Not available.

Source: United Nations, *Human Development Report*, 1995: Tables 12, 15, 16.

7.4). For each of them, the demographic transition, and a population brought into positive balance with its resources, are relatively distant goals.

One way of speeding up progress towards the realization of these goals is to markedly reduce the birth rate by artificial or natural means. However, Table 7.4 shows that six of the ten most populous countries in the world have relatively low contraceptive prevalence rates, varying from a low of 6 percent for Nigeria to a high of 53 percent for Mexico and Vietnam. Included among the reasons for these figures are the economic value of children as workers who contribute to the household income or food supply; the perceived value of children as their caretakers when their parents grow old and have no other sources of income, food. or shelter to rely on; the social and emotional value of children; the wish to have male children and to keep on having children until they have the desired number of male children; and lack of information about birth control and/or access to condoms, intrauterine devices, abortions, vasectomies, and other birth control methods.

The structure of households has also changed in ways that may undermine the hypothesized effects of the demographic transition. For example, with increases in material prosperity, extended families composed of grandparents, parents, and children and perhaps other close kin, are giving way to nuclear families composed of parents and children. This means that a country that has 300,000 extended households now has 580,000 nuclear households. To the extent that larger extended family households consume fewer food, energy, and other resources because it is more economical to feed, heat, and shelter a larger number of persons in the same household, increasing the number of households composed of fewer persons (nuclear families) will result in the consumption of a larger amount of the resources available. This will decrease the average level of material prosperity and leave fewer resources that can be invested in future economic growth (Mackellar et al., 1995).

Table 7.4 also reveals that poverty levels are relatively high. If these poverty levels are indicative of the relative absence of social and material prosperity, then, says Homer-Dixon, their demographic transition is "in doubt" (1991: 103).

Another factor placing the demographic transition in doubt, at least in the shorter run (i.e., within a generation), is the fact that developing countries have experienced massive urbanization without markedly increased industrialization of cities and towns. Indeed, Curran and Renzetti identify urbanization—the concentration of populations in cities—as "a major social problem" (1996). For example, between over one quarter (Nigeria) and three-quarters (China) of the population of the developing countries listed in Table 7.4 live in cities of 750,000 or more persons. Located in five of these countries are five of the world's largest metropolitan urbanized areas: Mexico City, Mexico (25 million); Sao Paulo, Brazil (22 million); Shanghai, China (17 million); Bombay, India (15 million); and Jakarta, Indonesia (14 million). Hunger, poor nutrition, unemployment, and a desperately poor quality of life are experienced by a large proportion of agricultural workers and others who migrate to cities. Instead of contributing to economic development, major cities in a number of developing countries appear to retard it.

Taken together, the factors listed here tend to retard or undermine the demographic transition in developing countries. Cleland reviewed the relevant research literature and came to the conclusion that "Demographic transition theory has been fatally damaged by...empirical scrutiny" (1994:353).

What Is to Be Done About Population and the Environment?

With the exception of advocates of human ingenuity and enterprise (market) solutions, and some supporters of the inalienable right of developing countries to determine the size of their own populations and do whatever it takes to reach levels of material prosperity enjoyed by industrial countries, there appears to be a consensus on one point: the size of the world's population has reached, or soon will reach, the point where it will cross the resources-available-to-sustain-it threshold. To prevent this from happening and, more optimistically, to change a negative population-resource balance to a positive one, we must do three things. First, we must decrease population growth and shrink the size of populations. Second, we must increase resources using environmentally friendly technologies and practices. Third, consumption levels, especially in the world's wealthiest societies, must be reduced or changed in ways that lead to a reduced demand for products that damage and degrade the environment.

Underlying these specific suggestions is a more general one that is derived from a power/inequality-commons theoretical perspective: acceptance of this perspective requires consideration of strategies that bring about changes in the motivational structure underlying the problem of environmental degradation.

We also advocate the formation of social movements whose objectives include protection of the environment in general, and environmental discrimination based on social class and race/ethnicity in particular. The claims-making activities of members of these groups also help bring about changes in the motivational structure underlying the problem of environmental degradation. Specifically, they raise the economic costs to polluters and degraders of engaging in activities that increase their profits but harm global, national, and local commons.

Decreasing Population Growth

Population growth can be decreased in a number of ways, and achieving material prosperity is one of them. After all, increasing the relative size of material prosperity did help lower the birth rate in Europe and North America. In fact, demographic transition theorists specifically identify the attainment of a threshold level of material prosperity as one way of lowering the birth rate in developing countries. To the extent that material prosperity includes the provision of old age benefits, couples in these countries may decide to have fewer children in order to ensure that

FIGURE 7.6
The Demographic Transition: Process and Outcome

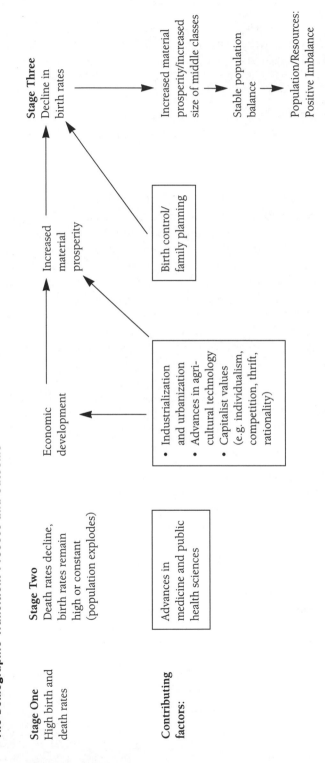

they will be taken care of when they are too old to look after each other, or themselves.

In addition to material prosperity, or independently of it, population growth may be slowed by emancipating women, implementing and enforcing a behavior management system. We shall assume that opportunities for controlling births (e.g., condoms, intrauterine devices, abortions) are available, provided either from domestic sources or by international aid and development agencies. The model presented in Figure 7.7 identifies the preferences/choices of people as the significant intervening factor.

Female Emancipation

Following Lappo and Schurman (1990: 30) and the authors of the United Nations Human Development Report (1995), we believe that full female emancipation will influence the reproductive choices of women in ways that lead to a decrease in population growth. This hypothesis is central to what we shall call the "gender emancipation transition" thesis. This transition involves three stages, each moving women from the margins to the center of economic and political power. In stage one (some Arab states' stage), gender inequality favoring males is significant and pervasive. In all major institutions, public as well as private (e.g., employment, government, education, legal, family), women are subordinate. Female life expectancy at birth is relatively low, an average of 67 for Syria, Iran, Iraq, and Egypt, and maternal mortality is high, averaging 162 per 100,000 live births (UN, 1995: Table A 2.2).

In stage two (Canada and Mexico), gender inequality decreases in areas and institutions that are not the real focus of power in society (e.g., education and health). Thus, "while doors to education and health opportunities have opened rapidly for women, the doors to political and economic opportunities are barely ajar" (UN, 1995 : 4). Female life expectancy at birth is high, averaging 80 years, and the maternal mortality rate is low, averaging approximately 7 per 100,000 live births (UN 1995, Table A 2.2).

Stage three is the Nordic (Sweden, Finland, Norway, Denmark) stage (See Box 7.4). In these countries, gender equality has spread to political and economic institutions, albeit without its full achievement. Life expectancy at birth is high, averaging approximately 80 years, and infant mortality is low, averaging 7 per 100,000 live births.

Findings cited in the United Nations (1995: 2) Report indicate that many industrial and developing countries have a long way to go to fully achieve stage two status. For example, of the 130 countries ranked on the basis of their gender-related development index (GDI), in none of them, not even Sweden (ranked number one), "do women enjoy the same opportunities as men." Around the world, women are greatly over-represented among those in poverty, the unemployed, those whom banks assume have no collateral to offer when seeking loans, and the lowest-paid wage earners. Almost everywhere, female workers are paid less than men for doing equal work. Finally, women are greatly underrepresented among corporate administrators and managers and in governments (Sivard, 1995).

BOX 7-4

A Leader in Gender-Balanced Politics

One of the first countries to grant women suffrage, Norway enjoys a well-deserved reputation as having one of the world's most gender-balanced political systems. Its multiparty system has consistently produced one of the most gender-balanced cabinets in the world, with about 40 percent women. Only very recently did Finland and Sweden surpass this ratio. From 1986 to 1989 and from 1990 on, the head of Norway's Labor Party, Gro Harlem Brundtland, has been the prime minister.

A long tradition of egalitarianism and a strong women's movement helped improve women's socio-economic status and political participation. Consultative rather than confrontational politics helped focus political competition on issues. A lively democracy, in which more than 80 percent of the electorate turns out to vote in national elections, ensures the political representation of diverse interests, including women's.

Women's movements since the turn of the century have sought political empowerment to promote gender-fairness policies. This politics-first strategy departs from women's employment-first or policy-first strategies used elsewhere. The 1960s and early 1970s witnessed the greatest leap of women's political representation. Between 1963 and 1967, women increased their representation in local councils from 5 percent to 12 percent and conducted voter education campaigns to teach women procedures and talk with them about issues.

Women in political parties and in women's organizations used the slogan "women representing women" as a means to the ends they sought. Parties began instituting quotas for female representation in the mid-1970s, and leftist and centrist parties continue to do so. Even in the major parties without quotas, women's representation exceeds 25 percent. The election of women was further aided by an electoral system based on proportional representation.

Increased female political participation has not made Norway a women's utopia. Women still do not enjoy equal rights with men in every area. And women's movements are now addressing such critical issues as large wage differences, job segregation and violence against women.

Source: United Nations (1995: 41), *Human Development Report, 1995.* Copyright © 1995 by United Nations Development Programme. Used by permission of Oxford University Press, Inc.

FIGURE 7.7
Population Growth Reduction Strategies

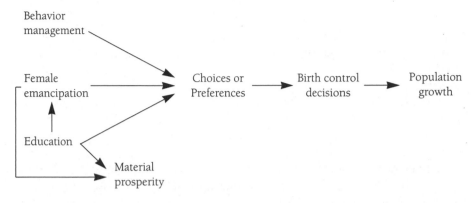

The authors of the United Nations Report (1995: 7) believe that "the market" cannot be relied upon to bring about the transition to stage three in a timely manner, if ever. Structural barriers, in the form of male dominated economic, political, educational, and religious institutions, effectively block or retard progress (See Figure 7.7). Instead, governments must intervene, and their interventions must take the form of "concrete strategies for accelerating progress" towards gender equality.

Specific, concrete strategies include

➤ reserving at least 30 percent of national decision making positions for women;

➤ increasing labor force participation for women, and passing/enforcing, pay-equity legislation;

➤ mounting campaigns aimed at pressuring all countries to unconditionally ratify the Convention on the Elimination of all Forms of Discrimination Against Women (90 UN member states have not yet done this);

➤ establish gender-equality targets and create national/global non-governmental organizations that would monitor progress, prepare reports, and mobilize bias in favor of reaching them;

➤ setting time-based targets for achieving legal equality;

➤ removing restrictions on women's collateral for bank loans, and pressuring banks to extend more credit to women; and

➤ devoting 20 percent of national budgets towards providing basic education, primary health care, family planning services, and nutrition for those in poverty or close to it.

Taken together, these interventions will, if effectively implemented around the world, usher in stage three of the global female emancipation transition. Stage three women are women who control their own fertility. Women who control their own fertility "are cornerstones of population and development-related programs" (International Conference on Population and Development, Cairo, September, 1994).

Reproductive Behavior Management

In addition to public education and exhortation, and making birth control methods generally available, reproductive behavior management systems emphasize coercion in which compliance is based on fear of punishment, or inducement in which benefits are made contingent upon compliance.

For a variety of political, social, economic, and religious reasons, the Quebec government is vitally interested in increasing the annual rate of population growth among French-Canadians. For primarily economic reasons, the Japanese government is also interested in increasing the rate of population growth of Japanese people. To this end, monetary incentives, based on the number of children, with a special bonus for four-children families, have been implemented. Conversely, the government of Indonesia is attempting to reduce its huge Muslim population's **annual growth rate** by offering a free trip to Mecca to married couples of reproductive age who practice birth control for a defined (lengthy) period of time (Curran and Renzetti, 1993: 190). Salient rewards can, it seems, be used to increase or decrease population growth rates. Policy makers who are interested in the latter outcome, must make the benefits made contingent with the extended and regular use of birth control practices greater than the present and expected future benefits of not using them or using them inconsistently.

For well over 125 years, China has been the country with the world's largest population. Ryan and Flavin point out that China "is roughly the same size as the United States but has four and a half times as many people," and that in 1994, "more people lived [in China] than in all of Europe, Russia, the United States, Canada, Japan, and Australia combined" (1995: 115).

Chairman Mao, revolutionary leader of the Chinese people, was very proud of the huge size of the Chinese population. For example, in 1949 he wrote, "It is very good thing that China has a big population even if China's population multiplies many times, she is fully capable of finding a solution, the solution is production" (cited in Ryan and Flavin, 1995: 115). Yet, by the year 2000, the annual growth of China's population is expected to be less than one percent, and it will come very close to achieving a national policy objective of reducing the size of the population by 1.2 billion!

In 1979, thirty years after the establishment of the Chinese People's Republic, government officials responsible for China's population policy realized that a more stringent population objective than the two-child limit and a more salient reward system would have to be implemented if China was going to reach its objective of reducing its population by 1.2 billion by the year 2000. To this end they issued one-child certificates. Compliance was rewarded with a variety of social and material benefits. In the following year, 1980, a birth quota system was implemented (local officials were made responsible for ensuring that the number of children born in their areas did not exceed the permitted number), and penalties were imposed on couples who had more than one child. Penalties included heavy fines and public humiliation.

Overall, the reproductive behavior management system implemented by the Chinese was remarkably successful. Thus, during the period 1992–2000 China's annual population growth rate is estimated to be 1.0 percent. The comparable figures for Canada and the United States are 1.1 and 0.9, respectively. The population of seven (of 151) developing countries is not expected to double until 2054—thirty years longer than the doubling year for all developing countries—and China is one of them (UN 1995: Table 16).

Earlier in this chapter we drew attention to the importance of actually studying why/how individuals make their fertility decisions. Li's (1995) study reveals that peasant and non-agricultural worker couples reacted very differently to the government measures—based partly on self-interested calculations, and partly on compliance with traditional cultural norms favoring the birth of sons. These differences, together with the fact that the government had far greater control over the lives of non-agricultural (e.g., government) workers than peasants, meant that compliance with the one-child policy, and the child-spacing policy was far greater among the former than the latter.

The perceived seriousness of the population size problem, growth in relation to resources and a willingness to violate individual rights in order to solve it, and a set of national values ranking the collective good over the good of individual, would appear to be the pre-conditions necessary for the effective implementation of coercive-punitive population control policies.

Technology/Production

In addition to decreasing the size of human population, technologies that contribute significantly to material prosperity must also be the focus of interventions aimed at achieving or maintaining sustainable global and societal environments. The primary reason for such a focus is the damage done to the environment by technologies of production. Chairman Mao, you may recall, was convinced that production was the solution to sustaining China's large population. Production in other words, would bring population and resources into balance.

China's implementation of a technology-driven, capitalist market solution to the problem of increasing the material prosperity level of its huge population within a relatively short period of time has also been remarkably successful (Ryan and Flavin, 1995). The environment, however, has been seriously damaged in the process. For example, China is a developing country (ranked 111 out of 174 in the United Nations Development Index), and if present trends continue, China will join the United States as "leading contributors to many global [environmental] problems" (Ryan and Flavin, 1995: 114). China's impact on the rest of the world is great now, and will become even greater as its economy expands. From its experience we can derive strategies that will contribute significantly to the goal of a sustainable environment for China and the rest of the world.

First and foremost, the energy demands of a country must be mainly, if not exclusively, met by modern technologies using natural gas, solar energy, and wind power as energy sources. Coal, especially when it is used to produce energy by directly burning it, is a major contributor to pollution, acid rain, and global warming. Perhaps, then, we need an international agreement requiring that no more than 30 percent of a country's primary energy needs are met by directly burning coal.

Second, legislation aimed at preventing deforestation beyond defined limits should be accompanied by implementing a behavior management system that rewards people for not cutting down trees, and planting new ones. Beyond this, reforestation policies on a large scale should be implemented, and extant laws against tree cutting should be strictly enforced.

Third, educational campaigns, aimed at encouraging people to use non-polluting means of travel (e.g., bicycles rather than private cars), should be initiated on a recurring basis. If polluting means of travel must be used, limit the damage done to the environment by relying mainly on public transportation systems using non-leaded fuels and catalytic converters.

Fourth, limits should be set on the amount of arable land that can be diverted to other than food-producing uses, and the results of scientific research to overcome impediments to increasing the productivity of the arable land that has been preserved (e.g., how to extend the period during which the crop returns from increasing fertilizer use begin to set in, use high-yielding crop strains etc) must be relied on.

Fifth, laws preserving the quantity and quality of fresh water, establishing thresholds beyond which fresh water cannot be diverted to non-farm uses should be enacted and then strictly enforced. This should be part of a more general sustainable water resource policy.

Affluence/Consumption

Erhlich and Erhlich identify "lowering per capita consumption" as one of the three interrelated strategies for achieving a sustainable global society (1991: 181). The United States and Canada contain approximately five percent (306 million) of the world's population. However, they jointly account for a disproportionate share of the damage done to the environment because the impact of a relatively small population is multiplied by the world's highest affluent/consumption levels sustained by the use of environmentally damaging technologies.

In this connection, Erhlich and Erhlich cite figures indicating that an American baby "represents twice the destructive impact on Earth's ecosystems and the services they provide as one born in Sweden, 3 times one born in Italy, 13 times one born in Brazil, 35 times one born in India, 140 times one born in Bangladesh, 280 times one born in Chad, Rwanda, Haiti, or Nepal" (1991: 134).

From cradle to grave, the growing American and Canadian baby can make a significant contribution to a **sustainable society** by consuming less, and by consuming environmentally friendly products. Socialization in families and schools, as well as public education campaigns are the mechanisms that could help bring about cultural changes which change consumption levels and patterns (Eitzen and Bacca Zinn, 1997). To these, one may have to add higher "sumptuary taxes" on products and practices that are clearly harmful to the environment (e.g., large autos and "sport-utility" vehicles that consume an enormous amount of gas, large pleasure-boats that pollute waterways). Just as the freedom to smoke cigarettes anywhere and to advertise them for sale to anyone has been constrained by socialization, public education, and legislation, the individual's freedom to consume more and more and more may have to be constrained in the interest of a sustainable society.

What, you may ask is a sustainable society? A sustainable society is one that does not exceed the capacity of its natural resource bases (land and water) to keep on producing a constant or increasing yield of products needed or wanted by its members. Thus, if corn was the staple food of a society, its corn-producing soil is viewed as "capital" (resource base), and the corn it produces is viewed as "interest," then this society would be self-sustaining with respect to food when enough corn (interest) is produced to satisfy human demand without decreasing the productive capacity of the soil (capital).

Given the centrality of consumption to economic growth and to the sense of self worth among individuals and families, it is going to be difficult to reduce and change levels of consumption (Eitzen and Bacca Zinn, 1997). Perhaps a necessary condition for achieving these objectives is a catastrophic consequence clearly tied to specific over-consumption patterns, such as the closing of all Atlantic coast beaches due to the accumulation of raw sewage, medical water, and solid non-biodegradable garbage, or the rapid loss of all non-domestic sources of oil.

Social Movements

Social change is an objective shared by social movements all over North America. A number of sociologists specializing in the study of social movements distinguish between **equity movements** which involve "the gradual mobilization of long standing grievances such as those by African-Americans, Native Americans and women," and **technology movements** associated with "an environmental threat which precipitates the rapid mobilization of local residents and their supporters against the industry in question" (Walsh et al., 1993: 25). Unlike equity protests which "seldom have to contend with scientific experts who argue against their position, technology protests typically have to mobilize challenges against mainstream scientific opponents" (1993: 25).

Against the background of these conceptual differences, research cited by Capek (1993) suggests that the effectiveness of social movements aimed at preventing or decreasing technologically induced environmental degradation may be increased by them adopting an environmental justice frame that includes claims against racism, sexism, and ageism wherever these forms of discrimination are evident. The environmental justice frame, in other words, can be used by members of both equity and technology movements.

Given the adoption of an environmental justice frame, what is the best way of bringing about social changes that protect the environment? Should social movements hire their own experts to challenge the evidence of experts hired by polluters/degraders with greater financial resources? Political (direct action) approaches are likely to be more effective than scientific or legal approaches that rely heavily on expert testimony. Politics, it seems, can overcome credentials (Capek, 1993).

Finally, members of many social groups are "underdogs." That is to say, they are members of relatively powerless groups. Compared with the claims of the "top-dog" groups they challenge, they own or control far fewer resources such as property, wealth, income, influence with governments, and credentials. The control of or ownership of resources is not the only, nor necessarily the most important, factor in influencing the outcome of social struggle between social movements and their opponents (Capek, 1993). How the resources available to each group are actually used is at least as, if not more, important. Thus, the Carver Terrace Community Action Group and the two British activists "won" their struggles against the EPA and McDonald's because they used their resources more effectively.

In sum, social movements are effective in bringing about social changes that protect the environment. The most effective social movements are likely to be those that

➤ adopt an environmental justice frame;

➤ adopt a political approach; and

➤ seek advice from local and national environmental groups whose members are highly skilled in using the resources that are available to them.

Summary

In this chapter, major concepts used in discussions and analyses of population problems and environmental degradation were defined. This was followed by the identification of global warming, ozone layer depletion, acid rain, deforestation, overuse/poisoning of land and water resources, and overpopulation as significant social problems. Case studies and statistics were used to describe the prevalence, seriousness, and complexity of these problems, and also to illustrate the point that human beings form or join social movements aimed at preventing or decreasing environmental degradation. An effective environmental social movement is likely to be one that does three things: (1) adopts an environmental justice frame, (2) takes a political (direct action) approach, and (3) seeks advice on strategy and tactics from experienced activists.

Statistical data reveal that Canada and the United States, two countries ranked first and second in the United Nations Human Development Index (n = 147 countries), make a disproportionately high contribution to global warming, ozone layer depletion, and hazardous waste production. Within the United States, the health risks associated with the distribution of hazardous toxic waste are borne unequally by members of different social groupings, with members of low-income groups and African-Americans being exposed to the highest level of risk.

A motivational structure central to commons theory was used to explain why business corporations, governments, and individuals degrade the environment. Power and inequality are implicated in why they continue to do so.

Overpopulation was identified as a source of environmental degradation and conflict. Malthus' explanation of overpopulation was examined, and although a number of valid criticisms of it were described, contemporary "ecological Malthusians" believe that Malthus' predictions will be confirmed if/when two conditions are met: (1) all or most of the world's developing countries (n = 151) become industrial countries (presently n = 22), and (2) each individual in the newly industrialized countries does as much damage to the environment as does each individual in long established industrial countries such as the United States and Canada.

The solutions we proposed in this chapter are derived from, or are not inconsistent with, an integrated commons theoretic/power and inequality perspective. Specifically, we proposed decreasing population growth, contributing to female emancipation, use of more environmentally friendly technologies of production and distribution, decreasing per capita consumption, especially in developed countries, and citizen participation in environmental social movements.

KEY TERMS

Annual growth rate of a population
Composition of a population
Cornucopians
Ecosystem
Environmental degradation
Greenpeace
Ideologies
Minamata disease
Neo-Malthusians
Population size
Social custom
Social movement
Sustainable society
Threshold crossings

DISCUSSION QUESTIONS

1. "Protecting the natural environment is more important than providing jobs or maintaining a high standard of living." Discuss and debate this statement with other students.
2. Technology is a major cause of environmental damage. Can technology also be used to clean up the environment or at least prevent further damage?
3. Why is overpopulation one of the most significant causes of environmental degradation and violent conflict?

4. How can overpopulation be solved by increasing gender equality?
5. Describe and critically evaluate how commons theory explains environmental degradation.
6. Why can't environmental problems be solved without decreasing the size of human populations?
7. How does inequality contribute to the degradation of the environment as well as differences in the risks of harm to which people are exposed?
8. What are the strengths and limitations of China's one-child policy?

PROBLEM SOLVING SCENARIOS

1. You are a Minister in the government of Bangladesh, charged with the responsibility of setting and achieving a reduction in the growth of your country's population by the year 2030. Describe your plan and its rationale.
2. You are Professor Erhlich, who has been asked to advise the United States and Canadian governments on a strategy to reduce the damage done to the environment. What advice would you give, bearing in mind the criticism of Professor Simon?
3. The United Nations wants to present a policy for reducing environmental degradation based on the theory that overpopulation is its major cause. You are asked for your advice. What advice would you offer? What evidence would you cite?

WEB EXERCISES

1. Write a term paper on the significance of the "Montreal Protocol." Begin your research at

   http://www.greenpeace.org/~ozone/indices/reports.html

2. Using the points made in this chapter and those at the website below, hold a debate over the following statement: "Overpopulation will create a global disaster."

   http://www.carnell.com/population/index.html

SUGGESTED READINGS

Beck, U. *Risk Society: Towards a New Modernity*. Thousand Oaks, CA: Sage, 1992.
This book is about the impact of global social changes on the environment. Driven by science and technological knowledge, the global economy is producing a "risk society," in which the risks of harm caused by damage to the environment are more likely to be experienced by some social groupings than others.

Kane, J. *Savages*. Toronto: Douglas and McIntyre, 1995.
The Huaroni are a small band of warriors. Their home is the Amazon (Ecuador). *Savages* describes their successful fight to make the transition from their traditional way of life to a new, modern way of life in their own way and on their own terms.

Vidal, J. *McLibel: Burger Culture on Trial*. London: Macmillan, 1997.
Over the past three years, two Greenpeace activists published information alleging that McDonald's U.K. was harming people directly by serving them unhealthy food, and indirectly by degrading the environment. McDonald's charged them with libel. The trial, which ended in June 1997, was the longest in British legal history, lasting 313 days. This book tells the story of that trial.

ENDNOTES

1   A threshold crossing is a point, level of activity, or change which, when exceeded or decreased, brings about other self-sustaining changes that occur relatively quickly, or even abruptly. For an interesting discussion of a threshold effect called "tipping," see Schelling (1978: 90-96). Threshold effects applied to the environment are discussed by Homer-Dixon (1991: 79-82).

2   A useful Internet source of information on McDonald's impact on the environment is McSpotlight. McSpotlight's environmental homepage address is http://www.enviroweb.org/mcspotlight-na/issues/environment/index.html

3   For a good discussion of the scarcity of fresh water resources, see Gleick (1993), Postel (1993), and for a theory linking water scarcity to "acute conflicts" see Homer-Dixon (1991), Rubin and Faure (1993), and Renner (1996).

Chapter 8

Drug Abuse in North America

I started smoking like a wildman. Before I knew anything I was damn near broke. I just barely had my head on top of the water. Like, I see a lot of my partners—they sunk, lost their cribs, their cars, their wife, they sold everything out from their house and all that kind of shit. I wasn't at that stage yet...but I could see it coming. I guess it might have been for the best that I got busted. (Leroy, a 44-year-old, inner-city, African-American cited in Ouellet et al., 1993: 78)

OBJECTIVES

In this chapter we focus on the topics

1. What is drug abuse?
2. How much drug abuse is there in North America?
3. Who uses cocaine, crack, and heroin in North America?
4. Why do people use and deal hard drugs?
5. What is to be done about hard drug abuse and drug dealing in North America?

Introduction

When Ouellet et al. (1993) interviewed Leroy, he was addicted to crack, "the fast food analog of cocaine" (Inciardi et al., 1993: 9). Today, disenfranchised, inner-city, African-American people like him, and the ways in which they are dealt with by agents of social control (e.g., police, doctors, etc.) are subjected to an unprecedented "feeding frenzy" of media coverage (Orcutt and Turner, 1993). Consider the popular television show *Cops*. Rarely will you watch an episode in which an economically disadvantaged African-American or Hispanic person is not arrested for possession of crack or some other illegal drug. Moreover, U.S. talk shows, such as *Oprah* and *Jerry Springer*, frequently focus on the horrors of crack use and dealing in inner-cities (Kappeler et al., 1996). Thus, it is not surprising that many people view the typical drug addict as a poor African-American or Hispanic person who jeopardizes relations with his or her family, sells his or her belongings, and who constantly punishes his or her body in pursuit of the "American pipe dream" (Chitwood et al., 1996).

Of course, many parts of North America, especially the urban "dead zones," such as the South Side of Chicago (Chitwood et al., 1996), must deal with unprecedented and endemic crack use and dealing among the "truly disadvantaged" (Wilson, 1987). Further, after two decades of the drug war, this problem is worse than ever before (Currie, 1993). As sociologists, we are well aware of the fact that the media often distort reality; however, the crack problem is "real" and not simply a function of moral panics created by elite opinion makers or media "hype." For example, between 1985 and 1989, cocaine-related deaths tripled in the United States as a whole; increased more than four times in Los Angeles, seven times in Chicago, and about nine times in Philadelphia; and cocaine-related medical emergencies quadrupled nationally in the same time period, rising sixfold in Chicago and Washington, tenfold in Philadelphia, and thirteenfold in Atlanta (Currie, 1993: 27).

These and other data presented in this chapter show that many disenfranchised people are addicted to cocaine in one form or another, and over 40 years of research shows that hard drug use is strongly associated with social and economic inequality (Currie, 1993). However, there are many more addicts than you can probably imagine, most of whom are generally considered to be "normal, respectable citizens." In fact, Canada and the United States are "high societies" (Boyd, 1991). These are nations where most people, regardless of their socioeconomic status, take an extraordinary variety of drugs to relieve stress, go to sleep, wake up, cure physical and psychological ailments, alter their moods, speed up, slow down, heighten their sensitivities, partake in religious rituals, or celebrate achievements (Boyd, 1991; DeKeseredy and Schwartz, 1996).

What was the first thing you did this morning? Well, if you are like many hard-working people such as Walter DeKeseredy and Shahid Alvi, you had what they refer to as an "Alvi breakfast." This "nutritious way to start your day" includes two cups of coffee and a cigarette. Believe it or not, cigarette smoking is more addicting than cocaine, more likely to addict a new smoker, and harder to quit once addicted. Furthermore, unlike heroin use, cigarette smoking leads to heart disease and cancer (Reiman, 1998). Thus, we, Reiman (1998), and many medical professionals ask, "Shouldn't those who have 'Alvi breakfasts' and who continue to smoke all day be defined as addicts?" Why haven't politicians and criminal justice officials officially designated them "drug abusers" and "junkies?" Why haven't federal, provincial, and state governments criminalized tobacco and declared a war on this substance? These are important questions when you take into account that: (1) tobacco causes at least 350,000 to 500,000 deaths annually in the United States alone, and (2) tobacco consumption costs at least $28 billion a year in medical costs and lost work productivity (DeKeseredy and Schwartz, 1996).

By now, some readers might be saying to themselves, "Well, I agree with you. I hate smoking and what it does to people. At least I'm not addicted to it." Okay, maybe you are not a smoker; however, you might be like other "legitimate" members of our society who "cannot get started without a caffeine fix in the morning and those who, once started, cannot slow down without their alcohol fix in the evening" (Reiman, 1998: 34). Did you know that there are at least 15 million alcoholics in the United States (Reiman, 1998)? Did you know that more than 25,000 Americans die each year from cirrhosis of the liver, a direct cause of alcohol abuse? Did you know that tens of thousands of people die each year in alcohol-related accidents? Did you know that alcohol is one of the key correlates of most of the violent crimes addressed in Chapter 5? Are those who abuse alcohol not addicts, and why, given the major threat this substance poses to our social order, should alcohol consumption and sales not be criminalized?

It is beyond the scope of this chapter to describe the myriad of so-called "legitimate drugs" that are extremely harmful to you and others. The most important point to consider here is that what drugs do to those who take them is rarely as important as the social context in which they are ingested and sold (DeKeseredy and Schwartz, 1996). Following labeling theorists like Becker (1973), we contend that if no behavior is inherently deviant or criminal, the same can be said about drugs. As Henslin (1994: 105) correctly points out, "The view that a particular drug is good or evil is a matter of social definition that, in turn, influences how people use and abuse drugs and whether or not a drug will be legal or illegal."

What Is Drug Abuse?

Before one can attempt to answer this question, it is first necessary to define the term "drug." What is a drug? At first glance, this seems like an absurdly easy question to answer (Goode, 1989). For example, when we ask our second year criminology and deviance students this question, most of them state that it is a chemical substance that temporarily or permanently alters one's physiological or psychological makeup. This is what Goode (1989: 22) refers to as an **objectivistic** definition, one that assumes that specific characteristics are intrinsic or dwell within substances that these students call drugs.

Objectivistic definitions such as the above are popular and widely used. However, from a sociological standpoint, they are not valid for several reasons. First, there is no psychological or physical effect common to all "drugs" that at the same time is not shared by "nondrugs" (Goode, 1989). For example, some drugs alter your mental processes (e.g., crack), while others, such as vitamin C, have no or little psychological impact. Furthermore, some drugs can prevent you from dying, while others can kill you. According to Goode (1989: 23), "there is no conceivable characteristic that applies to all substances considered drugs."

Second, there is widespread disagreement over what is and what is not a drug, regardless of its physical and psychological effects. For example, at the time of writing this chapter, Walter DeKeseredy frequented a local pub to relax, interact with friends, and to occasionally dull the pain associated with writing this book. Periodically, some of the patrons who knew he was a professor and author of books would ask him about his current research. One evening, when he discussed writing this chapter, one person said, "Based on my conversations with other parents, I consider myself to be extremely lucky. My kids don't do drugs. They just stick to beer." Another person, while puffing away on a cigarette, added to the conversation by saying "I hate people who use drugs. They should be shot and killed." Despite the fact that beer and cigarettes have psychopharmacological effects, these people and many other members of the North American general population do not define beer and cigarettes as "drugs" or dangerous substances.

Walter DeKeseredy's conversation and a large literature support the sociological view that a "drug" is something that is socially defined (Akers, 1992). Indeed, a drug is "something that has been arbitrarily defined by certain segments of society as a drug" (Goode, 1989: 23). In other words, when we talk about drugs, we are talking about labels. The effects of a substance such as LSD may be real; however, "Nothing is a drug but naming it makes it so" (Barber, 1967: 166). For these and other reasons too numerous to describe here, like Goode (1989), we contend that a **subjective** definition is superior to an objective one. Subjectively defined, a drug is a name or label that is not "in" a substance but is external to it. The label becomes attached to a drug during the course of social interaction.

If there are objective and subjective definitions of drugs, the same can be said about "drug abuse." Consider the debate surrounding marijuana use. Do you smoke it? If so, according to an objective definition formulated by the American Medical Association (AMA), you are a drug abuser because marijuana is not approved for medicinal purposes by the most "credible" doctors (Goode, 1989). Similarly, according to the government's objective definition, you are a criminal because smoking marijuana is against the law. If the police catch you smoking "grass" or "pot," you may end up like the Canadian musician featured in Box 8.1.

Subjectively defined, the term "drug abuse" is nothing more than behavior successfully labeled as such. Sociologists maintain that this definition is more useful than those formulated by the state or AMA because it is not the objective facts associated with using a substance that actually determine who is and who is not defined as an abuser. In other words, the labels "drug" and "drug abuser" are not completely determined by questions of public health (DeKeseredy and Schwartz, 1996). Ironically, the people who are labeled drug abusers and who are most strictly controlled, such as the musician featured in Box 8.1, are much less dangerous than those who consume vast quantities of alcohol and other "legitimate" substances (Eitzen and Baca Zinn, 1994).

BOX 8-1

Busted: How I Became a Criminal

It is February, it is freezing, and I am immersed in another night of the glamour of independent rock. [M]y band is playing an average dive, the kind of place that, for reasons known only to the patrons, appeals to sophomores and the working class alike.

As is usual with these events, there is no stage, no sound system, no microphones (the band supplies these), and at least at the start, no one listening. My cut will be around $10, or 24 cents a song. To help me get through the night—and dodge any unexpected projectiles—I have the camaraderie of my bandmates, the surreality of the venue, a modicum of free beer, and the love of my craft.

And I also have one joint of marijuana. The first set is not a complete disaster. We sell a couple of CDs, and a few brave souls are creating the illusion of an audience. With half our song list, most of our energy and all of our free beer expended, I head to the van to light up. We "spark up" what's known as a pin joint or "pinner." Pulling out the pinner is the non-verbal method of stating "I am out of pot ("dry") but I found these scraps ("shake") at the bottom of the decorative container ("happy box") I keep my dope in.

Even wildly inflating the worth of the joint, I would estimate my pinner had a street value of $1. Unfortunately, *de minimus non curat lex*—the law is not concerned with minutia—is not a defense known to... law.

Not that I would know. I do not buy drugs on the street. In fact, I abhor the seamy side of recreational drugs. I only buy direct from the growers—often farmers, people who are just trying to support their families. That is one of the problems with the drug trade: it is too often administered by people I regard as criminals. Or victims of the class struggle. In either case, people to whom I would not lend my bike.

I am about to take my first drag ("haul") of the joint when—out of nowhere—there is a sudden bang on the door and a huge flashlight shining in the window.

"Open up," demands a peace officer.

I comply.

"Having a little smoke, are we, boys?" asks the larger of the two cops.

"Yeah, I guess you got me," I reply. "I was smoking it."

For the record, I don't remember saying exactly that, but I must have, because my official arrest report would quote me on it. I'm positive the cop asked me if I was having "a little smoke," but that was officially recorded as "what are you doing?"

As you can imagine, this is when things begin to go quite badly.

Call me naïve, but until this point, I had always assumed I was a law-abiding person. Like almost anyone else I've known, I was a recreational user of marijuana. The mundane prevalence of the drug made our anti-marijuana laws seem vaguely unreal—certainly nothing that could ever seriously muck up my life. But now, with one tap on the window, I am on the wrong side of the law.

Source: Hamilton (1997: B1-B3).

BOX 8-2

For a Few, Marijuana Is the Best Medicine

Patients Struggle To Ease their Pain as Debate Drags on

When Irvin Rosenfeld was 10, he contracted a rare cancer.

Today, 33 years later, his muscles and blood vessels stretch over tumors on the ends of his arm and leg bones.

To relieve the pain and dangerous muscle tension, the stockbroker from Boca Raton, Florida, smokes 10 to 15 marijuana cigarettes a day, courtesy of the U.S. government. He's one of eight people in the U.S. with that privilege.

"There's not as much tension, not as much pain," says Rosenfeld, who has also tried such prescription drugs as Dilaudid and morphine. "Quite frankly," he says, "this is the best medicine I've discovered."

Legal marijuana may stop with Rosenfeld's group of eight. In November voters in California and Arizona gave doctors the right to prescribe marijuana for some patients, but earlier this month Washington just said no.

At a joint press conference, drug czar Barry McCaffrey, Health and Human Services Secretary Donna Shalala, and Attorney General Janet Reno said that doctors who prescribed marijuana risked losing their licenses to prescribe drugs and might face prosecution.

Few doctors think marijuana is the panacea that some advocacy groups argue it is, but many want to be able to give their patients the legal right to buy and possess it.

The case for medical marijuana has its merits, and a history.

In their book, *Marijuana: The Forbidden Medicine*, Harvard psychiatrists Lester Grinspoon and James Bakalar describe a dozen of marijuana's possible benefits, which include easing nausea and vomiting from cancer chemotherapy and improving the appetite of people with AIDS.

Rigorous research is still lacking, but illicit clinical use still continues. Many glaucoma and AIDS sufferers still rely on marijuana, and in a 1991 study of oncologists, 48 per cent said they would prescribe it if they could and 44 per cent said they had recommended it to patients.

Those against legalization say marijuana shouldn't be for anyone. The administration fears that any sanctioned use would lead to further liberalization of drug laws, which could in turn lead to increased drug use.

Others argue that newer drugs and therapies have filled the niches marijuana once might have. They point out that smoking marijuana is harmful to the lungs and may cause hormonal and reproductive problems.

By stopping legalization, the government has eliminated any impetus for further study. "I don't care what makes me survive," says Irvin Rosenfeld. "I just want the best care."

To the very sick, neither politics nor science really matters.

BOX 8-2

For example, there have been many reports over the past 17 years of the discovery of a variety of health hazards from marijuana, but "careful checking of these findings—either by repeating the experiment or by devising a better one—has found no damage from marijuana use" (Thio, 1995: 355). Believe it or not, research shows that there has never been a single cannabis-related death—approximately 70 million Americans have used marijuana and not one user reported an overdose—and that marijuana is much safer than many foods we commonly eat (Kappeler et al., 1996: 172; Trebach, 1989).

According to Kappeler et al. (1993: 156), "the real danger to marijuana smokers comes from marijuana which has been tainted by government drug control programs, such as the spraying of paraquat and other herbicides on marijuana crops." Moreover, there is no direct relationship between marijuana consumption and interpersonal violent crime (Boyd et al., 1991). It should also be noted that some doctors regard marijuana as a legitimate and effective way to minimize the pain and suffering associated with AIDS, cancer, and other serious ailments (see Box 8.2). Some people even view it as "one of the safest therapeutically active substances known to man" (Kappeler et al., 1996: 172).

On the other hand, drinking large amounts of alcohol over time is strongly associated with cirrhosis of the liver, hepatitis, heart disease, high blood pressure, brain dysfunction, neurological disorders, sexual dysfunction, and a host of other major medical problems (Akers, 1992). There is also a large literature showing a strong connection between alcohol and violent crimes, such as murder and sexual assault (Boyd, 1988; Boyd et al., 1991; Schwartz and DeKeseredy, 1997). If these findings don't alarm you, consider the following U.S. data uncovered by Eitzen and Bacca Zin (1997: 526):

➤ Over 50 percent of all traffic deaths occurred in alcohol-related accidents, and car accidents involving drunk drivers are the leading cause of death among teenagers.

➤ Alcoholics have a suicide rate six to 15 times greater than the rate for the general population, and they are 10 times more likely to die in fires than nonalcoholics.

➤ About 7 out of every 10 drowning victims were drinking before they died.

➤ Hundreds of billions are lost through job absenteeism, lost production, medical expenses, and accidents resulting from alcohol use.

➤ Problem drinking is strongly associated with disrupted families, family violence, desertion, and many other emotional problems. In fact, a 1992 Gallup poll found that one in five families reported alcohol as a serious problem in the household (McAneny, 1992: 47).

➤ Youths who drink excessively are more likely to engage in vandalism, racist acts, predatory street violence, and sexual assault.

In March, 1997, Walter DeKeseredy presented these and other alarming data on alcohol use to his second year criminology students. Several responded by saying, "Something is wrong here! Why doesn't the government do something about this?" Good question! Why don't the government, the AMA, and other agents of social control declare a "War on Alcohol" and define those who drink it as drug abusers? It is to this issue that we now turn.

The Politics of Criminalizing Drugs

Why are only certain drugs such as marijuana, cocaine, and heroin criminalized? Whom does it benefit to have certain drugs criminalized? How did a group's negative view of some drugs make its way into the law? Drug use and other behaviors do not get labeled as social problems or crimes unless there are some political, moral, and ideological reasons (Goode, 1989), and one major factor in the decision to make drugs illegal is when their use becomes associated with minority groups (DeKeseredy and Schwartz, 1996). For example, according to Musto (1973: 244–245),

"The most passionate support for legal prohibition of narcotics has been associated with fear of a given drug's effect on a specific minority. Certain drugs were dreaded because they seemed to undermine essential social restrictions which kept these groups under control: cocaine was supposed to enable blacks to withstand bullets which would kill normal persons and to stimulate sexual assault. Fear that smoking opium facilitated sexual contact between Chinese and white Americans was also a factor in its total prohibition. Chicanos in the Southwest were believed to be incited to violence by smoking marijuana. Heroin was linked in the 1920s with a turbulent age-group: adolescents in reckless and promiscuous urban gangs. Alcohol was associated with immigrants crowding into large

and corrupt cities. In each instance, use of a particular drug was attributed to an identifiable and threatening minority group."

A similar criminalization process occurred in Canada, a nation, like the United States, that is characterized by **systemic** or **structural discrimination** (Weinfeld, 1995). For example, during the late 1800s, many Chinese were brought to Canada to work on railroads and mines, and all of them worked at about half the wages of whites (Boyd, 1991). In addition to providing cheap labor, the Chinese operated many perfectly legal "opium dens," which provided both whites and Chinese with comfortable settings to "get high" and/or escape the hassles of everyday life. Anti-Chinese feelings, however, soon emerged after the railroads were finished and the economy started to deteriorate. Then many white working-class people rallied against poorly paid Chinese immigrants by arguing that these "aliens" were threatening white employment by working for very low wages. In 1908, the Canadian federal government, led by Prime Minister William Lyon MacKenzie King, responded to this labor crisis by outlawing opium smoking. This was Canada's first criminal prohibition of a drug (Comack, 1986).

Based on her historical research, Comack (1986: 86) contends that the Canadian anti-opium laws were more anti-Chinese than a concern for public health:

"There appears to be a clear and inescapable connection between legislation aimed at the "immoral" habit practised by the Chinese and the ideology that an 'alien element' was responsible for the deteriorating situation in British Columbia. Opium-smoking became an easy symbol for the dangers and evils embodied in the fantasy of the 'Yellow Peril,' and the opium legislation helped to affirm Oriental immigrants as a major cause of social problems. Consequently, one could argue that the drug legislation was not so much directed at the Chinese but rather helped to identify them as a major source of the problems confronting B.C. society."

In sum, in both Canada and the United States, the drugs of visible minority groups are the objects of a massive war on drugs, while the drugs of the white middle-class, such as alcohol, are freely available. Thus, it is not surprising that some criminologists contend that the war on drugs as we know it today is a modern and insidious way of enforcing racial segregation and discrimination (DeKeseredy and Schwartz, 1996; Mann, 1993). For example, recent data released by the U.S. Bureau of Justice Statistics (1995) show that 12 percent of the white inmates are behind bars for drug violations, as opposed to 25 percent of African-Americans and 33 percent of Hispanics.

Some of whom Reiman (1998) defines as "The Defenders of the Present Legal Order" may respond to our analysis of the racist nature of drug enforcement by arguing that since research shows that most of the American "hard drug" users are African-Americans and Hispanics, it is not surprising that you would find a higher number of them incarcerated for using or dealing these substances. In other words, more are in the "joint" or "big house" because more of them take and/or deal drugs. As we show in a subsequent section of this chapter, the unemployed, the subemployed, African-Americans, and Hispanics are more likely to use heroin and crack (Currie, 1993). Nevertheless, do you think that if most of the hard drug users were suddenly middle-class whites, the number of white people incarcerated for drug use and dealing would be greater than the number of minority people imprisoned for similar behavior? We don't think so! Given that North American society is dominated by white people of European descent who have more voting power, do you think that politicians would either eliminate or significantly tone down their war on drugs? Thio (1995: 375) thinks so and contends that "politicians would switch the drug war's priority from anti-drug-user law enforcement to user-friendly education and treatment." What do you think?

How Much Drug Abuse Is There in North America?

There are so many illegal drugs currently available in North America and it is beyond the scope of this chapter to describe how many people use each one. Instead, we will limit our discussion on the extent of drug abuse to two substances that appear to be of major concern to the media and most politicians, criminal justice officials, health care providers, and the general public: cocaine and heroin.

Cocaine

Cocaine is a stimulant, one that is occasionally referred to as "the champagne of drugs" or "caviar among drugs" (Thio, 1995). It is extracted from the leaves of the coca plant grown in the hills of Peru and Bolivia, but processed and prepared for smuggling in Colombia. In the Peruvian and Bolivian hills, Indians have cultivated and used this plant for thousands of years. Its leaves were, and still are, chewed by natives of the Andes Mountains for recreational, cultural, and medicinal purposes. The effect of chewing coca is similar to what one experiences after drinking a strong cup of black coffee (Nicholl, 1985).

Unlike South American mountain people, most North Americans who use coca do not do so for spiritual or medicinal purposes. Rather they smoke, inject, or inhale refined derivatives of the coca plant mainly to "get high" or because they are "hooked" or addicted to cocaine. In fact, in the United States, most clinicians estimate that about 10 percent of those who start using cocaine "socially" or "recreationally" will eventually become heavy users or addicts (NIDA, 1997a). Most users today purchase cocaine in powder form and inhale it through their nostrils. The major physical and psychological effects of "snorting" are as follows:[1]

➤ a temporary (for example, thirty-minute) sense of pleasure, well-being, and euphoria;

➤ a possible physical addiction and a strong psychological addiction;

➤ inhibition of appetite, and an increase in blood pressure and respiration rate;

➤ in low doses, an increase in energy and a reduction of fatigue;

➤ nervousness, excitability, agitation, and paranoia;

➤ hypersensitivity, mood swings, insomnia, impotence, and memory problems;

➤ increase in body temperature; and

➤ vomiting, cold sweats, tremors, muscle twitches, heart attacks, strokes, convulsions, and death.

Some people prefer to inject cocaine into their veins because they get a faster and more intense "high" (Currie, 1993). As with any other drug, intravenous (IV) injection is very dangerous practice for users who share "dirty" needles with those with the AIDS virus (McCoy et al., 1996). Despite media campaigns and public education efforts to sensitize people to the dangers of sharing needles, many IV drug users do not take precautions, even when they are readily available (DeKeseredy and Schwartz, 1996). Thio (1995) suggests that, for many of these people, the very attraction of taking dangerous drugs is to prove themselves daring in the face of danger, in which case personal safety would not be a concern.

How many people snort and inject cocaine? Some estimates generated by survey research are presented here; however, they underestimate the true extent of cocaine use for several reasons. Think about it. How would you go about gathering data on the extent of cocaine use in your community? Would you administer a survey to college or high school students? Or would you try to conduct door-to-door, face-to-face interviews? Maybe you would examine medical records or police statistics. Regardless of what research method you use, it will always underestimate the true extent of cocaine use because many people do not want others to know that they use it despite attempts to guarantee anonymity and confidentiality. Given the current American government's war on drugs, many people want to avoid embarrassment, going to prison, and being labeled a "junkie" (Currie, 1993). They don't really know that you won't "rat" on them, so that they can be sent to prison, get kicked out of school, or lose their job (DeKeseredy and Schwartz, 1996).

Still, although it is impossible to gather totally accurate data on cocaine use, some researchers strive to generate the most reliable estimates they can. In the United States, for example, the National Institute on Drug Abuse (NIDA), a branch of the U.S. Department of Health and Human Services, has sponsored two major surveys on illicit drug use: (1) the *National Household Survey On Drug Abuse* (NHSDA), and (2) the *Monitoring The Future Study* (MFS). Recent NHSDA data gathered from U.S. household residents age 12 and older show that in 1994 about 22 million people had tried cocaine at least once in their lifetime; approximately 3.7 million used cocaine in the past year; and more than 1.3 million used cocaine in the past month (NIDA, 1997a).

The MFS attempts to assess the extent of drug use among American adolescents and young adults. This study found that in 1995

➤ 1.8 percent of high school seniors (grade 12) used cocaine in the past year.

➤ 6.0 percent of these students used cocaine at least once in their lifetime.

➤ 4.2 percent of 8th-graders had tried cocaine at least once in their lifetime; 2.6 percent used it in the past year; 1.2 used it in the past month; and 0.1 percent used it daily.

➤ 5.0 percent of 10th-graders reported ever using cocaine; 3.5 percent used it in the past year; 1.7 percent used it in the past month; and 0.1 percent used it daily.

➤ Of 1994 full-time college students included in the study (one to four years beyond high school), 2.0 percent used cocaine in the past year and 0.6 percent used it in the past month (NIDA, 1997a, 1997b, 1997c).

A much smaller percentage of Canadians report using cocaine. For example, the 1993 *General Social Survey* (GSS) found that 0.3 percent of the Canadian general population reported using cocaine or crack in the past year (Single et al., 1997). What can we conclude from these data and those generated in the United States? At first glance, it appears that the North American cocaine problem is not as bad as politicians, the media, and criminal justice officials make it out to be. Indeed, the evidence presented here does not support former New York Governor Mario Cuomo's assertion that "The cocaine problem is sounding throughout the nation. There is no escape anywhere...We are truly dealing with an epidemic of unprecedented proportions" (cited in Brownstein, 1996: 46). Keep in mind, however, that the major drawback to the surveys cited here is that the people most likely to use hard drugs such as cocaine are excluded from these studies, such as the economically disadvantaged who live in urban ghettos (Currie, 1993). These surveys also exclude people who are in drug rehabilitation or AIDS clinics, hospitals, "crack houses," prisons, and "boot camps" (DeKeseredy and Schwartz, 1996). When we turn our empirical attention to these other kinds of North Americans, "the picture is much grimmer" (Currie, 1993), especially when it comes to determining the extent of crack-cocaine use.

Crack-Cocaine

Contrary to popular belief, crack is not a new drug. Even so, most North Americans believe it is a new threat to our public health and social order because, as Incidari et al. (1996) point out, the first media report on this substance appeared in a November 17, 1985 edition of the *New York Times* (Boundy, 1985: B12). After this story, "crack suddenly took on a life of its own" (Inciardi et al., 1996: 1). For example, in less than 11 months after this story, a "feeding frenzy" of media coverage emerged (Orcutt and Turner, 1993), with major newspapers and magazines, such as the *Los Angeles Times* and *Newsweek* collectively providing Americans with more than 1,000 stories on crack (Inciardi et al., 1996). At this time, according to Gladwell (1986: 11), there was "coverage feeding coverage, stories of addiction and squalor multiplying across the land."

Crack was first reported in the literature in the early 1970s (Chitwood et al., 1996). During this time, it was only available in drug communities for a short period because freebase users considered it to be an inferior product. According to one Miami "coke user" who was interviewed in 1986:

"Of course crack is nothing new. The only thing that's new is the name. Years ago it was called rock, base, or freebase, although it really isn't true "freebase." It was just an easier way to get something that gave a more potent rush, done the same way as now with baking soda. It never got too popular among the 1970s cokeheads because it was just not as pure a product as conventional freebase" (cited in Inciardi et al., 1996: 6).

Unfortunately, today, for reasons described further in this chapter, many people view crack, crack use, and crack distribution are much more than simply names or labels. For them, these problems are prominent elements of the continuing degradation of inner-city life (Devine and Wright, 1993; Wilson, 1996). Before we present data on the extent of crack use in the United States and Canada, it is first necessary to define crack and then discuss the physical, psychological, and social consequences of using it.

What is Crack?

Defining crack is the subject of debate among those who use it. In fact, many crack users don't know what it is and don't care (Inciardi et al., 1996). Nevertheless, crack is a much cheaper type of cocaine, one that is smoked, easy to manufacture, handle, sold in inexpensive quantities, and provides an intense, quick high (Bourgois, 1995; Brownstein, 1996; Inciardi et al., 1993). In fact, crack is a product of "clever marketing" and was "invented" to provide a market for the oversupply of high quality and expensive cocaine available during the 1980s (Brownstein, 1996). According to Witkin (1991: 44), "What turned crack into a craze was mass marketing that would have made McDonald's proud." For example, during the course of his ethnographic study of crack in New York, Williams found that:

"Crack offered a chance to expand sales in ways never before possible because it was packaged in small quantities that sold for as little as two to five dollars. This allowed dealers to attract a new class of consumer: the persistent poor. Crack was sold on street corners, bringing the drug to people who could not pay entrance fees to after-hours clubs or who would have been uncomfortable with the free-spending ambiance in those places. In a very short time, crack was readily available in most poor neighborhoods" (1992: 9).

Unlike cocaine, the high from smoking "rock" lasts only for three to five minutes, followed by a powerful state of depression. This alone has made it highly addictive, as many people reach yet for another "rock" to climb out of the depressive state. In fact, most crack users rarely have a single "hit." They typically spend between $50 to $500 during a "mission," also referred to as a three- to four-day binge. During this time, they constantly "beam up" and smoke between three to fifty rocks a day (Inciardi et al., 1996). For example, a recovering crack user told Inciardi et al. (1993: 11):

"I smoked it Thursday, Friday, Saturday, Monday, Tuesday, Wednesday, Thursday, Friday, Saturday—on that cycle. I was working at that time. I would spend my whole $300 check. Everyday was a crack day for me. My day was not made without a hit. I could smoke it before breakfast, don't even eat breakfast, or I don't eat for three days."

Although crack is highly addictive, research reviewed by Currie (1993) shows that it is not necessarily "the all-consuming drug" often portrayed by the media. Many people either use it sparingly or stop using it altogether after a few hits (DeKeseredy and Schwartz, 1996). Nevertheless, people who binge on crack eventually experience major health problems because they get little sleep, rarely, if ever, eat, and they neglect basic hygiene. According to Inciardi et al. (1996: 12–13), many bingers experience the following health problems:

➤ scabs on their faces, arms, and legs as a result of burns and attempts to remove insects perceived to be crawling under the skin;

➤ burned facial hair from carelessly lighting smoking paraphernalia;

➤ burned lips and tongues from hot pipe stems;

➤ respiratory problems; and

➤ sexually transmitted diseases resulting from the tendency to engage in unsafe sex, particularly in crack houses.

Contrary to popular belief, however, there is no strong relationship between crack use and violent crime (Smart, 1986). Indeed, research shows that the "crisis of crack related violence" was the result of a moral panic created by conservative politicians and journalists (Brownstein, 1996; Reinarman and Levine, 1989). Regardless of the exaggerated claim made by U.S. criminal justice officials that cocaine and crack use cause many homicides, most American cocaine-related homicides involve young, disenfranchised, inner-city African-American or Hispanic males fighting over "distribution rights," debt collection, territory, and the quality of the drug (Blumstein, 1995). For example, based on their analysis of 414 homicides in New York City in 1988, Goldstein et al. (1989) found that only three were directly related to crack or cocaine consumption, and two of these cases also involved the consumption of large amounts of alcohol—a major correlate of violent crime (DeKeseredy and Schwartz, 1996).

This is not to say that crack use and its distribution should be trivialized. These social problems deeply concern many inner-city residents, and their fear of drug-related problems is well-founded. Consider the following 17-year-old African-American student's description of how drugs such as crack have contributed to several problems in his West Side Chicago community, an area characterized by extreme poverty:

"When I first moved over here this neighborhood was quite OK. After six o'clock, you wouldn't see anybody on the street in this neighborhood, you know, even if it was summertime. People might be in the park, but if you walk down the street you may see somebody sitting on the porch, and they wasn't no lot of loud noise, and—and didn't many cars pass by. But, when drugs start flowing in, people start having drug fights and you couldn't sleep because here were cars coming up and down the street all night long. And, you know, that's bad 'cause that makes your community look bad" (cited in Wilson, 1996: 10).

Although crack consumption is not a major cause of violence, it is a real and frightening consequence of what happens "when work disappears" in inner-city areas (Wilson, 1996). So is the emergence of a relatively new crack-related problem: sex-for-crack exchanges. Even though there is nothing about crack that makes it more attractive to women than men, a growing number of inner-city women exchange sex for crack. On the street, they are usually referred to as "strawberries," "skeezers," "chickenheads," "rock prostitutes," or "crack whores," addicted women who have few options for getting the money they need to buy crack (Mahan, 1996). These women are also "almost universally disdained" by those who exploit them (e.g., dealers and prostitutes) and they often exchange sex for crack in sexually oriented crack houses (Ratner, 1993), where, as described by Inciardi in Box 8.3 (1993: 39-40), some women reach a level of degradation that you probably cannot imagine.

In addition to putting themselves at risk of becoming "crack whores," some female crack users jeopardize their children's physical and psychological well-being (Mahan, 1996). For example, Inciardi et al. (1993), suggest that as many

---

BOX 8-3

Sex-for-Crack Exchanges in a Miami Crack House

At the outset of this study, I was already well acquainted with the Miami crack scene, having studied it extensively since 1986. My first direct exposure to the sex-for-crack market came in 1988, during an initial visit to a North Miami crack house. I had gained entry through a local drug dealer, who had been a key informant of mine for almost a decade. He introduced me to the crack house door man as someone "straight but OK." After the door man checked us for weapons, my guide proceeded to show me around.

Upon entering a room in the rear of the crack house (what I later learned was called a freak room), I observed what appeared to be the gang-rape of an unconscious child. Emaciated, seemingly comatose, and likely no older than 14 years of age, she was lying spread-eagled on a filthy mattress while four men in succession had vaginal intercourse with her. After they had finished and left the room, however, it became readily clear that it had not been forcible rape at all. She opened her eyes and looked about to see if anyone was waiting. When she realized that our purpose there was not for sex, she wiped her groin with a ragged beach towel, covered herself with half of a tattered sheet affecting a somewhat peculiar sense of modesty, and rolled over in an attempt to sleep. Almost immediately, however, she was disturbed by the door man, who brought a customer to her for oral sex. He just walked up to her with an erect penis in hand, said nothing to her, and she proceeded to oblige him.

Upon leaving the crack house, a few minutes later, the dealer/informant explained that she was a house girl, a person in the employ of the crack house owner. He gave her food, a place to sleep, and all the crack she wanted in return for her providing sex—any type and amount of sex—to his crack house customers.

Source: Inciardi (1993: 39-40). Reprinted by permission of The Rowman & Littlefield Publishing Group.

as 400,000 crack-exposed babies are born each year in the United States, and that a substantial number of those exposed to cocaine and crack in the womb experience major health problems such as the following:

➤ abnormally small heads and brains;

➤ sudden infant death syndrome or crib deaths;

➤ deformed genital organs and urinary tracts;

➤ neurological damage leading to extraordinary irritability and learning disorders; and

➤ premature birth and low weight.

Of course other drugs, such as alcohol, jeopardize unborn children's health. It should also be noted that many infants exposed to cocaine and crack in the womb recover with good medical care and go on to lead healthy lives (Trebach, 1993). According to Dr. Ira Chasnoff, the children of "crack mothers" are "no different from other children growing up. They are not the retarded imbeciles people talk about...As I study the problem more and more, I think the placenta does a better job of protecting the child than we do as a society" (quoted in Sullum, 1992: 14).

This is not to say that we are condoning mothers using crack and putting their children at risk of birth defects, etc. However, we, like several other sociologists, are opposed to the "criminalization of crack pregnancies" (Maher, 1990), a government response that does little, if anything, to address the broader social and cultural factors that motivate women to engage in behaviors that have the risk of injuring their offspring (Mahan, 1996). These factors include poverty, joblessness, and the inadequate provision of prenatal health care and education (Currie, 1993; Humphries, 1993; King, 1993; Wilson, 1996).

How many people use crack and put themselves at risk of experiencing the above and other problems associated with "beaming up?" Again, for reasons described previously, it is impossible to obtain totally accurate data on the extent of crack use in North America, especially since most frequent crack users are excluded from mainstream surveys. With these limitations in mind, the U.S. NHSDA found that in 1994, among those age 12 and older, about four million people had used crack at least once in their lives, and about 1.2 million people had used crack in the past year (NIDA, 1997a). MFS 1995 data show that (NIDA, 1997b, 1997c)

➤ 2.7 percent of 8th graders; 2.8 percent of 10th graders, and 3.0 percent of 12th graders had used crack at least once in their lives.

➤ 1.6 percent of 8th graders, 1.8 percent of 10th graders, and 3.0 percent of 12th graders used crack within the preceding year.

➤ 0.7 percent of 8th graders; 0.9 percent of 10th graders, and 1.0 percent of 12th graders had used crack within the preceding month.

➤ Of the 1994 full-time college students (one to four years beyond high school), 0.5 percent used crack in the year preceding the study and 0.6 percent used it in the preceding month.

Unfortunately, the 1993 Canadian national General Social Survey (GSS) does not provide precise data on crack use because the sample was not large enough to yield reliable estimates (Wolff and Pottie Bunge, 1996). Again, the GSS cocaine estimate described previously (0.3 percent) includes those who used both crack and other forms of cocaine. Some smaller studies, however, have found that crack use is not a statistically significant problem in Canada. For example, a recent survey of Ontario students in Grades 7, 9, 11, and 13 found that about one percent of the respondents stated that they used crack in the year before the survey (Adlaf et al., 1994).

Heroin

If crack is highly addictive, the same can be said about heroin, one of the "world's most potent painkillers" (Boyd, 1991). Heroin is an opiate derived from poppy plants generally grown in Burma, Thailand, Laos, Pakistan, Afghanistan, Iran, and Mexico (Thio, 1995). It was used for centuries as a painkiller, and before crack came on the North American scene, heroin was considered the most feared, the most dreaded, and the "hardest" illicit drug (Kaplan, 1983). In fact, this substance is still viewed by many as the most dangerous illegal drug, regardless of the massive amount of state, media, and academic attention devoted to crack. According to Erich Goode, one of North America's leading sociological experts on drugs:

"Heroin is still the substance the American public is most likely to point to as an example of a dangerous drug; disapproval of any level of use is higher for heroin than it is for any other drug; opposition to legalization is higher for heroin than it is for any other drug; and heroin users are the most stigmatized of all drug users. Heroin is the epitome of the illicit street drug. Its association in the public mind with street crime, even today, in spite of strong competition from crack, is stronger than for any other drug. The stereotype of the "junkie" is that he or she is by nature a lowlife, an outcast, a dweller in the underworld, an unsavory, untrustworthy character to be avoided at almost any cost. This fact alone makes heroin an immensely fascinating drug to study." (1989: 226).

Heroin "flourished" in inner-city America after World War II (Currie, 1993). Like crack, it is mostly used by disenfranchised, inner-city, male ghetto residents, and there is evidence to suggest that it is replacing crack or powder cocaine as the drug of choice in urban areas characterized by poverty and social disorganization (Hanson and Venturelli, 1995). The relationship between heroin use, crack consumption, and inequality is addressed in greater detail later in this chapter.

Why are people so concerned about heroin? Of course, heroin use can be harmful to your health; however, of all the various drugs, legal or illegal, heroin has the fewest harmful effects associated with it (Inciardi, 1992). For example, although many years of government and media propaganda have convinced most North Americans that this drug is very dangerous, not one study has been able to demonstrate cell or organ damage directly related to heroin use, and no one has found that heroin use directly results in disease (DeKeseredy and Schwartz, 1996; McCaghy, 1976). In fact, many steady heroin users are "normal" people, such as physicians, who hold legitimate jobs for many years (Goode, 1989). Nevertheless, you are asking for trouble if needles are shared with someone who has AIDS or HIV, or if you overdose.

What happens when individuals ingest heroin? When people first use it, they typically have an unpleasant experience (e.g., nausea). However, once mastered, heroin generates a strong sense of euphoria and content, and then users develop a much higher level of tolerance (Currie, 1993). If, however, people inject heroin into their veins, the high is much stronger. Even so, only the first few injections result in euphoria, as former heroin addict and drug dealer Ron Santiago points out in Box 8.4.

In addition to sharing experiences similar to Ron Santiago's, IV heroin users can get addicted to "tragic magic" (the street term for heroin) and suffer from some major health problems, such as AIDS and HIV infection. Although most North Americans are now well aware of the fact that these ailments can be spread through sexual relations, the only risk factor associated with about 25 percent of the more than 200,000 diagnosed AIDS cases in the United States is intravenous drug use (Currie, 1993). In other words, approximately 25 percent of AIDS cases apparently developed because of shared needles in illegal drug use. In fact, the second most common route of HIV transmission in the United States is through sharing intravenous needles for illegal drug use (Herek and Glunt, 1995). Of course, this problem could be minimized substantially by providing clean, sterile needles to

BOX 8-4

One Man's Experience with Heroin

Only in the beginning and a very few other times during my life did I really get high—experience that fantastic euphoric feeling. Looking back at it now, every shot after the first shot that I ever took of heroin, I tried to get the same effect I got the first time. That dream kept me strung out for years, trying to get back to that point. But you lose something in the process, because you go straight from being sick to just being okay or nodding out off of the drug. There is no in-between level anymore, and this is what I tried to find. I always tried to find that level where I could float. Yet there were very few times where I could manage to get that feeling. When I had money I would just come home and I would shoot the dope. First it would take the sickness off and then I would wait for that good feeling to come down on me, but it seems like I would take the express elevator. I would either start nodding, or I would just be feeling okay. Not good enough for everything around me to blend in like it used to when I first started getting high. I no longer could experience that feeling of serenity and well-being. There was no feeling of being at peace with the world; no longer that special dreamy sensation of floating and total relaxation. It seems like after a while that middle point just leaves you. And there are very, very few times where I was high and enjoyed it after the first few years of shooting heroin.

Source: Cited in Hills and Santiago, (1992: 3). © 1992. Reprinted with permission of Wadsworth Publishing, a division of Thomson Learning. Fax 800-730-2215.

those who use heroin and other drugs. This strategy would also be much cheaper than the medical costs of dealing with only a handful of AIDS cases, as has been proven throughout Europe and Australia. In response to U.S. conservatives opposed to distributing clean needles to IV drug users, Wright and Devine (1994: 75) contend:

"It appears that we would prefer to let HIV infection spread among the drug-using population and shoulder the ensuing costs of treating the infection, rather than do something cheap and effective to arrest the spread of the disease in the first place."

In addition to putting themselves at risk of acquiring AIDS and HIV, those who routinely inject heroin into their veins can overdose. This problem is becoming more acute because many users are ingesting high potency white heroin that is relatively cheap and very lethal (National Institute of Health, 1994). For example, in the United States, approximately 2,500 people die each year from heroin overdoses, despite research showing that the number of heroin users is going down. It seems, then, that a smaller number of users are consuming more potent heroin (Goode, 1994).

Parts of Canada are facing the same problem. For example, in Toronto, there were 63 heroin-related deaths in 1993, surpassing the "record high" of 60 such deaths in 1992. According to the Metro Toronto Research Group on Drug Use (1997), this increase is partly the result of the distribution and consumption of higher potency heroin. Similarly, in 1995, Vancouver, British Columbia, experienced an epidemic of lethal overdoses due in large part to the use of high potency "China White" heroin. In response to this problem, some members of the provincial New Democratic government seriously considered decriminalizing heroin to lower the number of overdoses (DeKeseredy and Schwartz, 1996).

If IV heroin users don't get HIV and AIDS, or overdose, there is a good chance that they could experience other serious health problems, such as hepatitis, heart infections, and sores. No examination of IV heroin use is complete without a discussion on the problems associated with withdrawal. These include sweating, chills, abdominal cramps, diarrhea, etc. (Currie, 1993). What do IV heroin users feel like when they go through withdrawal? In Box 8.5, Ron Santiago describes what it was like for him.

Highly sensitive to the above and other dangers associated with IV heroin use, although the precise number is unknown, some researchers speculate that a growing number of North Americans now prefer to "chase the dragon." In other words, they smoke heroin. This technique also makes heroin easier to handle at a psychological level because smokers can view getting high as an "unproblematic extension of more conventional pursuits," such as smoking cigarettes (Auld et al., 1986: 175). Others who want to avoid the problems associated with IV heroin use either "sniff" or "snort" it (Currie, 1993).

Regardless of how they ingest heroin, crack, or powder cocaine, many addicts turn to crime to support their habit, a problem that also poses a health risk to them and their victims. In fact, many people don't start committing crimes once they become addicts. Rather, people who engage in predatory street crimes are more

BOX 8-5

The Pain and Suffering Associated with Withdrawal

Every once in a while in the beginning you try to play this game, this psychological game with dope, about how you don't really need it. So I guess your mind is trying to tell your body, don't get sick. Or you're feeling the symptoms, but mentally you're telling yourself you're not feeling them or you won't give in. You'll deal with the pain even though it is a light pain at first. You'll deal with it until you can't deal with it anymore. There were times when physically I had to get high almost every two hours, because otherwise I would get violently ill to the point where my hands were shaking. You know, I was starting to fall apart. My muscles weren't really coordinated and I would start to convulse. And the longer you are abstinent, away from the drug, the worse these symptoms become. But again, there were times I'd have to play mind games, because I didn't have the money for the dope, and I was out in the street and I had to hustle or scramble to do something. I knew it was going to take me three or four hours and I just had to deal with the pain of the withdrawal symptoms. So there were many days when I woke up in the morning or even during the day and I was sick as a dog but I had to go out.

Source: Cited in Hills and Santiago, (1992: 2). © 1992. Reprinted with permission of Wadsworth Publishing, a division of Thomson Learning. Fax 800-730-2215.

likely to use drugs such as heroin (DeKeseredy and Schwartz, 1996). For example, Faupel's qualitative study of 13 heroin addicts, like other studies (e.g., Inciardi, 1992) challenges the "drugs cause crime" thesis. Based on interviews with 13 heroin addicts with extensive criminal histories, Faupel found that criminal activities cause or at least facilitate drug use. Consider the following excerpt from his interview with "Stephanie" (1996: 180):

"'The better I got at crime,' remarked Stephanie, 'the more money I made, the more drugs I used.' She went on to explain, 'I think that most people that get high, the reason it goes to the extent that it goes—that it becomes such a high degree of money—is because they make the money like that. I'm saying if the money wasn't available to them like that, they wouldn't be into drugs as deep as they were.'"

When heroin addicts commit crimes such as robberies and burglaries, they are always placing themselves into dangerous situations that could result in them being arrested, knifed, or shot (DeKeseredy and Schwartz, 1996). Moreover, during the course of committing crimes, some heroin users use extreme forms of violence. Consider Ron Santiago—when he was addicted to heroin, he and a friend pistol-whipped a woman during a bank robbery. In fact, Ron did many "stickups" with a weapon when he was a heroin addict, and he had no compassion for his victims:

"I never knew personally the people that I robbed, so there was never a relationship built up. To me they were just objects. I never shot anybody that I robbed. I never really violently hurt anybody that I robbed. There were instances where I had to shoot someone to discipline them but that was an occupational hazard—one of my runners, one of my dope dealers. But I didn't develop any type of attachment towards the people that I robbed. It was the dope that was telling me: get the money. So I really didn't have time or energy to think about what these people felt or what they thought. Because I was living for three things: getting money to buy dope to get high. Nothing else in my life came in between those three things. I didn't care about anything or anybody except getting money to buy dope to get high" (cited in Hills and Santiago, 1992: 37).

How many North Americans use heroin? Unfortunately, people who lead a lifestyle similar to Ron Santiago's when he was addicted are excluded from the North American survey data on heroin use described here. Again, like the cocaine and crack figures described previously, the following data greatly underestimate the extent of heroin use in Canada and the United States.

In the United States, the 1993 NHSDA found that among those age 12 or older 0.1 percent reported using heroin in the past year, and 1.1 percent used it at least once in their lifetime (Maguire and Pastore, 1995). MFS 1995 data show that 1.1 percent used it at least once in their lifetime, while 0.1 percent of college students reported using heroin in the past 12 months and not one student reported using it in the past 30 days (NIDA, 1997b, 1997c).

Like their U.S. counterparts, Canadian surveys do not reveal a major heroin problem. For example, the 1993 GSS, which does not provide precise data on heroin use due to sampling limitations and other problems discussed previously, shows that 0.3 percent of respondents reported using either LSD, speed, or heroin. The 1989 National Alcohol and Other Drugs Survey (NADS) conducted by Statistics Canada for Health and Welfare Canada obtained a similar estimate (0.4 percent) (Eliany, 1994).

Summary

What can we conclude from the North American survey research on the use of cocaine, crack, and heroin? Well, at first glance, it appears that there is no empirical support for former Canadian Prime Minister Brian Mulroney's claim that "Drug abuse has become an epidemic that undermines our economic as well as our social fabric" (cited in Erickson, 1996: 67-68). These data also challenge former American President Ronald Reagan's claim that "Drugs are menacing our society..." (cited in Erickson, 1996: 67). It is true that so-called "hard drug" use is not a widespread problem. Even so, at the risk of sounding repetitive, the surveys described here and in other sources do not tell an accurate story. They exclude those most likely to use hard drugs, such as those whom Wilson (1987) refers to as "the truly disadvantaged." Alternative methods must be used to gather data on those who are most at risk of consuming these substances, such as interviewing people in institutions, on the streets, and in Native reserves (Hewitt et al., 1997). Indeed, future research requires using a variety of methods in order to obtain a more comprehensive understanding of drug use in North America.

Who Uses Cocaine, Crack, and Heroin in North America?

Here, answers to this question are situated under four categories: (1) sex, (2) age, (3) socioeconomic status, and (4) race/ethnicity.

Sex

In both Canada and the United States, men are more likely to use cocaine, crack, and heroin than are women (Barkan, 1996; DeKeseredy and Schwartz, 1996). For example, the 1989 National Alcohol and Other Drugs Survey (NADS) found that 2.0 percent of Canadian men reported using cocaine or crack in the year before the study, while only 0.8 percent of the female participants reported using these drugs (Eliany, 1994). In the United States, the NHSDA found that in 1994, men reported a higher rate of cocaine use than did women (0.9 percent and 0.4 percent respectively) (NIDA, 1997d). These findings do not surprise us and others who have devoted a substantial amount of time and energy to studying crime, deviance, and social control, because men are more likely generally to engage in criminal and deviant activities (Thio, 1995). However, there is evidence suggesting that crack dependence is higher among women than men in some U.S. communities (Barkan, 1996; Inciardi et al., 1993).

Although most of the drug research focuses on men, a few studies on female hard drug use show that women's use of heroin and cocaine stems from the same factors related to male use (Taylor, 1993). For example, inner-city female drug users resemble male users in their poverty, family backgrounds, and so on (Barkan, 1996; Mahan, 1996). Moreover, like economically disadvantaged males addicted to hard drugs such as heroin, disenfranchised female addicts often cannot see a way out. Working and lower-class women

"have at least the socially integrative and productive option of motherhood (a role often taken for granted). Women addicts lose even this option as their career in heroin progresses and their options regress. Thus, due to the nature of their careers, women addicts experience the opposite of liberation. They are, in fact, more oppressed than other women: They lose not only their work options but their options for a traditional career in wife and motherhood" (Rosenbaum, 1981: 135-136).

Some studies, however, found that men are more likely than women to use drugs for excitement, while women are more likely than men to use heroin, crack, etc. to cope with depression and other psychological problems, often related to sexual abuse (Barkan, 1996; Chesney-Lind, 1995; Inciardi et al., 1993). According to Barkan (1996: 429), "To the extent this gender difference exists, it reflects women's greater sense of powerlessness and the greater psychological distress they suffer in a sexist society and internalize instead of expressing through anger."

In short, women are markedly less likely to use crack, heroin, and other hard drugs than men. Why, then, is there such a moral panic about female drug users? Perhaps this societal reaction is a function of the anti-feminist "backlash" against the growing number of women entering the workplace. For example, many people believe that women's work-force participation leads to new pressures and temptations, such as crack use, because women are taking on male gender role characteristics (Erikson and Murray, 1989; Inciardi et al., 1993). This belief, to say the least, is wrong because there is no evidence showing that women are more drawn to hard drugs than men are and there is no evidence that female rates of crack, cocaine, and heroin use are growing faster than those of male rates (Erikson and Murray, 1989). One thing, however, we are sure of is that many women are incarcerated for drug offenses. In fact, about one-third of all women in American state prisons are there for drug offenses, compared to 21 percent of the men (BJS, 1995).

Age

Young adults, especially males, are most likely to use hard drugs in both Canada and the United States (DeKeseredy and Schwartz, 1996; Eliany, 1994; Single et al., 1997). For example, the U.S. NHSDA (1997d) found that in 1994, 1.2 percent of those 18 to 25 years old and 1.3 percent of those 26 to 34 years old used cocaine, whereas only 0.3 percent of youth 12 to 17 years old and 0.4 percent of adults 35 and older used it.

What accounts for the relationship between age and drug use? According to several sociologists and criminologists, to answer this question adequately, the negative consequences of urban unemployment must be taken into account. For example, Canada and the United States have alarmingly high levels of youth unemployment (Tanner, 1996),[2] especially in the inner-cities (Wilson, 1996). Many unemployed youths who live in urban under-class ghettos also have unemployed parents who cannot afford to buy them compact discs, "nice clothes," and so on. And even if these young people are working, many find that that the financial rewards do not enable them to buy these and other "commodified" badges and symbols of status created primarily by advertising (DeKeseredy and Schwartz, 1996). Consequently, many truly disadvantaged youths turn to either using or selling drugs as pointed out below by a 17-year-old African-American male who lives in a West Side Chicago ghetto neighborhood:

"Well, basically, I feel that if you are raised in a neighborhood and all you see is negative things, then you are going to be negative because you don't see anything positive...Guys and black males see drug dealers on the corner and they see fancy cars and flashy money and they figure: 'Hey, If I get into drugs I can be like him'" (cited in Wilson, 1996: 55).

Unfortunately, while most ghetto residents endorse mainstream norms against drug dealing, this behavior has become widely accepted as a legitimate response to economic barriers in their communities (Wilson, 1996). Needless to say, child labor laws do not apply to illegal drug dealing and such "jobs" are widely available to youths wanting money.

Socioeconomic Status

As we pointed out earlier in this chapter, North America is a continent of drug users. For example, about 80 percent of the North American population ingest caffeine, two-thirds drink alcohol, and 30 percent regularly use nicotine (Boyd,

1991; Goode, 1989). A substantially lower number of Canadians and Americans use cocaine, crack, and heroin; however, those who do are typically subemployed and unemployed (McKenzie and Williams, 1997; Peterson and Harrell, 1992). In fact, over 40 years of research shows that hard drug use and socioeconomic inequality "are closely and multiply linked" (Currie, 1993: 77). For example, the NHSDA found that 3.5 percent of unemployed U. S. adults used cocaine in 1994, compared with only 0.7 percent of adults who were employed (NIDA, 1997d).

Jobless North Americans, especially those living in large, urban areas, are also more likely to deal hard drugs due to the decline of conventional work opportunities. What would you do if you couldn't find a full-time job and had a family to support? Perhaps you would deal drugs like the 25-year-old unmarried father of one child interviewed by Wilson (1996: 58-59):

"Four years I been out here trying to find a steady job. Going back and forth all these temporary jobs and this `n` that. Then you know you gotta give money at home, you know you gotta buy your clothes which cost especially for a big person. Then you're talking about my daughter, then you talking about food in the house too, you know, things like that...Well, lately like I said I have been trying to make extra money and everything. I have been selling drugs lately on the side after I get off work and, ah, it has been going all right...Like I was saying you can make more money dealing drugs than your job, anybody. Not just me but anybody, for the simple fact that if you have a nice clientele and some nice drugs, some nice `caine or whatever you are selling then the money is going to come, the people are going to come...I can take you to a place where cars come through there like this all day—like traffic—and it got so trafficky that people got to seeing it and they got to calling the police and the police got to staking out the place, raiding the place and all this kind of stuff."

At the time of writing this chapter, Walter DeKeseredy was fascinated by William Julius Wilson's (1987, 1996) research on the relationship between joblessness, drug use, and dealing, and other symptoms of structured social inequality in urban ghettos. Thus, like many other sociologists who discover new, path-breaking research, he enthusiastically discussed Wilson's work with several colleagues and students, most of whom responded by stating, "Canada is not like the United States. We don't have the same levels of poverty, joblessness, and drug dealing." Chapters 2 and 3, however, show that a substantial number of Canadians fall under the category of "under-class" and there are Canadian inner-city ghettos riddled with drug use and dealing, such as the Jane-Finch Corridor located in North York, Ontario.

Also referred to as the "Jane Jungle," most of the people who reside in this community are new immigrants with low-paying jobs or no jobs at all. As in many U.S. disenfranchised urban areas, drug dealing is common in this "frontier of despair" (McLaren, 1980). Unfortunately, there are places in the "Jane Jungle" that resemble the "trafficky" setting described above by the 25-year-old father, and you don't need extensive training in ethnographic research techniques to find out where they are. In fact, there are places where you cannot avoid coming into contact with young drug dealers, such as at a small shopping center located on

Driftwood Avenue. Here, you are likely to find buyers slowly driving through the shopping center parking lot with their car windows rolled down, periodically nodding their heads. Several young drug dealers will then quickly approach the car and compete with one another to sell "clients" small packages of drugs. Once the transaction is complete, the dealers run behind a nearby wall and the buyers speed off to their destinations (DeKeseredy and Schwartz, 1996).

Similarly, Erickson (1996) discovered hundreds of crack users in one section of inner-city Toronto, and there were from five to ten dealers at any one time on street corners and several more in a nearby public housing complex. She also found that thousands of individual drug transactions were taking place in this area on a daily basis. The lesson to be learned from this Canadian study and the growing body of research on the relationship between joblessness and crack use is that Canadians should not be "complacent about the potential of an already existing crack market to offer a tempting avenue for prosperity to some youth in transition" (1996: 326).

Race/Ethnicity

In the United States, the highest rates of crack, cocaine, and heroin use are found among African-Americans and Hispanics. For example, the NHSDA found that in 1994, 1.3 percent of African-Americans, 1.1 percent of Hispanics, and 0.5 percent of whites used cocaine (NIDA, 1997d). If some visible minority groups are at greater risk of using hard drugs in the U.S., the same can be said about some Canadian racial/ethnic groups. According to the 1990 Yukon Alcohol and Drug Survey, 16 percent of Native people (e.g., Cree, Mohawk, Inuit, Huron) reported using cocaine at some time in their lives compared to about four percent of the rest of Canada (McKenzie, 1997; Yukon Bureau of Statistics, 1990).

Why are people who belong to these visible minority groups at greater risk of using hard drugs? The answer to this question does not depend on their biological makeup, skin color, or culture. Rather, many African-Americans and Hispanics live in jobless ghettos characterized by a major lack of legitimate or conventional opportunities and resources, inadequate formal and informal social control mechanisms, and family disruption (Sampson, 1987; Wilson, 1987). Of course, where whites are exposed to such factors, rates of drug use and dealing rise dramatically (Currie, 1993; DeKeseredy and Schwartz, 1996). In fact, rates of drug use in deprived white communities are higher than in "better off" minority communities. Regardless, then, of your race or ethnicity, high levels of drug activity in a community are a function of joblessness and other economic-related problems that negatively affect social organization. However, no other group in the United States experiences the levels of segregation, isolation, and poverty concentration as do African-Americans (Wilson, 1996), and thus it is not surprising that the highest rates of hard drug use are found among them.

Like their African-American and Hispanic counterparts, many inner-city Canadian Native people are at high risk of using cocaine, heroin, and so on because they

➤ are the least connected to families and communities;

➤ are poorer, less skilled, and less educated than other Canadians;

➤ have been involved in systems of social control at an earlier age and more often;

➤ live in areas characterized by staggering levels of poverty, joblessness, and segregated housing; and

➤ have been victimized more frequently and seriously than other Canadians (LaPrairie, 1995: 40).

In sum, skin color has nothing to do with drug use and dealing. Rather, African-Americans, Hispanics, and Native Canadians report higher rates of hard drug use because a substantial number of them live in "the world of the new urban poor" (Wilson, 1996). Indeed, to adequately understand drug use among these groups, society has to take into account the ways in which rapidly escalating rates of joblessness and other social problems that plague inner-city ghetto neighborhoods influence these groups to violate conventional social norms.

Why Do People Use and Deal Hard Drugs?

Why do people ingest substances that threaten their physical and psychological health? Why do people deal drugs, a criminal activity that makes many people fear for their lives and retreat to the safety of their homes (Wilson, 1996)? Here, we discuss three widely read and cited sociological answers to these questions. We begin our review by describing strain theories developed by Merton (1938, 1957) and Cloward and Ohlin (1960), and their contributions are variations of the structural functionalist perspective described in Chapter 1.

Strain Theory

Some of the data presented in previous sections of this chapter show that inner-city, disenfranchised people are at greater risk of using and dealing drugs than their more affluent counterparts. These behaviors are not the "sick" outcome of defective personalities or deviant biological structures (Messner and Rosenfeld, 1997). Nor are they the products of what James Q. Wilson (1985) refers to as a "wicked human nature." To understand why poor people take and/or deal hard drugs, according to Merton and other strain theorists (e.g., Messner and Rosensfeld, 1997), we must critically examine the wider structure of North American society.

For example, a goal that virtually all North Americans share and that is completely socially acceptable is economic success and the accompanying status, also referred to as the "American Dream" (Messner and Rosenfeld, 1997). "Money," according to Merton, "has been consecrated as a value in itself over and above its expenditure for articles of consumption or its use for the enhancement of power" (1957: 136). From a very early age, North Americans are socialized to strive for a lifestyle that will enable them to buy expensive commodities such as a BMW, a Sony home theater system, and a luxurious suburban home. Such material desires are promoted and legitimized in many contexts, such as the school, the church, and, most obviously, the media. In these and other contexts of socialization, we are constantly told to strive for the American Dream. How many times have you heard the following messages: "Become rich! Become powerful! Become prestigious! Everybody can do it. Any child can become President. Everyone should try" (Pfohl, 1994: 262).

These messages are probably familiar. In fact, you are probably reading this chapter because you are working towards a college or university degree that you hope will lead you to economic success. According to strain theorist Robert Merton, you have the legitimate means of acquiring the above dominant cultural goals because you are a post-secondary school student with a promising future. Indeed, the institutionalized means for success in North America include getting a good education, working hard in a job to get a raise or promotion, and perhaps marrying into an influential family like the Kennedys (DeKeseredy and Schwartz, 1996). Unfortunately, many North Americans do not even have the opportunity to attend school.

Moreover, many young people, even if they can attend post-secondary school, are unemployed or subemployed. You don't have to have a Ph.D. to know that North America is a continent with high levels of unemployment, poverty (see Chapters 3 and 4), homelessness, and other symptoms of class inequality. For example, federal government statistics show that Canada's youth unemployment rate is an alarming 20 percent. This estimate constitutes just the tip of the iceberg, because it does not include youths who have stopped searching for jobs due to frustration, anger, depression, fatigue, and so on (Alvi and DeKeseredy, 1997).

You often hear people say, "What do you mean there are no jobs out there? There is plenty of work for young people if they want it!" Yes, there are jobs, most of which are defined by career-oriented youths as either "bad," "low-level," or "low-paying." Here, we are referring to jobs provided by "lower-tier" industries, such as fast food chains, retail, etc. These jobs are often characterized by drudgery, low pay, and minimal opportunities for advancement.

In addition, Human Resources Development Canada data indicate that in 1992, youth under 25 years of age collected $2.5 billion in Unemployment Insurance benefits (UIC) and made up 17 percent of UIC recipients. In the same year, youth under 25 received over $2 billion in social assistance and represented 21 percent of social assistance cases (Alvi and DeKeseredy, 1997). These and other disenfranchised youths want the same material things as you, and the status associated with financial success. However, their social condition means that they will not achieve the "American Dream." In sum, while the general goals of society are held out for everyone to meet, the opportunities to reach these goals are not evenly and equally distributed.

Those who cannot achieve financial success through conventional means experience a great deal of **strain** because of this disjunction. There are a number of deviant or criminal ways of dealing with this strain, and Merton outlined four "modes of adaptation." The one of central concern in this chapter is **retreatism**, whereby people give up on both the goals and the legitimate means of acquiring them and instead become drug users. According to Chein (1966: 137, 140), they get high because heroin, crack, cocaine, and the like:

"... offer a quick and royal route to meeting the challenge of living. Heroin and its related subculture gives them a sense of well-being and of social acceptability and participation. If the price is a terrible one to pay...the pseudo-rewards, especially in the 'honeymoon stage,' are far more glittering than anything else their environment offers them."

A variant of "ghetto-related behavior," drug use then, according to strain theory, does not occur because people are psychologically weak or morally deficient. Rather, drug use, especially in inner-city slum areas, represents a particular cultural adaptation to the blockage of legitimate opportunities in poor urban areas and North American society as a whole (Wilson, 1996). Most inner-city drug users are in fact normal people facing an abnormal situation—that in some parts of society it is impossible to get the education and jobs necessary to achieve middle-class status. Retreating into drugs offers a series of real rewards (DeKeseredy and Schwartz, 1996).

Cloward and Ohlin (1960) modified Merton's theory to take into account the problems of access to both legitimate and deviant opportunities in socially disorganized ghetto neighborhoods. These theorists were primarily concerned with explaining the development of delinquent subcultures in these settings, and they argued that disenfranchised youths who cannot achieve status through either the legitimate or illegitimate opportunity structure develop a **retreatist subculture**. They are "double failures" and turn to drugs for solutions to their problems and withdraw from the broader community.

In sum, strain theories contend that the denial of legitimate opportunities to achieve the American Dream is one of the key factors that motivates disenfranchised, inner-city people to use hard drugs as a mode of adaptation. However, like all theoretical perspectives on drug use reviewed in this chapter and other sources (e.g., Akers, 1992), the strain theories reviewed here cannot adequately explain all drug use by all people. For example, they cannot account for why affluent people with an apparent high stake in conformity use heroin and cocaine (Thio, 1995). Nevertheless, some progressive sociological criminologists assert that since hard drug use among the middle- and upper-class is both steadily decreasing and generally manageable, the alarming rate of heroin, cocaine, and crack use among the under-class requires most of our empirical, theoretical, and political attention. Unfortunately, as Currie (1993: 4) correctly points out, "After two decades of the drug war, endemic hard-drug use among the poor and near-poor of the U.S. is higher than ever before."

Social Bond Theory

The authors of this text primarily teach criminology and deviance courses which emphasize acquiring a rich understanding of a diverse range of theoretical perspectives on various types of "crime and disrepute" (Hagan, 1994). Typically, after our lectures on causal theories (e.g., strain perspectives), several students respond by stating, "Why do you always dwell on the factors that influence people to commit crimes or deviant acts? What about those who adhere to conventional social norms? Can't you explain why they don't deviate?" These questions are valid and reflect sensitivity to the fact that most of us are not criminals, an issue of central concern to social bond theorists such as Hirschi (1969). They organize their research around the question, "Why don't most people take hard drugs?" They assert that most North Americans abstain from using these substances because they have a strong bond to conventional society. However, if their bond is broken or weakened, they are more likely to "shoot up" or "beam up."

Hirschi (1969) argued that the social bond has four elements: attachment, commitment, involvement, and belief. The first element, **attachment**, refers to the degree to which people have close emotional ties to conventional "significant others" such as parents, friends, teachers, ministers, and so on. The more attached young people are to these conventional members of society, the more likely they are to take their concerns, feelings, wishes, and expectations into account, which, in turn, inhibits drug use and dealing. However, youths who are isolated or detached from conforming members of society are less likely to respect the norms, values, and wishes of these people. Thus, there is a greater chance that they will engage in drug use and dealing.

Consider Chicago's ghetto neighborhoods. As noted previously, many people who reside there are either unemployed or subemployed, and consequently, they are less likely than more affluent people to belong to mainstream or conventional institutions and have conventional friends who are educated, work, and are married (Wilson, 1996). Thus, according to social bond theorists, it is not surprising that drug use and dealing are endemic to these urban areas.

People may be detached from significant others but still conform because they have a strong **commitment** to the conventional social order or a stake in conformity. Some people think of this in terms of "What do you have to lose?" If you have nothing, you have nothing to lose, and you might not be inhibited from taking or dealing drugs. For example, having nothing is often used as a justification for dealing drugs, as pointed out by an unemployed 35-year-old Chicago ghetto resident:

"And what am I doing now? I'm a cocaine dealer 'cause I can't get a decent-ass job. So, what other choices do I have? I have to feed my family...do I work? I work. See, don't...bring me that bullshit. I been working since I was fifteen years old. I had to take care of my mother and father and my sisters. See, so can't, can't nobody bring me that bullshit about I ain't looking for no job" (cited in Wilson, 1996: 58).

On the other hand, if you have a solid conventional reputation, a good job, relationships you might lose if you are branded a drug addict or drug dealer, job prospects, or other commitments, you have a lot to lose. For example, in the late 1980s, one of the authors of this text had non-academic friends who spent almost their entire weekends drinking and getting high. Since he was obsessed with completing his Ph.D. thesis and getting a tenure-track university job, he spent little time with these people and his family, and a substantial amount of time writing and interacting with scholars at both conferences and at a large Southern Ontario university. At this time, he believed that the enormous amount of time and effort invested in getting his Ph.D. and an Assistant Professor position could be jeopardized by a criminal conviction and/or the negative health effects of consuming drugs and "booze." So, he "kept his nose clean."

The third element of the social bond is **involvement**. This refers to the amount of time one spends engaging in conventional or legitimate activities such as studying, playing or watching sports, doing volunteer work, and so on. If you are busy working, studying, or playing sports day and night, you (by definition) won't be hanging out with hard drug users and dealers. On the other hand, "the devil plays with idle hands," especially in under-class communities characterized by high levels of joblessness and social disorganization. For example, according to one resident of a high-jobless community located in the South Side of Chicago:

"Our children, you know, seems to be more at risk than any other children there is, because there's no library for them to go to. There's not a center they can go to, there's no field house that they can go into. There's nothing. There's nothing at all" (cited in Wilson, 1996: 64).

The fourth element of the social bond, **belief**, refers to an acceptance of conventional social norms and values. Because they believe that obeying laws prohibiting drug use and dealing is "the right thing to do" and that law enforcement officials are exercising proper authority, many people refrain from pursuing the "American pipe dream" (Chitwood et al., 1996), "chasing the dragon," or "shooting up." On the other hand, what if you don't happen to strongly hold these beliefs? According to Hirschi (1969: 26), "The less a person believes he should obey the rules, the more likely he is to violate them." Furthermore, people are even less likely to believe in obeying laws prohibiting the use and distribution of drugs if a large number of people in their community tolerate or legitimate drug use and dealing (Wilson, 1996).

In sum, a large number of young, male, inner-city ghetto youths take or deal hard drugs because their bond to conventional society is broken or weakened due in large part to the blockage of legitimate job opportunities. But what about middle- and upper-class drug users? For example, powder cocaine is often referred to in terms such as "the luxurious drug of the middle-class" (Beirne and Messerschmidt, 1995). How can social bond theory explain their hard drug use? Compared with under-class inner-city residents, middle- and upper-class people apparently have a lot more to lose if they are caught using or dealing crack, heroin, and other illicit drugs. Nevertheless, some of them are willing to take this risk. Maybe this can be explained by the fact that some affluent people consider periodic drug use to be either acceptable or only mildly deviant behavior (DeKeseredy and Schwartz, 1996). Regardless of why some economically privileged people use drugs, we do know for sure that a strong bond to the conventional social order does not absolutely preclude us from using drugs. Even so, it does put people at lower risk of doing so.

An alternative explanation for drug use in affluent communities is provided by Currie. He argues that "The absence of available or concerned adults, and the pervasiveness of an insistent consumer culture" can make middle-class and upper-class people vulnerable to drug use (1993: 103). However, Currie does not provide reliable evidence to support this assertion.

Inequality and Drugs

Nostradamus (1503-1566), a French physician and astrologer, is one of the Western world's most famous predictors of the future. Many people have found some of his predictions to be accurate foretellings of major wars and other world events. However, Nostradamus had nothing on drug historian David Musto (1988). He predicted the emergence of a two-tiered drug culture in which hard drug use among economically deprived inner-city residents becomes endemic, while middle-class suburban use will decline. Well, a substantial amount of recent research confirms Musto's prediction (e.g., Currie, 1993), and unfortunately, the situation has become much worse than he anticipated. For example, we are now experiencing "perverse situations" in which youths are making their living by selling crack and other hard drugs to their elders in cities suffering from high poverty concentrations (Peterson and Harrell, 1992). What makes this "American nightmare especially frightening is that, like a fire that continues to rage after we have cut down half the forest to contain it, it has withstood the most extraordinary efforts at control" (Currie, 1993: 13-14).

Why do those whom Kasarda (1992) refers to as the "severely distressed" use and sell drugs as a means of adapting to the disruption of traditional job networks in inner-city communities? Elliott Currie contends that four theoretical models help answer this question: (1) the status model, (2) the coping model, (3) the structure model, and (4) the saturation model.

Like the strain perspectives described previously, the **status model** argues that poor people are denied legitimate means of achieving status in North American society. Therefore, some under-class people view hard drug use as an alternative means of attaining esteem, a sense of respect, and a sense of community. These motives are made explicit below by a methamphetamine, or "crank," user interviewed by Currie:

"I like the stuff, actually...Cause it gives you a high, you know, and ...it makes you look bigger (emphasis in original), you know? Makes you look big time, you know, when you got an 8-ball of crank in your pocket, and two hundred dollars in your other pocket, and you're walking around town and you've got nice clothes on and stuff like that, and you whip out the 8-ball, you snort a line and you're all—your eyes get all big, you're running around? [laughs] It's really fun, it's really cool. I like it" (1993: 107).

Status is also a concern for many female hard drug users (Morgan and Joe, 1997). For example, on the street, heroin is reputed to be the most dangerous drug, and thus this substance bestows on its users a reputation as the most serious outlaws (DeKeseredy and Schwartz, 1996). In fact, a growing number of bored and alienated women find this reputation attractive (Rosenbaum, 1981).

It should also be noted in passing that some women peddle hard drugs, such as methamphetamine, to enhance their self-esteem, as stated below by a female dealer interviewed by Morgan and Joe (1997: 102):

"I have very high self esteem. I'm sure about who I am. It's painful to see people who are beat down behind it. I understand it...Women especially, have very serious self esteem problems. Speed accentuates the deficit. You have to be comfortable inside your person. You're locked in this body for the duration."

The **coping model** views drugs as substances that minimize the stress and strain of living in economically distressed communities. For example, the "truly disadvantaged" have difficulties coping with life on a daily basis (Wilson, 1987). Needless to say, being poor or homeless "virtually insures a life of chronic hassles" (Currie, 1993: 113), such as inadequate school systems, day care, and transportation (Wilson, 1996); domestic violence and other family-related problems (e.g., ill-timed pregnancies and unstable marriages) (Furstenberg, 1993); and if they can find them, jobs characterized by drudgery, low pay, and minimal advancement (Alvi and DeKeseredy, 1997).

Given these and other alarming problems facing the working poor and the under-class, it is not surprising that many members of these marginalized groups use drugs to get a "momentary high that affords escape and pleasure in an otherwise dismal life" (Devine and Wright, 1993: 163-164). According to a female heroin user interviewed by Rosenbaum,

"It's just a good feeling. At that particular time, shit, you don't have a problem in the world. Nothin'. I heard a doctor say right here in this jail that heroin preserves people. You are not sick. You don't feel pain. Fuck the rent, fuck the food, fuck the phone, fuck the kids, fuck how you look. Really, it's just an 'aw, fuck it' attitude. At the time you are loaded nothing bothers you" (1981: 44).

People use drugs for coping purposes more than those who use them for other reasons (e.g., social and recreational) (DeKeseredy and Schwartz, 1996). Why, then, should we expect those who lives are characterized by extreme poverty to abstain from using hard drugs even if "shooting up" or smoking crack only gives them an illusion of well-being? Devine and Wright (1993: 164) ask us to seriously think about the following challenging questions: "Is this fleeting illusion not preferable to the cold realities of inner city life? Is there really a 'free will' choice to be made between momentary euphoria and endless misery?" What do you think and how would you cope with the day-to-day hassles of urban poverty? Research suggests that if you became one of the truly disadvantaged, you would be likely to move beyond simply smoking cigarettes or drinking alcohol, especially if you felt that there was no chance of escaping persistent poverty.

The **structure model** asserts that drugs provide disenfranchised people with a sense of structure and purpose to their lives, especially if they don't have meaningful jobs. Being jobless, for example, and particularly being unemployed with absolutely no hope of ever getting a job generates boredom and a sense of monotony. Drugs alleviate these problems. Put simply, what else is there to do? According to Eighner (1993: 162), "In a life that seems utterly without meaning and purpose, the quest for the daily dose is something to do, a reason to keep putting one foot in front of the other."

The **saturation model** is an extension of the structure model. For example, Wilson (1987, 1996) and other progressive sociologists (e.g., Devine and Wright, 1993) found that after decades and generations of limited economic opportunity, some inner-city communities are characterized by pervasive hopelessness. Consequently, drug use becomes more and more widespread until it virtually saturates the entire community. People don't really make a conscious effort to become drug users or drug dealers, but just seem to drift into doing what everyone else is doing, as pointed out by an inner-city Chicago ghetto resident interviewed by Wilson (1996: 55-56):

"And I think about how, you know, the kids around there, all they see, OK, they see these drug addicts, and then what else do they see? Oh, they see thugs, you know, they see the gangbangers. So, who do they, who do they really look, model themselves after? Who is their role model? They have none but the thugs. So that's what they wind up being, you know...They [the children in the neighborhood] deal with the only male role model that they can find and most of the time that be pimps, dope dealers, so what do they do? They model themselves after them. Not intentionally trying to but if, you know, that's the only male you're around and that's the only one you come in close contact with, you tend to want to be like that person. And that's why you have so many young drug dealers."

Moreover, in a community riddled with drug use and dealing, quitting is almost impossible. According to one of Goode's informants, "Whenever I saw my friends, they were shooting up, too...The problem with kicking heroin...is that all of your friends aren't kicking at the same time" (1989: 252).

Currie points out that these four models are not mutually exclusive. In fact, the nature and extent of disenfranchised people's drug use and dealing activities are not static but fluid (Morgan and Joe, 1997). For example, an under-class person may use crack or heroin for all of the reasons described here. He or she may want peer group status, be "stressed out" or bored, and be surrounded by other users and dealers. Further, the motives for his or her drug use may change at different stages in life. In sum, people's shifting roles in the illicit drug world are linked to changes in resources and social support, intimate relationships with romantic partners and family members, to criminal activities, and to employment and broader economic forces (Morgan and Joe, 1997).

Of the four models reviewed in this section, however, Currie argues that the status model best explains the early stages of drug use. As people get older, they do not derive as much excitement from using or dealing drugs, and they experience related long-term health problems. Even so, they continue to take drugs because they either need some method of coping with the hassles of poverty or need to manage their habit. These problems are exacerbated by their criminal status and addiction, and often hard drug addicts cannot see a way out of their desperate situation (Rosenbaum, 1981).

In sum, although the factors that motivate poor inner-city residents to use and deal hard drugs shift over time, the most important point to consider here is that the key source of their involvement in the illegal drug economy is social and economic marginality. What about affluent drug users and dealers? What influences

them to take and/or peddle drugs? These are important questions often raised by
the media, students, criminal justice officials, politicians, and so on. Of course,
many upper- and middle-class people use and/or deal drugs. For example, referred
to as "citizens," included in Morgan and Joe's (1997) sample of 141 female
methamphetamine users were a group of women who lived in "good" communities,
had husbands and children, had money, and who sometimes had conventional
jobs. According to Thio (1995), Currie's "unifactor theory" cannot account for
why these and other economically advantaged people ingest or sell drugs.

In fairness to Currie, he did not intend to address this concern. For him, the
ghetto poor's use and distribution of hard drugs warrants most of our empirical,
theoretical, and political attention because: (1) drug use among the affluent is
manageable and decreasing, and (2) the under-class drug problem has grown
significantly despite the U.S. government's war on drugs. Unfortunately, the U.S.
inner-city drug problem is much worse than it was when this war started, and the
future is bleak. Moreover, contrary to popular belief, illegal drug use actually
increases during periods in which U.S. governments aggressively enforce harsh
criminal penalties (Kappeler et al., 1993).

What Is to Be Done About Hard Drug Abuse and Drug Dealing in North America?

Like most of the other chapters in this text, this one provides data showing that the
United States and, to a lesser extent, Canada are in a "terrible mess" (Currie, 1992).
Can we clean it up? Can we lower the alarming rates of drug use described in this
chapter and other sources? Can we prevent disenfranchised people from selling
highly addictive drugs to their neighbors, friends, and relatives? The answer to
all of these questions is "yes." However, in order to minimize or overcome the
North American hard drug problem, we must choose a progressive path, one that
moves beyond simply doing more of the same, such as declaring yet another war
on drugs. If prisons and other harsh punishments do not deter the violent crimes
described in Chapter 5, the same can be said about drugs. Below, according to
several criminologists (e.g., Kappeler et al., 1993), is perhaps the best evaluation
of the harsh law and order strategy advanced by the U.S. government:

*"In baseball a player with three strikes is out. But after three dismal failures in trying to
stop the use of alcohol, opiates, and marijuana, the United States government still stands
at the plate determined to smash the hell out of the drug problem. Unlike ballplayers, who
adjust to the peculiarities of various pitchers and who put past experience to use, United
States legislators subscribe to a single-minded philosophy — if you don't hit it, you're
not swinging hard enough" (McCaghy, 1985: 298).*

The metaphor of war is also used by Canadian politicians and criminal justice
officials (Boyd, 1995). For example, in June 1985, Ontario Supreme Court Justice
Eugene Ewaschuk sentenced a person to 20 years imprisonment for importing

"grass." To justify this punishment, he told *Globe and Mail* reporters that, "Drug traffickers exploit the weak...Drug traffickers profit from the misery and crime of drug users. Drug traffickers live off the avails of other people's crimes and are thus social blood-suckers...The drug importer is a pernicious criminal" (cited in Boyd, 1995: 376).

Does this sound like a soft sentence to you? Imagine what this judge would have done if the accused were a crack or heroin dealer! For reasons described in Chapter 5, regardless of the severity of penalties imposed on drug users and dealers, little, if anything, will change unless we target the most powerful determinants of involvement in the illegal drug world identified in this chapter: joblessness, wage inequality, and related social problems such as fading inner-city families and inadequate education (Currie, 1993; Devine and Wright, 1993; Harrell and Peterson, 1992; Wilson, 1996).

Since we devoted a substantial amount of attention to job creation strategies and adequate social services in previous chapters, these proposals will not be repeated here. Rather, in the following section, we focus on ways in which we can restructure the North American secondary school system. Research shows that these initiatives constitute "one important weapon in the fight against acute joblessness in the inner-city ghetto" (Wilson, 1996: 218).

Youth Unemployment, Education, and Entrepreneurial Culture: Improving the Odds[3]

There are many things that sociologists like us do not know. However, what we do know is that factors influencing the rise of unemployment and underemployment in socially distressed inner-cities and other communities include a network of factors well beyond the control of North American public, high school, and post-secondary school teachers and students. To name but a few of these factors: globalization; "corporate anorexia;" the rise of the "contingent" work force; the North American Free Trade Agreement (NAFTA); transnational corporations moving operations to Third World countries to use cheap labor; the implementation of high technology in workplaces; and the shift from manufacturing to a service-based economy.[4]

The sheer magnitude and complexity of these factors in relation to employment means that ideally, a complex, progressive, multi-agency and multidimensional response is required. In other words, we must avoid what Elliott Currie (1985) sees as the tendency to compartmentalize social problems along bureaucratic lines. For example, many people think that schools should only deal with education, while the private sector should only address employment and broader economic issues. This is an incorrect and short-sighted way of looking at the issues raised here. Now is the time for a diverse range of formal institutions and stakeholders to consider the ways in which increasing class size, closing factories, cutting funds to government-sponsored youth employment initiatives, etc. all affect youth unemployment and underemployment, as well as the negative consequences of these problems such as youths' involvement in the illicit drug economy.

Unfortunately, due to space limitations here, we must limit our focus to just one, albeit important, "part of the puzzle;" that is, how the North American educational system, can, with the assistance of government agencies and members of the private sector, help overcome youth economic marginality and, ultimately, drug use and dealing by teaching students entrepreneurial and job-related skills.

North American Students' Employment Concerns

The higher one's educational achievement, the more likely one is to get a meaningful and rewarding job. For example, while the rate of unemployment in inner-city communities is the highest in businesses with low educational requirements, we are currently witnessing massive job growth in industries that require high levels of education, such as the computer industries (Wilson, 1987, 1996). Indeed, only a few Fortune 500 corporations hire young people fresh out of high school. This is not to say that high school graduates are completely ignored by these companies. The ones who are eventually hired are those who are in their mid-twenties, have work experience, and who have demonstrated what Matza (1964) refers to as "maturational reform" (e.g., married) (Marshall, 1994; Wilson, 1996).

Thus, many people argue that we must, with the help of government agencies, the private sector, and others, do everything in our power to ensure that students stay in school. Even so, staying in school is not enough anymore. For example, Shahid Alvi and Walter DeKeseredy teach sociology and criminology courses at Carleton University, a place where more and more students come to them with major concerns about what they are going to do when they graduate. Their anxieties, fears, and stresses are, in our opinion, indicators of the fact that many students know that they will eventually face great difficulties finding "decent jobs," especially in Ottawa. Also referred to as the "Silicone Valley of the North," Ottawa is the home of major "high tech" companies such as Corel, a corporation that is apparently not interested in hiring people with degrees in sociology or criminology unless they can demonstrate outstanding expertise in software development.

It is true that a few high school "drop outs" end up achieving something akin to the "American Dream." However, consider the following fact—the unemployment rate for Canadian youths with a high school degree is around 30 percent, compared to 10 percent for young people with a university or college degree. These data tell us, not surprisingly, that young people should stay in school. Even given these alarming data, the question still arises: how can they balance the realities of today's labor market with the importance of achieving high levels of educational attainment? One answer that is increasingly proposed is to provide youths with entrepreneurial and work-related skills.

Introducing Entrepreneurial Skills into the Curriculum

With the exception of community colleges or technical schools, the role of the teacher was never formally designed to facilitate the acquisition of a job or building a lucrative business. These functions, however, are certainly part of what social scientists refer to as the hidden curriculum, in that schools have implicitly (and sometimes explicitly) trained students for particular roles in the labor market. Why not, then, "come clean" and make teaching entrepreneurial and job-related skills part and parcel of the curriculum? After all, most students do not go to school primarily to become Plato, Socrates, or sociology professors. Emphasizing only reading, writing, and mathematics, and a few hours of career counseling is no longer enough to ensure a person's economic viability. And, if we continue along these heavily traveled paths, we will simply repeat past mistakes.

One way to enhance the educational experience, then, is to provide students with a background in math, history, languages, social sciences, and so on, and to make the linkage between these subjects and working world part of the *raison d'etre* of schooling. As Devine and Wright (1993: 209) point out, except for a few North American schools, most urban high schools have not tried to help students who don't want to go to college or university master "a single useful skill that would assist them in the transition from school to work. It seems...that next to the basic skills, some sort of marketable skill, craft, or trade is the minimum 'payoff' any student should expect to receive from his or her high school education."

Students should also be exposed to the realities associated with both the school-to-work transition (e.g., deadlines, punctuality, etc.) and starting their own business. In addition, public and high schools, colleges/universities, and other centers of higher learning should invite prominent, successful entrepreneurs, small business owners, and corporate executives to provide seminars and workshops on ways in which students can apply their academic skills in the "business world" and public sector. Ignoring this approach has serious consequences. For example, according to Wilson (1996: 217),

"[I]t removes our best corporations and their important learning systems from involvement in the process of molding young workers; it eliminates a natural communication network for feeding employer information to schools about the changing skills required in the workplace; and, most important, it disconnects achievements in school from rewards in the workplace, thereby undermining the incentive for academic success."

Youths who are not university/college bound and who are not given rich employment advice, career counseling, and job placement assistance are typically left to "sink or swim" (Wilson, 1996), and research described in this chapter and elsewhere shows that hopelessness and anger generated by joblessness often results in drug use and/or dealing.

The workshops proposed here should not involve only one or two "quick and dirty" presentations and group discussions. One-shot seminars or workshops are typically trivialized by students and teachers alike, and they only provide a superficial understanding of the issues, hassles, and efforts associated with finding employment and being an entrepreneur. Instead, weekly or bi-weekly events are necessary and should be mandatory as long as they are integrated with curricula in meaningful ways (Alvi and DeKeseredy, 1997).

In addition to teaching students entrepreneurial and work skills, however, presenters and workshop coordinators should emphasize how academic and entrepreneurial skills go hand-in-hand. One is not more important than the other. In other words, students should not be given the impression (as they often are) that what they learn in the classroom has no bearing on what they do in the workplace, or how they go about developing a business (Devine and Wright, 1993). Creating a successful business or finding an upper-tier job generally requires the development of sharp analytical writing and reading proficiency. Unfortunately and under-standably, many students find the process of acquiring these skills uncomfortable or boring. However, if entrepreneurial and job-related seminars, workshops, and other related events stress the importance of a broad-based education, students might become more motivated to pursue their traditional studies if they feel that their academic work will eventually lead to financial success or a stable job (Alvi and DeKeseredy, 1997).

Finally, we need to understand that creating successful business opportunities and skill sets for youths requires an integrated and cooperative approach similar to the School-to-Work Opportunities Act (SWOA) passed by the U.S. Congress in the spring of 1994. As in Germany and Japan, the SWOA emphasizes government, business, and education partnerships in local communities and stresses the private-sector investment in education (Wilson, 1996). However, this strategy should proceed upon the recognition that it is not just the individual who needs to be "motivated" and "provided with skills," but that structural barriers, such as racial/ethnic, gender, regional, language, and economic disparities need to be overcome as well.

Creating Linkages Between Schools, Private Business, and Government Agencies

There is much more to teaching students entrepreneurial and occupational skills than having them sit in a classroom and listen to people. Hands on strategies are also necessary. Most teachers already know that the best way to learn something is to actually do it. Thus, educational institutions, government agencies, and private business should work together to help students get summer and/or part-time jobs where they can learn and apply their entrepreneurial skills and gain some job experience. This is not an easy task, since many companies are downsizing and a substantial number of inner-city jobs are being eliminated due to global economic reorganization. Nevertheless, it is the long-term gain that should concern us. A few dollars spent now have the potential to make a growing number of North American youth avoid participating in the illicit drug economy, and helping them eventually become productive members of society.

It is either pay now or pay much more, later. For example, if the problems of youth unemployment and underemployment become more acute in North America, we and several other sociologists predict a substantial increase in drug consumption and dealing, homelessness, family violence, teen pregnancy, and the like. As described in Box 8.6, some sociologists, such as William Julius Wilson, even predict an inner-city scenario that resembles civil war. Can our governments, communities, school, and businesses afford to cope with the staggering rates of hard drug use and trafficking, as well as the problems raised in Box 8.6? We don't think so. In fact, the financial costs of sending people to prison, youth detention centers, and drug rehabilitation programs are much higher than the cost of providing youths with programs aimed at developing and applying entrepreneurial skills or (even better) creating the social and economic environment in which young inner-city people can flourish.

BOX 8-6

America's Formidable Enemy Within

When the Under-class Has Had Enough, the Result Will Resemble Civil War

It is just after 10 p.m. in downtown Seattle when the evening is suddenly punctured by a man's scream. Far below the hotel window, in a well-lit alleyway, two young African-Americans are trying to separate a middle-aged white man from his wallet.

The man flails wildly, kicking the shin of one of his assailants, knocking him backwards, but it is his unrelenting, attention-attracting shouting that finally drives them away.

They race down the alleyway and disappear into the drizzling night. But long after they have gone, the man—violated yet relatively unharmed—keeps shouting a torrent of racist invective against his attackers.

"Go back to your cages," he howls. But he doesn't report the attack to the police. "What's the use?" he says. "This is normal now."

The next morning, inside the same hotel, William Julius Wilson, a leading Harvard sociologist and respected African-American academic, looks and sounds frustrated as he talks about "America's disintegrating social fabric." The incident outside the hotel has become normal, routine, unexceptional in a nation where murder often hardly raises an eyebrow.

Wilson has long argued that crime and drug use in America's urban ghettos, particularly among blacks and Latinos, is linked to the disappearance of jobs in inner-city neighborhoods. He says U.S. society is responding to the problem of a growing under-class "by simply not addressing it."

"So far, we don't have the dramatic story. Millions of people in America live in ghettos and millions more ignore that fact. It's only when the worst case scenario happens, when large numbers of homeless families with kids move out to live on the streets, that maybe people will say enough is enough."

Wilson and other leading sociologists have come to Seattle to discuss America's under-class. They say the huge ghettos and barrios of Los Angeles, New York, Chicago, Boston and Miami are growing so quickly and America's poor are becoming so angry that rioting and massive social unrest are increasingly likely in the decade.

Paul Jargowsky, a University of Texas social scientist who specializes in poverty and has written the book *Poverty in Place*, says the population of U.S. high-poverty neighborhoods has risen from four million to eight million over the past 10 years. There are 2.5 million children "growing up in intolerable conditions," he adds.

Jargowsky says riots and even a form of civil war are possible. "It's unthinkable, I know, but the anger and frustration are growing every day. The ghettos are socially and economically isolated from American society. They're breeding grounds for the development of dysfunctional behavior. And there's no escape."

"America doesn't have any external enemies now, but it may have the most powerful internal enemy of all: itself. We're already seeing massive crime spilling out of these areas because of what amounts to racial and economic segregation. Concentrated poverty makes people increasingly hostile. The question is, how long will it take before it erupts."

Wilson and Jargowsky argue that enlightened self-interest rather than compassion should move America to take more action on the ghettos.

Wilson, author of *The Truly Disadvantaged*, a book that argues that businesses should be encouraged to relocate in troubled areas to help them rebuild, says useful community jobs also have to be created. "Kids have to be paid to clean streets, fill manholes, tear down dangerous buildings. We have to rebuild the community infrastructure."

But Wilson says the Clinton administration is now obsessed with a balanced budget rather than solving the problems of the poor. Wilson says a middle-of-the-road conservative agenda means the ghettos are falling lower on the priority list.

Ghettos have become a fact of life in America's largest inner-cities, but are also growing in such mid-size cities as Seattle, San Francisco, Atlanta, and New Orleans. They are increasingly isolated from the communities around them.

Street gangs have become an institution within the ghettos, according to Sudhir Alladi Venkatesh, a Harvard associate professor who lived for a time in a high-poverty neighborhood in Chicago.

The gangs, he said, have become the unofficial police forces of the ghettos. "They have become a resource for the community. They are a contradiction. On the one hand, they perpetrate crime. On the other, they help the local community enforce local rules. They bring thieves to unofficial courts made up of representative grassroots groups. They ferret out men who commit physical abuse or sexual harassment. They provide escort services through dangerous neighborhoods."

Venkatesh said this represents the sole positive side of street gangs. He likens them to the Mafia with the equivalent of local dons or leaders, but said there is one significant difference: drugs. "The prevalence of drug use in these neighborhoods is astronomical. The white Mafia used to keep drugs out of their neighborhoods. The street gangs bring them in and send them out. They're their life blood."

The problems of the black under-class, says Wilson, are exacerbated by the exodus of the black middle class from central cities to the white suburbs, "leaving the black poor more isolated and concentrated than ever before in urban history."

Increasingly, there is an image that black men are threatening and dangerous, says Wilson, and people would rather not come into contact with them. This image carries over into the workplace, he says.

BOX 8-6

Many conservative commentators have laughed off Wilson's idea of reviving poor black communities through job creation. They say street-gang kids—those who even black employers are unwilling to hire—are unsuitable to work as library aides or street cleaners.

There is also little sympathy in the U.S. mainstream for an under-class that is perceived as causing its own problems. The abject poor are not viewed so much as victims than as miscreants who behave badly because they do not abide by middle-class or mainstream moral values.

Some conservatives have even argued, somewhat controversially, that African-Americans have a cultural heritage that prepares them for failure rather than success. Pouring money into ghettos will be useless, they say, claiming that dysfunctional ghettos will never be eliminated.

Jargowsky is pessimistic about the future. In an economy where skill requirements are increasing, poorer neighborhoods are becoming ever more distant from the mainstream.

"It's a recipe for spiraling inequality...At some point, I strongly believe, it will all burst open."

Source: Haysom (1997: A4).

BOX 8-6

Summary

As described in Box 8.6 and elsewhere, youth unemployment and under-employment have contributed to an inner-city drug problem that is slowly ripping sections of North America apart. These problems will not go away on their own, and the policies currently in place, such as "three strikes and you're out" and government cutbacks to social services and education, are not working. Creating more "McJobs" and simply "getting tough" with young people are salient examples of being "penny wise and pound foolish." More substantial and effective progressive investments in our young people's future are necessary.

How do we know that the progressive, balanced, educational model suggested here will result in more people getting jobs, make communities safer and drug-free, improve the North American economy, and help people develop a stronger bond with the conventional social order? This is an empirical question that can only be answered by evaluating the outcome of the suggestions raised in this section. Why not put them into practice? What do we have to lose? Traditional pedagogical techniques are no longer working. It is time for policy makers, employers, educators, students, and others to mutually consider new directions such as those briefly addressed in this chapter. At the very least, they should be the subject of considerable dialog and debate within a framework of understanding that simple, "individualistic" solutions to North America's hard drug problem are doomed to failure (Currie, 1993).

Summary

A key objective of this chapter was to explain why only certain drugs are officially designated as major threats to our social, economic, psychological, and physical well-being. The potential for harm does not appear to be as important as the characteristics of the people generally associated with abusing a drug. In fact, a major factor in the decision to make drugs illegal is when their use is associated with minority groups, such as African-Americans, Orientals, and Hispanics. After all, if harm were the major concern, then alcohol and cigarettes would probably be outlawed.

Data reviewed throughout this chapter also show that Americans are more likely to use hard drugs (e.g., cocaine, crack, heroin) than Canadians. However, like disenfranchised African-American and Hispanic-American ghetto residents, poor Native people who live in Canadian inner-cities are at very high risk of ingesting these substances. Involvement in the illicit drug economy is a salient example of what happens "when work disappears" in North American urban areas.

Two of the three theories reviewed here heavily emphasize the influence of structured social inequality. These perspectives and the data that inform them sensitize us, once again, to the importance of developing progressive policies that target the ways in which broader social, economic, and cultural forces influence marginalized people to engage in deviant and/or criminal behavior.

What is to be done about hard drug use and dealing in socially distressed communities? The answer to this question is definitely more of what we are already doing. "Swinging the bat harder" does little, if anything, to prevent economically and socially disadvantaged people from peddling and using crack, heroin, and so on. What we need now is an alternative agenda, one that involves "making peace in the war on drugs" (Kappeler et al., 1996: 184). This approach involves aggressive attempts to eliminate joblessness in inner-cities and improving youths' preparation for work in the new global economy (Wilson, 1996). Together with the progressive policies advanced elsewhere in this book (e.g., Chapters 4 and 6), creating linkages between schools, private business, and government agencies is a step in the right direction.

KEY TERMS

Cocaine
Crack
Heroin
Hidden curriculum
Objectivistic definitions of drugs
Retreatism
Retreatist subculture
Social learning
Strain
Subjective definitions of drugs
Systemic discrimination

DISCUSSION QUESTIONS

1. Why are only certain drugs officially designated as dangerous?
2. What are the strengths and limitations of using mainstream survey research techniques to gather data on drug use?
3. Why are under-class, inner-city residents at the greatest risk of using and selling cocaine, crack, and heroin?
4. What is the relationship between education and involvement in the illicit drug economy?
5. What are the limitations of the policy proposals advanced in this chapter?

PROBLEM SOLVING SCENARIOS

1. As a class, divide into small groups of six people. Devise a plan of action that you can undertake to prevent disenfranchised, inner-city youths from becoming involved in the illicit drug economy.
2. Suppose some television journalists asked you to help them produce a documentary on the realities of drug use in North American society. What would you do to assist them?
3. Create your own theory of drug use and trafficking in inner-city ghetto neighborhoods. What assumptions have you made about race, class, gender, and the role of society in creating and/or perpetuating hard drug use and its distribution?
4. Suppose you were given money to test Elliott Currie's coping model. What research methods would you use to achieve this goal?
5. In a group, discuss the ways in which your local government has dealt with drug use and dealing in your community. Did it contribute to a reduction in the structural inequities that nourish these social problems?

WEB EXERCISES

1. Beginning at the following site, pull together enough information to hold a debate on the statement: "The war on drugs is not working."

    http://www.ncjrs.org/drgshome.htm

2. One issue not covered in this chapter is the abuse of so-called "legitimate" drugs. Beginning at the site given below, gather evidence to support or dispute the contention that "the abuse of legitimate drugs is more harmful to society than abuse of illegal drugs."

    http://www.arf.org/isd/info.html

SUGGESTED READINGS

Boyd, Neil. *High Society: Legal and Illegal Drugs in Canada.* Toronto: Key Porter Books, 1991.
This is one of the few books that provides students and researchers with a comprehensive, intelligible overview of drug use in Canada.

Currie, Elliott. *Reckoning: Drugs, the Cities, and the American Future.* New York: Hill and Wang, 1993.
Currie explains why hard drug use is endemic to the United States. He also points out the pitfalls of the war on drugs, and he offers progressive, short-term control and prevention strategies.

Mahan, Sue. *Crack Cocaine, Crime, and Women: Legal, Social, and Treatment Issues.* Thousand Oaks, CA: Sage, 1996.
Historically, sociologists and criminologists have ignored female drug users, and especially those who use crack. This book provides a detailed, empirically informed analysis of women who are addicted to cocaine and the ways in which they are dealt with by agents of social control.

Ratner, Mitchell S. (ed.) *Crack Pipe as Pimp: An Ethnographic Investigation of Sex-For-Crack Exchanges.* New York: Lexington Books, 1993.
This collection of articles is the result of an 18-month study funded by the National Institute on Drug Abuse. It includes rich, albeit depressing, descriptions of the world of sex-for-crack in various U.S. cities such as Miami, Philadelphia, and Chicago.

Wilson, William Julius. *When Work Disappears: The World of the New Urban Poor.* New York: Alfred A. Knopf, 1996.
This book is a "must read" for anyone interested in developing a rich sociological understanding of the relationship between joblessness and drugs in U.S. urban ghettos.

ENDNOTES

1   This list is derived from information published by Boyd (1991), Currie (1993), and DeKeseredy and Schwartz (1996).

2   For example, at the time of writing this chapter, the Canadian youth unemployment rate is about 20 percent (Alvi and DeKeseredy, 1997).

3   This section includes modified sections of an article published previously by Alvi and DeKeseredy (1997).

4   See Wilson (1987, 1991, 1996) for a more detailed analysis of the ways in which these factors have contributed to inner-city poverty and its related problems, such as violent crime and illegal drug use.

Chapter 9

The Information Revolution: Privacy, Pornography, and Alienation

So widespread and deep-rooted is the belief that technological advance is a self-evident good that men [sic] have largely failed to look into the conditions of society *under which* this is indeed the case. *(Robert K. Merton, 1968: 63)*

OBJECTIVES

In this chapter we focus on the topics

1. The information revolution in historical context
2. The growth of computer use in North America
3. What types of people and institutions use computers and who does not have access to computer technology?
4. The positive and negative consequences of the information revolution
5. Sociological theories of the information revolution
6. The future of computers in everyday life

Introduction

We cannot listen to the radio, read a magazine or book, or watch television without being bombarded with the notion that an "information revolution" has occurred. At work and at school, you will undoubtedly have some, if not constant, contact with a personal computer that helps you gather, organize, analyze, and disseminate information. Even if you never touch a computer keyboard, you will most certainly use equipment that relies heavily on a microchip of some sort. Try a simple experiment. Watch television for a few days and count the number of commercials portraying computerized solutions to everyday problems. You will probably see actor Denis Leary yelling at us to "work the web," innumerable advertisements for hardware, software, and, of course, the ever-present Microsoft, Apple, and IBM. The results of your experiment will no doubt show that the technologically driven information revolution is not only around us, but penetrates almost every conceivable area of life.

It should not be a surprise, then, that technology "shows up" as an important factor in almost every chapter of this book. Technological innovations have been important to the rise and reproduction of unemployment (Chapter 3). Technology is often touted as a boon to families (Chapter 6), and often, we assume that technology will either save us from, or alleviate the suffering associated with, many health problems (Chapter 4).

It is certainly true that if it were not for technology, many of us would probably suffer more than we do today. When people lament some of the problems associated with technological development, (some of which you will read about in this chapter), it is common to encounter differing opinions as to whether technology is "good" or "bad." For example, a few years ago one of the authors of this book was having a discussion with a friend about the wisdom of increasingly relying on technological medicine when so many health problems are related to structural issues such as poverty or drug addiction. He was arguing that many of the health problems people face could be resolved if we took a more preventative approach to health instead of always looking for a new drug, new therapy, or expensive technological solution. His friend, who completely disagreed, simply stated "yeah right, wouldn't it be great to be dying of the plague?" He felt that were it not for modern medical technology, our society would be much worse of in terms of the general health of the population. It was clear in this conversation that when it comes to technology, there are those who question its positive image, and those who embrace it wholeheartedly.

If we take a sociological perspective on the personal opinions expressed in this conversation, we could argue that it represents a more fundamental issue, namely, the debate over whether technology contributes to "progress." Robinson and Pennington (in Alcorn, 1997: 207) for example, argue that World War II can be "thought of as a motivating factor driving the general population to a period of increased productivity and innovation." They contend that regardless of the millions of people who died in that war, and the incalculable devastation, pain and suffering it caused, most important modern technological developments (such as improved communications) have their roots in the war years. For them, technology not only

BOX 9-1

What Is the Internet?

Originating in the late 1960s as an experimental network designed to facilitate military research, what is now known as the Internet became a cooperative effort between the U.S. Department of Defense, certain defense contractors, and other major corporations, research institutions, and selected major universities to create an information-sharing system that would be able to run even in the event of a major military attack. Information could be routed any number of ways to reach a given destination; if one node were knocked out, information could be routed over other nodes. During the 1970s and 1980s, this network grew enormously by adding first hundreds of computer systems in a few countries, then later thousands of computer systems all around the world, to the network. In fact, the Internet is actually a network of networks. Calls to other computers can involve several "bounces" from one network to another for no charge beyond whatever costs the user incurs to access the Internet computer site thousands of miles away.

Source: http://www.ntia.doc.gov/opadhome/mtdpweb/Internet.htm

originates from social structural conditions, but it also contributes to and indeed defines "progress."

However, others argue that while technology has given us many things we generally take to be useful, such as cars, television sets, computers, and dishwashers, it is quite another argument to suggest that technology is synonymous with progress. Think of the automobile for instance. It is now almost impossible to imagine life without the car—cars take us everywhere in good and bad weather, allow us to get to our jobs (though not always quickly), and for some of us, even help to define who we are. But cars also contribute to pollution, diminish natural resources, and cause thousands of deaths each year. Obviously, progress and technology are not the same thing. Those taking this position, such as Braun (1995), suggest, however, that unfortunately, technological progress has come to stand for progress in general. However, Braun urges us to consider whether technology has eliminated poverty, inequality, discrimination, crime, and wars. He asks us to assess whether technology has "increased the happiness of people and led to individual fulfillment and social harmony." In effect, he points out that the idea of progress is a value judgement because there can be many different kinds of progress. Principally, we need to differentiate between **social progress** "including the state of society, politics, economic activity, culture, and so forth; and **scientific-technical progress**" (1995: 3). As we will see in a later section, this distinction is at the core of the different theoretical approaches used by social scientists to analyze and assess the impact of technology on society.

In this chapter we could not possibly provide you with an understanding of the continuing sociological impact of technological developments in the twenty-first century. We have chosen to focus on what we consider to be the most important recent development—the transformation of society by the "information revolution" characterized by the widespread use of computers in everyday life and, more recently, the Internet (see Box 9.1). In addition to the debates over the real and potential impacts of the information revolution, we will confine our attention to the issues of privacy, pornography (or "cyberporn"), and education.

The Information Revolution in Historical Context

Defining Technology

To begin, we want you to think about the many ways **technology** can be defined. How would you go about providing sociological answers to the question "what is technology?" A common functionalist definition comes from the fields of physical anthropology or archaeology. This approach maintains that technology refers to the physical manipulation of the environment, the capacity of tools to alter an individual's or social group's surroundings (Terry and Calvert, 1997). They further specify that technology is an aspect of "culture and civilisation, distinguishing man [sic] from other species and providing evidence of 'his' superior relation to the natural world....[and illustrating] 'his' innate faculty of rationality." As we will see, this functionalist definition tends not only to see technology as "rational progress," that is, as a good thing in itself, but also in decidedly male terminology. For example, although Merton was writing many years ago, the quotation at the beginning of this chapter implies that it has only been men who have developed or been affected by technology.

A second definition takes a **relational approach**, one that states that technology encompasses relationships between the designers and users of technology, and the technology itself (Balabanian, 1980). This approach forces us to recognize that technology cannot be understood outside the context in which it has been developed. For instance, if we simply think of the technology associated with splitting the atom without understanding its negative implications (total nuclear annihilation, for example), we would be missing a very important part of the reality of technology, and would be implying that technology exists outside of human relationships. Thus, we need to account for the fact that defining technology involves understanding the interface between human beings (particularly their relationships with one another) and the technology itself. Obviously, if we take this approach, we need to study the ways in which the uses of technology are conditioned by the use and reproduction of power relationships (Penley and Ross, 1991). In keeping with the orientation of this text, the remainder of this chapter emphasises the relational approach.

The Information Revolution

If today's computers are tools allowing us to quickly manipulate vast quantities of information, what are the characteristics of this "information revolution"? In the early 1970s, sociologist Daniel Bell remarked that information would become a commodity—something that could be bought and sold on the market—with the coming of what he called "post-industrial" society. He argued that as industrial societies evolved from the production and sale of goods to the production and sale of information and services, "what will count is not raw muscle power, or energy, but information" (1973: 127). He was right.

Put in the simplest of ways, "information is power." Moreover, the revolution that has taken place with respect to information has to do with the fact that the North American economy is increasingly built around the buying and selling of information. For instance, running a government, planning for the future, developing new drugs, designing products, finding educational opportunities, and education itself are all activities heavily dependent on the flow of information. Accordingly, access to information is a critical issue for all of us. In addition, computers have allowed us to access and to create new kinds of information, and if there is one thing we know for certain, there is a lot of information "out there."

The Growth of Computer Use in North America

If technology has been one of the main factors affecting the organization of human societies, in the last 50 years, it has become more so. In many ways, computers now "think" for us, and most computer scientists now agree that by the turn of the century, computers will be able to "out-think" the average human mind. Of course, there is some controversy over this view, since some critics maintain that no computer can ever replicate human creativity. Nevertheless, the point is that computers are now capable of almost anything. Moreover, they are everywhere. By the turn of the century, there will be more than one billion computers in use worldwide (Rifkin, 1995).

It is clear that the growth of computer use has been exponential in North America, but so has the growth of the Internet. Figure 9.1 shows that world-wide, the density of Internet hosts is particularly high in North America, with only Australia and some Scandinavian countries achieving such levels.[1] Although many argue that this places North America in a good position (in terms of accessibility, the capacity to use the Internet for business, and ultimately for competitive advantage) relative to the rest of the world, this privileged position may not last much longer. The main reason for this is that Internet use around the world is growing quickly, though there are still many inequalities between and within nations as far as access to computers and the Internet are concerned. It is to this issue that we now turn.

FIGURE 9.1
World-Wide Distribution of Internet Host Sites

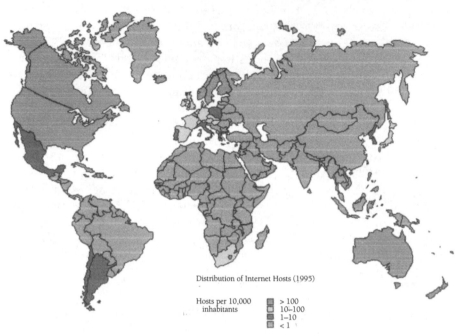

Distribution of Internet Hosts (1995)

Hosts per 10,000 inhabitants
- > 100
- 10–100
- 1–10
- < 1

Source: http://www.ntia.doc.gov/opadhome/mtdpweb/Internet.htm

What Types of People and Institutions Use Computers, and Who Does Not Have Access to Computer Technology?

Computers and information technology are critical to the "new economy." As we have pointed out elsewhere in this text, typically, capitalist societies are not "level playing fields" in which equal opportunities of access to the tools and knowledge one needs to be "successful" in the labor market are provided to each and every citizen. It will not surprise you, then, to learn that access to computer technology (and certainly information technology) depends on where you live, as well as your gender, class, and racial background. In Chapter 3, we presented a table showing how different racial and age groups have unequal access to computers. In this section, we provide additional data which helps to give us a more complete picture of who uses computers and the Internet.

One of the defining characteristics of the emergence of computer and information technology is the incredible hype and sense of urgency that surrounds its use. Indeed, we only have to think of the arguments made by many employers that computer literacy is a key aspect of employability in the new economy, that we must learn to harness the power of computers (or be condemned to the scrap heap of obsolescence), or that to be truly effective in our lives we must obtain the latest software or hardware upgrade. In the midst of such enthusiasm, it would seem logical that if we are not already using computers, many of us are scrambling to buy and learn how to use computers.

However, fully two-thirds of North Americans do not have access to computers in their home, and this seems to be equally true for men and women (GSS, 1994). Despite the fact that such data is good news for those interested in making a career in the field of computers because the "market" is virtually untapped, these data present a further set of interesting questions. One of the most important of these is—what are the characteristics of the small number of privileged North Americans who use computers and the Internet?

Although we cannot be completely sure due to a lack of comprehensive data, Table 9.1 provides us with some basic answers to this question. The table shows that the higher one's household income, the more likely one is to have a computer in the home. In fact, at least half of all people with a total household income of over $60,000 report that they have a computer in the household. The income level of users is directly tied to the costs of accessing the Internet, which is expensive. As Table 9.2 shows, according to the Organization for Economic Co-operation and Development (OECD), the average price for accessing the Internet in industrialized countries is almost $82 per month, though North Americans pay considerably less.

Table 9.1
Income Levels and Share of Internet Users, United States, 1995

Income	Share of Users (percent)
Less than 15 000	5
15-25 K	9
25-35 K	12
35-50 K	24
50-75 K	27
75-100 K	11
100-150 K	9
Greater than 150 000	3

Source: "Defining the Internet Opportunity," survey conducted by O'Reilly & Associates, U.S.A., November 1, 1995. Reprinted with permission.

Table 9.2
Average Cost for 20 Hours per Month Access to the Internet: Various Countries, 1997

United States	$39.77
Canada	$28.26
Australia	$33.23
Average for Industrialized Countries	$81.54

Source: Organization for Economic Co-operation and Development, Paris, France, March 20, 1997. Reprinted with permission.

While income is obviously an important factor in determining who does and does not use computers and the Internet, it is not the most powerful predictor. That distinction belongs to the level of education one possesses (see Figure 9.2), a factor that in itself is related to income—that is, the more money one has in a family unit, the more likely one is to have access to, and to complete, higher education such as university and college. In addition, the younger one is, the more likely one is to use computers and the Internet (see Table 9.3).

Here are some other important characteristics of computer and Internet users:

➤ According to a study conducted by the Rand Corporation, in the United States approximately 13 percent of African-American, Latino, and Native American households have computers, compared to 31 percent of white, and 37 percent of Asian American households.

➤ Only 9 percent of U.S. public schools, and 28 percent of its libraries, have access to the Internet (American Library Association, obtained from the *Montreal Gazette*, October 16, 1996).

➤ Of the Canadian population aged 18 and over, 29 percent "personally access the Internet" as of May 1997. This represents an increase of 7 points in 7 months, from 22 percent in October 1996. On an annualized basis, the penetration of the Internet is growing at a rate of 50 percent. (Nielsen Canadian Internet Survey, Spring 1997).

➤ The average household income of Internet users in the United States is $58,000. Europe has a higher percentage of users with incomes less than $10,000 which is not surprising since many European users are students.

➤ The number of Canadians aged 12 and over who use the Internet represents almost 8 million people, over 30 percent of the population.

➤ In Canada, females are now joining the community of Internet users in greater numbers than males. The percentage of male users fell from 57 percent in October 1996 to 55 percent in May 1997. In the United States, 33 percent of Internet users are female.

➤ About 39 percent of Internet users in the United States have used the Internet to make purchases at least a few times. Nevertheless, finding research and reference material on the World Wide Web continues to be the number one reason for using the Internet, with about one-third of U.S. users accessing information several times per week.

➤ Worldwide advertising on the Internet exceeded $300 million in 1996, approximately ten times the previous year's number (*Forbes* magazine, 1997).

Most Internet users are white. Data from a survey of over 17,000 World Wide Web users in Canada, the United States, and Mexico show that the overwhelming majority of users identify themselves as white (see Figure 9.3). African-Americans, Hispanics, Asians, and Indigenous people together made up just over five percent of all users surveyed (GVU Seventh WWW User Survey, April, 1997).

What can we conclude from these data? We can say with some confidence that the vast majority of people with access to computers and the Internet are

FIGURE 9.2
Canadians with Access to a Personal Computer in the Home, by Household Income

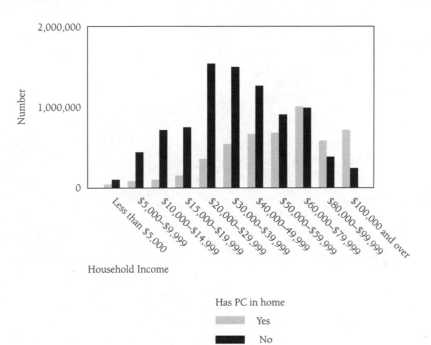

Source: Unpublished data, General Social Survey, Statistics Canada, 1994.

Table 9.3
Distribution of Internet users in the United States (1995)

Age Group	Share of Users
18-24	23 percent
25-29	17 percent
30-34	15 percent
35-44	25 percent
45-54	15 percent
55-64	3 percent
65+	1 percent

Source: "Defining the Internet Opportunity," survey conducted by O'Reilly & Associates, U.S.A., November 1, 1995. Reprinted with permission.

FIGURE 9.3
Race of Internet Users in North America (N = 17064)

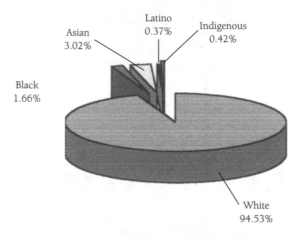

white, highly educated, and financially well off (Rheingold, 1996). Further, we may conclude that a kind of "computer and information segregation" now exists in North America. Given the importance of computers to everyday life, and particularly the centrality of computers to work and even basic literacy, it is hard not to agree with Ofori (cited in Ginchild-Abeje, 1996), who argues that unequal access "will contribute to the economic decline of impoverished city neighborhoods and create isolated islands of information have nots."

There are other negative consequences of unequal access to information technology for disadvantaged people. Mosco (1989) argues that as computer technology has penetrated almost every aspect of economic life, it has sped up the **commodification** process, so that more and more transactions are financial ones. Increasingly, everything is becoming "pay per view," "pay per keystroke," or "pay per bit of information," a situation that makes life for the poorer segments of society far more expensive and difficult. More fundamentally, the "digitization of everything" makes it easier for large multinational business "to shape market and pricing mechanisms to their maximum benefit" (Mosco, 1989: 35). Accordingly, probably one of the most important issues (from a sociological standpoint) emerging from the hype surrounding the information revolution is just how "worldwide" the Internet really is, and to what extent "real" communities sharing common interests will actually evolve. Moreover, because accessing cyberspace is expensive, at the moment, it seems only to be for middle- and upper-class whites (Lockard, 1997).

The Positive and Negative Consequences of the Information Revolution

Even before computers became common, new technological developments contributed both to the development of society, and to the demise of old ways of life. For instance, consider the fact that at the turn of the century, most North Americans were farmers. Less than one hundred years later, less than two percent of us make our living through farming. This massive shift caused tremendous job displacement, and the creation of a large class of individuals who had to look for other ways of making a living. Why the rapid change? The most significant reason lies in the introduction of machinery that could make farming more efficient and cost effective, which in turn eventually ensured that only those with the biggest, most efficient, and most expensive machinery could afford to farm any longer.[2]

Sometimes, technological change is also characterized by vigorous resistance. For example, between 1811 and 1816, a group of textile workers—the Luddites—routinely smashed their employer's machinery to protest the lowered wages and increased unemployment stemming from the introduction of these new technologies (Alcorn, 1997).

The point of these examples is to illustrate that technological change has almost always had a profound effect on human life, but it has not always been embraced with open arms. Indeed, many people feel more comfortable resisting change and "maintaining the status quo" when it comes to technology.

In the same way as Luddites fought against the introduction of technology into their working lives, today's "neo-Luddites" are just as uncomfortable with the rapid deployment and seemingly blind acceptance of the technological revolution. A very recent example of an extreme neo-Luddite who caused much pain and suffering is Theodore Kaczynski, known as "The Unabomber," whose 18-year mail bombing campaign terrorized Americans (see Box 9.2).

In addition to the fact that people simply "don't like change," there are other factors behind the resistance of many to technology. Alcorn (1997: 22-29) lists some of these as being

- ➤ fear of the unknown;

- ➤ anxiety and adjustment: the feelings one gets when having to learn the unfamiliar, and the corresponding sense that it is not all right to feel anxiety as one adjusts to the new situation;

- ➤ psycho-physiological restructuring: changes that affect our world view also create a mindset of conflicting information, a kind of "cognitive dissonance";

- ➤ chauvinistic conditioning: many of us are conditioned to believe that technology is an "out-of-control" monster; and

- ➤ specialization: as our society has developed a division of labor that is highly specialized, we have also created people who understand technology (such as engineers) and those who do not.

BOX 9-2

Introduction to the "Unabomber Manifesto"

1. The Industrial Revolution and its consequences have been a disaster for the human race. They have greatly increased the life expectancy of those of us who live in "advanced" countries, but they have destabilized society, have made life unfulfilling, have subjected human beings to indignities, have led to widespread psychological suffering (in the Third World to physical suffering as well) and have inflicted severe damage on the natural world. The continued development of technology will worsen the situation. It will certainly subject human beings to greater indignities and inflict greater damage on the natural world, it will probably lead to greater social disruption and psychological suffering, and it may lead to increased physical suffering even in "advanced" countries.

2. The industrial-technological system may survive or it may break down. If it survives, it MAY eventually achieve a low level of physical and psychological suffering, but only after passing through a long and very painful period of adjustment and only at the cost of permanently reducing human beings and many other living organisms to engineered products and mere cogs in the social machine. Furthermore, if the system survives, the consequences will be inevitable: There is no way of reforming or modifying the system so as to prevent it from depriving people of dignity and autonomy.

3. If the system breaks down the consequences will still be very painful. But the bigger the system grows the more disastrous the results of its breakdown will be, so if it is to break down it had best break down sooner rather than later.

4. We therefore advocate a revolution against the industrial system. This revolution may or may not make use of violence: it may be sudden or it may be a relatively gradual process spanning a few decades. We can't predict any of that. But we do outline in a very general way the measures that those who hate the industrial system should take in order to prepare the way for a revolution against that form of society. This is not to be a POLITICAL revolution. Its object will be to overthrow not governments but the economic and technological basis of the present society.

5. In this article we give attention to only some of the negative developments that have grown out of the industrial-technological system. Other such developments we mention only briefly or ignore altogether. This does not mean that we regard these other developments as unimportant. For practical reasons we have to confine our discussion to areas that have received insufficient public attention or in which we have something new to say. For example, since there are well-developed environmental and wilderness movements, we have written very little about environmental degradation or the destruction of wild nature, even though we consider these to be highly important.

In effect, the relationship between technology and society is a "contested terrain," characterized by friction between powerful and weak actors, fear and resistance, but also approval, excitement and acceptance. What is also clear is that the information revolution is changing our relationship between technology and society. In what follows we deal with several issues that highlight often neglected but important aspects of the problematic relationship between information technology and people.

Academic Dishonesty

Cyber-cheating refers to the deviant use of computer-based communications media to meet academic course requirements. Of course, post-secondary school students have always plagiarized and engaged in other forms of academic dishonesty (e.g., cheat or "crib" notes, stand-ins for exams, etc.) and they will continue to do so in the future. For example, some studies estimate that at least 50 percent of U.S. college students cheat (LaBeff et al., 1995). Others suggest that the incidence of some form of academic dishonesty among students may be as high as 90 percent (Chidley, 1997). Will the Internet make cheating and other forms of academic dishonesty easier than ever?

Some professors, journalists, students, and campus administrators contend that the Internet and other types of computer technology will make it easier to break academic rules. For example, lazy, desperate, or dishonest students intent on cheating can now quickly and easily use "services" such as those provided by writemyessay.com, a term-paper service that charges $20 for the first page, $10 for each additional page, and accepts all major credit cards. You will find the following message when or if you go to this website:

"Thank you for choosing writemyessay.com. At writemyessay.com, we are confident that you will receive the highest quality custom paper available anywhere. Our expert writers are all college graduates and all have an emphasis in writing. Their expertise will help you in further understanding your assignment and completing it with a high grade" (cited in Chidley, 1997: 78).

How many North American people rely on websites such as the above to get through university or college? Your guess is as good as anybody else's, because no one knows the exact extent and distribution of this problem. Box 9.3, however, strongly suggests that websites such as writemyessay.com and the Evil House of Cheat may increase the scope of academic dishonesty in universities and colleges. Do you know anyone who has engaged in cyber-cheating, and can you estimate the incidence and prevalence of this problem at your school? More pointedly, why do you think students are using the Internet to cheat?

Until we have more conclusive data, we cannot determine whether the Internet has contributed or will contribute to more plagiarism and other forms of academic dishonesty. What the Internet and websites such as School Sucks have definitely done, however, is encourage some college professors to give their students more creative assignments rather than the same ones they have used for years. For example, York University professor Mark Webber (see Box 9.3), now makes his

BOX 9-3

"Why Do I Always Leave it to the Last Minute to Buy My Essay?"

Is the Internet Making Cheating Easier Than Ever?

Business is good for Kenny Sahr—booming, in fact. And why not? When he launched his new website last year, the Houston-based entrepreneur knew he had tapped into a gold mine. "One day, it just hit me that no one had done this yet," says Sahr, 26. The idea was simple: post university essays on the World Wide Web—a veritable treasure trove of other people's ideas and words to inspire and inform students all around the world. A year and a half after launching his site, School Sucks, Sahr claims it attracts as 5,000 to 6,000 Web-surfers a day, with as much as 20 percent from Canada. He has already launched another site in Hebrew. Within 16 months, he estimates, the service will be available in 15 languages. As for what surfers do with the more than 2,500 essays on the site, Sahr, who makes most of his money selling ad space to video-game companies, publishers, and other youth-oriented retailers, insists that 99 percent of them "are using School Sucks for decent purposes." Sure, he concedes, a handful of college students have been caught printing up essays and handing them in as their own. "But they don't belong in school anyway," Sahr adds. "The universities should thank me for helping them find these people."

In the plugged-in Nineties, essay-writing services—once the denizens of college-town back alleys and benighted basements—are digitized, sophisticated, and just a mouse-click away. Dozens of them—and most are American—are now available to Canadian students on the Internet. Some, like School Sucks and the Evil House of Cheat, make papers available at no cost, but usually require students to upload their own papers before they are given full access to the essay database. The majority of services, however, expect money for their product. Prices vary: Professor Korn, operated out of Brooklyn, N.Y., advertises rates "as low as $5 a page," while others demand fees of $35 per page. "It's kind of tempting, because if you're in a rush you can just order an essay up," says Stacey Brown, 21, a fourth-year history/Native studies major at Brandon University in Manitoba. "But your conscience says no, I have to just write the paper."

The scope of the problem is anybody's guess. A university official in Manitoba says that in her six-plus years representing students, she has not seen any cases where the charge has involved buying an essay. "On the other hand, how do we know?" she asks. "It's difficult to quantify."

Universities, of course, take the threat very seriously. In late October, Boston University launched an unprecedented lawsuit against several Internet-based essay mills in the United States, charging them in federal court with wire fraud, mail fraud, racketeering and violating a Massachusetts law that bans the sale of term papers. The case, legal experts say, is a touchstone for the future of essay-writing services on the Internet.

But in the past, shutting down such companies has proven problematic. The services' standard defense is that the essays are intended as research tools. And most of the Internet mills post dire warnings about the consequences of plagiarism. Sahr has an entire Web page on his service devoted to telling students why they should not hand in School Sucks essays. "The essays are free, so students should know their professors also have access to them," he says. Prof. Mark Webber has heard such arguments before. Essay services "always say they're not doing anything wrong," says Webber, co-director of the Canadian Centre for German and European Studies at York. But it's very clear to anyone who's talked to these people, or to the students that hire them, that they know damned well what they're doing."

BOX 9-3

Source: Excerpted from Chidley (1997: 76–78, 79). Reprinted by permission.

students submit their papers to him in stages, from outlines to first drafts to finished manuscript. According to Webber, "If they tried to buy all that work from someone else, it would break the bank" (cited in Chidley, 1997: 79).

Unfortunately, regardless of whether Webber's pedagogical approach simultaneously deters many students from cheating and promotes better writing skills, academic dishonesty will always be with us. For the authors of this text and many other professors, this problem is a monster that never really goes away. It just changes its shape and form, and adapts to the changing world.

Cyberporn

Another negative and highly controversial consequence of new computer technologies is **cyberporn**. Defining pornography is the subject of much debate, and although there is no way a social scientist can apply one single definition to pornography (Schwartz and DeKeseredy, 1997), cyberporn is defined here as sexual material (pictures, words, etc.) distributed on the Internet that uses women for the purpose of sexually exciting men.[3]

The precise number of North American websites featuring pornographic material is unknown and probably will remain so; however, some researchers estimate that pornography occupies less than 20 percent of the Internet's overall content (Cavazos and Morin, 1995; Chidley, 1995; Ferguson, 1996).[4] Regardless of how much of it is actually available, our perusal of various websites leads us and other researchers to conclude that North American society is currently experiencing a rapid growth of pornography disseminated on the Internet, electronic Bulletin Board Systems (BBS), etc. As Ferguson (1996: 3), one of Canada's leading experts on cyberporn, points out, "Now, unlike ever before, anyone can produce and disseminate offensive data to a global public."

What is the nature and content of cyberporn? It is impossible to provide a simple answer to this question because cyberporn is very diverse. In other words, there are thousands, perhaps millions, of different pornographic images, audio clips, texts, etc. located in cyberspace. Nevertheless, most of the images, videos, audio clips, and text files available on the Internet are acceptable by legal standards. For example, most of these files include pictures of naked men and women, and of couples and groups engaged in consensual sexual activity, and are not distinct from those found in other pornographic media, such as magazines, video tapes, CD-ROMs, and so on (Ferguson, 1996).

Many images and texts, however, are extremely violent, regardless of whether they include women. For example, Ferguson "visited" one website and found a digitized image file that included

"...an individual lying down on a concrete slab, with his hands and feet bound. The individual is surrounded by five other nude humanoids with reddish skin, skull faces, horns extruding from the top of their heads, and talons protruding from their hands and feet. The five demonic figures appear to be preparing to sodomize the bound individual" (1996: 18).

In addition to providing men with many opportunities to view or read about sexual violence against women and other people, new cyberspace technology enables men to engage in the on-line victimization of women (DeKeseredy and Schwartz, 1988c). This involves men "virtually assaulting" or "virtually raping" women who use pornographic, real-time communications media such as Internet Relay Chat (IRC), teleconferencing, and videoconferencing, and so on. Ferguson (1996) found that many female "virtual victims" experience substantial psychological pain and suffering, as if they had actually been physically assaulted.

The consumption and distribution of cyberporn also seems to be a male subcultural phenomenon. For example, based on their review of preliminary investigations into the nature, content, and use of pornographic material on the Internet, DeKeseredy and Schwartz (1988b) suggest that there is evidence of the emergence of pro-abuse cyberspace male peer support groups. Ferguson's (1996) exploratory research shows that many men, most of whom probably never had face-to-face contact with each other, share violent pornographic material through human interfaces such as IRC channels, UseNet, and e-mail. These men are by no means innocent users who accidentally come across images, voices, texts, etc. Nor are they "continually bombarded" with this material. Rather, they choose to consume and distribute "cyberporn," and unfortunately, as described in Box 9.4, some of these "consumers" commit lethal violent acts.

DeKeseredy and Schwartz (1998c) hypothesize that, like sexist cultural artifacts (e.g., life-size blowup dolls, ice cubes in the shape of women) used on ritual occasions when males gather to affirm their relationships with other men (e.g., stag parties and other variants of "boys' night out"), the sharing of cyberporn helps to create and maintain sexist male peer groups.[5] DeKeseredy and Schwartz further hypothesize that this sharing reinforces attitudes that reproduce and reconstitute ideologies of male dominance, by approvingly presenting women as objects to be conquered and consumed. Future research needs to identify the reasons men join and participate in such cyber peer groups, and how they locate those who are like-minded.

BOX 9-4

The Deadly Consequences of Cyberporn

In late October, 1996, the body of a woman from Hampton, Maryland was pulled from a shallow grave outside the trailer of her lover in Lenoir, North Carolina. The incident occurred shortly after the victim had traveled to Lenoir to meet her lover for the first time following an anonymous e-mail liaison conducted using the pseudonyms "Nancy" and "Slowhand." During this liaison, the two had constructed and participated in several cyber-sexual scenarios involving sadomasochistic practices, torture, and snuff. The victim's lover was charged with her murder, but claims that her death was an accident that occurred while the two were living out the sexual fantasies conceived during their e-mail liaison.

Source: Ferguson (1996: 17).

Unfortunately, the problem may be that the very nature of electronic communication may make the problems identified in this section worse than they are in person (DeKeseredy and Schwartz, 1998c). According to several researchers such as Ferguson (1996), most cyberporn is easily accessible if people know where to find it and make a conscious decision to locate it. Further, the medium itself encourages people to adopt false identities and to act out any strange fantasy in their heads. For example, America On-Line (AOL), one of the most popular North American commercial Internet providers, allows subscribers to assume any of many false identities so as to carry on these fantasies.

How many people like "Nancy" (see Box 9.4) take on false identities they made for themselves on the Internet, and how did they do it? So far, we don't have reliable data that answer this question. Even so, there are some people who claim that the urge is very seductive. Consider Lynn Darling (1997), a 45-year-old professional writer who created the identity of "Pirategrrl" to test her reaction to participating in the OTK ("over the knee," or spanking) culture. She reports (1997: 44):

"Gradually, I began to recognize Pirategrrl. She had come along at a nervous moment in my own life, one that found me between identities, unsure of my own place in the world. I began to realize that, much more than I wanted to admit, Pirategrrl was a way to be in a world when I wasn't really sure who I was. I found myself turning to her personality—cocky, flip, straightforward—whenever the unreality in my own life became a little too frightening. Pirategrrl was visible when I was invisible, and increasingly I turned to her voice."

Could you lose yourself like Lynn Darling? DeKeseredy and Schwartz (1998c) contend that it does not seem unlikely that a number of others are doing the same thing. They further argue that what is worrisome about this is that there are large numbers of men who feel guilty because they are not more macho, masculine, assertive with women, and powerful (Connell, 1995). Thus it would be reasonable to suppose that a typical male fantasy would include more aggression towards women. DeKeseredy and Schwartz (1998c) worry that with the support of other men on the Internet, these men might find this personality a more attractive one to act out than their own.

Another important question that warrants attention here is: "Does cyberporn cause male sexual and physical violence against women?" Several studies show that consuming various types of pornography is strongly associated with woman abuse in intimate heterosexual relationships (DeKeseredy and Schwartz, 1998a; Harmon and Check, 1989; Russell, 1992); however, these studies cannot determine a direct causal relationship between pornography and male-to-female victimization, and they didn't focus specifically on cyberporn. Thus, to adequately answer the above question, we need long-term and expensive longitudinal research. For all we know right now, the factors that cause men to abuse women may also cause them to consume or purchase cyberporn and other types of pornography. Nevertheless, research shows that male attempts to get women to imitate scenes in pornographic media, including those on the Internet, are a component of the problem of woman abuse (DeKeseredy and Schwartz, 1998a).

Computers and Education

We had to choose among a range of important social problems to keep this book manageable, which meant we had to exclude some issues deserving in-depth coverage. One of the most important of those not covered explicitly in this book is education. Nevertheless, you will have noticed that educational issues figure prominently in most of the social problems we discuss. Obviously, we cannot engage here in the numerous debates associated with the definition, purposes, and future of education. Nevertheless, since there is currently a great deal of discussion on the implications of the information revolution for education, we briefly touch on some of these issues.

Depending on the sociological perspective one takes, education can be defined as a process of socialization in which people learn cultural values as well as how to become productive members of society; a process of social control and personal development which differs according to one's social class, race, or gender, or a process in which individuals are selected, trained, and placed into society (Ballantyne, 1997).

One of the main reasons for current interest in the technology and education relationship is the widespread dissatisfaction among taxpayers, parents, employers, and governments over the accessibility and quality of education in North America. Those interested in these issues take a variety of positions over "what's wrong with education." Some insist that quality of education is hampered by lack of financial resources. Others indict the educational system for focusing on learning strategies that detract from the basics of reading, writing, and arithmetic. Still others blame "burnt-out" teachers, teachers' unions, or disinterested parents and students. Regardless of what the "real problem" with education is (and more than likely the problem is a composite of these and other issues), computer technology is increasingly being touted as "the solution."

The debate over the uses of computer technology in education basically falls into two camps. There are those who argue that computers and software will increase accessibility and improve quality, and those who fear that quality, accessibility, and job security will suffer because of such technology. Each of these positions deserves some in-depth consideration.

Those who argue that computer-based learning is the way of the future maintain that the general public, schools, and students will make tangible gains through the introduction of computers and information technology (Papert, 1996). They point out that schooling in North America is expensive (think of the costs of buildings and staff alone), and that this issue is at the heart of attempts to restructure and "cheapen" the cost of education in most North American jurisdictions. Given that one of the most important aspects of computerization is its labor saving quality, it is not surprising that people in this camp argue that computers in the classroom can potentially save millions of dollars by reducing the number of staff needed to run schools, or by replacing paper with digitized books. But their arguments are directed at more than saving money. They also contend that computerization will actually improve the quality of education by creating synergies with young people's seemingly "innate" attraction to computers and software. Further, they say that the capabilities of the Internet, CD-ROMs, and other technologies have the potential to increase access to education for students around the world, and particularly in remote areas. Indeed, this seems to be happening already. Increasingly, university-level courses are being taught via television, videotape, and the Internet. It is even possible now to get a degree without ever attending a class. A good example of this approach is in a recent joint report by the National Academy of Science and National Academy of Engineering, on the importance of bringing technology into the classroom. The key argument in this document seems to be that children are already highly technologically literate because they are used to playing computer video games, which is why they are sometimes called "the Nintendo generation." The document argues that if we are to improve education, and therefore create better, more productive citizens, we should be tying young students' interests in video games to learning strategies in the classroom. This perspective is reflected in the following quotations from the report (1995: 2):

"We must take advantage of students' interests in technology....We must learn to use the technology students play with daily as educational resources.

The coming levels of interactive technology hold the potential—if we take advantage of it—to create order-of-magnitude changes in productivity in American education.

[Ki]ds are much more motivated to play games and use computers outside of school because of the level of interactivity. They have to make decisions frequently—every second or so—so they stay in charge. In school, if you're listening to a teacher lecture, you may only have to make a decision every half hour."

The other side of this debate takes a more skeptical view of the capacity of computer technology to improve education (Roszak, 1994; Talbott, 1995). Whether computers will improve education is a contentious issue because no one is sure how teachers, textbooks, and traditional time schedules will be affected, and these are the core elements of the learning experience. As well, it is by no means certain that substituting teacher-student interaction with a technology-student-teacher relationship will improve anything, given the evidence from decades of educational research showing that what seems to count is a quality curriculum, adequate resources, smaller classes, and satisfied teachers.

On the other hand, it is clear that one of the most important skills one can acquire today is expertise with computers, and the ability to deal with vast quantities of information. What is not clear is whether simply placing computers in the classroom, or actually replacing a good portion of teaching with computerized "interactive learning" will actually provide students with the critical skills required to understand the difference between "good" and "bad" information.

Computers and Privacy

Because information has become more and more commodified, corporations have a vested interest in controlling access to it, as well as its distribution and sale. However, they also have to ensure that people will actually use new information technologies such as the Internet to buy whatever information or products they are selling. One of the ways that the Internet is being marketed to get more people to use it is through corporate and government assurances that the individual's privacy is guaranteed. Why have they focused on privacy issues?

The answer is very simple. Most North Americans are worried that the Internet makes vast amounts of personal information accessible to others who might abuse their personal privacy. For example, about 83 percent of the general public in the United States are very concerned about privacy issues as they pertain to the Internet (Harris and Associates and Alan Westin, 1990, 1992). According to a major survey conducted in 1997, the top two issues for current Internet users are privacy and censorship (see Figure 9.4). If we boil this anxiety down to its basic elements, we can easily argue that the concern is really about personal freedom. The concern over privacy is about the perceived danger of too much personal information being given out without permission. It is about the capacity of computerized systems to control or limit personal freedom, or to use personal information for commercial purposes, as a result of "knowing everything" about the individual. Think, for a moment, about how information about your buying habits, your income, gender, personal preferences, and age would be coveted by marketers. Censorship is about the capacity of individuals to say and look at whatever they like (including cyberporn), thus, it is also about personal freedom.

Accordingly, we are dealing here with concerns over the "inflow" and "outflow" of information and, as Rhodes (cited in Samarajiva: 1997) puts it, outflows are the "none-of-your-business" aspect of privacy, while concerns over inflow of information are the "leave-me-alone" aspect of privacy.

There are basically two main schools of thought when it comes to the problem of computers and privacy. Some people worry that the presence of one's personal

FIGURE 9.4
Main Concerns of Internet Users Worldwide (N = 19 493)

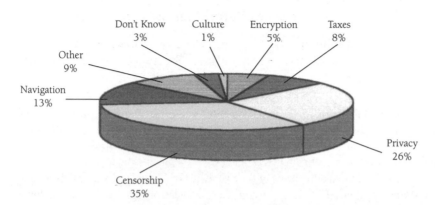

and confidential information on a computer hard drive also presents opportunities for criminals or governments to gain access to this information through the Internet. The implications of such access are serious—government interference in your personal life, criminal victimization, and the possibility that employers could terminate your services based on a negative assessment of your (supposedly confidential) medical records. Indeed, there are already many examples of privacy invasion which suggests that we should not trust government or employer run computer information systems (see Box 9.5).

The second approach, exemplified by people such as Negroponte (1996), contends that those concerned about the negative impact of the Internet on privacy are also paranoid. Negroponte (1996: 175) puts the point bluntly:

"... the virtual world is a far safer, more private, and less dangerous place than the real world...when people tell me they would never type their credit card number into the Internet, I try to suppress a laugh. These same people gleefully recite it over the telephone or hand their credit card to a lascivious-looking waiter, who disappears with it for a few minutes..."

He goes on to say that the most important aspect of privacy is not the technology of computers itself, but the policies associated with privacy. For instance, the U.S. government is currently attempting to outlaw the use of cryptography— a technology designed to code messages and other data so that no one without a code breaking "key" can decode it. The White House maintains that such laws are necessary in the interest of national security. According to Hoffman (1993, cited in Samarajiva, 1997), the FBI has been lobbying Congress to amend existing communications legislation so that communications services (such as telephone

BOX 9-5

Privacy Horror Stories

Small-scale privacy atrocities take place every day. Ask Dr. Denise Nagel, executive director of the National Coalition for Patient Rights, about medical privacy, for example, and she rattles off a list of abuses that would make Big Brother blush. She talks about how two years ago, a convicted child rapist working as a technician in a Boston hospital rifled through 1,000 computerized records looking for potential victims (and was caught when the father of a nine-year-old girl used caller ID to trace the call back to the hospital). How a banker on Maryland's state health commission pulled up a list of cancer patients, cross-checked it against the names of his bank's customers and revoked the loans of the matches. How Sara Lee bakeries planned to collaborate with Lovelace Health Systems, a subsidiary of Cigna, to match employee health records with work-performance reports to find workers who might benefit from anti-depressants.

Not to pick on Sara Lee. At least a third of all Fortune 500 companies regularly review health information before making hiring decisions. And that's nothing compared with what awaits us when employers and insurance companies start testing our DNA for possible imperfections. Farfetched? More than 200 subjects in a case study published last January in the journal Science and Engineering Ethics reported that they had been discriminated against as a result of genetic testing. None of them were actually sick, but DNA analysis suggested that they might become sick someday. "The technology is getting ahead of our ethics," says Nagel, and the Clinton Administration clearly agrees. It is about to propose a federal law that would protect medical and health-insurance records from such abuses.

But how did we arrive at this point, where so much about what we do and own and think is an open book?

Source: "Privacy Horror Stories," excerpted from *Time* Magazine, August 25, 1997. © 1997 Time Inc. Reprinted by permission.

companies or Internet Service Providers) will be required to build in modifications to allow surveillance by law-enforcement agencies with proper court orders. Similarly, the National Security Agency is proposing that a special chip be built into communications devices to allow for government to access information without the knowledge of the user.

While many of these proposals ride upon the issue of "protecting the nation" they seem awkward in light of the decreased significance of the cold war. Moreover, governments and other powerful actors are caught in a difficult dilemma—they seem to equate advances in society with advances in the information revolution, which in turn are tied to increased development and use of the Internet. At the same time, however, they realize that the Internet is not controlled by anyone, and that as long as this situation persists, there will be privacy concerns which will either force people to use their own encryption techniques, or prevent people from using the Internet altogether.

As the Internet becomes an integral component of everyday life, there will continue to be debates and concerns expressed over privacy and censorship policies and even the very definition of privacy. To conclude this section, we want you to consider privacy in light of what we think is one of the most central issues of the information revolution—the **commodification** of information. We know that when individual rights of any kind—such as those over protection of personal information—become a commodity, they generally remain a right only for those who can afford it (Mosco, 1989: 38). What this means for privacy in the information age, particularly in light of the pervasive inequality in North America, will continue to challenge the public, policy makers, and social scientists.

Sociological Theories of the Information Revolution

A friend of ours was once asked what kind of computer he had. He thought for a moment, then replied "beige." On one level he was right—computers are somewhat benign, inanimate objects. But this does not mean that the uses to which these machines are put are neutral. In this section, we provide you with some theoretical frameworks that you might use as a standpoint from which to do your own research and investigation on aspects of the information revolution.

Functionalist Theories

Functionalist approaches to theorizing the information revolution essentially maintain that the existence of new technologies is part of the "evolution of society," and that such developments, because they are presumed to be functional, or useful to society, are natural. As we will see, to some extent, this idea is shared by some other, more critical, theorists such as Marx. What differentiates the functionalist approach from critical theories is the acceptance of the inevitability of change without questioning the basis, purpose, or effects of that change.

As you may have noted, for example, popular media accounts assume that the World Wide Web will be the precursor of a new type of cyber-community, and that this community will be accessible to all. Based on the data presented in this chapter, however, this perception is clearly false. As you have seen, Internet time, and the hardware required to access it, are still relatively expensive, and this has imposed restrictions that are clearly defined by where one lives, as well as one's race and class.

Functionalist accounts of the information revolution tend to romanticize reality because they focus uncritically on the usefulness and purposes of this technology. Moreover, because functionalist theories generally assume that inequality is an outcome of individual failure, issues such as accessibility are presumed to be resolvable by simply increasing the availability of computers without concern for the very nature of developments like the Internet itself.

This is not to say, however, that the Internet or computers do not have the potential to create greater equality for North Americans, more effective democracy, or more accessible education. For example, Schmitz (1997) has documented how people in Santa Monica, California, were able to set up a community computer network which included access for the city's homeless. By gaining access to influential and powerful people who also participated in the on-line community, these severely disadvantaged people raised funding for a project providing them with clean clothes, showers, and lockers.

Despite success stories such as these, the vast majority of Internet activity is employed for commercial purposes, a fact that tends to be downplayed in functionalist frameworks. And, given that the bulk of information disseminated via technologies such as the World Wide Web is commercial information (the Internet is probably the world's biggest mall), it is clear that priorities have already been set as to its function and purposes, and that these are by no means neutral. Moreover, it is unclear whether simply "jumping on the technology bandwagon" will result in "trickle down" benefits to the majority of people in society (Rifkin, 1995).

Critical Theories: Marxist and Feminist Approaches

As we have noted, the idea that technology is responsible for the development of society is held by many, including those who may or may not believe that such technological development is an indicator of "progress."

Regardless of one's position on the notion of progress, those who take the position that technology is responsible for creating social relations are said to be **technological determinists**. Although there is some controversy about his position, many regard Marx to be one of the first sociologists to take the technological determinist position. This is not surprising, given that Marx was prone to making arguments such as "The windmill gives you society with the feudal lord: the steam-mill, society with the industrial capitalist" (Marx, 1847). For some interpreters of Marx, this statement and others like it place Marxist theories of technology squarely within the camp of technological determinism.[6] At the very least, Marx emphasized the relationship between technology, power, and control in society.

Contemporary Marxist approaches to the analysis of technology emphasize the ways in which phenomena like the Internet, computerization and, more broadly, automation are conditioned by the logic of capitalist society. That logic is, of course, to reproduce the power of the capitalist class by virtue of exploiting and controlling the labor power of middle-, working- and under-classes.

As we have seen, functionalists maintain that institutions, relationships, and other aspects of society only exist because they are functional for society—in other words, computers and the information they deal with exist "everywhere" today because they serve important, "positive" purposes. Critical theorists believe this to be a rather simplistic approach to understanding the impact of computers and information technology, mostly because it does not account for the essentially unequal nature of the relationship between classes, races, genders, and technology.

Given the transformation of society into a service and information based economy, the information revolution can probably be more adequately understood in terms of the increasing trend towards the commodification of information. According to Mosco (1996), two interrelated forces have accelerated the trend towards information as a commodity. The first is the great advances in technology discussed earlier. Computers are very good at sorting, analyzing, and operating with complex information, they are much less costly than they used to be, and will become cheaper. The second factor is the demand for information generated by government and corporations. To understand the nature and prevalence of information technology we must recognize that these two forces interact. "For example, businesses recognize the profit potential in marketable information and hence promote the development of technologies that enhance marketability" (Mosco, 1996: 26). In other words, the information revolution exists in the form it does because it is profitable. Moreover, the profit motive is the most important aspect of the information revolution, despite any potential it might have for creating a more equal, democratic society.

Another important characteristic of information technology is that it is an excellent tool for social control. Unless you are an anarchist, it is obvious that some form of social control is always necessary for societies to exist. However, the important question here is control over whom and for what?

As you saw in our discussion of privacy issues, it is already becoming clear that the information revolution has made it much easier for people in positions of power (such as police or employers), to maintain and even extend power over those who are powerless.

In addition, as the data in this chapter make clear, the current shape of the information revolution is decidedly **exclusionary** in that many (mostly subordinate) social groups are being systematically prevented from accessing the most important information technology resources—computers and the Internet.

Feminist scholarship on technology also provides important critical insights into the information revolution. As Terry and Calvert (1997: 3) point out, technology has traditionally been defined in terms of "objects" or "tools" that imply an objective existence apart from the creators and users of that technology. Put another way, the notion that technology is neutral and autonomous allows the designer to be "off the hook for what the tool actually does in the world."

To address this issue, these commentators take a similar position to that outlined here, namely that first, technology must be understood in historical and cultural context and second, that it encompasses social relationships among users, designers, and machines. As one might expect, one of the principal concerns here is the ways in which male domination and patriarchal structures have been, and continue to be, created and reproduced via technological "advancements."

Terry and Calvert (1997) point to a number of additional important questions to be asked by feminist and pro-feminist scholars of the information revolution:

1. Are technologies gendered? In what ways does it make sense to say that guns are "masculine" and curling irons are "feminine"?

2. Why is it that men are associated with "high technology" (e.g., computers and cars) while women tend to be associated with "low technology" (e.g., hair dryers and breast pumps)?
3. In what ways are women and men "situated differently" in relation to technologies such as computers? Why are there differences in the kinds of access women have to technology?
4. What are the different uses to which women and men put machines?

These are merely a few of the questions only now beginning to be analyzed in relation to the gendered aspects of the information revolution. Given the fact that the information revolution will increasingly become a defining characteristic of social life, research and policy reflecting the gendered nature of the world we live in will become increasingly crucial.

The Future of Computers in Everyday Life

As you might expect, the future of computers in everyday life is a topic of intense debate. **Hopeful optimists** such as Negroponte (1995) argue that technology has the potential to advance human society and relationships to levels we can only imagine today. He cites the potential of information technologies to enhance democracy, commerce, and communication. Yet we must keep in mind that when electricity became available around the late 1800s, many people thought that:

"... its widespread use would make the cities green, heal the breach between the classes, create a wealth of new goods, extend night into day, cure age-old diseases, and bring peace and harmony to the world" (Rifkin, 1995: 43)

For others—let's call them **skeptical pessimists**—increased computer, e-mail, and Internet use signals the rise of a "virtual" society, one that is less like a physical community of shared interests with high levels of human interaction and more like a society of faceless, nameless, digital interchange. For commentators such as Stoll (1995) who are dismayed by such scenarios, the simple solution is to turn off one's computer. Similarly, authors such as Sale (1995) point to the lessons people can learn from the Luddites discussed earlier in this chapter. In effect, he suggests that the best thing we can do to prevent the digitization of everything is to resist the pressure of computer technologies as much as possible.

Still others, the **rational analysts**, believe that the future will be neither a digital wonderland nor a dark, alienated cyber-society (Dery, 1995). They start with the premise that technology is essentially neutral. It is the uses to which computer technology is put, and the kinds of people employing it, that are important. To understand what the future may look like, we have to engage in rational analysis of technology within the context of the political and social environment in which it has developed historically, and in which it exists today.

So in terms of "big pictures" of the future of computers in everyday life, there is considerable diversity of opinion. In the more short-term future, there are some intriguing possibilities. For example, currently, several large computer organizations as well as the U.S. Department of Justice, are concerned about the increasing dominance of Microsoft in the computer operating system (OS), software, and Internet access markets. Some of these organizations are arguing that Microsoft is engaging in uncompetitive practices resulting in limited consumer choices, and difficulties for alternative OS and software providers. As of this writing, several of these companies are pursuing legal action against Microsoft to limit their size and domination of the industry. If these lawsuits are successful, it could mean the breakup of the company that currently overwhelmingly dominates the software market—which might create opportunities for other products. Such a scenario might conceivably change the face of computing in directions we cannot fully understand yet.

Another important issue is the "Year 2000 problem." Sometimes known as the millennium bug, this problem with the original design of computers has the potential to plunge business, government, and daily life into chaos.

In addition, here are several other possibilities for the future of computers in everyday life:

1. As computers become more of a "taken for granted" feature of everyday life (much like the telephone did a century or so ago), it will be interesting to observe whether we will see it as a tool for solving social problems, or whether it will become more of an instrument for the reproduction of social relationships as they now stand. In particular, it will be important to evaluate whether the hype over new information technologies gives way to rational concern over the capacity of such technologies to solve everyday problems. For instance, will technologies help us to solve urban problems, crime, environmental degradation, or to generate meaningful employment? Will we even be asking such questions? For many social scientists, and for those concerned about the relationship between everyday life (as mediated by the use of computers and information technology) and larger social questions, such issues are critical.

2. At the moment, computer technologies are very much tied to the workings of free markets. As Braun (1995) points out, most new technologies are thought to be important because they are "manipulated by excessive salesmanship....[particularly] that of the mass media." However, Braun explains that if media and advertising strategies characterizing free market capitalism place particular limits on the kinds of technologies that are deemed important enough to get to market, then there are some technologies that are not getting to market. For example, while we spend

millions on computer technology to make cars more efficient, or to reduce toxic emissions from industrial plants, we spend considerably less on research and development focusing on alternative forms of energy.

3. As Internet commerce develops, what will happen to the mass of people whose job it is to act as the "middle person" in most transactions? For example, if you buy an automobile today, you invariably go to a car dealer to make your choice and purchase. However, as the Internet becomes more accessible (assuming it will) and more sophisticated, it will be possible for General Motors or Ford to sell you the car you want directly from the manufacturing plant. This might sound like a good thing for the consumer and the car companies because prices will be lowered and sales volume would increase. However, it also means that car salespeople will face new roles or, more likely, lose their jobs altogether. When we think of the many, many individuals whose job involves mediating between the customer and the producer, the implications are profound (Negroponte, 1997).

4. Some observers are alarmed by the implications of advances in computer technology for communities and ultimately for social interaction. Slouka (1996) for example, maintains that the capacity for people to believe and interact in their own "on-line" world, as opposed to "the real world" is increasingly becoming possible. For example, the Internet now makes it possible for people to become globally connected, so much so that it is conceivable that our sense of individuality may be disappearing. Aside from the ramifications for both the study and definition of "society," there are important connotations for other social problems discussed in this text. What will be the implications for crime, for our understanding of poverty or social responsibility, for instance? As we have seen in this chapter, if people can interact in a virtual community without physical contact, the worst aspects of human behavior can easily avoid mechanisms of social control (think of cyberporn for example). As Slouka points out, "morality matters only within the bounds of the physical world. In cyberspace, nobody can hear you scream."

5. The current state of the information revolution provides North Americans, and indeed people around the world, with an important opportunity to

expand democracy, and make it more effective. Imagine the possibilities if every member of the general public was networked, with access to the information regarding the rationale behind government decisions. Think about how voting patterns would be affected if people could hold referenda "on-line." The most important factor here is control over the Internet and the information it contains. At the moment, no one really "owns or controls" the Internet—a situation that has both its good and bad points.

6. However, there is a danger that very soon, some organization, possibly government, could stake and enforce the claim that the Internet needs to be controlled. How will ordinary people respond? In what ways will we need to change our views on taken-for-granted concepts such as democracy, voting, politics, privacy, and so on? We believe that these and other, related, questions will be central ones for social scientists in the coming decades.

Summary

Because the information revolution is a relatively new development, this has been the most speculative chapter in this text. We have probably raised more questions than answers, and we leave it to you to make your own judgments as to the implications of the information revolution for North American society.

We have emphasized the fact that technology is integrally connected to the development of social relations, indeed, this has always been the case. We have shown how the notion of technological "advances" should be questioned carefully and not taken at face value. This cautionary approach is particularly important in light of the fact that North America is dominated by the logic of free markets, commodities, and individualism. The questions we raise have to do with how basic concepts of society, such as "rights," "freedoms," and "individuality," might be reconfigured by the persistent and powerful impact of the information revolution.

In addition, we have highlighted several social problems related to the development of computer technology and the Internet. These problems are really extensions of dilemmas that have always been with us, but which are now taking on new dimensions and meanings in light of technological shifts. For example, the debate over cyberporn is connected to age-old debates about pornography. Similarly, the changing nature of education in the information age is part of an ongoing discussion within the sociology of education about the nature and purposes of education itself.

To be sure, the social impact of the technologies discussed in this chapter cannot be ignored, for they have the potential to make North American society very different from what it is now. The question is, will these changes be positive, in the sense that they have the potential for better democracy and reduced inequality, or will they simply reflect, in new ways, deeply rooted historical patterns of suffering and disparity?

KEY TERMS

Commodification
Cyber-cheating
Cyberporn
Post-industrial society
Relational definition of technology
Social Progress
Technological determinism

DISCUSSION QUESTIONS

1. What would you argue to be the four most important social impacts of the information revolution? Why? Have these impacts been equal for all people?
2. Why are there such worldwide disparities in the use of computer technologies? What are the implications of this?

PROBLEM SOLVING SCENARIOS

1. Set up a debate among your fellow students on the following questions: "What would happen if all the information stored on the world's computers were accessible via the Internet to anyone? Who would own it? Who would control it? Who would protect it from abuse?"
2. Write a position paper on the question "Should access to the Internet be a right or a privilege?"
3. With other students, put together a project plan for an Internet homepage that disseminates information on social problems you consider to be very important. If you have the time and tools, put your plan into action.
4. Using interview techniques, determine why younger people seem to have more of an affinity for computers and the Internet than older people.

WEB EXERCISES

1. To get a sense of the debate over cyberporn, point your browser at the site below, and read the cover story on cyberporn. Think about the extent to which the facts in this article might be true or misleading. Now click on some of the links in the article and try to identify at least three key sociological aspects of cyberporn that are important to you.

   http://www.pathfinder.com/time/magazine/domestic/1995/950703/950703.cover.html

2. Hold a class discussion over this question: "To what extent does technology determine society and social change?" A good place to start your research is

   http://www.aber.ac.uk/~dgc/tdet01.html

SUGGESTED READINGS

James Brook and Iain A. Boal, eds. *Resisting the Virtual Life: The Culture And Politics of Information.* San Francisco: City Lights, 1995.

Clifford Stoll. *Silicon Snake Oil: Second Thoughts on the Information Highway.* New York: Doubleday, 1995.
Both these books provide a somewhat refreshing perspective on the information revolution, arguing that much of today's Internet mania is simple hype. Both authors contend that computer technology, particularly in relation to the Internet and World Wide Web, has the potential to increase alienation by decreasing face-to-face human contact.

Neil Postman. *Technopoly—The Surrender of Culture to Technology.* New York, Vintage Books, 1992.
Postman, who could be called a "neo-Luddite," argues that we are being overwhelmed by our own technologies. Written in an engaging and witty style, the book provides an excellent overview of the issues and much food for thought.

George Ritzer, *The McDonaldization of Society,* Pine Forge Press, Thousand Oaks, California, 1996.
Ritzer's notion of "McDonaldization" is an interesting metaphor for the continued North American obsession with efficiency, convenience, prediction, and control. The book focuses on workplace issues, but is essential reading for anyone interested in the pervasive degrading influence of technology on everyday life.

Joseph Weizenbaum. *Computer Power and Human Reason: From Judgment to Calculation.* New York, W.H. Freeman, 1976.
This is a classic book in which the author argues that there are essential differences between human and artificial intelligence, and that we need to protect what is essentially "human" from the driving logic of new technological developments.

ENDNOTES

1   Although there is no precise way of knowing how many people use the Internet, counting the number of "hosts"—a permanent connection that is likely used by several people—is one of the accepted ways of measuring Internet activity (Clipboard magazine, Summer 1996).

2   There are, of course, other important reasons for the demise of farming, including the rise of large "agri-business" firms, and the influence of banks and loan companies which gradually forced many farmers to foreclose on their mortgages because they could not pay back loans.

3   This is a modified version of Jensen's (1996) definition of pornography.

4   It is interesting to note, though, that *Playboy's* website records about five million hits (number of people logging on to their site) a day, making it the biggest draw on the information highway (Globe and Mail, May 22, 1996).

5   See DeKeseredy and Schwartz (1998c), Miller and Schwartz (1992), and Schwartz and DeKeseredy (1997) for more detailed analyses of the relationship between pro-abuse male peer support and the commodification of women as sexual objects.

6   Others, however, maintain that Marx had a dialectical or reciprocal view of the relationship between technology and society, that is, that society is influenced by technology and vice versa.

Chapter 10

Conclusion

Social problems in the United States are worsening. Since 1970 Marc Miringoff of Fordham University has compiled an "Index of Social Health" for U.S. society (Miringoff and Miringoff, 1995). This index, which is kind of a Dow Jones (stock market) average for social problems, has declined from a composite score of 74 (out of 100) in 1970 to 41 in 1992. Among those indicators which im-  *proved during those twenty-two years were infant mortality, high school dropouts, and poverty among those over 65. Among the declining indicators are the number of children in poverty, average weekly earnings, health insurance coverage, and the gap between the rich and the poor. (Eitzen and Leedham, 1998: 3)*

OBJECTIVES

In this chapter we focus on the topics
  1. What do we know about North American social problems?
  2. What social problems do we need to consider in the future?
  3. New methods of studying social problems
  4. New theoretical directions
  5. The need for new solutions

Introduction

Within the context of a sociological approach that links North Americans' personal experiences with broader social, economic, and political forces, this text attempted to help students answer important questions, such as the following:

➤ What is sociology and what are social problems?

➤ What is the extent and distribution of various social problems that plague North Americans (e.g., poverty, violent crime, etc)?

➤ Which sociological theories are commonly used to explain the issues described in Chapters 2 to 9?

➤ What are the most effective solutions to poverty, unemployment, violent crime, and so on?

The text also sensitized readers to what Coleman and Cressey (1987) refer to as a "depressingly long" list of North American social problems. Did we miss anything and what should we consider in the future? Do we need to think about new methods of studying social problems, new theoretical directions, and new solutions? Are things getting better or worse in North America? The main purpose of this chapter is to address these questions. Before we do, however, it is first necessary to briefly review some of the main arguments presented throughout this text.

What Do We Know About North American Social Problems?

Obviously, there are many answers to this question. However, perhaps the most important one is that social problems are constantly evolving and never-ending. It is to this issue that we turn first.

Social Problems Are Constantly Evolving and Never-Ending

Throughout history, we have consistently witnessed how **private troubles** (Mills, 1959), or what Neubeck and Neubeck (1997) refer to as **privately recognized problems**, eventually get the status of **public issues** (Mills, 1959; Ross and Staines, 1972). Consider anti-personnel land mines, military weapons that have harmed or killed people for decades. Until recently, those who were maimed or killed by them were primarily seen as suffering from a personal problem, despite the fact that more than 25,000 people, mostly civilians, are killed or maimed each year by land-mines. Further, there are at least 110 million land-mines in about 70 countries around the world (Greenaway, 1997).

Now, however, due in large part to the political efforts of activists, such as the late Diana, Princess of Wales, some politicians and popular musicians (e.g., Bruce Cockburn and Jackson Browne), and all the people involved with the early December, 1997 Ottawa summit conference to enact a treaty banning land-mines, these arms are now seen as both a public issue and a global social problem. The amount of world attention currently being devoted to banning land-mines is illustrated in Box 10.1.

BOX 10-1

Activists Celebrate Land-Mines Ban

Delegates Gather In Ottawa For Treaty Signing (December 2, 1997)

A tiny, tattered Canadian flag. Popping champagne corks. And seven "Raging Grannies" singing about the evil of land-mines.

It was all part of the warmup event yesterday before the serious business begins with the opening today of a three-day international conference to sign a new treaty banning anti-personnel mines.

In a party atmosphere, activists converged on the federal Conference Centre to celebrate the arrival of a team that had spent the past five weeks travelling across the United States in a minivan, campaigning against land-mines.

A handful of weary campaigners rolled out of the van after their 10,000 kilometre odyssey.

They were welcomed by Foreign Affairs Minister Lloyd Axworthy, Erik Derycke, Belgium's foreign minister, and Jody Williams, co-ordinator of the International Campaign to Ban Land-Mines and 1997 winner of the Nobel peace prize.

In the background, the seven Raging Grannies sang anti-land-mines tunes.

The travellers sprinkled the welcoming committee with champagne, shared a toast with Ms. Williams and presented Mr. Axworthy with the tattered Canadian flag.

It had flown from the van's aerial since the group left Berkeley, California, on Oct. 23.

"You've done one hell of a job," a beaming Mr. Axworthy declared.

Surrounded by activists from Europe, Australia and Canada, Ms. Williams oozed with glee and pride.

"It's breathtaking," she said, referring to the speed from which the treaty went from being a dream to being a reality.

"I think those of us who have put blood, sweat and tears into this campaign should take a day or two to feel damn proud of what we've done."

"The real surprise of this campaign is this damn treaty," she told reporters.

The conference has attracted at least 155 government delegations, more than a dozen led by foreign ministers, and about 300 representatives from non-government humanitarian and human rights groups from more than 60 countries.

The treaty—banning the use, production, stockpiling and transfer of land-mines —is open for signing beginning tomorrow following speeches by Prime Minister Jean Chretien and United Nations Secretary General Kofi Annan.

BOX 10-1

Mr. Axworthy said the treaty was still winning converts on the eve of the conference.

Venezuela announced yesterday it will sign.

Foreign Affairs officials say they expect at least 110 countries to sign, a number the grassroots campaign sees as too pessimistic.

Ms. Williams repeatedly predicted as many as 121 countries would sign.

At the same time, Ms. Williams played down the import of such countries as the United States, China, Russia, India and Pakistan not signing.

She argued that the treaty has stigmatized land-mines as unacceptable weapons.

Mr. Axworthy has adopted a similar line. The minister said in an interview he no longer considers getting the U.S. signature on the treaty as important as he once did.

The tables have turned, he said, and Washington is now on the defensive.

"As a result, I think they're bending over backwards to find money, to get involved in the post-Ottawa process."

U.S. officials have been promoting an initiative to raise the annual level of global spending on de-mining to $1 billion by 2010.

Mr. Axworthy also said he considered it a major step that such mine-using countries as Israel, Jordan and Syria are attending as observers.

He argued that involving them in joint de-mining programs could "draw" them into eventually signing the treaty.

Source: Excerpted from Greenaway (1997: A3). Reprinted with permission of *The Ottawa Citizen*.

Like land-mines, we are likely to see other "private troubles" transform into public issues or social problems in the near future. However, it takes much more than simply the efforts of activists and politicians to mobilize this change. For example, the following process described by Ross and Staines (1972: 18) must occur:

"Private or interest group recognition of the social problem; political recognition of the problem as an appropriate issue for public discussion; public debate and social conflict about the causes of the problem; a set of political outcomes of this consequence."

The media also play a key role in making problems like land-mines visible and in determining their significance and legitimacy (Neubeck and Neubeck, 1997). The media can even help transform statistically insignificant problems into major social problems, and this is another constantly evolving and never-ending concern for sociologists who study social problems. The next section addresses this issue.

Creating Social Problems: The Contribution of Media-Generated Moral Panics

Throughout history, we have seen examples of a relatively minor or harmless condition, episode, person, or group of persons come to be defined as a major threat to the dominant social order. This is referred to as a **moral panic** (Cohen, 1980). The media often describes these "threats" in detail, albeit inaccurately, and various journalists, community leaders, and politicians "jump on the bandwagon" with their own claims to be defending the moral fabric of society. Sociologists and other "experts" (e.g., lawyers) then quickly join the fray with diagnoses and solutions (DeKeseredy and Schwartz, 1996).

Generally, the objects of media-generated moral panics have been people such as anti-war protestors, "punk rockers," motorcycle gangs, or any other group likely to provoke the moral indignation of the community. However, the target can also be a harmless object or a movie, such as Oliver Stone's controversial and extremely violent film *Natural Born Killers*. For example, as ridiculous as this may sound, the popular children's water gun, the "Super Soaker," was such a target in May, 1992. During this time, an Ottawa, Ontario, resident filled his Super Soaker with bleach and sprayed an innocent bystander in the tourist-oriented Ottawa Market. Shortly before this incident, a water gun fight in Boston escalated into a handgun shooting incident. While the pain and suffering caused by these events should not be trivialized, it is the media's response that is of primary concern here.

One of Canada's leading newspapers devoted a substantial amount of attention to the "criminal" or "deviant" use of the Super Soaker, even though less than a handful of such injurious events occurred in both Canada and the United States. Further, a news reporter expressed great alarm over the potential hazards associated with the Super Soaker. The most important point to consider here is that the media suddenly and dramatically created a social problem. This water gun changed from a popular, harmless toy to an "instrument of criminal victimization." Maybe we are overstating the case to say that the mass media created public fears about the Super Soaker; however, we can certainly state that the media amplified such fears (DeKeseredy and Schwartz, 1996).

What difference does it make that fears about the Super Soaker were amplified? According to Cohen (1980), it makes a big difference because the public concern, anxiety, indignation, or panic caused by the media can result in the creation of new rules or laws. For example, U.S. politicians called for a ban on the Super Soaker, and some communities and stores refused to sell it. Do you think that these are rational responses based on a careful assessment of the true risk of criminal danger? Obviously, although this is a minor example, it highlights the role of the media in creating moral panics and social problems (DeKeseredy and Schwartz, 1996).

Socioeconomic Inequality Is Endemic to North America

After reading all or most of the chapters in this text, you are probably aware that the United States and Canada are both characterized by gross economic and social inequality, and that those at the bottom of North America's socioeconomic ladder are the ones most likely to be victimized by crime, be impoverished, experience high levels of unemployment, take and deal drugs, have lower levels of education, and so on. Unfortunately, we live in a society that is "distinctly unequal" (Fischer et al., 1996: 8). This is not by any means an accident, and the North American social, economic, and political structure we have today did not evolve from random events, carelessness, or bureaucratic inefficiency. Rather, the levels and types of inequality described throughout this text are by design (Fischer et al., 1996). For example, because of the high value that the U.S. general public and politicians place on competitive individualism, and the fact that the Democratic and Republican parties are financed by multinational corporations and wealthy individuals who want low taxes and minimal, if any, social programs, the United States has done very little to buffer its citizens from poverty and a host of other pressing social problems (Eitzen and Leedham, 1998).

"But why," some skeptics may ask, "would anyone want to construct or maintain a society characterized by extreme levels of poverty and social disorganization? Aren't these strong indicators of failure? Don't these social problems make the United States and Canada look bad?" According to Reiman (1998), it seems that for economic and political elites, "nothing succeeds like failure." For example, there are powerful people who reap large profits under the current inequitable social order, and they are fundamentally opposed to eliminating a capitalist patriarchal system that enabled them to achieve the American or Canadian Dream at the expense of others. For them, the North American social system's failure is only in the eye of those who are victimized by it. Indeed, according to those who gain from giving people low wages, maintaining high levels of unemployment, and providing inadequate health and maternity benefits, the system is a "roaring success" (Reiman, 1998: 40).

Some people may respond to this argument by saying, "Come on! Don't you think the problem is that we simply don't know what causes the social problems described in this text and therefore we lack adequate solutions?" Like Reiman (1998), Currie (1985), and other progressive sociologists, our response to this question is that the "we just don't know" excuse is, to say the least, lame. We do, in fact, know what the causes are and we do know what to do about them. If we didn't, this book would be much shorter. Recall Elliott Currie's (1985: 19) statement at the end of Chapter 5. He argues that social problems like violent crime and drugs are not "overwhelmingly mysterious," and we do know effective ways of curbing them. Unfortunately, many North Americans, especially those opposed to universal social services and giving people decent wages, have decided that the rewards of eliminating poverty, crime, unemployment, etc. are not worth the costs.

As silly as this may sound, there are also many people, including politicians, who simply don't want to hear about the key sources and progressive ways of solving major social problems. Consider the following experience described by Alfred Blumstein (1995: 13), former President of the American Society of Criminology, and a Carnegie Mellon University professor:

"There was a recent action by a House Judiciary subcommittee on a proposal that 1 percent of the crime bill money be allocated to research—just 1 percent to at least start

to find out what the effects of a variety of things we're advocating would have on crime. That was voted down on a straight party-line vote. There seems to be a determined view that even though we don't know, don't tell us, we don't want to be confused by the facts, we want to make decisions based on our ideological positions."

Many Social Problems Are Shaped by Racial/Ethnic, Class, and Gender Inequality

The roots of most of North American social problems can be traced to one or more of the above types of inequality. Thus, some people may ask, "Are these the only social problems that we should study because they are the key sources of all other social evils?" As Schwartz (1997: 276) asks,

"[M]ust social problems be inverately plural, because anxieties themselves migrate according to historical fronts and political climate? Should public policy be shaped to confront the one, remorseless, objective problem of inequity, or should it be shaped to confront a host of problems, each a subjective expression of social structure, current events, and physical reality" (Jones et al., 1988: 22)?

What do you think? Is it logical to presume that if socioeconomic inequality is the major source of most, if not all, contemporary social problems, sociologists should, then, devote most, if not all, of their time, grant money, and intellectual energy to studying this problem and offering solutions to it? In our opinion, we should not necessarily prioritize one topic over the other; but, it is important to recognize that socioeconomic inequality and many other social problems are inextricably linked. In other words, you are not likely to develop a rich sociological understanding of crime, drugs, poverty, etc. without understanding their relationship to broader social, political, and economic forces that foster social inequality and its negative outcomes.

Canadian and U.S. Social Problems Vary in Degree—Not Kind

In a subsequent section of this chapter, we present data showing that Canada is in some ways better off than the United States. Who knows, however, what will happen in the future? Perhaps you will live to see Canada becoming more like the United States or vice versa. Or, both countries could become homogenized due to the effects of the North American Free Trade Agreement (NAFTA) and other economic, political, and cultural factors (Dreier and Bernard, 1998). No matter what the future holds, it is clear that both countries are currently experiencing similar social problems. For example, drugs are dealt on both sides of the border, and murders occur in both countries. The key difference, though, is that many of the social problems described in this text are more common in the United States. This is because Canada has, as pointed out by several studies (e.g., Dreier and Bernard, 1998; Eitzen and Leedham, 1998; Shapiro, 1992), developed and, until recently maintained, different and somewhat progressive ways of coping with social problems (e.g., universal health care, greater access to education, etc.).

What Social Problems Do We Need to Consider in the Future?

Since we have written chapters on a variety of social problems, we, to a certain extent, accept the notion that social problems are "inveterately plural" (Schwartz, 1997). Moreover, we could have written a much longer text that includes conceptual, empirical, theoretical, and political discussions on a much wider range of the social problems plaguing North American society. Perhaps after reading this text, some will argue that the social problems covered in it constitute just the tip of the iceberg. We purposely excluded chapters on issues such as militarism, racism, education, and so on—not because we think them unimportant or of little social consequence. Rather, as noted in our introduction, we decided to replace the standard "cafeteria concept"—a little bit of many kinds of social problems—with the concept of *table d'hôte*, or a few selected offerings.[1] Again, the offerings are limited in number so that each topic can be covered in some depth.

Further, within the social problems literature, what has been conspicuously absent has been the study of the various intersections among class, race, and gender. Thus, following Anderson and Collins (1992), and Schwartz and Milovanovic (1996), who contend that race, gender, and class are interlocking categories and are the basis of many social problems, we wanted to avoid "ghettoizing" race, class, and gender issues into single chapters. For example, some social problems texts are longer than this one because they include separate and distinct chapters on racism, gender, and class-related issues. To some degree, this text takes this approach by providing distinct chapters on unemployment, poverty, and the family; however, the ways in which these and other problems are related to the above key sociological variables is made explicit in every chapter.

Let's assume, for a minute, that there is a major need to address a wider range of social problems in the future. Based, then, on your life experiences and your understanding of the social problems literature, what do you think we need to consider in the twenty-first century? Perhaps you, like many other North Americans, are deeply worried about a major war. This fear of war is, indeed, well-founded, because in the United States, and other parts of the world, the "institutional forces promoting militarism are...formidable" (Neubeck and Neubeck, 1997: 117).

Others are concerned about the negative consequences of the "information revolution" described in Chapter 9 and elsewhere. For example, while robotics, the "information highway," and other technological changes have generated new jobs, they are also making many obsolete. Unfortunately, in both Canada and the United States, we are currently witnessing a "widening gap" between technologically skilled and unskilled workers (Wilson, 1996). Further, technological change and joblessness go hand-in-hand, and thus we must be prepared to deal with this problem. Are you prepared? Are you comfortable using a computer and working with sophisticated software? Many of our students are not, and they are likely to face grim job prospects when they graduate.

Technological change also influences educational policy at all levels (e.g., primary, secondary, and post-secondary schools). Increasingly, throughout North

America, school boards, teachers, principals, university/college administrators, and professors are being formally and informally pressured to place stronger emphasis on teaching students "high tech skills," and the provision of computer facilities and computer training is regarded by many to be more valuable than giving students a holistic education sensitizing them to the importance of a wide range of disciplines, including the classics, languages, and comparative literature. For example, on December 5, 1997, Carleton University, located in Ottawa, Ontario, announced the closure of several important Arts Programs due to budget constraints. If Carleton has major budget problems, why, then, did its administration devote more money to the "high tech" programs? For example, its contribution to the "High Technology" faculties recently increased by $150,000 (Carleton University, December 4, 1997). Will you be affected by changes such as these? Will your liberal arts education be considered meaningless in the near future, and should we define this issue as a social problem?

Another negative consequence of bringing "high tech" into the school system is cheating (see Chapter 9), a problem familiar to most students. Should the Internet's contribution to academic dishonesty be considered a social problem? What about the threat of the "professorless" or "teacherless" classroom? Do you foresee sterile, quiet classrooms devoid of energetic debate and discussion, and should we be worried about these possible threats to traditional pedagogical approaches (e.g., lectures, seminars, and tutorials)? And what will be the effect of these learning approaches on students' ability to think critically? To interact with others and to learn inter-personal communication skills? To get a job where these skills are essential?

If you follow the model taken by social problems researchers such as Curran and Renzetti (1996), then you might also call for more in-depth analyses of issues such as mental illness; the "graying of the world's population;" heterosexism; and the numerous problems experienced by our children. Indeed, anyone familiar with most of the social problems texts published in this continent knows that the list of North American social problems described here could go on and on.

Because of rapid technological change and other factors (e.g., the globalization of the economy), many people now view the world as a "global village." In fact, most of us know that the events and policies unfolding in one part of our world often positively or negatively influence people in other parts of the planet (Soroka and Bryjack, 1995). Thus, doesn't it make sense to take a global or cross-cultural approach to studying the issues reviewed in this text and other social problems books? After all, as one person who works for the United Nations Development Program pointed out, "In the age of global interdependence, human crisis anywhere is a human threat everywhere" (cited in Soroka and Bryjack, 1995: xii).

New Methods of Studying Social Problems

Another issue to consider in the future is new methods of studying social problems. Researchers will always use survey technology, participant observation procedures, and other "mainstream methods;" however, we are likely to see more researchers develop techniques of generating data on a wide range of topics from those who use communications media such as Internet Relay Chat (IRC), teleconferencing, videoconferencing, and so on. For example, as described in Chapter 9, researchers like Ferguson (1996) are now studying the ways in which men share violent pornographic material with other men through human interfaces such as IRC channels, UseNet, and e-mail.

Means of eliciting "cyberspace" data will also be used together with mainstream research methods. In fact, many sociologists are now using e-mail and other communications media to conduct surveys. For example, the authors of this text were concerned about which material to add or delete from each chapter. So, we sent questionnaires out over various e-mail networks to approximately 50 of our North American colleagues who have either taught social problems courses, or who have a firm grasp of the relevant literature, or both. We received a wealth of valuable information from these people, and they quickly responded to our questionnaire.

Unfortunately, some social problems cannot be adequately studied using sophisticated communications technology. Consider poverty and unemployment. Many disadvantaged people do not have access to computers either at home or in formal institutions such as schools. Thus, for the time being at least, researchers may only be able to use communications technology to generate social problems data from mainly middle- or upper-class respondents.

New Theoretical Directions

After taking a variety of social science courses and reading different texts, journal articles, and scholarly monographs, students recognize that many social scientists "claim one disciplinary stance, favoring either a single theoretical model or a multiparadigm orientation" (Barak, 1998: xi). For example, although we are required to teach courses in an interdisciplinary criminology program that includes sociology, law, and psychology students, many students enrolled in this program complain that there is little overlap between the courses taught by sociologists, legal scholars, and psychologists. Also, many of these students often state that there seems to be much competition and tension between the different disciplinary perspectives on crime and its control.

What these criminology students and others attending different centers of higher learning frequently encounter is

"... something akin to the Tower of Babel. They will not be offered one answer but a series of competing and contradictory visions of the nature of man, deviation, and the social order. Very typically, they will be informed that their questions cannot even be discussed because they are not correctly phrased: they must first reconstruct the problem so that it can be placed with others in one of the master theories of deviance" (Downes and Rock, 1988: 2).

There is also considerable intellectual tension and competition for status among North American sociologists. For example, at conferences and departmental meetings, you will often see heated arguments between post-modernists, Marxists, feminists, symbolic interactionists, etc. about the scholarly value of various theoretical perspectives, research methods, and policies. It would be nice if, as a result of many generations of exhaustive research and deep thinking, we could provide a straightforward, easily understood explanation for poverty, why people kill and sell drugs, unemployment, and so on. Unfortunately, few sociologists would be so bold as to declare that we are now ready to conclusively answer that question. If anyone does claim to have an answer, many other sociologists would be quick to find fault with it (DeKeseredy and Schwartz, 1996).

What is to be done about this problem? Well, it is not likely to be minimized or overcome in the near future. Nevertheless, we are currently seeing a growing number of sociologists (e.g., Barak, 1998) who contend that the study of social problems and other topics should become more interdisciplinary in nature. Consider Sharon Bell (1994: 3), a social scientist who wrote a book that specifically combined "the disciplines of political theory, feminist theory, philosophy, comparative politics, literary theory, the politics of new social movements, and aspects of public policy." Similarly, to enhance a broader understanding of crime and its control, sociologist Gregg Barak (1998) recently attempted to combine the knowledge provided by biology, psychology, sociology, law, and economics with the interdisciplinary studies of mass media, public policy, culture, gender, and ethnicity.

It is beyond the scope of this chapter to fully describe an interdisciplinary theoretical approach to explaining or studying one or more social problems. In fact, one could write an entire book on this topic. Nevertheless, it is clearly time for sociologists and others who study social problems to appreciate the strengths of different "knowledges," and their theories, research methods, interests, and points of view (Barak, 1998).

The Need for New Solutions

In addition to thinking about new topics, new research methods, and new theories, we need to seriously consider new solutions to the social problems identified in this text and elsewhere. What we need, in fact, is a "broader vision" (Wilson, 1996), one that is specifically designed to target the ways in which broader social, political, cultural, and economic forces contribute to poverty, unemployment, substandard education, and other social problems. Conservative tinkering with the capitalist patriarchal status quo, such as building new prisons and creating workfare programs, does little, if anything, to eliminate inequality—a key determinant of many social problems. Such approaches are also unidimensional responses that are not helpful to most disenfranchised people. In fact, the social problems described throughout this text are multifaceted problems requiring multifaceted responses (DeKeseredy and MacLeod, 1997), such as those described in the policy sections of Chapters 2 to 9.

Rather than repeat or summarize the progressive policy proposals outlined in these chapters, we would like to ask you an important question: "Now that you have read this text, what do you think North American politicians, corporations, schools, the general population, and so on need to do to alleviate the pain and misery described here?" Like it or not, you are part of the evolving story of North American social problems. The topics covered in this text are part of your history, directly or indirectly. They will also affect your future. What part will you choose to play to make your country or community a better place?

Are Things Getting Better or Worse?

Shortly after your friends, relatives, co-workers, acquaintances, etc. experience two or more traumatic life events or tragedies in a short period of time (e.g., being fired, getting divorced, etc.), you will often hear them say, "Things couldn't get worse!" Unfortunately, for many North American citizens, especially those at the bottom of the socioeconomic ladder, nothing could be further from the truth. For example, due to factors such as rapid technological change, for the first time in this century, most adults in many inner-city communities are unemployed and they are not likely to get decent jobs in the near or distant future (Wilson, 1996).

Some readers may respond to this pessimistic interpretation of social conditions in North America by saying, "Come on! Why do sociologists always have to paint a "gloom and doom" picture of society? Can't you look for the good things in our country?" This is a valid point. After all, most contemporary sociologists are trained to be critical of the dominant social order and their own and others' definitions of social problems, research, theories, and policy proposals.

Since most of this book is devoted to telling a negative story of social, economic, and political conditions in North America, we will address the above criticism by briefly describing some of the positive features of North American society. Consider the following data generated by Shapiro (1992). He found that, compared to 19 other major industrial nations,[2] the United States ranks number one in

- real wealth;
- the number of billionaires;
- the amount of space in homes;
- defense spending and military capability;
- corporate executive salaries;
- doctors' salaries;
- multiculturalism or ethnic diversity;
- the number of people who have access to clean drinking water; and
- the percentage of people enrolled in higher education (cited in Eitzen and Leedham, 1998: 3–4).

Based on these data, many people, especially conservative defenders of the capitalist patriarchal status quo (e.g., Rush Limbaugh), might say, "See! Life is good here. What are you complaining about?" Our sociological and political backgrounds prevent us from only seeing what popular Canadian folk singer

Gordon Lightfoot refers to as "the summer side of life."[3] For example, if the United States ranks number one in the above indicators examined by Shapiro (1992), the same can be said about an alarming number of social problems indicators, many of which are addressed in previous chapters. These indicators are, according to Eitzen and Leedham (1998: 4):

"murder rate, reported rapes, robbery rate, incarceration rate, the number of drunken driving fatalities, cocaine use, greenhouse gas emissions, contributing to acid rain, forest depletion, hazardous waste per capita, garbage per capita, the number of cars per capita (and the use of cars rather than public transportation), the number of children and elderly in poverty, homelessness, inequality of wealth distribution, bank failures, military aid to developing countries, divorce, single-parent families, reported cases of AIDS, infant mortality, the death of children younger than five, and teenage pregnancy."

So, in many cases, being ranked first is not something to be proud of. It should also be noted that the United States ranks last on providing several important social services to disenfranchised people. For example, of the 19 countries in Shapiro's (1992) sample, the United States is at the bottom in providing financial aid to the poor; fully immunizing preschoolers against polio, DTP (diphtheria-tetanus-pertussis), and measles; providing humanitarian aid to developing nations; the number of people with medical insurance; and providing paid maternity leave (cited in Eitzen and Leedham, 1998: 4). Box 10.2 provides some salient examples of the severity of United States social problems compared to other industrialized countries. As Eitzen and Leedham (1998: 5) correctly point out: "the United States has more serious social problems than what is found in those countries most similar to it."

Need we say more? The United States is, to say the least, in a "terrible mess" (Currie, 1992). What about Canada? Many people, especially Canadian nationalists and progressive academics, think that Canada is "a more humane, liveable society than the U.S." (Dreier and Bernard, 1998: 13). To a certain extent, as described in Box 10.3, Canada is what former U.S. President George Bush defines as a "kinder, gentler nation." Further, according to the sixth annual United Nations Human Development Report (1995), Canada is the best country in the world to live in. For example, in overall human development, measured by a combination of indicators such as life expectancy, education, and income, Canada topped 174 nations for the second straight year (Beauchesne, 1995). The Canadian rate of predatory street violence (see Chapter 5) is also much lower than that of the U.S., and therefore many outside observers and Canadians regard Canada as a "peaceable kingdom" (DeKeseredy, 1997b; DeKeseredy and Schwartz, 1998a; Silverman, 1992).

However, Canadians should not be so smug, because Chapter 2 shows that the Canadian poverty rate (17.8 percent of the total population) is higher than that of the United States (13 percent), and the UN Report also states that Canadian women do not fare as well as men. In fact, Canada is one of four industrial countries that has a "sharply lower" ranking on the "gender development index" than on the "human development index." Canada is also indicted as a nation where many heterosexual women experience a substantial amount of physical and psychological

BOX 10-2

The Severity of U.S. Social Problems Compared to Other Industrialized Nations

Consider the following "fast facts."

The U.S. has the highest rate of poverty and the poor experience the longest period in poverty. The U.S. also provides the lowest amount of income security to its poor citizens (Children's Defense Fund, 1996; Danzier and Gottschalk, 1995).

Out of 18 industrialized nations studied by Rainwater and Smeeding (1995), the U.S. ranked sixteenth in poor children's living standards.

The U.S. is the only industrialized nation to deny its citizens some form of universal health care.

The U.S. ranks first among industrialized nations in the percentage of children born with low birth weight, in the proportion of children who die before the age of five, and in the percentage of children who are not immunized (Shapiro, 1992: 16-21).

The U.S. ranks fifteenth in life expectancy (Shapiro, 1992: 4-5).

Based on his path-breaking research on joblessness and other social problems that plague U.S. disenfranchised inner-city residents, William Julius Wilson (1996: 218) contends that "None of the other industrialized democracies has allowed its city centers to deteriorate as has the United States."

Like Portugal, Italy, Ireland, Spain, and Greece, the U.S. provides the least generous child benefit packages (Bradshaw et al., 1993).

Source: Eitzen and Leedham (1998: 4–5).

BOX 10-3

National Well-being in Canada and the United States

In many cases, Canada's social problems are less severe than those of the United States. For example:

The U.S. spends more on health care (12.4 percent of its Gross National Product (GNP), $2,566 per capita) than any country in the world, while not providing coverage for all of its citizens. Canada, on the other hand, spends nine percent of its GNP ($1,795 per capita) on health care and provides universal coverage for all its citizens.

The U.S. does not have a national maternity leave policy, while Canadian women receive 17-18 weeks of paid maternity leave.

The U.S. is the "murder capital of the world" (approximately 9.4 murders per 100,00 population). Compared to the rest of the world, Canada is not much better. In fact, it ranks third with 5.5 murders per 100,000 population.

In the late 1980s, the U.S. produced the largest amount of hazardous waste in the world (110,000 tons per 100,000 people), while Canada ranked second with less with 12,500 tons per 100,000 people. In other words, Canada generated one eighth of the amount of toxic waste produced by the U.S.

The U.S. spends 4.77 percent of its Gross Domestic Product (GDP) in public dollars on education, while Canada spends 6.53 percent of its GDP on education.

In 1991, corporate CEOs in U.S. companies (in firms with sales over $250 million) received renumeration of $747,500, 25 times the average pay of manufacturing employees. Canadian CEOs received $407,600, 12 times the average pay of manufacturing workers.

Of the 19 industrial nations included in Shapiro's (1992) sample, the U.S. gives its workers 10.8 paid vacation days per year. The U.S. ranks last and Canada ranks second last, with 14.7 paid vacation days per year.

The U.S. has one of the lowest voter turnouts of any industrialized democracy. For example, only 53 percent of eligible voters voted in the 1980s for presidential elections. The Canadian rate of voter turnout among eligible voters is typically 20 points higher.

BOX 10-3

Source: Adapted from Dreier and Bernard (1998: 14); includes data reported by Shapiro (1992), Teixera (1992), and The World Almanac (1992).

pain in a variety of intimate and domestic relationships. To support this assertion, the UN cites statistics generated by several major Canadian studies, such as those uncovered by the Canadian national survey on woman abuse in university/college dating relationships (DeKeseredy and Kelly, 1993; DeKeseredy and Schwartz, 1998) and Statistics Canada's national Violence Against Women Survey (Johnson, 1996). In addition, according to Hajnal (1995), Canada has proportionally more people in concentrated urban poverty than the United States.

In sum, Canada typically outperforms the United States on a large number of social indicators (Dreier and Bernard, 1988); however, Canada is currently facing several major threats to the maintenance of its universal social services, its economy, and its citizens' overall physical, material, and psychological well-being. Thus, many Canadian sociologists are currently asserting that if social problems in the United States are worsening, the same can be said about Canada.

Summary

We know many things about the North American social problems covered in this text. For example, most of them are directly linked to socioeconomic inequality. We also know that social problems are never-ending and constantly evolving. Still, there is much more to learn about the pressing social concerns facing North Americans and those who live in other parts of the world. We also need to consider new methods of gathering social problems data, and must begin to appreciate the knowledge generated by other disciplines. After all, sociologists do not have a monopoly on understanding poverty, crime, unemployment, and so on.

Again, we would like you to seriously consider the role that you will play in the broader struggle to eliminate or minimize the social problems facing North Americans today and in the future. Do you have the courage to help change our social structure, our ways of living, playing, loving, working, and caring for others? We believe that the prevention and elimination of the social problems covered in this text is both a profound act of courage and dramatic act of revolution, and we invite you to take part in the struggle to make North America kinder and gentler.

Are things improving or deteriorating? For reasons described here, social problems, especially those in the United States, are worsening and that country seems to be worse off than Canada. Keep in mind, however, that the social problems that plague Canada and the United States differ only in degree, not kind.

KEY TERMS

Broader vision
Index of social health
Interdisciplinary theory
Mainstream methods
Moral panic
Newsmaking criminology

DISCUSSION QUESTIONS

1. Why are North American social problems getting worse?
2. In what ways can Canada be considered "kinder and gentler" than the United States?
3. What is the value of taking a global approach to understanding the social problems described in this text?
4. What are the strengths and limitations of using communications technology to study social problems?
5. What is the value of taking an interdisciplinary approach to understanding social problems?

PROBLEM SOLVING SCENARIOS

1. In a group, develop an interdisciplinary theory of one or more of the social problems described in this text.
2. When you watch television and/or read the newspaper over the next week, note the ways in which the media help to create a social problem.
3. Develop a research design, one that involve the use of communications technology, to study one or more of the social problems covered in this text.
4. As a class, divide into groups to discuss ways in which you and others can individually help to minimize or overcome one or more of the social problems reviewed in this text.
5. In a group, make a list of social problems that are likely to warrant sociological attention in the near future, and provide a rationale for examining each one in your list.

WEB EXERCISES

1. Identify the assumptions (about society, the role of government, and the role of individuals) in relation to what can be done to improve social conditions at

   http://www.heritage.org/.

2. Point your browser at the site below and pick one of the many futuristic scenarios, then write a sociological analysis of the issues you encounter. Be sure to focus on the ways in which the notion of "private troubles and public issues" can inform your analysis.

   http://www.uio.no/~oleg/

SUGGESTED READINGS

Barak, Gregg. *Integrating Criminologies.* Boston: Allyn & Bacon, 1998.
Why should we seriously consider moving towards an interdisciplinary understanding of social problems, such as crime? Written by one of North America's most widely read and cited sociological criminologists, this book provides some compelling answers to this important question.

Eitzen, D. Stanley, and Craig S. Leedham (eds.). *Solutions to Social Problems: Lessons From Other Societies.* Boston: Allyn & Bacon, 1998.
This collection of readings sensitizes students and researchers alike to how and why social problems are worsening in the United States, and to the policy implications of examining social problems from a cross-cultural standpoint.

Schwartz, Martin D., and Dragan Milovanovic (eds.). *Race, Gender, and Class in Criminology: The Intersection.* New York: Garland, 1996.
This book is an excellent model for those seeking to develop a rich understanding of the intersection of class, gender, and race in criminology. It may also be a valuable resource for those seeking ways of addressing the intersection of these three important variables in other fields of inquiry, such as poverty, unemployment, and education.

Soroka, Michael P., and George J. Bryjak. *Social Problems: A World at Risk.* Boston: Allyn & Bacon, 1995.
Most North American social problems texts are parochial. In other words, they restrict their focus to macro- and micro-level crises experienced by those living in the United States. The authors of this book offer a refreshing alternative to this dominant method of examining social problems by providing a critical, comprehensive overview of various social problems from a global, cross-cultural perspective.

ENDNOTES

1   A growing number of criminology textbook authors, such as DeKeseredy and Schwartz (1996), Ellis (1987), and Ellis and DeKeseredy (1996), are also providing in-depth coverage of a smaller number of issues.
2   The nations included in his sample are: Australia, Austria, Belgium, Canada, Denmark, Finland, France, Germany, Ireland, Italy, Japan, the Netherlands, New Zealand, Norway, Spain, Sweden, Switzerland, the United Kingdom, and the United States.
3   This is the title of one of his songs.

REFERENCES

Abramovitz, J. 1993. "Sustaining Freshwater Ecosystems." Pp. 60–77 in *The State of the World*. Washington, DC: Worldwatch Institute.

ACNielsen. 1997. "Startling increase in internet shopping reported in new Commercenet/ Nielsem Media research survey." At http:// www.commerce.net/work/pilot/nielsen96/ press97.html.

Adlaf, E. M., R. G. Smart, and G. W. Walsh. 1994. *Ontario Student Drug Survey*. Toronto: Addiction Research Foundation.

Adler, P. 1994. "Between Legalization and War: A Reconsideration of American Drug Policy." Pp. 255–268 in *Drug Use in America: Social, Cultural, and Political Perspectives*, edited by P. Venturelli. Boston: Jones and Bartlett.

Ageton, S. 1983. *Sexual Assault Among Adolescents*. Lexington, MA: D.C. Heath.

Akers, R. L. 1992. *Drugs, Alcohol, and Society: Social Structure, Process, and Policy*. Belmont, CA: Wadsworth.

Alario, M. 1995. "Risk-Society Model, Environmental Destruction and Social Asymmetry: Environmental Justice and Equity Issues." Paper presented at annual meeting of the American Sociological Association, Washington, DC. (August 19–23).

Albrecht, G. L. 1992. *The Disability Business: Rehabilitation in America*. Newbury Park, CA: Sage.

Alcorn, P. A. 1997. *Social Issues in Technology: A Format for Investigation*. 2nd ed. Upper Saddle River, N. J.: Prentice Hall.

Alexander, M. B. 1996. "Foster Dad, Birth Mom Renew War." *Daily News* 11 April, 3.

Althusser, L. 1971. *Lenin and Philosophy and Other Essays*. New York: New Left Books.

Alvi, S. 1994a. *Health Costs and Competitiveness*. Ottawa: Conference Board of Canada.

Alvi, S. 1994b. "Professional Power and Proletarianization? A Class Analysis of Canadian Physicians." Carleton University, Department of Sociology and Anthropology: Unpublished doctoral dissertation.

Alvi, S. 1994c. *The Work-family Challenge: Issues and Options*. Ottawa: Conference Board of Canada/Canada Committee for the International Year of the Family.

Alvi, S. 1995. *Eldercare and the Workplace*. Conference Board of Canada Report # 150–95.

Alvi, S., and W. S. DeKeseredy. 1997. "Youth Unemployment and Entrepreneurial Culture: Improving the Odds?" *Teach* (March/April): 38–40.

ALVI Social Research. 1996. *Health Effects of Working at Home: A Review of the Literature*. Ottawa: Health Canada.

American Federation of Labor and Congress of Industrial Organizations. 1993. *The Workplace: America's Forgotten Environment*. Washington, D.C.: AFL-CIO.

Anderson, A. (1994). "The Health of Aboriginal People in Saskatchewan: Recent Trends and Policy Implications." Pp. 313–322 in *Racial Minorities, Medicine, and Health*, edited by B. Singh. Bolaria & R. Bolaria. Saskatoon/Halifax: SRU/Fernwood.

Anderson, M. L., and P. H. Collins. 1992. *Race, Class, and Gender: An Anthology*. Belmont, CA: Wadsworth.

Anderson, O. W., and J. J. Feldman. 1956. *Family Medical Costs and Voluntary Health Insurance: A Nationwide Survey*. New York: McGraw-Hill.

Archer, D., and R. Gartner. 1984. *Violence and Crime in Cross-National Perspective*. New Haven: Yale University Press.

Aronowitz, S., and W. DiFazio. 1994. *The Jobless Future: Sci-Tech and the Dogma of Work*. Minneapolis: University of Minnesota Press.

Auld, J., N. Dorn, and N. South. 1986. "Irregular Work, Irregular Pleasures: Heroin in the 1980s." Pp. 166–187 in *Confronting Crime*, edited by R. Matthews and J. Young. London: Sage.

Babbie, E. 1992. *The Practice of Social Research*. 6th ed. Belmont, CA: Wadsworth.

Bachman, R. 1993. "The Double Edged Sword of Violent Victimization Against the Elderly: Patterns of Family and Stranger Perpetration." *Journal of Elder Abuse and Neglect* 5: 59–76.

Bachman, R. 1994. *Violence Against Women: A National Crime Victimization Survey Report*.

Washington, D.C.: Bureau of Justice Statistics, National Institute of Justice.

Bachman, R., and L. Saltzman. 1995. *Violence Against Women: Estimates from the Redesigned Survey.* Washington, D.C.: Bureau of Justice Statistics, National Institute of Justice.

Bachman, R., and B. M. Taylor. 1994. "The Measurement of Family Violence and Rape by the Redesigned National Crime Victimization Survey." *Justice Quarterly* 11: 499–512.

Badgett, M. V. L. 1994. "Rising Black Unemployment—Changes In Job Stability Or In Employability?" *Review of Black Political Economy* 22: 55–75.

Bailey, R. Ed. 1995. *The True State of The Planet.* New York: Free Press.

Balabanian, N. 1980. "Presumed Neutrality of Technology." *Society* 17: 7–14.

Balbus, I. 1977. "Commodity Form and Legal Form: An Essay on the 'Relative Autonomy' of the Law." *Law and Society Review* 11: 571–588.

Ballantyne, J. H. 1997. *The Sociology of Education: A Systematic Analysis.* 4th ed. New Jersey: Prentice-Hall.

Banfield, E. C. 1974. *The Unheavenly City Revisited.* Boston: Little Brown.

Bank, S. P., and M. D. Kahn. 1982. *The Sibling Bond.* New York: Basic Books.

Barak, G. 1986. "Is America Really Ready for the Currie Challenge?" *Crime and Social Justice* 25: 200–203.

Barak, G. 1988. "News-Making Criminology: Reflections on the Media, Intellectuals, and Crime." *Justice Quarterly* 5: 565–88.

Barak, G. 1991. *Gimme Shelter: A Social History of Homelessness in Contemporary America.* New York: Praeger.

Barak, G. 1995. *Media, Process and the Social Construction of Crime: Studies in Newsmaking Criminology.* New York: Garland.

Barak, G. 1998. *Integrating Criminologies.* Boston: Allyn and Bacon.

Barber, B. 1967. *Drugs and Society.* New York: Russell Sage Foundation.

Barkan, S. E. 1997. *Criminology: A Sociological Understanding.* Upper Saddle River, NJ: Prentice Hall.

Barnett, O. W., C. L. Miller-Perrin, and R. D. Perrin. 1997. *Family Violence Across the*

Lifespan: An Introduction. Thousand Oaks, CA: Sage.

Barrett, M., and M. McIntosh. 1982. *The Anti-Social Family.* London: Verso.

Bartlett, D., and J. Steele. 1992. *America: What Went Wrong?* Kansas City: Andrews and McMeel.

Bastian, L. D., and M. M. DeBerry Jr., (Eds.). 1994. *Criminal Victimization in the United States, 1992.* Washington, D.C.: U.S Department of Justice, Bureau of Justice Statistics.

Beauchesne, E. 1995. "Canada Best Place to Live—With a Catch." *Ottawa Citizen* 18 August, A1–A2.

Beauchesne, E. 1997. "StatsCan Can't Draw Poverty Line: Agency Laments Widespread Misuse of Income Numbers." *Ottawa Citizen* 26 August, A1–A2.

Beck, U. 1992. *Risk Society: Towards a New Modernity.* Thousand Oaks, CA: Sage.

Becker, H. 1967. "Whose Side Are We On?" *Social Problems* 14: 239–267.

Becker, H. 1973. *Outsiders: Studies in the Sociological Study of Deviance.* New York: Free Press.

Beeghley, L. 1984. "Illusion and Reality in the Measurement of Poverty." *Social Problems* 31: 322–333.

Beehr, T. A., and R. S. Bhagat. 1985. "Introduction to Human Stress and Cognition in Organizations." Pp. 3–19 in *Human Stress and Cognition in Organizations: An Integrated Perspective*, edited by T. A. Beehr, and R. S. Bhagat. New York: Wiley.

Beirne, P., and J. W. Messerschmidt. 1991. *Criminology.* Toronto: Harcourt Brace.

Beirne, P., and J. W. Messerschmidt. 1995. *Criminology.* 2nd ed. Toronto: Harcourt Brace.

Bell, D. 1973. *The Coming of Post-industrial Society: A Venture in Social Forecasting.* New York: Basic Books.

Bell, S. 1994. *Reading, Writing, and Rewriting the Prostitute Body.* Bloomington: Indiana University Press.

Bennett, L. 1993. "There's Been a Misunderstanding About the Sixties." Pp. 40–52 in *On Prejudice: A Global Perspective*, edited by D. Gioseffi. New York: Doubleday.

Bennett, R. R., and J. P. Lynch. 1990. "Does a Difference Make a Difference: Comparing Cross-National Crime Indicators." *Criminology* 28: 153–181.

Bereleson, B. 1978. "Prospects and Programs for Fertility Reduction: What? Where?" *Population and Development Review*, 4: 579–616.

Bernstein, J. 1981. *The Analytical Engine: Computers—Past, Present and Future.* New York: William Morrow.

Betcherman, G., N. Leckie, K. McMullen, and C. Caron. 1994. *The Canadian Workplace in Transition.* Kingston: IRC Press.

Blau, J. R., and P. M. Blau. 1982. "The Cost of Inequality: Metropolitan Structure and Violent Crime." *American Sociological Review* 47: 114–129.

Blumstein, A. 1995a. "An Interview with Professor Alfred Blumstein of Carnagie Mellon University." *Law Enforcement News* 21: 13.

Blumstein, A. 1995b. "Violence by Young People: Why the Deadly Nexus?" Pp. 2–9 in *National Institute of Justice Journal.* Washington,D.C.: U.S. Department of Justice.

Bly, R. M. 1994. *Sibling Violence: Prevalence, Risk Markers and Protective Factors.* North York, ON: LaMarsh Research Centre on Violence and Conflict Resolution, York University.

Bograd, M. 1988. "Feminist Perspectives on Wife Abuse: An Introduction." Pp. 11–27 in *Feminist Perspectives on Wife Abuse*, edited by K. A. Yllo and M. Bograd. Beverly Hills: Sage.

Bohmer, C., and A. Parrot. 1993. *Sexual Assault on the College Campus: The Problem and the Solution.* Toronto: Maxwell Macmillan.

Bolaria, B. S., and H. D. Dickinson. 1994. *Health, Illness and Health Care in Canada.* 2nd ed. Toronto: Harcourt Brace and Company, Canada.

Bolger, N., A. DeLongis, R. C. Kessler, and E. Wethington. 1989. "The Contagion of Stress Across Multiple Roles." *Journal of Marriage and the Family* 51: 175–83.

Bottomore, T., L. Harris, and R. Miliband, (Eds.). 1983. *A Dictionary of Marxist Thought.* Cambridge, MA: Harvard University Press.

Bourgois, P. 1995. *In Search of Respect: Selling Crack in El Barrio.* Cambridge, UK: Cambridge University Press.

Bowermaster, J. 1993. "A Town Called Morrisonville." *Audubon*, 95 (July/August): 42–51.

Bowker, L. H. 1983. *Beating Wife-Beating.* Lexington, MA: Lexington.

Boyd, M., J. Goyder, F. Jones, H. McRoberts, P. Pineo, and J. Porter. 1985. *Ascription and Achievement.* Ottawa: Carleton University Press.

Boyd, N. 1988. *The Last Dance: Murder in Canada.* Toronto: Prentice Hall.

Boyd, N. 1991. *High Society: Legal and Illegal Drugs in Canada.* Toronto: Key Porter Books.

Boyd, N. 1995. "Legal and Illegal Drug Use in Canada." Pp. 361–379 in *Canadian Criminology: Perspectives on Crime and Criminality*, edited by M. A. Jackson and C. T. Griffiths. Toronto: Harcourt Brace.

Boyd, N., L. Elliott, and B. Gaucher. 1991. "Drug Use and Violence: Rethinking the Connections." *Journal of Human Justice* 3: 67–83.

Bradshaw, J., J. Ditch, H. Holmes, and P. Whitford. 1993. "A Comparative Study of Child Support in Fifteen Countries." *Journal of European Social Policy* 3: 255–271.

Brandt, A. M. 1985. *No Magic Bullet: A Social History of Venereal Disease in the United States Since 1880.* New York: Oxford University Press.

Brannen, J., G. Meszaros, P. Moss, and G. Poland. 1994. *Employment and Family Life: A Review of Research in the UK (1980–1994).* Sheffield: Employment Department.

Braun, E. 1995. *Futile Progress: Technology's Empty Promise.* London: Earthscan Publications Ltd.

Bread. 1992. "Poverty Amongst U.S. Children." *Bread for the World Newsletter* March, 3.

Breines, W., and L. Gordon. 1983. "The New Scholarship on Family Violence." *Signs: Journal of Women in Culture and Society* 8: 491–533.

Breslin, P. 1995. "The South Bronx Bounces Back." *Smithsonian* 26(1): 100–113.

Brickman, J., and J. Briere. 1984. "Incidence of Rape and Sexual Assault in an Urban Canadian Population." *International Journal of Women's Studies* 7: 195–206.

Brillon, Y. 1987. *Victimization and Fear of Crime Among the Elderly.* Toronto: Butterworths.

Brinkerhoff, M. and E. Lupri. 1988. "Interspousal Violence." *Canadian Journal of Sociology* 13: 407–434.

Brown, L. 1995. "Nature's Limits." Pp. 9–20 in *The State of the World*, edited by L. Brown Associates. Washington, DC: Worldwatch Institute.

Brown, L. 1996. "The Acceleration of History." Pp. 1–20 in *The State of the World*. Washington, DC: Worldwatch Institute.

Browne, A. 1987. *When Battered Women Kill.* New York: Free Press.

Browning, J. J., and D. G. Dutton. 1986. "Assessment of Wife Assault with the Conflict Tactics Scale: Using Couple Data to Quantify the Differential Reporting Effect." *Journal of Marriage and the Family* 48: 375–379.

Brownstein, H. H. 1996. *The Rise and Fall of a Violent Crime Wave: Crack Cocaine and the Social Construction of a Crime Problem.* New York: Harrow and Heston.

Bryant, B., and P. Mohai, (Eds.). 1992. *Race and the Incidence of Environmental Hazards.* Boulder, Co: Westview Press.

Bryant, C. D. 1972. *The Social Dimensions of Work.* Englewood Cliffs: Prentice Hall.

Brym, R. J., (Ed.). 1996. *Society in Question: Sociological Readings for the 21st Century.* Toronto: Harcourt Brace Canada.

Bureau of Labor Statistics. 1996. *Occupational Outlook Handbook.* Washington, DC: US Department of Labor.

Bureau of Labor Statistics. 1998a. "Employment Status of the Civilian Population by Race, Sex, Age, and Hispanic Origin." At http://stats. bls.gov/news.release/empsit.t02.htm.

Bureau of Labor Statistics. 1998b. "The Employment Situation." At http://www.bls. census.gov/cps/pub/empsit0498.htm, April.

Bureau of the Census. 1995a. "Sixty-five Plus in the United States." U.S. Department of Commerce Economics and Statistics Administration.

Bureau of the Census. 1995b. "Women in the United States: A Profile." July, U.S. Department of Commerce, Economics and Statistics Division.

Bureau of the Census. 1995c. "Women in the United States: A Profile." Statistical Brief SB/95–19RV: 2.

Bystydzienski, J. M. 1993. "Marriage and Family in the United States and Canada: A Comparison." *The American Review of Canadian Studies* 23: 565–82.

Canada. Department of the Environment. 1996. *The Life Cycle of the Hamburger.* Ottawa, Ontario: Government of Canada.

Canadian Council on Social Development. 1997. "Poverty Rates." Canadian Council on Social Development. At http://www.achilles.net/ ~council/fslic96.html.

Canadian Labour Congress. 1993. "National Day of Mourning for Workers Killed and Injured on the Job: Action Checklist for Local Unions and Labour Councils." Otttawa: CLC. Health, Safety and Environment Department.

Canadian Labour Congress. 1997. "Women's Work: A Report." Ottawa, Canada, March.

Canadian Labour Congress. 1993. "Fight for the Living, Mourn for the Dead." Ottawa: CLC, Health, Safety and Environment Department.

Canadian Press. 1996. "Don't Spank Your Children, Pediatric Society tells Parents." *Ottawa Citizen* 8 October, A2.

Cantor, B., N. L. Barrand, R. A. Dsonia, A. B. Cohen, and J. C. Merrill. 1991. "Datawatch." *Health Affairs* 10: 755–78.

Capek, S. 1993. "The 'Environmental Justice' Frame: A Conceptual Discussion and an Application." *Social Problems*, 40: 5–24.

Caringella-MacDonald, S., and D. Humphries. 1998. "Guest Editors' Introduction." *Violence Against Women* 4: 3–9.

Carleton University. 1997. "A Report to Senate on Strategic Restructuring from the Academic and Research Committee and Senate Academic Planning Committee." *This Week at Carleton,* 4 December: 1–4.

Carpenter, E. S. 1980. "Children's Health Care and the Changing Role of Women." *Medical Care* 18: 1208–18.

Carson, R. 1962. *The Silent Spring.* Greenwich, Conn: Fawcett.

Casper, L. M., S. S. McLanahan, and I. Garfinkel. 1994. "The Gender Poverty Gap: What We Can Learn from Other Countries." *American Sociological Review* 59: 594–605.

Caston, R. J. 1997. *Life in a Business-oriented Society: A Sociological Perspective.* Boston: Allyn and Bacon.

Cavazos, E. A., and G. Morino. 1995. *Cyber-Space and the Law: Your Rights and Duties in the On-Line World.* Cambridge, MA: MIT Press.

Chambliss, W. 1973. "The Saints and Roughnecks." *Society* 11: 22–31.

Chambliss, W., and R. Seidman. 1982. *Law, Order, and Power.* 2nd ed. Reading, MA: Addison-Wesley.

Chappell, N. 1995. "Health and Health Care." Pp. 11.1–11.21 in *New Society: Sociology for the 21st Century*, edited by R. J. Brym. Toronto: Harcourt Brace.

Chase-Lansdale, P. L., and J. Brooks-Gunn. 1995. *Escape form Poverty: What Makes a Difference for Children?* New York: Cambridge University Press.

Chein, I. 1966. "Narcotics Use Among Juveniles." Pp. 123–141 in *Narcotic Addiction*, edited by J. O'Donnell and J. Ball. New York: Harper and Row.

Chesney-Lind, M. 1995. "Girls, Delinquency, and Juvenile Justice: Toward a Feminist Theory of Young Women's Crime." Pp. 71–88 in *The Criminal Justice System and Women: Offenders, Victims and Workers.* 2nd ed. New York: McGraw-Hill.

Chidley, J. 1997. "Tales Out of School: Cheating Has Long Been a Great Temptation, and the Internet Makes it Easier Than Ever." *MacLean's* November 24: 76–79.

Children's Defense Fund. 1996. *The State of America's Children Yearbook 1996.* Washington, D.C.: Children's Defense Fund.

Chitwood, D. D., J. E. Rivers, and J. A. Inciardi, (Eds.). 1996. *The American Pipe Dream: Crack Cocaine and The Inner City.* New York: Harcourt Brace.

Clarke, J. 1990. *Health, Illness and Medicine in Canada.* Toronto: McClelland and Stewart.

Cleland, J. 1994. "Demographic Transition Theory." In *Population—The Complex Reality: A Report of the Population Summit of the World's Scientific Academies*, edited by F. Graham-Smith. Golden, CO: North American Press.

Clement, W., and J. Myles. 1994. *Relations of Ruling.* Montreal: McGill-Queens University Press.

Clinard, M., and P. Yeager. 1980. *Corporate Crime.* New York: Free Press.

Cloward, R., and L. Ohlin. 1960. *Delinquency and Opportunity: A Theory of Delinquent Gangs.* New York: Free Press.

Coburn, D. 1993. "Professional Powers in Decline: Medicine in a Changing Canada." Pp. 92–103 in *The Changing Medical Profession: An International Perspective*, edited by F. Hafferty, and J. McKinley. New York: Oxford University Press.

Cochran, J. K., and R. L. Akers. 1989. "Beyond Hellfire: An Exploration of the Variable Effects of Religiosity on Adolescent Marijuana and Alcohol Use." *Journal of Research on Crime and Delinquency* 26: 198–225.

Cohen, S. 1980. *Folk Devils and Moral Panics.* 2nd ed. Oxford: Basil Blackwell.

Cole, T. B. 1997. "Editor's Note." *Journal of the American Medical Association* 9 July. At http://www.ama-assn.org/sci-pubs/journals/archive/jama/vol278/no2/joc5b67a.htm.

Coleman, J. W., and D. R. Cressey. 1987. *Social Problems.* 3rd ed. New York: Harper and Row.

Comack, E. 1986. "We Will Get Some Good Out of This Riot Yet: The Canadian State, Drug Legislation and Class Conflict." Pp 67–90 in *The Social Basis of Law: Critical Readings in the Sociology of Law*, edited by S. Brickey and E. Comack. Toronto: Garamond.

Comack, E., and S. Brickey. 1991. "Theoretical Approaches in the Sociology of Law." Pp. 15–32 in *The Social Basis of Law: Critical Readings in the Sociology of Law*, edited by E. Comack and S. Brickey. Halifax: Garamond.

Commission for Racial Justice. 1987. *Toxic Waste and Race in the United States: A National Report on the Racial and Socioeconomic Characteristics of Communities With Hazardous Waste Sites.* New York: United Church of Christ.

Conference Board Inc. 1993. *Work-Family Policies: The New Strategic Plan.* Report No. 949. New York: The Conference Board Inc.

Congressional Budget Office. 1998. *The Economic and Budget Outlook: Fiscal Years 1999-2008: Projections of National Health Expenditures: 1997-2008*, Appendix H. At http://www.cbo.gov/showdoc.cfm?index=316&sequence=13. Washington, DC: Congressional Budget Office, U.S. Congress.

Connell, R. W. 1995. *Masculinities.* Berkeley: University of California Press.

Cook, T. D., and T. R. Curtin. 1987. "The Mainstream and the Underclass: Why are the Differences So Salient and the Similarities So Unobtrusive?" Pp. 217–264 in *Social Comparison, Social Justice, and Relative Deprivation*, edited by J. C. Masters and W. P. Smith. Hillsdale, NJ: Lawrence Erlbaum Associates.

Corin, E. 1994. "The Social and Cultural Matrix of Health and Disease." Pp. 93–132 in *Why Are Some People Healthy and Others Not?*, edited by R. G. Evans, M. L. Barer, and T. R. Marmor. New York: Aldine de Gruyter.

Corporate Crime Reporter. 1988. no title 11/88 ed. Washington DC: Corporate Crime Reporter.

Coser, L. W. 1977. *Masters of Sociological Thought: Ideas in Historical and Social Context.* 2nd ed. New York: Harcourt Brace Jovanovich.

Covich, A. 1993. "Water and Ecosystems." In *Water in Crisis: A Guide to the World's Freshwater Resources*, edited by P. H. Gleick. New York: Oxford University Press.

Crawford, M., and R. Gartner. 1992. *Woman Killing: Intimate Femicide in Ontario, 1974-1990.* Report prepared for the Women We Honour Action Committee and the Ontario Women's Directorate, Toronto.

Crichton, A. 1976. "The Shift from Entrepreneurial to Political Power in the Canadian Health Care System." *Social Science and Medicine* 10: 59–66.

Crutchfield, R. 1989. "Labor Stratification and Violent Crime." *Social Forces* 68: 589–612.

Crysdale, S. 1991. *Families Under Stress: Community, Work and Economic Change.* Toronto: Thompson Educational Publishing Inc.

Curran, D. J., and C. M. Renzett. 1994. *Theories of Crime.* Boston: Allyn and Bacon.

Curran, D. J., and C. M. Renzetti. 1993. *Social Problems: Society in Crisis.* 3rd ed. Boston: Allyn and Bacon.

Curran, D. J., and C. M. Renzetti. 1996. *Social Problems: Society in Crisis.* 4th ed. Boston: Allyn and Bacon.

Currie, D. H., and B. D. MacLean. 1994. "Preface." Pp. 5–6 in *Social Inequality, Social Justice: Selections from the 32nd Annual Meetings of the Western Association of Sociology and Anthropology*, edited by D. H. Currie and B. D. MacLean. Vancouver: Collective Press.

Currie, E. 1985. *Confronting Crime: An American Challenge.* New York: Pantheon.

Currie, E. 1992. "Retreatism, Minimalism, Realism: Three Styles of Reasoning on Crime and Drugs in the United States." Pp. 88–97 in *Realist Criminology: Crime Control and Policing in the 1990s*, edited by J. Lowman and B. D. MacLean. Toronto: University of Toronto Press.

Currie, E. 1993. *Reckoning: Drugs, the Cities and the American Future.* New York: Hill and Wang.

Curtis, J., and L. Tepperman. 1988. *Understanding Canadian Society.* Toronto: McGraw-Hill Ryerson.

Daly, K., and M. Chesney-Lind. 1988. "Feminism and Criminology." *Justice Quarterly* 5: 497–538.

Danziger, S., and P. Gottschalk. 1995. *America Unequal.* New York: Russell Sage Foundation.

Darling, L. 1997. "Dear Ravager: I've Never Done This Before..." *Esquire* 128(1): 40–45, 100–101.

Darwin, C. 1968. *The Origin of Species.* New York: Penguin.

Das Gupta, T. 1996. *Racism and Paid Work.* Toronto: Garamond.

Davis, K. 1937. "The Sociology of Prostitution." *American Sociological Review* 5: 523–535.

Davis, K. 1945. "The World Demographic Transition." *Annals of the American Academy of Political and Social Science*, 237: 1–11.

Davis, K., and M. Bernstram, (Eds.). 1991. *Resources, Environment and Population.* Toronto: Oxford University Press.

Deber, R., and G. Thompson. 1992. "Purchasing Hospital Capital Equipment: What Role for Technology Assessment?" Pp. 213–22 in *Restructuring Canada's Health Services System: How Do We Get There from Here?*, edited by R. Deber, and G. Thompson. Toronto: University of Toronto Press.

DeKeseredy, W. S. 1990. "Male Peer Support and Woman Abuse: The Current State of Knowledge." *Sociological Focus* 23: 129–139.

DeKeseredy, W. S. 1992. "In Defence of Self-Defence: Demystifying Female Violence Against Male Intimates." Pp. 245–252 in *Crosscurrents: Debates in Canadian Society*, edited by R. Hinch. Scarborough, ON: Nelson.

DeKeseredy, W. S. 1993. *Four Variations of Family Violence: A Review of Sociological Research.* Ottawa: National Clearinghouse on Family Violence, Health Canada.

DeKeseredy, W. S. 1996a. "The Canadian National Survey on Woman Abuse in University/ College Dating Relationships: Biofeminist Panic Transmission or Critical Inquiry." *Canadian Journal of Criminology* 38: 81–104.

DeKeseredy, W. S. 1996b. "Patterns of Family Violence." Pp. 249–272 in *Families: Changing Trends in Canada.* 2nd ed., edited by M. Baker. Toronto: McGraw-Hill Ryerson.

DeKeseredy, W. S. 1997a. "Guest Editor's Introduction." *Violence Against Women* 3: 563–565.

DeKeseredy, W. S. 1997b. "Measuring Sexual Abuse in Canadian University/College Dating Relationships: The Contribution of a National Representative Sample." Pp. 43–53 in *Researching Sexual Violence Against Women: Methodological and Personal Perspectives*, edited by M. D. Schwartz. Thousand Oaks, CA: Sage.

DeKeseredy, W. S. 1998. "The Anti–Feminist Backlash Against Woman Abuse Surveys: Some Canadian Examples." Paper presented at the annual meeting of the Academy of Criminal Justice Sciences, Albuquerque, NM.

DeKeseredy, W. S., H. Burshtyn, and C. Gordon. 1992. "Taking Woman Abuse Seriously: A Critical Response to the Solicitor General of Canada's Crime Prevention Advice." *International Review of Victimology* 2: 157–167.

DeKeseredy, W. S., and D. Ellis. 1988. "Sibling Violence: A Review of Canadian Sociological Research and Suggestions for Further Empirical Research." *Humanity and Society* 21: 397–411.

DeKeseredy, W. S., and C. Goff. 1992. "Corporate Violence Against Canadian Women: Assessing Left Realist Research and Policy." *Journal of Human Justice* 4: 55–70.

DeKeseredy, W. S., and R. Hinch. 1991. *Woman Abuse: Sociological Perspectives.* Toronto: Thompson Educational Publishing.

DeKeseredy, W. S., and R. Hinch. 1994. "Corporate Violence and Women's Health at Home and in the Workplace." Pp. 326–44 in *Health, Illness and Health Care in Canada.* 2nd ed., edited by B. S. Bolaria, and H. D. Dickinson. Toronto: Harcourt Brace Canada.

DeKeseredy, W. S., and K. Kelly. 1993a. "The Incidence and Prevalence of Woman Abuse in Canadian University and College Dating Relationships." *Canadian Journal of Sociology* 18: 137–159.

DeKeseredy, W. S., and K. Kelly. 1993b. "Woman Abuse in University and College Dating Relationships: The Contribution of the Ideology of Familial Patriarchy." *Journal of Human Justice* 4: 25–52.

DeKeseredy, W. S., and B. D. MacLean. 1990. "Researching Woman Abuse in Canada: A Left Realist Critique of the Conflict Tactics Scale." *Canadian Review of Social Policy* 25: 19–27.

DeKeseredy, W. S., and B. D. MacLean. 1998. "'But Women Do it Too': The Contexts and Nature of Female-to-Male Violence in Canadian Heterosexual Dating Relationships." Pp. 23–30 in *Unsettling Truths: Battered Women, Policy, Politics, and Contemporary Research in Canada*, edited by K. D. Bonnycastle and G. S. Rigakos. Vancouver: Collective Press.

DeKeseredy, W. S., and L. MacLeod. 1997. *Woman Abuse: A Sociological Story.* Toronto: Harcourt Brace.

DeKeseredy, W. S., D. G. Saunders, M. D. Schwartz, and S. Alvi. 1997. "The Meanings and Motives for Women's Use of Violence in Canadian College Dating Relationships: Results from a National Survey." *Sociological Spectrum* 17: 199–222.

DeKeseredy, W. S., and M. D. Schwartz. 1993. "Male Peer Support and Woman Abuse: An Expansion of DeKeseredy's Model." *Sociological Spectrum* 13: 393–414.

DeKeseredy, W. S., and M. D. Schwartz. 1996. *Contemporary Criminology.* Belmont, CA: Wadsworth.

DeKeseredy, W. S., and M. D. Schwartz. 1997. "How Does Woman Abuse Vary?: The Role of Male Peer Support, Region, Language and School Type." Paper presented at the annual meeting of the American Society of Criminology, San Diego, California.

DeKeseredy, W. S., and M. D. Schwartz. 1998a. *Woman Abuse on Campus:Results from the Canadian National Survey.* Thousand Oaks, CA: Sage.

DeKeseredy, W. S., and M. D. Schwartz. 1998b. "Measuring the Extent of Woman Abuse in

Intimate Heterosexual Relationships: A Critique of the Conflict Tactics Scales." U.S. Department of Justice Violence Against Women Grants Office Electronic Resources. At http://www.vaw.umn.edu/research.asp.

DeKeseredy, W. S., and M. D. Schwartz. 1998c. "Male Peer Support and Woman Abuse in Postsecondary School Courtship: Suggestions for New Directions in Sociological Research," Pp. 83–96 in *Issues in Intimate Violence*, edited by Raquel Kennedy Berge. Thousand Oaks, CA: Sage.

DeKeseredy, W. S., M. D. Schwartz, and K. Tait. 1993. "Sexual Assault and Stranger Aggression on a Canadian University Campus." *Sex Roles* 28: 263–277.

de Koninck, M. 1991. "Double Work and Women's Health." Pp. 235–41 in *Continuity and Change in Marriage and Family*, edited by J. Veevers. Toronto: Holt, Rinehart and Winston Canada.

de la Cour, L., and R. Sheinin. 1990. "The Ontario Medical College for Women, 1883 to 1906: Lessons from Gender Separatism in Medical Education." Pp. 112–20 in *Despite the Odds: Essays on Canadian Women and Science*, edited by M. Goszto nyi Ainley. Montreal: Vehicule Press.

Department of Indian Affairs and Northern Development. (1980). *Indian Conditions: A Survey*. Ottawa: Minister of Supply and Services.

Dery, M. 1996. *Escape Velocity: Cyberculture at the End of the Century*. New York: Grove Press.

Desroches, F. J. 1995. *Force and Fear: Robbery in Canada*. Scarborough, ON: Nelson.

Devine, J. A., and J. D. Wright. 1993. *The Greatest of Evils: Urban Poverty and the American Underclass*. New York: Aldine de Gruyter.

deWolff, A. 1994. *Strategies for Working Families*. Toronto, ON: Ontario Coalition for Better Child Care.

Dexter, L. A. 1958. "A Note on the Selective Inattention in Social Science." *Social Problems* 6: 176–182.

Dickinson, H. 1995. "Work and Unemployment as Social Issues." Pp. 296–317 in *Social Issues and Contradictions in Canadian Society*. 2nd ed., edited by B. S. Bolaria. Toronto: Harcourt Brace.

Dobash, R. E., and R. Dobash. 1979. *Violence Against Wives: A Case Against the Patriarchy*. New York: Free Press.

Dobash, R., R. E. Dobash, M. Wilson, and M. Daly. 1993. "The Myth of Sexual Symmetry in Marital Violence." *Social Problems* 39: 71–91.

Downes, D., and P. Rock. 1988. *Understanding Deviance: A Guide to the Sociology of Crime and Rule Breaking*. 2nd ed. New York: Oxford University Press.

Downey, D. B. 1995. "When Bigger is Not Better: Family Size, Parental Resources, and Children's Educational Performance." *American Sociological Review* 60: 746–61.

Doyal, L. 1995. *What Makes Women Sick? Gender and the Political Economy of Health*. London: McMillan.

Dreier, P., and E. Bernard. 1998. "Canada: A Kinder, Gentler Nation." Pp. 13–25 in *Solutions to Social Problems: Lessons from Other Societies*, edited by D. S. Eitzen and C. S. Leedham. Boston: Allyn and Bacon.

Drug Programs Reform Secretariat. 1992. "Summary of the Background Papers for Public Discussion." Ontario: Ministry of Health.

Duncan, G. J. 1984. *Years of Poverty, Years of Plenty: The Changing Economic Fortunes of American Workers and Families*. Ann Arbor, MI: Institute for Social Research, University of Michigan.

Durham, W. 1979. *Scarcity and Survival in Central America: The Ecological Origins of the Soccer War*. San Francisco: Freeman.

Durkheim, E. 1933. *The Division of Labour*. New York: Macmillan. (Originally published in 1893).

Durkheim, E. 1951. *Suicide*. Glencoe, ILL: Free Press (Originally published in 1897).

Duxbury, L., C. A. Higgins, and C. M. Lee. 1992. *Balancing Work and Family: a Study of Canadian Private Sector Employees*. London: University of Western Ontario.

Duxbury, L., C. Higgins, C. Lee, and S. Mills. 1992. "Time Spent in Paid Employment." *Optimum: The Journal of Public Sector Management* 23: 38–45.

Edelman, M. W. 1994. "Quotation". P. xxi in *Wasting America's Future: The Children's Defense Fund's Report on the Costs of Child Poverty*, written by A. Sherman. Boston: Beacon.

Edleson, J. L., and M. P. Brygger. 1986. "Gender Differences in Reporting of Battering Incidences." *Family Relations* 34: 377–382.

Ehrenreich, B. 1990. *Fear of Falling: The Inner Life of the Middle Class*. New York: HarperPerennial.

Ehrlich, P., and A. Ehrlich. 1991. *The Population Explosion*. New York: Simon and Schuster.

Eichler, M. 1988. *Families in Canada Today: Recent Changes and Their Policy Consequences*. 2nd ed. Toronto: Gage Educational Publishing.

Eichler, M. 1997. *Family Shifts: Families, Policies and Gender Equality*. Toronto: Oxford University Press.

Eigner, L. 1993. *Travels with Lizbeth: Three Years on the Road and on the Streets*. New York: St. Martin's Press.

Eitzen, D. S., and M. Bacca Zinn. 1994. *Social Problems*. 6th ed. Boston: Allyn and Bacon.

Eitzen, D. S., and M. Bacca Zinn. 1997. *Social Problems*. 7th ed. Boston: Allyn and Bacon.

Eitzen, D. S., and C. S. Leedham. 1998. "U.S. Social Problems in Comparative Perspective." Pp. 3–12 in *Solutions to Social Problems: Lessons from Other Societies*, edited by D. S. Eitzen and C. S. Leedham. Boston: Allyn and Bacon.

Eliany, M. 1994. "Alcohol and Drug Use." Pp. 407–414 in *Canadian Social Trends*, Volume 2, edited by Thompson Educational Publishing. Toronto: Thompson Educational Publishing.

Elliot, D., S. Odynak, and H. Krahn. 1992. "A Survey of Unwanted Sexual Experiences Among University of Alberta Students." Research Report prepared for the Council on Student Life, University of Alberta. Population Research Laboratory, University of Alberta.

Ellis, D. 1987. *The Wrong Stuff: An Introduction to the Sociological Study of Deviance*. Toronto: Collier Macmillan.

Ellis, D. 1995. *Spousal Violence: Who Hurts Whom, How Often and How Seriously?* North York, ON: LaMarsh Research Centre on Violence and Conflict Resolution, York University.

Ellis, D., and W. S. DeKeseredy. 1994. *Pre-Test Report on the Frequency, Severity and Patterning of Sibling Violence in Canadian Families: Causes and Consequences*. Ottawa: Health Canada.

Ellis, D., and W. S. DeKeseredy. 1996. *The Wrong Stuff: An Introduction to the Sociological Study of Deviance*. 2nd ed. Scarborough, ON: Allyn and Bacon.

Ellis, D., and W. S. DeKeseredy. 1997. "Rethinking Estrangement, Interventions, and Intimate Femicide." *Violence Against Women* 3: 590–609.

Ellis, D., and N. Stuckless. 1996. *Mediating and Negotiating Marital Conflicts*. Thousand Oaks, CA: Sage.

Embassy of Canada, 1997. "United States-Canada: The World's largest Trading Relationship." At http://www.cdnemb-washdc.org, March 22, 1999.

Engels, F. 1963. "Eulogy." Pp. 258–260 in *Marx's Concept of Man*, edited by E. Fromm. New York: Frederick Ungur.

Engels, F. 1975. *The Condition of the Working Class in England. Marx Engels Collected Works*, IV. London: Lawrence and Wishart.

Ensor, G. 1818. *An Inquiry Concerning the Population of Nations: Containing a Refutation of Mr. Malthus's Essay on Population*. London: Effingham Williamson.

Erickson, K. 1985. Foreword to A. Shklinyk, *A Poison Stronger Than Love*. New Haven, CT: Yale University Press.

Erikson, P. 1996. "The Selective Control of Drugs." Pp. 59–77 in *Social Control in Canada: Issues in the Social Construction of Deviance*, edited by B. Schissel and L. Mahood. Toronto: Oxford University Press.

Erikson, P., and G. Murray. 1989. "Sex Differences in Cocaine Use and Experiences: A Double Standard Revived?" *American Journal of Drug and Alcohol Abuse* 15: 135–152.

Eshleman, J. R. 1997. *The Family*. 8th ed. Boston: Allyn and Bacon.

Evans, J., and R. Chawla. 1990. "Work and Relative Poverty." *Perspectives on Labour and Income* (Summer): 33–43.

Evans, R. G., M. L. Barer, and C. Hertzman. 1991. "The 20 Year Experiment: Accounting for, Explaining and Evaluating Health Care Cost Containment in Canada and the United States." *Annual Review of Public Health* 12: 481–518.

Evans, R. G., M. Barer, and T. Marmor, (Eds.). 1994. *Why Are Some People Healthy and Others Not? The Determinants of the Health of Populations*. New York: Aldine de Gruyter.

Faludi, S. 1991. *Backlash: The Undeclared War Against American Women*. New York: Crown.

Faupel, C. E. 1996. "The Drugs-Crime Connection Among Stable Addicts." Pp. 180–188 in In Their Own Words, edited by P. Cromwell. Los Angeles: Roxbury.

Faure, G., and J. Rubin. 1993. "Water Resources: Some Introductory Observations." In Culture and Negotiation, edited by G. Faure, and J. Rubin. Thousand Oaks, CA: Sage.

Federal Bureau of Investigation. 1995. "1994 Crime Statistics." Bureau of Justice Statistics, National Institute of Justice. At http://www.ojp.usdog.gov/bjs/.

Federal Bureau of Investigation. 1996. "Victims Report 9 Percent Fewer Violent Crimes Last Year." Bureau of Justice Statistics, National Institute of Justice. At http://www.ojp.usdog.gov/bjs/.

Fekete, J. 1994. Moral Panic: Biopolitics Rising. Montreal: Robert Davies.

Feldman, D. C. 1996. "The Nature, Antecedents and Consequences of Underemployment." Journal of Management 22: 385–407.

Felson, M. 1994. Crime and Everyday Life. Thousand Oaks, CA: Pine Forge Press.

Ferguson, I. 1996. "A Preliminary Investigation into Offensive and Illegal Content on the Internet: Deviant Criminal Pornography." Report prepared for Scott Clark, Principle Researcher, Criminal Law and Young Offenders Unit, Research, Statistics, and Evaluation Directorate, Department of Justice Canada. Ottawa: Justice Canada.

Findlay, D. A., and L. J. Miller. 1995. "Through Medical Eyes: The Medicalization of Women's Bodies and Women's Lives." Pp. 276–306 in Health, Illness and Health Care in Canada. 2nd ed., edited by B. S. Bolaria, and H. D. Dickinson. Toronto: Harcourt Brace and Company Canada.

FIND/SVP. 1995. The American Internet User Survey. December. Researched and developed by FIND/SVP, presented in association with HSF Consulting and C+C Data, Inc., and sponsored by thirty major companies with diverse interests in the Internet.

Finkelman, L. 1992. Report of the Survey of Unwanted Sexual Experiences Among Students of U.N.B.-F. and S.T.U. Fredericton, NB: University of New Brunswick Counselling Services.

Finnie, R. 1993. "Women, Men and the Economic Consequences of Divorce: Evidence from Canadian Longitudinal Data." Canadian Review of Sociology and Anthropology 30: 205–41.

Fischer, C. S., M. Hout, M. Sanchez Jankowski, S. R. Lucas, A. Swidler, and K. Voss. 1996. Inequality by Design: Cracking the Bell Curve Myth. Princeton, NJ: Princeton University Press.

Fitzpatrick, D., and C. Halliday. 1992. Not the Way to Love: Violence Against Young Women in Dating Relationships. Amherst, NS: Cumberland County Transition House Association.

Fitzpatrick, K., M. LaGory, and F. Fitchey. 1993. "Criminal Victimization Among the Homeless." Justice Quarterly 10: 353–368.

Flavin, C. 1996. "Facing Up to the Risks of Climatic Change." Pages 21–39 in The State of The World, Washington, DC: Worldwatch Institute.

Foot, D. K. 1996. Boom, Bust, and Echo. Toronto: Macfarlane, Walter and Ross.

Forcese, D. 1997. The Canadian Class Structure. 4th ed. Toronto: McGraw-Hill Ryerson.

Fox, A. 1980. "The Meaning of Work." Pp. 139–91 in The Politics of Work and Occupations, edited by G. Esland, and G. Salaman. Toronto: University of Toronto Press.

Fox, B. 1995. "The Family." Pp. 9.1–9.29 in New Society: Sociology for the 21st Century, edited by R. J. Brym. Toronto: Harcourt Brace.

Fox, B. 1997. "Another View of the Sociology of the Family in Canada." Canadian Review of Sociology and Anthropology 34: 93–99.

Frank, J. W., and J. F. Mustard. 1995. "The Determinants of Health from a Historical Perspective." Daedalus (Fall), 123.

Frank, N., and M. J. Lynch. 1992. Corporate Crime, Corporate Violence: A Primer. New York: Harrow and Heston.

Franklin, R. S. 1991. Shadows of Race and Class. Minneapolis: University of Minnesota Press.

Freund, P. E. S., and M. B. McGuire. 1995. Health, Illness and the Social Body: A Critical Sociology. 2nd ed. New Jersey: Prentice Hall.

Frone, M. R., M. Russell, and M. L. Cooper. 1991. "Relationship of Work and Family Stressors to Psychological Distress: The Independent Moderating Influence of Social Support, Mastery, Active Coping, and Self-focused Attention." Journal of Social Behaviour and Personality 6: 227–50.

Fry, J., (Ed.). 1984. *Contradictions in Canadian Society.* Toronto: John Wiley and Sons.

Fulton, J. 1993. *Canada's Health Care System: Bordering on the Possible.* Washington, DC: Faulkner and Gray.

Furstenberg, F. F., Jr. 1993. "How Families Manage Risk and Opportunity in Dangerous Neighborhoods." Pp. 231–258 in *Sociology and the Public Agenda*, edited by W. J. Wilson. Newbury Park, CA: Sage.

Gabor, T., M. Baril, M. Cusson, D. Elie, M. Leblanc, and A. Normadeau. 1987. *Armed Robbery: Cops, Robbers, and Victims.* Springfield: Charles C. Thomas.

Gaillard, A. W. K., and C. J. E. Wientjes. 1994. "Mental Load and Work Stress as Two Types of Energy Mobilization." *Work and Stress* 8: 141–52.

Galinsky, E., D. Hughes, and J. David. 1990. "Trends in Corporate Family-supportive Policies." *Marriage and Family Review* 15: 75–95.

Gallagher, C. 1994. *American Ground Zero: The Secret Nuclear War.* New York: Random House.

Galloway, G. 1996. "Job Hazards Being Kept Secret, CLC Head Charges." *Ottawa Citizen* 8 October, C8.

Garabino, J., and K. Kostelny. 1994. "Family Support and Community Development." Pp. 32–68 in *Putting Families First*, edited by S. Kagan and B. Weissbourd. San Francisco: Jossey-Bass.

Gartner, R. 1995. "Homicide in Canada." Pp. 186–222 in *Violence in Canada: Sociopolitical Perspectives*, edited by J. I. Ross. Toronto: Oxford University Press.

Gartner, R., and A. N. Doob. 1994. *Trends in Criminal Victimization: 1988-1993.* Ottawa: Canadian Centre for Justice Statistics.

Gee, E. M. 1992. "Only Children as Adult Women: Life Course Events and Timing." *Social Indicators Research* 26: 183–97.

Gelles, R. J. 1980. "Violence in the Family: A Review of Research in the Seventies." *Journal of Marriage and the Family* 42: 873–885.

Gelles, R. J., and C. P. Cornell. 1985. *Intimate Violence in Families.* Beverly Hills: Sage.

Gelles, R. J., and M. A. Straus. 1988. *Intimate Violence: The Causes and Consequences of Abuse in the American Family.* New York: Simon and Schuster.

Gerth, H., and C. W. Mills. 1959. *From Max Weber.* London: Routledge.

Gibbons, D. 1995. "Unfit for Human Consumption: The Problem of Flawed Writing in Criminal Justice and What to Do About It." *Crime and Delinquency* 41: 246–266.

Gilliomm, J. 1994. *Surveillance, Privacy and the Law: Employee Drug Testing and the Politics of Social Control.* Ann Arbor: University of Michigan Press.

Gilpin, A. 1977. *Dictionary of Economic Terms.* London: Butterworths.

Ginchild-Abeje, R. 1996. "Grappling with the Net: The Need for Universal Access." *Third Force Magazine* (July/August). At http://www.digitalsojourn.org/profiles/access.html.

Gladwell, M. 1986. "A New Addiction to an Old Story." *Insight* (October, 27): 8–12.

Glaser, W. 1991. "Paying the Hospital: American Problems and Foreign Solutions." *International Journal of Health Services* 21: 389–99.

Glass, B. L. 1988. "A Rational Choice Model of Wives' Employment Decisions." *Sociological Spectrum* 8: 35–48.

Glass, J. L., and S. B. Estes. 1997. "The Family Responsive Workplace." *Annual Review of Sociology* 23: 289–313.

Gleick, P. H. (Ed.) 1993. *Water in Crisis: A Guide to the World's Fresh Water Resources.* New York: Oxford University Press.

Glick, P. C., and A. J. Norton. 1980. "Marriage and Married People." Pp. 307–21 in *Family in Transition.* 3rd ed., edited by A. Skolnick, and J. H. Skolnick. Boston, MA: Little, Brown and Company.

Goffman, E. 1961. *Asylums: Essays on the Social Situation of Mental Patients and Other Inmates.* New York: Anchor.

Gold, D., C. Lo, and E. O. Wright. 1975. "Recent Developments in Marxist Theories of the Capitalist State." *Monthly Review* 27: 29–51.

Golden, R. 1997. *Disposable Children: America's Child Welfare System.* 1st ed. Belmont, CA: Wadsworth.

Goldstein, P. J., H. H. Brownstein, P. J. Ryan, and P. A. Bellucci. 1989. "Crack and Homicide in New York City, 1988: A Conceptually Based Event Analysis." *Contemporary Drug Problems* (Winter): 651–687.

Gonick, C. 1978. *Out of Work.* Toronto: James Lorimer and Company.

Gonyea, J. G., and B. K. Googins. 1997. "The Restructuring of Work and Family in the United States: A New Challenge for American Corporations." Pp. 63–78 in *The Work Family Challenge: Rethinking Employment*, edited by S. Lewis, and J. Lewis. London: Sage.

Goode, E. 1989. *Drugs in American Society.* 3rd ed. New York: Knopf.

Goode, E. 1994. *Deviant Behavior.* Englewood Cliffs, NJ: Prentice-Hall.

Goodwin, L. 1969. *Do the Poor Want to Work?* Washington, D.C.: The Brookings Institution.

Gordon, D., R. Edwards, and M. Reich. 1982. *Segmented Work, Divided Workers.* New York: Cambridge University Press.

Gordon, M., and P. Berger. 1996. "Public Debate on Private Medicine: Response." *Canadian Medical Association Journal* 155: 1662–63.

Gortmaker, S. L., and P. H. Wise. 1997. "The First Injustice: Socioeconomic Disparities, Health Services Technology, and Infant Mortality." *Annual Review of Sociology* 23: 147–171.

Goulding, M. 1993. "Hooded Forests of the Amazon." *Scientific American* (March).

Graham-Smith, F. (Ed.) 1994. *Population—The Complex Reality: A Report of the Population Summit of the World's Scientific Academies.* Golden, Co: North American Press.

Grant, S., and J. Barling. 1994. "Linking Unemployment Experiences, Depressive Symptoms, and Marital Functioning: A Mediational Model." Pp. 311–27 in *Job Stress in a Changing Workforce*, edited by G. P. Keita, and J. J. Hurrell. Washington, DC: American Psychological Society.

Gray, G., and N. Guppy. 1994. *Successful Surveys.* Toronto: Harcourt Brace.

Grayson, J. P. 1983. "Shutdown Canada." Pp. 285–90 in *Working Canadians: Readings in the Sociology of Work and Industry*, edited by G. S. Lowe, and H. J. Krahn. Toronto: Methuen.

Greenaway, N. 1997. "Activists Celebrate Land-Mines Ban: Delegates Gather in Ottawa for Treaty Signing." *Ottawa Citizen* 2 December, A3.

Greenberg, D., (Ed.). 1981. *Crime and Capitalism: Readings in a Marxist Criminology.* Palo Alto, CA: Mayfield.

Greenhaus, J., and N. Beutell. 1985. "Sources of Conflict Between Work and Family Roles." *Academy of Management Review* 10: 76–88.

Greenstein, R. 1985. "Losing Faith in 'Losing Ground'." *New Republic* (March 25): 12–17.

Greider, W. 1994. "Why the Mighty GE Can't Strike Out." *Rolling Stone* (April 21): 36.

Grescoe, P. 1972. "We Asked You Six Questions." *Canadian Magazine* (April 28): 12–14.

Gronau. A. 1985. "Women and Images: Feminist Analysis of Pornography." Pp. 48–62 in *Women Against Censorship*, edited by C. Vance and V. Burstyn. Toronto: Douglas and McIntyre.

GSS. 1994. "General Social Survey." Unpublished data, Statistics Canada.

Gubrium, J., and J. Holstein. 1990. *What is a Family?* Mountain View, CA: Mayfield.

Gurr, T. R. 1995. "Foreword." Pp. viii–xvii in *Violence in Canada: Sociopolitical Perspectives*, edited by J. I. Ross. Toronto: Oxford University Press.

Gutierres, S. E., D. S. Saenz, and B. L. Green. 1994. "Job Stress and Health Outcomes Among White and Hispanic Employees: A Test of the Person-Environment Fit Model." Pp. 107–25 in *Job Stress in a Changing Workforce*, edited by G. Puryear Keita, and J. Hurrell. Washington: American Psychological Association.

Gwyn, R. 1997. *The Power of the Market.* Toronto: The Toronto Star.

Haas, L., and P. Hwang. 1995. "Corporate Culture and Men's Use of Family Leave Benefits in Sweden." *Family Coordinator* 44: 28–36.

Hagan, F. 1993. *Research Methods in Criminal Justice and Criminology.* 3rd ed. New York: Macmillan.

Hagan, J. 1985. *Modern Criminology: Crime, Criminal Behaviour, and Its Control.* Toronto: McGraw-Hill.

Hagan, J. 1994. *Crime and Disrepute.* Thousand Oaks, CA: Pine Forge Press.

Hagedorn, J. 1994. "Homeboys, Dope Fiends, Legits, and New Jacks." *Criminology* 32: 197–220.

Hajnal, Z. L. 1995. "The Nature of Concentrated Urban Poverty in Canada and the United States." *Canadian Journal of Sociology* 20: 497–556.

Hale, S. 1995. *Controversies in Sociology.* Toronto: Copp Clark Ltd.

Hall, E., and P. Flannery. 1984. "Prevalence and Correlates of Sexual Assault Experiences in Adolescents." *Victimology* 9: 398–406.

Hallowell, L., and R. I. Meshbesher. 1977. "Sports Violence and the Criminal Law." *Trial* 13: 27–32.

Hamilton, W. 1997. "Busted: How I Became a Criminal." *Ottawa Citizen* 25 January, B1–B3.

Hampton, R. L., P. Jenkins, and T. P. Gullotta, (Eds.). 1996. *Preventing Violence in America.* Thousand Oaks, CA: Sage.

Handy, C. 1984. *The Future of Work.* Worcester: Basil Blackwell.

Hanmer, J., and S. Saunders. 1984. *Well-Founded Fear: A Community Study of Violence to Women.* London: Hutchinson.

Hanson, G., and P. Venturelli. 1995. *Drugs and Society.* 4th ed. Boston: Jones and Bartlett.

Hardert, R. A., Gordon, L., Laner, M., and Reader, M. 1984. *Confronting Social Problems.* San Francisco: West.

Hardin, G. 1968. "The Tragedy of the Commons." *Science,* 162: 1243–1248.

Harding, J. 1986. "Mood Modifiers and Elderly Women in Canada: The Medicalization of Poverty." Pp. 51–86 in *Adverse Effects: Women and the Pharmaceutical Industry*, edited by K. McDonnell. Toronto: Women's Educational Press.

Hareven, T. 1982. "American Families in Transition: Historical Perspectives on Change." in *Normal Family Processes*, edited by F. Walsh. New York: Guilford Press.

Harman, L. D. 1989. *When a Hostel Becomes a Home: Experiences of Women.* Toronto: Garamond.

Harmon, P. A., and J. V. P. Check. 1989. *The Role of Pornography in Woman Abuse.* North York, ON: LaMarsh Research Programme on Violence and Conflict Resolution, York University.

Harris, L., and A. F. Westin. 1990. *The Equifax Report on Consumers in the Information Age.* Atlanta, GA: Equifax Inc.

Harris, L., and A. F. Westin. 1992. *Harris-Equifax Consumer Privacy Survey.* Atlanta, GA: Equifax Inc.

Harrison, T., and H. Krahn. 1995. "Populism and the Rise of the Reform Party in Alberta." *Canadian Review of Sociology and Anthropology* 32: 25–53.

Haveman, R. H. 1987. *Poverty Policy and Poverty Research: The Great Society and the Social Sciences.* Madison, WI: University of Wisconsin Press.

Hawken, P. 1994. *The Ecology of Commerce: How Business Can Save the Planet.* Toronto: Harper-Collins.

Hayford, A., and S. Crysdale. 1994. "Families Under Stress: Community, Work and Economic Change." *Journal of Comparitive Family Studies* 25: 426–27.

Haysom, I. 1997. "America's Formidable Enemy Within: When the Underclass Has Had Enough, the Result Will Resemble Civil War." *The Ottawa Citizen,* 23 February, A4.

Health Information Division. 1993. *Economic Burden of Illness in Canada, 1993.* Ottawa: Health Canada, Health Protection Branch.

Hecht, S. 1992. "Development or Destruction? The Livestock Sector in Latin America." In *Development or Destruction: The Conversion of Tropical Forest to Pasture in Latin America*, edited by H. Pearson. Colorado: Westview.

Hecht, S. 1996. "Witness Statement." McLibel Case. Presented in court on February 21st.

Henslin, J. 1994. *Social Problems.* 3rd ed. Englewood Cliffs, NJ: Prentice Hall.

Henslin, J. M., and A. Nelson. 1997. *Essentials of Sociology: A Down to Earth Approach.* Scarborough, ON: Prentice-Hall Canada.

Herek, G. M., and E. K. Glunt. 1995. "An Epidemic of Stigma: Public Reaction to AIDS." Pp. 25–36 in *AIDS: Readings on a Global Crisis*, edited by E. R. Bethel. Boston: Allyn and Bacon.

Herrnstein, R. J., and C. Murray. 1994. *The Bell Curve: Intelligence and Class Structure in American Life.* New York: Free Press.

Hewitt, D. G. Vinje, and P. Macniel. 1997. "Young Canadians' Alcohol and Other Drug Use: Increasing Our Understanding." Executive Summary of a report prepared for Health Canada. Canadian Centre on Substance Abuse. At http://www.ccsa.ca/horiz3e.htm.

Hewlett, S. 1991. *When the Bough Breaks: The High Cost of Neglecting Our Children.* New York: Basic Books.

Hibbard, J. H., and C. R. Pope. 1993. "The Equality of Social Roles as Predictors of Morbidity and Mortality." *Social Science and Medicine* 36: 217–25.

Hill, G. B. 1978. "Preventive Strategy and Problems of Intervention." *Canadian Journal of Public Health* 69: 191–96.

Hills, S., and R. Santiago. 1992. *Tragic Magic: The Life and Crimes of a Heroin Addict.* Chicago: Nelson-Hall.

Hinch, R. 1992. "Conflict and Marxist Theories." Pp. 267–291 in *Criminology: A Canadian Perspective*, edited by R. Linden. Toronto: Harcourt Brace Jovanovich.

Hinch, R. 1994. "Introduction: Theoretical Diversity." Pp. 1–26 in *Readings in Critical Criminology*, edited by R. Hinch. Scarborough, ON: Prentice Hall.

Hirschi, T. 1969. *Causes of Delinquency.* Berkeley, CA: University of California Press.

Hobbes, T. 1965. *Leviathan.* Toronto: Penguin. Originally published in 1651.

Hochschild, A. R. 1989. *The Second Shift.* New York: Viking.

Hochschild, A. R. 1997. *The Time Bind: When Work Becomes Home and Home Becomes Work.* New York: Metropolitan Books.

Holmes, R. M., and S. T. Holmes. 1994. *Murder in America.* Thousand Oaks, CA: Sage.

Homer-Dixon, T. 1991. "On the Threshold: Environmental Changes as Causes of Acute Conflict." *International Security*, 16: 70–116.

Hornosty, J. M. 1996. "A Look at Faculty Fears and Needed University Policies Against Violence and Harassment. Pp. 31–56 in *Violence: A Collective Responsibility*, edited by C. Stark-Adamec. Ottawa: Social Science Federation of Canada.

Hornung, C., B. McCullough, and T. Sugimoto. 1981. "Status Relationships in Marriage: Risk Factors in Spouse Abuse." *Journal of Marriage and the Family* 43: 675–692.

Hotaling, G. T., and D. B. Sugarman. 1986. "An Analysis of Risk Markers and Husband to Wife Violence." *Violence and Victims* 1: 101–124.

Howell, J. C., B. Krisberg, J. D. Hawkins, and J. J. Wilson, (Eds.). 1995. *A Sourcebook: Serious, Violent, and Chronic Juvenile Offenders.* Thousand Oaks, CA: Sage.

Hughes, B. 1985. *World Futures: A Critical Analysis of Alternatives.* Baltimore: Johns Hopkins University Press.

Humphries, D. 1993. "Crack Mothers, Drug Wars, and the Politics of Resentment." Pp. 31–48 in *Political Crime in Contemporary America*, edited by K. D. Tunnell. New York: Garland.

Hurst, C. E. 1995. *Social Inequality: Forms, Causes, and Consequences.* 2nd ed. Boston: Allyn and Bacon.

Huston, A., V. McLoyd, and C. G. Coll. 1994. "Children and Poverty: Issues in Contemporary Rsearch." *Child Development* 65: 275–276.

Illich, I. 1976. *Medical Nemesis: The Expropriation of Health.* New York: Pantheon.

Inciardi, J. A. 1992. *The War on Drugs II: The Continuing Epic of Heroin, Cocaine, Crack, Crime, AIDS and Public Policy.* Palo Alto, CA: Mayfield.

Inciardi, J. A. 1993. "Kingrats, Chicken Heads, Slow Necks, Freaks, and Blood Suckers: A Glimpse at the Miami Sex-for-Crack Market." Pp. 37–68 in *Crack Pipe as Pimp: An Ethnographic Investigation of Sex-For-Crack Exchanges*, edited by M. S. Ratner. New York: Lexington.

Inciardi, J. A., D. Lockwood, and A. E. Pottieger. 1993. *Women and Crack-Cocaine.* New York: Macmillan.

Inciardi, J. A., H. L. Surratt, D. D. Chitwood, and C. B. McCoy. 1996. "The Origins of Crack." Pp. 1–14 in *The American Pipe Dream: Crack Cocaine and The Inner City*, edited by D. D. Chitwood, J. A. Rivers, and J. A. Inciardi. New York: Harcourt Brace.

International Labour Organization. 1993. *World Labour Report.* Geneva: International Labour Office.

International Monetary Fund. 1990. *Government Finance Statistics Yearbook 1990.* Washington, D.C.: International Monetary Fund.

Irwin, J., and J. Austin. 1994. *It's About Time: America's Imprisonment Binge.* Belmont, CA: Sage.

Jackson, S. E., S. Zedeck, and E. Summers. 1985. "Family Life Disruptions: Effects of Job-induced Structural and Emotional Interference." *Academy of Management Journal* 28: 574–86.

Jaggar, A. 1983. *Feminist Politics and Human Nature.* Totowa, NJ: Roman and Littlefield.

Jecker, N. S. 1994. "Can an Employer Based Health Insurance System be Just?" Pp. 259–75 in *The Politics of Health Care Reform*, edited by J. S. Morone, and G. S. Belkin. Durham: Duke University Press.

Jensen, R. 1996. "Knowing Pornography." *Violence Against Women* 2: 82–102.

Joffe, J. 1997. "The Secret of U.S. World Domination." *Foreign Affairs Journal*, 4: 4–15.

Johnson, H. 1996a. *Violent Crime in Canada*. Ottawa: Canadian Centre for Justice Statistics.

Johnson, H. 1996b. *Dangerous Domains: Violence Against Women in Canada*. Scarborough, ON: Nelson.

Johnson, R., and H. Toch, (Eds.). 1982. *The Pains of Imprisonment*. Beverly Hills, CA: Sage.

Jones, A., and M. Butler. 1980. "A Role Transition Approach to the Stresses of Organizationally-Induced Family Role Disruption." *Journal of Marriage and the Family* 42: 367–376.

Jones, B. 1982. *Sleepers Wake*. Brighton: Wheatsheaf Books.

Jones, B. J., B. J. Gallagher III, and J. A. McFalls Jr. 1988. *Social Problems: Issues, Opinions, and Solutions*. New York: McGraw-Hill.

Jones, T., B. D. MacLean, and J. Young. 1986. *The Islington Crime Survey*. Aldershot, UK: Gower.

Jouriles, E. N., and K. N. O'Leary. 1985. "Interspousal Reliability of Reports of Marital Violence." *Journal of Consulting and Clinical Psychology* 53: 419–421.

Kalish, C. B. 1988. *International Crime Rates: Special Report*. Washington, D.C.: U.S. Department of Justice, Bureau of Justice Statistics.

Kanter, R. 1977. *Work and Family in the United States: A Critical Review and Agenda for Research and Policy*. New York, NY: Sage Publications.

Kaplan, J. 1983. *The Hardest Drug: Heroin and Public Policy*. Chicago: University of Chicago Press.

Kaplan, R. 1994. "The Coming Anarchy." *The Atlantic Monthly* (February): 44–76.

Kaplan, R. 1997. "History Moving North." *The Atlantic Monthly* (February): 34–44.

Kappeler, V. E., M. Blumberg, and G. W. Potter. 1993. *The Mythology of Crime and Criminal Justice*. Prospects Heights, IL: Waveland Press.

Kappeler, V. E., M. Blumberg, and G. W. Potter. 1996. *The Mythology of Crime and Criminal Justice*. 2nd ed. Prospect Heights, IL: Waveland Press.

Karasek, R., and T. Theorell. 1990. *Healthy Work: Stress, Productivity and the Reconstruction of Working Life*. New York: Basic Books.

Karmen, A. 1996. *Crime Victims*. 3rd ed. Belmont, CA: Wadsworth.

Kasarda, J. D. 1992. "The Severely Distressed in Economically Transforming Cities." Pp. 45–98 in *Drugs, Crime, and Social Isolation: Barriers to Urban Opportunity*, edited by A. V. Harrell and G. E. Peterson. Washington, D.C.: Urban Institute Press.

Katz, L. 1978. "Work: It's More Dangerous for Public Employees." *The Public Employee* 1:6.

Katz, M. B. 1975. *The People of Hamilton, Canada West*. Cambridge, MA: Harvard University Press.

Kaufman Kantor, G., and M. A. Straus. 1990. "The 'Drunken Bum' Theory of Wife Battering." Pp. 203–224 in *Physical Violence in American Families: Risk Factors and Adaptations to Violence in 8,145 Families*, edited by M. A. Straus and R. J. Gelles. New Brunswick, NJ: Transaction.

Kelly, K. 1991. "Visible Minorities: A Diverse Group." Statistics Canada. At http://www.statcan.ca/Documents/English/SocTrends/vismin.html.

Kelly, K. D., and W. S. DeKeseredy. 1994. "Women's Fear of Crime and Abuse in College and University Dating Relationships." *Violence and Victims* 9: 17–30.

Kelly, L. 1988. *Surviving Sexual Violence*. Minneapolis: University of Minnesota Press.

Kennedy, L., and D. G. Dutton. 1989. "The Incidence of Wife Assault in Alberta." *Canadian Journal of Behavioural Science* 21: 40–54.

Keyfitz, N. 1972. "Population Theory and Doctrine: A Historical Survey." Pp. 41–69 in *Readings in Population*, edited by W. Peterson. New York: Macmillan.

Keyfitz, N., and K. Lindahl-Kiessling. 1994. "Inequality and Population Growth." Pp. 32–46 in *Population—The Complex Reality: A Report of the World's Scientific Academies*, edited by F. Graham-Smith. Golden, Co: North American Press.

King, P. 1993. "Helping Women Helping Children: Drug Policy and Future Generations." Pp. 291–318 in *Confronting Drug Policy: Illicit Drugs in a Free Society*, edited by R. Bayer and G. Oppenheimer. New York: Cambridge University Press.

Kinsella, W. 1994. *Web of Hate: Inside Canada's Far Right Network*. Toronto: HarperCollins.

Kipelman, R., J. Greenhaus, and T. Connolly. 1983. "A Model of Work, Family and Interrole Conflict: A Construct Validation Study." *Organizational Behavior and Human Performance* 32: 198–215.

Kirchmeyer, C. 1992. "Perceptions of Nonwork to Work Spillover: Challenging the Common View of Conflict-ridden Domain Relationships." *Basic and Applied Social Psychology* 13: 231–49.

Kirkey, S. 1997. "There's No Place Like Work: Parents Flee to Office to Escape Children's Cries for Time and Attention." *Ottawa Citizen's Weekly* (June 22): 11.

Kirkwood, C. 1993. *Leaving Abusive Partners: From the Scars of Survival to the Wisdom for Change*. Newbury Park, CA: Sage.

Klein, N. 1997. "McLibel Trial Deep-fries Image of Fast Food Giant." *The Toronto Star*, 16 June.

Koenig, D. J. 1996. "Conventional Crime." Pp. 385–422 in *Criminology: A Canadian Perspective*. 3rd ed., edited by R. Linden. Toronto: Harcourt Brace.

Kolzon, J. 1997. "Foreward." Pp. ix–x in *Disposable Children: America's Child Welfare System*, written by R. Golden. Belmont, CA: Wadsworth.

Kopelman, R., J. Greenhaus, and T. Connolly. 1983. "A Model of Work, Family and Interrole Conflict: A Construct Validation Study." *Organizational Behaviour and Human Performance* 32: 198–215.

Kornblum, W., and J. Julian. 1995. *Social Problems*. Englewood Cliffs, New Jersey: Prentice-Hall.

Kornblum W. 1997. *Sociology in a Changing World*. 4th ed. New York: Harcourt Brace.

Koss, M. P. 1989. "Hidden Rape: Sexual Aggression and Victimization in a National Sample of Students in Higher Education." Pp. 145–168 in *Violence in Dating Relationships: Emerging Social Issues*, edited by M. A. Pirog-Good and J. E. Stets. New York: Praeger.

Kurz, D. 1993. "Physical Assaults by Husbands: A Major Social Problem." Pp. 88–103 in *Current Controversies on Family Violence*, edited by R. J. Gelles and D. R. Loseke. Newbury Park, CA: Sage.

LaBeff, E. E., R. E. Clark, V. J. Haines, and G. M. Diekhoff. 1995. "Situational Ethics and College Student Cheating." Pp. 331–336 in *Readings in Deviant Behavior*, edited by A. Thio and T. Calhoun. New York: HarperCollins.

Labour Canada. 1998. "Historical Summary of Occupational Injuries and Their Cost: Canada 1970–1995." At http://info.load-otea.hrdc-drhc.gc.ca/~oshweb/oicc9195/table1e.htm. Ottawa: Human Resources Development Canada.

Lappe, F. M., and Schurman, R. 1990. *Taking Population Seriously*. San Francisco: The Institute for Food and Development Policy.

LaPrairie, C. 1995. "Seen But not Heard: Native People in Four Canadian Inner Cities." *Journal of Human Justice* 6: 30–45.

Lasch, C. 1977. *Haven in a Heartless World: The Family Besieged*. New York: Basic Books.

Lauer, R. H. 1998. *Social Problems and the Quality of Life*. 7th ed. Boston: McGraw-Hill.

Laxer, G. 1989. *Open for Business: The Roots of Foreign Ownership in Canada*. Toronto: Oxford University Press.

Laxer, J. 1993. *False God: How the Globalization Myth has Impoverished Canada*. Toronto: Lester.

Lea, J., and J. Young. 1984. *What Is to Be Done About Law and Order*. New York: Penguin.

Ledwitz-Rigby, F. 1993. "An Administrative Approach to Personal Safety on Campus: The Role of the President's Advisory Committee on Woman's Safety on Campus." *Journal of Human Justice* 4: 85–94.

Lemert, E. 1951. *Social Pathology*. New York: McGraw-Hill.

Lero, D. S., and L. M. Brockman. 1993. "Single Parent Families in Canada: A Closer Look." Pp. 98–107 in *Single Parent Families: Perspectives on Reserach and Policy*, edited by J. Hudson, and B. Galaway. Toronto: Thompson Educational Press.

Leroux, T. G., and M. Petrunik. 1989. "The Construction of Elder Abuse as a Social Problem: A Canadian Perspective." Paper presented at the annual meeting of the Society for the Study of Social Problems, Berkeley, CA.

Levinson, D. 1989. *Family Violence in Cross-Cultural Perspective*. Newbury Park, CA: Sage.

Lewis, O. 1966. "The Culture of Poverty." *Scientific American* (October): 19–25.

Lewis, S. 1997. "Rethinking Employment: An Organizational Culture Change Framework." Pp. 1–19 in *The Work Family Challenge: Rethinking Employment*, edited by S. Lewis, and J. Lewis. London: Sage Publications.

Lewis, S., and J. Lewis, (Eds.). 1997. *The Work Family Challenge: Rethinking Employment*. London, England: Sage Publications.

Li, J. 1995. "China's One-Child Policy: How and How Well it Worked? A Case Study of Hebei Province, 1979-1988." *Population and Development Review*, 21: 563–585.

Liebow, E. 1995. *Tell Them Who I Am: The Lives of Homeless Women*. New York: Penguin.

Lockard, J. 1997. "Progressive Politics, Electronic Individualism and the Myth of Virtual Community." Pp. 219–32 in *Internet Culture*, edited by D. Porter. London: Routledge.

Loftin, C., and R. H. Hill. 1974. "Regional Subculture and Homicide: An Examination of the Gastil-Hackney Thesis." *American Sociological Review* 39: 714–724.

Lowe, G. S. 1987. *Women in the Administrative Revolution: The Feminization of Clerical Work*. Toronto: University of Toronto Press.

Lowe, G. S., and H. J. Krahn, (Eds.). 1984. *Working Canadians: Readings in the Sociology of Work and Industry*. Toronto: Methuen.

Lundgren-Gaveras, L. 1996. "The Work-Family Needs of Single Parents—a Comparison of American and Swedish Policy Trends." *Journal of Sociology and Social Welfare* 23: 131–47.

Lupri, E. 1990. "Male Violence in the Home." Pp. 170–172 in *Canadian Social Trends*, edited by C. McKie and K. Thompson. Thompson Educational Publishing.

Lyman, M. D., and G. W. Potter, (Eds.). 1996. *Drugs in Society: Causes, Concepts and Control*. 2nd ed. Cincinatti, OH: Anderson Press.

Lynch, M. J., and W. B. Groves. 1989. *A Primer in Radical Criminology*. 2nd ed. New York: Harrow and Heston.

MacKellar, F., W. Lutz, C. Prinz, and A. Goujon. 1995. "Population, Households and CO2 Emissions." *Population and Development Review* 21: 849–65.

MacMillan, H. L., J. E. Fleming, N. Trocme, M. H. Boyle, M. Wong, Y. A. Racine, W. R. Beardslee, and D. Offord. 1997. "Prevalence of Child Physical and Sexual Abuse in the Community: Results from the Ontario Health Supplement." *Journal of the American Medical Association Abstracts*—July 9, 1997. At http//www.ama-assn.org/scipubs/journals/archive/jama/vol278/no2/joc5b67a.htm.

Maguire, K., and A. L. Pastore, (Eds.). 1995. *Sourcebook of Criminal Justice Statistics—1994*. Washington, D.C.: Department of Justice, Bureau of Justice Statistics.

Maguire, P. 1987. *Doing Participatory Research: A Feminist Approach*. Amherst, MA: The Center for International Education.

Mahan, S. 1996. *Crack Cocaine, Crime, and Women: Legal, Social, and Treatment Issues*. Thousand Oaks, CA: Sage.

Mahar, L. 1990. "Criminalizing Pregnancy—The Downside of a Kinder, Gentler Nation?" *Social Justice* 17: 111–135.

Malthus, T. 1798. *An Essay on the Principle of Population*. London: J. Johnson.

Malthus, T. 1830. *A Summary View of the Principle of Population*. London: J. Murray.

Mandryk, M. (1990). "Sandy Bay: Frustration and an Unhealthy Isolation." *Leader-Post*, 3 March, A17.

Manga, P. 1981. "Income and Access to Medical Care in Canada." In *Health and Canadian Society: Sociological Perspectives*, edited by D. Coburn, C. D'Arcy, P. New, and G. Torrance. Toronto: Fitzhenry and Whiteside.

Mann, C. R. 1993. *Unequal Justice: A Question of Color*. Bloomington: Indiana University Press.

Mann, E. A. 1990. "L.A.'s Smogbusters." *The Nation* (September 17): 257, 268–274.

Mann, S. A., M. D. Grimes, A. A. Kemp, and P. J. Jenkins. 1997. "Paradigm Shifts in Family Sociology—Evidence from 3 Decades of Family Textbooks." *Journal of Family Issues* 18: 315–49.

Marmot, M. 1994. "Social Differentials in Health Within and Between Populations." *Daedalus* 123: 197-215.

Marmot, M. 1996. "The Social Pattern of Health and Disease." Pp. 42–70 in *Health and Social Organization*, edited by D. Blane, E. Brunner, and R. Wilkinson. London: Routledge.

Marmot, M. G., G. Davey Smith, S. Stansfeld, C. Patel, F. North, J. Head, I. White, E. Brunner, and A. Feeney. 1991. "Health Inequalities Among British Civil Servants: The Whitehall II Study." *Lancet* 337: 1387–92.

Marmot, M., and T. Theorell. 1988. "Social Class and Cardiovascular Disease: The Contribution of Work." *International Journal of Health Services* 18: 659–74.

Maroney, H. J., and M. Luxton, (Eds.). 1987. *Feminism and Political Economy: Women's Work, Women's Struggles.* Toronto: Methuen.

Marshall, B., U. Brandenburg, and K. Lippmann. 1994. "Health Promotion at Worksite—Health Promotion and Work Design." *Homeostasis in Health and Disease* 35: 37–42.

Marshall, R. 1994. "School-to-Work Processes in the United States." Paper presented at the Carnagie Corporation/Johann Jacobs Foundation, Marbach Castle, Germany.

Marx, K. 1975. "The Poverty of Philosophy." In *Marx/Engels Collected Works*, Vol. VI. London: Lawrence and Wishart. (Originally published in 1847).

Marx, K. 1963. *The Economic and Philosophical Manuscripts.* Translated by T. Bottomore. New York: Frederick Ungar (Originally Published in 1844).

Marx, K., and F. Engels. 1939. *German Ideology.* New York: International Publishers (Originally published in 1846).

Marx, K., and F. Engels. 1975. *The Communist Manifesto.* Great Britain: C. Nickolls (Originally published in 1872).

Mason, M. A. 1988. "The Equality Trap." *Working Mother*: 120.

Matza, D. 1964. *Delinquency and Drift.* New York: John Wiley and Sons.

May, P. A., and J. R. Moran. 1995. "Prevention of Alcohol Misuse." *American Journal of Health Promotion* 9: 288–299.

McAneny, L. 1992. "Number of Drinkers on the Rise Again." *Gallup Poll Monthly* 317: 43–47.

McCaghy, C. H. 1976. *Deviant Behavior.* New York: Macmillan.

McCaghy, C. H. 1985. *Deviant Behavior.* 2nd ed. New York: Macmillan.

McCoy, C. B., L. R. Metsch, and J. A. Inciardi, (Eds.). 1996. *Intervening with Drug-Involved Youth.* Thousand Oaks, CA: Sage.

McDaniel, S. 1997. "Toward Healthy Families Vol. 3." Ottawa: National Forum on Health. At http://wwwnfh.hc-sc.gc.ca/publicat/execsumm/mcdaniel.htm.

McKenzie, D. 1997. "Alcohol, Tobacco and Other Drugs: Aboriginal People." Canadian Centre on Substance Abuse. At http://www.ccsa.ca/cpnate.htm.

McKenzie, D., and B. Williams. 1997. "Canadian Profile: Alcohol, Tobacco and Other Drugs." Canadian Centre on Substance Abuse. At http://www.ccsa.ca/cpdruge.htm.

McKie, C., and K. Thompson, (Eds.). 1990. *Canadian Social Trends.* Toronto: Thompson educational publishing.

McLoyd, V., T. Jayaratne, R. Ceballo, and J. Borquez. 1994. "Unemployment and Work Interruptions Among African American Single Mothers: Effects on Parenting and Adolescent Socioemotional Functioning." *Child Development* 65: 563.

McLuhan, M. 1964. *Understanding Media: The Extensions of Man.* New York: McGraw-Hill.

McNeely, R. L., and G. Robinson-Simpson. 1987. "The Truth About Domestic Violence: A Falsely Framed Issue." *Social Work* 32: 485–490.

McQuaig, L. 1987. *Behind Closed Doors.* Toronto: Penguin.

Mead, G. H. 1934. *Mind, Self and Society.* Chicago: University of Chicago Press.

Mechanic, D., and D. A. Rochefort. 1996. "Comparative Medical Systems." *Annual Review of Sociology* 22: 239–270.

Menaghan, E. G. 1991. "Work Experiences And Family Interaction Processes: The Long Reach Of The Job?" *Annual Review of Sociology* 17: 419–444.

Merton, R. 1938. "Social Structure and Anomie." *American Sociological Review* 3: 672–682.

Merton, R. 1957. *Social Theory and Social Structure.* New York: Free Press of Glencoe.

Mesquida, C., and N. Wiener. 1996. *Human Collective Aggression: A Behavioural Ecology Perspective.* La Marsh Report 084-9749. York University, Ontario, Canada: La Marsh Research Centre on Violence and Conflict Resolution.

Messerschmidt, J. W. 1986. *Capitalism, Patriarchy, and Crime: Toward a Socialist Feminist Criminology.* Totowa, NJ: Roman and Littlefield.

Messerschmidt, J. W. 1993. *Masculinities and Crime: Critique and Reconceptualization of Theory.* Lanham, MD: Roman and Littlefield.

Messner, S. F., and R. Rosenfeld. 1997. *Crime and the American Dream.* 2nd ed. Belmont, CA: Wadsworth.

Messner, S. F., and K. Tardiff. 1986. "Economic Inequality and Levels of Homicide: An Analysis of Urban Neighborhoods." *Criminology* 24: 297–318.

Metro Toronto Research Group on Drug Use. 1997. "Drug Use in Metropolitan Toronto 1995." Metro Toronto Research Group on Drug Use. At http://www.ccsa.ca/statstor.htm.

Michalowski, R. J. 1983. "A Progressive Agenda for Crime Control." *Crime and Social Justice* 19: 13–23.

Michalowski, R. J. 1985. *Order, Law, and Crime: An Introduction to Criminology.* New York: Random House.

Michalowski, R. J. 1991. "'Niggers, Welfare Scum and Homeless Assholes': The Problems of Idealism, Consciousness and Context in Left Realism." Pp. 31–38 in *New Directions in Critical Criminology*, edited by B. D. MacLean and D. Milovanovic. Vancouver: Collective Press.

Micklin, P. 1992. "The Aral Crisis: Introduction to the Special Issue." *Post-Soviet Geography* (May).

Micklin, P. 1993. "Touring the Aral: Visit to an Ecological Disaster Zone." *Soviet Geography* (February).

Miliband, R. 1969. *The State in Capitalist Society.* London: Wiedenfeld and Nicholson.

Miliband, R. 1983. *Class Power and State Power.* London: Verso Press.

Miller, J., and M. D. Schwartz. 1992. "Lewd Lighters and Dick-ee Darts: The Commodification of Women Through Sexual Objects." Paper presented at the annual meetings of the American Society of Criminology, New Orleans.

Miller, L. J. 1990. "Violent Families and the Rhetoric of Harmony." *British Journal of Sociology* 41: 419–423.

Mills, C. W. 1956. *The Power Elite.* New York: Oxford University Press.

Mills, C. W. 1959. *The Sociological Imagination.* New York: Oxford University Press.

Miringoff, M., and M. L. Miringoff. 1995. "America's Social Health: The Nation's Need to Know." *Challenge* 38: 19–24.

Morgan, P., and K. A. Joe. 1997. "Uncharted Terrain: Contexts of Experience Among Women in the Illicit Drug Economy." *Women and Criminal Justice* 8: 85–109.

Morone, J. A., and G. S. Belkin, (Eds.). 1994. *The Politics of Health Care Reform: Lessons from the Past, Prospects for the Future.* Durham: Duke University Press.

Morris, B. 1997. "Is Your Family Wrecking Your Career? (And Vice Versa)." *Fortune Magazine*, March 17: 70.

Mosco, V. 1989. *The Pay-per Society: Computers, and Communication in the Information Age.* Toronto: Garamond.

Muir, B.L. (1991). *Health status of Canadian Indians and Inuit 1990.* Ottawa: Minister of Supply and Services Canada.

Murray, C. 1984. *Losing Ground: American Social Policy, 1950-1980.* New York: Basic Books.

Musto, D. 1973. *The American Disease: Origins of Narcotic Control.* New Haven, CT: Yale University Press.

Musto, D. 1988. *The American Disease: Origins of Narcotic Control.* Exp. ed. New York: Oxford University Press.

Myers, N., and J. Simon. 1994. *Scarcity or abundance?* New York: W. W. Norton.

Myrdal, G. 1987. "Challenge to Affluence—The Emergence of an 'Under-Class'." Pp. 151–155 in *Structured Social Inequality: A Reader in Comparative Stratification*, edited by C. S. Heller. New York: Macmillan.

National Academy of Science, and National Academy of Engineering. 1996. *Reinventing Schools: The Technology is Now.* Washington: National Academy of Sciences.

National Center for Health Statistics. 1994. *Health, United States 1994.* Huntsville, Maryland: U.S. Department of Health and Human Services, National Center for Health Statistics.

National Center for Health Statistics. 1995. *Health, United States, 1994.* Washington D.C.: U.S. Government Printing Office.

National Institute of Health. *Epidemiologic Trends in Drug Abuse.* National Institute of Health. At http://www.ccsa.ca/statsus.htm.

National Institute on Drug Abuse NIDA. 1997. *Patterns of Substance Use in 1994.* National Institute on Drug Abuse. At http://www.health.org/pubs/94hhs/patterns.htm.

National Institute on Drug Abuse NIDA. 1997. *Cocaine Abuse.* National Institute on Drug Abuse. At http://www.nida.nih.gov/nidacapsules/nccocaine.html.

National Institute on Drug Abuse NIDA. 1997. *Facts About Teenagers and Drug Abuse.* National Institute on Drug Abuse. At http://165.112.78.61/nidacapsules/ncteenagers.html.

National Institute on Drug Abuse NIDA. 1997. *Prevalence for Various Types of Drugs.* National Institute on Drug Abuse. At http://www.nida.nih.gov/nidacapsules/nccollege.html.

National Institute on Drug Abuse NIDA. 1997. *Trends in Drug Use Among College Students.* National Institute on Drug Abuse. At http://www.nida.nih.gov/nidacapsules/nccollege-trends.html.

National Safety Council. 1992. *Accident Facts.* Washington, D.C.: National Safety Council.

National Safety Council. 1995. *Accident Facts.* Itasca, Il. National Safety Council.

National Victim Center. 1992. *Rape in America: A Report to the Nation.* Charleston, NC: Department of Psychiatry and Behavioral Sciences, Medical University of South Carolina.

Navarro, V. 1976. *Medicine Under Capitalism.* New York: Prodist.

Navarro, V. 1986. *Crisis, Health and Medicine: A Social Critique.* New York: Tavistock.

Naylor, C. D. 1986. *Private Practice, Public Payment.* Kingston: McGill-Queens University Press.

Negroponte, N. 1995. *Being Digital.* New York: Vintage Books.

Negroponte, N. 1996. "Been Digital—What's the Next Big Thing." *Forbes* (Suppl. S, December 2): 174–75.

Negroponte, N. 1997. "Psst, Transactions." *Forbes* 160: 166–67.

Nett, E. 1981. "Canadian Families in Social-historical Persective." *Canadian Journal of Sociology* 6: 3.

Network Wizards. 1996. "Network Wizards." *Clipboard Magazine.* At http://www.media-awareness.ca/eng/ISSUES/STATS/usenet.htm.

Neubeck, K. J., and M. A. Neubeck. 1997. *Social Problems: A Critical Approach.* 4th ed. New York: McGraw-Hill.

Nicholl, C. 1985. *The Fruit Palace.* London: Heinemann.

Nickerson, C. 1994. "Canada, U.S. Share Much but Part Ways on Crime." *The Boston Globe* 4 September, 1, 24.

O'Connor, J. 1973. *The Fiscal Crisis of the State.* New York: St. Martin's Press.

O'Hare, W. P. 1985. "Poverty in America: Trends and Patterns." *Population Bulletin* 40: 1–42.

Okun, L. 1986. *Woman Abuse: Facts Replacing Myths.* Albany: State University of New York Press.

Olweus, D. 1980. "The Consistency Issue in Personality Psychology Revisited —With Special Reference to Aggression." *British Journal of Social and Clinical Psychology* 19: 377–390.

Orcutt, J. D, and J. B. Turner. 1993. "Shocking Numbers and Graphic Accounts: Quantified Images of Drug Problems in the Print Media." *Social Problems* 40: 190–206.

Organization for Economic Cooperation and Development. 1997. *Health Data 97.* OECD, Paris. At http://www.oecd.org/publications/observer/figures/heala.pdf.

Ouellet, L. J., W. W. Wiebel, A. D. Jimenex, and W. A. Johnson. 1993. "Crack Cocaine and the Transformation of Prostitution in Three Chicago Neighborhoods." Pp. 69–96 in *Crack Pipe as Pimp: An Ethnographic Investigation of Sex-For-Crack Exchanges,* edited by M. S. Ratner. New York: Lexington.

Pagelow, M. D. 1985. "The 'Battered Husband Syndrome': Social Problem or Much Ado About Little?" Pp. 45–62 in *Marital Violence,* edited by N. Johnson. London: Routledge and Kegan Paul.

Panitch, L., (Ed.). 1977. *The Canadian State: Political Economy and Political Power.* Toronto: University of Toronto Press.

Papert, S. 1996. *The Connected Family—Bridging the Digital Generation Gap.* Atlanta: Longstreet Press.

Pappas, G., S. Queen, W. Hadden, and G. Fisher. 1993. "The Increasing Disaparity in Mortality Between Socioeconomic Groups in the United States, 1960 and 1986." *New England Journal of Medicine* 329: 103–9.

Paris, H. 1989. *The Corporate Response to Workers with Family Responsibilities*. Report 43–89. Ottawa: Conference Board of Canada.

Parker, R. N. 1989. "Poverty, Subculture of Violence, and Type of Homicide." *Social Forces* 67: 983–1007.

Parrillo, V., J. Stimson, and A. Stimson. 1996. *Contemporary Social Problems*. 3rd ed. Boston: Allyn and Bacon.

Parsons, T. 1937. *The Structure of Social Action*. New York: McGraw Hill.

Parsons, T. 1972. "Definitions of Health and Illness in Light of American Values and Social Structure." Pp. 165–87 in *Patients, Physicians and Illness*. 2nd ed., edited by E. G. Jaco. New York: Free Press.

Parsons, T., and R. Bales. 1955. *Family Socialization and Interaction*. New York: The Free Press.

Pateman, C. 1988. *The Sexual Contract*. Cambridge: Polity Press.

Pearce, F. 1989. *The Radical Durkheim*. Boston: Unwin Hyman.

Pederson, J. 1995. Drought, Migration and Population Growth in the Sahel: The Case of Malian Gourma, 1900-1991. *Population Studies*, 49: 111–126.

Pence, D., and R. Ropers. 1995. *American Prejudice: With Liberty and Justice for Some*. New York: Plenum Press.

Penley, C., and A. Ross. 1991. *Technoculture*. Minneapolis: University of Minnesota Press.

Pescosolido, B. A., and J. J. Kronenfeld. 1995. "Health, Illness and Healing in an Uncertain Era: Challenges from and for Medical Sociology." *Journal of Health and Social Behavior* (extra issue): 5–35.

Peterson, G. E., and A. V. Harrell. 1992. "Introduction: Inner-City Isolation and Opportunity." Pp. 1–26 in *Drugs, Crime, and Social Isolation*, edited by A. V. Harrell and G. E. Peterson. Washington, D.C.: Urban Institute Press.

Peterson, R. D., and L. J. Krivo. 1993. "Racial Segregation and Black Urban Homicide." *Social Forces* 71: 1001–1028.

Pfohl, S. 1994. *Images of Deviance and Social Control: A Sociological History*. 2nd ed. New York: McGraw-Hill.

Pillemer, K. A., and D. Finkelhor. 1988. "Prevalence of Elder Abuse: A Random Sample Survey." *The Gerontologist* 28: 51–57.

Pirog-Good, M. A., and J. E. Stets. 1989. *Violence in Dating Relationships: Emerging Social Issues*. New York: Praeger.

Piven, F. F., and R. A. Cloward. 1979. *Poor People's Movements*. New York: Vintage.

Platt, A. 1969. *The Child Savers: The Invention of Delinquency*. Chicago: University of Chicago Press.

Plotnick, R. D., and F. Skidmore. 1975. *Progress Against Poverty: A Review of the 1964-1974 Decade*. New York: Academic Press.

Podnieks, E. 1990. *National Survey on Abuse of the Elderly*. Toronto: Ryerson Polytechnical Institute.

Polsky, N. 1969. *Hustlers, Beats, and Others*. New York: Doubleday.

Popenoe, D. 1994. "Family Decline and Scholarly Optimism." *Family Affairs* 6: 9–10.

Population Reference Bureau. 1993. *1993 World Population Data Sheet*. Washington D.C.: Population Reference Bureau.

Postel, S. 1992a. *Last Oasis: Facing Water Scarcity*. New York: W. W. Norton.

Postel, S. 1992b. *The State of the World*. Washington, D.C.: Worldwatch Institute.

Postel, S. 1996. "Forging a Sustainable Water Strategy." Pp. 40–59 in *State of The World*. Washington, D.C.: Worldwatch Institute.

Poulantzas, N. 1973. *Political Power and Social Class*. Atlantic Fields, NJ: Humanities Press.

Punch, M. 1985. *Conduct Unbecoming: The Social Construction of Police Deviance and Control*. London: Tavistock.

Rainwater, L., and T. Smeeding. 1995. "Doing Poorly: The Real Income of American Children in Comparative Perspective." *Luxembourg Income Study Working Paper* Number 127 (August).

Randall, M., and L. Haskell. 1995. "Sexual Violence in Women's Lives: Findings from the Women's Safety Project, a Community-Based Survey." *Violence Against Women* 1: 6–31.

Ratner, M. S. (Ed.) 1993. *Crack Pipe as Pimp: An Ethnographic Investigation of Sex-For-Crack Exchanges*. New York: Lexington.

Rawlings, S., and A. Saluter. 1995. "Household and Family Characteristics: March 1994." *Current Population Reports: Populations Characteristics*, p20-483. U.S. Department of Commerce, Econmics and Statistics Administration, Bureau of the Census.

Reasons, C., L. Ross, and C. Patterson. 1981. *Assault on the Worker.* Toronto: Butterworths.

Reener, M. 1996. *Fighting for Survival.* New York: W. W. Norton.

Rees, W. 1996. "Two Earths." Paper presented at the annual meeting of the American Association for the Advancement of Science (Baltimore, February 9).

Reiman, J. 1998. *The Rich get Richer and the Poor get Prison: Ideology, Class, and Criminal Justice.* Boston: Allyn and Bacon.

Reinarman, C., and H. G. Levine. 1989. "Crack in Context: Politics and Media in the Making of a Drug Scare." *Contemporary Drug Problems* 16: 535–577.

Reiss, A. J., and J. A. Roth, (Eds.). 1993. *Understanding and Preventing Violence.* Washington D.C.: National Research Council.

Renzetti, C. M. 1993. "On the Margins of the Malestream (Or, They Still Don't Get It, Do They?): Feminist Analyses in Criminal Justice Education." *Journal of Criminal Justice Education* 4: 219–234.

Renzetti, C. M. 1994. "On Dancing With a Bear: Reflections on Some of the Current Debates Among Domestic Violence Theorists." *Violence and Victims* 9: 195–200.

Renzetti, C. M., and D. J. Curran. 1998. *Living Sociology.* Boston: Allyn and Bacon.

Rheingold, H. 1996. "A Slice of my Life in my Virtual Community." Pp. 413–36 in *High Noon on the Electronic Frontier: Conceptual Issues in Cyberspace*, edited by P. Ludlow. Cambridge: MIT Press.

Rice, M. 1990. "Challenging Orthodoxies in Feminist Theory: A Black Feminist Critique." Pp. 57–69 in *Feminist Perspectives in Criminology*, edited by L. Gelsthorpe and A. Morris. Philadelphia: Open University Press.

Richardson, C. J. 1992. "Family Law Research in a Decade of Change." Pp. in *Sociology for Canadians: A Reader*, edited by A. Himelfarb, and C. J. Richardson. Whitby: McGraw Hill.

Richardson, C. J. 1996. *Family Life: Patterns and Perspectives.* Toronto: McGraw-Hill Ryerson.

Richmond-Abbott, M. 1992. "Women Wage Earners." Pp. 135–49 in *Feminist Philosophies*, edited by J. A. Kourany, J. P. Sterba, and R. Tong. New Jersey: Prentice Hall.

Rifkin, J. 1994. *The Rise and Fall of the Cattle Culture.* London: Thorsons.

Rifkin, J. 1996. *The End of Work: The Decline of the Global Labor Force and the Dawn of the Post-market Era.* New York: Tarcher/Putnam.

Riley, M. W., R. L. Kahn, and A. Foner. 1994. *Age and Structural Lag.* New York: Wiley.

Roberts, J. 1994. *Criminal Justice Processing of Sexual Assault Cases.* Ottawa: Canadian Centre for Justice Statistics.

Rodgers, K. 1994. *Wife Assault: The Findings of a National Survey.* Ottawa: Canadian Centre for Justice Statistics.

Rodgers and Associates. 1995. "DuPont Employee Study on Work-Life Initiatives." At http://www.wfd.com/worklife/industrynews3fr.htm.

Rogers, A. 1997. "Seeing Through the Haze: Can Marijuana Ever Be Good Medicine?" *Newsweek*, 13 January, 60.

Roscoe, B., M. P. Goodwin, and D. Kennedy. 1987. "Sibling Violence and Agonistic Interactions Experienced by Early Adolescents." *Journal of Family Violence* 2: 121–137.

Rosenbaum, M. 1981. *Women on Heroin.* New Brunswick, NJ: Rutgers University Press.

Ross, D. P. and E. R. Shillington. 1996. *The Canadian Fact Book on Poverty 1994.* Ottawa: Canadian Council on Social Development.

Ross, D. and E. R. Shillington. 1997. *A Working Definition of Statistics Canada Low Income Cut-Offs (LICOs).* Canadian Council on Social Development. At http:// www.ccsd.ca/fspovbk.htm.

Ross, D. P. and E. R. Shillington. 1989. *The Canadian Fact Book on Poverty 1989.* Ottawa: Canadian Council on Social Development.

Ross, J. I. 1995. *Violence in Canada: Sociopolitical Perspectives.* Toronto: Oxford University Press.

Ross, R., and G. L. Staines. 1972. "The Politics of Analyzing Social Problems." *Social Problems* 20: 18–40.

Roszak, T. 1994. *The Cult of Information—A Neo-Luddite Treatise on High-Tech, Artificial Intelligence, and the True Art of Thinking.* Berkeley: University of California Press.

Rothschild, E. 1995. "Echoes of the Malthusian Debate at the Population Summit." *Population and Development Review* 21: 351–359.

Rouse, L. 1988. "Abuse in Dating Relationships: A Comparison of Blacks, Whites, and Hispanics." *Journal of College Student Development* 29: 312–319.

Russell, D. E. H. 1975. *The Politics of Rape.* New York: Stein.

Russell, D. E. H. 1990. *Rape in Marriage.* 2nd ed. Bloomington: Indiana University Press.

Ryan, M., and C. Flavin. 1995. "Facing China's Limits." Pp. 113–31 in *The State of the World*, edited by Worldwatch Institute. Washington, DC: Worldwatch Institute.

Sacco, V. F., and W. Kennedy. 1994. *The Criminal Event.* Scarborough, ON.: Nelson.

Sale, K. 1995. *Rebels Against the Future: The Luddites and Their War on the Industrial Revolution.* Reading: Addison-Wesley.

Samarajiva, R. 1994. "Privacy In Electronic Public Space: Emerging Issues." *Canadian Journal of Communication* 19: 87–89.

Sampson, R. J. 1985. "Neighborhood and Crime: The Structural Determinants of Personal Victimization." *Journal of Research in Crime and Delinquency* 22: 7–40.

Sampson, R. J. 1986. "Neighborhood Family Structure and the Risk of Personal Victimization." Pp. 58–72 in *The Social Ecology of Crime*, edited by J. Byrne and R. J. Sampson. New York: Springer-Verlag.

Sampson, R. J. 1987. "Urban Black Violence: The Effect of Male Joblessness and Family Disruption." *American Journal of Sociology* 93: 348–382.

Sampson, R. J. 1989. "The Promises and Pitfalls of Macro-Level Research." *The Criminologist* 14: 6–11.

Sampson, R. J., and W. B. Groves. 1989. "Community Structure and Crime: Testing Social Disorganization Theory." *American Journal of Sociology* 94: 774–802.

Sanday, P. R. 1996. *A Woman Scorned: Acquaintance Rape on Trial.* New York: Doubleday.

Sartre, J. P. 1969. *The Words.* New York: Braziller.

Saunders, D. G. 1986. "When Battered Women Use Violence: Husband-Abuse or Self-Defense?" *Violence and Victims* 1: 47–60.

Saunders, D. G. 1988. "Wife Abuse, Husband Abuse, or Mutual Combat?: A Feminist Perspective on Empirical Findings. Pp. 99–113 in *Feminist Perspectives on Wife Abuse*, edited by K. Yllo and M. Bograd. Newbury Park, CA: Sage.

Saunders, D. G. 1989. "Who Hits First and Who Hurts Most?: Evidence for the Greater Victimization of Women in Intimate Relationships." Paper presented at the annual meeting of the American Society of Criminology, Reno, Nevada.

Scanzoni, J. 1982. *Sexual Baragaining: Power Politics in the American Marriage.* 2nd ed. Chicago: University of Chicago Press.

Scheingold, S. A. 1984. *The Politics of Law and Order.* New York: Longman Inc.

Schelling, T. 1978. *Micromotives and Macrobehaviour.* New York: W. W. Norton.

Schiller, B. R. 1989. *The Economics of Poverty and Discrimination.* Englewood Cliffs, NJ: Prentice Hall.

Schmitz, J. 1997. "Structural Relations, Electronic Media, and Social Change: The Public Electronic Network and the Homeless." Pp. 102–32 in *Virtual Culture: Identity and Communication in Cybersociety*, edited by S. G. Jones. London: Sage.

Schnaiberg, A., and K. Gould. 1994. *Environment and Society: The Enduring Conflict.* London: St. Martin's Press.

Schulman, M. A. 1979. *A Survey of Spousal Violence Against Women in Kentucky.* Study No. 792701 conducted for the Kentucky Commission on women. Washington, DC: U.S. Government Printing Office.

Schur, E. M. 1984. *Labeling Women Deviant: Gender, Stigma and Social Control.* New York: Random House.

Schwartz, H. 1997. "On the Origin of the Phrase 'Social Problems.'" *Social Problems* 44: 276–296.

Schwartz, M. D. 1988. "Ain't Got No Class: Universal Risk Theories of Battering." *Contemporary Crises* 12: 373–392.

Schwartz, M. D. 1991. "The Future of Criminology." Pp. 119–124 in *New Directions in Critical Criminology*, edited by B. D. MacLean and D. Milovanovic. Vancouver: Collective Press.

Schwartz, M. D., and W. S. DeKeseredy. 1993. "The Return of the 'Battered Husband Syndrome' Through the Typification of Women as Violent." *Crime, Law and Social Change* 20: 249–265.

Schwartz, M. D., and W. S. DeKeseredy. 1997. *Sexual Assault on the College Campus: The Role of Male Peer Support.* Thousand Oaks, CA: Sage.

Schwartz, M. D., and D. Milovanovic. 1996. *Race, Gender, and Class in Criminology: The Intersection.* New York: Garland.

Schwartz, M. D., and V. L. Pitts. 1995. "Exploring a Feminist Routine Activities Approach to Explaining Sexual Assault." *Justice Quarterly* 12: 9–31.

Schwarzer, R., A. Hahn, and R. Fuchs. 1994. "Unemployment, Social Resources, and Mental and Physical Health: A Three Wave Study on Men and Women in a Stressful Life Transition." Pp. 75–87 in *Job Stress in a Changing Workforce: Investigating Gender, Diversity and Family Issues,* edited by G. Puryear Keita, and J. J. Hurrell. Washington, DC: American Psychological Association.

Schwendinger, H., and J. Schwendinger. 1993. "Giving Crime Prevention Top Priority." *Crime and Delinquency* 39: 425–466.

Schwendinger, J., and H. Schwendinger. 1983. *Rape and Inequality.* Newbury Park, CA: Sage.

Scott, J., D. F. Alwin, and M. Braun. 1996. "Generational Changes in Gender-role Attitudes: Britain in a Cross National Perspective." *Sociology* 30: 471–92.

Selke, W. 1993. *Prisons in Crisis.* Bloomington: Indiana University Press.

Shapiro, A. L. 1992. *We're Number One! Where America Stands—and Falls in the New World Order.* New York: Random House.

Sheley, J. 1985. *America's "Crime Problem": An Introduction to Criminology.* Belmont, CA: Wadsworth.

Sherman, L. 1974. "Moral Careers of Corrupt Policeman." Pp. 191–205 in *Police Corruption,* edited by L. Sherman. New York: Doubleday.

Sherman, L., and R. Berk. 1984. "The Specific Deterrence Effects of Arrest for Domestic Assault." *American Sociological Review* 49: 261–272.

Sherman, L., and E. Cohn. 1989. "The Impact of Research on Legal Policy: The Minneapolis Domestic Violence Experiment." *Law and Society Review* 23: 117–144.

Sherman, L., P. Gartin, and M. Buerger. 1989. "Hot Spots and Predatory Crime: Routine Activities and the Criminology of Place." *Criminology* 27: 27–55.

Shkllnyk, A. 1985. *A Poison Stronger than Love.* New Haven, CT: Yale University Press.

Shoham, S., and J. Hoffman. 1991. *A Primer in the Sociology of Crime.* New York: Harrow and Heston.

Shortt, S. E. D. 1983. "Physicians, Science and Status: Issues in the Professionalization of Anglo-american Medicine in the Nineteenth Century." *Medical History* 27: 50–72.

Shragge, E. 1997. *Workfare: Ideology for a New Under-Class.* Toronto: Garamond.

Silverman, R. A. 1992. "Street Crime." Pp. 236–277 in *Deviance: Conformity and Control in Canadian Society,* edited by V. F. Sacco. Scarborough, ON: Prentice Hall.

Silverman, R., and L. Kennedy. 1993. *Deadly Deeds: Murder in Canada.* Scarborough, ON: Nelson.

Simon, D. R. 1996. *Elite Deviance.* Boston: Allyn and Bacon.

Simon, J. 1996. "The State of Humanity Steadily Improving." Pp. 354–59 in *Taking Sides,* edited by K. Einsterbusch, and G. McKenna. Guilford, Conn.: Dushkin.

Simon, J., and H. Kahn, (Eds.). 1984. *The Resourceful Earth: A Response to Global 2000.* Oxford: Basil Blackwell.

Single, E. W., J. M. Brewster, P. MacNeil, J. Hatcher, and C. Trainor. 1997. *Alcohol and Drug Use: Results from the 1993 General Social Survey.* Canadian Centre on Substance Abuse. At http://www.ccsa.ca/gsseng.htm.

Sinom, J. 1981. *The Ultimate Reason.* New Jersey: Princeton University Press.

Sivard, R. L. 1985. *Women: A World Survey.* New York: Carnegie, Ford, and Rockefeller foundations.

Sklar, H. 1990. "American Dreams, American Nightmares." *Z* (November): 41–42.

Skolnick, A. S. 1991. *Embattled Paradise: The American Family in an Age of Uncertainty.* New York: Basic Books.

Slouka, M. 1995. *War of the Worlds: Cyberspace and the High-Tech Assault on Reality.* New York: Basic Books.

Smandych, R. 1985. "Marxism and the Creation of Law: Re-Examining the Origins of the Canadian Anti-Combines Legislation, 1890-1910." Pp. 87–99 in *The New Criminologies in Canada: State, Crime, and Control*, edited by T. Fleming. Toronto: Oxford University Press.

Smeeding, T. M. 1988. "Why the U.S. Antipoverty System Doesn't Work Very Well." Pp. 33–43 in *Solutions to Social Problems*, edited by D. S. Eitzen and C. S. Leedham. Boston: Allyn and Bacon.

Smith, A. 1793. *The Theory of Moral Sentiments*. London: Augustus B. Kelley Publishers.

Smith, D., and G. Jarjoura. 1988. "Social Structure and Criminal Victimization." *Journal of Research in Crime and Delinquency* 25: 27–52.

Smith, H. J. 1994. *Managing Privacy: Information Technology and Corporate America*. Chapel Hill: University of North Carolina Press.

Smith, M. D. 1979. "Hockey Violence: A Test of the Violent Subculture Thesis." *Social Problems* 27: 235–247.

Smith, M. D. 1983. *Violence and Sport*. Toronto: Butterworths.

Smith, M. D. 1986. "Effects of Question Format on the Reporting of Woman Abuse: A Telephone Survey Experiment." *Victimology* 11: 430–438.

Smith, M. D. 1987. "The Incidence and Prevalence of Woman Abuse in Toronto." *Violence and Victims* 2: 173–187.

Smith, M. D. 1989. "Woman Abuse in Toronto: Incidence, Prevalence and Sociodemographic Risk Markers." *The LaMarsh Research Programme on Violence and Conflict Resolution*. Report No. 18. North York, ON: York University.

Smith, M. D. 1990a. "Patriarchal Ideology and Wife Beating: A Test of a Feminist Hypothesis." *Violence and Victims* 5: 257–273.

Smith, M. D. 1990b. "Sociodemographic Risk Factors in Wife Abuse: Results from a Survey of Toronto Women." *Canadian Journal of Sociology* 15: 39–58.

Smock, P. J. 1993. "The Economic Costs of Marital Disruption for Young Women over the Past Two Decades." *Demography* 30: 353–71.

Smock, P. J. 1994. "Gender and the Short-run Economic Consequences of Marital Disruption." *Social Forces* 73: 243–62.

"Social Problems." 1993. *Environmental Justice*, 40: whole volume.

Solicitor General of Canada. 1990. *Woman Alone*. Ottawa: Ministry of the Solicitor General of Canada.

Sommer, R. 1988. "Beyond a One-Dimensional View: The Politics of Family Violence in Canada." Pp. 31–38 in *Unsettling Truths: Battered Women, Policy, Politics, and Contemporary Research in Canada*, edited by K. D. Bonnycastle and G. S. Rigakos. Vancouver: Collective Press.

Soroka, M. P., and G. J. Bryjak. 1995. *Social Problems: A World at Risk*. Boston: Allyn and Bacon.

Soros, G. 1997. "The Capitalist Threat." *The Atlantic Monthly* (February): 45–70.

Spear, S., and R. L. Akers. 1988. "Social Learning Variables and the Risk of Habitual Smoking among Adolescents: The Muscatine Study." *American Journal of Preventive Medicine* 4: 336–348.

Spencer, H. 1851. *Social Statistics*. London: Chapman.

Spencer, H. 1906. *The Principles of Sociology*, Vol. III. Westport, CT: Greenwood.

Spitzer, S. 1975. "Toward a Marxian Theory of Deviance." *Social Problems* (June): 638–651.

Staines, G. L. 1980. "Spillover Versus Compensation: A Review of the Literature on Work and Nonwork." *Human Relations* 33: 111–29.

Stanko, E. A. 1985. *Intimate Intrusions: Women's Experiences of Male Violence*. London: Routledge.

Stanko, E. A. 1990. *Everyday Violence: How Women and Men Experience Sexual and Physical Danger*. London: Pandora.

Stanko, E. A. 1995. "The Struggle Over Commonsense Feminism, Violence and Confronting the Backlash." Pp. 156–172 in *Proceedings of the Fifth Symposium on Violence and Aggression*, edited by B. Gillies and G. James. Saskatoon, Saskatchewan: University Extension Press, University of Saskatchewan.

Starnes, R. 1997. "Hopelessness Can Kill You, Medical Study Suggests." *Ottawa Citizen* 27 August, A1.

Starr, P. 1982. *The Social Transformation of American Medicine*. New York: Basic Books.

Statistical Abstract of the United States. 1995. *The National Data Book.* 15th edition. Maryland: Berman Press.

Statistics Canada. 1991. *Aboriginal Peoples Survey, Schooling, Work and Related Activities, Income Expenses and Mobility.* Ottawa: Statistics Canada.

Statistics Canada. 1992a. *Accidents in Canada: General Social Survey Analysis Series.* Ottawa: Statistics Canada.

Statistics Canada. 1993a. *Violence Against Women Survey.* Ottawa: Statistics Canada.

Statistics Canada. 1993b. *Basic Facts on Families in Canada, Past and Present.* Cat No. 89-516, Ottawa: Minister of Industry Science and Technology.

Statistics Canada. 1993c. *Schooling Work and Related Activities, Income, Expenses and Mobility.* Ottawa: Minister of Industry, Science and Technology.

Statistics Canada. 1994a. *Canada Year Book, 1994.* Ottawa: Statistics Canada.

Statistics Canada. 1994b. *Canadian Social Trends,* Vol. 2. Toronto: Thompson Educational Press.

Statistics Canada. 1995. *Women in Canada.* Third Edition. Ottawa: Statistics Canada.

Statistics Canada. 1996a. 1996 Census. Catalogue No. 93F0027XDB96007.

Statistics Canada. 1996b. *Income Distributions by Size in Canada,* 1995. Catalogue No. 13-207-XPB. Ottawa: Statistics Canada.

Stearns, P. J. 1986. "Old Age Family Conflict: The Perspective of the Past." Pp. 3–24 in *Elder Abuse: Conflict in the Family*, edited by K. A. Pillemer and R. S. Wolf. Dover, MA: Auburn House.

Steinmetz, S. K. 1977. "The Use of Force for Resolving Family Conflict: The Training Ground for Abuse." *The Family Coordinator* 26: 19–26.

Steinmetz, S. K. 1982. "A Cross-Cultural Comparison of Sibling Violence." *International Journal of Family Psychiatry* 2: 337–351.

Steinmetz, S. K. 1997-78. "The Battered Husband Syndrome." *Victimology* 2: 499–509.

Stets, J. E., and M. A. Straus. 1990. "Gender Differences in Reporting Marital Violence and its Medical and Psychological Consequences." Pp. 151–165 in *Physical Violence in American Families: Risk Factors and Adaptions to Violence in 8,145 Families*, edited by M. A. Straus and R. J. Gelles. New Brunswick, NJ: Transaction.

Stoll, C. 1995. *Silicon Snake Oil —Second Thoughts on the Information Highway.* New York: Doubleday.

Stone, S. 1991. "They Said I Was 'Young and Immature.'" Pp. 28–32 in *Dating Violence: Young Women in Danger*, edited by B. Levy. Seattle, WA: Seal Press.

Storey, R. 1991. "Studying work in Canada." *Canadian Journal of Sociology* 16: 241–64.

Straus, M. A. 1979. "Measuring Intrafamily Conflict and Violence: The Conflict Tactics CT Scales." *Journal of Marriage and the Family* 41: 75–88.

Straus, M. A. 1989. "Gender Differences in Assault in Intimate Relationships: Implications for the Primary Prevention of Spousal Violence." Paper presented at the annual meeting of the American Society of Criminology, Reno, Nevada.

Straus, M. A. 1990. "The Conflict Tactics Scale and Its Critics: An Evaluation and New Data on Validity and Reliability." Pp. 49–74 in *Physical Violence in American Families: Risk Factors and Adaptations to Violence in 8,145 Families*, edited by M. A. Straus and R. J. Gelles. New Brunswick, NJ: Transaction.

Straus, M. A. 1991. "Discipline and Deviance: Physical Punishment of Children and Violence and Other Crime in Adulthood." *Social Problems* 38: 133–154.

Straus, M. A. 1994. *Beating the Devil Out of Them: Corporal Punishment in American Families.* New York: Lexington Books.

Straus, M. A., and R. J. Gelles. 1986. "Societal Changes and Change in Family Violence from 1975 to 1985 as Revealed by Two National Surveys." *Journal of Marriage and the Family* 48: 465–479.

Straus, M. A., R. J. Gelles, and S. K. Steinmetz. 1981. *Behind Closed Doors: Violence in the American Family.* New York: Anchor.

Straus, M. A., S. Hamby, S. Boney-McCoy, and D. B. Sugarman. 1995. *The Revised Conflict Tactics Scales* (CTS2-Form A). Durham, NH: Family Research Laboratory, University of New Hampshire.

Struthers, G. 1990. "Infant mortality rates 'sicken' Native leader." *StarPheonix*, 27 January, A8.

Sullum, J. 1992. "The Cocaine Kids." *Reason* 24: 14.

Surette, R. 1998. *Media, Crime, and Criminal Justice.* Belmont, CA: Wadsworth.

Swanson, J. 1997. "Resisting Workfare." Pp. 149–170 in *Workfare: Ideology for New Underclass,* edited by E. Shragge. Toronto: Garamond.

Swift, E. M. 1994. "Anatomy of a Plot." *Sports Illustrated* 80(6): 28–41.

Talbott, S. 1995. *The Future Does Not Compute—Transcending the Machines in Our Midst.* Sabestapol: O'Reilly and Associates.

Tanner, J. 1996. *Teenage Troubles: Youth and Deviance in Canada.* Scarborough, ON: Nelson.

Tarazuk, V. (1994). "Poverty, Homelessness and Health." Pp. 53–65 in *Racial Minorities, Medicine, and Health,* edited by B. Singh Bolaria and R. Bolaria. Saskatoon/Halifax: SRU/Fernwood.

Taylor, C. 1993. *Girls, Gangs, Women, and Drugs.* East Lansing, MI: Michigan State University Press.

Taylor, I. 1983. *Crime, Capitalism and Community: Three Essays in Socialist Criminology.* Toronto: Butterworths.

Taylor, I., P. Walton, and J. Young. 1973. *The New Criminology.* London: Routledge and Kegan Paul.

Teixeira, R. A. 1992. *The Disappearing American Voter.* Washington, D.C.: Brookings Institution.

Terry, D. 1991. "As Medicaid Fees Push Doctors Out, Chicago Patients Find Fewer Choices." *New York Times* 12 April: A10.

Terry, J., and M. Calvert, (Eds.). 1997. *Processed Lives: Gender and Technology in Everyday Life.* London: Routledge.

Thio, A. 1995. *Deviant Behavior.* 4th ed. New York: HarperCollins.

Thio, A. 1998. *Deviant Behavior.* 5th ed. New York: Longman.

Thompson, L. 1992. "Feminist Methodology for Family Studies." *Journal of Marriage and the Family* 54: 3–18.

Thorne-Finch, R. 1992. *Ending the Silence: The Origins and Treatment of Male Violence Against Women.* Toronto: University of Toronto Press.

Thorpe, K. E. 1993. "The American States and Canada: A Comparative Analysis of Health Care Spending." *Journal of Health Politics, Policy and Law* 18: 477–88.

Tomaszewski, A. In press. "Review Essay on William Julius Wilson's *When Work Disappears.*" *Justice Quarterly.*

Tong, R. 1989. *Feminist Thought.* Boulder, CO: Westview.

Trebach, A. S. 1989. "Drug Policies for the Democracies." Statement before the Public Hearing on Drug Control, Interior Committee of the Deutscher Bundestag, The Parliament of the Federal Republic of Germany, March 13.

Trebach, A. S. 1993. "Contemplating the Future under Legislation." Pp. 99–125 in *Legalize It?: Debating American Drug Policy,* edited by A. S. Trebach and J. A. Inciardi. Washington, D.C.: American University Press.

Trevethan, S. 1992. *Elderly Victims of Violent Crime.* Ottawa: Canadian Centre for Justice Statistics.

Tunnell, K. D. 1995. "Worker Insurgency and Social Control: Violence By and Against Labour in Canada." Pp. 78–96 in *Violence in Canada: Sociopolitical Perspectives,* edited by J. I. Ross. Toronto: Oxford University Press.

Turner, J. 1997. *Social Problems in America.* New York: Harper and Row.

Uchitelle, L. 1991. "Insurance Linked to Jobs: System Showing its Age." *New York Times* 1 May, A1, A14.

United Nations. 1995. *Human Development Report 1995.* Toronto: Oxford University Press.

U.S. Bureau of Census, Population Division. 1994. Household and Family Characteristics. U.S. Bureau of Census.

U.S. Department of Commerce, Bureau of the Census. 1995. "Income and Job Mobility in the Early 1990's." Statistical Brief SB/951:2.

U.S. Bureau of Census. 1996. *Poverty 1995: Highlights.* U.S. Bureau of Census. At http://www.census.gov./hhes/poverty/pov95/pov95hi.htm.

U.S. Bureau of Census. 1996. *Poverty 1995: Source and Accuracy of Estimates.* U.S. Bureau of Census. At http://www.census.gov/hhes/poverty/pov95/pov95src.htm.

U.S. Bureau of Justice Statistics. 1995. *Drugs and Crime Facts, 1994.* Washington, D.C.: U.S. Government Printing Office.

U.S. Bureau of Labor Statistics. 1996. New data on contingent and alternative employment examined by BLS. Bureau of Labor Statistics News Releases. At http://stats.bls.gov/news. release/conemp.toc.htm.

U.S. Department of Commerce, Bureau of the Census. 1995a. "Income and Job Mobility in the Early 1990's." Statistical Brief SB/951: 2.

U.S. Department of Commerce, Bureau of the Census. 1995b. "Women in the United States: A Profile." Statistical Brief SB/95-19RV: 2.

U.S. Department of Commerce, Bureau of the Census. 1997. Money Income in the United States: 1996.

U.S. Department of Commerce, Economics and Statistics Administration. 1997. Bureau of the Census.

U.S. Department of Labor. 1992. *Bureau of Labor Statistics Reports on Survey of Occupational Injuries and Illnesses in 1991*. Washington, D.C.: U.S. Department of Labor.

U.S. News and World Report. 1979. "Battered Families: A Growing Nightmare." *U.S. News and World Report* (January 15): 60–61.

Utech, M. R., and R. R. Garrett. 1992. "Elder and Child Abuse: Conceptual and Perceptual Parallels." *Journal of Interpersonal Violence* 7: 418–428.

Vance, C. 1984. *Pleasure and Danger: Exploring Female Sexuality*. London: Routledge and Kegan Paul.

van Dijk, J., and P. Mayhew. 1992. *Criminal Victimization in the Industrial World*. The Netherlands: Ministry of Justice.

Vanier Institute of the Family. 1994. *Profiling Canada's Families*. Ottawa: Vanier Institute of the Family.

Vanwijk, C., K. P. Vanvliet, and A. M. Kolk. 1996. "Gender Perspectives and Quality of Care: Towards Appropriate and Adequate Health Care for Women." *Social Science and Medicine* 43: 707–20.

Vedder, R. K., and L. E. Gallaway. 1994. "American Unemployment In Historical-Perspective." *Journal of Labor Research* 15: 1–17.

Verbrugge, L. M. 1985. "Gender and Health: An Update on Hypotheses and Evidence." *Journal of Health and Social Behavior* 26: 156–82.

Vold, G., and T. Bernard. 1986. *Theoretical Criminology*. 3rd ed. New York: Oxford University Press.

Waitzkin, H. 1983. *The Second Sickness: Contradictions of Capitalist Health care*. New York: The Free Press.

Walker, L. 1979. *The Battered Woman*. New York: Harper and Row.

Walker, L. 1984. *The Battered Woman Syndrome*. New York: Springer.

Walker, S., C. Spohn, and M. DeLone. 1996. *The Color of Justice: Race, Ethnicity and Crime in America*. Belmont: Wadsworth.

Walklate, S. 1989. *Victimology: The Victim and the Criminal Justice Process*. London: Unwin Hyman.

Wallace, H. 1996. *Family Violence: Legal, Medical, and Social Perspectives*. Toronto: Allyn and Bacon.

Walsh, E., R. Warland, and D. Smith. 1993. "Backyards, NIMBY's and Incinerator Sitings: Implications for Social Movement Theory." *Social Problems* 40: 25–38.

Walters, V. 1991. "Beyond Medical and Academic Agendas: Lay Perspectives and Priorities." *Atlantis* 17: 28–35.

Walters, V. 1994. "Women's Perceptions Regarding Health and Illness." Pp. 307–25 in *Health, Illness and Health Care in Canada*, edited by B. S. Bolaria, and H. D. Dickinson. Toronto: Harcourt Brace Canada.

Waquant, L. J. D., and W. J. Wilson. 1989. "The Cost of Racial and Class Exclusion in The Inner-City." *The Annals of the American Academy of Political and Social Science* 501: 8–25.

Warr, P. 1983. "Work, Jobs and Unemployment." *Bulletin of the British Psychological Society* 36: 4–28.

Warshaw, R. 1988. *I Never Called It Rape*. New York: Harper and Row.

Weaver, C. N., and M. D. Matthews. 1996. "What Workers Want from Their Jobs." *Personnel Journal*. At http://cdnet.icpsr.umich.edu/GSS/ bib/bib2859.htm.

Webb, E., D. Campbell, R. Schwartz, and L. Sachrest. 1966. *Unobtrusive Measures: Non-Reactive Research in the Social Sciences*. Chicago: Rand McNally.

Wechsler, H., A. Davenport, G. Dowdall, B. Moeykens, and S. Castillo. 1994. "Health and Behavioral Consequences of Binge Drinking in College." *Journal of the American Medical Association* 272:1672–1677.

Weiner, M. 1983. The Political Demography of Assam's Anti-Immigrant Movement. *Population and Development Review* 9: 279–292.

Weinfeld, M. 1995. "Ethnic and Race Relations." Pp. 4.1–4.29 in *New Society: Sociology for the 21st Century*, edited by R. J. Brym. Toronto: Harcourt Brace.

Weiss, G. L., and L. E. Lonnquist. 1997. *The Sociology of Health, Healing and Illness*. 2nd ed. New Jersey: Prentice Hall.

Wellman, B., D. Dimitrova, L. Garton, M. Gulia, C. Haythornwaite, and J. Salaff. 1996. "Computer Networks as Social Networks: Collaborative Work, Telework, and Virtual Community." *Annual Review of Sociology* 22: 213–38.

Wells, L. E., and J. H. Ranken. 1991. "Families and Delinquency: A Meta-analysis of the Impact of Broken Homes." *Social Problems* 38: 71–93.

Whiteis, D. G. 1997. "Unhealthy Cities: Corporate Medicine, Community Economic Underdevelopment, and Public Health." *International Journal of Health Services* 27: 227–42.

Wiehe, V. R. 1990. *Sibling Abuse: Hidden Physical, Emotional, and Sexual Trauma*. Lexington, MA: Lexington Books.

Wilentz, S. 1996. "Jobless and Hopeless." *The New York Times Book Review* 29 September, 7.

Wilkins, R., and O. B. Adams. 1981. "Health Expectancy in Canada, Late 1970s: Demographic, Regional and Social Dimensions." In *Health and Canadian Society: Sociological Perspectives*, edited by D. Coburn, C. D'Arcy, G. Torrance, and P. New. Markham: Fitzhenry and Whiteside.

Wilkins, R., G. J. Sherman, and P. A. F. Best. 1991. *Birth Outcomes and Infant Mortality by Income in Urban Canada 1986*. Health Reports, Statistics Canada, Catalogue no. 82-003, Vol. 3-1 pp 7–31.

Wilkinson, R. G. 1986. "Income and Mortality." Pp. 88–114 in *Class and Health: Research and Longitudinal Data*, edited by R. Wilkinson. London: Tavistock.

Williams, D. R., and C. Collins. 1995. "US Socioeconomic and Racial Differences in Health: Patterns and Explanations." *Annual Review of Sociology* 21: 349–386.

Williams, T. 1992. *Crackhouse—Notes from the End of the Line*. New York: Penguin.

Wilson, F. D., M. Tienda, and L. Wu. 1995. "Race And Unemployment—Labor-Market Experiences Of Black And White Men." *Work and Occupations* 22: 245–70.

Wilson, J. Q. 1985. *Thinking About Crime*. New York: Vintage.

Wilson, M., and M. Daly. 1994. *Spousal Homicide*. Ottawa: Canadian Centre for Justice Statistics.

Wilson, W. J. 1987. *The Truly Disadvantaged: The Inner City, the Underclass and Public Policy*. Chicago: University of Chicago Press.

Wilson, W. J. 1991. "Studying Inner-City Social Dislocations: The Challenge of Public Agenda Research, 1990 Presidential Address." *American Sociological Review* 56: 1–14.

Wilson, W. J. 1996. *When Work Disappears: The World of the New Urban Poor*. New York: Knopf.

Windle, M. 1991. "Alcohol Use and Abuse: Some Findings from the National Adolescent Student Health Survey." *Alcohol Health and Research World* 15: 5–10.

Witkin, G. 1991. "The Men Who Created Crack." *U.S. News and World Report* (August): 44–53.

Wolff, L., and V. Pottie Bunge. 1996. "Illicit Drugs." Pp. 217–230 in *Crime Counts: A Criminal Event Analysis*, edited by L. W. Kennedy and V. F. Sacco. Scarborough, ON: Nelson.

Wolfgang, M. E., and F. Ferracuti. 1967. *The Subculture of Violence: Towards and Integrated Theory in Criminology*. London: Tavistock.

World Almanac. 1992. *World Almanac*. New York: Pharos Books.

World Bank. 1991. *World Development Report 1991*. New York: Oxford University Press.

World Health Organization. 1958. *The First Ten Years of the World Health Organization*. Geneva: WHO.

Worling, J. R. 1995. "Adolescent Sibling-Incest Offenders: Differences in Family and Individual Functioning when Compared to Adolescent Nonsibling Sex Offenders." *Child Abuse and Neglect* 19: 633–643.

Wotherspoon, T., and V. Satzewich. 1993. *First Nations: Race, Class, and Gender Relations.* Scarborough, ON: Nelson.

Wotherspoon, T. (1994). Colonization, Self-determination and the Health of Canada's First Nations Peoples. Pp. 247–268 in *Racial Minorities, Medicine, and Health* , edited by S. Bolaria and R. Bolaria. Halifax: Fernwood.

Wright, C. 1995. *Risk of Personal and Household Victimization: Canada, 1993.* Ottawa: Canadian Centre for Justice Statistics.

Wright, J., and J. Devine. 1994. *Drugs as a Social Problem.* New York: HarperCollins.

Wrong, D. 1994. *The Problem of Social Order.* Cambridge, Mass: Cambridge University Press.

Yllö, K. A. 1993. "Through a Feminist Lens: Gender, Power, and Violence." Pp. 47–62 in *Current Controversies in Family Violence*, edited by R. J. Gelles and D. R. Lseke. Newbury Park, CA: Sage.

York, G. 1987. *The High Price of Health.* Toronto: James Lorimer and Company.

Young, J. 1992. "Ten Points of Realism." Pp. 24–68 in *Rethinking Criminology: The Realist Debate*, edited by J. Young and R. Matthews. London: Sage.

Yukon Bureau of Statistics. 1990. *Yukon Alcohol and Drug Survey, 1990*, Volume 1. Technical Report. Yukon Executive Office: Bureau of Statistics.

INDEX